6JP100

PRESERVED BUSES

By The PSV Circle Publications Team

MARCH 2012

PRESERVED BUSES (P)

This publication lists all known preserved buses in the United Kingdom, the Republic of Ireland, the Isle of Man and the Channel Islands. It contains all known information as at January 2012 and is current to the PSV Circle British Journal 865.

The main list includes buses which are fully restored, under restoration, awaiting restoration and those preserved buses in active use with PSV operators. Appendices cover preserved trams, horse buses, self-powered miniature psvs, preserved commercial vehicles on psv chassis and British-operated buses known to be preserved abroad. A further appendix lists the buses and trams normally on display at each bus or transport museum.

Although the list is as complete as possible, it is hoped that readers will notify any additions or amendments to ensure that the PSV Circle can continue to maintain a comprehensive register of preserved buses.

The PSV Circle wishes to extend its thanks to the many organisations and people, within and outside the PSV Circle, enthusiasts and bus owners, who have contributed to this publication since the previous edition - especially Glasgow Vintage Vehicle Trust, Kevin Pankhurst, Don Vincent and John Wakefield. It also acknowledges the use of numerous bus preservation-related websites - notably Bristol Commercial Vehicle Enthusiasts (Rob Sly), British Trams On Line, Classic Buses (Dick Gilbert), Ian's Bus Stop (Ian Smith) and Kells Transport Museum.

CONTENTS

All enquiries, comments, suggestions and additional information should be sent to:
The PSV Circle (6JP100), Unit 1R, Leroy House, 436 Essex Road, LONDON N1 3QP;
or by e-mail to: publications.manager@psv-circle.org.uk

Details of how to join The PSV Circle and a list of all our publications can be obtained from The PSV Circle website - www.psv-circle.org.uk.

ISBN: 978-1-908953-00-1
Published by the PSV Circle.

LAYOUT / INFORMATION GUIDE

This list contains the following information:

(1)	Optional prefix		(a)	vehicle for ancillary use
			(q)	vehicle for resale
			(r)	vehicle for spares
			(z)	vehicle used as store / messroom
(2)	Registration			
(3)	Chassis manufacturer, type and number			
(4)	Body manufacturer and number			
(5)	Body configuration and seating capacity	Before seating capacity	AB	articulated single deck bus
			B	single deck bus
			C	coach (single deck unless used with H or L)
			CO	convertible open top
			DP	single deck dual purpose
			Ch	charabanc
			F	full front (where not normally fitted)
			H	highbridge double deck
			HD	half deck coach
			L	lowbridge double deck
			M	minibus (van conversion)
			O	permanent opentop
			PO	partial opentop
			R	observation coach (raised roofline)
			T	toastrack
		Seating capacity		For double deckers, upper saloon capacity / lower saloon capacity
			RV	recovery vehicle
			TW	tower wagon
		After seating capacity	C	central entrance
			D	dual entrance
			F	front entrance
			L	fitted with a chairlift
			M	mail compartment
			O	outside stairs
			R	rear entrance
			RD	rear entrance with platform doors
			T	three entrance
			T	(as second letter) fitted with a toilet

(6) Date new; this is usually the date first licensed unless the vehicle is known to have been built earlier and stored.
(7) Original operator; where a vehicle has been rebodied or rebuilt, this will be the first operator after rebodying or rebuilding.
(8) Current owner or custodian.

GUIDE TO OTHER ABBREVIATIONS USED IN THIS PUBLICATION

ACB	Associated Coachbuilders
ACTD	Aberdeen Corporation Transport Department
AEC	Associated Equipment Company (AEC Ltd from 1948)
BaMMOT	Birmingham & Midland Motor Omnibus Trust
BEC	British Electric Car Comapny
BEEC	British Electrical Engineering Company
BRCW	Birmingham Railway Carriage & Wagon
BUT	British United Traction
CIE	Coras Iompair Eireann
CRV	Commercial Road Vehicles
CSC	Coventry Steel Caravans
DUT	Dublin United Tramways
ECW	Eastern Coach Works
ERTCW	Electrical Railway & Tramway Carriage Works
FoKAB	Friends of King Alfred Buses
GFOC	Gosport & Fareham Omnibus Company
GNR	Great Northern Railway (Ireland)
GNSR	Great North of Scotland Railway
JMT	Jersey Motor Transport
LCC	London County Council
Leyland-NGT	Leyland - Northern General Transport
Leyland-PCT	Leyland - Preston Corporation Transport
LGOC	London General Omnibus Company
LNER(GC)	London & North Eastern Railway (Great Central)
LNWR	London & North Western Railway
LPTB	London Passenger Transport Board
MCW	Metro-Cammell-Weymann
Midland RCW	Midland Railway Carriage & Wagon
NGT	Northern General Transport
NIRTB	Northern Ireland Road Transport Board
NZMB	New Zealand Motor Bodies
PCT	Preston Corporation Transport
PMT	Potteries Motor Traction
SBS	Singapore Bus Services
SCWS	Scottish Co-operative Wholesale Society
SELB	Southern Education & Library Board
RTS	Road Transport Services
SHMD	Stalybridge Hyde Mossley & Dukinfield
SMT	Scottish Motor Traction
UCC	Union Construction Company
UEC	United Electric Car Company
UTA	Ulster Transport Authority
WELB	Western Education & Library Board

COUNTY / AREA CODES

In the final column reference is made to owners who are actually licenced operaters. These are designated by the inclusion of a two character 'County' or Area Code in brackets as follows. An X prefix to the county code denotes a non-PSV operator. (Q) denotes a dealer.

BD - Bedfordshire
BE - Berkshire
BK - Buckinghamshire
CA - Cumbria
CC - South Central Wales
CD - Cleveland
CH - Cheshire
CI - Channel Islands
CM - Cambridgeshire
CN - North Wales
CO - Cornwall
CS - South East Wales
CW - Mid & West Wales
DE - Derbyshire
DM - Durham
DN - Devon
DT - Dorset
EI - Republic of Ireland
ES - East Sussex
EX - Essex
EY - East Yorkshire
GL - Gloucestershire
GM - Greater Manchester
HA - Hampshire
HR - Herefordshire
HT - Hertfordshire
IM - Isle of Man
IS - Isles of Scilly
IW - Isle of WIght
KT - Kent
LA - Lancashire
LE - Leicestershire
LI - Lincolnshire
LN - Greater London
MY - Merseyside
ND - Northumberland
NG - Nottinghamshire
NI - Northern Ireland
NK - Norfolk
NO - Northamptonshire
NY - North Yorkshire
OX - Oxfordshire
SE - Scotland East
SH - Shropshire
SK - Suffolk
SN - Scotland North
SO - Somerset
SR - Surrey
SS - Scotland South
ST - Staffordshire
SW - Scotland West
SY - South Yorkshire
TW - Tyne & Wear
WI - Wiltshire
WK - Warwickshire
WM - West Midlands
WO - Worcestershire
WS - West Sussex
WY - West Yorkshire

PRESERVED BUSES (P)

	Registration	Make	Model	Chassis no	Body	Body no	Layout	New	First owner	Current owner
	A 9164	→ see LN 314 *Overseas*								
	AA 8330	Fiat	2B	29757B2	Rickett		B12	-/15	station bus, Reading	Banfield, Staplehurst
	AG 6470	Reo	FB	FB1708	Economy		B20F	3/31	Liddell, Auchinleck	Emerton, Nantwich
(r)	AG 8604	Gilford	168OT	12121	*chassis only*			6/33	Western SMT 604	Holt, Lydd
	AH 9282		*body only*		?		Ch??	-/20	Sadler, Sheringham	Banfield, Staplehurst
			(see also commercial vehicles section)							
	AH 9737	Ford	T	-?-	?		B14	-/22	lorry chassis	Brett, Guyhirn
	AV 9963	Leyland	Titan TD5	17479	Leyland		L27/26RD	4/38	Sutherland, Peterhead 68	McKerracher, Stirling
	AZ 5078	Leyland	Lion LT2	51113	--		lorry	6/30	CIE GT6	Transport Museum Society of Ireland
	BC 4476	Daimler	Y	17570	*chassis only*			-/15	How, Leicester	Banfield, Staplehurst
	BD 209	Leyland	G7	12301	Dodson	6500	Ch/B32D	10/21	United Counties B15	Sutcliffe, Totternhoe
	BF 4729	Albion	A16DC	902A	replica		ch18	-/19	unknown	-?-, -?-
					(replica body by5/09)					
	BF 4812	Dennis	Low Loader	7370	replica		T17	9/28	fire engine chassis	Parsons, Ambleside (CA)
			(ex RD 111)		*(replica body built 1970/1 on fire engine chassis)*					
			(may be ex-RD 2000 new 7/30)							
	BG 8557	Guy	Arab II	FD26388	Massey	2093	H31/26R	1/44	Birkenhead 242	Whittingham & Anderson, Birkenhead
					(rebodied 8/53)					
	BG 9225	Leyland	Titan PD1	460599	Massey		H30/26R	12/46	Birkenhead 105	Wirral Borough Council
	BH 4081	→ see SV 6354								
	BK 2136	Dennis	2-ton	875105	replica		T14	-/22	lorry chassis	Herring, Fringford
					(replica body -/75)					
	BK 2986	Thornycroft	J	7457	Dodson		O18/16RO	8/19	Portsmouth 10	Portsmouth Museums
					(rebodied 11/26 with body new c1920)					
	BL 539	Panhard-Levassor	E	8781	Coward (Maidenhead)		B8	-/04	wagonette	Vincent, -?-
	BM 2856	Commer	WP3	WP3/290	Commer		ch13	-/13	Earl of Lonsdale	Tappin, Didcot (OX)
	BP 9822	Shelvoke & Drewery	Freighter	92:950	replica		B18F	-/29	dustcart chassis	Amberley Museum
			(ex CV 784)		*(replica body -/96)*					
	BR 6496	ADC	416A	416743	Wyatt		C30D	4/28	Northern General D376	group, Sheffield
					(replica body 8/79)					
	BR 7132	Leyland	Lion LT1	50381	Leyland		B34F	5/29	Sunderland 2	Southdown Omnibus Trust
			(ex J 9008, BR 7132)							
	BT 9420	Ford	T	-?-	Fentiman		B14	-/19	Fentiman, Seaton Ross	Kemp, -?-
					(body probably dates from -/26)					
	BU 7108	Leyland	Titan TD2	911	Massey		H--/--R	3/32	Oldham 69	Moores, Diseworth
	BV 5741	Tilling Stevens	HA39A7	8788	*chassis only*			5/36	Cronshaw, Hendon	Newman, Maidstone
	BW 2057	→ see YYJ 555								
	C 56	All-American		106-25/30	Barrow (Rothwell)		Ch20	-/13	-?-, -?-	Preston, Hutton Rudby
					(replica body -/73)					
	C 78	Austin	40hp	576	?		B?	-/11	estate bus	Corner, Leyburn
	C 2367	Leyland	G2	9961	Phoenix		O23/20RO	6/21	Todmorden 14	Sutcliffe, Totternhoe

CC 1087	Leyland	S4.36.T3	S568/1627	Leyland		Ch32	7/14	LNWR 59	Sutcliffe, Totternhoe
		(ex XA 8086, LP 8597, CC 1087)							
CC 7745	SOS	QL	647	Brush		B37F	5/28	Royal Blue, Llandudno	BaMMOT, Wythall
CC 8670	Dennis	G	70442	J Roberts		T19	2/29	Llandudno	Fitzpatrick, Queensferry
CC 8671	Dennis	G	70443	J Roberts		T19	3/29	Llandudno	Southampton University Engineering Faculty Society
CC 9305	Dennis	GL	70608	J Roberts		T19	2/30	Llandudno	Smith, Rye
CC 9424	Dennis	GL	70621	J Roberts		T19	4/30	Llandudno	Smith {Northern Star}, Pickering (NY)
CD 4867	Tilling Stevens	TS3A	2550	*chassis only*			5/22	Southdown 67	Glue, Littlehampton
		(ex XH 9297)							
CD 5125	Leyland	N	10975	Short		O27/24RO	1/21	Southdown 125	Southdown Omnibus Trust
				(*rebodied 7/28*)					
CD 7045	Leyland	N Special	12347	Short		O27/24RO	6/22	Southdown 135	Southdown (WS) 19945
				(*rebodied 12/28*)					
CD 7104	Vulcan	VSD	73	Peskett		B18F	6/22	Southdown 174	Lee {World of Country Life}, Exmouth
				(*replica body 9/95*)					
CF 4994	Ford	T	7900874	Mann Egerton	C805	B9	-/??	estate bus	Reliance Garage, Glossop
CG 9607	AEC	Regal 4	O642131	Reading/GFOC		FB35F	12/34	Gosport & Fareham 24	Whitaker, Waltham Cross
				(*rebodied -/62*)					
CH 7156	Tilling Stevens	TS6	3796	*chassis only*			12/27	Derby 11	Moore, Coulsdon
CJ 5052	Maxwell	25cwt	752	Maxwell		Ch14	4/22	Williams, Bromyard	National Motor Museum, Beaulieu
CK 3825	Leyland	Lion LSC1	45570	Ribble		B31F	3/27	Ribble 295	Ribble (LA) 39945
				(*replica body -/82*)					
CK 4474	Leyland	Tiger TS3	61555	Leyland		B--F	-/31	Ribble 1117	Ribble Vehicle Preservation Trust
CK 4518	Leyland	Lion LT2	51383	Leyland		B--F	3/31	Ribble 1161	Ashcroft, Lostock Hall
CK 4649	Leyland	Lion LT5	1005	English Electric		B32R	7/32	Preston 76	Broatch, Chicklade
CN 2870	SOS	Q	420	Brush		B37F	5/27	Northern General 321	BaMMOT, Wythall
CN 4740	SOS	IM4	1455	Short		B34F	3/31	Northern General 540	North East Bus Preservation Trust
CN 6100	Northern General	SE6	65	Short		B44F	6/34	Northern General 604	Northern Omnibus Trust, Durham
CS 3364	Leyland	Cheetah LZ2	8621	Alexander	1496	FB--F	4/36	Western SMT	Pettie, Dunfermline
CU 4488	AEC	Regal	O6623494	*chassis/cab*			5/40	Northern General 968	Smith, Hexham
CU 4740	Leyland	Tiger PS1	470575	Burlingham	2899	C--F	-/47	Hall, South Shields	-?-, Aberdeen
CY 5981		*body only*		?Brush?		O54RO	-/23	South Wales	Banfield, Staplehurst
CZ 4803	Leyland	Tiger TS6	3882	NIRTB		B34R	5/34	NIRTB 714	Miller, Ballyclare
		(ex PIF 240, CZ 4803)		(*rebodied 3/44*)					
CZ 7013	Dennis	Lancet	170761	Harkness		B31F	12/35	Belfast 102	Ulster Folk & Transport Museum
				(*rebodied 1/50*)					
D 1959	→ see LC 3185 *Overseas*								
D 8650	Hallford	3-ton	258	Tilling		O18/16RO	11/12	Maidstone & District	Herbert, Slade Green
DB 2243	Crossley	20/25	5109A	Spendlove		B12F	-/15	Irish country bus	Smith, Wilmslow
		(ex BI 5014)		(*replica body new c1968/69*)					
DB 5062	Tilling Stevens	TS6	3635	*chassis/body remains*			-/25	North Western 162	Weatherhead, Woburn Sands
DB 5070	Tilling Stevens	TS6	3606	Wyatt		O54RO	4/25	North Western 170	Cook, Worfield
				(*replica body -/84*)					
DD 475	Ford	TT	5406464	Healey		B14	3/22	Freeman, Ashleworth	Cook, Worfield
DD 1770	Dearborn	FX	1728B	Constable		B14F	1/23	Pritchett, Bibury	Charlett, Yarnton
DF 8420	Leyland	Tiger TS2	60320	Duple	53306	C33F	8/29	Jennings, Bude	Smith, Whaley Bridge
				(*rebodied -/49*)					

	Reg	Chassis	Chassis no	Body	Body no	Layout	New	First operator	Current owner
	DL 621	Straker-Squire U	889	*chassis only*			5/12	Cannon, Worthing	Thornycroft, West Norwood
	DL 2610	Leyland C1	19125	*chassis only*			3/22	Nash, Ventnor	Golding, Ryde
	DL 5084	Daimler CK	2686	Dodson	6708	B26D	4/27	Dodson, Cowes 11	Golding, Wellow
				(believed to have reconditioned -/19 chassis; body believed built -/22)					
	DL 9015	Dennis Ace	200216	Harrington		B20F	7/34	Southern Vectis 405	Priddle, Farnham
	DL 9706	Dennis Lancet	170955	ECW	8356	B36R	7/35	Southern Vectis 516	Hinson, Potterspury
				(rebodied -/44)					
	DM 2583	Leyland SG7 40hp	12535	Leyland		FB40D	5/23	Brookes, Rhyl	Sutcliffe, Totternhoe
	DM 6228	Leyland Lioness LTB1	50261	Burlingham		C26D	5/29	Brookes, Rhyl 7	Stanier, Luddesdown
		(ex J 2975, DM 6228)							
	DP 7680	Morris-Commercial T/2	15317	replica		B10D	12/26	-?-, -?-	Ritchie D, Hetton-le-Hole
				(replica body built 1980-85)					
	DR 4902	Leyland Titan TD1	70549	Leyland		L51RO	3/29	National 2849	Science Museum, Wroughton
(r)	DR 7100	Leyland Lion LT2	50957	Mumford		B--R	6/30	Southern National 3000	Shears C, Winkleigh
				(rebodied 7/38)					
	DS 7132	→ see XWV 942A *Overseas*							
	DS 7422	Morris-Commercial 1-Ton	7484T	Harris (Clanfield)		B10D	12/26	-?-, -?-	Payne, Great Sampford
				(original body rebuilt by6/86)					
	DS 7922	→ see Unregistered Vehicles							
	DS 8637	Ford TT	11277113	Anstiss		B10R	-/25	-?-, -?-	Jackson, Bishops Stortford
				(replica body -/88)					
	DS 9751	Thornycroft J2	7731J	Peskett		Ch30	7/19	lorry chassis	Lee {World of Country Life}, Exmouth
		(ex -?-)		*(replica body 4/92)*					
	DU 4838	Daimler Y	4305	City of Oxford Electric Tramways		B--R	10/20	City of Oxford 39	Taylor, Oxford
				(ex lorry chassis new -/17)					
	DV 7890	Leyland Lion LT2	51273	?Burlingham?		C31F	1/31	Pridham, Lamerton	Snaith, Otterburn (ND)
				(rebodied or rebuilt -/49)					
	DX 3426	Ford TT	5413857	?		B??	1922	Halstead Omnibus Co	Kemp, Billericay
	DX 6591	Tilling Stevens Express B9A	5524	Eastern Counties	3060	B36R	7/27	Eastern Counties P78	Ipswich Transport Museum
				(rebodied 3/34)					
	DX 7657	Tilling Stevens Express B10B2	5939	*chassis only*			12/28	Eastern Counties P113	Newman, Maidstone
	DX 7812	Tilling Stevens Express B10A2	6368	*chassis only*			3/29	Eastern Counties P116	Ipswich Transport Museum
	DX 9547	Gilford AS6	12001	Taylor		B20F	12/31	Rivers, Ipswich	Skevington, Leighton Buzzard
	DX 9764	Bedford WLB	108221	Waveney		C20F	3/32	Smith, Ipswich	Dickerson, Thorrington
	DY 5029	Karrier JKL	10631	London Lorries		C26D	5/28	Timpson 117	Golcar Transport Museum, Huddersfield
	EA 4181	Dennis ES	17664	Dixon		B32F	11/29	West Bromwich 32	32 Group, Birmingham
	EC 634	Commer RC	M114	?		B12	-/09	Lord Lonsdale	Sloan, Tunbridge Wells
	EC 8852	Vulcan Duchess	20	Vulcan		B26D	7/29	Dallam Motor Services 7	Emerton, Nantwich
(r)	ED 6141	Leyland Titan TD1	71573	Massey	C780	H--/--R	9/30	Warrington 22	Ensign, Purfleet (EX)
				(lower deck remains only)					
	EE 8128	Albion PM28	7038G			TW	9/28	Grimsby 32	-?-, Kent
	EF 7380	Leyland Titan TD7	307898	Roe	GO747	H26/22C	7/42	West Hartlepool 36	Kell, Durham
	EK 8867	Leyland Tiger TS4	1730	Santus		B32R	10/32	Wigan 81	Hoare, Chepstow (CS)
	EL 5454	Tilling Stevens TS3	2156	*chassis only*			9/20	Bournemouth	Bournemouth Heritage Transport Collection
	EN 9965	Leyland Titan PD2/4	495870	Weymann	M7334	RV	1/50	Bury 165	Mitchell, Manchester
	EO 9051	Leyland Titan PD2/3	491238	Park Royal	B33057	RV	10/49	Barrow 124	Hambler, Barrow

EO 9177	Leyland	Titan PD2/3	494532	Roe	GO4915	H31/28RD	3/50	Barrow 147	Barrow Transport Museum
				(rebodied 3/60)					
EP 1673	Ford	TT	4569364	Ruston & Hornsby		B13	3/21	Owen, Meifod	Onions, Shrewsbury
ER 7449	Ford	T	30280	replica		B6	-/22	-?-, -?-	-?-, -?-
				(replica body built -/72)					
ES 5150	Albion	C20	3003K	Harvey		B13F	12/22	Tighauloan Hotel, Fearnan	Biggar Albion Foundation
ES 8640	Chevrolet	X	X10093	replica		Ch??	6/26	Melville, Kirk Michael	Jordan, Chelmsford
				(replica body built -/??)					
EU 9722	Leyland	Tiger PS1	492480	Lydney		B--F	7/49	Griffin, Brynmawr 122	Reason Rees & Woodward, Cardiff
EX 885	Ford	TT	7403596	Bush & Twiddy		Ch??	-/22	Page, Gorleston	Meakin, Norwich
EX 1128	Guy	BB	BB1497	United		B--D	6/24	Great Yarmouth 4	East Anglia Transport Museum
EX 6566	Leyland	PD2/1	495964	Leyland		H30/26R	1/50	Great Yarmouth 66	East Anglia Transport Museum
EX 6644	Crossley	SD42/7	98136	Yeates	157	C35F	1/50	Felix, Great Yarmouth 7	Plant, Brereton
EX 9779	AEC	Reliance	MU3RV906	Duple	1066/34	C41C	8/56	Seagull, Great Yarmouth	Coach Hire, Freckleton (LA)
EY 5218	Thornycroft	Lightning GC/SC6	24689	*chassis & body frame*			5/35	Jones, Menai Bridge	Hampshire Museums, Winchester
EY 9025	→ see WFF 583 *Overseas*								
EY 9194	Crossley	SD42/7	97849	Gurney Nutting	C1204	FC35F	6/49	Jones, Menai Bridge	Plant, Brereton
				(rebodied 3/51)					
EY 9392	→ see WFF 582 *Overseas*								
FA 9716	Guy	Arab III	FD36252	Massey	2373	H33/28R	12/50	Burton 16	Burton Arab Preservation Society
				(rebodied 1/60)					
FB 8772	Ford	AA	AF3591004	?		B?	10/30	Estate bus, Bath	Edmonds, Leamington Spa
FC 2602	Daimler	Y	7195	LGOC		O18/16RO	-/17	City of Oxford	Taylor, Oxford
		(ex lorry chassis)		*(body new -/06)*					
FF 889	Ford	T	3899885	?		B10F	3/22	Griffiths, Dyffryn	-?-, -?-
FG 5854	Maudslay	ML6	4811	Duple	4056	C29	3/30	Fallowfield & Britten	Gerring, Fleet
				(rebodied 5/34)					
FJ 6154	Maudslay	ML3B	4514	Northern Counties		B33D	3/29	Exeter 5	West Country Historic Omnibus & Transport Trust
FJ 8967	Bristol	H5G	H160	Bristol		B35R	7/33	Western National 137	Billington, Maidenhead
				(rebodied 11/42)					
FM 6397	Leyland	Titan TD1	71556	Leyland		L--/--R	-/31	Crosville 45	Moores, Diseworth
FM 6435	Leyland	Lion LT2	51307	Leyland		B32F	-/31	Crosville 474	Moores, Diseworth
FM 6858	Leyland	Tiger TS4	105	ECW	6060	C28R	9/31	Crosville 168	James, Blaenporth
				(rebodied -/39)					
FM 7443	Leyland	Cub KP2	982	Brush		B20F	12/32	Crosville 716	Moores, Diseworth
FM 9984	Leyland	Tiger TS7	8184	Harrington		C32F	-/36	Crosville K101	Moores, Diseworth
FN 6050	Daimler	Y	5775	*chassis only*			1/24	East Kent	Weatherhead, Woburn Sands
FS 1116	Albion	Valkyrie PW65	16007H	Cowieson		B--F	10/31	SMT A98	Struthers, East Kilbride
FS 8000	→ see YTA 415L								
FV 4548	AEC	Regal	6621547	English Electric		C18R	3/34	Ribble D81	-?-, -?-
				(rebodied c12/48 with body new 5/34)					
FV 5737	Leyland	Tiger TS7	6726	Duple	53826	C31F	1/36	Ribble 753	Hoare, Chepstow (CS)
				(rebodied 5/50)					
FV 9044	Leyland	Tiger TS7	13010	Burlingham		FB--C	7/37	Blackpool 7	Burchell, Billingshurst
FW 2378	Bedford	WLG	114010	Rainforth		B20F	7/31	Gosling, Mareham-le-Fen	Lincolnshire Aviation Heritage Centre

	Reg	Make	Model	Chassis no	Body	Body no	Layout	New	First owner	Current owner
	FW 5696	Leyland	Tiger TS7	6410	Burlingham	4241	B35F	4/35	Lincolnshire 368	Marshall, Sutton-on-Trent (NG)
					(rebodied 3/50)					
	FW 5698	Leyland	Tiger TS7	6412	Burlingham	-?-	B35F	4/35	Lincolnshire 370	Lincolnshire Vintage Vehicle Society
					(rebodied -/49)					
	GA 3560	Ford	TT	3384273	?		Ch??	-/19	-?-, -?-	Myreton Motor Museum, Aberlady
	GE 2446	Leyland	Titan TD1	70203	SBG Engineering		L27/24RO	9/28	Glasgow 111	Pettie & Hoare, Dunfermline
					(replica body new -/89)					
	GJ 2098	AEC	Regent	661660	Tilling		H27/25RO	11/30	London Transport ST922	London Bus Preservation Trust
	GK 434	Leyland	Tiger TS3	61383			RV	-/30	Western SMT	-?-, -?-
	GK 3192	AEC	Regent	6611481	LGOC	15490	H28/20R	3/31	London General ST821	London Transport Museum
	GK 5323	AEC	Renown	663166	LGOC	12796	H33/23R	1/31	London General LT165	London Transport Museum
	GK 5486	AEC	Regal	662715	Duple	2106	C30F	1/31	Green Line T219	London Transport Museum
	GM 5875	Leyland	Titan PD2/10	531122	Leyland		RV	12/53	Alexander Midland ML245	Karlsberg, New Ferry
	GM 6384	Leyland	Titan PD2/10	541019	Leyland		L27/28R	10/54	Central SMT L484	L484 Preservation Group, Glasgow
	GM 9287	→ see TVS 367								
	GN 8242	AEC	Regal	662630	Weymann	M274	B--F	1/31	London Transport T357	London Bus Preservation Trust
					(rebodied 3/35)					
	GO 5170	AEC	Renown	664070	LGOC	12961	B--F	5/31	London General LT1059	London Bus Preservation Trust
	GO 5198	AEC	Renown	664087	LGOC	12414	B35F	5/31	London General LT1076	London Transport Museum
	GR 7100	Crossley	Mancunian	91946	Blagg		B--F	10/39	Sunderland 22	Green, Thompson & Moodie, Reading
	GR 9007	Crossley	DD42/3	93893	Crossley		H30/26R	-/47	Sunderland 13	Jackson & Melia, Wormingford
	GV 1173	Bedford	WLB	108489	Duple	2849	B20F	4/32	Cross, Bury St Edmunds	Matthews, Bellingdon
	GW 713	Gilford	168OT	11584	Weymann	W801	C30D	12/31	Valliant, Ealing	Marshall, New Haw *(on loan from Science Museum, Wroughton)*
	GZ 783	Bedford	OWB	10204	Ulsterbus		B32F	11/42	NIRTB V957	Ulsterbus (NI) V957
					(replica body new -/85)					
	GZ 1882	Daimler	CWA6	11826	Harkness		H30/26R	12/44	Belfast 214	Ulster Folk & Transport Museum
	GZ 2248	Bedford	OWB	22415	Mulliner		B28F	12/44	NIRTB X337	Martin, Penkridge
					(rebodied by7/00 with body new -/49)					
	GZ 4696	Leyland	Tiger PS1	462166	*chassis only*			-/46	NIRTB Z800	Ulster Folk & Transport Museum
	GZ 6106	Leyland	Tiger PS1	470148	NIRTB		B34R	5/47	NIRTB A515	Ulsterbus (NI) 515
	GZ 7585	Leyland	Tiger PS1	471781	NIRTB		B34R	-/47	NIRTB A8517	Begley, Lisburn
	GZ 7588	→ see KID 154 *Ireland*								
	GZ 7624	Leyland	Tiger PS1	472604	NIRTB		B34R	-/47	NIRTB A8556	Alexander, Baldrine
	GZ 7628	Leyland	Tiger PS1	472656	NIRTB		B34R	1/48	NIRTB A8560	Montgomery W, Ballymena
	GZ 7638	Leyland	Tiger PS1	472686	NIRTB		B34R	-/47	NIRTB A8570	Transport Museum Society of Ireland
	HA 3501	SOS	S	196	Ransomes	513	B28F	10/25	BMMO 564	BaMMOT, Wythall
	HA 4963	SOS	RR	1348	*chassis/cab*			-/30	BMMO A1189	Shaw, Warley
(r)	HA 6203	SOS	IM4	1430	*chassis only*			-/30	BMMO 1273	North East Bus Preservation Trust
	HA 8047	SOS	REDD	1673	Metro-Cammell	BB2030	H--/--R	-/33	BMMO 1418	BaMMOT, Wythall
	HA 9483	SOS	CON	1836	Short		B38F	-/34	BMMO A1532	Digbeth S12 Group
	HB 4060	Bedford	WLB	108190	Davies		C20F	12/31	Williams, Blaina	Jenks, Churt
	HC 8643	Leyland	Lion LSC3	46861	Leyland		B32R	6/28	Eastbourne 58	Brown, Milton Keynes
	HD 7905	Leyland	Tiger PS1	480750	Brush		B34F	3/48	Yorkshire Woollen 622	Brooke, Leeds
	HE 12	Leyland	S3.30.T	S253/1020	Brush		B27F	5/13	Barnsley & District 5	Sutcliffe, Totternhoe

	Reg	Make	Model	Chassis no	Body	Body no	Layout	Date	First operator	Owner
	HE 6762	Leyland	Tiger TS7	6538	Weymann	C9396	B34F	4/35	Yorkshire Traction 492	South Yorkshire Transport Museum
					(rebodied 4/50)					*(on loan from Yorkshire Traction (SY))*
	HG 9651	Leyland	Tiger PS1/1	462709	Brush		B34R	7/48	Burnley Colne & Nelson 10	Leighton, Keighley
	HK 7553		*lower deck body remains only*		Dodson	7647	O--/--RO	7/26	National 2056	Doggett P, Purley
	HK 9421		*body only*		Hurst Nelson		O34RO	c-/17	Laindon & District	Banfield, Staplehurst
			(ex LA 9802)							
(r)	HL 1803	Bristol	4-ton	1563	*chassis only*			4/24	West Riding 142	Donaldson, Wrenthorpe
	HL 7538	Leyland	Cub KPZ2	5903	Roe	GO6057	B24F	10/36	West Riding 464	Emerton, Nantwich
	HL 9261	Leyland	Cub SKPZ2	8735	Roe	GO166	B20F	4/39	West Riding 560	Shackell, Ducklington
	HO 8312	Leyland	RAF	21811	Eastbourne Aviation		B40F	-/21	Stoneham, Eastleigh 5	Hubbuck, Petersfield
	HT 3506	Bristol	4-ton	1336	Bl		B--F	5/21	Bristol Tramways	Donaldson, Wrenthorpe
					(body ex HL 1803)					
	HU 6618	Bristol	2-ton	0303	*chassis only*			-/26	Bristol Tramways	M Shed, Bristol
	HW 6634	Bristol	B	B557	*chassis only*			-/29	Bristol Tramways	Walker & Curtis, Wells
	IB 552	Tilling Stevens	TS3	351	Newman		O22/18RO	12/14	Worthing Motor Services	Southdown Omnibus Trust
			(ex CD 4952, IB 552)		*(body new -/09)*					
	IL 2849	Leyland	Cheetah LZ1	13986	*chassis only*			-/37	Cassidy, Enniskillen	Ulster Folk & Transport Museum
	J 2503	Dodge	50	-?-	Osborne		O18/14RO	3/88	Gateshead Tramways (replica)	North of England Open Air Museum
			(replica of 1913 Daimler CC/Dodson)							
	JA 5506	Dennis	Lancet	170892	Eastern Counties	3609	B31R	-/35	North Western 706	Moores, Diseworth
	JA 5515	Leyland	Tiger TS7	9487	Windover	7129	C32F	3/36	North Western 380	Docherty, Auchterarder (SE)
					(rebodied -/50)					
	JA 5528	Bristol	JO5G	JO5G209	Brush		B31R	6/36	North Western 728	Moores, Diseworth
					(rebodied -/46)					
	JA 7585	Leyland	Tiger TS7	12418	English Electric		B35C	12/36	Stockport 185	Museum of Transport, Manchester
	JA 7591	Leyland	Tiger TS7	12424	English Electric		B35C	1/37	Stockport 191	Hoare, Chepstow (CS)
	JA 7626	Crossley	DD42/3	93872	*chassis only*			-/46	Stockport 226	Darwen Transport Museum Trust
	JC 2772	Guy	Wolf	CFP11365	J Roberts		B20F	6/35	Llandudno	-?-, -?-
	JC 4557	Commer	PN3	46579	Waveney		B20F	6/37	Llandudno	Walters, Talke
	JC 5313	Guy	Wolf	CFP13451	Waveney	1669	B20F	3/38	Llandudno	Golcar Transport Museum, Huddersfield
	JC 8344	Guy	Wolf	NLW31094	Barnard		B21F	4/48	Llandudno	Conwy County Borough Council
	JC 9735	Guy	Wolf	NLW40302	Barnard		B21F	5/49	Llandudno	Castleman, Stanbridge
	JC 9736	Guy	Wolf	NLW40300	Barnard		B21F	5/49	Llandudno	Voel, Dyserth (CN)
	JD 1981	Gilford	168OT	11268	Wycombe	1229	C26F	3/32	Hillman, Romford	Banfield, Staplehurst
	JF 2378	AEC	Regal	6621120	Burlingham		C32R	12/31	Provincial, Leicester	Morley, Leicester
	JG 669	Tilling Stevens	Express B10C2	7013	Brush		B37R	2/30	East Kent	Newman, Maidstone
(a)	JG 683	Tilling Stevens	Express B10C2	7027	Brush		B--R	3/30	East Kent	Thornycroft, West Norwood
			(used as a mess room by the Amberley Museum bus group)							
	JG 691	Tilling Stevens	Express B10C2	7035	Brush		B--R	4/30	East Kent	Newman, Maidstone
(r)	JG 4234	Dennis	Ace	200107	*chassis only*			-/34	East Kent	Emerton, Nantwich
	JG 8720	Dennis	Lancet II	175292	Park Royal	B34029	B35R	7/37	East Kent	Thomas, Bexleyheath
					(rebodied 9/49)					
	JG 9938	Leyland	Tiger TS8	16594	Park Royal	B4902	C32R	12/37	East Kent	Quantock, Bishops Lydeard (SO)
	JH 6699	→ see KSK 466								
	JJ 4379	AEC	Regent	6612307	Chalmers		van	6/33	London Transport 832J	Dyckhoff, Smith & Burton, Ealing

	Reg	Make	Model	Chassis No	Body	Body No	Layout	New	First operator	Owner
	JK 5605	Leyland	Titan TD4	11079	Leyland		O28/24R	7/36	Eastbourne 95	Hoare, Chepstow (CS)
	JK 8418	Leyland	Lion LT9	303392	Leyland		B32F	8/39	Eastbourne 12	Bryden, Crowhurst
	JK 8421	→ see LMG 184								
	JK 9115	Leyland	Titan PD1	461661	East Lancs	4090	O30/26R	5/47	Eastbourne 17	Hoare, Chepstow (CS)
	JN 5783	AEC	Q	762158	*chassis only*			6/35	Westcliff-on-Sea Motor Services	Armour et al, Derby
	JO 5032	AEC	Regal 4	642017	*chassis only*			7/32	City of Oxford 41	Taylor, Oxford
			(ex J 1418, JO 5032)							
	JO 5403	AEC	Regent	6611865	Brush		O28/24R	8/32	City of Oxford 16	Taylor, Oxford
	JP 2248	Leyland	Cheetah LZ2	13463	Thurgood	455	B35F	5/37	JMT 62	Price, Newcastle
			(ex NMY 156, J 8545, JP 2248) (but may be ex JP 2191)				*(rebodied 4/48)*			
	JP 4712	Leyland	Titan TD7	306293	Leyland		L27/26R	7/40	Wigan 70	Williams, Fazeley
	JP 6032	Leyland	Titan PD1A	471599	Leyland		L27/26R	8/47	Wigan 34	Blackman, Halifax
	JP 7538	Crossley	SD42/7	97790	Duple	223/2	FC35F	3/49	Liptrot, Bamfurlong	Emerton, Nantwich
					(rebodied -/55)					
	JR 3520	Gilford	168SD	12267	Wycombe	1405	C26F	-/31	Robson, Hexham	Francis, Broughton
			(chassis new -/31 but bodied 7/35; converted to forward control)							
	JS 1972	Ford	T	9954481	MacLeod		B14	4/24	Mackay, Stornoway	Macleod, South Shawbost
	JS 8089	Bedford	OB	89529	Duple	52291	B30F	10/48	Mitchell, Stornoway	McLeod, North Tolsta
	JT 8077	Bedford	WTB	111587	Duple	2329	C25F	10/37	Sheasby, Corfe Castle	Woodhams, Ryde (IW)
	JU 963	Leyland	Cub KP3	712	Willowbrook	2581	C20F	7/32	Brown, Sapcote	Beadles, Newtown
	JV 9901	AEC	Regent III	O961215	Roe	GO2248	H31/25R	1/47	Grimsby 81	Pitcher, Nottingham
	JX 7046	AEC	Regent	O6616358	Park Royal	-?-	H30/26R	2/39	Halifax 80	Blackman et al, Halifax
	JX 9106	AEC	Regal I	O6624935	Weymann	C9076	RV	8/46	Hebble L4	Blackman L, Halifax
	JY 124	Tilling Stevens	Express B39A7	8681	Beadle	364	B--R	5/32	Western National 3379	Cook, Exeter
					(rebodied 3/47)					
	KB 9656	Ford	T	324965680	?		B??	-/22	-?-, -?-	Molyneux, Ulverston
	KD 3185	Karrier	WL6	42117	*chassis only*			12/28	Liverpool	Golcar Transport Museum, Huddersfield
	KD 5296	Leyland	Tiger TS2	60134	Harrington		C31F	3/29	James, Wavertree	Webster, Lower Southrepps
					(rebodied 6/39)					
	KE 4771	Dennis	4-ton	20016	*chassis only*			5/21	Cooperabancs, Kent	Giles, Gamlingay
	KE 9677	→ see UV 6025 *Preserved commercial vehicles on PSV chassis*								
	KF 1040	Thornycroft	FC	19909	Liverpool CT		B37R	1/31	Liverpool	Merseyside County Museums
(r)	KJ 1930	Leyland	Titan TD1	72276	*chassis only*			-/31	Maidstone & District 236	Plunkett, Ashurst
(r)	KJ 2578	Leyland	Titan TD1	72057	LCPT		B--C	7/31	Liverpool CL4	Ensign, Purfleet (EX)
					(body fitted 10/51)					
	KK 980	Ford	TT	5413757	Bakers (Tonbridge)		-14-	8/22	village cricket team bus	Hussey, Horsham
			(open lorry-bus wagonette)							
	KL 7796	Tilling Stevens	TS6	3702	Short		O--/--RO	7/25	Maidstone & District 73	Thornycroft, West Norwood
	KO 54	Albion	PM28	7003L	Beadle		B--R	3/27	Redcar A54	Herbert, Slade Green
	KO 63	Albion	PM28	7004I	Vickers		B--R	3/27	Redcar A63	-?-, Kent
	KO 7311	Tilling Stevens	Express B9A	5365	Short		B--R	3/28	Maidstone & District 461	Newman, Redhill
	KR 66	→ see WX 2658								
	KR 1728	Leyland	Titan TD1	71348	Short		H--/--R	5/30	Maidstone & District 321	Ensign, Purfleet (EX)
	KR 8385	Leyland	Tiger TS2	61346	Burlingham		B--F	5/31	Maidstone & District 665	Ensign, Purfleet (EX)
					(rebodied 12/43)					
	KU 2923	Fiat	F2	174375			wagonette	-/17	estate bus	Hutt, St Annes-on-Sea

	Reg	Make	Model	Chassis no	Body	Body no	Layout	Date	First operator	Owner
	KW 474	Leyland	Lion LSC1	45532	Leyland		B31F	3/27	Blythe & Berwick,Bradford	Lincolnshire Vintage Vehicle Society
			(ex J 6825, KW 474)							
	KW 1961	Leyland	Lion LSC3	45974	Leyland		B35F	7/27	Blythe & Berwick,Bradford	Aire Valley Transport Group
			(ex J 7278, KW 1961)							
	KW 2260	Leyland	Lion LSC3	46020	Leyland		B36R	9/27	Bradford 325	Keighley Bus Museum Trust
	KW 7604	Leyland	Badger TA4	65603	Plaxton		B20F	1/30	Bradford 023	Lincolnshire Vintage Vehicle Society
(r)	KX 1923	Gilford	166OT	10498	*chassis only*			2/29	Amersham & District 17	Jones, Kessingland
	KY 9106	AEC	Regent	O6613183	Weymann	M318	lorry	2/35	Bradford 046	Blackman A, Halifax
										(*on loan from Bradford Industrial Museum*)
	LA 9802	AEC	B	B214	LGOC		O18/16RO	-/11	London General B214	Ward, Harrogate
	LA 9802	(*previous body*) → see HK 9421								
	LA 9825	AEC	B	B237	*chassis only*			-/11	London General B237	Ward, Harrogate
	LA 9928	AEC	B	B340	LGOC	4502	O18/16RO	5/11	London General B340	London Transport Museum
	LC 3701	de Dion	L	L7	*chassis only*			-/06	London General L7	London Transport Museum
	LC 4393	Commer	RC	RC801	Dodson		B16R	-/05	Boyer, Rothley	Duffin, Mountsorrell
	LD 3204	Renault	?	-?-	?		B12	-/06	estate bus	Bygones Museum Collection, Holkham Hall
	LE 7487	Chase	3/4ton	1435	?		B--F	c-/15	-?-, -?-	Cook, Worfield
			(ex -?-)							
	LE 9819	AEC	B	B1056	*chassis only*			3/12	London General B1056	Ward, Harrogate
	LF 8375	AEC	B	B1609	LGOC?		O18/16RO	-/12	London General B1609	Weatherhead, Woburn Sands
	LF 9205	Daimler	-?-	444	*chassis only*			-/12	Metropolitan Electric Tramways	Cook, Worfield
	LF 9967	Leyland	S3.30.T	S209/954	Birch		O20/16RO	7/13	Wellingborough MOC	Sutcliffe, Totternhoe
	LG 2637	Crossley	Arrow	90207	Crossley		B32R	10/29	Jackson, Crewe	Plant, Brereton
	LH 8518	AEC	B	B5103	LGOC		B20R	-/19	London General B5103	Banfield, Staplehurst
	LJ 500	Karrier	WL6/1	42147	Hall Lewis		B40D	10/29	Bournemouth 33	Bournemouth Heritage Transport Collection
	LJ 9501	Albion	Valiant SpPV70	11509B	Harrington	136	C32F	3/34	Charlies Cars 57	Farrall, Chester
					(*rebodied 8/47*)					
	LN 4743	AEC	B	B43	LGOC	2840	O18/16RO	-/11	London General B43	Imperial War Museum, London
	LN 7270	Leyland	X2 35hp	X2.64	Tilling		O18/16RO	6/08	London Central 14	Sutcliffe, Totternhoe
	LU 8318	AEC	K	20110	*chassis/body remains*			1/20	London General K110	Banfield, Staplehurst
	LU 8360	AEC	K	20241	*chassis/body remains*			-/20	London General K241	Doggett P, Purley
	MJ 4549	Dennis	Lancet	170209	Short		B32F	6/34	Smith, Westoning	Miles, Chessington
	MO 9324	Tilling Stevens	Express B9A	5280	replica		B32R	6/27	Thames Valley 152	Southdown Omnibus Trust
					(*replica body built1994-98*)					
	MR 3879	Reo	Speedwagon	115729	?		C14D	5/25	Harrington, Fordingbridge	Black Country Living Museum
	MS 172	Daimler	4hp	1197	Stirling		wagonette	1897	Wright, Bainsford	Loder, Battle
	MS 9157	Leyland	Lion LT1	50469	Alexander		B32F	7/29	Alexander N39	McKerracher, Stirling
					(*rebodied 2/36 with body new -/32*)					
	MV 8996	Bedford	WLB	108002	Duple	2367	C20F	11/31	Duple demonstrator	North East Bus Preservation Trust
	MY 57	Gilford	166SD	10816	Carriage & Wheel Works		C26D	6/29	Ewer, London	Holt, Lydd
	MZ 1929	Leyland	Tiger PS2/1	492929	UTA		B37F	-/49	UTA C8858	Montgomery T, Ballymena
	MZ 7384	Guy	Arab III	FD70114	Harkness		B31F	2/50	Belfast 286	Miller, Ballyclare
	MZ 7396	Guy	Arab III	FD70326	Harkness		B31F	3/50	Belfast 298	Transport Museum Society of Ireland
	MZ 7444	Guy	Arab III	FD70654	Harkness		H28/26R	2/51	Belfast 346	Bell, Belfast
	MZ 7789	Leyland	Titan PD2/1	501239	UTA		L27/26RD	10/50	UTA D927	Miller, Ballyclare

Reg	Make	Model	Chassis No	Body	Body No	Layout	New	First operator	Owner
NG 1109	Reo	Pullman	GE230	Taylor		C23D	6/31	Reynolds, Overstrand	Golding, Wellow
NG 2414	Bedford	WLB	108384	Economy		B20F	4/32	Jarvis, Swaffham	Rambler, Hastings (ES) 1
NG 7491	Morris-Commercial	C	339C11912	Mann Egerton		B9	8/34	estate bus	Peel, Pocklington
NH 8048	Crossley 20.9hp		40781	Grose		B??	11/27	Whitton, Northampton	Beanland, Nottingham
				(body newer than chassis)					
NH 9189	Guy	FCX	FCX23259	Grose		H--/--R	6/29	Northampton 29	Walmsley, Burnham-On-Crouch
NN 373	Locomobile 45hp		-?-	LGOC		O18/16RO	-/15	London General (body)	Caister Castle Motor Museum
		(chassis ex US Army, rebuilt c1963 with c1911 body)							
NV 30	→ see PSL 234								
O 9926	Tilling Stevens	TS3/7	2836	Tilling		O18/16RO	-/23	Birmingham District	BaMMOT, Wythall
		(body & registration date from 1913)							
OC 527	Morris-Commercial	Imperial	O53HD	Metro-Cammell		H--/--R	-/33	Birmingham 527	BaMMOT, Wythall
OD 5489	Vauxhall	Cadet VY	17180	Mount Pleasant		B--	8/33	Davies, Rockbeare	Shears C, Winkleigh
				(body new -/46)					
OD 5868	Leyland	Lion LT5	2605	Weymann	W953	B31F	6/33	Devon General 68	Shears C, Winkleigh
OD 7497	AEC	Regent	O6612445	Short		O31/24R	1/34	Devon General DR210	Greet, Broadhempston
OD 7500	AEC	Regent	O6612448	Brush		H30/26R	1/34	Devon General DR213	Shorland, Exeter
				(rebodied -/49)					
OJ 9347	Morris-Commercial	Dictator	131H	Metro-Cammell		B--F	5/33	Birmingham 47	Aston Manor Road Transport Museum
OP 237		*body only*		Short		H--/--R	-/26	Birmingham 208	Shaw, Warley
OP 3655	AEC	S	507095	*chassis only*			-/27	Birmingham 215	Shaw, Warley
		(may have either Brush or Biuckingham H—body)							
OT 8283	Dennis	F	80052	*chassis only*			4/28	Aldershot & District D210	Aldershot & District Omnibuses Rescue & Restoration Society
		(rebuilt to Dennis E specification 3/32)							
OT 8592	Dennis	E	17448	Strachan & Brown	J2477	B--R	5/28	Aldershot & District D217	Aldershot & District Omnibuses Rescue & Restoration Society
OT 8898	Dennis	E	17483	Strachan & Brown		B--R	6/28	Aldershot & District D226	Aldershot & District Omnibuses Rescue & Restoration Society
OT 8902	Dennis	E	17507	Dennis		B--R	6/28	Aldershot & District D235	Aldershot & District Omnibuses Rescue & Restoration Society
OT 9698	Morris-Commercial	1-ton	17100T	Morris		B10	-/28	estate bus	Jordan, Chelmsford
OU 7352	Ford	AA	3950684	?		B12	1/31	estate bus	Crockett, Nonington
OU 7951	Tilling Stevens	Express B10A2	6953	*chassis only*			6/31	Aldershot & District TS15	Newman, Maidstone
OU 9286	Dennis	30cwt	56455	Short		B18F	8/31	King Alfred, Winchester	FoKAB, Winchester
		(ex TP 6404, OU 9286)							
OV 4090	Morris-Commercial	Dictator	097H	Metro-Cammell		B34F	-/31	Birmingham 90	BaMMOT, Wythall
OV 4486	AEC	Regent	6611648	Metro-Cammell		H27/21R	12/31	Birmingham 486	BaMMOT, Wythall
OZ 6686	Daimler	CVG6DD	18118	Harkness		H30/26R	10/53	Belfast 432	Transport Museum Society of Ireland
OZ 6700	Daimler	CVG6DD	18132	Harkness		H30/26R	11/53	Belfast 446	Miller, Ballyclare
PP 8805	Morris Commercial	D	371SW	Morgan (Leighton Buzzard)		B12	-/26	estate bus	Myreton Motor Museum, Aberlady
				(bodied as a bus -/28)					
PS 1805	Austin	K2SL	135527	Federated Industries		C20F	6/49	Watt, Reawick	Dudding, St Mary's Bay
PS 2001	→ see YSK 763								

Registration	Chassis	Chassis no	Body	Body no	Layout	New	First operator	Current owner
PT 2053	Daimler CJK22	4268	Robson(?)		B20F	1/24	Baker, Quarrington Hill	Sullivan & Greaves, Annitsford
								(*operates as Greaves, Annitsford (TW)*)
PU 8156	AEC YC	9277	Dodson(?)		B31R	-/18	National 2226	Doggett P, Purley
PV 9371	Bedford OB	109693	Duple	48307	C27F	7/49	Mulley, Ixworth	Ipswich Transport Museum
PW 8605	ADC 415	415078	United		B--F	9/26	United E61	Sutcliffe & Weatherhead, Totternhoe
PY 6170	Morris-Commercial 15.9hp	525	?		ch16	-/26	Robinson, Scarborough	Buckingham, West Bridgford
PZ 4874	Leyland Tiger Cub PSUC1/5	534683	Saunders-Roe	-?-	B44F	-/54	UTA H301	Sherry, Ballinderry
RA 3829	Albion SpPB24	4247G	?		B??	8/27	Duke of Devonshire	Smith, Leeds
RA 7589	Austin 20	11986	?		B??	-/28	estate bus	Rushton, Chertsey
RB 4757	Commer Centaur	46038	Reeve & Kenning		B14D	3/32	Fox, Alfreton	Golcar Transport Museum, Huddersfield
			(*new with -/29 body*)					
RB 5509	Morris-Commercial Dictator	090H	Metro-Cammell		B32F	3/32	Chesterfield 51	Walmsley, Burnham-on-Crouch
RC 2721	SOS DON	2125	Brush		B--F	7/35	Trent 321	Lincolnshire Vintage Vehicle Society
RC 4248	Daimler COG5	9721	Brush		RV	10/36	Derby 48	Anthony, Burton-on-Trent
RC 4615	AEC Regal	O6622059	Willowbrook	50796	B35F	5/37	Trent 714	BaMMOT, Wythall
			(*rebodied 6/50*)					
RC 6562	Daimler COG5	10574	Brush		TW	9/38	Derby 62	Anthony, Burton-on-Trent
RC 7927	BMMO SON	2884	Trent		B34F	5/40	Trent 417	Trent (DE) A417
			(*replica body -/78*)					
RC 9012	AEC Regal I	O6625055	*chassis only*			11/46	Trent 746	Quantock, Bishops Lydeard (SO)
RD 111	→ see BF 4812							
RD 7127	AEC Regent	O6613647	Park Royal	-?-	L26/26R	7/35	Reading 47	British Trolleybus Society
RG 1173	Albion PMA28	7061B	Walker		B31R	4/30	Aberdeen 79	Aberdeen & District Transport Preservation Trust
	(ex TSK 716, RG 1173)							
RH 206	Leyland Tiger TS2	60930	Ransomes	1134	C26R	6/30	East Yorkshire 157	Bluebird Vehicles, Scarborough
RH 4758	AEC Regal	6621190	*chassis only*			3/32	Hull 8	Hull 245 Group
RL 2727	Thornycroft A1	12377	Carlton		Ch20	12/25	Warner, Tewkesbury	Warner, Tewkesbury
			(*replica body by12/82*)					
RN 7588	Leyland Tiger TS7	6680	Burlingham	-?-	B35F	3/35	Ribble 209	Ribble Vehicle Preservation Trust
			(*rebodied -/49*)					
RN 7824	Leyland Cheetah LZ2	9371	Brush		C31F	6/36	Ribble 1568	Ribble Vehicle Preservation Trust
RN 8622	Leyland Titan TD5	301400	Alexander	3573	L27/26R	3/39	Ribble 2057	Bignell & Butler, Pangbourne
			(*rebodied -/49*)					(*on loan to Ribble Vehicle Preservation Trust*)
RR 3116	Guy BA	2301	*chassis only*			3/26	South Notts 1	-?-, Wolverhampton
RT 2975	Ford T	14394906	replica		B14F	4/27	Bickers, Coddenham	Bickers, Coddenham
			(*replica body by12/00*)					
RT 4539	Dennis 30cwt	53308	replica		T14	5/28	Abbott, Ashfield-cum-Thorpe	-?-, East Yorkshire
			(*replica body -/03*)					
RU 2266	Shelvoke & Drewery Freighter	51:191	*chassis only*			12/25	Bournemouth 9	Shears D, Winkleigh
RU 8678	Leyland Lion LSC3	47819	Leyland		B35F	1/29	Hants & Dorset 268	Scoular, Edinburgh
			(*replacement period body by8/07; original body retained as separate exhibit*)					
RU 8805	AEC Reliance	660021	Beadle		C28R	3/29	Elliott, Bournemouth	Billington, Maidenhead
			(*rebodied 11/35*)					
RV 720	Crossley Condor	90803			RV	10/31	Portsmouth 74	Portsmouth Museums
RV 3411	Leyland Titan TD2	2874	English Electric		RV	7/33	Portsmouth TW1	Portsmouth Museums
	(ex DSV 101, RV 3411)							

	RV 3412	Leyland	Titan TD2	2875	English Electric		RV	7/33	Portsmouth TW2	Dorey, Old Bolingbroke (LI)
	RV 6358	Leyland	Titan TD4	7148	English Electric		CO26/24R	7/35	Portsmouth 5	McFarlane, Sandling
	RV 6360	Leyland	Titan TD4	7150	English Electric		O26/24R	7/35	Portsmouth 6	North West Museum of Transport
	RV 6367	Leyland	Titan TD4	7157	English Electric		O26/24R	7/35	Portsmouth 7	City of Portsmouth Preserved Transport Depot
	RV 6368	Leyland	Titan TD4	7158	English Electric		O26/24R	7/35	Portsmouth 8	Portsmouth Museums
	RX 5577	Leyland	Lion LT1	50776	Brush		B29R	2/30	Thames Valley 215	Pribik, Winnersh
	SB 5348	Guy	Wolf	CFP12560	Martin		C17F	1/37	McConnacher, Ballachulish	Emerton, Nantwich
	SB 8155	Guy	Wolf	FLW42349	Ormac		C20F	7/50	McConnacher, Ballachulish	Niblett, Birmingham
	SJ 1340	Bedford	OB	145785	Duple	56604	C29F	6/51	Gordon, Lamlash	George, Dalgety Bay
	SL 6069	Bedford	SB3	63456	Plaxton	2326	C41F	6/58	Halley, Sauchie	Adam, Dunblane
	SL 7809	Ford	570E	510E66919	Duple	1139/299	C41F	6/61	Gray, Clackmannan	Gray, Clackmannan
	SL 9483	Bedford	SB5	94190	Duple	1170/381	C41F	5/64	Halley, Sauchie	Mackie, Alloa (SE)
	SL 9806	→ see Unregistered Vehicles								
	SN 6524	Ford	BB	5305060	Martin		B14F	1/35	Lawson, Kirkintilloch 62	Mackie, Glasgow
	SO 3740	Leyland	Tiger TS2	60381	Alexander	1116	B32F	11/29	Alexander P36	Pettie, McKerracher & Thomson, Dunfermline
					(rebodied 3/34)					
	SR 1266	Maudslay	Subsidy A	2784	*chassis only*			11/16	Royal Flying Corps	Coventry Transport Museum
					(to receive replica bus body)					
	SS 7376	Bedford	OB	121153	Duple	54209	C29F	11/49	McKinley, Prestonpans	East Yorkshire (EY) 100
			(ex KSU 381, 1949 MN, SS 7376)							
	SS 7486	Bedford	OB	130194	Duple	54879	C29F	2/50	Stark, Dunbar B12	George, Dalgety Bay
	SS 7501	Bedford	OB	132317	Duple	56030	C29F	3/50	Fairbairn, Haddington	George, Dalgety Bay
	ST 2614	Ford	T	3531055	replica		B6	2/21	station bus, Inverness	-?-, Yorkshire
					(replica body new -/??)					
	SV 6009	Ford	TT	9851990	replica		B9	-/24	-?-, USA	-?-, -?-
			(ex -?-)		*(replica body probably new by5/96)*					
	SV 6107	Leyland	Titan TD1	70682	Leyland		L24/24R	1/31	JMT 24	Stanier, Luddesdown
			(ex MJX 222J, J 1199, OV 1175)							
	SV 6354	Ford	T	218868	Pitt (Barton Stacey)		B14	-/14	Dovey, Owslebury	-?-, -?-
			(ex BH 4081)		*(bodied as a bus 6/21)*					
	SV 6820	Ford	TT	13798325	replica		ch??	-/26	-?-, -?-	-?-, Hertfordshire
			(ex -?-)		*(replica body probably new by7/97)*					
	SV 8005	Ford	T	10461442	?		Ch14	9/24	-?-, France	Scott, Windermere
	SV 8236	Morris Commercial	T	9209T	Ritchie		Ch12	-/26	-?-, -?-	Ritchie C, Hetton-le-Hole
			(ex TY 7368)		*(replica body begun by Charlton & completed by Ritchie -/00)*					
	SV 8280	Morris-Commercial	LT	LT1939	?		B??	-/26	-?-, -?-	Matthewson, Thornton Dale (Q)
	SV 8322	Ford	T	10418951	?		B6	-/??	station wagon, USA	Weatherhead, Royston
(r)	SW 8039	Bedford	OB	123682	*chassis only*			3/50	Campbell, Gatehouse of Fleet	Staniforth, Stroud
	SX 7693	Morris	JR	JR12912	Morris		B??	8/52	-?-, -?-	Suds'r'Us, Edinburgh (XSS)
	TE 2896	Leyland	Lion LSC1	46393	Leyland		B--F	2/28	Furness, Dalton	Stokes, West Wellow
	TE 5110	Leyland	Lion LSC3	47446	*chassis only*			-/28	Colne 22	Transport Museum Society of Ireland
	TE 5780	Karrier	WL6	42135	English Electric		B32F	11/28	Ashton 8	Golcar Transport Museum, Huddersfield
	TE 7870	Dennis	ES	17654	Wyatt		B29D	-/29	Accrington 57	Buckland, Hacheston (SK)
					(replica body built -/74)					
	TE 8318	Chevrolet	LQ	51377	Spicer		C14D	6/29	Jardine, Morecambe	Lincolnshire Vintage Vehicle Society

Reg	Make	Model	Chassis no	Body	Body no	Layout	New	First operator	Owner
TF 818	Leyland	Lion LT1	50828	Roe	GO1538	B30F	3/30	Lancashire United 202	Lincolnshire Vintage Vehicle Society
		(ex J 4229, TF 818)							
TF 6860	Leyland	Lion LT3	51764	Leyland		B36R	12/31	Rawtenstall 61	Keighley Bus Museum Trust
TH 1451	International Harvester SL-34		41234	Agenda Coachworks		B20F	3/31	Davies, Pencader	Williams, Brecon (CW)
				(replica body built 8/00)					
TJ 836	Dennis	Dart	75794	Duple	3231	C20R	3/33	Entwistle, Morecambe	Alexander Dennis, Guildford
TJ 6760	Leyland	Lion LT5A	5154	Leyland		B32R	10/34	Leyland demonstrator	Calrow, Bolton
TK 617	→ see VW 203								
TL 6863	Ford	78	3261	?		B??	9/37	-?-, -?-	Fisher, Wimborne
TM 9347	Bedford	WHB	100001	Waveney		C14F	8/31	Woodham, Melchbourne	Vauxhall Heritage Centre, Luton
TN 1795	AEC	411	411063	Strachan & Brown		B30F	9/25	Newcastle 64	Webb, Tenbury Wells
TP 6404	→ see OU 9286								
TS 9379	Citroen-Kegresse B2		-?-	-?-		B8	-/29	Bell, Pitlochry	Stewart, Strathmiglo
		(estate bus with tracked rear wheels for grouse shooting parties)							
TV 4949	AEC	Regent	6611707			RV	10/31	Nottingham 509	Notts Vehicle Preservation Society
TV 6749	AEC	Regent	6611857			TW	7/32	Nottingham 503	Cook, Worfield
		(rebuilt to normal control)							
TY 2896	Chevrolet	LM	15767	General Motors		B14	4/27	Storey, Long Horsley	Buxton, Hayes
TY 9608	AEC	Regal	6621331	Strachan		B--R	6/32	Orange, Bedlington 42	Hunter, Leeds
UB 7931	Dennis	Lance	125038			RV	10/31	Leeds 111	Tramway Museum Society
UC 2208	ADC	416A	416821	*chassis only*			3/28	London General AD51	Stagg, Offham
UF 1517	Dennis	30cwt	51600	Short		B19R	6/27	Southdown 517	Amberley Museum
UF 4813	Leyland	Titan TD1	70477	Brush		O27/24RO	6/29	Southdown 813	Southdown (WS) 19913
UF 6473	Leyland	Titan TD1	71414	Leyland		H24/24R	7/30	Southdown 873	Southdown Omnibus Trust
UF 6805	Tilling Stevens Express B10A2		6909	Short		B31R	10/30	Southdown 1205	Southdown Omnibus Trust
UF 7403	Leyland	Titan TD1	71822	*chassis only*			-/31	Southdown 903	-?-, -?-
UF 7407	Leyland	Titan TD1	71826			RV	-/31	Wilts & Dorset 243	Stokes, West Wellow
UF 7428	Leyland	Titan TD1	71981	Short		H26/24R	7/31	Southdown 928	Southdown Omnibus Trust
UF 8837	Leyland	Tiger TS4	1560			RV	7/32	Southdown L2	Hoare, Chepstow (CS)
UL 1771	Bean	30cwt	1753/11/W	Birch		B14R	1/29	Turner, Wandsworth	Best, Bredgar
UM 5137	Morris-Commercial	A	2929T	replica		OB13F	5/26	lorry chassis	-?-, -?-
				(replica body built -/??)					
UO 1477	Austin	SPL	14593	Dowell		T13	3/27	Dagworthy, Sidmouth	Griffiths & Eley, Sidmouth
				(rebodied 3/40 with c1921 body)					
UO 2331	Austin	SPL	14697	Tiverton		B13F	4/27	Dagworthy, Sidmouth	Shears D, Winkleigh
				(rebodied 8/40 with body new c-/34)					
UP 551	SOS	QL	600	replica		B37F	3/28	Northern General 338	North of England Open Air Museum, Beamish
				(replica body -/97)					
UP 2941	Crossley	Hawk	90301	Hosfield		B--F	5/29	Blaydon A, Blaydon	Farrall, Chester
US 6798	Albion	SpLB41	14183D	?		B14F	6/34	Glasgow convent	Jones, Andreas
									(in the care of Farrall, Chester)
UT 7836	Gilford	AS6	11542	Willowbrook	2466	B20F	10/30	Whetton, Coalville	Sargent, Henley
UU 6646	AEC	Regal	662058	LGOC	10253	B29R	12/29	London General T31	London Bus Preservation Trust
UY 6596	Thornycroft A2/FB4		18660	United		B28D	10/29	Worcester College for the Blind	Longden, Frodsham
				(rebodied by6/96 with body new -/28)					
UZ 318	Leyland	Tiger Cub PSUC1/5	566128	UTA		B43F	11/56	UTA 318	Bell, Belfast
UZ 334	Leyland	Tiger Cub PSUC1/5	567037	UTA		B43F	12/56	UTA 334	Poots, Tandragee

	Reg	Make	Model	Chassis no	Body	Body no	Layout	New	First owner	Current owner
	VA 5777	AEC	Renown	413149	Metcalfe		B25R	12/26	GOC, Hamilton 22	Saunders, Lower Stondon
	VD 3433	Leyland	Lion LT5A	3697	Alexander	2992	B34F	7/34	Alexander P721	Pettie, Dunfermline
					(rebodied 11/45)					
	VE 4201	Leyland	Titan TD1	71529	ECW	5906	H--/--R	9/30	Eastern Counties A19	Deeks, -?-
					(rebodied 4/39)					
	VF 2788	ADC	425A	425098	Eastern Counties	3362	B36R	6/28	Eastern Counties J9	Ipswich Transport Museum
					(rebodied 12/34)					
	VF 6618	Chevrolet	LQ	55772	Bush & Twiddy		C14F	7/29	Reynolds, Overstrand	Banfield, Staplehurst
	VF 8157	Chevrolet	LQ	57441	Bush & Twiddy		C14D	3/30	Final, Hockwold	Ipswich Transport Museum
					(rebodied with body new 7/30)					
	VG 5541	Bristol	GJW	G113	Weymann	C564	O28/26R	6/33	Norwich Omnibus 43	Burdett, Corley
	VH 2088	Karrier	ZA	ZA30461	?		B14F	3/29	-?-, -?-	Golcar Transport Museum, Huddersfield
	VH 6217	AEC	Regent	661289			TW	-/34	Bournemouth 12	Hearn, Bideford
	VK 5401	Dodge	UF30A	8343143	Robson		B14F	9/31	Baty, Rookhope	VK Club, Prudhoe-on-Tyne
	VL 1263	Leyland	Lion LT1	50320	Applewhite		B33R	7/29	Lincoln 5	Lincolnshire Vintage Vehicle Society
	VO 6806	AEC	Regal	6621015	Cravens		B32F	11/31	Red Bus, Mansfield	Science Museum, Wroughton
	VO 8846	Leyland	Lion LT5	1669	Willowbrook	2584	DP32F	1/33	South Notts 17	Nottingham Transport Heritage Centre
	VR 5742	Leyland	Tiger TS2	60858	Manchester CTD		B30R	-/30	Manchester 28	Museum of Transport, Manchester
	VV 5696	Bristol	JO5G	JO5G389	ECW	3069	B35R	3/37	United Counties 450	Chelveston Preservation Society
					(rebodied -/49)					
(r)	VV 7255	Bristol	L5G	46122	*chassis only*			11/38	United Counties 490	Ipswich Transport Museum
	VV 8934	Daimler	CWD6	12186	Duple	40610	H30/26R	6/45	Northampton 129	Childs et al, Lincoln
(r)	VV 9141	Crossley	DD42/3	93287	Roe	GO2226	H--/--R	11/46	Northampton 141	Jackson & Melia, Wormingford
	VV 9142	Crossley	DD42/3	93289	Roe	GO2222	H31/25R	11/46	Northampton 142	Haining, Dalkeith
	VV 9145	Crossley	DD42/3	93292	Roe	GO2228	H31/25R	11/46	Northampton 145	Haining, Dalkeith
	VV 9146	Crossley	DD42/3	93293	Roe	GO2229	H31/25R	11/46	Northampton 146	Jackson & Melia, Wormingford
	VW 203	Leyland	Lion LSC3	45896	Mumford		B--R	6/27	National Omnibus & Transport 2407	Thames Valley & Great Western Omnibus Trust
			(displays incorrect registration TK 617 - rebodied 2/36)							
	VW 657	Chevrolet	LM	17143	?		B??	7/27	Furze, Tiptree (as lorry)	Ricketts, Charlton Marshall
					(replica body by3/02)					
	VY 957	Leyland	Lion LSC3	47695	Ribble		B32R	5/29	York 2 / Ribble 296	Ribble (LA) 39957
					(replica body -/84)					

	Reg	Make	Model	Chassis no	Body	Body no	Layout	New	First owner	Current owner
	W 963	Daimler	CJA	4397	Barton		ch22	-/23	Barton	Barton Cherished Vehicle Collection
			(ex NW 7341)		*(body new 5/53)*					
	WF 1029	ADC	416	416097	Bell		B--F	12/27	Bridlington & District	Banfield, Staplehurst
	WG 540	Albion	Valkyrie PW65	16005G	Cowieson		B--F	7/31	Alexander 121	McKerracher, Stirling
	WG 1448	Albion	Valkyrie PW65	16017B	Alexander	927	B34F	12/32	Alexander F55	Mackie, Glasgow
	WG 1620	Gilford	Hera L176S	12185	*chassis only*			5/34	Alexander Y49	Scottish Vintage Bus Museum
	WG 2338	Leyland	Lion LT5B	4072	Burlingham	-?-	B35F	3/34	Alexander P290	McKerracher, Stirling
					(rebodied -/46)					
	WG 2361	→ see SU 5861 *Preserved commercial vehicles on PSV chassis*								
	WG 2365	Leyland	Lion LT5B	4139	Alexander		RV	7/34	Alexander 161	McKerracher, Stirling
	WG 2373	Leyland	Lion LT5B	4126	Burlingham	2363	B35F	8/34	Alexander P169	Jones, Glasgow
					(rebodied 8/47)					
	WG 3260	Leyland	Lion LT5A	6564	Alexander	3000	B--F	3/35	Alexander P705	Pettie, Dunfermline
					(rebodied 12/45)					

	WG 4445	Leyland	Tiger TS7	8807	Alexander	3641	B35F	2/37	Alexander P331	McKerracher, Stirling
					(rebodied 4/49)					
	WG 8107	Leyland	Tiger TS8	300307	Alexander		RV	6/39	Alexander 205	Heathcote, Edinburgh
	WG 8790	Leyland	Tiger TS8	302749	Alexander	2063	B39F	6/39	Alexander P573	Scottish Vintage Bus Museum
	WG 9180	Leyland	Titan TD7	303762	Leyland		L27/26R	3/40	Alexander R266	Pollard & Davis, Scotland
	WG 9754	Leyland	Tiger TS11	307820	Willowbrook	4053	B34F	8/42	Alexander P684	McKerracher, Stirling
	WG 9833	Bedford	OWB	11872	Duple	127/3	C29F	1/43	Alexander W120	Chandler, Elton
					(rebodied -/53)					
	WH 1553	Leyland	Titan TD1	70322	Leyland		L27/24RO	3/29	Bolton 54	Lincolnshire Vintage Vehicle Society
	WP 6114	Commer	Centaur	46269	Carmichael		C20F	6/34	Burnham, Worcester	Emerton, Nantwich
	WS 4522	Leyland	TS7	7223	Cowieson		B--R	8/35	SMT H110	Pettie, Dunfermline
					(body new 6/34 ex FS 8584 c12/04)					
	WS 5169	Bedford	WLB	110087	*chassis only*			7/35	Ord, Alnwick	Matthews, Bellingdon
	WT 9156	Karrier	JH	10187	Strachan & Brown		B??F	-/25	Premier, Keighley	Golcar Transport Museum, Huddersfield
	WV 1209	Bedford	WLB	108517	Waveney		B20F	5/32	Alexander, Devizes	Ipswich Transport Museum
	WW 4271	Tilling Stevens	Express B10A	5586	Tilling		B31R	-/28	West Yorkshire 228	Butler, Harrietsham
	WX 2658	Dennis	30cwt	55259	Short		B16F	10/29	Jackson, Westgate-on-Sea	Emerton, Nantwich
			(ex AJM 26A, KR 66)							
	WX 3567	Gilford	168SD	11272	Fielding & Bottomley		C26D	3/30	Oade, Heckmondwike	Jones & King, Kessingland
	WX 9288	Garner	-?-	632583	Jenings		B12F	-/25	estate bus	Shipley, Scunthorpe
	WZ 659	Leyland	Titan PD2/10C	473501	UTA/Metro-Cammell		H32/28RD	-/48	UTA 659	Miller, Ballyclare
	XA 2802	Rolls Royce	Silver Ghost	5UB	Salmons (Newport Pagnell)		B14	-/14	estate bus	-?-, -?-
					(body new -/30)					
	XC 8025	AEC	K	20221	*chassis/body remains*			-/20	London General K414	Doggett P, Purley
	XC 8059	AEC	K	20424	Brush		O24/22RO	11/20	London General K424	London Transport Museum
	XC 8117	AEC	K	20502	Short		O24/22RO	6/20	London General K502	Weatherhead, Woburn Sands
					(body probably new -/25)					
	XG 9304	Leyland	Titan PD1A	462995	Northern Counties	4078	L27/26R	6/47	Middlesbrough 52	-?-, -?-
	XH 9297	→ see CD 4867								
	XH 9298	Tilling Stevens	TS3A	2551	*chassis only*			5/22	Tilling 929	Banfield, Staplehurst
	XL 1204	Tilling Stevens	TS3A	2559	replica		O22/26RO	7/22	Tilling 935	Banfield, Staplehurst
					(replica body by12/96)					
	XL 8940	AEC	S	21687	LGOC		B--R	10/22	London General S433	Weatherhead, Woburn Sands
	XL 8962	AEC	S	21708	Dodson		O28/26RO	10/22	London General S454	Banfield, Staplehurst
	XM 7399	AEC	S	21996	Ransomes		O28/26RO	4/23	London General S742	London Transport Museum
	XO 1038	AEC	NS	22293	*chassis only*			3/23	London General NS1414	London Bus Preservation Trust
			(may be NS174 : XO 1048)							
(r)	XO 7696	AEC	NS	22673	*chassis only*			3/23	London General NS524	London Bus Preservation Trust
	XR 9961	AEC	K	20571	LGOC		O--/--RO	5/24	London General K1077	Banfield, Staplehurst
	XU 7498	Leyland	LB5	12920	Dodson	7072	O26/22RO	8/24	Chocolate Express B6	Sutcliffe, Totternhoe
	XW 9892	Tilling Stevens	TS7	3421	Tilling		B30R	10/25	Tilling	Weatherhead, Woburn Sands
	XX 9591	Dennis	3-ton	40347	Dodson		O26/22RO	4/25	London Public D142	London Bus Preservation Trust
	YC 37	Graham	?	-?-	Fay		B15F	-/27	Pearce, Yatton	Ferguson, Avening
	YD 3193	Bedford	WLB	108107	Willowbrook		C20F	10/31	Hanks, Bishops Lydeard	Chivers, Shirley
					(body may be Waveney)					

	YD 9533	Dennis	Ace	200178	Dennis		B20F	5/34	Sully, Ilminster	Newton, Aylesford
	YF 714	Guy	FBB	22251	Vickers		B35R	3/27	Great Western Railway 1268	Thames Valley & Great Western Omnibus Trust
	YG 7831	Leyland	Tiger TS6	4829	Northern Counties		RV	6/34	Todmorden 15	Sutcliffe, Totternhoe
(r)	YH 1173	AEC	409	409112	*chassis only*			1/27	BAT (British) 527	London Bus Preservation Trust
	YL 740	Morris-Commercial	1-ton	11731	replica		Ch14	-/25	-?-, -?-	Chew, Cookham
					(replica body built -/84)					
(r)	YN 3772	AEC	NS	24020	*chassis/body remains*			7/26	London General NS1849	London Bus Preservation Trust
	YR 3844	AEC	NS	24191	LGOC	9637	H28/24RO	2/27	London General NS1995	London Transport Museum
	YT 33	Rolls Royce	Silver Ghost	89RM	-?-		B??	-/24	Sir Mallaby-Deeley, Mitcham	-?-, -?-
			(ex PD 3078)				*(rebodied -/63 with body of unknown date)*			
	YT 3738	Leyland	Lioness LC1	45932	Leyland		C26F	7/27	King George V	Gresty, Northwich
			(ex J 8462, YT 3738)		*(rebuilt by Thurgood -/38)*					
	AAA 756	Albion	Victor PK114	24001C	Abbott		C20C	6/35	King Alfred , Winchester	Hurley D, Worthing
	AAX 27	Leyland	Beaver TSC9	5548	*chassis only*			7/35	West Monmouthshire 13	Hoare, Chepstow (CS)
	ABH 358	Leyland	Cub KP3	1303	Duple	3452	C20F	5/33	Oborne, Aylesbury	Emerton, Nantwich
	ABL 766	Leyland	Titan TD4	12614	Brush		L55R	2/37	Thames Valley 336	Green, Reading
	ABR 433	Crossley	DD42/4	94838	Crossley		H--/--R	3/49	Sunderland 100	Buckley & Minto, Newcastle-upon-Tyne
	ACB 902	Guy	Arab II	FD28338	Northern Coachbuilders		H--/--R	3/47	Blackburn 74	Blackman, Halifax
	ACB 904	Guy	Arab II	FD28341	Northern Coachbuilders		RV	3/47	Blackburn 502	Parry Roberts & Williams, Heswall
	ACC 88	Bedford	OB	108625	Duple	49225	C29F	6/49	Davies & Jones, Deiniolen	McAlinden, Winsford
	ACC 629	Bedford	OB	131392	Duple	55471	C29F	3/50	Penmaenmawr Motor Company	Bibby, Ingleton (NY)
			(ex TRN 618A, ACC 629, J 3617, ACC 629)							
	ACC 712	→ see Unregistered Vehicles								
	ACH 441	AEC	Regal III	O682012	Windover	6790	C32F	4/48	Trent 611	Quantock, Bishops Lydeard (SO)
	ACH 627	Daimler	CVD6DD	13537	Brush		H30/26R	11/47	Derby 27	Clark & Benson, Derby
	ACK 796	Guy	Arab II	FD26592	Northern Counties	3550	L27/26R	3/44	Ribble 2413	Ribble Vehicle Preservation Trust
	ACW 645	Leyland	Titan PD2/1	494246	Leyland		H30/26R	1/50	Burnley Colne & Nelson 63	Hanson, Padiham
	ADR 813	Leyland	Titan TD5c	15945	Leyland		L27/26R	1/38	Plymouth 141	Shears C, Winkleigh
					(rebodied -/53)					
	ADV 128	Bristol	JO5G	JO5G128	Beadle		B--R	2/36	Western National 222	Cook, Exeter
					(rebodied 9/49)					
	ADX 1	AEC	Regent III	9612E4633	Park Royal	B34240	H30/26R	5/50	Ipswich 1	Ipswich Transport Museum
	AEK 514	Leyland	Royal Tiger PSU1/13	530812	Northern Counties	4762	B44F	9/53	Wigan 101	-?-, Manchester
	AEK 516	Leyland	Royal Tiger PSU1/13	530814	Northern Counties	4764	B43F	9/53	Wigan 103	Collier, Lattimore & Whipperly, Ince
	AEP 849	Bedford	OB	98950	Duple	43776	C--F	2/49	Owen, Berriew	Kinchin-Smith, Banbury
			(ex 159 GMO, AEP 849)							
	AFT 930	Leyland	Titan PD3/4	580546	Metro-Cammell		H41/32R	6/58	Tynemouth 230	Hines, Seaburn
	AFY 971	Leyland	Titan TD3	4997	English Electric		O26/25R	11/34	Southport 43	North West Museum of Transport
	AGX 520	AEC	Regent	6612314	Chalmers		van	6/33	London Transport 738J	Stagg, Offham
	AHA 582	SOS	DON	2065	Brush		B36F	-/35	BMMO 1703	BaMMOT, Wythall
	AHC 411	AEC	Regal III	6821A532	East Lancs	4605	DP30R	7/50	Eastbourne 11	Eastbourne (ES) 39911
	AHC 442	AEC	Regent III	9613A5636	Bruce		H30/26R	11/50	Eastbourne 42	Eastbourne Regent Preservation Group
	AHE 163	Leyland	Titan PD1	460687	Roe	GO2194	H31/25R	9/46	Yorkshire Traction 726	Milner, Lincoln
	AHF 850	Leyland	Titan PD2/1	500311	Metro-Cammell		H30/26R	3/51	Wallasey 54	Greenwood, Birkdale
	AHL 694	Leyland	Tiger PS1/1	462139	Barnaby		B35F	2/47	Bullock, Wakefield 284	Ford, Churston Ferrers (DN)

	AHU 803	Bristol	JO5G	J134	Bristol		B35R	4/34	Bristol 2355	Bristol Vintage Bus Group, Bristol
					(rebodied 6/47)					
	AIG 280	Leyland	Leopard PSU3E/4R	8030336	Alexander (Belfast)	-?-	B53F	6/82	Ulsterbus 280	Thompson, Newtownards
			(ex FEZ 7746, AXI 280)							
	AIG 286	Leyland	Leopard PSU3E/4R	8030380	Alexander (Belfast)	752/11	B53F	7/82	Ulsterbus 286	Nogues, Bangor
			(ex GEZ 8109, AXI 286)							
	AJA 118	Bristol	L5G	4670	Burlingham	4746	B35R	9/38	North Western 364	Preston, Kington
					(rebodied -/50)					
	AJA 132	Bristol	L5G	4684	Burlingham	4754	B35R	3/39	North Western 372	Quantock, Bishops Lydeard (SO)
					(rebodied -/50)					
	AJA 152	Bristol	K5G	49065	Willowbrook	51957	L27/26R	5/39	North Western 432	Pollock & Gaskell, Manchester
					(rebodied -/51)					
	AJB 635	Bedford	WS	100765	Churchill		B11F	4/37	estate bus	Annetts & Porter, Innersdown (HA)
			(ex J 8588, AJB 635)							
	AJC 550	Guy	Wolf	FLW42959	Metalcraft	122	FB24F	6/51	Llandudno	Cookson, Shrewsbury
	AJD 959	Morris-Commercial	CV11/40	51040	Stocker		C16F	7/45	Stocker, St Margarets	Crankshaw, Meltham
					(rebodied -/59 ex van)					
	AJN 825	Bristol	K5G	4787	ECW	6339	L27/26R	3/39	Westcliff-on-Sea Motor Services	825 Preservation Group, Harwich
	AJT 176	Bedford	WTB	3372	Willmott		C20F	5/39	Vincent, Thorncombe	Prosser, Bastonford
	AJX 369	AEC	Regent III	9612E1303	Park Royal	B32980	H33/26R	12/48	Halifax 243	Blackman A, Halifax
(r)	AKN 44	Albion	Victor PHB49	15004E	*chassis*			6/32	Albion demonstrator	Hurley D, Worthing
	AMR 739	Bedford	WS	98913	Churchill		B14F	12/36	estate bus	Dewarth, Silfield
	ANB 851	Crossley	Mancunian	91701	Crossley/Manchester CTD		H--/--R	-/34	Manchester 436	Museum of Transport, Manchester
					(rebodied -/38)					
	ANH 154	Daimler	CVG6DD	13738	Northern Coachbuilders		H30/26R	6/47	Northampton 154	154 Preservation Society, Northampton
	ANW 678	AEC	Regent	6612740	Roe	GO4074	H30/26R	6/34	Leeds 135	Dearnley, Halifax
	ANW 682	AEC	Regent	6612744	Roe	GO4084	H30/26R	9/34	Leeds 139	Keighley Bus Museum Trust
	AOG 638	Daimler	COG5	9271			lorry	1/35	Birmingham 51	Hawketts, Birmingham
	AOG 642	Daimler	COG5	9275			lorry	3/35	Birmingham 3	Thomas, Kidderminster
	AOG 679	Daimler	COG5	9312	Riverlee		van	3/35	Birmingham 83	Aston Manor Road Transport Museum
					(rebodied 2/47)					
	AOW 383	AEC	Regal	6622198	Harrington	711	C33F	-/37	Summerbee, Southampton	Annetts & Porter, Innersdown (HA)
					(rebodied -/50)					
(r)	APV 128	Austin	CXC	175597	Mann Egerton		FC32F	5/52	Norfolk, Nayland	Norfolk, Nayland
	ARA 475	AEC	Q	762028	Willowbrook	2679	C37C	7/34	Woolliscroft, Darley Dale	British Motor Industry Heritage Trust
										(on loan to Armour et al, Derby)
	ARN 392	Leyland	Titan PD1A	460931	Alexander	3032	H30/26R	10/46	Preston 88	Richardson, Thetford
(r)	ARU 179	Leyland	Tiger TS7	7040	*chassis/cab*			4/35	Hants & Dorset F482	Ribble Vehicle Preservation Trust
	ASF 365	Leyland	Tiger TS7	13207	Duple	106/4	C33F	6/37	Alexander P808	Paterson, Dufftown
					(rebodied -/51)					
	ASV 900	Dennis	Lancet III	570J3	Reading	6345	C33F	6/49	Gunn {Safeway}, South Petherton	Gunn, Lopen
			(ex ETP 184)							
	ATD 683	Leyland	Lion LT7	8925	Massey	C927	B32R	12/35	Widnes 39	North West Museum of Transport
	ATF 477	Leyland	Tiger TS7T	9302	Fowler		C39F	4/36	Singleton, Leyland	West of England Transport Collection
	ATS 408	Bedford	OB	86011	Duple	52136	C29F	9/48	Meffan, Kirriemuir	Simpson, Killamarsh
										(*operates as Simpson & Smith, Killamarsh (DE)*)
	ATS 689	→ see ZV 50203 *Ireland*								

	Reg	Make	Model	Chassis no	Body	Body no	Layout	New	First operator	Owner
	ATT 922	Bristol	JJW6A	JJW208	Beadle		B35R	8/35	Western National 172	Cook, Exeter
					(rebodied 5/49)					
	AUF 666	Leyland	Titan TD3	4731	Beadle		H54R	6/34	Southdown 966	Newman, Ryde
					(rebodied 5/49)					
	AUF 670	Leyland	Titan TD3	4909	East Lancs	-?-	H26/26R	7/34	Southdown 970	Hawketts, Birmingham
					(rebodied -/46)					
	AUI 4122	→ see IH 408 *Ireland*								
	AUX 296	Gilford-HSG		H1502	Cowieson		B32R	1/39	Sentinel demonstrator	-?-, Cheshire
	AWG 393	Guy	Arab III	FD35970	Cravens		H30/26R	5/48	Alexander RO607	Pettie, Dunfermline
	AWG 623	AEC	Regal I	O6625340	Alexander	3313	C31F	8/47	Alexander A36	Mitchell & Souter, Bridge of Allan
	AWG 639	AEC	Regal I	O6625476	Alexander		C35F	5/47	Alexander A52	Mitchell, Huddersfield
	AWS 965	Bedford	BYC	844072	?		B8	6/37	estate bus	Harris, Croydon
	AXI 280	→ see AIG 280								
	AXI 285	Leyland	Leopard PSU3E/4R	8030379	Alexander (Belfast)	752/10	B53F	6/82	Ulsterbus 285	Dixon, Waringstown
	AXI 286	→ see AIG 286								
	AXI 319	→ see GEZ 8118								
	AXI 2259	Leyland	PSU3E/4R	8030829	Wright	B147	C49F	9/82	Ulsterbus 259	Irish Transport Heritage
	AXI 2531	→ see 84-C-3716 *Ireland*								
	AXI 2533	Bristol	RELL6G	RELL-3-2690	Alexander (Belfast)	753/4	B45F	5/82	Citybus 2533	Graham, Kesh
	AXI 2534	Bristol	RELL6G	RELL-3-2691	Alexander (Belfast)	753/7	B45F	6/82	Citybus 2534	Hussey et al, Basingstoke
	AXI 2538	→ see 84-DL-2360 *Ireland*								
	AXI 2539	Bristol	RELL6G	RELL-3-2696	Alexander (Belfast)	753/10	B48F	4/84	Citybus 2539	Nash, Ockley
			(ex 84-DL-2356 *Ireland,* AXI 2539)							
	AXI 2542	Bristol	RELL6G	RELL-3-2699	Alexander (Belfast)	753/13	B45F	10/82	Citybus 2542	Transport Museum Society of Ireland
	AXI 2547	Bristol	RELL6G	RELL-3-2704	Alexander (Belfast)	753/17	B16F	9/84	Citybus 2547	Menagh, Belfast
			(ex 84-DL-2363 *Ireland,* AXI 2547)							
	AXI 2548	Bristol	RELL6G	RELL-3-2705	Alexander (Belfast)	753/19	B45F	2/83	Citybus 2548	Richman, Kidsgrove
(r)	AXI 2551	Bristol	RELL6G	RELL-3-2708	Alexander (Belfast	753/24	B45F	11/83	Citybus 2551	Stroud RE Group
	AXJ 857	Leyland	Titan TD3	5349	*chassis only*			-/34	Manchester 526	Museum of Transport, Manchester
	AXM 649	AEC	Regent	6612610	Chalmers		van	4/34	London Transport 830J	London Transport Museum
					(rebodied 3/50)					
	AXM 693	AEC	Regent	6612661	LPTB	14503	H30/26R	6/34	London Transport STL441	London Bus Preservation Trust
	AYH 93	Maudslay ML3		5152	*chassis only*			-/34	Lewis, Greenwich	York, Cogenhoe
	AYJ 379	Daimler	CVD6DD	15892	Croft		H30/26R	9/49	Dundee 127	Dundee City Council
	AYJ 666	Bedford	OB	131963	Duple	56016	C29F	3/50	Fyffe, Dundee	McNeill, Todmorden
	AYV 651	AEC	Regent	6612789	LPTB	14252	H30/26R	7/34	London Transport STL469	London Transport Museum
	BAS 287	Leyland	Atlantean PDR1/1	591704	Metro-Cammell		H44/31F	5/60	Hull 142	Mould, Chase Terrace
			(ex 6342 KH)							
	BBA 560	AEC	Regent	O6616609	Park Royal	-?-	H26/22R	12/39	Salford 235	Museum of Transport, Manchester
	BBW 291	Bedford	OWB	10568	Duple	31827	B32F	12/42	House, Watlington	Wilks, Lincoln
	BBZ 6818	Leyland-DAB	07-1735B2220SY	8500203	DAB		ADP67D	8/85	South Yorkshire PTE 2013	South Yorkshire Transport Trust
			(ex C113 HDT)							
	BCB 340	→ see EAS 956								
	BCB 341	Leyland	Tiger PS1	472994	Crossley		B32F	-/48	Blackburn 8	Young, Faversham
	BCF 802	Austin	CXB	115176	Plaxton	539	C29F	12/48	Beeston, Hadleigh	Munson, Hadleigh
	BCP 671	AEC	Regent III	9612E5018	Park Royal	B34233	H33/26R	3/50	Halifax 277	Blackman, Halifax (WY)

	Reg	Chassis make	Model	Chassis no	Body	Body no	Layout	New	First operator	Owner
	BDF 273	Bedford	WTB	110741	Willmott		C26R	9/36	Dingle, Quenington	Higgs, Cheltenham
	BDJ 67	AEC	Regent III	O9615608	Park Royal	B34500	H30/26R	6/50	St Helens D67	Scottish Vintage Bus Museum
	BDJ 807	AEC	Regent III	O9617137	Park Royal	B35158	H30/26RD	1/52	St Helens D7	Fowler, Burntwood
(r)	BDJ 808	AEC	Regent III	O9617138	Park Royal	B35159	RV	1/52	Harper, Heath Hayes 10	Aire Valley Transport Group
	BEN 177	AEC	Regent III	9613S2696	Weymann	M4430	H30/26R	10/52	Bury 177	Stubbins, Rawtenstall
	BEP 882	Bedford	OB	144844	Duple	54165	B29F	3/51	Mid Wales, Newtown	Owen, Yateley
	BFE 419	Leyland	Titan TD7	306844	Roe	GO562	H31/25R	2/41	Lincoln 64	Lincolnshire Vintage Vehicle Society
	BFM 144	Leyland	Tiger TS7	12352	ECW	4568	B32F	4/37	Crosville KA27	Moores, Diseworth
(r)	BGA 97	Daimler	COG6	10144	*chassis/cab*			1/38	Glasgow 531	Slater, Wideopen
	BGV 845	Bedford	OB	112837	Duple	54251	C29F	8/49	Norfolk, Nayland	Wootton, Great Horwood
	BHE 442	Leyland	Tiger PS1	480991	replica		B32F	4/49	Yorkshire Traction 781	Batley, Scholes
					(replica body built -/??)					
	BHG 755	Leyland	Tiger PS2/14	531167	East Lancs	4957	B39F	12/53	Burnley Colne & Nelson 36	Bensted, Dagenham
	BHG 756	Leyland	Tiger PS2/14	531168	East Lancs	4955	B39F	-/53	Burnley Colne & Nelson 37	Kirkup, Burnley
	BHL 682	Leyland	Titan PD2/1	483605	Leyland		L27/26R	10/48	West Riding 640	West Riding Omnibus Preservation Society
	BHN 254	Bristol	JO5G	JO5G190	*chassis only*			-/36	United BJO59	Hunter, Leeds
	BIL 763	→ see YJI 9932								
	BJA 425	Bristol	L5G	61096	Willowbrook	52056	B38R	12/46	North Western 922	Museum of Transport, Manchester
					(rebodied -/58 with body new -/52)					
	BJA 441	Bristol	L5G	63034	*chassis/cab*			-/47	North Western 141	Staniforth, Stroud
	BJA 442	Bristol	L5G	63035	ECW	1470	B--R	5/47	North Western 142	Marsh & Pixton, Stockport
	BJV 590	Bedford	OB	142125	Duple	44991	C24F	8/50	Blackburn, Grimsby	Taw & Torridge, Merton (DN)
	BKZ 2460	Leyland	Tiger TRCTL11/2R (ex RMO 202Y)	8201600	Plaxton	8311LTP1X514	C53F	3/83	Reading 202	-?-, Skelton
	BMS 206	Leyland	Tiger PS1	471459	Alexander	3329	C35F	9/47	Alexander PA44	Ainsworth, Great Yarmouth
	BMS 222	Leyland	Royal Tiger PSU1/15	520077	Alexander	4203	C41C	5/52	Alexander PC1	Stagecoach Scotland (SE) 59922
	BMS 405	Daimler	CVD6SD	14512	Burlingham	2873	C33F	3/48	Alexander D10	Tennant, Livingston
	BMS 414	Daimler	CVD6SD	14532	Burlingham	2882	C33F	3/48	Alexander D19	Sargent, Henley
	BMS 415	Daimler	CVD6SD	14525	Burlingham	2883	C33F	3/48	Alexander D20	Duffill, Hatton & Mould, Chase Terrace
	BMS 848	Guy	Arab III	FD32920	Guy		B35F	2/48	Alexander G78	McKerracher, Stirling
	BOI 1392	Leyland	Leopard PSU3A/4R	7004576	Alexander (Belfast)		DP49F	2/71	Ulsterbus 1392	Begley, Lisburn
	BOR 767	AEC	Regent	O6614417	Park Royal	B4409	H30/26R	9/36	Gosport & Fareham 35	Whitaker, Waltham Cross
	BOT 303	Dennis	Lancet II	175251	*chassis only*			5/37	Aldershot & District D452	Aldershot & District Omnibuses Rescue & Restoration Society
	BOW 162	Bristol	L5G (6LW)	461			RV	7/38	Hants & Dorset 9081	Shears & Hearn, Winkleigh
	BOW 169	Bristol	L5G	468			RV	7/38	Wilts & Dorset 9082	Hoare, Chepstow (CS)
	BPV 8	AEC	Regal IV	9822E1594	Park Royal	B36036	B42D	8/53	Ipswich 8	Guess, Byfleet
	BPV 9	AEC	Regal IV	9822E1595	Park Royal	B36037	B40D	8/53	Ipswich 9	Ipswich Transport Museum
	BRM 596	Leyland	Titan TD4	11399	ECW	3898	L27/28R	10/36	Cumberland 291	Quantock, Bishops Lydeard (SO)
					(rebodied -/50)					
	BRN 654	Bedford	OB	67375	Duple	49141	C29F	1/48	Barnes, Preston	Mackirdy, Battersea
	BRS 37	Daimler	CWD6	12210	Duple	40621	H30/26R	7/45	Aberdeen 155	Aberdeen Bus Preservation Society
	BSD 470	Albion	KP71NW	64000B	Scottish Aviation		C30C	-/51	Albion demonstrator	McKerracher, Stirling
					(first licensed 6/52)					
	BTA 59	Dennis	Ace	240037	Eastern Counties	3450	B26F	12/34	Southern National 668	Billington, Maidenhead
	BTB 928	Leyland	Lion LT7c	11383	Leyland		B34R	10/36	Lytham St Annes 34	Lancastrian Transport Trust
	BTF 24	Leyland	Lion LT7c	12116	Leyland		B34R	3/37	Lytham St Annes 44	Higgins W, Tarvin
	BTF 25	Leyland	Titan TD4c	12109	Leyland		FH30/24R	3/37	Lytham St Annes 45	Calrow, Bolton

	Reg	Make	Model	Chassis No	Body	Body No	Layout	Date	First Operator	Current Owner
	BTN 113	Daimler	COS4	8116	Northern Coachbuilders		B--R	5/35	Newcastle 173	Slater, Wideopen
(r)	BTW 488	Dennis	Lancet	170795	*chassis only*			6/35	Eastern National 3549	Hinson, Potterspury
	BUS 181	AEC	Regent	O6616225	Crossley		RV	7/38	Glasgow 615	Glasgow City Council
					(rebodied 3/51)					
	BWG 39	Bedford	OB	73977	SMT		C25F	5/48	Alexander W218	George & Renilson, Dalgety Bay
(r)	BWG 246	Bedford	OB	76466	*chassis only*			7/48	Alexander W231	George & Renilson, Dalgety Bay
(r)	BWG 528	Leyland	Tiger PS1	471311	Alexander	3531	C35F	3/49	Alexander PA123	Quantock, Bishops Lydeard (SO)
	BXD 576	AEC	Q	O762116	BRCW		B35C	9/35	London Transport Q55	London Transport Museum
	BXD 628	Leyland	Cub KPO3	3961	Short		B20F	4/35	London Transport C4	Ensign, Purfleet (EX)
	BXD 661	Leyland	Cub KPO3	3993	Short		B20F	6/35	London Transport C36	Jenner, Offham
(r)	BXD 675	Leyland	Cub KPO3	4012	Short		B20F	7/35	London Transport C50	Jenner, Offham
	BXI 326	→ see MEZ 1493								
	BXI 328	→ see FEZ 8628								
	BXI 333	→ see GEZ 8821								
	BXI 334	Leyland	Leopard PSU3F/4R	8131412	Alexander (Belfast)	750/34	DP49F	6/83	Ulsterbus 334	Haughey, Forkhill
	BXI 337	→ see FEZ 8629								
	BXI 338	Leyland	Leopard PSU3F/4R	8131425	Alexander (Belfast)	750/38	DP49F	9/83	Ulsterbus 338	Kells Transport Museum, Cork
	BXI 339	Leyland	Leopard PSU3F/4R	8131450	Alexander (Belfast)	750/37	DP49F	3/84	Ulsterbus 339	Irish Transport Heritage
	BXI 2563	Bristol	RELL6G	RELL-3-2720	Alexander (Belfast)	780/3	B52F	6/83	Citybus 2563	Nu-Venture, Aylesford (KT)
	BXI 2565	Bristol	RELL6G	RELL-3-2722	Alexander (Belfast)	780/6	B52F	7/83	Citybus 2565	Bartram & Budden, Shanklin
	BXI 2569	→ see 84-DL-2349 *Ireland*								
	BXI 2570	Bristol	RELL6G	RELL-3-2727	Alexander (Belfast)	780/7	B52F	5/84	Citybus 2570	Stewart, Shenfield
			(ex 84-DL-2329 *Ireland*, BXI 2570)							
	BXI 2573	Bristol	RELL6G	RELL-3-2730	Alexander (Belfast)	780/13	B52F	3/84	Citybus 2573	Green Triangle, Atherton (GM)
	BXI 2583	Bristol	RELL6G	RELL-3-2740	Alexander (Belfast)	754/4	B51F	11/82	Ulsterbus 2583	Irish Transport Heritage
	BXI 2588	Bristol	RELL6G	RELL-3-2745	Alexander (Belfast)	754/8	B52F	2/83	Ulsterbus 2588	Tether, Bilston
	BXI 2589	Bristol	RELL6G	RELL-3-2746	Alexander (Belfast)	754/7	B52F	12/82	Ulsterbus 2589	Haughey, Forkhill
	BXI 2590	Bristol	RELL6G	RELL-3-2747	Alexander (Belfast)	754/10	B52F	2/83	Ulsterbus 2590	Carroll, Cardiff
	BXI 2595	→ see 83-DL-1651 *Ireland*								
	BXI 2598	Bristol	RELL6G	RELL-3-2755	Alexander (Belfast)	754/19	B52F	5/83	Ulsterbus 2598	Green Triangle, Atherton (GM)
	BXI 2599	Bristol	RELL6G	RELL-3-2756	Alexander (Belfast)	754/17	B52F	3/83	Ulsterbus 2599	Nash, Ockley
	BXM 568	Bedford	WTL	875523	Duple	5058	C20F	6/35	Blunt, Mitcham	Lodge, High Easter (EX)
			(ex CMN 986, BXM 568)							
	CAH 923	Dennis	Ace	200577	ECW	6686	B20F	1/38	Eastern Counties D3	Ipswich Transport Museum
					(rebodied -/65 with body new 12/41)					
	CAP 229	Bristol	K5G	55069	ECW	6930	CO33/26R	10/40	Brighton Hove & District 6352	Butler, Northampton
	CAP 234	Bristol	K5G	55067	ECW	6929	O30/26R	10/40	Brighton Hove & District 6350	Priddle, Farnham
	CAX 390	Albion	Valkyrie SpPV141	44016H	Duple	2291	C32F	5/38	Red & White 390	Hoare, Chepstow (CS)
	CAZ 3693	Bedford	SB5	DW453282	Plaxton	74SB014	C41F	9/74	Barnes, Aldbourne	Bowyer, Biddulph
			(ex SHR 780N)							
	CBC 921	AEC	Renown	0664277	Northern Counties		H32/32R	3/39	Leicester 329	Leicestershire Museums
	CBR 539	Guy	Arab III	FD71552	Roe	GO3549	H33/25R	12/52	Sunderland 139	North East Bus Preservation Trust
	CBV 431	Guy	Arab III	FD36221	Crossley		H30/26R	7/49	Blackburn 131	Darwen Transport Museum Trust
	CBV 433	Guy	Arab III	FD36222	Crossley		H30/26R	9/49	Blackburn 133	Darwen Transport Museum Trust
(r)	CBV 857	Bedford	OB	116065	*chassis only*			9/49	Barnes, Rishton	Glover, Shirebrook
	CBW 864	Dennis	Lancet III	156J3	Plaxton	602100	FC37F	4/47	Chiltern Queens,Woodcote	Ryan, Farnborough
					(rebodied 8/60)					

	Reg	Chassis	Model	Chassis No	Body	Body No	Layout	Date	First operator	Current owner
	CCB 300	Albion	Victor FT39N	72869A	Duple	54034	C31F	-/50	Cronshaw, Hendon	Leary, Pilsley
	CCB 861	Bedford	OB	144490	Duple	50983	C29F	1/51	Ribblesdale, Blackburn	Golynia & Warnack, Long Melford (SK)
	CCC 596	Guy	Otter	LOD45485P	Roe	GO3851	B25F	4/54	Llandudno	Hughes {Alpine}, Llandudno (CN)
	CCD 940	Leyland	Titan TD4	9276	East Lancs	4610	H--/--R	5/36	Southdown 140	Bluerbird Vehicles, Scarborough
					(rebodied 3/50)					
	CCF 574	Austin	CXB	143819	Mann Egerton		FC31F	2/50	Norfolk, Nayland	Norfolk, Nayland
	CCF 648	Bedford	OB	129693	Duple	55878	C27F	1/50	Theobald, Long Melford	Woodhams, Ryde (IW)
	CCF 669	Bedford	OB	137848	Duple	48972	C29F	6/50	Chambers, Bures	Falmouth Coaches, Falmouth (CO)
	CCF 777	Vulcan	6PF	4517	Dutfield		C29F	3/50	Goldsmith, Sicklesmere	Brewster, Sicklesmere
	CCK 346	Leyland	Titan PD2/3	483409	Leyland		RV	8/48	Alexander Midland ML242	Robbins, Leatherhead
	CCK 359	Leyland	Titan PD2/3	483585	Leyland		L27/26R	9/48	Ribble 2584	Quantock, Bishops Lydeard (SO)
	CCK 368	Leyland	Titan PD2/3	483598	Leyland		RV	9/48	Alexander Midland ML240	Robbins, Leatherhead
	CCK 663	Leyland	Titan PD2/3	493185	Brush		L27/26R	11/49	Ribble 2687	Lancastrian Transport Trust
	CCX 777	Daimler	CWA6	12193	Duple	41151	L27/28R	7/45	Huddersfield 217	Quantock, Bishops Lydeard (SO)
	CCX 801	Guy	Arab II	FD27925	Roe	GO3715	L27/26R	9/45	County 70	East Pennine Transport Group
					(rebodied 9/53)					
	CCZ 5919	Leyland	Leopard PSU3E/4R (ex ROI 107)	7705846	Alexander (Belfast)	360/2	RV	4/78	Ulsterbus 4107	Jurby Transport Museum, Jurby
	CDB 206	Bristol	L5G	79020	Weymann	C9302	B35R	4/50	North Western 206	Burdett, Corley
	CDB 224	Leyland	Titan PD2/1	472868	Leyland		L27/26R	1/48	North Western 224	Pollock & Gaskell, Manchester
	CDH 501	Dennis	Lance II	126097	Park Royal	-?-	H--/--R	12/35	Walsall 110	Hatton, Chase Terrace
	CDJ 878	Leyland	Titan PD2/10	531763	Davies		H--/--R	3/54	St Helens E78	North West Museum of Transport
	CDL 792	Bedford	WTB	18122	Duple	6362	C26F	6/39	Shotter, Brighstone	Woodhams, Ryde (IW)
	CDL 899	Bristol	K5G	51100	ECW	6462	O30/26R	7/39	Southern Vectis 702	Southern Vectis (IW) 602
	CDL 920	Bedford	WTB	20066	Duple	6826	C26F	7/39	Holmes, Cowes	Brett, Guyhirn
	CDR 679	Guy	Arab II	FD26342	Duple	41620	H30/26R	10/43	Plymouth 249	Souter, Perth
					(rebodied by7/01, ex VV 9135 - body new 3/46)					
	CDX 516	AEC	Regent III	9613E7963	Park Royal	B37083	H30/26R	5/54	Ipswich 16	Bedford, Finchley
	CEO 956	Leyland	Titan PD2/40	573471	Park Royal	B33339	H33/28R	10/58	Barrow 169	Hambler, Barrow
	CEO 957	Leyland	Titan PD2/40	573472	Park Royal	B33340	H33/28R	10/58	Barrow 170	Hambler, Barrow
	CFK 340	AEC	Regal III	6821A121	Burlingham	3427	C33F	5/48	Burnham, Worcester	Burdett, Corley
	CFM 354	Leyland	Titan TD5	16366	ECW	5242	L26/26R	2/38	Crosville M52	Peers, Bradford
	CFN 104	Leyland	Tiger PS1/1	471303	Park Royal	B32610	C32R	3/48	East Kent	Jones, High Wycombe
	CFN 121	Dennis	Lancet III	552J3	Park Royal	B33964	B35R	6/49	East Kent	Thompson, Retford *(operates as Sly, Retford (NG))*
	CFN 136	Dennis	Lancet III	236J3	Park Royal	B32641	B35R	7/47	East Kent	Adams, Goudhurst
	CFN 154	Dennis	Lancet III	359J3	Park Royal	B32659	B35R	3/48	East Kent	Hamshere, Guildford
	CFV 851	Bedford	OB	68894	Duple	49151	C29F	3/48	Wood, Blackpool	Payne, Thundersley
	CGJ 188	AEC	Q	O762136	BRCW		B35C	10/35	London Transport Q83	London Bus Preservation Trust
	CHF 565	Leyland	Titan PD2/10	541851	Burlingham	3984	H30/26R	1/56	Wallasey 106	Wirral Borough Council
					(new with body built -/49)					
	CHG 540	Leyland	Tiger PS2/14	540923	East Lancs	5042	B39F	12/54	Burnley Colne & Nelson 40	Townsley, Leeds
	CHG 541	Leyland	Tiger PS2/14	541010	East Lancs	5040	B39F	12/54	Burnley Colne & Nelson 41	-?-, -?-
(r)	CHG 543	Leyland	Tiger PS2/14	541049	*chassis only*			12/54	Burnley Colne & Nelson 43	Heaps, Bradford
	CHG 545	Leyland	Tiger PS2/14	541059	East Lancs	5039	B39F	12/54	Burnley Colne & Nelson 45	Heaps, Bradford
	CHL 687	Bedford	OB	143984	Duple	50570	C--F	8/50	Belle Vue, Wakefield	Chandler, Elton
	CHL 772	Daimler	CVD6SD	17462	Willowbrook	50808	B35F	5/50	Bullock, Wakefield 342	Irvine, Law (SW)
	CIB 9520	Albion	Viking EVK55CL	51798J	Alexander (Belfast)	-?-	B45F	1/78	Southern Education & Library Board	Boyd, Enniskillen

CIL 5626	Leyland	Tiger TRCTL11/3R	8300021	Plaxton	8312LTP1X544	C53F	5/83	United Counties 103	Garnham, Coventry
		(ex NBD 103Y, 8779 KV, NBD 103Y)							
CIW 708	Dennis	Dorchester	SDA807/131	Duple	8366/0414	C53FT	7/84	Hestair Dennis demonstrator	Arnold, Warrington
		(ex A767 HPF)							
CJG 959	Leyland	Titan PD1A	472857	Leyland		L27/26R	12/47	East Kent	East Kent Heritage, Dover
CJP 813	→ see RSJ 422								
CJT 185	Bedford	OB	58446	Duple	44003	C27F	9/47	Gibbs, Beaminster	Witham, Wilden
CJY 299	Leyland	Titan PD1	460583	Roe	GO2154	L27/28R	6/46	Plymouth 89	Greet, Broadhempston
CKE 64	Morris-Commercial	C	508C18324	*chassis only*			7/35	Guildford Hotel, Sandwich	Simmonds, Sussex
CKO 988	Leyland	Titan TD4	9692	Weymann	M610	RV	3/36	Maidstone & District 310	Murphy, Bearwood
CLE 122	Leyland	Cub KPO3	4482	Weymann	M578	B20F	5/36	London Transport C94	London Transport Museum
CLJ 566	Austin	20	-?-	Caseley		T13	-/36	estate bus	Austin, Raunds
				(rebodied c-/65 with prewar body)					
CLX 548	Leyland	Cub SKPZ2	5735	Park Royal	B4190	RC18F	10/36	London Transport C111	Cross, Solihull
CLX 550	Leyland	Cub SKPZ2	5737	Park Royal	B4192	RC--F	10/36	London Transport C113	Rubery, Epsom
CMG 30	Bedford	WLB	110051	Duple	5401	C20R	5/35	Garner, Ealing	Rambler, Hastings (ES)
		(ex JTA 608, CMG 30)							
CMS 9	→ see TSK 736								
CMS 200	Leyland	Tiger PS1	483094	Alexander	3703	C35F	6/49	Alexander PA132	Blair, Paisley
CMS 201	Leyland	Tiger PS1	482844	Alexander	3704	C35F	6/49	Alexander PA133	St Margarets School Transport Society, Aigburth
CMS 371	→ see DRS 198A								
CNH 699	Bristol	KSW6B	84013	ECW	5092	L27/28R	-/52	United Counties 699	Staniforth, Stroud
CNH 860	Bristol	LWL5G	87020	ECW	5396	B39R	3/52	United Counties 860	Brown, Rushden
CNH 861	Bristol	LWL5G	87021	ECW	5397	B39R	-/52	United Counties 861	Salmon, South Benfleet
CNH 862	Bristol	LWL6B	87022	ECW	5398	DP33R	4/52	United Counties 862	Chelveston Preservation Society
COI 919	Leyland	Atlantean PDR2/1	7102448	Alexander (Belfast)	451/8	H48/37F	9/71	Ulsterbus 919	Begley, Lisburn
CRC 911	Crossley	DD42/8A	95309	Brush		H30/26R	2/52	Derby 111	Harpurs, Derby (DE)
CRD 259	AEC	Regent II	O6617940	Park Royal	B32746	L26/24RD	3/47	Reading 65	British Trolleybus Society (Reading Area)
CRG 811	Daimler	CVD6SD	13604	Alexander	5538	B35F	7/47	Aberdeen 11	Mills, Aberdeen
				(rebodied 6/58)					
CRN 79	Leyland	Tiger PS1/1	462445	East Lancs	4164	B34R	6/49	Preston 74	Kidswheels, Liverpool (XMY)
CRN 80	Leyland	Tiger PS1/1	462685	East Lancs	4165	B34R	6/49	Preston 75	Hamer & Morriss, Ravenstonedale (CA)
CRN 984	Leyland	Tiger PS2/5	493029			RV	3/50	Ribble BD3	Higgins W, Tarvin
CRN 993	Leyland	Tiger PS2/5	493202	Burlingham	4304	OB35F	3/50	Southport 12	Glass, Holywell
CRR 819	Leyland	Cub KPZ2	7001	Brush		C20F	1/37	Barton 284	Barton Cherished Vehicle Collection
CRS 834	Daimler	CVD6SD	13608	Walker/ACTD		B31F	7/48	Aberdeen 14	Souter, Bridge of Allan
CSF 226	Leyland	Tiger TS8	302686	Alexander		RV	4/39	Alexander 199	McKerracher, Stirling
CSL 469	Karrier	Q25	91A2444	Reading	-?-	C12F	7/57	Derbyshire Hospitals	Stone, Hungarton
		(ex 600 ERA)							
CSL 498	AEC	Regent III	O9611390	Weymann	W1691	H30/26R	9/48	London Transport RT981	Carousel Buses, High Wycombe (BK)
		(ex JXN 9)							
CSL 643	Bedford	CAV	13227	Martin Walter	UD14146	M9	9/53	non-PSV	Wheeler, Bradford
		(ex NOG 560)							
CSV 253	Leyland	Tiger TRCTL11/3R	8100822	Duple	135/5458	C50FT	8/81	Morris, Pencoed	-?-, Milton Keynes
		(ex LKG 19X)							
CTF 423	Leyland	Tiger TS8	14960	Roe	GO7145	DP30F	4/38	Lancashire United 114	Aire Valley Transport Group
CTP 200	Bedford	OWB	13424	Ulsterbus		B32F	5/44	Portsmouth 170	Working Omnibus Museum Project
				(replica body by3/93)					

	Reg	Make	Model	Chassis no	Body	Body no	Type	New	First operator	Owner
	CTW 210	Dennis	Ace	200442	Dennis		FB20C	1/36	Eastern National 3614	James, Blaenporth
			(ex J 11668, CTW 210)							
	CUF 404	Leyland	Cub KPZ1	5854	Harrington		C20F	7/36	Southdown 4	Stokes, West Wellow
	CUH 856	Leyland	Tiger PS1	471209	ECW	1551	B35R	8/47	Western Welsh 856	856 Trust, Cardiff
	CUT 465	Bedford	OWB	21060	Duple	127/2	C29F	7/44	Jacques, Coalville	Dew, Somersham (CM)
					(rebodied -/52)					
	CVF 842	Bristol	LL5G	48048	ECW	8430	B39R	6/39	Southern National 377	Group 94, Coventry
					(rebuilt & rebodied 11/54)					
	CVF 874	Bristol	L5G	50022	ECW	6280	B35R	8/39	Eastern Counties LL74	Ipswich Transport Museum
	CVP 122	Daimler	COG5	9931	Metro-Cammell		lorry	7/37	Birmingham 12	1685 Group, Birmingham
	CVP 207	Daimler	COG5	10073	Metro-Cammell		H30/24R	11/37	Birmingham 1107	1685 Group, Birmingham
					(rebodied 6/50 with body built in -/39)					
	CVR 760	Crossley	Mancunian	92247	Metro-Cammell/Crossley		H--/--R	11/36	Manchester 558	Shaw, Warley
	CWB 987	Leyland	Titan TD4C	10733	Metro-Cammell		H--/--R	8/36	Crosville M511	Armour, Derby
					(rebodied -/52 with body new -/37)					
	CWG 206	Leyland	Tiger PS1	483215	Alexander	3935	C35F	3/50	Alexander PA164	Crankshaw, Meltham
	CWG 273	Leyland	Tiger PS1	485293	Alexander	3984	C35F	8/50	Alexander PA171	Aberdeen & District Transport Preservation Trust
	CWG 283	→ see DRS 122A								
	CWG 286	Leyland	Tiger PS1	495570	Alexander	3972	C35F	6/50	Alexander PA184	Hamer & Morriss, Ravenstonedale (CA)
	CWH 717	Leyland	Titan PD2/4	483231	Leyland		TW	9/48	Bolton 367	Museum of Transport, Manchester
	CWJ 410	AEC	Regent	O6614433	Weymann	M985	TW	1/37	Sheffield TW58	Tramway Museum Society, Crich
	CWX 671	Bristol	K5G	4723	Roe	GO3063	L27/28R	12/38	Keighley-West Yorkshire K383	Fearnley & Wilde, Harrogate
					(rebodied 4/50)					
	CXX 171	AEC	Regal	O6621997	Weymann	M777	C30F	6/36	London Transport T448	London Bus Preservation Trust
	CXX 457	AEC	Regent	O6614337	Weymann	M628	O--/--F	11/36	London Transport 971J	London Bus Company, Northfleet (KT)
	CYC 476	Morris-Commercial	CS11/30	1023C31884	Real Medland & Wells		B12F	5/37	Jenkins, Goathurst	Cooke, Reepham
					(body may be by Taylor (Cringleford))					
	CYF 663	Daimler	57hp	-?-	Hooper		B8R	-/24	Sandringham Estate	Sandringham Museum
			(first registered c6/36)							
	CYJ 252	AEC	Regent III	9613E7723	Alexander	4349	H32/26R	8/53	Dundee 137	Pettie & Fraser, Dunfermline
	DBE 187	Bristol	K6A	W3173	ECW	1042	H30/26R	-/46	Lincolnshire 661	Milner, Lincoln
	DBL 154	Bristol	K6A	62014	ECW	1180	L27/28R	9/46	Thames Valley 446	Jones, High Wycombe
	DBN 311	Leyland	Titan PD2/4	484778	Leyland		H32/26R	1/49	Bolton 408	Lister, Bolton
	DBN 978	Crossley	SD42/7	98140	Crossley		B32R	9/49	Bolton 8	Oakes-Garnett, Saddleworth
	DBU 246	Leyland	Titan PD1/3	470808	Roe	GO2349	H31/25R	7/47	Oldham 246	Museum of Transport, Manchester
	DBU 889	Bedford	OB	51611	Duple	43842	C27F	6/47	Shearing,Oldham	Golynia & Warnack, Long Melford (SK)
	DBW 613	Bedford	OB	82194	Duple	44185	C29F	7/48	Oliver, Long Hanborough	Oxford Bus Museum Trust
(r)	DCB 305	AEC	Regal IV	9821E1280	*chassis only*			5/52	Ribblesdale, Blackburn 49	Selt, Colchester
	DCC 125	Bedford	SB	37662	Duple	1055/369	C34F	6/55	Williams, Waunfawr	Lloyd-Williams, Fyfield
	DCK 219	Leyland	Titan PD2/3	501756	East Lancs	4666	FCL27/22RD	1/51	Ribble 1248	Souter, Perth
	DCN 83	Beadle-AEC		JCB334	Beadle		C35F	4/54	Northern General 1483	North East Bus Preservation Trust
	DCS 616	Daimler	CVD6DD	16519	Massey	2300	O32/28RD	11/50	A1, Ardrossan	Heathcote, Edinburgh
					(rebodied 3/58)					
	DDG 393	Bedford	WTB	18413	Duple	5914	C26F	6/39	Ellis & Bull, Moreton-in-Marsh	Boath, Norwood Green
	DDL 50	Bristol	K5G	55001	ECW	6685	O30/26R	1/40	Southern Vectis 703	Priddle, Farnham
	DDM 652	Maudslay	Marathon II	60024	Duple	42530	C33F	1/47	Rhyl United, Rhyl	Emerton, Nantwich
					(rebodied -/56 with body new 6/46)					

DDR 414	Leyland	Titan PD1A	463028	Weymann	M3136	L27/26R	11/47	Plymouth 114	Armour, Derby
DDV 446	AEC	Regal rebuild	O6623326	Weymann	M6196	H--/--R	4/39	Devon General DR716	Hulme, Yatton
				(rebuilt and rebodied -/53)					
DED 797	Leyland	Titan PD1	461006	Alexander	3040	H30/26R	11/46	Warrington 18	Arnold, Warrington
DEK 106	Leyland	Titan PD2/20	571197	Massey	2280	H32/26RD	10/57	Wigan 4	Wigan Transport Trust
DFE 383	Guy	Arab III	FD35956	Guy/Park Royal	106/B33419	H31/25R	11/48	Lincoln 23	Lincolnshire Vintage Vehicle Society
DFP 496	Albion	Victor PH115	25026I	Reading	2908	B32F	4/39	Watson, St Martins	Bowring, Lydney
		(ex 653)		*(rebodied -/53)*					
DFV 146	Leyland	Titan PD2/5	492148	Burlingham	3223	FH--/--CD	12/49	Blackpool 246	Lancastrian Transport Trust
DFX 932	Bedford	OB	105190	Mulliner	T397	B28F	5/49	Abbott, Piddletrenthide	Milligan, West Lavant
DFZ 8200	Leyland	Tiger TR2R62V16Z4	TR01163	Alexander (Belfast)	B37.01	B53F	4/92	Ulsterbus 1400	Kells Transport Museum, Cork
		(ex WXI 1400)							
DGS 536	Leyland	Tiger PS1/3	500255	McLennan		C39F	5/51	McLennan, Spittalfield	Martin-Bates, St Madoes
DGS 625	Leyland	Tiger PS1/3	500249	McLennan		C39F	6/51	McLennan, Spittalfield	Stagecoach Scotland (SN) 39925
DHD 177	AEC	Regent V	2LD3RA479	Metro-Cammell		H39/31F	1/59	Yorkshire Woollen 797	Turner, Tingley
DHE 353	Leyland	Royal Tiger PSU1/9	504256	Brush		B43F	5/51	Yorkshire Traction 917	Taylor, Barnsley
DHN 475	Bristol	L5G	48169	ECW	5336	B35R	-/39	United BLO11	Hunter, Leeds
				(rebodied -/47 with body new 4/38)					
DHR 192	Guy	Arab II	FD25969	Weymann	C7905	H30/26R	7/43	Swindon 51	Science Museum, Wroughton
DIB 2407	Albion	Viking EVK55DL	51823A	Alexander (Belfast)	450/2	B45F	5/78	SELB, Northerm Ireland	-?-, -?-
DJF 349	Leyland	Titan PD1	460693	Leyland		H--/--R	12/46	Leicester 248	LNER (GC) Heritage Trust, Ruddington
DJI 3195	Albion	Viking EVK55L	51795H	Alexander (Belfast)	-?-	B53F	11/77	WELB, Northern Ireland	Graham, Kesh
DJP 754	Leyland	Titan PD2/30	581260	Northern Counties	5261	H33/28R	11/58	Wigan 115	Heaton, Stirrup & Wall, Wigan
DJR 264	Bedford	OB	134665	Duple	50084	C29F	4/50	Jordan, Bedlington	Machin, Church Lawton
DJT 376	Bedford	OB	111797	Duple	54270	C27F	7/49	Budden, Wimborne	Wootton, Great Horwood
DJY 945	Leyland	Titan PD2/1	472960	Leyland		L27/26R	1/48	Plymouth 315	Greet, Broadhempston
DJY 965	Crossley	DD42/5	94102	Crossley		L27/26R	4/48	Plymouth 335	Barlow et al, Penarth
DKT 11	Leyland	Tiger TS7	13439	Harrington	753	C32F	6/37	Maidstone & District 553	Peers, Bradford
DKT 16	Leyland	Tiger TS7	13444	Harrington	762	C32F	6/37	Maidstone & District 558	Gibbons, Maidstone
DKT 20	→ see YKT 959B								
DLU 92	AEC	Regent	O6615520	LPTB	91	H30/26R	6/37	London Transport STL2093	Ensign, Purfleet (EX)
				(rebodied 4/49 with body new 3/39)					*(on long term loan from London Bus Preservation Trust)*
DMS 130	AEC	Regal III	6821A512	Alexander	4035	C35F	5/51	Alexander A104	Braga, Lower Dean
DMS 820	Leyland	Tiger OPS2/1	481803	Alexander	4099	C35F	12/51	Alexander PB7	Gascoine, Blackridge
DMS 823	Leyland	Tiger OPS2/1	481806	Alexander	4090	C35F	12/51	Alexander PB10	Davis, Scotland
DNC 599	Leyland	Cub SKPZ2	7080	Burlingham	2687	C27F	3/37	Burnham, Worcester	Field, Dudley
				(rebodied c-/47)					
DNF 204	Crossley	Mancunian	91937	Metro-Cammell/Crossley		B32R	7/37	Manchester 129	Finch, Manchester
DNH 197	Daimler	CVG6DD	15187	Park Royal/Roe	GO3676	H30/26R	12/53	Northampton 197	197 Preservation Group, Northampton
DOD 474	AEC	Regal	O6623452	Weymann	C5577	B35F	2/40	Devon General SR474	Shorland, Exeter
DOD 518	Bristol	L5G	52029	Beadle		B36R	7/40	Western National 333	333 Bus Group, Cheltenham
				(rebodied 4/50)					
DOI 1571	Leyland	Leopard PSU3A/4R	7201586	Alexander (Belfast)	450/41	B53F	6/72	Ulsterbus 1571	Shannon, Newtownards
DPR 518	Seddon	Mk IV	3805	Santus		C30F	12/49	Vincents, Thorncombe	Plant, Brereton
DPT 848	Leyland	Tiger TS8	301322	Roe	GO114	B32F	3/39	Sunderland District 159	Kell, Durham
DPY 335	Leyland	Tiger PS1/1	461229	Plaxton	37	C33F	3/47	Smith, Thirsk	Smith, Thirsk (NY)
DRD 820	Bedford	OB	107763	Duple	44505	C29F	5/49	Smith, Reading	Brett, Guyhirn
DRN 289	Leyland	Titan PD2/3	505598	Leyland		L27/26RD	12/50	Ribble 1349	Ribble Vehicle Preservation Trust

	Reg	Chassis make	Model	Chassis no	Body	Body no	Layout	Date	First owner	Current owner
	DRS 360	→ see WTS 937A								
(r)	DRS 369	Daimler	CVG6DD	16189	*chassis only*			3/51	Aberdeen 169	Mills, Aberdeen
	DSG 169	Leyland	Titan TD5	307829	Leyland		L27/26R	7/42	SMT J66	Pettie & Dawson-Smith, Dunfermline
	DSL 540	AEC	Routemaster	RM1033	Park Royal	L4299	H30/26R	11/61	London Transport RM1033	Comfort, Basingstoke
			(ex 33 CLT)							
	DSL 856	AEC	Reliance	2U3RA4155	Plaxton	728901	C49F	7/62	East Kent	Richards, Guist (NK)
			(ex LAH 817A, 521 FN)		*(rebodied 7/72)*					
	DSV 101	→ see RV 3411								
	DSV 335	→ see 692 AEH								
	DSV 715	Morris-Commercial	PV	PV5929	Reading		C13F	-/49	ice cream van	-?-, -?-
			(ex 43 EBK, ERV 34)							
(r)	DTF 269	Leyland	Tiger TS8	302169	*chassis only*			3/39	Lancashire United 504	Pettie, Dunfermline
	DTJ 58	Leyland	Tiger TS8c	302714	Leyland		B36R	-/39	Rawtenstall 50	Higgins W, Tarvin
	DTP 823	Leyland	Titan PD1	460431	Weymann	M2981	H30/26R	1/48	Portsmouth 189	Working Omnibus Museum Project
	DUD 522	Bedford	OB	104625	Duple	46247	C29F	4/49	Taylor, Bicester	Hunter, Tarleton
	DUF 179	Leyland	Tiger TS7	11973	Harrington		C32R	6/37	Southdown 1179	Ensign, Purfleet (EX)
	DUK 278	Guy	Arab II	FD28083	Roe	GO3353	H31/25R	1/46	Wolverhampton 378	Guy Owners Club / West Midlands Bus Preservation Society
					(rebodied 2/52)					
	DUX 655	Daimler	CVD6SD	13611	Metalcraft	137	FC33F	10/47	Smith, Trench	DUX 655 Group, Hereford
					(rebodied 3/48)					
	DVD 248	Leyland	Titan PD2/1	482835			RV	-/48	Central SMT S26	Ferguson, East Kilbride
	DVH 752	Leyland	Tiger PS1	482939	Roe	GO2664	B32R	12/48	County 73	Batley, Scholes
	DWG 521	Leyland	Royal Tiger PSU1/15	520746	Alexander	4227	C41C	6/52	Alexander PC25	Reid, Newmachar
	DWG 526	Leyland	Royal Tiger PSU1/15	515309	Leyland		C41C	5/52	Alexander PC30	Wallace, Edinburgh
	DWG 917	Leyland	Titan PD2/12	521425	Alexander	4136	L27/26R	6/53	Alexander RB161	Hoare, Chepstow (CS)
	DXI 3341	Leylland	Tiger TRBTL11/2RP	8300591	Alexander (Belfast)	980/2	DP53F	1/84	Ulsterbus 341	Begley, Lisburn
	DXI 3343	Leyland	Tiger TRBTL11/2RP	8300603	Alexander (Belfast)	980/4	DP53F	2/84	Ulsterbus 343	Irish Transport Heritage
	DXI 3363	Leyland	Tiger TRBTL11/2RP	8300697	Alexander (Belfast)	981/3	B53F	6/84	Ulsterbus 363	Shannon, Newtownards
	DXI 3370	Leyland	Tiger TRBLXCT/2RP	8300790	Alexander (Belfast)	980/16	DP53F	6/84	Ulsterbus 370	Nash, Ockley
	DYG 53	Albion	Valkyrie CX13	58023A	Burlingham	3737	C33F	11/41	South Yorkshire 51	H-S Transport Collection, Leeds
					(rebodied -/58 with body new 1/50)					
	EAJ 679	Bedford	OB	68823	Plaxton	698	C29F	2/48	Howard, Whitby	Lockett, Henfield
	EAS 956	Leyland	Tiger PS1	473263	Crossley		B32F	3/48	Blackburn 7	Thomas, Holyhead
			(ex BCB 340)							
	EAV 458	Leyland	Tiger PS1	473433	Duple	48395	C35F	3/48	Sutherland, Peterhead 117	Graveling, Bourne
	EBO 900	Crossley	DD42/7	94855	Alexander	3650	L27/26R	6/49	Cardiff 46	National Museum of Wales
	ECB 687	Bedford	SBG	26685	Yeates	418	C--F	3/54	Ribblesdale, Blackburn 55	Staniforth, Stroud
	ECD 524	Leyland	Cub KPZ2	8377	Park Royal	-?-	B20F	12/37	Southdown 24	Southdown Omnibus Trust
	ECK 179	Leyland	Royal Tiger PSU1/15	511940	Leyland		C41C	10/51	Ribble 899	Hunter, Tarleton
					(rebodied with body ex ECK 147 12/85)					
	ECT 912	Bedford	OB	135037	Duple	43457	C29F	4/50	Sharpe, Heckington	Jones, Llanfaethlu (CN)
	ECX 425	AEC	Regent III	9612E4144	Northern Coachbuilders		L29/26R	6/49	Huddersfield 225	Blackman A, Halifax
	EDB 549	Leyland	Titan PD2/1	510318	Leyland		O28/20R	8/51	Stockport 295	Quantock, Bishops Lydeard (SO)
	EDB 562	Leyland	Titan PD2/1	510445	Leyland		H30/26R	-/51	Stockport 308	Museum of Transport, Manchester
	EDB 575	Crossley	DD42/7	95322	Crossley		H30/26R	-/51	Stockport 321	Museum of Transport, Manchester
	EDL 657	Bristol	K5G	64050	ECW	1722	L27/28R	10/47	Southern Vectis 721	Hunt, Rookley

EDP 757	Bedford	OB	126680	Duple	44507	C15F	2/50	Smith, Reading	Whitehead, Reading
EDT 703	Leyland	Titan PD2/1	472364	Roe	GO4069	H34/28R	11/47	Doncaster 94	Doncaster Omnibus & Light Railway Society
				(rebodied 1/64 with body new -/55)					
EED 5	Leyland	Titan PD1	460995	Alexander	3042	H30/26R	11/46	Warrington 17	Clark, Hull
EED 8	Leyland	Titan PD1	451572	Alexander	3051	H30/26R	2/47	Warrington 38	Hughes R, Warrington
EEL 46	Bedford	WTB	112173	*chassis only*			5/38	Bournemouth 2	Kenzie, Shepreth (CM)
		(ex TAC 480 *Cyprus*, EEL 46)							
EFJ 92	Bedford	WTB	112122	Heaver		C25F	6/38	Taylor, Exeter	West Country Historic Omnibus & Transport Trust
EFJ 241	Leyland	Titan TD5	300639	Leyland		O30/26R	7/38	Exeter 26	Shears C, Winkleigh
EFJ 666	Leyland	Tiger TS8	300628	Cravens		B32R	12/38	Exeter 66	Shears C, Winkleigh
EFM 581	Leyland	Tiger TS8	304015	ECW	6654	B32F	1/40	Crosville KA158	Moores, Diseworth
EFN 182	Guy	Arab III	FD36270	Park Royal	B33475	L27/26R	5/50	East Kent	Jones, Herne Bay
EFN 562	Dennis	Falcon	117P3	Dennis		B--F	3/50	East Kent	Walton, Woore
EFN 568	Dennis	Falcon	132P3	Dennis	39556	B20F	7/50	East Kent	Hamshere, Guildford
EFN 584	Dennis	Lancet III	832J3	Park Royal	B34316	C32F	5/50	East Kent	Thompson, Retford
EFN 592	Dennis	Lancet III	864J3	Park Royal	B34325	C32F	6/50	East Kent	Lead A, Finglesham
EFN 595	Dennis	Lancet III	874J3	Park Royal	B34327	DP32F	6/50	East Kent	Wilkinson, Scarborough
EFV 300	Leyland	Titan PD2/5	502509	Burlingham	4699	FH29/23C	12/51	Blackpool 300	Hinchliffe, Huddersfield
EGA 79	Albion	Venturer CX37S	60103C	Croft		H30/26R	6/49	Glasgow B92	Glasgow City Council
EGO 426	AEC	Regent	O6615804	LPTB	17813	H30/26R	11/37	London Transport STL2377	London Bus Preservation Trust
EHA 775	SOS	SON	2636	*chassis/cab*			-/38	BMMO A2207	Shaw, Warley
EHL 335	Leyland	Tiger PS2/13A	515267	Roe	GO3508	C35F	11/52	West Riding 724	Hudson & Lawson, Bradford
EHL 336	Leyland	Tiger PS2/13A	515268	Roe	GO3509	C35F	11/52	West Riding 725	Burdett, Corley
EHL 344	Leyland	Tiger PS2/12A	520140	Roe	GO3521	B39F	7/52	West Riding 733	West Riding Omnibus Preservation Society
EHO 228	Guy	Arab I	FD25532	Reading	4512	H30/26R	10/42	Gosport & Fareham 55	First Hampshire & Dorset (HA)
				(rebodied -/55)					
EHO 869	Guy	Arab II	FD26207	Reading	1889	CO30/26R	9/43	Gosport & Fareham 57	Provincial Society, Fareham
				(rebodied -/53)					
EHV 65	Bedford	OB	146572	Duple	56061	B29F	2/51	East Ham Education	EHV65 Preservation Group, Portsmouth
EIB 8234	Bristol	LH6L	LH-280	Northern Counties	6957	B39D	1/70	Lancashire United 335	LUT Society
		(ex UTD 298H)							
EJD 510	Bedford	SB	3946	Duple	1006/330	C33F	-/52	Essex County, Stratford	Towler, Emneth (NKp)
EJI 2573	Albion	Viking EVK55DL	51831H	Alexander (Belfast)	564/5	B53F	4/79	WELB, Northerm Ireland	Graham, Kesh
EJN 638	Bristol	LS6G	89032	ECW	5745	C39F	1/53	Westcliff-on-Sea Motor Services	Mahoney I, Brentwood
EJR 791	→ see ZV 2428 *Ireland*								
EKV 966	Daimler	CWA6	11789	Roe	GO3305	H31/25R	8/45	Coventry 366	Coventry Transport Museum
				(rebodied 2/51)					
EKY 558	Leyland	Titan PD2/3	491998	Leyland		H33/26R	7/49	Bradford 558	Welburn, Guiseley
ELP 223	AEC	Regal	O6622646	LPTB	18141	C--F	7/38	London Transport T499	Ensign, Purfleet (EX)
ELP 228	AEC	Regal	O6622651	LPTB	18127	C30F	5/38	London Transport T504	London Bus Preservation Trust
EMW 284	Bristol	L6B	65089	Beadle		C32R	3/49	Wilts & Dorset 279	Tancock, Temple Cloud
		(ex YSV 610, EMW 284)							
EMW 893	Daimler	CVD6SD	13437	Park Royal	B32662	B35C	11/47	Swindon 57	Shears D, Winkleigh
ENG 707	Bristol	L5G	54043			TW	10/42	Eastern Counties X39	Howard & Oliver, Nottingham
ENT 778	Leyland	Tiger PS1	481412	Burlingham	3383	C33F	6/48	Gittins, Crickheath	Lediard, Morpeth
EOI 4857	Daimler	Fleetline CRG6LX-33	66645	Alexander (Belfast)	-?-	H49/37F	1/73	Citybus 2857	Ulster Folk & Transport Museum
				(rebodied 4/76)					
EOO 590	Bristol	Lodekka FLF6G	199146	ECW	13136	H38/32F	9/62	Eastern National 1622	Western Greyhound, Summercourt (CO)

	EOR 875	Guy	Arab II	FD27469	Reading	4907	FH30/26R	4/45	Gosport & Fareham 17	Provincial 17 Group, Fareham
					(rebodied -/58)					
	EPV 24	AEC	Regent III	9613E8261	Park Royal	B39345	H33/28R	7/56	Ipswich 24	Culverwell, Southampton
	ERD 154	Crossley	DD42/8	94932	Crossley		L26/26RD	11/50	Reading 85	Green & Thompson, Reading
	ERG 164	Bedford	OB	145540	Duple	56575	C29F	3/51	Paterson, Aberdeen	Simpson, Killamarsh
	ERN 700	Leyland	Royal Tiger PSU1/13	522281	Leyland		B8FL	10/52	Ribble 377	Ribble Vehicle Preservation Trust
(r)	ERN 709	Leyland	Royal Tiger PSU1/13	522209	Leyland		B44F	11/52	Ribble 386	Ribble Vehicle Preservation Trust
(r)	ERN 723	Leyland	Royal Tiger PSU1/13	522567	*chassis only*			12/52	Ribble 400	Hunter, Tarleton
	ERU 513	Bristol	L5G	48144			RV	3/39	Hants & Dorset 9083	Staniforth, Stroud
	ESG 652	Guy	Arab III	FD29364	Metro-Cammell		B35R	9/48	Edinburgh 739	Pettie, Fraser & Heathcote, Dunfermline
	ESS 989	→ see YYJ 914								
	ESU 912	AEC	Reliance (ex XER 134T)	6U3ZR37347	Plaxton	7912ACM011	C57F	1/79	Miller, Foxton	Harrogate Coach, Green Hammerton (NY)
	ESV 106	Bedford	WS (probably ex CXV 784)	97274	-?-		B??	-/36	estate bus	Cook, Worfield
	ESV 215	Albion	Victor FT39KAN (ex 8230)	73838A	Reading	2365	B35F	4/58	Guernsey Railway 61	Mitcham, Burwell
	ESV 811	AEC	Regal III (ex II-14-49 *Portugal*)	0963428	Weymann /CCFL	M3411	B20D	5/48	Lisbon Electric Tramways 17	Carris AEC Preservation Group, Croydon
	ETA 280	Dennis	Ace	200566	Dennis		B16F	2/37	Hydro Hotel, Torquay	Emerton, Nantwich
	ETJ 108	Leyland	Tiger TS11	306692	Roe	GO498	RV	12/40	Leigh 79	Offley & Abrahams, Dalgety Bay
	ETL 221	Bedford	OB	134198	Plaxton	579	C29F	6/50	Blankley, Colsterworth	Edwards, Llanon
	ETL 373	Bedford	OB	140636	Duple	56260	C29F	8/50	Delaine, Bourne	Atkin, North Owersby
	ETP 184	→ see ASV 900								
	ETS 964	Daimler	CVG6DD	18840	Metro-Cammell		H37/28R	11/55	Dundee 184	Taybus Vintage Vehicle Society
	ETT 946	Bristol	L5G	4313	Beadle		B--R	6/38	Southern National 280	Hague, Kings Nympton
					(rebodied 3/50)					
	ETT 956	Bristol	LL5G	4381	ECW	8427	B39R	6/38	Western National 262	Cotswold PSV Group, Stroud
					(rebuilt & rebodied 8/55)					
	ETT 995	AEC	Regent	O6615343	Saunders-Roe	648	H30/26R	7/37	Devon General DR705	Cope, Longton
					(rebodied -/53)					
	EUF 181	Leyland	Titan TD5	17088			RV	5/38	Southdown 0181	Nicholas, Portsmouth
	EUF 182	Leyland	Titan TD5	17089			RV	5/38	Southdown 0182	Shears D, Winkleigh
	EUF 184	Leyland	Titan TD5	17091			RV	5/38	Southdown 0184	Southdown Omnibus Trust
	EUF 196	Leyland	Titan TD5	17105	Beadle	721	L26/26R	6/38	Southdown 196	Newman, Ryde
	EUF 198	Leyland	Titan TD5	17107			RV	6/38	Southdown 0198	Peers, Bradford
	EUF 204	Leyland	Titan TD5	17584	Park Royal	B33661	H28/26R	7/38	Southdown 204	Blackman A, Halifax
					(rebodied -/49)					
	EUI 530	→ see B11 CTB								
	EUX 959	Commer	Commando	17A0975	Harrington	490	C30F	2/49	Smith, Trench	Emerton, Nantwich
	EVA 324	Guy	Arab III	FD70158	Guy		B33R	6/50	Central SMT K24	Miller, Ballyclare
	EVC 244	Daimler	COG5-40	8558	Park Royal	B5804	B38F	4/40	Coventry 244	Burdett, Corley *(on long term loan from Derby Museums)*
	EVD 406	Crossley	DD42/7	94758	Roe	GO4026	H31/25R	6/49	Wood, Mirfield 20	Quantock, Bishops Lydeard (SO)
					(rebodied 4/55)					
	EVD 580	Leyland	Tiger PS1/1	473258	Plaxton	168	C33F	5/49	Hutchison, Overtown	Snape, Leyland
	EVH 664	Bedford	OB	136406	Duple	50360	C29F	4/50	Chatman, Huddersfield	Hissey, Sale
	EWM 358	Daimler	CWA6	11984	Duple	40557	H30/26RD	2/45	Southport 62	North West Museum of Transport

	Registration	Make	Model	Chassis no.	Body	Body no.	Layout	Date	First owner	Current owner
	EWO 467	Guy	Arab I	FD25519	Bristol		L27/28R	10/42	Red & White 467	Allen, Ross-on-Wye
					(rebodied -/50)					
	EXG 892	Guy	Arab IV	FD72776	Northern Counties	4930	H33/28R	12/55	Middlesbrough 92	Larkin, Peterborough
	EXI 6301	Leyland	Leopard PSU3E/4R	8030722	Duple	133/5160	C53F	3/81	Excelsior, Dinnington	Crosby, Nottingham
			(ex THE 442W, HIL 8670, KWG 131W)							
	EYA 923	Leyland	Cheetah LZ5	201440	Harrington		C31F	3/39	Porlock Blue, Minehead	Clayton, Baynards
	EYE 599	Bedford	WTB	112281	Duple	5165	C25F	5/38	Underwood, Orsett	EYE 599 Restoration Society, Orsett
	EYK 396	AEC	Regent III	O9611144	LPTB	18246	H30/26R	3/49	London Transport RT1	London Bus Preservation Trust
			(chassis ex JXC 183 by5/79)		*(rebodied 6/56 with body new 2/39)*					
	FAE 60	Bristol	L5G	4366			TW	6/38	Bristol W75	Staniforth, Stroud
	FAM 2	Bristol	L6B	71010	Beadle		C32R	6/49	Wilts & Dorset 285	Staniforth, Stroud
(r)	FAP 9	Bedford	OB	122946	Duple	54271	C27F	1/50	Killick & Vincent, Dallington	Gamlen, Pensford
	FAS 982	Albion	Victor FT39KAN	73842F	Reading	2246	B35F	2/58	JMT 5	Graham, Aspatria (CA)
			(ex J 1359)							
	FAV 827	AEC	Regent III	9612E4331	Massey	2020	L27/26RD	9/49	Sutherland, Peterhead 124	McKerracher, Stirling
	FAW 334	Crossley	SD42/7	97797	Plaxton	257	C33F	12/48	Davies, Acton Burnell	Davies, Acton Burnell
	FBG 910	Leyland	Titan PD2/40	571367	Massey	2268	H31/28R	1/58	Birkenhead 10	201 Restoration Group, Wallasey
	FBU 827	Crossley	DD42/8	95306	Crossley		H30/26R	7/50	Oldham 368	Museum of Transport, Manchester
	FCK 844	Leyland	Tiger Cub PSUC1/1	534290	Saunders-Roe	1457	B44F	1/54	Ribble 412	Anglesey Vintage Equipment Society
	FCK 884	Leyland	Tiger Cub PSUC1/1	534968	Saunders-Roe	1497	B44F	3/54	Ribble 452	Ribble Vehicle Preservation Trust
	FDB 500	Atkinson	Alpha PM746H	FC2737	Weymann	M5464	B42R	6/52	North Western 500	Gaskell, Irlam
	FDL 676	Bedford	OB	87567	Duple	50039	C29F	3/49	Southern Vectis 216	Tucker, Boroughbridge
										(on loan to Isle of Wight Bus Museum)
	FDL 842	Bedford	OB	96558	Duple	46338	C29F	1/49	Pearce, Ryde	Dorey, Old Bolingbroke (LI)
	FDM 724	Foden	PVD6	28790	Massey	2018	H30/26R	7/49	Phillips, Holywell	BaMMOT, Wythall
	FDO 573	AEC	Regent III	9613E4332	Willowbrook	53087	H32/28RD	2/53	Camplin, Donington	Milner, Lincoln
	FEA 156	Daimler	CVG5SD	14364	Metro-Cammell		B38R	3/52	West Bromwich 156	156 Group, West Bromwich
	FEF 462	Bedford	SB3	62608	Plaxton	2341	C41F	7/58	Beeline, Hartlepool	Paterson, Dufftown
	FEL 216	Bedford	WTB	16366	Burlingham		DP25F	6/39	Bournemouth 13	Salter, Wareham
(r)	FEL 218	Bedford	WTB	16493	Burlingham		DP25F	6/39	Bournemouth 15	Salter, Wareham
	FEV 178	Leyland	Titan TD5	14438	ECW	3148	L27/26R	7/37	Eastern National 3709	-?-, -?-
					(rebodied 9/49)					
	FEZ 8166	Leyland	Leopard PSU3E/4R	7801709	Alexander (Belfast)	360/17	RV	8/78	Ulsterbus 126	Kells Transport Museum, Cork
			(ex ROI 126)							
	FEZ 8628	Leyland	Leopard PSU3F/4R	8131331	Alexander (Belfast)	750/27	DP49F	12/82	Ulsterbus 328	Graham, Kesh
			(ex BXI 328)							
	FEZ 8629	Leyland	Leopard PSU3F/4R	8131424	Alexander (Belfast)	750/40	DP49F	9/83	Ulsterbus 337	Kells Transport Museum, Cork
			(ex BXI 337)							
	FFN 382	Guy	Arab III	FD70790	Park Royal	B33525	O30/26R	5/51	East Kent	Laming, Ramsgate
	FFN 399	Guy	Arab III	FD70817	Park Royal	B33539	H32/26R	6/51	East Kent	Lead A, Finglesham
	FFN 446	Beadle-Leyland		JCB240	Beadle		C35F	6/51	East Kent	Perry, Southampton
	FFN 451	Leyland	Royal Tiger PSU1/13	505584	Park Royal	B34582	C37C	6/51	East Kent	Hirst, Herne Bay
	FFS 867	Bedford	OB	59326	Burlingham	5511	C24F	11/47	SMT C167	Forsyth, Braidwood
					(rebodied -/53)					
	FFS 871	Bedford	OB	67468	Burlingham	5515	FC--F	2/48	SMT C171	Bluebird Vehicles, Scarborough
					(rebodied -/53)					

FFU 860	AEC	Regal III	9621E439	Willowbrook	9592	DP35F	4/49	Enterprise, Scunthorpe 60	Milner, Lincoln
FFW 830	Bristol	L5G	79097	ECW	4072	B35R	5/50	Lincolnshire 749	Bulmer, North Stainley (NY)
FFX 458	Bedford	MLC	220822	Lee		C14F	4/52	Dorset County Council	Aish, Poole
FFY 401	Leyland	Titan PD2/3	471486	Leyland		O30/26R	11/47	Southport 84	Blackman, Halifax (WY)
FFY 402	Leyland	Titan PD2/3	472246	Leyland		O30/26R	11/47	Southport 85	BaMMOT, Wythall
FFY 403	Leyland	Titan PD2/3	472322	Leyland		O30/26R	11/47	Southport 86	Blackman, Halifax (WY)
FFY 404	Leyland	Titan PD2/3	472323	Leyland		O30/26R	11/47	Southport 87	North West Museum of Transport
FHF 451	Leyland	Atlantean PDR1/1	582372	Metro-Cammell		H44/33F	12/58	Wallasey 1	201 Restoration Group, Wallasey
FHF 456	Leyland	Atlantean PDR1/1	590547	Metro-Cammell		H--/--F	9/59	Wallasey 6	North West Museum of Transport
FHN 833	Bristol	L5G	54080	ECW	6859	B35F	1/41	United BG147	Lincolnshire Vintage Vehicle Society
FHN 923	Bristol	K5G	55018			RV	5/40	United EDO23	Aycliffe & District Bus Preservation Society
FHT 112	Bristol	K5G	45130	ECW	5806	O30/26R	9/38	Bristol C3209	Boughton, Brightwell
FIB 1763	Leyland	National 1151/2R/0401	00189	Leyland National		B48D	11/72	Ribble 372	Ribble Vehicle Preservation Trust
		(ex PTF 718L)							
FJB 267	Bedford	OB	119697	Duple	54859	C29F	12/49	Townsend, Crowthorne	Sleep, Eversley (HA)
FJF 193	Leyland	Titan PD2/1	502647	Leyland		H33/29R	12/50	Leicester 154	Gill, Rugeley
FJJ 764	Leykand	FEC	301690	*chassis only*			6/39	London Transport TF67	London Bus Preservation Trust
FJJ 774	Leyland	FEC	301700	LPTB	55	B34F	7/39	London Transport TF77	London Transport Museum
FJT 86	Bedford	MLC	225739	Lee		B16F	7/52	Dorset County Council	Whittaker, West Bromwich
FJU 818	Crossley	SD42/7	98082	Burlingham	4154	C33F	7/49	Adams,Market Harborough	Hunt, Lavendon
FJW 322	AEC	Rebuild	E36/0/48	Burlingham	3348	C33F	5/48	Everall, Wolverhampton	Quantock, Bishops Lydeard (SO)
FKL 611	Bristol	K5G	4783	Weymann	M904	L24/24R	11/38	Maidstone & District 273	Howe, Polegate
				(new with body built 12/36)					
FKO 223	Leyland	Titan TD5	301873	Weymann	M1745	H28/26R	6/39	Maidstone & District 293	Gibbons, Maidstone
FLJ 538	Bristol	K5G	55043	ECW	7590	O32/28R	5/40	Hants & Dorset 1086	Isle of Wight Bus Museum
				(rebodied 4/54)					
FMO 938	Bristol	LL6B	81121	ECW	4711	B39R	8/50	Thames Valley 556	Tyler, Worcester
FMO 949	Bristol	LL6B	83130	ECW	4722	B39F	12/51	Thames Valley 567	Rampton, Reading
FMO 983	Bristol	KSW6B	80117	ECW	4382	L27/28R	-/51	Thames Valley 601	Rampton, Reading
FMS 815	Albion	Victor FT3AL	70886A	Harvey		B30F	-/54	Falkirk Hospital Board	Struthers, East Kilbride
FNV 557	Leyland	Tiger PS2/3	496026	Whitson		FC33F	2/50	Church, Pytchley	Burdett, Corley
FNV 705	Bedford	OB	130083	Duple	46567	C29F	3/50	KW, Daventry	Glover, Shirebrook
FNY 933	Bristol	K6A	W1051	Park Royal	B28693	H30/26R	12/44	Pontypridd 40	Boughton, Brightwell
FOI 1629	Bristol	LH6L	LH-691	Alexander (Belfast)	838/1	B45F	5/73	Ulsterbus 1629	Irish Transport Heritage
FON 630	Leyland	Titan TD7	307058	*chassis only*			7/42	Birmingham 1330	Shaw, Warley
FOP 429	Daimler	CWA6	11994	Duple	40562	O33/26R	2/45	Southend 244	Castle Point Transport Museum
FRC 956	Leyland	Titan PD2/12	541780	Leyland		H32/26RD	12/54	Trent 1256	BaMMOT, Wythall (WO)
FRJ 511	Daimler	CVG6DD	15389	Metro-Cammell		H30/24R	10/51	Salford 511	4100 Group, Manchester
FRP 692	Bristol	KS5G	80181	ECW	4393	L27/28R	10/50	United Counties 692	Ledger, Northampton
FRP 828	Bristol	LL5G	83151	ECW	4952	B39R	12/50	United Counties 828	Ledger, Northampton
FRU 224	Guy	Arab II	FD26420			mobile crane	2/44	Bournemouth 40	Bournemouth Heritage Transport Collection
FRU 305	Bristol	K6A	W1060	Hants & Dorset		FO31/28R	3/45	Hants & Dorset 1108	Transport Museum Society of Ireland
				(rebodied 5/52)					
FSA 232	Bedford	OB	120606	Duple	55052	C27F	10/49	Watt, Tarland	Adkins, Upper Boddington
FSC 182	Daimler	CVG6DD	13822	Metro-Cammell		H31/25R	5/49	Edinburgh 135	City of Edinburgh Council *(on loan to Lothian Bus Consortium)*
FSV 424	→ see JWU 307								
FTA 634	Bristol	K5G	55097	ECW	7204	L30/26R	3/41	Western National 345	Billington, Maidenhead

	Reg	Make	Model	Chassis No	Body	Body No	Layout	New	Original operator	Current owner
	FTB 11	Leyland	Titan TD7	307809	Northern Coachbuilders		L27/26R	12/41	Leigh 84	Museum of Transport, Manchester
	FTO 614	AEC	Regent	O6616460			TW	7/39	Nottingham 802	Sandtoft Transport Centre
	FTR 511	Guy	Arab III	FD36019	Park Royal	B32957	O30/26R	3/49	Southampton 64	Southampton City Council
										(in care of Southampton & District Transport Heritage Trust)
	FTR 514	Guy	Arab III	FD36066	Park Royal	B32960	O30/26R	3/49	Southampton 67	Ashbee, Southampton
	FTT 704	Bristol	K6A	W1132	ECW	8418	L27/28R	7/45	Western National 353	Bristol Vintage Bus Group
					(rebodied 6/55)					
	FUF 63	AEC	Regent	O6616435	Weymann	M1910	H30/26R	3/39	Brighton 63	Pye & Nicholson, West Drayton
	FUF 181	Dennis	Falcon	280013	Harrington		B30C	5/39	Southdown 81	Priddle, Farnham
	FUN 319	Crossley	SD42/7	97893	Burlingham	4108	C33F	5/49	Peters, Llanarmon	Wright, Nenthead (CA)
	FUT 58	Bedford	OB	122911	Duple	46605	C29F	3/50	Smith, Syston	Winstanley, Bedford
	FVA 854	Albion	Valiant CX39N	60315D	Duple	54032	C33F	6/50	Hutchison, Overtown	Albion Vehicle Preservation Trust
	FVH 1	Guy	Arab UF	UF70909	Guy/Park Royal	B35089	B43F	11/51	Huddersfield 1	Stoneywood Motors, Sowerby Bridge
	FWG 846	Bristol	LS6G	107024	ECW	8303	B45F	3/55	Alexander E11	Fife Bus Group
	FWW 596	Bedford	OB	52924	Duple	46808	C26F	7/47	West Yorkshire 646	Hudson, Bradford
	FWX 799	Leyland	Tiger PS1/1	462347	Barnaby		RV	6/47	Felix, Hatfield 25	Adkins, Upper Boddington
	FXI 400	→ see KEZ 3555								
	FXI 401	→ see JEZ 4092								
	FXT 120	Leyland	REC	201981	LPTB	228	B20F	11/39	London Transport CR14	Nicholson, Cippenham
	FXT 122	Leyland	REC	201983	LPTB	239	B20F	11/39	London Transport CR16	Skevington, Leighton Buzzard
(r)	FXT 142	Leyland	REC	202003	*chassis only*			6/46	London Transport CR36	Skevington, Leighton Buzzard
	FXT 183	AEC	Regent	O6616756	LPTB	339	H30/26R	5/39	London Transport RT8	Ensign, Purfleet (EX)
	FXT 219	AEC	Regent	O6616792	LPTB	286	H30/26R	1/40	London Transport RT44	Wood, Marchwood
	FXT 229	AEC	Regent	O6616802	LPTB	296	H30/26R	3/40	London Transport RT54	Wood, Marchwood
	FXT 288	AEC	Regent	O6616861	LPTB	347	H30/26R	5/40	London Transport RT113	2RT2 Preservation Group, Southfields
	FXT 318	AEC	Regent	O6616891	*chassis only*			12/41	London Transport RT143	-?-, Beith
	FYS 8	Leyland	Titan PD2/24	582698	Glasgow City Transport		O29/28R	2/59	Glasgow L108	Glasgow City Council
			(ex HSK 953, LDS 388A, SGD 10)							
	FYS 998	Leyland	Atlantean PDR1/1	582374	Alexander	5595	H44/34F	12/58	Glasgow LA1	Glasgow City Council
	FYS 999	Daimler	CVD6-30DD	30003	Alexander	5377	H41/32R	3/58	Glasgow D217	Glasgow City Council
	GAA 580	Dennis	Lancet III	328J3	Strachan		B32R	6/48	Aldershot & District D657	-?-, Surrey
	GAA 616	Dennis	Lancet III	430J3	Strachan		C--R	6/48	Aldershot & District D693	Waller et al, Camberley
(r)	GAD 781	Bedford	OB	38307	Duple	43174	C27F	11/46	Harrison, Broadway	Price, Shobdon
	GAL 967	Bedford	OWB	18939	Duple	122/2	C29F	3/44	Gash, Newark B7	Johnson, Worksop (NG)
					(rebodied 5/52)					
	GAM 215	Bristol	L6B	73080	Portsmouth Aviation		C32R	1/50	Wilts & Dorset 296	Hoare, Chepstow (CS)
	GAM 216	Bristol	L6B	73087	Portsmouth Aviation		C32R	1/50	Wilts & Dorset 297	Lawson, Baildon
	GAV 254	Albion	Victor FT3AB	70791K	Duple	53997	C31F	-/49	Spence, Alford	Dale, Dunbar
	GAY 171	Leyland	Tiger PS1/1	496186	Willowbrook	50768	DP35F	5/50	Allen, Mountsorrel 43	Countryman, Ibstock (LE)
	GBJ 192	AEC	Regent	O6617945	ECW	1581	H30/26R	1/47	Lowestoft 21	East Anglia Transport Museum
	GBJ 195	AEC	Regent	O6617948	ECW	1584	H30/26R	1/47	Lowestoft 24	Mould, Chase Terrace
	GBL 200	→ see LJO 757								
	GCA 747	Bedford	OB	134639	Duple	49261	C29F	4/50	Owen, Rhostyllen	Martin, Penkridge
	GCC 3	Ford	570E	510E21626	Burlingham	6866	C41F	6/59	Creams, Llandudno	Grayscroft, Mablethorpe (LI)
	GCD 48	Leyland	Titan TD5	303341	Park Royal	B34367	H28/26R	8/34	Southdown 248	Stobart, Wimbledon
					(rebodied 3/50)					

	GCY 740	Daimler	CVD6DD	17381	Bruce/East Lancs	4628	H30/26RD	4/50	Swansea Motor Services 40	South Wales Transport Preservation Trust
	GDJ 435	AEC	Regent V	MD3RV432	Weymann	M7968	H33/28R	8/57	St Helens H135	North West Museum of Transport
	GDL 33	Crossley	SD42/7	98011	Whitson		C33F	6/49	Nash, Ventnor	Emerton, Nantwich
	GDL 137	Bedford	OB	110422	Duple	43628	C29F	6/49	Seaview Services 11	Pitcher, Henley-on-Thames
	GDL 667	Bedford	OB	133749	Duple	48795	C29F	3/50	Paul, Ryde	Alexcars, Cirencester (GL)
	GDL 764	Leyland	Titan PD2/1	501304	Leyland		L27/26R	5/50	Seaview Services 13	Hunt, Rookley
	GDM 494	Leyland	Tiger PS2/3	500266	Harrington	820	C33F	7/50	Wakley, Northop	Cowdery, East Markham
	GDT 421	Daimler	CVD6DD	16591	Roe	GO2636	L27/26R	6/49	Doncaster 112	Doncaster Omnibus & Light Railway Society
	GEA 174	Daimler	CVD6DD	17942	Weymann	M5090	H30/26R	3/52	West Bromwich 174	Black Country Museum Transport Group
	GED 797	Bedford	OB	144976	Duple	56530	C29F	10/50	Fairhurst, Warrington	Premier Auto Trim, Aspull
	GEN 201	Leyland	Titan PD3/6	580227	Weymann	M7556	H41/32RD	5/58	Bury 201	Stephenson J, Bolton
	GEZ 8109	→ see AIG 286								
	GEZ 8118	Leyland	Leopard PSU3F/4R	8131241	Alexander (Belfast)	752/28	B53F	10/82	Ulsterbus 319	Kells Transport Museum, Cork
			(ex AXI 319)							
	GEZ 8821	Leyland	Leopard PSU3F/4R	8131371	Alexander (Belfast)	750/36	DP49F	6/83	Ulsterbus 333	Montgomery T, Ballymena
			(ex BXI 333)							
	GFM 882	Bristol	L6A	67115	ECW	1946	B35F	4/48	Crosville KB73	MacEwan, Amisfield (SW)
	GFN 273	Beadle-Leyland		JCB309	Beadle		C35F	12/52	East Kent	Harris & Smith, Hawkinge
	GFO 641	Leyland	Titan PD2/1	484680	Leyland		H30/26R	2/49	Isle of Man Road Services 72	Freeman, Hampshire
			(ex KLE 80N, KMN 502 - may be displayed as HOR 493)							
	GFW 496	Foden	PVSC6	28752	Plaxton	2792	FC37F	7/50	Bullock, Cheadle	Bullock, Cheadle (GM)
					(rebodied 2/56)					
	GFW 849	Bristol	LL5G	83091	ECW	4700	B39R	12/50	Lincolnshire 788	Gallagher, Waddington
	GFY 406	Leyland	Titan PD2/3	501800	Leyland		H30/26R	5/50	Southport 106	Pearce, Worthing
	GGA 670	Foden	PVSC6	27346	Plaxton	721	FC32F	9/48	SCWS, Glasgow	Dickens, Goostrey
(a)	GHA 333	SOS	SON	2861			RV	-/40	BMMO 2415	BaMMOT, Wythall
	GHA 337	SOS	SON	2865	Brush		B38F	-/40	BMMO 2418	BaMMOT, Wythall
	GHD 215	Ford	570E	510E63864	Duple	1139/341	C41F	-/61	Yorkshire Woollen 871	Turner, Tingley
	GHD 765	Leyland	Titan PD3A/1	611461	Metro-Cammell		H39/31F	4/62	Yorkshire Woollen 893	Goldthorp, Batley
	GHE 27	Leyland	Tiger Cub PSUC1/1	534758	Willowbrook	54158	C39R	7/54	Yorkshire Traction 1027	Batley, Scholes
	GHN 189	Bristol	K5G	57029	ECW	3162	L27/26R	6/42	United BGL29	Aycliffe & District Bus Preservation Society
					(rebodied -/54 with body new -/49)					
	GHT 127	Bristol	K5G	53001	ECW	6529	O33/26R	3/41	Bristol C3315	First Somerset & Avon (SO) *(on loan to Bristol Vintage Bus Group)*
	GHT 154	Bristol	K5G	53035	Bristol		H30/26R	11/40	Bristol C3336	Bristol Vintage Bus Group
	GJB 251	Bristol	LWL6B	85042	ECW	5360	B39R	-/52	Thames Valley 613	-?-. -?-
	GJB 254	Bristol	LWL6B	85168	ECW	5363	B39R	-/52	Thames Valley 616	616 Preservation Group, Luton
	GJB 265	Bristol	LWL6B	87018	ECW	5374	B39R	3/52	Thames Valley 627	Bilbé, Green & Rampton, Reading
	GJB 279	Bristol	KSW6B	84046	ECW	5081	L--/--RD	11/51	Thames Valley 641	Karlsberg, New Ferry
	GJM 2	Bedford	SB3	77444	Plaxton	602938	C41F	3/60	Mallinson, Windemere	Brewster, Sicklesmere
	GJP 197	Bedford	SB1	85869	Yeates	863	C41F	10/60	Unsworth, Wigan	Unsworth, Wigan
	GJT 29	Leyland	Royal Tiger PSU1/16	531117	Leyland		C41C	12/53	Warwickshire Miners	Massingham, Slough
	GJX 331	Daimler	CVG6DD	19080	Roe	GO4230	H37/28R	11/56	Halifax 19	Keighley Bus Museum Trust (WY)
	GJZ 9575	Leyland	Atlantean AN68A/1R	7804916	Roe	GO8065	O43/28F	3/79	Plymouth 129	Wells & Hughes, Ipswich
			(ex STK 129T)							
	GKD 434	AEC	Regent II	O6617483	Weymann/Liverpool	M2725	H30/26R	11/46	Liverpool A233	Merseyside Transport Trust
	GKE 65	Bristol	K5G	49080	Weymann	M1687	RV	6/39	Chatham & District 871	Moores, Diseworth
	GKE 68	Bristol	K5G	49083	Weymann	M1690	H28/26R	6/39	Chatham & District 874	Friends of Chatham Traction

	Reg	Make	Model	Chassis	Body	Body no	Layout	Date	New to	Owner
	GKG 52	Leyland	Royal Tiger PSU1/15	512122	East Lancs	4770	B44F	-/52	Cardiff 135	Brewer, Cardiff
					(latterly converted to a railbus for Bord na Mona, Ireland)					
	GKV 94	Daimler	CVA6DD	14460	Metro-Cammell		H31/29R	8/50	Coventry 94	Burdett, Corley
	GKV 105	Daimler	CVD6SD	14466	Brush		B--F	9/49	Coventry 105	Group 94, Coventry
	GLJ 957	Leyland	Titan PD1A	472326	ECW	2307	L27/26R	1/48	Hants & Dorset PD959	Leatherdale, Milton Keynes
	GLJ 971	Bristol	K5G	64083	Hants & Dorset		FO31/28R	10/47	Hants & Dorset 1128	Froud, Verwood
					(rebodied 9/57 with body new 5/53)					
	GLX 913	Daimler	CWA6	11845	Massey	2131	L27/28RD	10/44	Southend 263	Ensign, Purfleet (EX)
					(rebodied 6/54)					
	GNU 750	Daimler	COG5-40	8485	Willowbrook	3208	C35F	5/39	Tailby & George, Willington DR5	Quantock, Bishops Lydeard (SO)
	GOE 486	Daimler	CVA6DD	12911	Metro-Cammell		H30/24R	7/47	Birmingham 1486	Hawketts, Birmingham
	GOU 732	Tilling Stevens	K6LA7	9276	Scottish Aviation		C33F	3/49	Warrens, Alton	Burdett, Corley
	GOU 845	Dennis	Lance III	131K3	East Lancs	4548	L25/26R	6/50	Aldershot & District 145	Stubbs, Burton-upon-Trent
	GPV 548	Bedford	CAV	97782	Martin Walter	U37995	M--	5/58	Cranfield Flour Mills, Ipswich	Bass, Ipswich
	GPW 679	Bristol	L5G	67050	ECW	1977	B35R	3/48	Eastern Counties LL679	Mahoney R, Brentwood
	GRH 193	Guy	Arab II	FD27169	Roe	GO3599	H30/26R	12/44	East Yorkshire 409	Ireland, Hull
					(rebodied 2/53)					
	GSD 779	Guy	Arab IV	FD72425	Roe	GO4024	H37/28RD	6/55	AA (Dodds), Ayr	Dodds, Ayr (SW)
	GSR 244	Commer	Q4	18B1670S	Scottish Aviation		C29F	4/50	Meffan, Kirriemiur	Thompson, Longframlington
	GSU 378	Albion	Venturer SpCX19W	60023C	Commonwealth Engineering		H33/28R	-/47	Sydney 1877	Sydney Albion Venturer Group
			(ex 648 XUA, 050 OJO *Australia*, mo.1877 *Australia*)							
	GSV 580	Leyland	Titan PD2/24	583145			RV	6/59	Glasgow L266	Ferguson, East Kilbride
			(ex SGD 268)							
	GTA 395	Bristol	LL5G	56010	Bristol		B39R	6/42	Southern National 373	373 Group, Plymouth
					(rebuilt & rebodied 2/54)					
	GTB 903	Leyland	Titan PD1	460805	Leyland		H30/26R	7/46	Lytham St Annes 19	Lancastrian Transport Trust
										(operates as Totally Transport, Blackpool(LA))
	GTJ 694	AEC	Regent II	O6617875	Park Royal	B32501	RV	5/47	Morecambe & Heysham 10	Blackman A, Halifax
(r)	GTP 986	Leyland	Titan PD2/10	521652	Leyland		H30/26R	8/52	Portsmouth 69	Howe, Polegate
	GTP 995	Leyland	Titan PD2/10	521759	Leyland		H30/26R	9/52	Portsmouth 78	Portsmouth 78 Group, Strood
	GTR 484	Guy	Arab III	FD70174	Park Royal	B33139	H30/26R	7/51	Southampton 222	Blair, Upham
	GTX 437	Leyland	Tiger PS1/1	471671	Neath		B39F	9/47	Llynfi, Maesteg 37	Swansea Industrial & Maritime Museum
					(rebodied -/57)					
	GUE 247	Leyland	Tiger PS1	483185	Northern Coachbuilders		B34F	12/48	Stratford Blue 41	BaMMOT, Wythall
	GUF 191	Guy	Arab II	FD27376	Northern Counties	3734	O30/26R	1/45	Southdown 451	Richardson, Worthing
			(ex AR88.141 *Denmark*, LR80.113 *Denmark*, GUF 191)							
	GUF 727	Leyland	Tiger PS1/1	461056	ECW	1654	B32R	4/47	Southdown 1227	Jefford, Hatton
	GUJ 356	Bedford	OB	144984	Duple	49262	C29F	10/50	Gittins, Crickheath	Meredith, Malpas (CH)
	GUJ 608	Sentinel	STC4	STC4/40/30	Sentinel		B40F	11/50	Sentinel demonstrator	Gray, Birmingham
	GUS 926	Maudslay	Marathon III	70512	Park Royal	B34217	C35F	8/49	MacBrayne 136	Hunter, Fordoun
	GUX 188	Bedford	OB	146262	Duple	43245	B30F	-/51	Lloyd, Oswestry	Transport Museum Society of Ireland
	GVA 635	Albion	Victor FT39N	73061A	Scottish Aviation		C31F	9/51	Duncan, Law	MacPherson, Donisthorpe (LE)
	GVD 47	Guy	Arab III	FD70577	Duple	53154	H31/26R	-/50	Hutchison, Overtown	McGill, Greenock (SW)
					(first licensed 2/52)					
	GVJ 190	Bedford	OB	119666	Duple	54483	C29F	10/49	Tummey, Llangarron	Miles & Turner, Tredegar
	GWG 94	→ see PVS 984								
	GWG 472	AEC	Monocoach	MC3RV130	Alexander	4710	B45F	6/55	Alexander AC68	North East of Scotland Bus Preservation Group
	GWJ 724	AEC	Regent	O6616981			gritter	6/41	Sheffield G54	South Yorkshire Transport Museum

	Reg	Make	Model	Chassis No	Body	Body No	Layout	Date	New to	Owner
	GWM 816	Crossley	SD42/7s	98213	Crossley		B32F	3/51	Southport 116	Wilkinson, Liverpool
	GWN 432	Dennis	Lancet III	868J3	Thurgood	978	FC37F	8/50	Modern Super, Tottenham	Bannister, Owston Ferry (LI)
					(rebodied 6/60)					
	GWS 139	Bedford	OB	111861	Duple	54299	C--F	7/49	Reid & Mackay,Edinburgh	Machin, Church Lawton
	GWT 630	Albion	Valkyrie CX13	58030E	Burlingham	2982	C33F	12/47	South Yorkshire 61	Lawson, Baildon (WY)
	GWU 12	Leyland	Titan PD2/1	472953	Leyland		L27/26R	2/48	Todmorden 2	Powell, Todmorden
	GWV 101	Bedford	OB	146973	Duple	44097	C29F	1/51	Leather, Maiden Bradley	Cooper, Maiden Bradley
	GWV 297	Bedford	OB	146963	Duple	45256	C29F	1/51	Athelstan, Malmesbury	Steeds, Radstock
	GXI 434	→ see KEZ 5806								
	GYE 98	Daimler	CWA6	12143	Harkness		H30/26R	6/45	Belfast 476	Montgomery W, Ballymena
					(rebodied -/56)					
	HAP 985	Bristol	KSW6G	98052	ECW	6712	H32/28R	7/53	Brighton Hove & District 447	Brighton & Hove (ES) 6447
	HAT 245	AEC	Regent II	O6617633	Weymann	M2895	H31/29R	10/46	Hull 245	Hull 245 Group
	HAW 302	Sentinel	SLC4	SLC4/35/54	Beadle	C321	C41F	5/51	Brown, Donnington Wood	Wheatley, Kenilworth
	HAW 373	Sentinel	SLC4	SLC4/35/22	Beadle	C315	C35C	5/51	Brown, Donnington Wood	Wheatley, Kenilworth
	HBL 68	Bristol	KSW6B	94055	ECW	5915	L27/28R	5/53	Thames Valley 666	Fowler, Holbeach Drove (LI)
	HCC 850	Bedford	SB3	73068	Duple	1120/17	C41F	4/60	Purple, Bethesda	Owens, Rhiwlas (CN)
	HCD 449	Leyland	Tiger PS1/1	462467	ECW	1644	C31R	3/47	Southdown 1249	Gray, Funtley
	HCZ 5695	Leyland	Leopard PSU3E/4R	7801537	Alexander (Belfast)	360/27	RV	10/78	Ulsterbus 120	Kells Transport Museum. Cork
			(ex ROI 120)							
	HDD 654	Bristol	L6G	67037	Duple	46102	C35F	3/48	Black & White B111	Black & White, Penton Mewsey (HA)
	HDG 448	Albion	Venturer CX19	60042L	Metro-Cammell		H30/26R	3/49	Cheltenham District 72	BaMMOT, Wythall
	HDJ 753	AEC	Regent V	D3RV514	Weymann	M8348	H33/28R	7/58	St Helens J153	McGarry, Widnes
	HDK 835	AEC	Regent III	9612E4961	East Lancs	4726	H31/28R	9/51	Rochdale 235	Dearnley, Halifax
	HDL 263	Bristol	KS5G	84072	ECW	5001	L27/28R	11/51	Southern Vectis 749	Handford, Bournemouth
	HDL 279	Bristol	LL5G	83337	ECW	5267	B39R	10/51	Southern Vectis 835	Steward, Apse Heath
	HDL 280	Bristol	LL5G	83338	ECW	5268	B39R	10/51	Southern Vectis 836	Priddle, Farnham
	HDL 285	Bristol	LL5G	83343	ECW	5273	B39R	3/52	Southern Vectis 841	Porter, Chandlers Ford
	HDM 473	Bedford	SB	4972	Duple	1006/396	C33F	2/51	Owen, Rhyl	Emerton, Nantwich
	HDZ 5419	Renault	S75	222690	Wright	L183	B28F	3/90	Centrewest RW19	GM Buses Group
	HDZ 5488	Leyland	PSU3/3R	7401140	Alexander	63AYS/1873/9	RV	5/74	Alexander Fife FPE59	Pearson, Kinghorn
			(ex 23 PTA, XXA 859M)							
	HEK 705	Leyland	Titan PD3A/2	610873	Massey	2447	H41/29F	7/61	Wigan 57	Museum of Transport, Manchester
	HEK 962	AEC	Reliance	2MU3RA3703	Plaxton	7410AC006S	C45F	7/61	Smith, Wigan	Forsyth, Braidwood
					(rebodied 6/74)					
	HER 27	AEC	Regent III	6811A083	Weymann	M4553	H30/26R	10/49	Pest Control, Bourn	Brown & Richman, Wateringbury
	HET 513	Crossley	DD42/8	95908	Crossley		H30/26R	8/53	Rotherham 213	Science Museum, Wroughton
	HFJ 142	Leyland	PD2/1	480632	Leyland		H30/26R	12/47	Exeter 15	Gobbin, St Austell
	HFJ 144	Leyland	PD2/1	480630	Leyland		H30/26R	12/47	Exeter 17	Robbins, Leatherhead
	HGC 130	Guy	Arab II	FD28104	Park Royal	B31034	H30/26R	2/46	London Transport G351	London Bus Preservation Trust
	HGC 225	AEC	Regent II	O6617501	Weymann	M2739	H30/26R	2/46	London Transport STL2692	Wickens, Walderslade
	HGE 219	Bedford	OB	137703	Duple	54759	C29F	7/50	SCWS, Glasgow	Taylor, Diss
	HGG 359	Thornycroft	Nippy HF/ER4	54290	Croft		B20F	7/50	MacBrayne 149	Hunter, Fordoun
	HHA 26	Guy	Arab II	FD27082	Weymann	C8294	H30/26R	10/44	BMMO 2574	BaMMOT, Wythall
	HHA 637	BMMO	S6	3036	Metro-Cammell		B40F	-/46	BMMO 3036	BaMMOT, Wythall
(r)	HHA 640	BMMO	S6	3039	Brush		B--F	-/46	BMMO 3039	BaMMOT, Wythall

	Registration	Make	Model	Chassis No	Body	Body No	Layout	Date	First Owner	Current Owner
	HHE 323	Leyland	Tiger PS1	461231Y	Roe	GO3976	H33/26R	7/47	Yorkshire Traction 1042	Batley & Braithwaite, Scholes
			(ex AHE 467)		*(rebodied 7/55)*					
	HHF 15	→ see BHT 677A								
	HHN 202	Bristol	L5G	63001	ECW	1069	B35R	2/47	United BG216	Northern Counties Bus Preservation Group
					(rebodied 3/57 with body new -/46)					
	HHP 755	AEC	Regal III	9621E612	Duple	51484	FC33F	9/48	Greenslades Tours	Quantock, Bishops Lydeard (SO)
	HIB 2138	→ see 84-G-659 *Ireland*								
	HIG 5681	Leyland	Titan TNLXB2RR	0603	Leyland		H44/27F	8/82	London Transport T553	Bamford, Ramsgate
			(ex NUW 553Y)							
	HIL 7081	Bedford	CFL	JY612266	Plaxton	79C011CF	C15F	4/79	Wilder, Feltham	Greet, Broadhempston
			(ex DJF 631T)							
	HIL 8418	Leyland	Tiger TRCTL11/3R	8300111	Plaxton	8312LTP1C088	C51F	8/83	Yorkshire Traction 57	Mason, Lincoln
			(ex MSV 922, 3141 HE, VHE 890, A 57 WDT)							
	HIL 8436	Leyland	Leopard PSU3E/4R	7930082	Willowbrook	91063	B53F	6/80	Dunstan & Bruckshaw, Davenport	Kells Transport Museum, Cork
			(ex BVP 794V, YBO 331, BVP 794V)		*(rebodied 10/91)*					
	HIL 8785	Ford	R192	BC04LJ51052	Plaxton	732463	C34F	11/72	Barrie, Balloch	Perkins, Workington
			(ex FSN 224L)							
	HJG 17	Dennis	Lancet UF	116LU2	Duple	190/9	C41C	4/54	East Kent	Webster, Lower Southrepps
	HJN 904	Morris	JR	JR22666	Morris		M9	7/54	Arnold, Leigh-on-Sea (as van)	Sanders, Kelvedon Hatch
					(converted to minibus -/55 by Brown, Great Easton)					
(r)	HJY 296	Leyland	Titan PD2/12	531699	Leyland		H30/26R	11/53	Plymouth 396	Robbins, Leatherhead
	HJY 297	→ see ADV 854A								
	HKE 867	Bristol	K6A	W2068	Weymann	M5666	H30/26R	10/45	Maidstone & District 159	Maidstone & District & East Kent Bus Club
					(rebodied 3/53)					
	HKF 820	AEC	Regent III	9612E1810	Weymann/Liverpool	M3515	H30/26R	3/49	Liverpool A344	Wirral Borough Council
	HKL 819	AEC	Regal I	O6624609	Beadle	391	OB34F	11/46	Maidstone & District OR1	Baker, St Neots
	HKL 826	AEC	Regal I	O6624616	Beadle	399	OB35F	9/46	Maidstone & District OR2	North East Bus Museum Trust
	HKL 836	AEC	Regal I	O6624920	Beadle	432	OB35F	3/47	Maidstone & District OR3	London Bus Company, Northfleet (KT)
	HKW 82	AEC	Regent III	9613E7099	East Lancs	4839	H33/28R	12/52	Bradford 82	Hudson & Lawson, Bradford
	HLJ 17	Bristol	K6A	68041	ECW	2569	L27/28R	9/48	Hants & Dorset	-?-, Yorkshire
	HLJ 44	Bristol	K6A	72080	ECW	2596	L27/28R	2/49	Hants & Dorset TD895	Ensign, Purfleet (EX)
	HLW 159	AEC	Regent III	O961047	Park Royal	L18	H30/26R	9/47	London Transport RT172	Leighton, Keighley
	HLW 177	AEC	Regent III	O9612735	Park Royal	L39	H30/26R	6/49	London Transport RT190	Stubbington & Peters, Welling
			(ex JXC 481)							
	HLW 178	AEC	Regent III	O961021	Weymann	W144	H30/26R	10/47	London Transport RT191	Scott, Romford
	HLW 214	AEC	Regent III	O961099	Park Royal	L76	H30/26RD	11/47	London Transport RT227	Mudie, Aberystwyth
	HLW 248	AEC	Regent III	O961243	Park Royal	L3221	H30/26R	1/48	London Transport RT261	Clements, Ditton
	HLX 146	AEC	Regent III	O961327	Park Royal	L177	H30/26R	2/48	London Transport RT329	Dale, Sherborne
	HLX 359	AEC	Regent III	O961334	Weymann	W1964	H30/26R	6/48	London Transport RT542	Wilkinson, Billericay
	HLX 403	AEC	Regent III	O961458	Park Royal	L2161	H30/26R	7/48	London Transport RT586	Tyburn, Bristol
	HLX 410	AEC	Regent III	O961442	Weymann	W189	H30/26R	7/48	London Transport RT593	Townsend & Plummer, Longfield
	HLX 421	AEC	Regent III	O9611091	Weymann	W1611	H30/26R	7/48	London Transport RT604	Purley Transport Preservation Group
	HLX 462	AEC	Regal III	9621E177	Mann Egerton		B31F	7/48	London Transport T792	Herting, Chorleywood
	HNT 49	Sentinel	SLC4	SLC4/35/63	Beadle	C328	DP41F	7/51	Brown, Donnington Wood	Wheatley, Kenilworth
	HOD 30	Bristol	L6A	71030	Beadle		C31F	10/48	Western National 1228	Lawson, Baildon (WY)
	HOD 55	Bedford	OB	116496	Duple	54551	C29F	6/49	Western National 566	Cedar, Bedford (BD)
	HOD 66	Beadle-Bedford		JCB67	Beadle	C215	B35R	8/49	Western National 2015	Greet, Broadhempston
	HOD 75	Bedford	OB	119577	Duple	54844	C29F	9/49	Western National 596	Annetts & Porter, Innersdown (HA)

	Registration	Chassis make	Chassis model	Chassis no.	Body	Body no.	Layout	Date	New to	Current owner
	HOD 76	→ see MSJ 606								
	HOI 1902	Leyland	Leopard PSU3C/4R	7401486	Alexander (Belfast)	-?-	RV	3/75	Ulsterbus 1902	Kells Transport Museum, Cork
	HOI 1904	Leyland	Leopard PSU3C/4R	7402282	Alexander (Belfast)	-?-	RV	4/75	Ulsterbus 1904	Begley, Lisburn
	HOI 2922	→ see 75-D-70 *Ireland*								
	HOI 2925	→ see 75-D-79 *Ireland*								
	HOI 2926	→ see 75-D-101 *Ireland*								
	HOR 493	→ see GFO 641								
	HOT 339	Bedford	OB	131034	Duple	46227	C27F	3/50	Grace, Alresford	Barton, Shenington
	HOU 904	Dennis	Lancet III	118J10	Strachan		B38R	11/50	Aldershot & District 178	MacPherson, Donisthorpe (LE)
	HOV 685	Leyland	Titan PD2/1	480794	Brush		H30/24R	10/48	Birmingham 1685	1685 Group, Birmingham
	HPW 108	Bristol	K5G	72089	ECW	2871	H30/26R	1/49	Eastern Counties LKH108	Appleton, Higham Ferrers
	HPW 133	Bristol	K5G	74152	ECW	2896	H30/26R	5/49	Eastern Counties LKH133	Gray, Lincoln
	HPY 844	Commer	Avenger I	23A0892	Plaxton	1752	C33F	4/52	Smith, Thirsk	Smith, Thirsk (NY)
	HRG 207	→ see UFF 178								
	HRG 209	AEC	Regent V	D2RVG080	Crossley		H35/29R	7/55	Aberdeen 209	Aberdeen & District Transport Preservation Trust
(r)	HRH 461	AEC	Regent III	O961674	*chassis only*			6/47	Hull 261	Hull 245 Group
(r)	HRN 31	Leyland	Titan PD2/13	550763	Metro-Cammell		H33/28RD	9/55	Ribble 1391	Farrelly & Douglas, Longton
	HRN 32	→ see ABV 784A								
	HRN 39	Leyland	Titan PD2/13	550840	Metro-Cammell		H33/28RD	10/55	Ribble 1399	Ousby & Berry, Morecambe
										(on loan to Ribble Vehicle Preservation Trust)
	HSK 953	→ see FYS 8								
	HSV 103	→ see TUH 7								
	HTB 656	Leyland	Tiger PS1	462440	Roe	GO2321	B35R	4/47	Ramsbottom 17	Museum of Transport, Manchester
	HTC 577	Bedford	OB	51163	Du	47990	C29F	6/47	Robinson, Great Harwood	Blake, West Mersea
	HTC 661	Bedford	OB	52711	Du	43493	C29F	6/47	Dean & Pounder, Morecambe	Countryman, Ibstock (LE)
	HTF 586	Bedford	OB	60781	SMT		C29F	12/47	Warburton, Bury	Museum of Transport, Manchester
	HTM 20	→ see 1949 MN *Isle of Man*								
	HTP 326	Austin	K8VC	20518	Reading		C14F	5/53	Field, Paulton	Wilson, Mullion
	HTT 487	AEC	Regal I	O6624813	Weymann	C9053	B35F	7/46	Devon General SR487	Greet, Broadhempston
	HUF 303	Leyland	Tiger PS1/1	471195	Park Royal	B33016	C32R	3/48	Southdown 1303	Hall S & Pixton P, Hazel Grove
	HUM 401	AEC	Regent	O6616910	Roe	GO336	H31/25R	3/40	Leeds 106	Keighley Bus Museum Trust
										((on long term loan from First West Yorkshire (WY))
	HUO 510	AEC	Regal I	O6625520	Weymann	C9188	B35F	3/48	Devon General SR510	Blackman A, Halifax
	HUP 236	Albion	Valiant CX39N	60303D	ACB		C33F	5/47	Economic, Whitburn 7	Purvis, Seaburn
(r)	HUS 675	Albion	Victor FT21N	71554J	*chassis only*			12/50	Glasgow Education	Roulston, Glasgow
	HUS 676	Albion	Victor FT21N	71554K	Bennett		B20F	1/51	Glasgow Education	Roulston, Glasgow
	HUY 655	Bedford	OB	116301	Duple	49921	C29F	9/49	Ketley, Stourport	Emerton, Nantwich
			(ex ASV 541, HUY 655)							
	HVH 234	AEC	Regent III	9613E4915	East Lancs	5064	L30/28R	9/54	Huddersfield 234	-?-, -?-
	HVH 710	Trojan	20	M5741	Trojan		B12	8/54	Wilson, Huddersfield (van)	Pratt, Woodlesford
	HVJ 203	Bedford	OB	145695	Duple	54500	C29F	2/51	Wye Valley, Hereford	Boulton, Cardington (SH)
	HVJ 583	Leyland	Tiger PS2/3	500453	Harrington	900	C35F	5/51	Wye Valley, Hereford	Wheatley, Kenilworth
	HVO 937	AEC	Regent II	O6618000	Weymann	M3346	H30/26R	11/47	Mansfield District 126	Peck, Mansfield Woodhouse
	HWO 323	Leyland	Tiger PS1/1	494728	Lydney		C33F	6/50	Red & White C350	Bowring, Lydney
	HWO 334	Guy	Arab III	FD70112	Duple	46077	L27/26RD	2/50	Red & White L1149	BaMMOT, Wythall
	HWO 342	Guy	Arab III	FD70168	Duple	47202	L27/26RD	3/50	Red & White L1749	Morgan, Ashford
(r)	HWS 775	Leyland	Royal Tiger PSU1/13	514762	*chassis only*			2/52	Edinburgh 810	Gascoine, Blackridge
	HWV 294	Bristol	KSW5G	92028	ECW	5968	L--/--R	9/52	Wilts & Dorset 365	Brown, Rushden

	HWY 36	Leyland	Titan PD2/1	496259	Leyland		L27/26R	1/50	Todmorden 18	Exelby, Bromyard
	HXB 521	Bedford	JC	JCV6699	Martin Walter		B??	10/46	non-PSV	Pearce, Worcester
	HXI 460	→ see JNZ 7487								
	HXI 468	→ see MEZ 5619								
	HXI 3007	→ see YEZ 2452								
	HYP 722	Bedford	OB	47814	Duple	44112	C29F	2/48	Birch, Kentish Town K22	Hamilton, Bow (DN)
			(This may carry LTA 755 for display purposes)							
	IBZ 3051	Mercedes-Benz	609D	66806320008513	Made to Measure		C24F	8/90	McEneaney, Crossmaglen	Houston, Newtownards
			(ex H904 XGA)							
	ICZ 3919	Leyland	Leopard PSU3E/4R	7801337	Alexander (Belfast)	360/14	RV	8/78	Ulsterbus 118	Kells Transport Museum, Cork
			(ex ROI 118)							
	IIL 4317	Auwarter	Cityliner N116	82-86-00	Auwarter		C16FT	8/82	Clevedon Motorways	Cocking, Basildon
			(ex MEU 603Y)							
	IIW 670	AEC	Reliance	6U3ZR23862	Willowbrook	90041	C53F	4/90	Lewis, Greenwich	Hearson, Chesterton
			(ex UMT 903M)							
	IJI 5367	Bristol	RELH6L	RELH-4-392	Plaxton	713884	C49F	5/71	Greenslade 300	Gray, Exeter
			(ex ARU 500A, ARU 80A, SNJ 611, HGC 233J, 240 MT, UFJ 229J)							
	IUI 2142	Leyland	Titan TNLXB2RR	0390	Leyland		H44/32F	11/81	London Transport T341	Brown, Romford
			(ex KYV 341X)							
	IUI 5036	Bristol	VRT/SL3/680	VRT/SL3/2779	ECW	24668	H43/31F	3/81	Southdown 266	Southdown Preservation Group
			(ex JWV 266W)							
	IUI 6410	AEC	Reliance	6U3ZR37602	Plaxton	7911AX521	C49F	2/79	Premier Travel 280	Buckley, Darwen
			(ex WEB 410T)							
	IUI 6411	AEC	Reliance	6U3ZR37593	Plaxton	7911AX522	C49F	3/79	Premier Travel 281	Hearson, Chesterton
			(ex WEB 411T)							
	IUI 9892	Mercedes-Benz	709D	6690032P042366	Dormobile	50590 632 90	B29F	10/90	McGibbons & Tipping, Paisley	Stafford, Renfrew (SW)
			(ex H124 YGG)							
	IXI 1000	→ see SEZ 9973								
	IXI 7015	Mercedes-Benz	609D	66806320762939	Ulsterbus		C18FL	3/87	Flexibus 15	Hudson, Donaghadee
	JAA 708	Leyland	Olympic HR40	502362	Weymann	L19	B40F	10/50	King Alfred, Winchester	FoKAB, Winchester
			(ex BIC 671, JAA 708)							
	JAB 661	→ see J 7247 *Jersey*								
	JAB 867	Bedford	OB	137672	Duple	49926	C29F	8/50	Wright, Kidderminster	Fortune, Watchet
	JAP 698	Harrington-Commer		48A5018	Harrington	INTEG00012	C41C	7/54	Harrington demonstrator	Webster, Lower Southrepps
	JAS 715	Bedford	CALV4	215316	Martin Walter	UT75008	M9	11/61	non-PSV	Simpson, Whittlesey
			(ex 9682 MT)							
	JAT 435	Leyland	Tiger PS1	471980	Brush		RV	7/48	East Yorkshire 467	Ireland, Hull
	JAX 354	Leyland	Tiger PS1	472692	Wilks & Meade		B35F	5/48	JMT 60	Robertson, Ashington (ND)
			(ex VVJ 675K, J 8535)							
	JBD 975	Bristol	KSW6B	98161	ECW	7114	L27/28R	10/53	United Counties 938	Ledger, Northampton
	JBN 153	Leyland	Titan PD2/13	551588	Metro-Cammell		H34/28R	5/56	Bolton 77	Museum of Transport, Manchester
	JBN 157	Leyland	Titan PD2/13	551650	Metro-Cammell		H34/28R	5/56	Bolton 81	-?-, -?-
	JBY 804	Bedford	OB	143735	Duple	54345	C29F	3/51	Barber, Mitcham	Kenzie, Shepreth (CM)
(r)	JCK 530	Leyland	Titan PD2/12	522377	Burlingham	6169	H33/28RD	7/56	Ribble 1455	Butler, Gosforth
										(on loan to Ribble Vehicle Preservation Trust)

JCK 542	Leyland	Titan PD2/12	556012	Burlingham	6181	H33/28RD	8/56	Ribble 1467	Butler, Gosforth
									(on loan to Ribble Vehicle Preservation Trust)
JCK 892	Leyland	Tiger Cub PSUC1/2	564004	Burlingham	5852	C25F	3/56	Ribble 980	Jones, Flint (CN)
JCY 870	AEC	Regal IV	9822E285	Burlingham	5078	C39C	4/53	Evans, Llangennech	Hawkins, Bridgend
JDC 599	Dennis	Loline I	140Y1A	Northern Counties	5340	H36/31RD	11/58	Middlesbrough 99	500 Group, Stockton
JDL 40	Bristol	KSW5G	94038	ECW	5897	L--/--RD	3/53	Southern Vectis 766	Priddle, Farnham
JDN 668	AEC	Regent III	6812A112	Roe	GO3828	H33/25RD	3/54	York Pullman 64	Lincolnshire Vintage Vehicle Society
JDV 754	Bedford	OB	65366	Duple	46411	C23F	12/47	Woolacombe & Mortehoe	Lewis, Henstridge (SO)
JDZ 2315	Dennis	Dart	8.5SDL3003/294	Wright	M168	B26F	1/91	Centrewest DW15	London Transport Museum
JEL 257	Bristol	K5G	76143	ECW	3585	L27/28R	12/49	Hants & Dorset 1238	Staniforth, Stroud
JEO 772	→ see BLV 755A								
JEZ 4092	Leyland	Tiger TRBTL11/2RP	8400439	Alexander (Belfast)	963/2	DP53F	4/85	Ulsterbus 401	Menagh, Belfast
		(ex FXI 401)							
JFH 760	→ see PFF 777								
JFJ 606	Daimler	CVD6DD	14982	Brush		H30/26R	1/49	Exeter 43	Hoare, Chepstow (CS)
JFJ 873	Daimler	CVD6SD	14993	Weymann	C9323	B35F	4/50	Exeter 73	Handford & Rymill, Solihull
JFJ 874	Daimler	CVD6SD	14994	*chassis / body remains*			4/50	Exeter 74	B&M Bus Project, Hyde
JFJ 875	Daimler	CVD6SD	14995	Weymann	C9328	B35F	4/50	Exeter 75	Shears D, Winkleigh
JFJ 939	Bedford	OB	105898	Duple	46962	mobile caravan	5/49	Greenslades Tours	Golynia, Long Melford
JFM 575	AEC	Regal III	6821A198	Strachan		B35R	11/48	Crosville TA5	Quantock, Bishops Lydeard (SO)
JFM 990	Beadle-Bedford		JCB32	Beadle	C180	B--R	-/50	Crosville SC18	-?-, -?-
JFV 527	Harrington-Commer		T48B6007	Harrington	00062	C41C	7/55	Abbott, Blackpool	Ashcroft & Williamson, Preston
JGD 426	Albion	Victor FT21N	71569B	?		B12	5/51	City of Glasgow Police	McKindless, Wishaw
JHA 890	BMMO	S8	3290	Metro-Cammell		B40F	-/49	BMMO 3290	Hudd, Eltham
JHL 670	Atkinson	Alpha CPL745H	FC4656	Plaxton	2966	C41C	7/56	Young, Hornchurch	O'Sullivan V, Hospital
JHL 701	Bedford	SBG	47306	Plaxton	2949	C41F	10/56	Moore, Jedburgh	Coach Hire, Freckleton (LA)
JHL 708	AEC	Reliance	MU3RV888	Roe	GO4308	B44F	11/56	West Riding 808	Bennett, Ossett
JHL 983	AEC	Reliance	MU3RV1009	Roe	GO4261	C41C	4/57	West Riding 803	West Riding Omnibus Preservation Society
JHT 122	Bristol	K6A	W3061	ECW	3207	H--/--R	3/46	Bristol 1546	Black & White, Penton Mewsey (HA)
				(rebodied 5/56 with body new 11/48)					
JHT 802	Bristol	K6A	W3151	ECW	3253	H31/28R	8/46	Bristol C3386	Walker, Wells
				(rebodied 4/57 with body new 8/49)					
JHT 827	Bristol	L5G	W4028	Bristol		B35R	8/46	Bristol 2174	Burt, Shaftesbury
				(rebodied 3/57 with body new 10/50)					
JIL 2157	Leyland	National 1151/1R/0402	00365	East Lancs	B8702	B49F	4/73	Midland Fox 2157	LeFevre & Spratley, Newhaven
		(ex NPD 142L - *fitted with a Volvo engine - rebodied 5/94*)							
JIL 2426	Leyland	Leopard PSU3E/4R	7930058	Plaxton	8011LC009	C53F	11/81	Marfleet, Binbrook	-?-, -?-
		(ex BTL 485X)							
JIW 4045	AEC	Reliance	6U3ZR38435	Plaxton	7912AC032	C57F	5/79	Randall, Willesen	Knight, Hemel Hempstead
		(ex EBM 459T)							
JJP 502	→ see PSJ 480								
JKC 178	Daimler	CVA6DD	15491	Northern Counties	4334	H--/--R	3/49	Liverpool D553	Merseyside Transport Trust
JLJ 401	Leyland	Tiger PS2/3	492220	Burlingham	3657	FC31F	8/49	Bournemouth 44	Quantock, Bishops Lydeard (SO)
JLJ 402	Leyland	Tiger PS2/3	492221	Burlingham	3656	FDP35F	8/49	Bournemouth 45	Mackin, Balderton
									(may promote Travel Wright, Newark (NG))
JLJ 403	Leyland	Tiger PS2/3	492222	Burlingham	3655	FDP35F	8/49	Bournemouth 46	Shears D, Winkleigh
JNA 467	Leyland	Titan PD1/3	492234	Metro-Cammell		H32/26R	8/49	Manchester 3166	Wotton, Littleborough
JNB 416	Maudslay	Marathon II	60093	Trans-United		C33F	1/48	Hackett, Manchester	Coventry Transport Museum

	JND 629	Leyland	Titan PD2/3	504815	Metro-Cammell		H32/26R	10/51	Manchester 3228	Stephenson & Holden, Bolton
	JND 646	Leyland	Titan PD2/3	510082	Metro-Cammell		H32/26R	10/51	Manchester 3245	Museum of Transport, Manchester
	JND 728	Daimler	CVG6DD	14832	Metro-Cammell		H32/26R	12/50	Manchester 4127	4100 Group, Manchester
	JND 791	Crossley	DD42/8s	94784	Crossley		H32/26R	1/49	Manchester 2150	Museum of Transport, Manchester
	JNN 384	Leyland	Titan PD1	460798	Duple	42690	L29/26F	12/47	Barton 467	Quantock, Bishops Lydeard (SO)
	JNZ 7487	Leyland	Tiger TRBTL11/2RP	8500214	Alexander (Belfast)	570/1	B53F	1/86	Ulsterbus 460	Kells Transport Museum, Cork
			(ex HXI 460)							
	JOH 262	→ see IY 1947 *Ireland*								
	JOJ 222	Leyland	Titan PD2/1	492326	Park Royal	B33392	H29/25R	-/50	Birmingham 2222	Shaw, Warley
	JOJ 231	Leyland	Tiger PS2/1	500279	Weymann	M4609	B34F	6/50	Birmingham 2231	Hawketts, Birmingham
	JOJ 245	Leyland	Tiger PS2/1	495582	Weymann	M4624	B34F	8/50	Birmingham 2245	Acocks Green Bus Preservation Group
	JOJ 255	Leyland	Tiger PS2/1	495583	Weymann	M4629	B34F	10/50	Birmingham 2255	Waldron, Bromsgrove
	JOJ 257	Leyland	Tiger PS2/1	495754	Weymann	M4637	B34F	10/50	Birmingham 2257	Hudd, Eltham
	JOJ 489	Crossley	DD42/6	95177	Crossley		H30/24R	7/50	Birmingham 2489	Harvey, Dudley
	JOJ 526	Guy	Arab IV	FD71000	Metro-Cammell		H30/24R	7/50	Birmingham 2526	Shaw, Warley
	JOJ 533	Guy	Arab IV	FD71007	Metro-Cammell		H30/24R	8/50	Birmingham 2533	Acocks Green Bus Preservation Group
	JOJ 548	Guy	Arab IV	FD71023	Metro-Cammell		H30/24R	10/50	Birmingham 2548	BCTS 2548 Group, Birmingham
	JOJ 555	Guy	Arab IV	FD71029	Metro-Cammell		H30/24R	10/50	Birmingham 2555	Waldron, Bromsgrove
	JOJ 707	Daimler	CVD6DD	17531	Metro-Cammell		H30/24R	9/51	Birmingham 2707	Hawletts, Birmingham
	JOJ 827	Daimler	CVG6DD	17844	Crossley		H30/25R	9/52	Birmingham 2827	Wilkins, Birmingham
	JOJ 847	Daimler	CVG6DD	17858	Crossley		H30/25RD	11/52	Birmingham 2847	Shaw, Warley
	JOJ 976	Guy	Arab IV	FD71281	Metro-Cammell		H30/25R	2/53	Birmingham 2976	BaMMOT, Wythall (WO)
	JOW 928	Guy	Arab UF	UF71420	Park Royal	B35214	B16F	1/55	Southampton 255	Southampton & District Transport Heritage Trust
	JPT 544	Daimler	CVD6SD	13315	Willowbrook	8386	B35F	-/48	Venture 156	Reed, Sunniside
	JPY 505	→ see C307 SAO								
	JPY 985	Commer	Avenger I	23A0927	Plaxton	2024	C33F	5/53	Heather, Robin Hoods Bay	Graveling, Bourne
(z)	JRA 634	Leyland	Tiger PS1	461133	Crossley		B32R	4/47	Chesterfield 47	BaMMOT, Wythall
	JRA 635	Leyland	Tiger PS1	461136	Crossley		B35R	4/47	Chesterfield 48	Watts, Chesterfield
	JRD 990	AEC	Reliance	MU3RV275	Duple	213/1	C--C	3/55	Smith, Reading	British Trolleybus Society (Reading Area)
	JRN 29	Leyland	Tiger Cub PSUC1/2	564092	Burlingham	6225	C41F	5/56	Ribble 963	Hunter, Tarleton
	JRR 404	Leyland	Titan PD1A	470111	Duple	42703	L29/26F	6/48	Barton 473	BaMMOT, Wythall
	JRR 930	Leyland	Titan PD1A	470453	Duple	42704	L29/26F	6/48	Barton 509	Barton Cherished Vehicle Collection
	JRX 823	Bristol	KSW6B	106026	ECW	7476	L27/28R	9/55	Thames Valley 748	Pribik, Winnersh
	JSJ 797	AEC	Routemaster	RM1174	Park Royal	L4180	H36/28R	3/62	London Transport RM1174	Bruce, Brentwood
			(ex 174 CLT)							
	JSL 317	Bedford	J4LZ2	66652	Plaxton	602114	C25F	8/60	Shellmex BP, Ellesmere Port	-?-, -?-
			(ex ACA 631A, 601 MMA)							
	JSU 173	Leyland	Titan TD5	15286	Leyland		O30/24R	12/37	JMT 23	Lister, Bolton
			(ex J 4540)							
	JTA 314	Guy	Arab II	FD26087	Roe	GO3318	H31/25RD	9/43	Devon General DG314	Blackman A, Halifax
					(rebodied -/51)					
	JTB 749	AEC	Regal III	O962313	Burlingham	2897	C33F	1/48	Florence, Morecambe	Hamer & Morriss, Ravenstonedale (CA)
	JTD 381	Leyland	Titan PD2/1	481225	Leyland		H30/26R	5/48	Lytham St Annes 10	Rydeheard, Blackpool
	JTE 546	AEC	Regent III	6811A090	Park Royal	B32869	H33/26R	9/48	Morecambe & Heysham 20	Quantock, Bishops Lydeard (SO)
	JUB 29	Leyland	Titan TD2	2124	Eastern Counties	2826	L27/26R	12/32	Keighley-West Yorkshire K451	Jenkinson, Queensbury
			(ex YG 2058)							
	JUE 349	Leyland	Tiger PS2/3	495827Y	Northern Counties	5839	H35/28F	4/50	Stratford Blue 51	BaMMOT, Wythall
					(rebodied 1/63)					

	JUE 860	Bedford	OB	132303	Duple	46694	C29F	3/50	Webb, Armscote	Kenzie, Shepreth (CM)
	JUI 4233	Leyland	Leopard PSU5D/4R	8031019	Plaxton	8012LC065	C53F	3/81	Southdown 1356	-?-, -?-
			(ex LPN 356W)							
	JUO 943	Bristol	LL6B	67074	ECW	10747	FB39F	8/48	Southern National 1211	Abbey Hill Steam Rally Committee, Yeovil
					(rebodied 4/58)					
	JUO 983	Bristol	LL6B	65078	ECW	10730	FB39F	8/48	Southern National 1218	Billington, Maidenhead
					(rebodied 4/58)					
	JUO 992	Leyland	Titan PD1A	471271	ECW	2301	L27/26R	12/47	Southern National 2932	Quantock, Bishops Lydeard (SO)
	JUP 233	AEC	Regal III	6821A125	Burlingham	3788	B35F	9/48	Baker, Quarrington Hill 26	Southam, Leicester
	JVB 908	Leyland	Royal Tiger PSU1/13	510075	Mann Egerton		HD24/26F	6/52	Homeland, Croydon	Jenkinson, Rickinghall
	JVF 528	Bedford	OB	102766	Duple	47678	C29F	2/49	Bensley, Martham	Oxford Bus Museum Trust
	JVH 373	AEC	Regent III	9613E4925	East Lancs	5104	L30/28R	6/55	Huddersfield 243	Munday, Huddersfield
	JVH 378	AEC	Regent III	9613E4927	East Lancs	5107	H33/28R	6/55	Huddersfield 178	Stoneywood Motors, Sowerby Bridge
	JVH 381	AEC	Regent III	9613E4932	East Lancs	5110	H33/28R	7/55	Huddersfield 181	-?-, -?-
	JVO 230	Leyland	Titan PD1A	470451	Duple	42708	L29/26F	7/48	Barton 507	Allen & Bairstow, Nottingham
	JVS 293	Bristol	MW6G	184045	ECW	12239	C--F	5/61	Western National 2266	Billington, Maidenhead
			(ex 55 GUO)							
	JVS 541	→ see RMS 714								
	JVW 430	Bristol	K5G	57087	ECW	8062	L27/28R	2/44	Eastern National 3885	Castle Point Transport Museum
	JVY 516	AEC	Regal III	6821A632	Barnaby		C39F	6/54	York Pullman 66	Bowman, Burthwaite (CA)
	JWB 416	Leyland	Tiger PS1	462095	Weymann	C9147	B34R	1/47	Sheffield 216	South Yorkshire Transport Museum
(r)	JWC 715	Bristol	Lodekka FLF6G	199177	*chassis only*			11/62	Eastern National 1629	Hughes, Hartley
	JWG 682	→ see YTS 916A								
	JWN 908	AEC	Regent III	9613S7945	Weymann	M6321	O30/26RD	3/54	South Wales 432	Hier, Swansea
	JWS 594	Guy	Arab Rebuild	195214	Duple/Nudd	130/12	H31/24R	7/43	Edinburgh 314	Pettie, Fraser & Heathcote, Dunfermline
			(ex GLL 577)		*(rebodied 3/53)*					
	JWU 307	Bedford	OB	132253	Duple	55879	C29F	4/50	Lunn, Rothwell	Hawkins, Clophill
			(ex J 9151, FSV 424, JWU 307)							
	JWU 886	Bristol	LL5G	83185	ECW	4828	B39R	5/51	West Yorkshire SGL16	Keighley Bus Museum Trust
	JXC 77	AEC	Regent III	0961588	Weymann	W1507	H30/26R	7/48	London Transport RT714	London Bus Company, Northfleet (KT)
	JXC 149	AEC	Regent III	O9611123	Park Royal	L2255	H30/26R	8/48	London Transport RT786	Biddell, Woodford Bridge *(operates as Imperial Bus, Romford (LN))*
	JXC 194	AEC	Regent III	O9611393	Cravens		H30/26R	5/49	London Transport RT1431	Ensign, Purfleet (EX)
	JXC 282	Leyland	Tiger PS1	483965	Mann Egerton		B30F	4/49	London Transport TD89	Pring, St Albans (HT)
	JXC 288	Leyland	Tiger PS1	484505	Mann Egerton		B30F	5/49	London Transport TD95	London Bus Preservation Trust
	JXC 311	Leyland	Tiger PS1	484910	Mann Egerton		B30F	8/49	London Transport TD118	Bole, Dover
	JXC 323	Leyland	Tiger PS1	490662	Mann Egerton		B30F	9/49	London Transport TD130	-?-, -?-
	JXC 432	AEC	Regent III	O9611174	Weymann	W1564	H30/26R	8/48	London Transport RT624	Ensign, Purfleet (EX)
	JXC 481	→ see HLW 177								
	JXI 1025	Leyland	Tiger TRBTL11/2RP	8600087	Alexander (Belfast)	782/6	DP53F	1/87	Ulsterbus 1025	Thompson & Shannon, Newtownards
	JXN 9	→ see CSL 498								
	JXN 46	AEC	Regent III	O9611478	Weymann	W1520	H30/26R	11/48	London Transport RT1018	Lloyd, Wigan
	JXN 135	AEC	Regent III	O9611576	Weymann	W1437	H30/26R	1/49	London Transport RT1107	Wilkinson, Billericay
	JXN 202	AEC	Regent III	O9617290	Park Royal	L433	H30/26R	7/53	London Transport RT824	Funnell, Hayes
			(ex NLE 989)							
	JXN 215	AEC	Regent III	O9611066	Weymann	W1285	H30/26R	9/48	London Transport RT837	Trumble, Greenhithe
	JXN 263	AEC	Regent III	O9611428	Park Royal	L2276	H30/26R	10/48	London Transport RT885	Saunders, Lower Stondon
	JXN 325	AEC	Regent III	O9611504	Weymann	W398	H30/26R	12/48	London Transport RT935	RT935 Preservation Group, Basingstoke

	Reg	Make	Model	Chassis No	Body	Body No	Layout	Date	New to	Owner
	JXN 366	Leyland	7RT	485283	Park Royal	L673	H32/25F	1/49	London Transport RTL43/A1, Ardrossan	Potter, Luton
	JXN 370	Leyland	7RT	485325	Park Royal	L2760	H30/26RD	1/49	London Transport RTL47	Platt, Pendlebury
	JXN 371	Leyland	7RT	485332	Park Royal	L2765	H30/26R	1/49	London Transport RTL48	London Bus Company, Northfleet (KT)
	JXU 548	Bedford	OB	91861	Duple	44532	C29F	3/49	Fallowfield & Britten	Wadley, Berrow
	JXX 487	Bedford	OB	114640	Duple	52668	B30F	1/50	Ministry of Supply	Phillips, Cilgerran
	JYC 855	Leyland	Tiger PS1	472198	Harrington	303	C33F	3/48	Porlock Weir Motor Services	Burdett, Corley
	KAD 882	Bedford	OB	141936	Duple	55995	C29F	8/50	Miles, Guiting Power	Cook, Wroxall
	KAG 856	Leyland	Titan PD2/20	571079	Alexander	5178	L31/28R	8/57	Western SMT 1375	McGowan & Walker, Glasgow
	KAH 407	Bristol	L4G	73185R	ECW	3407	B35R	8/49	Eastern Counties LL407	Ipswich Transport Museum
	KAH 408	Bristol	L4G	73186R	ECW	3411	B35R	9/49	Eastern Counties LL408	East Anglia Transport Museum
	KAL 551	Crossley	SD42/7	97672	Yeates	091	C35F	11/48	Gash, Newark CO1	Smalley, Worksop
	KAL 578	Daimler	CVD6DD	15226	Massey	2529	H33/28RD	11/48	Gash, Newark DD1	Johnson, Worksop (NG)
					(rebodied 12/62)					
	KAL 579	Daimler	CVD6DD	15227	Massey	2324	H33/28RD	11/48	Gash, Newark DD2	BaMMOT, Wythall
					(rebodied 10/58)					
	KAY 903	Tilling Stevens	L4MA8	9938	*chassis only*			-/54	N&S, Kibworth	Boultbee, Sheppey
	KBZ 7415	Ford	Transit	BDVYFA00657	Carlyle	CBS191	B16F	3/86	Alder Valley North 326	Rampton, Reading
			(ex D826 UTF, C326 RPE)		(Dormobile shell 4501 924 85)					
	KCD 697	Albion	Victor FT3AB	70790B	Harrington	663	C26F	11/49	St Dunstan's, Brighton	-?-, -?-
	KCF 711	Guy	Arab IV	FD73431	Roe	GO4318	L31/28R	1/57	Chambers, Bures	Salmon, South Benfleet
	KCH 106	→ see XMD 47A								
	KCH 112	→ see ABV 33A								
	KCK 869	Leyland	Titan PD3/4	571500	Burlingham	6449	FH41/31F	6/58	Ribble 1523	Butler, Gosforth *(on loan to Ribble Vehicle Preservation Trust)*
(r)	KCK 914	Leyland	Titan PD3/4	572501	Burlingham	6466	FH41/31F	6/58	Ribble 1553	Ribble Vehicle Preservation Trust
	KDB 651	Leyland	Tiger Cub PSUC1/1	555487	Weymann	M7371	B--F	3/56	North Western 651	Duffy, Macclesfield
	KDB 666	→ see KDB 499 *Overseas*								
	KDB 696	Leyland	Tiger Cub PSUC1/1	575806	Weymann	M7861	B44F	9/57	North Western 696	Flynn, Sprowston
	KDD 38	AEC	Regal III	9621A899	Harrington	801	FC33F	6/50	Soudley Valley, Soudley	Helliker, Stroud
	KDD 846	Bedford	OB	144940	Duple	56238	C27F	10/50	Miller, Cirencester	Lewis, Llanvihangel Crucorney
	KDJ 999	AEC	Regent V	2D3RA746	East Lancs	5615	H41/32F	12/59	St Helens K199	North West Museum of Transport
	KDT 393	AEC	Regent III	9613A5644	Roe	GO3368	H31/25R	9/51	Doncaster 122	Lincolnshire Vintage Vehicle Society
	KDZ 5805	Dennis	Dart	9SDL3011/534	Wright	N106	B45F	8/91	West Midlands 805	Davies, -?-
	KEL 94	Bedford	OB	137293	Duple	55875	C29F	5/50	Shamrock & Rambler	Padhurst, Llantrisant
			(ex ZV 9400 Ireland, KEL 94, WSL 115, KEL 95))							
	KEL 95	→ see KEL 94								
	KEL 110	Leyland	Titan PD2/3	496595	Weymann	M4267	FH33/25D	3/50	Bournemouth 110	Shears D, Winkleigh
	KEL 127	Leyland	Titan PD2/3	500169	Weymann	M4282	FH33/25D	5/50	Bournemouth 127	Shears D, Winkleigh
	KEL 131	Leyland	Titan PD2/3	500237	Weymann	M4289	FH33/25D	7/50	Bournemouth 131	Hawkins, Kingswear
	KEL 133	Leyland	Titan PD2/3	500239	Weymann	M4280	FH27/21D	5/50	Bournemouth 133	Shears D, Winkleigh
	KEL 405	Bristol	LL6B	73124	ECW	12780	FB37F	5/50	Hants & Dorset 677	Dale. Sherborne
					(rebodied 6/61)					
	KEL 679	Bedford	OB	142936	Duple	56156	C25F	9/50	Hants & Dorset 687	Adams, Clapton-on-the-Hill
			(ex J 5149, KEL 679)							
	KET 220	Daimler	CVG6DD	16810	Weymann	M6380	H30/26R	5/54	Rotherham 220	Taylor, Rotherham

	Reg	Chassis make	Model	Chassis no	Body make	Body no	Layout	Date	First owner	Current owner
	KEZ 3555	Leyland	Tiger TRBTL11/2RP (ex FXI 400)	8400437	Alexander (Belfast)	983/1	DP53F	4/85	Ulsterbus 400	Kells Transport Museum, Cork
	KEZ 5806	Leyland	Tiger TRBTL11/2RP (ex GXI 434)	8500029	Alexander (Belfast)	540/18	DP53F	10/85	Ulsterbus 434	Kells Transport Museum, Cork
(r)	KFM 1	Foden	PVSC6	27712	Plaxton	1	C33F	12/48	Taylor, Chester	Herefordshire Transport Collection
	KFM 766	Bristol	L5G	79066	ECW	4026	B35R	3/50	Crosville KG117	Brown, Rushden
	KFM 767	Bristol	L5G	79093	ECW	4027	B35R	3/50	Crosville KG118	Pratt {Crosville}, Weston super Mare (SO)
	KFM 774	Bristol	L5G	79130	ECW	4034	B20R	6/50	Crosville KG125	Ward, Etruria
	KFM 775	Bristol	L5G	79138	ECW	4035	B35R	6/50	Crosville KG126	BaMMOT, Wythall (WO)
	KFM 893	Bristol	L5G	79152	ECW	4040	DP35R	6/50	Crosville KG131	Quantock, Bishops Lydeard (SO)
	KFN 220	AEC	Reliance	MU3RV575	Weymann	M6950	DP41F	6/55	East Kent	Dwyer & Richman, Lancing
	KFN 239	AEC	Reliance	MU3RV594	Weymann	M6937	DP41F	5/55	East Kent	Burlingham, Ewell Minnis
	KGD 903	Bedford	OLAZ	246291	Duple	1027/3	C20FM	10/52	MacBrayne 162	MacBrayne Circle
	KGD 904	Bedford	OLAZ	246739	Duple	1027/4	C20FM	10/52	MacBrayne 163	McPherson & MacDonald, Howmore
	KGK 529	Leyland	6RT	493112	Leyland		H30/26R	8/49	London Transport RTW29	Adams, Bristol
	KGK 575	Leyland	6RT	494266	Leyland		H30/26R	9/49	London Transport RTW75	London Bus Company, Northfleet (KT)
	KGK 675	AEC	Regent III	O9612916	Weymann	W1391	H30/26R	8/49	London Transport RT1206	RT1206 Group, Little Hadham
	KGK 708	AEC	Regent III (ex NXP 971)	O9617594	Saunders		H30/26R	1/54	London Transport RT4686	Ensign, Purfleet (EX)
(r)	KGK 709	AEC	Regent III	O9613067	Weymann	W1811	H--/--RD	10/49	London Transport RT1240	London Bus Company, Northfleet (KT)
	KGK 758	AEC	Regent III	O9612892	Cravens		H30/26R	11/49	London Transport RT1499	Ensign, Purfleet (EX)
	KGK 803	Leyland	7RT	490868	Park Royal	L1010	H30/26R	3/49	London Transport RTL139	London Bus Preservation Trust
	KGK 938	AEC	Regent III	O9612756	Park Royal	L2768	H30/26R	3/49	London Transport RT2129	London Bus Company, Northfleet (KT)
	KGK 959	AEC	Regent III	O9612815	Weymann	W1938	H30/26R	4/49	London Transport RT2150	London Bus Company, Northfleet (KT)
(r)	KGN 204	Bedford	OB	96780	*chassis only*			4/49	Garner, Ealing	George, Dalgety Bay
	KGN 433	Bedford	OB	101690	Duple	49980	B29F	5/49	Metropolitan Police	Blue Motors, Blackpool (LA)
	KGU 4	Leyland	7RT	491072	Metro-Cammell		H30/26R	9/49	London Transport RTL554	Macbeth, York
	KGU 106	AEC	Regent III	O9612857	Weymann	W1557	H30/26R	5/49	London Transport RT2177	Herting, Chorleywood
	KGU 142	AEC	Regent III	O9612894	*chassis only*			6/49	London Transport RT2213	London Bus Preservation Trust
	KGU 162	AEC	Regent III	O9612942	Weymann	W751	H30/26R	6/49	London Transport RT2233	Biddell, Woodford Bridge
	KGU 235	AEC	Regent III	O9613035	Park Royal	L799	H3026R	7/49	London Transport RT961	London Bus Company, Northfleet (KT)
	KGU 284	Leyland	7RT	493427	Park Royal	L1179	H30/26R	8/49	London Transport RTL325	British Commercial Vehicle Museum
	KGU 290	AEC	Regent III	O9613057	Weymann	W722	H30/26R	8/49	London Transport RT1530	Barrett & Clarke, Ewell
	KGU 320	AEC	Regent III	O9613070	Park Royal	L2669	H30/26R	8/49	London Transport RT2291	Duker, Little Paxton
	KGU 322	AEC	Regent III	O9613085	Weymann	W1362	H30/26R	8/49	London Transport RT2293	Buckland, Nazeing
	KGU 434	Leyland	7RT	494183	Park Royal	L945	H30/26R	9/49	London Transport RTL358	Boughton, Brightwell
(r)	KGY 199	Bedford	OB	109972	Duple	44535	C29F	6/49	Fallowfield & Britten	George, Dalgety Bay
	KHA 301	BMMO	C1	3301	Duple	47501	C30C	11/48	BMMO 3301	3301 Preservation Group, Sutton Coldfield
	KHA 311	BMMO	C1	3311	Duple	47512	C30C	3/49	BMMO 3311	Hawketts, Birmingham
	KHA 341	BMMO	C1	3341	Duple	47542	C30C	-/49	BMMO 3341	Waldron, Bromsgrove
	KHA 352	BMMO	CL2	3352	Plaxton (*rebodied 4/62*)	622022	C--C	7/50	BMMO 3352	Bishop, Birmingham
	KHC 345	AEC	Regent V (ex XWV 416A, KHC 368)	2D3RV1263	East Lancs	5962	H32/28R	5/63	Eastbourne 68	Morgan & Vinall, Brighton
	KHC 366	AEC	Regent V (ex VSV 990, KHC 366	2D3RV1261	East Lancs	5965	RV	5/63	Eastbourne 98	Grindrod, Cornwall
	KHC 367	AEC	Regent V	2D3RV1262	East Lancs	5966	H32/28R	5/63	Eastbourne 67	Turner, Southampton
	KHC 368	→ see KHC 345								

	Reg	Make	Model	Chassis no	Body	Body no	Layout	Date	New to	Owner
	KHC 369	AEC	Regent V	2D3RV1264	East Lancs	5964	H32/28RD	5/63	Eastbourne 69	Wood, Hertford
	KHJ 999	AEC	Reliance	MU3RV398	Harrington	1631	C26C	5/55	Nicholls, Southend	Johnston, Sanderstead
	KHL 855	Guy	Arab IV	FD73875	Roe	G04544	L29/26RD	11/57	West Riding 855	Byard, Kirk Smeaton
	KHU 28	Bedford	OB	49630	Duple	43266	C--F	4/47	Maple Leaf, Bristol	Hawkins, Bridgend
(r)	KHU 620	Bristol	K6A	64024	ECW	1824	H30/26R	8/47	Bristol 3701	Staniforth, Stroud
	KHU 624	Bristol	K5G	64028	ECW	1591	L27/28R	9/47	Bristol L4103	Cook, Exeter
	KHW 630	Leyland	Titan PD1	471610	ECW	2320	H30/26R	1/48	Bristol C4019	Bristol Omnibus Vehicle Collection
	KHY 383	Bristol	L6B	65014	Bristol		B35R	3/48	Bristol 2382	-?-, West Midlands
					(rebodied 11/58 with body new 5/50)					
	KIB 7027	→ see EAP 937V								
	KIJ 4035	Dodge	KC6055	380202	Harkness		B28F	7/78	SELB, Northern Ireland	Ulster Folk & Transport Museum
	KJH 91	→ see MAS 427 *Overseas*								
	KJH 492	Bedford	OB	97489	Duple	50330	C27F	3/49	St Michael's Convent, Effingham	Chandler, Elton
	KJH 731	Bedford	OB	98856	Duple	44412	C29F	2/49	Kirby, Bushey Heath	Dorrington, Bath
	KKH 650	AEC	Regal III	9621E753	Weymann	C9333	B35F	8/49	Hull 5	Hull Museums Department
	KKN 752	Bedford	OB	76964	Duple	44272	C29F	6/48	Eglinton, Sittingbourne	Maynes, Buckie (SN)
			(ex KSU 362, KKN 752)							
	KLB 569	AEC	Regent III	O9613456	Saunders		H30/26R	2/50	London Transport RT1320	Platt, Pendlebury
	KLB 596	AEC	Regent III	O9613753	Weymann	W1124	H30/26R	4/50	London Transport RT1347	Black & White, Penton Mewsey (HA)
	KLB 648	Leyland	7RT	495918	Park Royal	L444	H30/26R	12/49	London Transport RTL453	Ensign, Purfleet (EX)
	KLB 662	AEC	Regent III	O9613407	Park Royal	L2777	H30/26R	12/49	London Transport RT1574	Blair, Upham
	KLB 716	AEC	Regent III	O9613507	Park Royal	L1448	H--/--RD	2/50	London Transport RT1594	Dale, Sherborne
	KLB 719	→ see LLU 804								
	KLB 721	AEC	Regent III	O9613515	Park Royal	L3066	H30/26R	2/50	London Transport RT1599	Adams, Bristol
	KLB 799	AEC	Regent III	O9613349	Weymann	W1442	H--/--RD	11/49	London Transport RT2420	Macey, Luton
(r)	KLB 828	AEC	Regent III	O9613392	*chassis only*			12/49	London Transport RT2449	Duker, Little Paxton
	KLB 881	Leyland	6RT	495951	Leyland		H30/26R	11/49	London Transport RTW151	Wright & Humphries, Dagenham
	KLB 908	Leyland	6RT	496243	Leyland		H30/26RD	10/49	London Transport RTW178	Stubbs, Burton-upon-Trent
	KLB 915	Leyland	6RT	496299	Leyland		H30/26R	10/49	London Transport RTW185	Clayton, Baynards
	KLJ 749	Bristol	LL6G	73132	Portsmouth Aviation		DP36R	11/50	Hants & Dorset 779	Tovey & Knight, Bristol
	KMA 553	Foden	PVSC6	27288	Plaxton	22	C33F	4/48	Bullock, Cheadle	Herefordshire Transport Collection
	KNG 374	Bristol	K6B	76039	ECW	3520	L27/28R	12/49	Eastern Counties LK374	Ipswich Transport Museum
	KNG 699	Bristol	L5G	79131	ECW	4258	DP31R	7/50	Eastern Counties LL699	Hughes & Wheble, Hartley
	KNG 711	Bristol	L5G	81010	ECW	4649	B35R	7/50	Eastern Counties LL711	Burnside, Norwich
	KNG 718	Bristol	LL5G	81176	ECW	4656	B39R	10/50	Eastern Counties LL718	Eastern Transport Collection
	KNN 254	Leyland	Titan PD1A	485820	Duple	45919	L29/26F	2/49	Barton 580	Nottingham Heritage Vehicles
	KNN 314	Bedford	OB	100400	Duple	-?-	C29F	4/49	South Notts, Gotham 38	Wilson, Haughley
	KNN 959	Daimler	CVD6DD	17161	Roberts		H30/26RD	8/49	Gash, Newark DD6	Brown, Hertford
	KNT 780	Leyland	Royal Tiger PSU1/16	532484	Burlingham	5108	C37C	1/54	Gittins, Crickheath	Boulton, Cardington (SH)
	KNU 446	AEC	Regal I	O6624654	Willowbrook	6160	DP35F	10/46	Woolliscroft, Darley Dale 4	Burton, Alfreton (DE)
	KNV 337	Bristol	KSW6B	102054	ECW	7219	L27/28R	9/54	United Counties 964	Chelveston Preservation Society
	KOD 585	AEC	Regent III	9612E2495	Weymann	M3787	H30/26R	8/49	Devon General DR585	Greet, Broadhempston
	KOD 965	Bedford	OB	114111	Duple	54113	C27F	8/49	Blue, Ilfracombe	Jenkins, Wells
	KOI 9961	Leyland	Leopard PSU3C/4R	7505787	Alexander (Belfast)	184/13	RV	2/65	Ulsterbus 1961	Kells Transport Museum, Cork
	KPT 909	Leyland	Titan PD2/1	494078	Leyland		L27/26R	8/49	Weardale, Frosterley	Science Museum, Wroughton
	KPW 986	Bedford	OB	122499	Duple	54099	C29F	7/50	Eagle, Castle Acre	Lewis, Henstridge (SO)
	KRH 338	AEC	Regent III	9612E4534	Weymann	M4335	H32/26R	12/49	Hull 328	Hull Museums Department
	KRN 422	Leyland	Titan PD2/10	571349	Crossley	5226	H33/29R	12/57	Preston 31	Barber, Chadderton

	KRR 255	AEC	Regal III	9621E481	Weymann	M4122	DP35F	5/50	Mansfield District 9	Peck, Mansfield Woodhouse
	KRU 961	Bristol	KSW6B	82105	ECW	5066	L27/28R	9/51	Hants & Dorset 1295	Froud, Verwood
	KSK 466	Renault	TN6C	610-539	STCRP		B??R	-/34	RATP (Paris) 2758	Dooner, Doncaster
	KSJ 622	→ see MXX 481								
			(ex JH 6699)							
	KSU 288	Albion	Victor FT39AN	73791K	Heaver		B35F	1/56	Guernsey Motors 70	Lighthouse & Transport Museum, Arran
			(ex 15141, 1982)							
	KSU 362	→ see KKN 752								
	KSU 381	→ see SS 7376								
	KSV 102	AEC	Regent III	9631E1694	Weymann	M6652	H37/28R	10/54	Lisbon Electric Tramways 255	Shearman, Tunbridge Wells
			(ex GB-21-07 *Portugal*)							
	KTB 672	Crossley	SD42/7	97759	Burlingham	3685	C33F	1/49	Warburton, Bury	Emerton, Nantwich
	KTC 615	→ see 831 XUW								
	KTD 768	Leyland	Titan PD2/1	485241	Lydney		L27/26R	2/50	Leigh 16	North West Museum of Transport
	KTF 587	→ see IY 1940 *Ireland*								
	KTF 589	AEC	Regent III	9612E4655	Park Royal	B33408	O33/26R	8/49	Morecambe & Heysham 60	Hoare, Chepstow (CS)
	KTF 591	AEC	Regent III	9612E4657	Park Royal	B33410	O33/26R	9/49	Morecambe & Heysham 62	Lord, Morecambe
										(operated as Lord & Smith, Morecamber (LA))
	KTF 594	AEC	Regent III	9621E4660	Park Royal	B33411	O33/26R	9/49	Morecambe & Heysham 65	Quantock, Bishops Lydeard (SO)
	KTJ 502	Leyland	Tiger PS1	492482	Burlingham	3744	B35F	9/49	Haslingden 2	Lediard, Morpeth
	KTL 780	Leyland	Titan PD2/20	550943	Willowbrook	56838	H35/28RD	4/56	Delaine, Bourne 45	Delaine, Bourne (LI) 45
	KTT 689	Guy	Vixen	LLV40298	Wadham		FC29F	1/49	Court, Torquay	Cope, Longton
	KTX 631	Leyland	Tiger PS2/3	501267	Massey	2076	B39F	6/51	Llynfi, Maesteg 59	-?-, Swansea
(r)	KUI 2269	Leyland	Atlantean PDR2/1	7101746	Northern Counties	-?-	DP42F	8/71	Fylde 4	Lancstrian Transport Trust
			(ex TKU 462K)		*(rebodied 6/93)*					
	KUI 6566	Mercedes-Benz	O303	30122521026760	Plaxton	8112MC004	C53F	4/81	Wahl, Camberwell	Webb, Armscote (WK)
			(ex XAM 229A, JJD 47W)							
	KUO 972	Bristol	K6B	80018	ECW	3738	L27/28R	7/50	Western National 959	Hoare, Chepstow (CS)
	KUP 234	Bedford	OB	118093	Duple	54726	C29F	10/49	Harrison, Wingate	Chandler, Elton
	KUP 799	Albion	Valiant CX39N	60311B	ACB		C33F	1/50	Economic, Whitburn 10	Sullivan & Dawson, Consett
	KUP 949	Leyland	Tiger PS1/1	496118	Burlingham	4113	C31F	2/50	Iveson, Cornsay Colliery	Bate, Horsforth
	KUX 774	MCW	Metroliner DR130/3	MB7572	MCW		CH57/23F	7/84	Ribble 120	Vals, Chase Terrace (ST)
			(ex A253 TPO, POR 1, SNU 122, A120 KBA)							
	KVS 601	AEC	Routemaster	RM471	Park Royal	L3852	H36/28R	11/60	London Transport RM471	Dobbing, Stibbington (CM)
			(ex EDS 394A, WLT 471)							
	KWE 255	AEC	Regent III	9612E2649			gritter	7/48	Sheffield G55	South Yorkshire Transport Museum
	KWG 564	→ see XYJ 890								
	KWG 655	Leyland	Titan PD3/3	581491	Alexander	5532	L35/32R	9/58	Alexander RB194	Assiph, Dundee
	KWJ 25	→ see OWJ 340A								
(r)	KWT 600	Daimler	CVD6DD	17179	*chassis only*			4/51	Rossie, Rossington	Marshall, Sutton-on-Trent (NG)
	KWU 383	Bristol	LWL6G	87007			RV	-/52	West Yorkshire Road Car 1037	Hunter, Leeds
			(ex NSU 375, KWU 383)							
	KWX 412	Bedford	SB	3743	Duple	56794	C33F	8/51	Kildare, Adwick-le-Street	Jamieson, Cullivoe (SN)
	KXV 562	Bedford	OB	125070	Mulliner		B30F	-/49	Ministry of Works	Shaw, Gilberdyke
	KXW 22	Leyland	7RT	496143	Metro-Cammell		H30/26R	2/50	London Transport RTL672	London Bus Company, Northfleet (KT)
	KXW 123	AEC	Regent III	O9613476	Weymann	W1464	O29/26R	1/50	London Transport RT2494	Cruise, Fulham
			(ex 54636 , KXW 123)							

	Reg	Make	Model	Chassis	Body	Body no	Layout	New	Original operator	Owner
	KXW 171	AEC	Regent III	O9613554	Saunders		H30/26R	2/50	London Transport RT3062	London Bus Company, Northfleet (KT)
	KXW 234	AEC	Regent III	O9613801	Weymann	W2104	H30/26R	4/50	London Transport RT3125	Taylor, Edgware
	KXW 304	AEC	Regent III	O9613778	Weymann	W1359	H30/26R	3/50	London Transport RT1658	London Bus Company, Northfleet (KT)
	KXW 429	Leyland	6RT	501712	Leyland		H30/26R	5/50	London Transport RTW329	Biddell, Woodford Bridge
	KXW 435	Leyland	6RT	501807	Leyland		H30/26R	6/50	London Transport RTW335	Ensign, Purfleet (EX)
	KXW 478	AEC	Regent III	O9613679	Weymann	W2045	H30/26R	6/50	London Transport RT1379	Cooper, Newquay
	KXW 488	AEC	Regent III	O9613967	Weymann	W1315	H30/26R	7/50	London Transport RT1389	London Bus Company, Northfleet (KT)
	KXW 495	AEC	Regent III	O9614013	Saunders		H30/26R	8/50	London Transport RT1396	Tamkin, Leighton Buzzard
										(operates as Alpha, Soulbury (BK))
	KYD 151	AEC	Regal III	6821A119	Harrington	425	C33F	3/49	Hawkins, Minehead	Waldron, Bromsgrove
	KYE 905	Bedford	OB	133670	Duple	52432	C27F	3/50	Grey Green, Stamford Hill	Padfield, Llantrisant
	KYW 335	Bedford	OB	143000	Whitson		B28F	2/50	Ministry of Supply	French, Arborfield
	KYY 527	AEC	Regent III	O9613656	Weymann	W724	H30/26R	4/50	London Transport RT1700	London Bus Company, Northfleet (KT)
	KYY 529	AEC	Regent III	O9613644	Park Royal	L1435	H30/26R	5/50	London Transport RT1702	1702 Preservation Society, Orpington
	KYY 532	AEC	Regent III	O9613819	Park Royal	L95	H30/26R	4/50	London Transport RT1705	Ackroyd & Evans, Send
	KYY 615	AEC	Regent III	O9613934	Park Royal	L2979	H30/26R	6/50	London Transport RT1777	Richards, Twickenham
	KYY 622	AEC	Regent III	O9613692	Park Royal	L341	H30/26R	6/50	London Transport RT1784	Hinson, Potterspury
	KYY 628	AEC	Regent III	O9614010	Park Royal	L3118	H30/26R	6/50	London Transport RT1790	Clarke, Dorking (SR)
	KYY 647	Leyland	7RT	502098	Park Royal	L1544	H29/23F	6/50	London Transport RTL1004	Ullmer, Enfield
			(ex 47312, 995, KYY 647)							
	KYY 653	AEC	Regent III	O9614047	Weymann	W1898	H30/26R	6/50	London Transport RT1798	Ricketts, Andover
	KYY 663	AEC	Regent III	O9613923	Weymann	W1027	H30/26R	6/50	London Transport RT1808	National Motor Museum, Beaulieu
	KYY 832	AEC	Regent III	O9614089	Park Royal	L3104	H30/26R	9/50	London Transport RT4229	Biddell, Woodford Bridge
	KYY 872	AEC	Regent III	O9613680	Weymann	W2007	H30/26R	5/50	London Transport RT3143	Brown, Hawkhurst (KT)
	KYY 877	AEC	Regent III	O9613671	Weymann	W852	H30/26R	5/50	London Transport RT3148	Country Bus Rallies, East Grinstead
	KYY 883	AEC	Regent III	O9613852	Park Royal	L1377	H--/--R	5/50	London Transport RT3154	Blackman A, Halifax
(r)	KYY 904	AEC	Regent III	O9613833	Weymann	W840	H30/26R	5/50	London Transport RT3175	Austin, Sidcup
	KYY 912	AEC	Regent III	O9613635	Weymann	W2075	H30/26R	6/50	London Transport RT3183	Powis, Tonbridge
			(ex BHJ 203S, KYY 912)							
	KYY 927	→ see KYY 967								
	KYY 957	AEC	Regent III	O9614044	Weymann	W1951	H30/26R	6/50	London Transport RT3228	London Bus Company, Northfleet (KT)
	KYY 961	AEC	Regent III	O9614081	Weymann	W1288	H30/26R	7/50	London Transport RT3232	Ensign, Purfleet (EX)
	KYY 967	AEC	Regent III	O9613913	Weymann	W1052	H30/26R	6/50	London Transport RT3198	London Bus Company, Northfleet (KT)
			(ex KYY 927)							
	KYY 970	AEC	Regent III	O9613971	Weymann	W1018	H30/26R	6/50	London Transport RT3241	McOwan, Ashen
	LAA 231	Dennis	Lancet III	177J10C	Strachan	51874	FC38R	6/53	Aldershot & District 196	Stubbs, Burton-upon-Trent
	LAE 13	Leyland	Titan PD1A	472861	ECW	2331	H30/26R	3/48	Bristol C4044	Bristol Vintage Bus Group
(r)	LAE 317	Bristol	K6B	66094	*chassis only*			7/48	Bristol 3743	Staniforth, Stroud
(r)	LAH 75	Bedford	OB	132882	Duple	55817	C29F	3/50	Parnell, West Rudham	Cobus, Bridlington
	LAO 630	Albion	Victor FT39N	73113F	Duple	110/4	C31F	-/51	Henderson, Alston	Easton, Stratton Strawless (NK)
(r)	LAS 948	Bristol	Lodekka FLF6G	199156	ECW	13095	O--/--F	10/62	Bristol G7066	Staniforth, Stroud
			(ex JSK 492, 511 OHU)							
	LAT 69	Leyland	Titan PD2/3	496402	Roe	G03207	H30/26R	10/50	East Yorkshire 541	Ireland, Hull
	LAX 333	AEC	Regal IV	9821E504	Burlingham	4907	C37C	7/51	Westbury, Bristol	MacPherson, Donisthorpe (LE)
			(ex OAE 949)							

	Reg	Make	Model	Chassis No	Body	Body No	Layout	Date	Original Operator	Current Owner
	LBP 500	Bedford	OB	121288	Duple	44873	C29F	-/49	Silver Queen, Worthing	Dealtop, Plymouth (DN)
	LCU 112	Daimler	CCG6DD	20099	Roe	GO5822	H35/28R	4/64	South Shields 140	Busways (TW) 19912
	LDA 890	Morris	JR	JR19464	Morris		B9	12/53	non-PSV	Thurstans, Stillington
	LDB 796	Leyland	Tiger Cub PSUC1/1	595379	Willowbrook	59347	DP43F	3/60	North Western 796	Butler, Gosforth
			(ex BE-21-96 *Netherlands*, LDB 796)							
	LDF 833	Bedford	OB	H&S3024	Duple	127/1	C29F	7/52	Bowles, Ford	Garaghty & Messenger, Desborough
	LDJ 985	Leyland	Titan PD2A/30	601241	Weymann	M9498	H30/5RD	8/60	St Helens K175	North West Museum of Transport
(r)	LDL 733	Bristol	Lodekka LD6G	108025	ECW	8083	H--/--RD	6/55	Southern Vectis 534	-?-, -?-
	LDN 96	AEC	Regent III	6812A127	Roe	GO4002	H33/27RD	5/55	York Pullman 67	Armour, Derby
	LDP 945	AEC	Regent III	6812A130	Park Royal	B38355	L31/26RD	1/56	Reading 98	Rampton, Reading
	LDV 483	Bedford	OB	124372	Duple	54905	C29F	3/50	Gourd, Kingsteignton	Higgs, Cheltenham
	LEC 214	Bedford	VAS2	1403	Plaxton	632642	C29F	6/63	Merseyside Regional Hospital Board	Jones, Llanfaethlu (CN)
	LEL 699	Karrier	Q25	32A0214	Reading		C--F	-/51	Priory, Christchurch	Clifford, Oswestry
	LEN 101	Guy	Wulfrunian	FDW74695	*chassis only*			12/60	Bury 101	West Riding Omnibus Preservation Society
	LEV 917	Leyland	Titan PD1/1	461011	Alexander	3045	O33/26R	2/47	City, Brentwood LD1	Springhill Vehicle Preservation Group, Tunbridge Wells
	LFF 875	AEC	Routemaster	RMC1456	Park Royal	L4725	H32/25RD	7/62	London Transport RMC1456	Michael, Stroud
			(ex 456 CLT)							
	LFM 302	Leyland	Tiger PS1/1	492489	Weymann	M4143	B35F	3/50	Crosville KA226	Quantock, Bishops Lydeard (SO)
	LFM 320	Leyland	Tiger PS1/1	494123	Weymann	M4146	B35F	3/50	Crosville KA244	Marsh & Pixton, Stockport
	LFM 329	Leyland	Tiger PS1/1	494217	Weymann	M4159	B--F	3/50	Crosville KA253	Quantock, Bishops Lydeard (SO)
	LFM 404	Bedford	OB	140988	Duple	56134	C29F	7/50	Crosville SL67	Price, Shobdon
	LFM 717	Bristol	L5G	79172	ECW	4562	B35R	7/50	Crosville KG136	Shears D, Winkleigh
	LFM 728	Bristol	L5G	81036	ECW	4573	B35R	7/50	Crosville KG147	Jones, Hawarden
	LFM 731	Bristol	LL5G	81082	ECW	4577	B39R	8/50	Crosville KG150	Bailey, Telford
	LFM 734	Bristol	LL5G	81085	ECW	4579	B39R	8/50	Crosville KG153	Braga, Lower Dean
	LFM 737	→ see FCI 323 *Ireland*								
	LFM 753	Bristol	L6B	81162	ECW	4884	DP31R	7/50	Crosville KW172	Jones, Hawarden
	LFM 756	Bristol	LL6B	81165	ECW	4582	B39R	10/50	Crosville KW175	Jones, Hawarden
	LFM 759	Bristol	LL6B	83005	ECW	4587	B39R	10/50	Crosville KW178	Oates, Mobberley
	LFM 767	Bristol	LL6B	83053	ECW	4597	B39R	11/50	Crosville KW186	Marsden, Cullingworth
	LFM 810	Bristol	LWL6B	85135	ECW	5286	B39R	2/51	Crosville KW229	Prince, West Kirby
(r)	LFS 418	Leyland	Titan PD2/20	540187	Metro-Cammell		H33/27R	6/54	Edinburgh 418	Roulston, Glasgow
	LFS 480	Leyland	Titan PD2/20	541200	Metro-Cammell		H34/29R	10/54	Edinburgh 480	City of Edinburgh Council (*on loan to Lothian Bus Consortium*)
	LFV 309	Leyland	Titan PD2/21	560766	Metro-Cammell		FH35/24R	6/57	Blackpool 309	Grimmer, Carlisle
	LFW 326	Bristol	Lodekka LD6B	104064	ECW	7345	H33/25RD	4/55	Lincolnshire 2318	Lincolnshire Vintage Vehicle Society
	LGV 994	Bedford	SB3	58898	Duple	1090/7	C41F	3/58	Burton, Haverhill	Hewitt, Watford
	LHN 823	Bristol	L5G	73025	ECW	4130	B35R	10/49	United BG381	Bulmer, North Stainley (NY)
	LHN 860	Bristol	L5G	79070	ECW	4166	B35F	12/50	United BG413	Aycliffe & District Bus Preservation Society
	LHT 911	Bristol	L5G	67128	Bristol		B35R	9/48	Bristol 2388	Amos, Nailsea
					(*rebodied 10/58 with body new 10/50*)					
	LHW 918	Bristol	L5G	71074	ECW	3274	B--R	7/49	Bristol 2410	Staniforth, Stroud
	LHY 937	Bristol	K6B	78084	ECW	3839	H31/28R	4/50	Bristol C3448	Law et al, Walthamstow
	LHY 976	Bristol	L5G	71173	ECW	4216	B33D	12/49	Bristol C2736	Walker & Curtis, Wells
	LHY 994	Bristol	L5G	73018	ECW	3986	B20R	11/49	Bristol 2447	Ward, Sandy
	LIL 7804	Merecedes-Benz	L608D	31041420567822	Plaxton	WO5438	C25F	4/83	Jackson, Altrincham	Golynia & Warnack, Long Melford (SK)
			(ex ANA 114Y)							

	Reg	Make	Model	Chassis No	Body	Body No	Layout	Date	First Owner	Current Owner
(r)	LIL 7960	Volkswagen	LT55	ZH021493	Optare	281	B25F	9/87	Yorkshire Rider 2018	Tindall, Huddersfeild
			(ex E218 PWY)							
	LIL 9929	Bedford	VAS5	JW458174	Plaxton	79PJK017	C29F	3/79	Blood Transfusion Service	Dickson, Dunfermline
			(ex CJU 998T)							
	LJH 665	Dennis	Lancet III	722J3	Duple	52015	C35F	12/49	Lee, Barnet	Quantock, Bishops Lydeard (SO)
	LJO 757	Bedford	OB	144971	Duple	55779	C29F	11/50	Chiltonian, Chilton Foliat	Howard, Upminster
			(ex GBL 200)							
	LJW 336	Guy	Arab LUF	LUF71567	Saunders-Roe		B44F	9/53	Guy demonstrator	Haines, Stafford
	LJX 198	AEC	Regent V	2D3RA727	Weymann	M9165	H39/32F	11/59	Hebble 307	Blackman, Halifax (WY)
	LJX 215	AEC	Regent V	2D3RA760	Metro-Cammell		H40/32F	2/60	Halifax 215	Blackman A, Halifax
	LKG 678	AEC	Regent V	MD3RV216	Park Royal	B38800	H--/--RD	6/56	Western Welsh 678	Cardiff Transport Preservation Group
	LKH 429	Bedford	OB	143909	Duple	49832	C29F	10/50	Grey-de-Luxe, Hull	Cook, Worfield
	LKN 550	Bedford	OB	106863	Mulliner	T413	B28F	6/49	Dineley, Margate	Staniforth, Stroud
	LKT 991	Bristol	L6A	79024	ECW	4086	B35R	3/50	Maidstone & District SO43	Smith, Hayes
(r)	LKZ 6715	Leyland	Leopard PSU3E/4R	7901952	Alexander (Belfast)	580/40	DP49F	6/80	Ulsterbus 187	Montgomery T, Ballymena
			(ex VOI 187)							
	LKZ 9307	Mercedes-Benz	O303	30031521039093	Jonckheere	19110	C51F	2/85	Mott, Stoke Mandeville	Webb, Armscote (WK)
			(ex B360 VLJ, A 5 UNX, B360 VLJ, SJI 8235, 9820 MT, B493 CBD)							
	LLU 610	AEC	Regent III	O9613955	Weymann	W2139	H30/26R	7/50	London Transport RT3251	Langley, Wethersfield
	LLU 613	AEC	Regent III	O9613978	Weymann	W1414	H30/26R	7/50	London Transport RT3254	Wills, Stevenage
(r)	LLU 642	AEC	Regent III	09615092	*chassis only*			8/50	London Transport RT3843	Duker, Little Paxton
	LLU 670	AEC	Regent III	O9615170	Park Royal	L3214	H30/26R	9/50	London Transport RT3871	London Bus Company, Northfleet (KT)
	LLU 693	AEC	Regent III	09615985	Weymann	W1012	H30/26R	9/50	London Transport RT3894	Cracknell, Dartford
	LLU 701	AEC	Regent III	O9615216	Park Royal	L1721	H--/--R	11/50	London Transport RT3902	Garbutt, Holbeach
	LLU 732	AEC	Regent III	O9615258	Park Royal	L3094	H30/26R	10/50	London Transport RT3933	London Bus Company, Northfleet (KT)
	LLU 770	AEC	Regent III	O9615089	Park Royal	L3085	H30/26R	8/50	London Transport RT1884	Topgood, Ramsey
	LLU 804	AEC	Regent III	O9613491	Park Royal	L3189	H29/23F	2/50	London Transport RT1597	Austin, Sidcup
			(ex KLB 719)							
	LLU 829	Leyland	7RT	504001	Park Royal	L1806	H30/26R	9/50	London Transport RTL1050	Thrower, Warrington
	LLU 957	Leyland	6RT	504335	Leyland		H30/26R	10/50	London Transport RTW467	RTW467 Group, Twickenham
	LLU 987	Leyland	6RT	504621	Leyland		H30/26R	11/50	London Transport RTW497	Potter, Luton
	LMA 284	Foden	PVSC6	27750	Lawton		C35F	4/49	Coppenhall, Sandbach	Bullock, Cheadle (GM)
					(*rebodied c6/60*)					(*on loan to Museum of Transport, Manchester*)
	LMG 184	Leyland	Lion LT9	303395	Leyland		B39F	8/39	Eastbourne 15	Canham, Whittlesey
			(ex JK 8421)							
	LMU 605	Ford	ET6	7267463	Bellhouse Hartwell	B228	C20FL	3/52	Friern Hospital, New Southgate	McGowan, Gunnerton
	LNA 367	Bedford	OB	141301	Duple	49748	C29F	4/50	Moss & Smith, Macclesfield	Moseley (PCV), South Elmsall
	LNN 353	Daimler	CVD6DD	16955	Duple	50194	L27/26RD	8/50	Gash, Newark DD7	Marshall, Sutton-on-Trent (NG)
	LNY 903	Leyland	Titan PD2/12	514801	Leyland		L27/28R	12/51	Caerphilly 3	Cardiff Transport Preservation Group
	LOD 495	Albion	Victor FT39N	72873F	Duple	54037	C31F	5/50	Way, Crediton	Carmel Coaches, Northlew (DN)
	LOD 529	Bedford	OB	137285	Duple	56050	C29F	5/50	Good, Beer	Sutton, Redgrave
	LOE 300	→ see RSK 615								
	LOG 301	Guy	Arab IV	FD71259	Saunders-Roe		H30/25R	11/52	Birmingham 3001	Shaw, Warley
	LOG 302	Daimler	CLG5DD	18335	Metro-Cammell		H30/25R	10/54	Birmingham 3002	-?-, -?-
	LOI 1859	Bedford	YLQ	FW453531	Alexander (Belfast)	-?-	B45F	3/77	Ulsterbus 1859	Curry, Pinxton
	LOI 1864	→ see 76-D-74 *Ireland*								
	LOI 1868	→ see 76-D-75 *Ireland*								
	LOI 1878	Bedford	YLQ	FW455852	Alexander (Belfast)	-?-	B--F	1/77	Ulsterbus 1878	Shannon, Newtownards

	LOU 48	Dennis	Lance III	118K4	East Lancs	4976	L28/28R	3/54	Aldershot & District 220	Stubbs & Spalding, Burton-upon-Trent
	LOW 217	Guy	Arab III	FD71962	Park Royal	B33570	H30/26R	9/54	Southampton 71	Southampton City Council
										(in care of Southampton & District Transport Heritage Trust)
	LPT 328	AEC	Regal III	9621E989	Burlingham	4186	C33F	5/50	Gillett, Quarrington Hill 31	Thomas, Holyhead
	LRA 907	AEC	Regal III	O962093	Duple	45398	C35F	12/47	Wolliscroft, Darley Dale 14	James, Blaenporth
	LRB 750	Bedford	OB	64154	Barnaby		C29F	3/48	Booth & Fisher, Halfway 11	McNeill, Todmorden
	LRC 454	Leyland	Titan PD3/4	572846	Willowbrook	57985	H41/32RD	3/58	Trent 1054	Trent (DE) 1054
	LRL 660	Bedford	OB	110509	Duple	52473	C29F	7/49	Willis, Bodmin	Ealson, Chertsey (SR)
	LRM 806	AEC	Regal III	9621A1545	Plaxton	2043	FC33F	3/53	Brownrigg, Egremont	Bowman, Burthwaite (CA)
	LRV 988	Leyland	Titan PD2/12	551131	Metro-Cammell		O33/26R	3/56	Portsmouth 6	Gradwell, Hyde
	LRV 991	Leyland	Titan PD2/12	551134	Metro-Cammell		O33/26R	3/56	Portsmouth 1	City of Portsmouth Preserved Transport Depot
	LRV 992	Leyland	Titan PD2/12	551157	Metro-Cammell		O33/26R	4/56	Portsmouth 2	Pearce & Jackson, Worthing
	LRV 996	Leyland	Titan PD2/12	551168	Metro-Cammell		O33/26R	4/56	Portsmouth 4	Working Omnibus Museum Project
	LSU 857	Bedford	OB	32426	Mulliner		B28F	3/47	JMT 57	Sleep, Eversley (HA)
			(ex LTR 336R, J 6986)							
	LSV 748	Albion	Victor FT39AN	73821F	Heaver		B31F	1/57	Guernsey Motors 73	Tidley, Wales
			(ex JPA 81V, 4029)							
	LTA 629	AEC	Regal III	9621A779	Duple	55182	C32F	5/50	Devon General TCR629	Cowdery, East Markham
	LTA 729	Bristol	LL6B	81038	Duple	54587	C37F	3/51	Western National 1250	Billington, Maidenhead
(r)	LTA 741	Bristol	LL6B	83165	*chassis only*			7/51	Western National 1303	Shears C, Winkleigh
	LTA 748	Bedford	OB	127745	Duple	54854	C29F	5/50	Western National 1409	Billington, Maidenhead
	LTA 750	Bedford	OB	127852	Duple	54858	C27F	5/50	Western National 1411	Wootton, Great Horwood
	LTA 752	Bedford	OB	135254	Duple	56053	B27F	5/50	Lincolnshire 2094 / Western National 1413	Lodge, High Easter (EX)
	LTA 755	Bedford	OB	135986	Duple	56056	C29F	5/50	Western National 1416	Hillier, Foxham (WI)
	LTA 755	→ see also HYP 722								
	LTA 772	Bristol	LWL5G	83222	ECW	5406	B39R	3/51	Western National 1613	West Country Historic Omnibus & Transport Trust
	LTA 813	Bristol	KS5G	80055	ECW	4419	L27/28R	9/50	Western National 994	Burdett, Corley
	LTA 893	Bristol	LL6B	81050	Duple	54576	C37F	3/51	Southern National 1264	Gooding, Stirchley
	LTA 895	Bristol	LL6B	81052	Duple	54578	C37F	4/51	Southern National 1266	Hawke, Newquay
	LTA 898	Bristol	LL6B	83103	Duple	54601	C37F	5/51	Southern National 1269	Burdett, Corley
	LTA 904	Bedford	OB	123031	Duple	54797	C27F	12/49	Southern National 1428	Edwards, Clanfield
	LTA 906	Bedford	OB	123634	Duple	54800	C29F	12/49	Southern National 1430	Greet, Broadhempston
										(operates as Nostalgic Transport, Broadhempston (DN))
	LTA 908	Bedford	OB	124001	Duple	54801	C27F	12/49	Southern National 1432	Tarrant, Colchester
(r)	LTA 924	Bedford	OB	134432	*chassis only*			6/50	Southern National 1448	Simpson, Killamarsh
	LTA 946	Bristol	KS6B	82025	ECW	4352	L27/28R	12/50	Southern National 1836	Billington, Maidenhead
	LTA 958	Bristol	LL6B	83219	Duple	56400	C37F	9/51	Southern National 1324	Hoare, Chepstow (CS)
	LTA 995	Bristol	KSW6B	92144	ECW	5889	L27/28R	1/53	Southern National 1852	Haynes Publishing, Sparkford
	LTB 907	Bedford	OB	125509	Duple	55677	C29F	1/50	Lamb, Upholland	Ingall, Rand
	LTF 254	AEC	Regent III	9612E5341	Park Royal	B34423	H33/26R	7/50	Morecambe & Heysham 69	Knott, Halifax
	LTT 913	Bedford	OB	118863	Duple	43367	C29F	11/49	Sunbeam, Torquay	Keaney, Hepworth
	LTU 670	Bedford	OB	117210	Duple	54367	C--F	1/50	Bullock, Cheadle	Machin, Church Lawton
	LTU 869	Commer	Avenger I	23A0260	Plaxton	1057	C33F	10/49	Thornley, Woodley	Transport Museum Society of Ireland
	LTV 702	AEC	Regal III	9621E844	East Lancs	4604	B35R	7/51	Nottingham 702	Blood, North Tawton
	LTX 311	Leyland	Tiger PS2/5	520623	Massey	2083	B35F	6/52	Caerphilly 1	Re-liance 1284 Preservation Group, Tredegar
	LUC 72	→ see LUC 250								
	LUC 187	AEC	Regent III	O9615539	Park Royal	L1225	H30/26R	1/51	London Transport RT4028	Copas, Redruth
	LUC 204	AEC	Regal IV	9821LT004	Metro-Cammell		B35F	5/51	London Transport RF4	Penfold, Meldreth

	Reg	Chassis	Model	Chassis No	Body	Body No	Layout	Date	First Operator	Current Owner
	LUC 210	AEC	Regal IV	9821LT010	Metro-Cammell		B35F	5/51	London Transport RF10	Kriesler, Wallington
	LUC 212	AEC	Regal IV	9821LT012	Metro-Cammell		B35F	5/51	London Transport RF12	Wealdsman Preservation Group, Headcorn
	LUC 213	AEC	Regal IV	9821LT013	Metro-Cammell		B35F	5/51	London Transport RF13	Wealdsman Preservation Group, Headcorn
	LUC 216	AEC	Regal IV	9821LT016	Metro-Cammell		B35F	5/51	London Transport RF16	Wealdsman Preservation Group, Headcorn
			(ex WI 8166, LUC 216)							
	LUC 219	AEC	Regal IV	9821LT019	Metro-Cammell		B35F	5/51	London Transport RF19	Selt, Colchester
(r)	LUC 220	AEC	Regal IV	9821LT020	Metro-Cammell		B35F	5/51	London Transport RF20	Penfold, Meldreth
	LUC 250	Leyland	7RT	504741	*chassis only*			11/50	London Transport RTL1073	Thrower, Hurst, Lloyd & Simmons, Warrington
			(ex AGS 72B, LUC 72)							
	LUC 253	Leyland	7RT	504832	Park Royal	L1885	H30/26R	12/50	London Transport RTL1076	London Bus Company, Northfleet (KT)
	LUC 289	AEC	Regent III	O9615516	Park Royal	L1224	H30/26R	12/50	London Transport RT2041	Stevens, Chilham
	LUC 291	AEC	Regent III	O9615527	Park Royal	L3273	H30/26R	12/50	London Transport RT2043	Stagg, Offham
	LUC 315	Leyland	7RT	504842	Park Royal	L2354	H30/26R	12/50	London Transport RTL1105	London Bus Company, Northfleet (KT)
	LUC 381	AEC	Regal IV	9821E323	ECW	5470	C39F	5/51	London Transport RFW6	London Bus Preservation Trust
	LUC 389	AEC	Regal IV	9821E331	ECW	5479	C39F	6/51	London Transport RFW14	RFW14 Group, Twickenham
	LUC 488	AEC	Regent III	O9615874	Weymann	W1315	H30/26R	5/51	London Transport RT4139	Addison, Whitstable
	LUD 606	Bedford	SBG	50294	Duple	1074/92	C41F	7/57	Worth, Enstone	Worth, Enstone (OX)
	LUF 242	Leyland	Titan PD2/12	515038	Leyland		H32/26RD	4/52	Southdown 742	Robbins, Leatherhead
	LUF 828	Leyland	Royal Tiger PSU1/15	512925	Harrington	1085	C41C	5/52	Southdown 828	Elliott & Burtenshaw, Chichester
	LUM 613	Bedford	OB	90130	Duple	50540	C29F	-/48	Wallace Arnold Tours	Herefordshire Transport Collection
	LUO 595	AEC	Regal III	6821A450	Weymann	C9389	B35F	5/50	Devon General SR595	Blackman, Newton Abbot
	LUO 694	Leyland	Tiger PS2/3	495756	Burlingham	4353	C35F	5/50	Pridham, Lamerton	Lawson, Baildon
	LUR 446	Bedford	OB	143368	Duple	49884	C29F	9/50	Kirby, Bushey Heath	Stevens, Great Bromley
(r)	LUW 615	Bedford	OB	146580	Duple	57763	C—F	5/50	Fallowfield & Britten	Kenzie, Shepreth (CM)
	LVK 123	Leyland	Titan PD2/1	484761	Leyland		H30/26R	12/48	Newcastle 123	Northern Counties Bus Preservation Group
	LVO 530	Austin	K8CVC	14844	Kenex		C12F	5/51	Lees, Worksop	Leach, Telford
	LVS 175	AEC	Reliance	2MU3RV2777	Alexander	6009	C--F	5/60	Highland B24	Macleod, Bettyhill
			(ex OST 502)							
	LWR 424	Bristol	KSW6G	94023	ECW	5955	RV	5/53	West Yorkshire Road Car 4044	
			(ex USU 623, LWR 424)							West Yorkshire Preservation Group, Baildon
(r)	LXI 1036	Mercedes-Benz	609D	66806320825448	Citybus		C19F	1/88	Flexibus 36	Houston, Newtownards
	LXI 1122	Leyland	Tiger TRBTL11/2RP	TR00056	Alexander (Belfast)	B02.08	B53F	1/88	Ulsterbus 1122	Kells Transport Museum, Cork
	LXI 1131	Leyland	Tiger TRBTL11/2RP	TR00081	Alexander (Belfast)	B04.02	B52F	4/88	Ulsterbus 1131	Kells Transport Museum, Cork
	LXI 6609	Leyland	Tiger TRBLXB/2RP	TR00256	Alexander (Belfast)	B03.10	B42F	9/88	Citybus 2609	Kells Transport Museum, Cork
	LXI 6610	Leyland	Tiger TRBLXB/2RP	TR00268	Alexander (Belfast)	B03.02	B42F	6/88	Citybus 2610	Kells Transport Museum, Cork
	LXI 7143	Leyland	Tiger TRBTL11/2RP	TR00146	Alexander (Belfast)	B05.04	DP53F	3/88	Ulsterbus 1143	Kells Transport Museum, Cork
	LXU 397	→ see 397 CLT								
	LYB 941	Bedford	OB	124672	Duple	55645	C29F	-/49	Tor, Street	School Bus Company, Kingston Bagpuize (OX)
	LYC 731	Bedford	OB	130805	Duple	55905	C29F	3/50	Blagdon Lioness,Blagdon	Jones, Penygroes (CN)
			(ex ZV 1460 *Ireland*, LYC 731)							
	LYD 87	Austin	K4SL	131712	Jeffreys		C29F	-/50	Blackie, Eyemouth	Barfoot S, West End
	LYF 21	AEC	Regent III	O9615770	Park Royal	L1758	H30/26R	1/51	London Transport RT2084	Wilkinson, Billericay
			(ex WSK 177, BKX 689A, LYF 22)							
	LYF 22	→ see LYF 21								
	LYF 104	Leyland	7RT	510599	Park Royal	L2068	H30/26R	3/51	London Transport RTL1163	Cousens & Hobbs, Abbotskerswell
	LYF 247	AEC	Regent III	O9615885	Weymann	W1697	H30/26R	6/51	London Transport RT4188	London Bus Company, Northfleet (KT)
	LYF 249	AEC	Regent III	O9615908	Weymann	W1415	H30/26R	6/51	London Transport RT4190	Money, Barking
	LYF 278	AEC	Regent III	O9615931	Park Royal	L235	H30/26R	6/51	London Transport RT2553	Carousel, High Wycombe (BK)

	LYF 281	AEC	Regent III	O9615904	Weymann	W1756	H30/26R	6/51	London Transport RT2556	Bole, Dover
	LYF 316	AEC	Regent III	O9615968	Park Royal	L1879	H30/26R	6/51	London Transport RT2591	Blackman, Halifax (WY)
	LYF 377	AEC	Regal IV	9821LT032	Metro-Cammell		B37F	10/51	London Transport RF26	Crowther, Silverstone
	LYF 379	AEC	Regal IV	9821LT034	Metro-Cammell		B39F	10/51	London Transport RF28	Catchpole et al, Halling
	LYF 387	AEC	Regal IV	9821LT042	Metro-Cammell		B37F	11/51	London Transport RF36	Henderson, Cambridge
	LYF 392	AEC	Regal IV	9821LT047	Metro-Cammell		B39F	12/51	London Transport RF41	Dale, Sherborne
	LYF 399	AEC	Regal IV	9821LT054	Metro-Cammell		B39F	11/51	London Transport RF48	Welch, London
										(on loan to Meadows, Crewe (CH))
	LYF 403	AEC	Regal IV	9821LT062	Metro-Cammell		B37F	12/51	London Transport RF52	Henderson, Cambridge
	LYF 430	AEC	Regal IV	9821LT094	Metro-Cammell		B35F	12/51	London Transport RF79	Henderson, Cambridge
	LYF 464	AEC	Regal IV	9821LT136	Metro-Cammell		B39F	1/52	London Transport RF113	Hood, Northwold
	LYH 624	Bedford	MLZ	134056	Reall		B22F	-/51	London County Council 1639	Smith, Barwell
	LYM 729	AEC	Regal IV	9821E276	ECW	12069	C39F	5/51	Tilling	Dolan A, Crook
					(rebodied -/60)					
(r)	LYM 731	AEC	Regal IV	9821E278	*(chassis only)*			5/51	Tilling	Dolan A, Crook
	LYM 732	AEC	Regal IV	9821E279	ECW	12071	C29F	5/51	Tilling	Mahoney I, Brentwood
					(rebodied -/60)					
	LYR 533	AEC	Regent III	O9616134	Park Royal	L2215	H30/26R	9/51	London Transport RT3314	Pickles, Keighley
	LYR 535	AEC	Regent III	O9615424	Park Royal	L2194	H30/26R	9/51	London Transport RT3316	Hobcraft, Hartfield
										(operates as Bolebrooke Castle, Hartfield (ES))
	LYR 542	AEC	Regent III	O9616053	Park Royal	L2247	H--/--RD	9/51	London Transport RT3323	Sandtoft Transport Centre
	LYR 672	AEC	Regent III	O9616142	Park Royal	L2327	H30/26R	9/51	London Transport RT2688	Padbury & Fisher, Southgate
	LYR 788	Leyland	7RT	514925	Park Royal	L2367	H30/26R	12/51	London Transport RTL1256	Biddell, Woodford Bridge
										(operates as Imperial, Romford (LN))
	LYR 826	AEC	Regent III	O9616343	Park Royal	L2417	H30/26R	1/52	London Transport RT2775	London Bus Preservation Trust
	LYR 854	AEC	Regent III	O9616327	Weymann	W1692	O30/26R	1/52	London Transport RT3435	London Bus Company, Northfleet (KT)
	LYR 877	AEC	Regent III	O9616387	Weymann	W1365	H30/26R	3/52	London Transport RT3458	Austin, Sidcup
	LYR 880	AEC	Regent III	O9616445	Weymann	W1598	H30/26R	2/52	London Transport RT3461	Sullivan, Potters Bar (HT)
	LYR 910	AEC	Regent III	O9616468	Park Royal	L2433	H30/26R	3/52	London Transport RT3491	Greene, Douglas-Lane & Wheeler, Newport
	LYR 915	AEC	Regent III	O9616518	Weymann	W205	H30/26R	4/52	London Transport RT3496	Dale, Luton
	LYR 964	AEC	Regent III	O9616375	Weymann	W1663	H30/26R	1/52	London Transport RT2794	Thrower, Warrington
	LYR 969	AEC	Regent III	O9616352	Weymann	W1470	H30/26R	2/52	London Transport RT2799	London Bus Company, Northfleet (KT)
	LYR 997	AEC	Regent III	O9616479	Weymann	W194	H30/26RD	2/52	London Transport RT2827	Patten, South Benfleet

MAF 544	Austin	CXB	139946	*chassis only*			9/49	Pollard, Fraddam	Cook, Exeter
MAH 744	Bristol	LSX4G	LSX002	ECW	4255	B41F	7/51	Eastern Counties LL744	Ipswich Transport Museum
MAL 310	Leyland	Royal Tiger PSU1/11	502461	Duple	56302	DP45F	5/51	South Notts, Gotham 42	Allen & Bairstow, Nottingham
MAZ 7584	Leyland	Royal Tiger RT	RTC87.11	Leyland		C49FT	4/87	Abbott, Leeming	Ferguson, Todmorden
		(ex MAZ 8728, D904 FHN)							
MBH 541	Dennis	Pax	989D2	Wadham		C29F	7/49	Lucas, Slough	Rawlings, Chelmsford
MBN 177	Leyland	Titan PD3/5	573921	East Lancs	5477	H41/33R	8/58	Bolton 122	Fitness, Rossett
MCO 658	Leyland	Titan PD2/12	561604	Metro-Cammell		O30/26R	9/56	Plymouth 58	Plymouth (DN) 358
		(ex ADV 935A, MCO 658)							
MCO 669	Leyland	Titan PD2/12	562071	Metro-Cammell		H--/--RD	11/56	Plymouth 69	Hoare, Chepstow (CS)
MCY 407	AEC	Regent V	MD3RV010	Weymann	M6709	H33/26RD	11/55	South Wales 447	South Wales Transport Preservation Trust
MCZ 8545	Leyland	Fleetline FE30ALR	7801552	Northern Counties	8493	H43/31F	3/79	Cleveland Transit H121	-?-, Dublin
		(ex YVN 521T)							

	Reg	Make	Model	Chassis No	Body	Body No	Layout	Date	First Owner	Current Owner
	MDE 666	Bedford	OB	140900	Duple	49265	C29F	8/50	Richards, Moylgrove	Cobus, Bridlington
	MDL 954	Bristol	Lodekka LD6G	116146	ECW	8616	O33/27R	5/56	Southern Vectis OT4	Priddle, Farnham
	MDT 222	AEC	Regal III	9621A588	Roe	GO3666	B39F	5/53	Doncaster 22	Doncaster Omnibus & Light Railway Society
	MEB 626	Trojan	19	1509825	Trojan	7903	C13F	5/61	Embling, Guyhirn	Embling, Guyhirn (CM)
	MED 168	Foden	PVD6	33858	Crossley		H30/28R	11/54	Warrington 102	Maiden, Wellington
	MEZ 1493	Leyland	Leopard PSU3F/4R	8131313	Alexander (Belfast)	750/29	DP49F	1/83	Ulsterbus 326	Kells Transport Museum, Cork
			(ex BXI 326)							
	MEZ 5619	Leyland	Tiger TRBTL11/2RP	8500222	Alexander (Belfast)	570/9	B52F	5/86	Ulsterbus 468	Kells Transport Museum, Cork
			(ex HXI 468)							
	MFB 724	Bedford	CAL	208361	Martin Walter		M10	7/60	private owner	Brooklands Museum
	MFF 578	AEC	Routemaster	RM329	Park Royal	L3599	H36/28R	7/60	London Transport RM329	York Pullman, York (NY)
			(ex WLT 329)							
	MFM 38	Bedford	OB	141575	Duple	56137	C29F	7/50	Crosville SL70	Marshopper, New Romney (KT)
	MFM 39	Bedford	OB	142625	Duple	56138	C29F	5/51	Crosville SL71	Smallwood, Churchill
	MFN 888	Guy	Arab IV	FD73239	Park Royal	B39153	H33/28RD	1/57	East Kent	Lines, Deal
	MFN 898	Guy	Arab IV	FD73436	Park Royal	B39163	H33/28RD	1/57	East Kent	Lines, Deal
	MHU 49	Bedford	OB	119935	Duple	54772	B29F	12/49	Bristol 207	Walker, Wells
	MHU 52	Bedford	OB	123166	Duple	54775	B30F	4/50	Bristol 210	Greet, Broadhempston
	MHU 193	Bedford	OB	116397	Mulliner	T492	B31F	10/49	Clifton College, Bristol	Walker, Wells
	MHU 992	Bedford	OB	121666	Duple	54834	C29F	3/50	Bristol 220	Smith J, Douglas
	MHY 1	AEC	Regal III	9621A1034	Plaxton	434	C33F	3/50	Westbury, Bristol 7	James, Blaenporth
	MHY 765	Leyland	Comet ECPO/1R	484221	Duple	48631	C32F	4/50	Orient, Bristol	Ellin, Sheffield
	MHY 904	Bedford	OB	138714	Duple	56162	C29F	6/50	Bristol Co-op	Hennessey, Redhill
(r)	MIB 4194	Bristol	RELH6L	RELH-4-763	Plaxton	7411BCR005	C49F	5/75	National Travel South East	Bissett, Westbury
			(ex JEU 508N, CSV 992, GJD 196N)							
	MIL 9372	Bristol	LHS6L	LHS-387	Plaxton	818BC008	C30F	5/81	Richmond, Epsom	Britishbus Preservation Group
			(ex XGO 225W)							
	MIW 5795	Volvo	B10M-61	000872	Plaxton	8112VCV923	C53F	8/81	Bebb, Llantwit Fardre	Dew, Somersham (CM)
			(ex LBO 11X)							
	MJB 481	Bedford	SBG *(diesel)*	46774	Duple	1060/230	C37F	5/56	Chiltonia, Clinton Foliat	Lodge, High Easter (EX)
	MJC 5	Ford	570E	L80B830582	Duple	1160/44	C41F	5/63	Creams, Llandudno	Jones, Blaenau Ffestiniog
	MJD 759	→ see RSL 383								
	MJI 7215	→ see NJI 3022								
	MJW 43	Morris	JR	JR21044	Morris		B??	3/54	non-PSV	Dracup, Rickmansworth
	MKB 994	AEC	Regent III	9613A6433	Crossley		H30/26R	1/52	Liverpool A801	Merseyside Transport Trust
	MKH 84	Leyland	Titan PD2/12	515197	Roe	GO3404	FH30/20RD	5/52	East Yorkshire 575	Hull 245 Group
	MKP 810	Bedford	OB	143025	Duple	54403	C29F	9/50	Jessop, Frinstead	Pursey, Wickford
(r)	MLF 348	Crossley	SD42/7	98137	Crossley		B35F	-/51	Molins Machine, Deptford	Ementon, Nantwich
	MLF 596	Bedford	SB	5572	Duple	57336	C33F	11/51	Timpson	Campbell & Broadley, Culloden
	MLL 523	AEC	Regal IV	9821LT113	Metro-Cammell		B39F	2/52	London Transport RF136	Macnamara, Merton Park
	MLL 528	AEC	Regal IV	9821LT1050	Metro-Cammell		B39F	3/52	London Transport RF202	Western Greyhound, Summercourt (CO)
			(ex UVS 678, XKR 164A, MLL 589)							
	MLL 533	AEC	Regal IV	9821LT159	Metro-Cammell		B39F	2/52	London Transport RF146	Huxford & Aves, Ewell
	MLL 554	AEC	Regal IV	9821LT1015	Metro-Cammell		B37F	3/52	London Transport RF167	Rawlins et al, -?-
	MLL 555	AEC	Regal IV	9821LT1016	Metro-Cammell		B39F	3/52	London Transport RF168	Friend, Heathfield
	MLL 564	AEC	Regal IV	9821LT1024	Metro-Cammell		B39F	3/52	London Transport RF177	Awain & Russell, Tunbridge Wells
	MLL 567	AEC	Regal IV	9821LT1028	Metro-Cammell		B39F	3/52	London Transport RF180	London Bus Company, Northfleet (KT)
	MLL 570	AEC	Regal IV	9821LT1029	Metro-Cammell		B37F	3/52	London Transport RF183	Alexander, Dover

	MLL 584	AEC	Regal IV	9821LT1045	Metro-Cammell		B37F	3/52	London Transport RF197	Hudd, Eltham
	MLL 589	→ see MLL 528								
	MLL 600	AEC	Regal IV	9821LT1061	Metro-Cammell		B39F	4/52	London Transport RF213	Burtenshaw, Stockwell
(z)	MLL 605	AEC	Regal IV	9821LT1066	Metro-Cammell		B39F	4/52	London Transport RF218	Barrett, Betchworth
	MLL 652	AEC	Regent III	O9616540	Weymann	W1546	H30/26R	5/52	London Transport RT2905	Henderson, Cambridge
	MLL 658	AEC	Regent III	O9616610	Park Royal	L2560	H30/26R	5/52	London Transport RT2911	London Bus Company, Northfleet (KT)
	MLL 665	AEC	Regent III	O9616611	Weymann	W1530	H30/26R	5/52	London Transport RT2918	Chapman, Penkridge
	MLL 685	Leyland	7RT	521293	Park Royal	L562	H30/26R	6/52	London Transport RTL1323	Blair, Upham
	MLL 696	AEC	Regent III	O9616654	Park Royal	L2227	H30/26R	7/52	London Transport RT2937	Express Bus, Dublin (EI)
	MLL 721	AEC	Regal IV	9822E1186	Park Royal	B35254	RDP37C	12/52	British European Airways 1079	Marshopper, New Romney (KT)
	MLL 722	AEC	Regal IV	9822E1188	Park Royal	B35255	RDP--C	12/52	British European Airways 1080	Seddon, -?-
	MLL 735	AEC	Regal IV	9822E1202	Park Royal	B35268	RDP--C	1/53	British European Airways 1092	Ensign, Purfleet (EX)
	MLL 738	AEC	Regal IV	9822E1210	Park Royal	B35271	RDP37C	2/53	British European Airways 1097	Marshopper, New Romney (KT)
	MLL 740	AEC	Regal IV	9822E1196	Park Royal	B35273	RDP37C	2/53	British European Airways 1095	Allmey, Eastcote
	MLL 763	AEC	Regal IV	9821LT1075	Metro-Cammell		B37F	4/52	London Transport RF226	London Bus Preservation Trust
	MLL 769	AEC	Regal IV	9821LT1080	Metro-Cammell		B32F	4/52	London Transport RF232	Sharland, Exeter
	MLL 792	AEC	Regal IV	9821LT1091	Metro-Cammell		B37F	6/52	London Transport RF255	Wealdsman Preservation Group, Headcorn
	MLL 806	AEC	Regal IV	9821LT1117	Metro-Cammell		B37F	6/52	London Transport RF269	Legg, Chatham
	MLL 808	AEC	Regal IV	9821LT1121	Metro-Cammell		B37F	8/52	London Transport RF271	Edgar, Heath Hayes
	MLL 817	AEC	Regal IV	9821LT1133	Metro-Cammell		B37F	8/52	London Transport RF280	Hinson & Wylie, Potterspury
	MLL 818	AEC	Regal IV	9821LT1135	Metro-Cammell		B39F	9/52	London Transport RF281	Beeson, Bishops Stortford
	MLL 933	AEC	Regal IV	9821LT683	Metro-Cammell		B39F	9/52	London Transport RF515	Kane, Gilford
	MLL 935	AEC	Regal IV	9821LT678	Metro-Cammell		B41F	9/52	London Transport RF517	Dale, Sherborne
	MLL 936	AEC	Regal IV	9821LT652	Metro-Cammell		B39F	10/52	London Transport RF518	Prescott, Rettendon
	MLL 943	AEC	Regal IV	9821LT664	Metro-Cammell		B39F	10/52	London Transport RF525	Ross, Gerrards Cross
	MLL 948	AEC	Regal IV	9821LT667	Metro-Cammell		B39F	10/52	London Transport RF530	Transport Preservation Trust, Beith (*operates as Roulston, Beith (SW)*)
(r)	MLL 949	AEC	Regal IV	9821LT674	Metro-Cammell		cab/flatbed	10/52	London Transport RF312	Dawes & Crouch, Headcorn
	MLL 952	AEC	Regal IV	9821LT708	Metro-Cammell		B39F	12/52	London Transport RF315	Osborne, Lincoln
	MLL 956	AEC	Regal IV	9821LT1132	Metro-Cammell		B39F	10/52	London Transport RF319	Ensign, Purfleet (EX)
	MLL 963	AEC	Regal IV	9821LT675	Metro-Cammell		B39F	11/52	London Transport RF326	Cheeseman, Walton-on-Thames
	MLL 969	AEC	Regal IV	9821LT701	Metro-Cammell		RV	11/52	London Transport RF332	Wealdsman Preservation Group, Headcorn
(r)	MLL 970	AEC	Regal IV	9821LT713	Metro-Cammell		B--F	11/52	London Transport RF333	Penfold, Meldreth
	MLL 974	AEC	Regal IV	9821LT705	Metro-Cammell		B41F	11/52	London Transport RF337	Reynolds, -?-
	MLL 991	AEC	Regal IV	9821LT716	Metro-Cammell		B23F	12/52	London Transport RF354	Lewis et al, St Lawrence
	MLL 992	AEC	Regal IV	9821LT725	Metro-Cammell		B39F	11/52	London Transport RF355	Brown, Romford
	MMB 861	Foden	PVFE6	30640	Metalcraft		FC37F	3/51	Hollinshead, Scholar Green 2	Foden Coach Preservation Group, Stroud
	MMR 552	Leyland	Tiger Cub PSUC1/2	553502	Harrington	1648	C41C	7/55	Silver Star, Porton Down 10	Silver Star 10 Group, Chandlers Ford
	MMR 553	Leyland	Tiger Cub PSUC1/2	553503	Harrington	1650	C41C	7/55	Silver Star, Porton Down 26	Dawes, Dewsbury (*on loan to Thornes, Hemingbrough)NY)*)
	MNW 86	Leyland	Tiger PS1	483353	Roe	GO2847	B36R	11/48	Leeds 28	Keighley Bus Museum Trust
	MOD 973	Bristol	LS6G	89088	ECW	6287	C41F	9/52	Southern National 1286	Billington, Maidenhead
	MOD 978	Bristol	LS6G	89103	ECW	6292	C41F	9/52	Southern National 1291	Grigg, Portishead
	MOF 9	Guy	Arab IV	FD71706	Metro-Cammell		H30/25R	7/53	Birmingham 3009	Wigley, Stourbridge
	MOF 35	Guy	Arab IV	FD71732	Metro-Cammell		H30/25R	7/53	Birmingham 3035	Wood, Birmingham
	MOF 90	Guy	Arab IV	FD71787	Metro-Cammell		H30/25R	6/54	Birmingham 3090	Shaw, Warley
	MOF 102	Guy	Arab IV	FD71797	Metro-Cammell		H30/25R	10/54	Birmingham 3102	Belle Vue, Heaton Chapel (GM)
	MOF 225	Daimler	CVG6DD	18186	Crossley		H30/25R	10/54	Birmingham 3225	West Midlands (WM) 3225

	Reg	Make	Model	Chassis No	Body	Body No	Layout	Date	Original operator	Owner
	MOI 2134	→ see 77-D-816 *Ireland*								
	MOO 177	Bristol	MW6G	195112	ECW	12628	B45F	9/62	Eastern National 556	Vince, Mattishall
	MOR 581	AEC	Reliance	MU3RV141	MCW		B40F	8/54	Aldershot & District 543	Tutty, Guildford
					(rebodied 1/67)					
	MPP 747	Dennis	Lancet III	779J3	Yeates	182	C35F	4/50	Dell, Chesham 16	Cedar, Bedford (BD)
	MPU 21	Bristol	K6B	66085	ECW	1631	L27/28R	5/48	Eastern National 3960	Brown, Rushden
	MPU 52	Leyland	Titan PD1A	472154	ECW	2297	L27/26R	-/47	Eastern National 1121	Gent, South Benfleet
	MPW 455	Bedford	SB	3671	Duple	56722	C33F	8/51	Stainsby, Heacham	Moseley (PCV), South Elmsall
	MRB 765	Bedford	OB	95361	Duple	-?-	C29F	1/49	Andrews, Tideswell	Simpson, Killamarsh
	MRD 146	AEC	Regent III	6812A135	Park Royal	B39044	L27/26RD	1/57	Reading 3	Wale, Burghfield
	MRD 147	AEC	Regent III	6812A136	Park Royal	B39045	L27/26RD	1/57	Reading 4	Rampton, Reading
	MRL 765	Austin	K8VC	8998	Tiverton		C12F	5/50	Hawkey, Wadebridge	Davey, East Huntspill
	MRL 865	Austin	C/VB	159325	Whitson	7613	C29F	5/50	Rowe, Dobwalls	Casburn, Corpusty
	MSD 407	Leyland	Titan PD3/3	590057	Alexander	5778	L35/32RD	7/59	Western SMT 1543	Cumming, Edinburgh
	MSD 408	Leyland	Titan PD3/3	590195	Alexander	5781	L35/32RD	7/59	Western SMT 1544	Cumming, Edinburgh
	MSJ 499	Leyland	Atlantean PDR1/1	602642	Metro-Cammell	H052698/1	O44/31F	5/61	Devon General DL925	Hawkins, Kingswear
			(ex ADV 299A, 925 GTA)							*(on loan to McAllister, Paignton (DN))*
	MSJ 606	Bedford	OB	120202	Duple	54843	C27F	11/49	Western National 597	Gamlen, Pensford
			(ex ZV 3839, MSJ 606, HOD 76)							
	MSJ 702	Vulcan	Countess	D40	Reading		FB32F	4/33	Watson, St Martins	Glover, Shirebrook
			(ex 3409)		*(rebodied postwar)*					
	MSL 292	Bedford	CASV	185161	Martin Walter	UW65672	M11	-/60	non-PSV	Wheeler, Bradford
			(ex PSU 414, -?-)							
	MSL 294	AEC	Regent III	O9612070	Northern Counties	4264	H30/26R	7/48	Douglas 63	Greet, Broadhempston
			(ex JMN 727)							
	MSV 412	Albion	Victor FT39AN	73787C	Heaver	2753	B35F	1/56	Guernsey Motors 68	Black & White, Penton Mewsey (HA)
			(ex 1463)							
	MTB 848	Leyland	Tiger PS2/1	500192	East Lancs	4658	B35R	9/50	Rawtenstall 55	Cotton, Manchester
	MTC 540	AEC	Regent III	9613E4333	Park Royal	B34489	H33/26R	10/50	Morecambe & Heysham 72	72 Group, Lancaster
	MTD 235	Leyland	Royal Tiger PSU1/15	502300	Leyland		C41C	-/51	Leyland demonstrator	Simpson {Pennine}, Skipton (NY)
	MTE 635	AEC	Regent III	6812A100	Weymann	M4683	H33/26R	2/51	Morecambe & Heysham 73	Wade, Burnley
	MTE 639	AEC	Regent III	6812A104	Weymann	M4684	H33/26R	2/51	Morecambe & Heysham 77	Armour, Derby
	MTG 172	AEC	Regal IV	9821S211	Burlingham	4980	C—F	3/53	Thomas, Port Talbot	South Wales Transport Preservation Trust
	MTG 884	AEC	Regal III	9621A1554	Longwell Green/Park Royal		B35F	3/53	Gelligaer 19	National Museum of Wales
	MTJ 84	Guy	Arab III	FD70606	Roe	GO3189	C31F	5/51	Lancashire United 440	Hamer & Morriss, Ravenstonedale (CA)
	MTL 750	Leyland	Tiger Cub PSUC1/2	578422	Yeates	660	DP43F	3/58	Delaine, Bourne 47	City of Leicester Museums
(r)	MTT 214	Bedford	OB	146068	*chassis only*			11/50	Court, Torquay	Simpson, Killamarsh
	MTT 640	Leyland	Titan PD2/1	511256	Leyland		L27/26R	3/51	Devon General DL640	Carmel Coaches, Northlew (DN)
	MTU 296	Foden	PVFE6	30624	Metalcraft		C37F	7/50	Coppenhall, Sandbach 16	Sample, Brereton
	MUF 488	Beadle-Leyland		JCB349	Beadle		B31F	5/53	Southdown 649	Gray, Funtley
	MVS 972	Leyland	Titan PD3/4	611384	Metro-Cammell		H39/31F	10/61	Preston 19	Chatterton, Foxham
			(ex PRN 911)							
	MWB 310	Bedford	OB	129432	Duple	55680	C29F	1/50	Sims, Sheffield	Dodd, Belton (LI)
	MWD 908	Bedford	SB	14378	Duple	1030/4	C35F	-/53	Hill, Stockingford	Curtis, Radstock
	MWV 840	Leyland	Leopard PSU5C/4R	8030117	Duple	935/5494	C53F	8/80	Maidstone & District 4165	Morgan & Vinall, Brighton
			(ex JKM 165V)							
	MXB 733	AEC	Regal rebuild	733	ECW	6285	FC35F	5/52	Tilling	Benson J Jnr, Little Waltham
	MXX 8	AEC	Regal IV	9821LT1131	Metro-Cammell		B41F	12/52	London Transport RF366	Andress, Chippenham

MXX 10	AEC	Regal IV	9821LT731	Metro-Cammell		B41F	12/52	London Transport RF368	-?-, -?-
MXX 12	AEC	Regal IV	9821LT736	Metro-Cammell		B—F	12/52	London Transport RF370	London Bus Company, Northfleet (KT)
MXX 23	AEC	Regal IV	9821LT750	Metro-Cammell		B39F	1/53	London Transport RF381	BaMMOT, Wythall
MXX 24	→ see NMN 355 *Isle of Man*								
MXX 25	AEC	Regal IV	9821LT746	Metro-Cammell		B39F	12/52	London Transport RF383	London Bus Company, Northfleet (KT)
MXX 71	Leyland	7RT	522155	Park Royal	L1365	H30/26R	11/52	London Transport RTL1348	Ladd, Iver
		(ex J 8629, MXX 71)							
MXX 219	Leyland	7RT	522892	Park Royal	L703	H30/26R	1/53	London Transport RTL1412	Wright & Humphries, Dagenham
MXX 223	AEC	Regent III	9613E6948	Weymann	M5526	L27/26R	10/52	London Transport RLH23	Pring, St Albans (HT)
MXX 229	AEC	Regent III	9613E6965	Weymann	M5533	L27/26R	10/52	London Transport RLH29	Pring, St Albans (HT)
MXX 232	AEC	Regent III	9613E6971	Weymann	M5534	L27/26R	10/52	London Transport RLH32	Pring, St Albans (HT)
MXX 244	AEC	Regent III	9613E6952	Weymann	M5543	L--/--CD	10/52	London Transport RLH44	Pring, St Albans (HT)
MXX 248	AEC	Regent III	9613E6970	Weymann	M5551	L27/26R	10/52	London Transport RLH48	Proctor, Buckland Filleigh
MXX 261	AEC	Regent III	9613E6984	Weymann	M5569	L27/26R	11/52	London Transport RLH61	Ensign, Purfleet (EX)
MXX 280	AEC	Regal IV	9821LT754	Metro-Cammell		B39F	1/53	London Transport RF392	Boxall & Welch, Beckenham
									(on loan to Meadows, Crewe (CH))
MXX 283	AEC	Regal IV	9821LT757	Metro-Cammell		B41F	1/53	London Transport RF395	London Bus Preservation Trust
MXX 289	AEC	Regal IV	9821LT763	Metro-Cammell		B39F	1/53	London Transport RF401	London Bus Company, Northfleet (KT)
MXX 292	AEC	Regal IV	9821LT767	Metro-Cammell		B--F	1/53	London Transport RF404	Griffiths, Royston
MXX 294	AEC	Regal IV	9821LT769	Metro-Cammell		B39F	1/53	London Transport RF406	Summers, -?-
MXX 301	Guy	Special	NLLVP44208	ECW	6347	B26F	10/53	London Transport GS1	Model Road & Rail, Worcester Park
MXX 302	Guy	Special	NLLVP44209	ECW	6348	B26F	10/53	London Transport GS2	Huxford, Ewell
MXX 312	Guy	Special	NLLVP44714	ECW	6361	B26F	11/53	London Transport GS12	Mantell, Leyton
MXX 313	Guy	Special	NLLVP44716	ECW	6356	B26F	10/53	London Transport GS13	Cartwright, High Wycombe
MXX 314	Guy	Special	NLLVP44718	ECW	6354	B26F	10/53	London Transport GS14	Boulton, Coulsdon
MXX 315	Guy	Special	NLLVP44720	ECW	6359	B26F	10/53	London Transport GS15	Speller, Bromley
MXX 317	Guy	Special	NLLVP44752	ECW	6362	B26F	11/53	London Transport GS17	Dobbing, Stibbington (CM)
MXX 319	Guy	Special	NLLVP44760	ECW	6365	B26F	11/53	London Transport GS19	Hudgell, Tiverton
MXX 326	Guy	Special	NLLVP44800	ECW	6372	B26F	11/53	London Transport GS26	Bubb, Whitchurch
MXX 332	Guy	Special	NLLVP44819	ECW	6373	B26F	11/53	London Transport GS32	Clarke, Aylesbury
MXX 334	Guy	Special	NLLVP44816	ECW	6407	B26F	12/53	London Transport GS34	London Bus Preservation Trust
MXX 336	Guy	Special	NLLVP44826	ECW	6385	B26F	12/53	London Transport GS36	Dale, Sherborne
MXX 340	Guy	Special	NLLVP44845	ECW	6386	B26F	12/53	London Transport GS40	Fuller & Bennett, West Bromwich
MXX 342	Guy	Special	NLLVP44856	ECW	6382	B26F	12/53	London Transport GS42	Heels, Ashtead
MXX 343	Guy	Special	NLLVP44862	ECW	6387	B26F	12/53	London Transport GS43	Bowden, Bromley
MXX 345	Guy	Special	NLLVP44868	ECW	6388	B26F	12/53	London Transport GS45	Smith, Melksham
MXX 352	Guy	Special	NLLVP44943	ECW	6403	B26F	12/53	London Transport GS52	O'Sullivan V, Hospital
MXX 355	Guy	Special	NLLVP44957	ECW	6399	B26F	12/53	London Transport GS55	Rivers, Ashford
MXX 356	Guy	Special	NLLVP44961	ECW	6401	B26F	12/53	London Transport GS56	Adams, Goudhurst
MXX 360	Guy	Special	NLLVP44979	ECW	6405	B26F	12/53	London Transport GS60	London Bus Company, Northfleet (KT)
MXX 361	Guy	Special	NLLVP44988	ECW	6410	B26F	1/54	London Transport GS63	Davies, Knighton
		(ex MXX 363)							
MXX 362	Guy	Special	NLLVP44985	ECW	6408	B26F	12/53	London Transport GS62	Charman, East Grinstead
MXX 363	→ see MXX 361								
MXX 364	Guy	Special	NLLVP44994	ECW	6409	B26F	12/53	London Transport GS64	London Transport Museum
MXX 367	Guy	Special	NLLVP44999	ECW	6412	B26F	1/54	London Transport GS67	Marshopper, New Romney (KT)
MXX 384	Guy	Special	NLLVP45066	ECW	6430	B26F	2/54	London Transport GS84	Miller, Ballyclare
MXX 398	AEC	Regal IV	9821LT776	Metro-Cammell		B39F	1/53	London Transport RF421	Shaftesbury & District, Shaftesbury (DT)

	MXX 406	AEC	Regal IV	9821LT796	Metro-Cammell		B39F	2/53	London Transport RF429	Country Bus Rallies, East Grinstead
	MXX 410	AEC	Regal IV	9821LT800	Metro-Cammell		B41F	2/53	London Transport RF433	Hinson, Potterspury
	MXX 419	AEC	Regal IV	9821LT809	Metro-Cammell		B39F	2/53	London Transport RF442	Chapman, Stevenage
	MXX 421	AEC	Regal IV	9821LT813	Metro-Cammell		B39F	2/53	London Transport RF444	Austin, Sidcup
	MXX 430	AEC	Regal IV	9821LT845	Metro-Cammell		B39F	2/53	London Transport RF453	Hinson, Potterspury
	MXX 434	AEC	Regal IV	9821LT722	Metro-Cammell		B39F	2/53	London Transport RF457	RF457 Preservation Group, Luton
	MXX 435	→ see 53-OY-20 *Ireland*								
	MXX 436	AEC	Regal IV	9821LT764	Metro-Cammell		B39F	2/53	London Transport RF459	Humphries, Dagenham
	MXX 439	AEC	Regal IV	9821LT806	Metro-Cammell		B39F	2/53	London Transport RF462	Henderson, Cambridge
	MXX 440	AEC	Regal IV	9821LT807	Metro-Cammell		B39F	2/53	London Transport RF463	Heighway, Preston
	MXX 442	AEC	Regal IV	9821LT812	Metro-Cammell		B--F	2/53	London Transport RF465	-?-, Essex
	MXX 445	AEC	Regal IV	9821LT817	Metro-Cammell		B39F	2/53	London Transport RF468	Tompkins, Kingsash
	MXX 456	AEC	Regal IV	9821LT833	Metro-Cammell		B39F	3/53	London Transport RF479	Jones, -?-
	MXX 457	AEC	Regal IV	9821LT837	Metro-Cammell		B39F	2/53	London Transport RF480	-?-, -?-
	MXX 463	AEC	Regal IV	9821LT847	Metro-Cammell		B39F	3/53	London Transport RF486	Osborn & Whitelegg, Dorking
	MXX 466	AEC	Regal IV	9821LT851	Metro-Cammell		B39F	3/53	London Transport RF489	Lennox-Kay, Aldington
	MXX 468	AEC	Regal IV	9821LT852	Metro-Cammell		B39F	3/53	London Transport RF491	Pring, St Albans (HT)
	MXX 472	AEC	Regal IV	9821LT859	Metro-Cammell		B39F	3/53	London Transport RF495	Hobcraft, Hartfield
	MXX 480	AEC	Regal IV	9821LT870	Metro-Cammell		B39F	3/53	London Transport RF503	Joseph, Ilford
	MXX 481	AEC	Regal IV	9821LT874	Metro-Cammell		B41F	3/53	London Transport RF504	Alpha, Soulbury (BK)
			(ex KSJ 622, MXX 481)							
	MXX 484	AEC	Regal IV	9821LT880	Metro-Cammell		B39F	3/53	London Transport RF507	Haining, Heathfield
	MXX 485	AEC	Regal IV	9821LT882	Metro-Cammell		B39F	3/53	London Transport RF508	Thrower, Warrington
	MXX 487	AEC	Regal IV	9821LT885	Metro-Cammell		B39F	3/53	London Transport RF510	Dale, Sherborne
	MXX 488	AEC	Regal IV	9821LT892	Metro-Cammell		B39F	3/53	London Transport RF511	Ladd, Iver
	MXX 489	AEC	Regal IV	9821LT915	Metro-Cammell		B41F	3/53	London Transport RF512	Wills, Stevenage
(r)	MYA 217	Albion	Valiant CX39N	60314L	*chassis only*			6/50	Alford, Coleford	Purvis, Seaburn
(r)	MYA 524	Bedford	OB	140818	Duple	48070	C29F	7/50	Wake, Sparkford	Atkin, North Owersby
(r)	MYA 525	Bedford	OB	141556	Duple	56478	C27F	7/50	Wake, Sparkford	Higgs, Cheltenham
	MYA 590	Leyland	Comet CPP1	495337	Harrington	813	C29F	7/50	Hawkins, Minehead	Batten & Prince, Stoneleigh
	MYB 33	Bedford	OB	145431	Duple	56553	C29F	10/50	Safeway, South Petherton	Jones, Moulton
	NAE 3	Bristol	L6B	81077	ECW	4907	FC31F	9/50	Bristol 2467	Walker, Wells
	NAH 941	Bristol	KSW5G	92116	ECW	6056	H32/28R	8/52	Eastern Counties LKH341	Eastern Transport Collection
	NBB 171	Bedford	OB	109758	Duple	50113	C29F	6/49	Tait, Morpeth	Staniforth, Stroud
	NBH 746	Bedford	OB	143848	Duple	48919	C29F	12/50	Sargeant, Slough	Telford, Coleraine (NI)
	NBN 436	Leyland	Titan PD3/4	583447	East Lancs	5541	H41/32F	4/59	Bolton 128	Bolton Bus Preservation Group
	NBU 494	Leyland	Titan PD2/20	562859	Roe	GO4360	H31/29R	4/57	Oldham 394	Museum of Transport, Manchester
	NCB 167	Guy	Arab IV	FD74974	East Lancs	5759	H35/28R	8/61	Blackburn 167	Darwen Transport Museum Trust
(r)	NCF 111	Bedford	SB3	69342	Plaxton	592568	C41F	6/59	Goldsmith, Sicklesmere	Brewster, Sicklesmere
	NCF 888	Bedford	C5Z1	4033	Duple	1111/33	C29F	7/59	Mulley, Ixworth	Mulley, Ixworth (SK)
	NCY 626	AEC	Reliance	MU3RV1287	Weymann	M7646	C37F	6/56	South Wales 1032	South Wales Transport Preservation Trust
	NDB 356	Leyland	Tiger Cub PSUC1/1	584041	Crossley		B44F	7/58	Stockport 403	Quantock, Bishops Lydeard (SO)
	NDG 172	Guy	Arab LUF	LUF72116	Duple	191/12	C37C	-/54	Black & White G172	Black & White, Penton Mewsey (HA)
	NDK 980	AEC	Regent V	D2RA6G103	Weymann	M7189	H33/28R	6/56	Rochdale 280	Museum of Transport, Manchester
	NDL 869	AEC	Reliance	MU3RV1326	Duple	1079/1	C41F	5/57	Shotter, Brighstone	MacEwan, Amisfield (SW)
	NEH 453	Leyland	Titan OPD2/1	492993	Northern Counties	4531	L27/26RD	12/49	Potteries L453	Parks, Guildford
					(rebodied 11/54 with body new 5/51)					

	NEH 466	Leyland	Titan OPD2/1	493181	Northern Counties	4846	L27/26RD	12/49	Potteries L466	Potteries Omnibus Preservation Society
					(*rebodied -/54*)					
	NFM 46	Bristol	LL6B	87050	ECW	5317	B39R	5/52	Crosville KW290	Black & White, Penton Mewsey (HA)
	NFM 67	Bristol	KSW6B	86085	ECW	5493	H32/28R	5/52	Crosville MW435	Chelveston Preservation Society
	NGK 245	Bedford	KZ	244053	Spurling		C7FM	9/52	Ministry of Supply	Campbell, Fochabers
	NGY 577	Leyland	Royal Tiger PSU1/14	522298	Duple	137/3	B54F	7/53	Ministry of Supply	Dodd, Dromara
	NHA 744	BMMO	S12	3744	Brush		B44F	10/50	BMMO 3744	BaMMOT, Wythall
	NHA 750	BMMO	S12	3750	Metro-Cammell		B44F	11/50	BMMO 3750	Digbeth S12 Group
	NHA 795	BMMO	D5B	3795	Brush		H30/26RD	12/50	BMMO 3795	BaMMOT, Wythall
	NHH 482	Commer	Avenger IV	94A0130	Blair & Palmer		B45F	5/59	Blair & Palmer, Carlisle	Herefordshire Transport Collection
	NHN 128	Bristol	LL6B	81154	ECW	4759	B39R	6/51	United BG460	Hudson, Bradford
	NHO 400	Commer	Avenger III	T85A0026	Duple	1057/30	C41F	-/55	Parlane, Bordon	Smith, Whitwell
	NHO 720	AEC	Reliance	MU3RV295	Duple	212/4	C43F	3/55	Creamline, Bordon	Spiers, Henley-on-Thames
	NHU 2	Bristol	LSX5G	LSX001	ECW	4978	B42D	1/51	Bristol 2800	Walker & Curtis, Wells
	NHY 947	Bristol	LWL6B	85097	ECW	5431	FC35F	9/51	Bristol 2815	Walker, Wells
			(ex BE-52-30 *Netherlands*, NHY 947)							
	NIB 5232	Leyland	Titan TNLXB2RR	1160	Leylland		O44/29F	9/84	London Transport T1100	South Yorkshire Transport Museum (SY)
(r)	NIL 5377	Bristol	LHS6L	LHS-325	Plaxton	788BC011	C31F	3/78	Miller, Foxton	Hitchens, Bristol
			(ex 533 FN, TCE 131S)							
	NIL 7242	Leyland	National 10351B/1R	06013	Leyland National		B44F	3/79	Cumberland 206	Campbell, Paisley
			(ex AHH 206T)							
	NIW 1639	→ see BJU 13T								
	NJI 3022	Dennis	Javelin	11SDA1932/532	Alexander (Belfast)	B25.08	B53F	3/90	WELB, Northern Ireland	Graham, Kesh
			(ex MJI 7215)							
	NJI 5505	→ see B 75 URN								
	NJO 703	AEC	Regal III	9621A624	Willowbrook	9584	DP32F	5/49	City of Oxford 703	Oxford Bus Museum Trust
	NJV 995	AEC	Bridgemaster	B3RA076	Park Royal	B44460	O41/27R	6/60	Grimsby-Cleethorpes 133	Black & White, Penton Mewsey (HA)
	NKD 536	AEC	Regent III	9613S7655	Crossley		H30/26R	11/53	Liverpool A36	Kelly, Liverpool
	NKD 540	AEC	Regent III	9613S7708	Saunders-Roe	408	H32/26R	11/54	Liverpool A40	Merseyside Transport Trust
	NKH 46	Leyland	Royal Tiger PSU1/15	515490	Plaxton	1715	C41C	7/52	Bluebird, Hull	Henley, Goudhurst
	NKN 650	Commer	Avenger I	23A0682	Harrington	885	C16F	4/51	Maidstone & District LC1	Harrington Society, Worthing
	NKO 953	Albion	Victor FT39N	73006K	Duple	54047	C31F	5/51	Fuggle, Benenden	Spiers, Henley-on-Thames
	NKR 529	Crossley	SD42/7	98123	Brockhouse		FC33F	9/49	Molins Machine, Deptford	Emerton, Nantwich
	NKT 875	Leyland	Titan PD2/12	510803	Leyland		H30/28R	5/51	Maidstone & District DH379	Yarnell, St Leonards
	NKT 896	Leyland	Titan PD2/12	512390	Leyland		H30/28RD	8/51	Maidstone & District DH400	Dicker Clifford & Coombs, Hastings
	NKY 161	Bedford	SBG	51465	Yeates	622	C41F	5/57	Fairways, Bradford	Don, Great Dunmow (EX)
(r)	NLE 515	AEC	Regal IV	9821LT784	Metro-Cammell		B—F	3/53	London Transport RF296	Huxford & Rivers, Ewell
	NLE 527	AEC	Regal IV	9821LT876	Metro-Cammell		B38F	4/53	London Transport RF308	RF308 Group, Luton
	NLE 528	AEC	Regal IV	9821LT877	Metro-Cammell		B38F	4/53	London Transport RF309	Henderson, Cambridge
	NLE 534	AEC	Regal IV	9821LT899	Metro-Cammell		B39F	4/53	London Transport RF534	Betterton, Tivetshall
	NLE 537	AEC	Regal IV	9821LT898	Metro-Cammell		B39F	4/53	London Transport RF537	London Transport Museum
	NLE 538	AEC	Regal IV	9821LT897	Metro-Cammell		B39F	4/53	London Transport RF538	RM40 Group, Manor Park
	NLE 539	AEC	Regal IV	9821LT901	Metro-Cammell		B39F	4/53	London Transport RF539	Narduzzo & Puddephatt, Marsworth
	NLE 551	AEC	Regal IV	9821LT906	Metro-Cammell		B38F	5/53	London Transport RF551	Gregory, Malvern
	NLE 556	AEC	Regal IV	9821LT913	Metro-Cammell		B39F	5/53	London Transport RF556	Henderson, Cambridge
	NLE 573	AEC	Regal IV	9821LT930	Metro-Cammell		B41F	5/53	London Transport RF573	Walters, Wimbledon
	NLE 580	AEC	Regal IV	9821LT937	Metro-Cammell		B39F	5/53	London Transport RF580	Miller, Twickenham
	NLE 600	AEC	Regal IV	9821LT957	Metro-Cammell		B41F	7/53	London Transport RF600	SRARFA, Reigate

	NLE 603	AEC	Regal IV	9821LT960	Metro-Cammell		B39F	6/53	London Transport RF603	Hutt, Finstock (OX)
	NLE 626	AEC	Regal IV	9821LT984	Metro-Cammell		B39F	7/53	London Transport RF626	Garbutt & Peacock, Holbeach
	NLE 627	AEC	Regal IV	9821LT985	Metro-Cammell		B39F	7/53	London Transport RF627	Eveleigh, Meriden
	NLE 633	AEC	Regal IV	9821LT992	Metro-Cammell		B41F	8/53	London Transport RF633	Country Bus Rallies, East Grinstead
	NLE 643	AEC	Regal IV	9821LT999	Metro-Cammell		B41F	8/53	London Transport RF643	Clarke, Maidenhead
	NLE 644	AEC	Regal IV	9821LT1007	Metro-Cammell		B39F	9/53	London Transport RF644	Cunnington & Shirley, Holmwood
										(operates as Red Baron, Holmwood (SR))
(r)	NLE 652	AEC	Regal IV	9821LT1321	Metro-Cammell		B39F	9/53	London Transport RF652	Stanley & Broad, East Grinstead
	NLE 667	AEC	Regal IV	9821LT1336	Metro-Cammell		B39F	9/53	London Transport RF667	Dale, Sherborne
	NLE 672	AEC	Regal IV	9821LT1342	Metro-Cammell		B41F	10/53	London Transport RF672	Morris & Jones, Carshalton
	NLE 673	AEC	Regal IV	9821LT1341	Metro-Cammell		B39F	9/53	London Transport RF673	Cartwright, High Wycombe
	NLE 676	AEC	Regal IV	9821LT1345	Metro-Cammell		B39F	10/53	London Transport RF676	Chalmers, Wilsonham & Philipson, Ilford
	NLE 679	AEC	Regal IV	9821LT1348	Metro-Cammell		B39F	10/53	London Transport RF679	Rivers, Ashford
	NLE 701	Leyland	7RT	524964	Park Royal	L416	H30/26R	2/53	London Transport RTLl427	Hammer, Beeding (WS)
	NLE 744	AEC	Regent III	O9616829	Park Royal	L772	H30/26R	3/52	London Transport RT2976	Pratt {Crosville}, Weston super Mare (SO)
	NLE 840	AEC	Regent III	O9616940	Weymann	W565	H30/26R	6/53	London Transport RT3733	Welch, London
	NLE 882	AEC	Regent III	O9617335	Park Royal	L2692	H30/26R	8/53	London Transport RT3775	Bluebell Railway, Sheffield Park
	NLE 918	AEC	Regent III	O9616915	Weymann	W578	H30/26R	5/53	London Transport RT3028	Brown, Hawkhurst (KT)
	NLE 939	AEC	Regent III	O9616939	Park Royal	L2585	H--/--R	5/53	London Transport RT4275	Hinson, Potterspury
	NLE 981	AEC	Regent III	O9617294	Park Royal	L2611	H--/--RD	7/53	London Transport RT4317	Hemmings & Young, Potton
	NLE 989	→ see JXN 202								
	NLJ 268	Leyland	Royal Tiger PSU1/13	532050	Burlingham	5643	B--F	1/54	Bournemouth 258	Shears D, Winkleigh
	NLJ 271	Leyland	Royal Tiger PSU1/13	532053	Burlingham	5646	B42F	2/54	Bournemouth 261	Quantock, Bishops Lydeard (SO)
	NLJ 272	Leyland	Royal Tiger PSU1/13	532054	Burlingham	5647	B42F	2/54	Bournemouth 262	Shears D, Winkleigh
	NLP 581	→ see Q995 CPE								
	NLP 645	AEC	Regal IV	9822E1495	Park Royal	B36853	RDP37C	9/53	British European Airways 1035	Science Museum, Wroughton
	NLT 4	→ see RBY 764K *Overseas*								
	NMS 358	AEC	Reliance	2MU3RV2264	Alexander	5829	C41F	3/60	Alexander AC147	Booth/West of Scotland Bus Group, Glasgow
	NMS 366	AEC	Reliance	2MU3RV2272	Alexander	5831	C41F	3/60	Alexander AC155	Mcleod, Bettyhill
	NMS 372	AEC	Reliance	2MU3RV2278	Alexander	5818	C41F	3/60	Alexander AC161	Transport Preservation Trust, Beith
	NNB 125	Leyland	Royal Tiger PSU1/13	530665	Northern Counties	4723	B41C	10/53	Manchester 25	Talbot & Stubbins, Leicester
	NNB 208	Leyland	Titan PD2/12	531524	Leyland		H32/28R	-/53	Manchester 3368	-?-, -?-
	NNJ 210	Trojan	19	0908967	Trojan		C13F	5/60	Moore, Scunthorpe	Warren, Martock
			(ex GSL 107, VFW 329)							
	NNN 968	Btn	BTS1	BTL30/52/1026			transporter	1/53	Barton 668	Barton Cherished Vehicle Collection
	NNW 492	AEC	Regent III	9612E2398	Roe	GO2987	H31/25R	1/50	Leeds 492	Keighley Bus Museum Trust
	NOG 560	→ see CSL 643								
	NOI 1968	→ see 77-D-824 *Ireland*								
	NOI 1981	Leyland	Leopard PSU3E/4R	7605950	Alexander(Belfast)	-?-	RV	6/77	Ulsterbus 1981	Kells Transport Museum, Cork
	NRA 708	Crossley	SD42/7	97702	Crossley		B35R	9/49	Chesterfield 8	Smalley, Worksop
	NRA 712	Crossley	SD42/7	97736	Crossley		B35R	9/49	Chesterfield 12	Smalley, Worksop
	NRN 586	Leyland	Atlantean PDR1/1	600553	Metro-Cammell		H44/33F	10/60	Ribble 1686	Ribble Vehicle Preservation Trust
	NSF 757	Leyland	Titan PD2/20	562184	Metro-Cammell		H34/29R	11/56	Edinburgh 757	Hunt, Fleetwood
	NSG 869	Albion	Nimbus MR9	82000A	Scottish Omnibuses		B32F	12/55	Albion demonstrator	Walters, Talke
	NSJ 502	AEC	Reliance	2MU3RV4229	Alexander	6863	C41F	6/62	Alexander Northern NAC205	Wallace, Broxburn
			(ex SRS 117)							
	NTF 9	Leyland	Titan PD2/15	512882	Leyland		H30/26R	11/51	Leyland demonstrator	Docherty, Irvine
	NTF 466	Daimler	CVG5SD	18003	Northern Counties	4619	B35F	2/52	Lancaster 466	North West Museum of Transport

	NTT 661	AEC	Regent III	9613A7155	Weymann	M5514	H30/26R	5/52	Devon General DR661	Platt, Dawlish Warren
	NTT 679	AEC	Regent III	9613A7173	Weymann	M5523	H30/26R	1/53	Devon General DR679	Greet, Broadhempston
										(operates as Nostalgic Transport, Broadhempston (DN))
	NTU 125	Foden	PVRF6	31232	Metalcraft	171	C41C	5/51	Hollinshead, Scholar Green	Burdett, Corley
	NTW 368	Bedford	OB	85220	Duple	48026	C29F	9/48	Hall, Maldon	Harrington, Bishops Itchington (WK)
	NTW 706	Bedford	OB	89535	Duple	46511	C25F	12/48	Dix, Dagenham	Harrington, Bishops Itchington (WK)
	NVE 748	Bedford	CAV	39630	?		M8	5/55	private owner	Jacobs, Burwell
	NVK 341	AEC	Regent III	9613A5303	Northern Coachbuilders		H30/26R	10/50	Newcastle 341	Northern Counties Bus Preservation Group
	NVL 165	→ see RFE 482								
	NVN 507	Trojan	-?-	M7362	Trojan		B??	3/56	private owner	Trojan Museum Trust, Fyfield
	NWO 122	Sentinel	SLC4	SLC4/27/1	Beadle	C331	C35C	4/55	Chapple, Raglan	Wheatley & Perry, Kenilworth
	NXI 1200	Leyland	Tiger TRBTL11/2RP	TR00410	Alexander (Belfast)	B09.01	B48F	11/88	Ulsterbus 1200	Kells Transport Museum, Cork
	NXI 4242	Leyland	Tiger TRBTL11/2RP	TR00588	Alexander (Belfast)	B11.33	DP53F	3/89	Ulsterbus 1242	McAlinney, Newtownards
	NXI 4247	Leylland	Tiger TRBTL11/2RP	TR00646	Alexander (Belfast)	B11.37	DP53F	4/89	Ulsterbus 1247	Haughey, Forkhill
	NXI 4624	Leyland	Tiger TRBLXB/2RP	TR00485	Alexander (Belfast)	B10.12	B42F	2/89	Citybus 2624	Kells Transport Museum, Cork
	NXI 4629	Leyland	Tiger TRBLXB/2RP	TR00527	Alexander (Belfast)	B10.17	B42F	4/89	Citybus 2629	Kells Transport Museum, Cork
	NXI 4635	Leyland	Tiger TRBLXB/2RP	TR00580	Alexander (Belfast)	B10.24	B42F	5/89	Citybus 2635	Shannon, Newtownards
	NXL 847	AEC	Regal III	6821A483	Duple	146/1	C39F	6/53	Eastern Belle, Bow	Burdett, Corley
	NXP 506	Bedford	SB	15840	Plaxton	2175	C33F	6/53	Halley, Sauchie	Moseley (PCV), South Elmsall
	NXP 775	AEC	Regent III	O9617801	Weymann	W2064	H30/26R	1/54	London Transport RT4421	Ensign, Purfleet (EX)
	NXP 778	AEC	Regent III	O9617351	Weymann	W1666	H30/26R	6/53	London Transport RT4424	London Bus Company, Northfleet (KT)
	NXP 796	AEC	Regent III	O9617557	Park Royal	L2825	H--/--R	12/53	London Transport RT4442	Bird, Burgess Hill (WS)
	NXP 847	AEC	Regent III	O9617824	Weymann	W1847	H30/26R	12/53	London Transport RT4683	Ryan, Clacton-on-Sea
			(ex NXP 935)							
	NXP 881	AEC	Regent III	O9617549	Park Royal	L2959	H18/26R	12/53	London Transport RT4628	Duker & Young, Little Paxton
	NXP 935	→ see NXP 847								
	NXP 971	→ see KGK 708								
	NXP 997	AEC	Regent III	O9617831	Park Royal	L3122	H30/26R	2/54	London Transport RT4712	London Transport Museum
	OBD 903	Bristol	LS6G	119050	ECW	9962	C41F	6/57	United Counties 116	Mahoney I, Brentwood
	OBY 362	Ford	E83W	C854685	Martin Walter		B7	-/55	non-PSV	Wickens, Iver
			(ex SSV 976, OBY 362)							
	OCD 772	Leyland	Titan PD2/12	542426	Park Royal	B37691	H31/26RD	5/55	Southdown 772	Osborne I, Fareham
	OCO 502	Leyland	Titan PD2/40	580215	Metro-Cammell		H30/26R	5/58	Plymouth 102	Hobcraft, Hartfield
	OCS 712	→ see XSL 945A								
	OCS 713	→ see XSN 25A								
	ODE 182	Sentinel	STC6	STC6/44/90	Sentinel		B44F	2/52	Edwards, Crymych	Hinchliffe, Huddersfield
	ODK 705	AEC	Regent V	D2RA6G088	Weymann	M7209	H33/28R	10/56	Rochdale 305	Dearnley, Halifax
	ODL 399	Bedford	SBG	50260	Duple	1074/270	C--F	5/57	Moss, Sandown	ODL400 Group, Binstead
	ODL 400	Bedford	SBG	50274	Duple	1074/274	C41F	5/57	Moss, Sandown	ODL400 Group, Binstead
	ODN 348	AEC	Regent V	MD3RV172	Roe	GO4495	H33/28RD	7/57	York Pullman 71	York Pullman, York (NY)
	OED 217	Foden	PVD6	39832	East Lancs	5214	H30/28R	3/56	Warrington 112	-?-, -?-
	OFC 205	AEC	Regal III	6821A423	Duple	51609	C32F	3/50	South Midland 66	Oxford Bus Museum Trust
	OFC 393	AEC	Regent III	9621A4665	Weymann	M4499	H30/26R	8/49	City of Oxford H393	Oxford Bus Museum Trust
	OFM 634	Bristol	KSW6B	92124	ECW	5818	L27/28R	2/53	Crosville MW476	Thorogood et al, Briantspuddle
	OFS 777	Leyland	Titan PD2/20	562389	Metro-Cammell		H34/29R	1/57	Edinburgh 777	Lothian Bus Consortium
(r)	OFS 795	Leyland	Titan PD2/20	570967	Metro-Cammell		H34/29R	10/57	Edinburgh 795	Roulston, Glasgow
	OFS 798	Leyland	Titan PD2/20	571029	Metro-Cammell		H34/29R	11/57	Edinburgh 798	Scoular, Edinburgh

	Reg	Make	Model	Chassis no	Body	Body no	Layout	Date	Original operator	Current owner
	OFW 795	Bristol	SC4LK	121045	ECW	8994	B35F	9/57	Lincolnshire 2446	Gallagher & Stopper, Waddington
	OFW 806	Bristol	SC4LK	121018	ECW	9981	DP33F	6/57	Lincolnshire 2609	Lincolnshire 2609 Group, Waddington
	OHK 432	Daimler	CVD6DD	15327	Roberts		H30/26R	4/49	Colchester 4	Milner & Childs, Lincoln
	OHR 919	Bristol	Lodekka LD6G	130047	ECW	8685	H33/27R	12/56	Wilts & Dorset 628	Three Counties Bus Preservation, Southampton
	OHY 938	Bristol	KSW6B	90063	ECW	5986	L27/28RD	9/52	Bath Tramways L8089	Walker, Wells
	OJF 191	Leyland	Tiger Cub PSUC1/1	565542	Weymann	M7704	B44F	10/56	Leicester 191	Leicester Transport Heritage Trust
	OJI 4371	Leyland	Atlantean AN68A/1R	7605985	Northern Counties	8160	H43/31F	11/77	Fylde 85	Lancastrian Transport Trust
			(ex EBV 85S)							*(operated by Totally Transport, Blackpool (LA))*
	OJO 727	AEC	Regal III	9621A1217	Willowbrook	50779	B32F	4/50	City of Oxford 727	Wareham, Kidlington
	OKH 337	AEC	Regent III	9613E7748	Weymann	M4395	H32/26R	10/53	Hull 337	Chaplin, Hull
	OKM 317	AEC	Regent III	9612E4661	Saunders-Roe		H30/26R	12/51	Maidstone & Districtt DH500	Dodds, Ayr (SW)
	OKP 980	Beadle-Leyland		JCB209	Beadle		C35F	3/52	Maidstone & District C0252	Thornes, Hemingbrough (NY)
			(ex VSJ 566, OKP 980)							
	OLD 559	AEC	Regent III	O9617989	Weymann	W1931	H30/26R	7/54	London Transport RT4772	London Bus Company, Northfleet (KT)
	OLD 564	AEC	Regent III	O9618023	Park Royal	L2939	H30/26R	7/54	London Transport RT4777	Shaftesbury & District, Shaftesbury (DT)
	OLD 566	AEC	Regent III	O9618034	Weymann	W1058	H30/26R	7/54	London Transport RT4779	RT4779 Group, Fordyce
	OLD 587	AEC	Regent III	O9617909	Saunders		H30/26R	4/54	London Transport RT4823	London Bus Company, Northfleet (KT)
	OLD 589	AEC	Regent III	O9617912	Park Royal	L2954	H30/26R	4/54	London Transport RT4825	London Transport Museum
	OLD 702	AEC	Regent III	O9617891	Saunders		H30/26R	3/54	London Transport RT4482	Bosher et al, Egham
	OLD 714	AEC	Regent III	O9617929	Weymann	W2089	H30/26R	4/54	London Transport RT4494	Gray & Chubb, Lincoln
	OLD 768	AEC	Regent III	O9618074	Park Royal	L2917	H30/26R	9/54	London Transport RT4548	London Bus Company, Northfleet (KT)
	OLG 855	Foden	PVRF6	31234	Plaxton	737	C41C	9/51	Foden Motor Works Band	Helliker, Stroud
	OLJ 291	Bedford	CAV	19973	Bedford		M12	4/54	non-PSV	Science Museum, Wroughton
	OMB 161	Daimler	CVD6DD	17993	Northern Counties	4609	H36/28R	3/52	SHMD 61	Chatterton, Foxham
	OMS 244	Albion	Nimbus NS3L	82058A	Alexander	6123	C29F	5/60	Alexander N11	Roulston, Glasgow
	OMS 253	→ see WSK 509								
	ONO 49	Bristol	L5G	79028	ECW	4050	B35R	2/50	Eastern National 309	Castle Point Transport Museum
(z)	ONO 59	Bristol	K5G	76073	ECW	3550	L--/--RD	11/49	Eastern National 4038	Lincolnshire Vintage Vehicle Society
	ONO 85	Bedford	OB	108741	Duple	54307	C29F	-/48	Eastern National 4064	Repton, Little Bookham (SR)
(r)	ONO 995	Bristol	LL6B	81134	ECW	4670	B39R	-/50	Eastern National 4081	Ledger, Northampton
	ONU 280	Guy	Arab III	FD70285	Weymann	M4203	L--/--R	3/50	Chesterfield 180	Smith, Whitwell
	ONV 425	Bristol	SC4LK	121001	ECW	9007	B35F	7/57	United Counties 125	Cook, Exeter
	OPB 536	Leyland	Comet CPP1	495305	Duple	48721	C32F	4/50	Brady, Forest Green	-?-, Bedfordshire
	OPN 807	Bristol	Lodekka LDS6B	138296	ECW	10177	H33/27R	5/59	Brighton Hove & District 7	Adair Terrill & Start, Brighton
	OPV 47	AEC	Regent V	2D2RA940	East Lancs	5800	H37/28R	3/62	Ipswich 47	London Bus Company, Northfleet (KT)
	ORB 277	Daimler	CVD6SD	17375	Duple	50201	C35F	7/50	Blue Bus, Willington DR12	BaMMOT, Wythall
(z)	ORF 130	Daimler	CVD6SD	14947	*chassis only*			-/48	Greatrex, Stafford 38	BaMMOT, Wythall
	ORL 357	Commer	Avenger I	23A0821	Harrington	976	C33F	3/51	Skinner, Millbrook	-?-, -?-
	ORR 140	AEC	Regent III	6812A087	Willowbrook	53142	L27/28R	1/54	West Bridgford 21	Howard & Oliver, Nottingham
	ORV 989	Leyland	Titan PD2/40	572237	Metro-Cammell		H30/26R	2/58	Portsmouth 112	Working Omnibus Museum Project
	ORV 992	Leyland	Titan PD2/40	572287	Metro-Cammell		H30/26R	2/58	Portsmouth 115	Blair, Upham
	OSC 711	→ see RMS 714								
	OSJ 512	Morris-Commercial	CVF13/5	72196	Wadham		FB27F	-/48	JMT 71	Payne, Great Sampford
			(ex J 11429)							
	OSK 831	Karrier	BFD3023	D98A0461	Plaxton	2149	C14F	1/58	Brocksbank, Bramley	Dixon (Alan), Thornton, Annfield Plain
			(ex BVH 157A, 6666 U)							
	OST 502	→ see LVS 175								
	OTT 43	Bristol	LS6G	97046	ECW	7098	C39F	8/53	Western National 2200	Burdett, Corley

OTT 55	Bristol	LS5G	97190	ECW	7140	B41F	1/54	Southern National 1701	Science Museum, Wroughton
OTT 85	Bristol	LS6G	101066	ECW	7165	C39F	9/53	Southern National 1376	Billington, Maidenhead
OTT 90	→ see SVS 904								
OTT 98	Bristol	LS6G	97089	ECW	7086	C39F	9/53	Southern National 1299	West Country Historic Omnibus & Transport Trust
OTV 137	AEC	Regent III	9613E4841	Park Royal	B34054	H30/26R	12/53	Nottingham 137	Needham, Carterton
OTV 161	AEC	Regent III	9613E4865	Park Royal	B34078	H30/26R	2/54	Nottingham 161	Allen & Bairstow, Nottingham
OTY 208	Bedford	C5Z1	3767	Duple Midland	489/30/18	B30F	1/59	Tait, Morpeth	Hughes, Llithfaen
OUH 107	AEC	Reliance	MU3RV1921	Harrington	1985	C39F	3/58	Western Welsh 107	Hawkins, Bridgend
OVB 345	Trojan	DT	M5808	Strachan	51941	C12F	9/54	Trojan demonstrator	Macdougall, East Devon
OVF 229	Bristol	Lodekka LD5G	100123	ECW	6737	H33/25RD	11/54	Eastern Counties LKD229	Eastern Transport Collection
OVL 465	Bristol	MW5G	164108	ECW	11851	B45F	10/60	Lincolnshire 2245	Milner, Lincoln
OVL 473	Bristol	Lodekka FS5G	155081	ECW	11623	H33/27RD	7/60	Lincolnshire 2378	Rolley, Quainton
		(ex PVS 315, LDS 448A, OVL 473)							
OVL 494	Bristol	SC4LK	158029	ECW	12014	B35F	6/60	Lincolnshire 2485	Tilly's, Southwold (SK)
OWE 116	AEC	Regent III	9613A2685	Roe	G03446	H33/25R	9/52	Sheffield 116	South Yorkshire Transport Museum
OWJ 112	AEC	Routemaster	RM1822	Park Royal	L5047	H36/28R	1/64	London Transport RM1822	English, Dover
		(ex EYY 772B, 822 DYE)							
OWS 620	Bristol	Lodekka LD6G	134053	ECW	9504	H33/27R	7/57	Scottish Omnibuses AA620	Gascoine, Walker, Thomas & Godfrey, Edinburgh
OWX 167	Bristol	Lodekka LD6B	108186	ECW	8122	H33/27RD	11/55	West Yorkshire DX23	Halliday, Shipley
OXI 1250	Leyland	Tiger TRBTL11/2RP	TR00462	Alexander (Belfast)	B16.01	DP53F	2/90	Ulsterbus 1250	Holden, Bude
OXI 1267	Leyland	Tiger TRBTL11/2RP	TR00721	Alexander (Belfast)	B12.08	B53F	6/89	Ulsterbus 1267	Kells Transport Museum, Cork
OXI 1274	Leyland	Tiger TRBTL11/2RP	TR00729	Alexander (Belfast)	B12.15	B53F	6/89	Ulsterbus 1274	Kells Transport Museum, Cork
OXI 1282	Leyland	Tiger TRBTL11/2RP	TR00741	Alexander (Belfast)	B12.23	B53F	7/89	Ulsterbus 1282	Kells Transport Museum, Cork
OXI 1299	Leyland	Tiger TRBTL11/2RP	TR00779	Alexander (Belfast)	B12.39	B53F	11/89	Ulsterbus 1299	Kells Transport Museum, Cork
OYL 220	Karrier	Q25	52A0138	Reading	3283	C14F	7/54	Karrier demonstrator	Dawson, Anerley

PBC 734	Karrier	Q25	91A0640	Reading		C14F	-/56	Leicester Council	Coventry Transport Museum
PBN 653	Leyland	Titan PD2/27	600530	Metro-Cammell		FH--/--F	4/61	Bolton 135	Norris & Bradley, Bolton
PBN 668	Daimler	CVG6-30DD	30082	East Lancs	5549	H41/32F	3/60	Bolton 150	Holden, Bolton
PCB 24	→ see TRN 851A								
PCK 370	Leyland	Titan PD3/5	603275	Metro-Cammell		FH41/31F	6/61	Ribble 1729	Snape, Leyland
PCK 618	Leyland	Leopard L2	610203	Harrington	2447	C32F	5/61	Ribble 1036	Prescott, Fulwood *(on loan to Ribble Vehicle Preservation Trust)*
PCN 762	AEC	Routemaster	3R2RH2171	Park Royal	B49992	H41/31F	4/64	Northern General 2099	North East Bus Preservation Trust
		(ex EDS 508B, RCN 699)							
PCW 957	Leyland	Tiger Cub PSUC1/11	L10896	East Lancs	5996	B43F	9/63	Burnley Colne & Nelson 57	Millington, -?-
PDH 808	Leyland	Royal Tiger PSU1/13	522577	Park Royal	B35149	DP40F	5/53	Walsall 808	BaMMOT, Wythall
PDL 515	Bristol	MW6G	135103	ECW	10085	C39F	4/58	Southern Vectis 315	Isle of Wight Bus Museum
PDL 518	Bristol	Lodekka LD6G	138106	ECW	10311	H8/16RD	6/58	Southern Vectis 558	Boughton, Brightwell
PDW 484	Leyland	Titan PD2/40	581934	Longwell Green	15135	H30/28R	10/58	Newport 178	Newport (CS) 178
PEF 21	Leyland	Leopard L1	L03800	Strachan	52126	B43D	3/64	West Hartlepool 21	Larkin, Peterborough
PEF 370	Bedford	VAL14	1469	Plaxton	642281	C--F	4/64	Beeline, West Hartlepool	Greet, Broadhempston
PFF 777	Bedford	KZ	232395	Spurling		B9F	2/52	Rotol, Cheltenham	Foster P, Darlington
		(ex JFH 760)							
PFN 858	AEC	Regent V	2LD3RA559	Park Royal	B42292	FH40/32F	4/59	East Kent	Blackman, Halifax (WY)
PFN 865	AEC	Regent V	2LD3RA566			RV	5/59	East Kent	Smith, Keighley

	Reg	Chassis	Model	Chassis No	Body	Body No	Layout	New	First Operator	Current Owner
	PFN 867	AEC	Regent V	2LD3RA568	Park Royal	B42316	FH40/32F	5/59	East Kent	Love et al, St Albans
										(in care of East Kent Heritage, Dover)
	PFN 868	AEC	Regent V	2LD3RA569	Park Royal	B42297	FH40/30F	4/59	East Kent	PFN868 Preservation Group, Berkhamsted
	PFN 874	AEC	Regent V	2LD3RA575	Park Royal	B42293	FH40/32F	4/59	East Kent	Chant, Herne Bay
	PFO 256	Bristol	MW6G	195026	ECW	12869	DP--F	5/62	Wilts & Dorset 717	Mahoney I, Brentwood
			(ex 675 AAM)							
	PFR 346	Leyland	Titan PD2/27	583394	Metro-Cammell		FH35/28RD	3/59	Blackpool 346	Lancastrian Transport Trust
	PFR 727	Karrier	BF3023	98A2867	Plaxton	592501	C14F	3/59	Abbott, Blackpool	Leach, Telford
	PFR 747	Bedford	SB1	67798	Harrington	2072	C--F	4/59	Abbott, Blackpool	Webster, Southrepps
	PFW 935	Bristol	SC4LK	141021	ECW	9001	B35F	12/57	Lincolnshire 2453	Lawrence, Winterton-on-Sea
	PFW 939	Bristol	SC4LK	141033	ECW	9005	B35F	2/58	Lincolnshire 2457	Simpson, Killamarsh
	PHJ 953	Leyland	Titan PD3/6	580831	Massey	2307	O41/33R	6/58	Southend 314	Atkins, Folkestone (KT)
	PHJ 954	Leyland	Titan PD3/6	580863	Massey	2308	L35/32R	6/58	Southend 315	Gent & Salmon, South Benfleet
	PHN 699	Guy	Arab III	FD70917	Roe	GO3430	B41C	5/52	Darlington 26	Blackman, Halifax (WY)
	PHN 829	Bristol	KSW6B	90071	ECW	6101	L27/28R	-/52	United BBL67	Dolan, Crook
	PHN 831	Bristol	LS5G	89014	ECW	5705	B45F	5/53	United BU2	Dolan M, Crook
	PIB 3673	Leyland	Leopard PSU5/4R	7300603	Plaxton	732322	C53F	6/73	Richmond, Epsom	Kells Transport Museum, Cork
			(ex KNR 328L)							
	PIB 5891	Leyland	Fleetline FE33ALR	8001733	Northern Counties	2006	H49/31D	6/81	Southend 232	-?-, -?-
			(ex MRJ 232W)							
	PIL 5863	Bedford	YMP	FT106810	Plaxton	858MQP2C015	C35F	1/86	Hurst, Wigan	Atkin, North Owersby
			(ex C724 LCP)							
	PIL 7013	Leyland	National NL116AL11/2R	07486	Leyland National		B47F	11/80	Crosville SNL2	Campbell, Paisley
			(ex AFM 2W)							
	PIL 9243	Leyland	Lynx LX1126LXCTZR1R	LX1243	Leyland		B45F	1/89	Northern General 4722	-?-, -?-
			(ex F722 LRG)							
	PIW 4791	Leyland	Atlantean AN68A/2R	7702694	Alexander	AL60/2775/44	H49/37F	5/78	Tyne & Wear PTE 276	Cartwright, Newcastle-upon-Tyne
			(ex SCN 276S)							
(r)	PJI 3534	AEC	Reliance	6U3ZR37085	Duple	843/5811	C57F	9/78	Baker, Weston super Mare	Forsyth, Braidwood
			(ex XHT 159T, 950 LYD, TOU 637T)							
	PJI 7756	Leyland	Leopard PSU5C/4R	7930146	Plaxton	8112LC002	C57F	2/81	Marchwood, Totton	Rodgers, Hamilton
			(ex LIL 9239, MRU 551W)							
	PJX 35	Leyland	Leopard L1	612074	Weymann	M330	B42F	8/62	Halifax 35	Waites et al, Huddersfield
	PJX 43	Leyland	Titan PD2/37	622180	Weymann	M308	H36/28F	11/62	Halifax 43	McAllister, Paignton (DN)
	PJX 232	Leyland	Leopard L1	612229	Weymann	M331	B44F	9/62	Halifax 232	Keighley Bus Museum Trust
	PJY 2	Leyland	Royal Tiger PSU1/15	511000	Plaxton	729025	C43F	-/51	Munden, Bristol	Herefordshire Transport Collection
			(ex EHY 111K, HMR 444) *(rebodied 4/72)*							
	PND 460	Leyland	Titan PD2/12	551984	Metro-Cammell		H36/28R	8/56	Manchester 3460	Talbot & Stubbins, Leicester
	POI 2151	→ see 77-D-214 *Ireland*								
	POI 2156	→ see 77-D-827 *Ireland*								
	POI 2180	→ see 78-D-825 *Ireland*								
	POI 2187	→ see 77-LH-519 *Ireland*								
	POI 2190	Bristol	RELL6G	RELL-3-2249	Alexander (Belfast)	-?-	B52F	12/77	Ulsterbus 2190	Hart et al, York
	POI 2192	→ see 77-D-213 *Ireland*								
	POI 2193	→ see 78-D-824 *Ireland*								
	POR 428	Dennis	Falcon II	123P5	Strachan	-?-	B30F	8/56	Aldershot & District 282	Falcon 282 Group, Aldershot
			(ex 29 HMN, POR 428)							
	POU 494	Leyland	Titan PD2/24	560374	East Lancs	5297	L27/28R	10/56	King Alfred, Winchester	FoKAB, Winchester

	Reg	Chassis	Model	Chassis no	Body	Body no	Layout	New	First owner	Current owner
	PPC 275	Bedford	OB	147359	Duple	48139	C29F	2/51	Howard, West Byfleet	McNeill, Todmorden
	PPF 492	AEC	Regal III	6821A375	Harrington	859	C37F	5/51	Surrey, Sutton 36	Hurley et al, Worthing
	PPH 698	Bedford	SB	2138	Duple	56702	C33F	6/51	Richmond, Epsom	Heels, Ashtead
	PRD 32	AEC	Reliance	MU3RV2140	Burlingham	6813	B34D	1/59	Reading 12	Stone, Reading
	PRN 145	Leyland	Atlantean PDR1/1	610601	Metro-Cammell		H44/33F	5/61	Scout, Preston 5	Ribble Vehicle Preservation Trust
	PRN 761	Leyland-PCT	PD3/6	PC61/3	Leyland-PCT		H38/32F	7/61	Preston 2	Gilroy, Alnwick (ND) 2
	PRN 906	Leyland	Titan PD3/4	611323	Metro-Cammell		H39/31F	10/61	Preston 14	Ribble Vehicle Preservation Trust
	PRN 908	→ see Q644 GFV								
	PRN 911	→ see MVS 972								
	PSJ 480	Leyland	Titan PD2A/27	622126	Massey	2505	H37/27F	10/62	Wigan 35	Wigan Transport Trust
			(ex JJP 502)							
	PSK 389	Leyland	Titan PD2/37	610409	Weymann	M9624	H37/27F	7/61	Brighton 10	McPherson, Walworth
			(ex 5010 CD)							*(on loan to London Bus Export Company, Lydney (XGL))*
	PSL 234	Maudslay	ML3BC/4LW	4988	Thurgood	506	C35F	4/31	Church, Pytchley	Shears, Winkleigh
			(ex ABD 812A, NV 30)		*(rebodied 10/48)*					
	PSU 414	→ see MSL 292								
	PTW 110	Bristol	L6B	81139	ECW	4719	FC31F	5/51	Eastern National 4107	Mara, Canvey
	PUF 647	Guy	Arab IV	FD72880	Park Royal	B38420	H33/26RD	6/56	Southdown 547	Morgan, Redhill
	PUJ 781	Leyland	Tiger Cub PSUC1/2	577966	Burlingham	6563	C41F	4/58	Whittle, Highley	Rogers, Kidderminster (WO)
	PUJ 783	Leyland	Tiger Cub PSUC1/2	578370	Burlingham	6565	C41F	4/58	Whittle, Highley	Bannister, Owston Ferry (LI)
	PVS 315	→ see OVL 473								
	PVS 984	AEC	Reliance	MU3RV549	Alexander	4698	B45F	6/55	Alexander AC43	Roulston, Glasgow
			(ex GWG 94)							
	PWL 413	AEC	Regent III	9613A5624	Weymann	M4676	L27/26R	1/51	City of Oxford L166	Oxford Bus Museum Trust
	PXE 761	Sentinel	SLC/6/30	SLC63013	Duple	215/1	C--C	1/55	Lewis, Greenwich	Spiers, Henley-on-Thames
	PXI 1300	Leyland	Tiger TR2R56V16Z4	TR00528	Alexander (Belfast)	B20.01	DP53F	3/90	Ulsterbus 1300	Kells Transport Museum, Cork
	PXI 1315	Leyland	Tiger TR2R56V16Z4	TR00916	Alexander (Belfast)	B22.16	DP53F	2/90	Ulsterbus 1315	Irish Transport Heritage
			(ex AXI 315, PXI 1315)							
	PXI 1320	Leyland	Tiger TR2R56V16Z4	TR00928	Alexander (Belfast)	B22.14	DP53F	2/90	Ulsterbus 1320	Kells Transport Museum, Cork
	PXI 5524	Leyland	Tiger TRCTL11/3ARZA	TR00861	Alexander (Belfast)	B17.11	C53F	5/90	Ulsterbus 2524	Irish Transport Heritage
	RAG 400	Bristol	Lodekka LD6G	177024	ECW	12156	H33/27RD	8/61	Western SMT 1634	Ritchie, Glasgow
	RAG 411	Bristol	Lodekka LD6G	177068	ECW	12167	H--/--RD	8/61	Western SMT 1645	Thomas, Glasgow
	RAG 578	Daimler	CVG6LX-30DD	30083	Northern Counties	5480	FH41/32F	12/60	A1, Ardrossan	Scottish Vintage Bus Museum
	RAL 334	→ see APR 167A								
	RAL 795	Daimler	CVG6DD	18688	Massey	2148	H33/28RD	7/54	Gash, Newark DD10	-?-, -?-
	RAO 733	Bristol	Lodekka LD6G	116135	ECW	8540	H--/--RD	6/56	Cumberland 369	Cumbria Omnibus Group
	RCD 735	Bedford	CAV	46087	Martin Walter	UB24159	M??	-/55	private owner	Mitchinson, York
	RCK 920	Leyland	Titan PD3/5	612585	Metro-Cammell		FH41/31F	5/62	Ribble 1775	Ribble Vehicle Preservation Trust
(r)	RCK 938	Leyland	Titan PD3/5	612783	Metro-Cammell		FH41/31F	3/62	Ribble 1793	Ribble Vehicle Preservation Trust
	RCM 493	Leyland	Leopard L1	L04497	Massey	2572	B44D	5/64	Birkenhead 93	Wirral Borough Council
	RCN 697	AEC	Routemaster	3R2RH2169	Park Royal	B49990	H--/--F	4/64	Northern General 2097	Dodds, Ayr (SW)
	RCN 699	→ see PCN 762								
	RCP 237	AEC	Regent V	2D3RA1131	Northern Counties	5765	H39/32F	10/62	Hebble 619	-?-, Paignton
	RCS 382	Leyland	Titan PD3A/3	610348	Alexander	6552	L35/32RD	7/61	Western SMT 1684	Western Buses (SW) 19982
	RCT 3	Leyland	Titan PD3/1	590945	Yeates	818	H39/34RD	7/60	Delaine, Bourne 50	Delaine, Bourne (LI) 50
	RDB 846	AEC	Reliance	2MU3RA3525	Alexander	6665	DP41F	5/61	North Western 846	Roberts, Stockport
	RDB 851	→ see TSY 337								

	Reg	Chassis	Model	Chassis No	Body	Body No	Layout	Date	First operator	Current owner
	RDB 867	AEC	Reliance	2MU3RA3258	Willowbrook	CF79	DP43F	4/61	North Western 867	Roberts, Stockport
	RDB 872	Dennis	Loline III	1011L3AF2D1	Alexander	6673	H39/32F	12/61	North Western 872	Preston, Kington
	RDH 505	Leyland	Titan PD2/12	530901	Roe	GO3707	FH33/23RD	7/53	Walsall 815	BaMMOT, Wythall
	RDJ 729	Leyland	Titan PD2A/30	621166	East Lancs	5859	H36/28R	6/62	St Helens L29	Johnson, Hillan & Dean, St Helens
	RDU 903	AEC	Reliance	MU3RV609	Burlingham	5917	C41C	-/55	BTS, Coventry	Wilfreda-Beehive, Adwick-le-Street (SY)
	REL 55	Bedford	SBO	33554	Duple	1055/59	C25FL	3/55	Shamrock & Rambler	Staniforth, Stroud
	REN 116	Leyland	Atlantean PDR1/1	621942	Metro-Cammell		H41/33F	4/63	Bury 116	Museum of Transport, Manchester
	REV 90	Bedford	OB	140203	Duple	47861	C29F	5/50	Dagenham Coach Services	Chandler, Elton
	RFE 416	Leyland	Titan PD2/41	603248	Roe	GO5278	H33/28R	6/61	Lincoln 89	Milner, Lincoln
	RFE 482	Bristol	SC4LK	172032	ECW	12739	B35F	8/61	Lincolnshire 2494	Lincolnshire (LI) 2494
			(ex NVL 165, OWJ 339A, RFE 482)							
	RFM 408	Bristol	Lodekka LD6B	100008	ECW	6553	H--/--R	3/54	Crosville ML663	Brown, Worthen
	RFM 641	Guy	Arab IV	FD71864	Massey	2113	H30/26R	6/53	Chester 1	North West Museum of Transport
	RFM 644	Guy	Arab IV	FD71905	Guy/Park Royal	B37000	H30/26R	12/53	Chester 4	Dennis, Chester
	RFO 361	AEC	Regent V	2D3RA1110	Park Royal	B48708	H41/32F	3/62	AERE, Harwell	Roselyn Coaches, Par (CO)
			(ex 241 AJB)							
	RFO 375	Albion	Victor FT39N	72874E	Heaver	9424	B8F	4/50	Guernsey Railway 36	Hart, Bodmin
			(ex Q402 JDV, 6436)							
	RFU 689	Bristol	SC4LK	141045	ECW	10709	DP33F	4/58	Lincolnshire 2611	Chelveston Preservation Society
	RGV 111	AEC	Reliance	2MU4RV3454	Harrington	2404	C37F	3/61	Mulley, Ixworth	Mulley, Ixworth (SK)
	RHK 843	→ see 1950 MN *Overseas*								
	RHN 548	Austin	K8CVC	25111	Plaxton	2000	C14C	10/52	Scotts Grey, Darlington	Kitching, Scarborough
	RIB 4407	Bedford	Venturer YNV	FT700437	Plaxton	8712NVP3C014	C53F	5/87	Hodge, Sandhurst	Kells Transport Museum, Cork
			(ex D556 DPG, 5226 PH)							
	RIB 8742	Bedford	YLQ	HT100714	Plaxton	878MSP3C015	C22F	4/87	Armchair, Brentford	Ealson, Chertsey (SR)
			(ex D642 ALR)							
	RIL 4827	Leyland	Tiger TRCTL11/3R	8301429	Duple	8441/0407	C57F	7/85	Smith, Sacriston	-?-, Moray
			(ex B997 JTN)							
	RIL 9158	Leyland	Atlantean AN68D/2R	8300123	East Lancs	A2612	H45/32F	5/83	Lancaster 222	Blackpool Transport Omnibus Group
			(ex BFV 222Y)							
	RIL 9168	→ see 81-C-1657 *Ireland*								
	RIW 8799	Mercedes-Benz	O303/15	30036523035760	Mercedes-Benz		C53F	4/83	Wahl, Camberwell	Webb, Armscote (WK)
			(ex ALJ 568A, PUL 91Y)							
	RJX 250	Albion	Nimbus NS3AN	82067B	Weymann	M835	DP31F	5/63	Halifax 250	Bell, Cross Hills
	RKC 262	Leyland	Titan PD2/20	541718	Alexander	4513	H32/26R	1/55	Liverpool L161	Merseyside Transport Trust
	RMB 240	AEC	Regal IV	9822E1647	Plaxton	2188	C41C	7/53	Altrincham Coachways	Meir, Stone
	RMS 678	Leyland	Titan PD3/3C	6081	Alexander	6583	L35/32R	2/61	Alexander Midland MRB246	McKerracher, Stirling
	RMS 714	Leyland	Tiger Cub PSUC1/2	614905	Alexander	6486	C41F	7/61	Alexander Fife PD225	Fricker {North Somerset}, Nailsea (SO)
			(ex OSC 711, JVS 541, RMS 714)							
	ROD 765	AEC	Regent V	MD3RV036	Metro-Cammell		H33/26RD	1/56	Devon General DR765	Blackman, Newton Abbot
(r)	ROD 767	AEC	Regent V	MD3RV038	Metro-Cammell		H--/--RD	7/56	Devon General DR767	South Wales Transport Preservation Trust
	ROI 107	→ see CCZ 5919								
	ROI 108	→ see SCZ 2658								
	ROI 117	→ see YAZ 6412								
	ROI 118	→ see ICZ 3919								
	RO1 120	→ see HCZ 5695								
	ROI 126	→ see FEZ 8166								
	ROI 129	→ see RUI 129								

ROX 184	AEC	Reliance	MU3RV427	Burlingham	6069	C41C	6/55	Winwood, Yardley	Adkins, Upper Boddington
RPU 100	Commer	Avenger I	23A0566	Allweather		C--F	9/50	Moore, Saffron Walden	Herefordshire Transport Collection
RRG 289	Daimler	CVG6DD	19806	Alexander	6643	H--/--R	5/61	Aberdeen 289	Aberdeen & District Transport Preservation Trust
RRN 405	Leyland	Atlantean PDR1/1	613689	Metro-Cammell		L39/33F	7/62	Ribble 1805	Lancastrian Transport Trust
RRN 423	Leyland	Atlantean PDR1/1	613281	Weymann	M346	CH--/--FT	5/62	Ribble 1274	Cherry, Bootle
RRN 428	Leyland	Atlantean PDR1/1	613394	Weymann	M342	CH39/20F	5/62	Ribble 1279	Bignell, Pangbourne
									(on loan to Ribble Vehicle Preservation Trust)
RRU 901	Leyland	Tiger Cub PSUC1/1	553637	Park Royal	B37662	B42F	10/55	Bournemouth 264	Roulston, Glasgow
RRU 903	Leyland	Tiger Cub PSUC1/1	553657	Park Royal	B37664	B42F	10/55	Bournemouth 266	Hawkins, Kingswear
RRU 904	Leyland	Tiger Cub PSUC1/1	553658	Park Royal	B37665	B42F	10/55	Bournemouth 267	Shears D, Winkleigh
RSJ 422	Bedford	SBG	49724	Duple	1074/34	C41F	4/57	Stringfellow, Wigan	Moseley (PCV), South Elmsall
		(ex CJP 813)							
RSJ 747	Albion	Victor FT39AN	73791J	Heaver		B35F	1/56	Guernsey Motors 69	Barlow, Penarth
		(ex 1529)							
RSK 615	Leyland	Royal Tiger PSU1/15	510265	Duple	59/11	C41F	8/51	Jackson, Castle Bromwich	Walsh, Ashton-under-Lyne
		(ex LOE 300)							
RSL 383	AEC	Reliance	MU3RV1995	Roe	GO4720	C41C	5/58	Essex County, Stratford	Atkin, North Owersby
		(ex MJD 759)							
RTC 822	Leyland	Titan PD2/12	532077	Leyland		H31/25R	10/53	Rawtenstall 18	Quantock, Bishops Lydeard (SO)
RTS 463	→ see CSF 25B								
RTT 996	Bristol	Lodekka LD6B	104025	ECW	7758	H33/25RD	11/54	Southern National 1877	Billington, Maidenhead
RUF 186	Leyland	Titan PD2/12	561606	Beadle	B146	H33/26RD	12/56	Southdown 786	Stobart, Wimbledon
RUF 205	Leyland	Titan PD2/12	563092	East Lancs	5261	H33/26RD	5/57	Southdown 805	Robbins, Leatherhead
RUI 129	Leyland	Leopard PSU3E/4R	7801952	Alexander (Belfast)	360/25	DP49F	10/78	Ulsterbus 129	McAlinney, Newtownards
		(ex FEZ 8627, ROI 129)							
RVS 305	Bedford	WLG	134625	Harris (Clanfield)		B12F	-/35	-?-, -?-	Childs, Barton-le-Clay
				(mock vintage body built by2/93)					
RWB 87	Leyland	Titan PD2/12	531484	Weymann	M5802	H32/26R	3/54	Sheffield 687	South Yorkshire Transport Museum (SY)
RWC 608	Bristol	Lodekka FLF6G	210014	ECW	13150	O38/32F	4/63	Eastern National 2300	Staniforth, Stroud
RWD 242	AEC	Reliance	MU3RV426	Burlingham	6068	C41C	-/55	Payne, Bedworth	Adkins, Upper Boddington
RXI 5598	Leyland	Tiger TRCTL11/3RZ	8400914	Van Hool	11703	C57F	3/85	Smith, Wigan	Kells Transport Museum, Cork
		(ex B310 UNB)							
SAB 784	AEC	Sabre	VP2R004	ECW	18786	C53F	10/80	Best, Ealing	Kemp, Cliftonville
		(ex CBU 636J)							
SAD 189	Guy	Arab LUF	LUF73039	Willowbrook	56748	C37C	-/56	Black & White G189	Black & White, Penton Mewsey (HA)
SBF 233	Leyland	Titan PD2/28	611321	Northern Counties	5685	RV	1/62	Harper, Heath Hayes 25	Potts, Birmingham
SCZ 2658	Leyland	Leopard PSU3E/4R	7705928	Alexander (Belfast)	360/8	RV	5/78	Ulsterbus 108	Jurby Transport Museum, Jurby
		(ex ROI 108)							
SDK 442	Leyland	Worldmaster RT3/2	570984	Plaxton	708082	C41F	3/58	Ellen Smith, Rochdale	Museum of Transport, Manchester
				(rebodied -/70)					
SDL 268	Bristol	Lodekka LD6G	150147	ECW	11019	H33/27R	6/59	Southern Vectis 563	Newman, Ryde
SDX 57	AEC	Regent V	2D2RA1199	Neepsend		H37/28R	8/63	Ipswich 57	Claydon, Corringham
SDX 60	AEC	Regent V	2D2RA1202	Neepsend		H--/--RD	7/63	Ipswich 60	Barlow, Penarth
SED 232	→ see 696 UXO								
SEV 777	Bedford	OB	143967	Duple	56593	C29F	1/51	Wiffen, Finchingfield	Brenson J Jnr, Little Waltham
SEZ 9973	Leyland	Tiger TRBTL11/2RP	8500696	Alexander (Belfast)	781/2	DP53F	9/86	Ulsterbus 1000	Kells Transport Museum, Cork
		(ex IXI 1000)							

	Reg	Make	Model	Chassis no	Body	Body no	Layout	Date	Original operator	Owner
(r)	SFC 609	AEC	Regal IV	9821S1221	*chassis only*			6/52	City of Oxford 609	Oxford Bus Museum Trust
	SFC 610	AEC	Regal IV	9821S1222	Willowbrook	52985	C37C	6/52	City of Oxford 610	Oxford Bus Museum Trust
	SFJ 904	Bedford	SBG	44731	Duple	1060/295	C41F	4/56	Greenslades Tours	Lewis, Henstridge (SO)
			(ex UJT 384, GRE 63T, J 9040, SFJ 904)							
	SFV 421	Leyland	Atlantean PDR1/1	592643	Weymann	M9406	CH34/16FT	6/60	Standerwick 25	Ribble Vehicle Preservation Trust
	SGD 10	→ see FYS 8								
	SGD 65	Leyland	Titan PD2/24	573528	Alexander	5341	H33/28R	10/58	Glasgow L163	Glasgow City Council
	SGD 239	Daimler	CVG6DD	19563	Alexander	5638	H33/28R	11/59	Glasgow D256	Roulston, Glasgow
	SGD 241	Daimler	CVG6DD	19567	Alexander	5640	H33/28R	11/59	Glasgow D258	Roulston, Glasgow
	SGD 268	→ see GSV 580								
	SGD 271	Leyland	PD2/24	583089			RV	6/59	Glasgow L269	Roulston, Glasgow
	SGD 407	Leyland	Titan PD3/2	600405	Alexander	6248	H41/31F	11/60	Glasgow L405	Stewart, Chelmsford
	SGD 448	Leyland	Titan PD3/2	600053	Alexander	6289	H41/31F	10/61	Glasgow L446	Glasgow City Council
	SGD 491	AEC	Regent V	2D2RA871	Alexander	6128	H--/--F	12/60	Glasgow A341	Transport Preservation Trust, Beith
	SGD 500	AEC	Regent V	2D2RA827	Alexander	6137	H41/31F	1/61	Glasgow A350	Jones, Glasgow
	SHA 431	Leyland	Titan PD2/12	525000	Leyland		H30/26RD	-/53	BMMO 4031	1685 Group, Birmingham
	SHE 166	Leyland	Tiger Cub PSUC1/1	595950	Metro-Cammell		B45F	4/61	Yorkshire Traction 1178	Taylor, Barnsley
	SHL 917	AEC	Reliance	2MU3RV3574	Plaxton	602297	C41C	1/61	West Riding 917	Atkin, North Owersby
	SHN 301	AEC	Regal IV	9821E1414	Burlingham	5139	C41C	3/53	Scotts Grey, Darlington 3	Leonard, Sunderland
	SHN 745	Bristol	LS5G	101026	ECW	6793	B45F	7/54	United BU55	Bulmer, North Stainley (NY)
	SHO 800	AEC	Reliance	MU2RA1627	Duple	1079/18	C41F	1/58	Creamline, Bordon	Thornes, Hemingbrough (NY)
			(ex TAS 975, SHO 800)							
	SIB 6706	Leyland	National NL106AL11/1R	07534	East Lancs	B4202	B41F	10/81	London Country (South West) 855	LeFevre, Newhaven
			(ex LFR 855X) *(fitted with a Gardner engine; rebodied 11/92)*							
	SIB 6711	Leyland	National 10351/1R/SC	02095	East Lancs	B4207	B41F	4/75	London Country (South West) 341	Owen., Bedlington
			(ex HPF 310N)		*(rebodied 12/92)*					
	SJI 6568	Leyland	Fleetline FE30AGR	7801212	Northern Counties	8496	H43/31F	3/79	Cleveland Transit H118	Kells Transport Museum, Cork
			(ex YYN 518T)							
	SJI 8515	Mercedes-Benz	709D	6690032N021562	Alexander (Belfast)	M31.04	B33F	11/94	WELB, Northern Ireland	Graham, Kesh
	SJW 515	Guy	Warrior	WU2168	Burlingham	6401	C41F	1/57	Guy demonstrator	Dodds, Ayr (SW)
	SKB 168	Leyland	Royal Tiger PSU1/13	541590	Crossley/Metro-Cammell		RC23/21F	10/56	Liverpool XL171	Merseyside Transport Trust
	SKB 224	Leyland	Titan PD2/20	550866	Crossley	4818	H32/26R	5/56	Liverpool L227	Merseyside Transport Trust
	SLT 56	AEC	Routemaster	RM1	Park Royal		H36/28R	9/54	London Transport RM1	London Transport Museum
			(ex OLD 862)							
	SLT 57	AEC	Routemaster	RM2	Park Royal		H36/28R	3/55	London Transport RM2	London Transport Museum
			(ex OLD 863)							
	SLT 58	Leyland	Routemaster	562092	Weymann	W2201	H36/28R	6/57	London Transport RML3	London Bus Preservation Trust
	SLT 59	Leyland	Routemaster	562093	ECW	8250	H32/25RD	7/57	London Transport CRL4	London Bus Company, Northfleet (KT)
	SME 526	Commer	Commando	17A0168	Park Royal	B31571	RC18C	7/47	British European Airways 1008	Rawsthorn, Bournemouth
	SOG 506	Morris-Commercial	CV11/40	-?-	Mulliner		B24F	11/55	Romsley Sanatorium	-?-, Ulverston
	SOI 3591	Leyland	Leopard PSU3E/4R	UBLE697801	Alexander (Belfast)	500/2	B53F	9/78	Ulsterbus 1591	Irish Transport Heritage
			(rebuilt from AOI 1347)							
	SOU 456	Dennis	Loline I	113Y1	East Lancs	5457	H37/31RD	5/58	Aldershot & District 348	Trevaskis, Pirbright
	SOU 465	Dennis	Loline I	122Y1	East Lancs	5451	H37/31RD	3/58	Aldershot & District 357	Trevaskis, Pirbright
	SOX 859	Commer	Avenger IV	85A0343	Duple	1062/41	C41F	5/56	Worthington, Birmingham	Herefordshire Transport Collection
	SPT 65	Guy	Arab LUF	LUF72678	Weymann	M7051	B44F	9/55	Northern General 1665	North East Bus Preservation Trust
	SPU 985	Leyland	Olympic HR44	512421	Weymann	L105	DP40F	10/51	Jennings, Ashen	Wingrove & Wilson, Strood
	SRB 424	Daimler	CD650DD	18332	Willowbrook	52037	L27/28RD	4/53	Blue Bus, Willington DR15	Coventry Transport Museum

	SRB 425	Daimler	CD650DD	18333	Willowbrook	52036	L27/28RD	2/53	Blue Bus, Willington DR16	Anthony, Burton-upon-Trent
	SRC 370	Leyland	Atlantean PDR1/1	592243	Weymann	M9339	L39/34F	3/60	Trent 1370	Brown, Wateringbury
	SRH 633	Leyland	Titan PD2/12	550199	Roe	GO4001	L28/28R	7/55	East Yorkshire 633	Ireland, Hull
	SRS 112	Albion	Lowlander LR1	62111H	Alexander	6877	H40/31F	4/63	Alexander Northern NRE2	Roulston, Glasgow
	SRS 117	→ see NSJ 502								
	SRU 981	Bristol	Lodekka LD6B	120054	ECW	8588	H--/--RD	8/56	Hants & Dorset 1368	Pratt {Crosville}, Weston super Mare (SO)
	STP 995	Leyland	Titan PD3/6	593939	Metro-Cammell		H--/--RD	7/59	Portsmouth 123	City of Portsmouth Preserved Transport Depot
			(ex VSV 560, STP 995)							
	SUG 19	Sentinel	SLC/6/30	SLC6304	Burlingham	5718	C41C	5/54	Metcalfe, Keighley	Herefordshire Transport Collection
	SUK 3	Guy	Arab IV	FD73468	Metro-Cammell		H33/27R	3/57	Wolverhampton 3	BaMMOT, Wythall
	SVA 438	Bedford	C5Z1	3069	Duple Midland	489/30/12	B30F	7/58	Hutchison, Overtown	Emerton, Nantwich
	SVS 281	Daimler	CWA6	12009	Duple	40577	H30/26R	1/45	Douglas 52	Sandtoft Transport Centre
			(ex FWW 188J, FMN 955)							
	SVS 904	Bristol	LS6G	101136	ECW	7170	C35F	1/54	Southern National 1381	Aire Valley Transport Group
			(ex OTT 90)							
	SWN 159	Bristol	Lodekka LD6G	150051	ECW	10348	O--/--R	6/59	United Welsh 323	Hier, Swansea
			(ex ACY 307A, ACY 178A, SWN 159)							
	SWO 986	Bristol	MW6G	135125	ECW	9932	C39F	5/58	Red & White UC758	Hier, Swansea
	SWS 671	AEC	Reliance	2MU3RV2291	Alexander	5796	C38F	5/59	Scottish Omnibuses B671	Wallace, Edinburgh
	SWS 715	AEC	Reliance	2MU3RV2308	Park Royal	B43187	C--F	6/59	Scottish Omnibuses B715	Wallace, Edinburgh
	SXI 2643	Leyland	Tiger TR2R56V16Z4	TR01044	Alexander (Belfast)	B26.08	B51F	2/91	Citybus 2643	Kells Transport Museum, Cork
	SXI 2648	Leyland	Tiger TR2R56V16Z4	TR01049	Alexander (Belfast)	B26.13	B51F	2/91	Citybus 2648	Kells Transport Museum, Cork
	SXI 2650	Leyland	Tiger TR2R56V16Z4	TR01051	Alexander (Belfast)	B26.15	B51F	3/91	Citybus 2650	Kells Transport Museum, Cork
	SXT 169	Bedford	SBO	51627	Mulliner		B31F	3/57	Ministry of Defence	McNeill, Todmorden
	SXT 387	Karrier	Q25	91A1257	Reading		C14F	11/56	Frames, London 99	Letts, Gillingham
	SYG 561	Bedford	SBG	50574	Duple	1074/172	C41F	3/57	Walton & Helliwell, Mytholmroyd	Turner, Tingley
	TAX 235	Bristol	Lodekka LD6G	138070	ECW	9463	H33/27RD	5/58	Red & White L358	Cardiff Transport Preservation Group
	TBC 162	→ see RVS 432 *Overseas*								
	TBC 163	Leyland	Titan PD3/1	581026	Park Royal	B41207	H--/--R	6/58	Leicester 163	Leicester 163 Preservation Group
	TBC 164	Leyland	Titan PD3/1	581015	Willowbrook	58994	H41/33R	7/58	Leicester 164	City of Leicester Museums
	TCK 465	Leyland	Leopard PSU3/1R	629320	Marshall	B3139	B53F	6/63	Ribble 465	Ribble Vehicle Preservation Trust
(r)	TCK 494	Leyland	Leopard PSU3/1R	L00575	Marshall	B3169	B53F	10/63	Ribble 494	Ribble Vehicle Preservation Trust
	TCK 726	Leyland	Leopard PSU3/3R	L00495	Harrington	2759	C49F	6/63	Ribble 726	Fenner, Fulwood *(on loan to Ribble Vehicle Preservation Trust)*
	TCK 821	Leyland	Titan PD3/5	629240	Metro-Cammell		FH41/31F	5/63	Ribble 1821	Reilly, Bootle
	TCK 841	→ see AAO 771A								
	TCK 847	Leyland	Titan PD3/5	L00042	Metro-Cammell		FH41/31F	6/63	Ribble 1847	Reilly, Bootle
	TCO 537	Leyland	Atlantean PDR1/1	600727	Metro-Cammell		H44/33F	6/60	Plymouth 137	Delbridge, Ivybridge
			(ex WSV 980, TCO 537)							
	TDJ 612	AEC	Reliance	2MU3RA4660	Marshall	B3186	B45F	4/63	St Helens 212	North West Museum of Transport
	TDK 322	AEC	Regent V	D2RA662	Weymann	M8766	H33/28RD	3/59	Rochdale 322	Wray, Sheffield
	TDL 998	Bristol	Lodekka FS6G	155036	ECW	11655	H33/27RD	6/60	Southern Vectis 565	Priddle, Farnham
			(ex ABK 832A, TDL 998)							
	TDT 344	AEC	Regent V	MD3RV061	Roe	GO4158	H34/28R	12/55	Doncaster 144	Hawley, Killamarsh
	TER 840	Bedford	VAS5	FT100618	Plaxton	858PJS4C003	C27F	5/85	Glynglen, London	Nolan, Kings Lynn
			(ex B157 FWJ)							
	TET 135	Daimler	CVG6-30DD	30037	Roe	GO4008	RV	3/59	Rotherham 135	South Yorkshire Transport Museum

TFA 987	Daimler	CCG5DD	20060	Massey	2559	H33/28R	1/64	Burton 87	Burton Daimler Group
TFF 251	Bristol	MW6G	135003	ECW	8433	RV	3/58	Crosville G341	Adams, Wellingborough
		(ex 811 DFM)							
TFJ 808	Guy	Arab IV	FD73287	Massey	2250	H30/26R	11/56	Exeter 50	Shears D, Winkleigh
TFO 249	Albion	Victor FT39KAN	73840J	Reading	2369	B35F	2/58	Guernsey Motors 78	Eastbourne Auction Rooms, Eastbourne
		(ex JPA 84V, 8228)							
TFU 90	Bedford	SB1	69944	Plaxton	592550	C41F	3/59	Hudson, Horncastle	Paterson, Dufftown
THA 82	BMMO	D7	4082	Metro-Cammell		H37/26RD	9/53	BMMO 4082	Waldron, Bromsgrove
THA 114	BMMO	D7	4114	Metro-Cammell		H37/26RD	-/53	BMMO 4114	Tucker, Birmingham
TIL 2878	Bedford	YMP	GT104112	Plaxton	868MQP2C007	C35F	7/86	British Aerospace, Warton	Young, Haddenham (CM)
		(ex C989 OFR)							
TIL 5977	Bedford	YMP	HT101280	Plaxton	879.5MQP3C003	C35F	6/87	Marton, West Drayton	Marshall, Haydon Bridge
		(ex D800 ALR)							
TJD 464	AEC	Reliance	2MU3RV3496	Duple	1135/19	C37C	5/61	Essex County, Stratford	Falmouth Coaches, Falmouth (CO)
TJI 1691	AEC	Reliance	6U3ZR34028	Duple	745/5800	C57F	6/77	Smith, Wigan	Hunt, Preston
		(ex REK 921R)							
TJI 4036	Volvo	B58-61	15957	Plaxton	8012VC089	C50F	8/80	Trathen, Yelverton	-?-, -?-
		(ex ADR 192W)							
TJI 6310	→ see UUF 328J								
TJI 7514	Leyland	Tiger TRCTL11/2R	8200103	ECW	25414	DP49F	7/82	London Country TL11	-?-, -?-
		(ex TPC 111X)							
TJI 8780	Leyland	Tiger TRCTL11/2R	8201635	Plaxton	8311LTP1C006	C49F	3/83	Southern Vectis 310	Berry, Bolton
		(ex WDL 142, WDL 310Y)							
TJI 8782	Leyland	Tiger TRCTL11/2R	8300651	Plaxton	8411LTP1C001	C51F	11/83	Southern Vectis 312	Lear, Ashbury Station
		(ex A312 BDL)							
TJV 100	→ see NAT 766A								
TKM 322	AEC	Reliance	MU3RV243	Harrington	1507	C37C	12/54	Maidstone & District CO322	Gibbons, Maidstone
TKZ 9780	Leyland	Olympian ONLXCT/1R	ON608	Northern Counties	2401	H43/30F	11/83	Greater Manchester PTE 3016	-?-, -?-
		(ex A581 HDB)							
TMM 788	Ford	WOT1	6150488	Mulliner		B14R	-/41	Royal Air Force	Royal Air Force Benevolent Fund
		(ex RAF 57630)							
TMY 700	Bedford	OB	103474	Duple	44048	C29F	4/49	Essex County, Stratford	Lodge, High Easter (EX)
TNA 496	Leyland	Titan PD2/40	572426	Burlingham	6375	H37/28R	2/58	Manchester 3496	Turnbull, Irlam
TNA 520	Leyland	Titan PD2/34	572450	Burlingham	6399	H37/28R	9/58	Manchester 3520	Crankshaw, Meltham
TNC 719	Bedford	CAV	64288	Kenex		M9	7/56	non-PSV	Bawden, Halifax
TOB 377	AEC	Reliance	MU3RV793	Burlingham	5928	C37C	3/56	Flights, Birmingham	Millington, Horsforth
TOI 2288	Bristol	RELL6G	RELL-3-2395	*chassis only*			6/79	Ulsterbus 2288	M Shed, Bristol
TOI 2306	Bristol	RELL6G	RELL-3-2412	Alexander (Belfast)	341/104	B52F	8/79	Ulsterbus 2306	Shannon, Newtownards
TOI 2316	Bristol	RELL6G	RELL-3-2423	Alexander (Belfast)	340/34	B52F	8/79	Citybus 2316	Stewart, Shenfield
TRJ 109	AEC	Reliance	2MU3RV3870	Weymann	M187	B45F	2/62	Salford 109	North West Museum of Transport
TRJ 112	Daimler	CVG6DD	19852	Metro-Cammell		H37/28R	2/62	Salford 112	Cooper & Platt, Manchester
TRN 731	Leyland	Leopard PSU3/3R	L02490	Plaxton	632773	C49F	3/64	Standerwick 731S	Ribble Vehicle Preservation Trust
TSD 285	→ see WSD 827								
TSJ 272	AEC	Bridgemaster	2B3RA115	Park Royal	B48746	H43/29F	6/62	East Yorkshire 725	Blackman L, Halifax
		(ex 9725 AT)							
TSK 716	→ see RG 1173								
TSK 736	Commer	Commando	17A0848	Scottish Aviation		C29F	6/49	Lawson C8	Hamer & Morriss, Ravenstonedale (CA)
		(ex CMS 9)							

	TSY 337	AEC	Reliance	2MU3RA3530	Alexander	6672	DP41F	5/61	North Western 851	Roberts, Stockport
			(ex RDB 851)							
	TTT 781	AEC	Regent V	MD3RV219	Metro-Cammell		H33/26RD	1/56	Devon General DR781	Blackman, Halifax (WY)
	TUE 132	Bedford	SBG	41422	Duple	1060/158	C37F	1/56	Hills, Stockingford	Howlett, Shepshed
			(ex 6 EBH, TUE 132)							
	TUG 20	→ see 344 XUK								
	TUH 7	Albion	Nimbus NS3N	82054D	Harrington	2254	DP30F	7/60	Western Welsh 7	Dixon (Alan), Annfield Plain
			(ex HSV 103, TUH 7)							
	TUH 13	Albion	Nimbus NS3N	82055D	Harrington	2260	DP30F	7/60	Western Welsh 13	-?-, -?-
	TUH 14	Albion	Nimbus NS3N	82055H	Harrington	2261	DP--F	7/60	Western Welsh 14	Young, Thurso
(r)	TUJ 261	Ford	570E	510E28397	Burlingham	6924	C--F	8/59	Whittle, Highley	Grayscroft, Mablethorpe (LI)
	TUO 492	Bristol	LS5G	111051	ECW	8165	B41F	1/56	Southern National 1776	Tresham, Leighton Buzzard
	TUO 497	Bristol	LS5G	111064	ECW	8170	B45F	2/56	Southern National 1781	Brown, Worthen
	TUP 859	AEC	Regent V	MD3RV261	Roe	GO4191	H35/28R	5/56	Hartlepool 4	Slater, Wideopen
	TVS 337	Bedford	J2SZ10	172795	Plaxton	632477	C20F	6/63	Harris, Cambridge 56	Henshaw, Rigside
			(ex NSG 970A, 522 CER)							
	TVS 367	Bristol	Lodekka LD6G	138102	ECW	10123	H33/27R	7/58	Central SMT B87	Strachan, Glasgow
			(ex GM 9287)							
	TWL 928	AEC	Regent III	9613S7214	Park Royal	B36028	H30/26R	6/53	City of Oxford H928	Shaw, Farmoor
	TWT 123	Bristol	MW5G	139025	ECW	9902	DP41F	5/59	West Yorkshire EUG71	Halliday, Shipley
	TWY 8	Albion	Valiant CX39N	60309D	Roe	GO4651	L27/26RD	1/50	South Yorkshire 81	West Riding Omnibus Museum Trust
			(ex JWT 112)			*(rebodied 5/58)*				
	TYD 888	AEC	Reliance	MU3RV390	Duple	225/1	C43F	5/55	Wake, Sparkford	Gascoine, Blackridge
	TYJ 424	Bristol	MW6G	164038	ECW	11925	RV	6/60	Crosville G386	Peake, Porthmadog
			(ex 302 PFM)							
	TYJ 916	Ford	E83W	4854476	?		B??	9/39	estate bus	Mould, Reading
			(ex 'WHM 92', 'MCA 888', BBD 407)							

	UAF 746	Bedford	SBG	36373	Duple	1055/289	C36F	4/55	Taylor, Falmouth	Falmouth Coaches, Falmouth (CO)
	UAS 430	AEC	Routemaster	RM597	Park Royal	L3820	H36/28R	1/61	London Transport RM597	-?-, -?-
			(ex WLT 597)							
	UAW 982	Ford	570E	510E34001	Burlingham	7022	C--F	1/60	Whittle, Highley	Maiden, Wellington
	UBN 902	Leyland	Titan PD3A/2	611934	East Lancs	5824	FH41/32F	4/62	Bolton 169	Bolton Bus Preservation Group
	UCK 875	Bedford	VAL14	1432	Plaxton	642170	C--F	4/64	Premier, Preston	Transport Museum Society of Ireland
	UCS 659	Albion	Lowlander LR7	62100B	Alexander	6976	H40/31F	5/63	Western SMT 1795	Western Buses (SW) 19959
	UCX 275	Guy	Wulfrunian	FDW74902	Roe	GO5267	H43/32F	9/61	County 99	West Riding Omnibus Preservation Society
	UCY 837	AEC	Bridgemaster	B3RA041	Park Royal	B43233	H41/31RD	10/59	South Wales 1203	South Wales Transport Preservation Trust
(r)	UCZ 1781	Leyland	Leopard PSU3E/4R	7902314	Alexander (Belfast)	580/28	DP49F	5/80	Ulsterbus 182	Thompson, Newtownards
			(ex VOI 182)							
	UDL 453	→ see WFF 599 *Overseas*								
	UDL 454	Bedford	SB3	81316	Duple	1120/517	C41F	6/60	West Wight, Totland Bay	Heal, Sandford
(r)	UFF 178	AEC	Regent V	D2RVG078	Crossley		H35/29R	7/55	Aberdeen 207	Aberdeen & District Transport Preservation Trust
			(ex HRG 207)							
	UFJ 292	Guy	Arab IV	FD73680	Massey	2252	H30/26R	6/57	Exeter 52	Shaw, Willington
	UFJ 296	Guy	Arab IV	FD73580	Park Royal	B39414	H31/26R	6/57	Exeter 56	Greet, Broadhempston
	UFX 718	AEC	Reliance	6U2R38584	Plaxton	8011AX501/S	C53F	11/79	London Country RS136	Bryce, Nottingham
			(ex EPM 136V)							

	UHA 255	BMMO	S14	4255	BMMO		B44F	4/55	BMMO 4255	BaMMOT, Wythall
	UHJ 842	Bedford	C4Z2	4214	Duple	1111/39	C29F	11/59	Rochford Hospital	Towler, Brandon
	UHY 359	Bristol	KSW6B	106043	ECW	7835	H32/28R	12/55	Bristol C8319	Staniforth, Stroud
	UHY 360	Bristol	KSW6B	106045	ECW	7836	H32/28R	12/55	Bristol C8320	Walker, Wells
	UHY 362	Bristol	KSW6B	106047	ECW	7838	H32/28R	1/56	Bristol C8322	Hunt, Stafford
	UHY 374	Bristol	KSW6B	106005	ECW	7850	H--/--R	-/55	Cheltenham District 90	Black & White, Penton Mewsey (HA)
	UHY 383	Bristol	KSW6G	106019	ECW	7859	H32/28RD	10/55	Bristol 8335	Ellis, Cambridge (Gloucs)
	UHY 384	Bristol	KSW6G	106020	ECW	7860	H32/28RD	10/55	Bristol 8336	Walker & Peters, Wells
	UIA 884	Bedford	J2SZ10	9T143303	Plaxton	702039	C15F	9/69	Rickards, Brentford 24	Wilkinson, Scarborough
			(ex KNK 369H)							
	UIB 3987	Leyland	Atlantean PDR2/1	7101753	Northern Counties	-?-	DP42F	8/71	Fylde 7	Lancastrian Transport Trust
			(ex TKU 469K)			*(rebodied 5/93)*				
	UIB 5303	MCW	Metroliner CR126/2	MB7230	MCW		C53F	5/83	East Kent 8846	Mackintosh, Birmingham
			(ex 572 RKJ, FKK 846Y)							
	UIL 2090	Scania	K112CRS	1806256	Jonckheere	18996	C51FT	6/84	Randall, Willesden	Young, Haddenham
			(ex GFX 175, A50 JLW)							
	UJI 6314	Leyland	Titan B15	7600668	Park Royal	B60769	H45/32F	11/75	Leyland demonstrator	Rimmer, Litherland
			(ex NHG 732P)							
	UJT 384	→ see SFJ 904								
	UKG 274	→ see 71 AHI *Ireland*								
	UKN 207	Harrington-Commer		T48B6021	Harrington	00054	B42F	10/55	Maidstone & District S207	Gibbons, Maidstone
(r)	UKN 210	Harrington-Commer		T48B6024	Harrington	00057	B42F	11/55	Maidstone & District S210	Gibbons, Maidstone
	UMA 370	Atkinson	PD746	FC3476	Northern Counties	4865	H35/24C	2/55	SHMD 70	Museum of Transport, Manchester
	UMB 2	→ see 878 UXO								
	UMP 227	AEC	Regal IV	U134974	Park Royal	B33954	B40F	5/49	AEC demonstrator	-?-, Cobham
	UMR 112	Daimler	CVG6DD	19686	Weymann	M9282	H36/28R	4/60	Swindon 112	Swindon Vintage Omnibus Society
	UNB 524	Leyland	Titan PD2/40	580004	Metro-Cammell		H37/28R	10/58	Manchester 3524	Lonergan, Stockport
	UNB 629	Leyland	Atlantean PDR1/1	580109	Metro-Cammell		H44/33F	4/60	Manchester 3629	Museum of Transport, Manchester
			(ex MO.7204 *Australia*, MO.4670 *Australia* , UNB 629)							
	UOI 2386	Bristol	RELL6G	RELL-3-2493	Alexander (Belfast)	561/25	B52F	7/80	Ulsterbus 2386	Roulston, Glasgow
	UOI 2390	Bristol	RELL6G	RELL-3-2497	Alexander (Belfast)	561/30	B52F	9/80	Ulsterbus 2390	Hart et al, York
	UOI 9163	Leyland	Leopard PSU3E/4R	7900209	Alexander (Belfast)	580/14	DP49F	3/80	Ulsterbus 163	Slevin, Monilea (EI)
	URE 281	AEC	Regal III	9621A1000	Harrington	808	FC33F	7/50	Lymer, Tean	Hine, Cheadle
	URR 865	AEC	Reliance	MU3RV1150	Plaxton	2923	C45F	4/56	Barton 765	Webb, Acton (Suffolk)
	USK 625	AEC	Routemaster	RM980	Park Royal	L3542	H36/28R	10/61	London Transport RM980	Warrener, Winchester
			(ex WLT 980)							
	USK 947	Bedford	BYC	841052	Huntley & Palmers		B??	7/35	estate bus	Izart, Kingswood
	USL 580	Leyland	Leopard PSU3/3R	620117	Alexander	7150	DP49F	5/62	North Western 916	Patterson, Seahouses (ND)
			(ex VDB 916)							
	USU 623	→ see LWR 424								
	USV 324	Leyland	Leopard PSU3E/4R	7901592	Plaxton	7911LX587	C49F	6/79	Southdown 1320	Jenkins, Horsham
			(ex 424 DCD, BYJ 920T)							
	UTC 672	AEC	Regent III	9613S4922	East Lancs	5072	L27/28RD	12/54	Bamber Bridge 4	Hamer & Morriss, Ravenstonedale (CA)
(r)	UTV 229	AEC	Regent V	D3RV088	Park Royal	B34136	H33/28R	3/56	Nottingham 229	Blackman, Halifax
	UUA 207	Leyland	Titan PD2/11	542403	Roe	GO3897	H33/25R	3/55	Leeds 207	Murray, Leeds
	UUA 212	Leyland	Titan PD2/11	550071	Roe	GO3884	H33/25R	3/55	Leeds 212	Briggs, Newcastle upon Tyne
	UUA 214	Leyland	Titan PD2/11	550154	Roe	GO3895	H33/25R	5/55	Leeds 214	Wild et al, Leeds
	UUB 402	Commer	Avenger III	T84A0024	Plaxton	2667	C35F	5/55	Wallace Arnold Tours	Simonds, Diss (NK)

	Registration	Chassis	Chassis no.	Body	Body no.	Layout	New	First owner	Current owner
	UUB 403	Commer Avenger III	T84A0025	Plaxton	2668	C35F	5/55	Wallace Arnold Tours	Simonds, Diss (NK)
	UUB 404	Commer Avenger III	T84A0027	Plaxton	2669	C35F	5/55	Wallace Arnold Tours	Simonds, Diss (NK)
	UUD 12	Bedford J2SZ7	121622	Plaxton	612918	C20F	12/61	Florey, Witney	Rambler, Hastings (ES)
	UUK 967	Turner	-?-	Whitson		B8	-/54	Turner demonstrator	-?-, -?-
	UUO 198	Bedford SBG	44399	Duple	1060/288	C41F	3/56	Hill, Stibb Cross	Falmouth Coaches, Falmouth (CO)
	UVB 389	Trojan -?-	-?-	Trojan		B??	-/59	private owner	Trojan Museum Trust, Fyfield
	UVS 678	→ see MLL 528							
	UWH 185	Leyland Atlantean PDR1/1	622842	East Lancs	5939	H45/33F	4/63	Bolton 185	Bolton Bus Preservation Group
	UYJ 654	AEC Routemaster	RM1224	Park Royal	L4272	H36/28R	12/62	London Transport RM1224	Bennett, East Grinstead
		(ex 224 CLT)							
	VBT 191	AEC Reliance	MU3RV823	Yeates	658	C41F	5/58	Boddy, Bridlington	Fowler, Holbeach Drove (LI)
	VBW 581	→ see AJH 241A							
	VCD 984	Bedford C4Z2	2558	Duple	1089/20	C29F	7/58	Alpha, Brighton	Falmouth Coaches, Falmouth (CO)
	VCS 391	→ see EDS 486A							
	VDB 916	→ see USL 580							
	VDV 749	Bristol LS6G	119020	ECW	9967	C39F	3/57	Western National 2206	Ensign, Purfleet (EX)
	VDV 752	Bristol Lodekka LDL6G	134102	ECW	9577	O37/33RD	11/57	Western National 1935	Quantock, Bishops Lydeard (SO)
	VDV 753	Bristol Lodekka LDL6G	134104	ECW	9578	O37/33RD	12/57	Western National 1936	Quantock, Bishops Lydeard (SO)
	VDV 760	Bristol Lodekka LD6G	138109	ECW	9585	H33/27RD	1/58	Western National 1943	Stevens, Sheffield
	VDV 789	Bristol MW5G	139095	ECW	9794	B--F	2/58	Southern National 1788	-?-, -?-
(r)	VDV 796	AEC Reliance	MU3RA1420	Weymann	M8020	B--F	7/57	Devon General SR796	Platt, Dawlish Warren
	VDV 798	AEC Reliance	MU3RA1415	Weymann	M8018	B41F	7/57	Devon General SR798	Platt, Dawlish Warren
	VDV 817	AEC Regent V	MD3RV321	Metro-Cammell		H33/26R	7/57	Devon General DR817	Platt, Dawlish Warren
	VDV 818	AEC Regent V	MD3RV322	Metro-Cammell		O33/26R	7/57	Devon General DR818	Greet, Broadhempston
									(*operates as Nostalgic Transport, Broadhempston (DN)*)
	VFJ 995	Leyland Titan PD2/40	581113	Weymann	M8049	H31/26R	5/58	Exeter 60	Shears D, Winkleigh
	VFW 329	→ see NNJ 210							
	VHO 200	Seddon Mk19	22003	Harrington	2071	C41F	4/59	Liss & District, Bordon	Thornes, Hemingbrough (NY)
	VHO 462	Bedford J4EZ1	6825687	Reading	2402C	B35F	7/66	Guernsey Railway 78	Cottrell, Goring Heath
		(ex 14867)							
	VIB 5069	→ see FYX 817W							
(r)	VIB 8319	Leyland National 10351A/2R	04854	Leyland National		B44F	1/78	London Transport LS130	Wright & Cole, Hornchurch
		(ex THX 130S)							
	VIL 8730	Talbot Pullman	428850	Talbot	141	DP20F	6/88	Barrow 100	Barrow Transport Museum
		(ex E571 MAC)							
	VJW 882	Commer Avenger IV	94A0160	Duple	1091/34	C41F	5/58	Everall, Wolverhampton	Hunt, Rookley
	VKB 711	Leyland Titan PD2/20	561039	Crossley	5287	H33/29R	11/56	Liverpool L255	Wilson, Bootle
	VKB 841	Leyland Titan PD2/20	562489	Crossley	5443	H--/--RD	9/57	Liverpool L320	Merseyside Transport Trust / Cammack, Liverpool
	VKB 900	AEC Regent V	D3RV267	Metro-Cammell		H33/29R	9/57	Liverpool A267	Merseyside Transport Trust
	VKH 44	AEC Regent V	MD3RV272	Willowbrook	56819	H30/26RD	11/56	East Yorkshire 644	East Yorkshire (EY) 644
	VKH 674	Albion Aberdonian MR11L	82503A	Park Royal	B40372	B39F	1/58	East Yorkshire 674	Ireland, Hull
	VKR 39	AEC Regent V	MD3RV166	Park Royal	B38238	L--/--RD	3/56	Maidstone & District DL39	Baker, Hail Weston
	VKR 470	AEC Regent V	MD3RV150	Park Royal	B38222	H33/26RD	6/56	Maidstone & District DH478	Cornford, Bexhill
	VLT 7	AEC Routemaster	RM7	Park Royal	L3818	H36/28R	6/59	London Transport RM7	Hurley, Goole
	VLT 8	AEC Routemaster	RM8	Park Royal	L3281	H36/28R	-/58	London Transport RM8	RM8 Club, Sidcup
	VLT 13	→ see KGJ 83A							

	VLT 14	→ see OYM 424A								
	VLT 16	AEC	Routemaster	RM16	Park Royal	L5166	H36/28R	3/60	London Transport RM16	Potter & Lewer, South Oxhey
	VLT 17	→ see WLT 675								
	VLT 24	AEC	Routemaster	RM24	Park Royal	L3332	H36/28R	6/59	London Transport RM24	Kilby, Corfe Mullen (DT)
	VLT 25	AEC	Routemaster	RM25	Park Royal	L4414	H36/28R	7/59	London Transport RM25	Ensign, Purfleet (EX)
			(ex 855 UXC, VLT 25)							
	VLT 40	AEC	Routemaster	RM40	Park Royal	L4004	H36/28R	8/59	London Transport RM40	RM40 Group, Manor Park
	VLT 44	AEC	Routemaster	RM44	Park Royal	L5168	H36/28R	9/59	London Transport RM44	Miles, South Benfleet
	VLT 54	→ see LDS 279A								
(a)	VLT 66	AEC	Routemaster	RM66	Park Royal	L3751	B--	11/59	London Transport RM66	South Wales Transport Preservation Trust
	VLT 70	AEC	Routemaster	RM70	Park Royal	L3920	H36/28R	12/59	London Transport RM70	Alucord, -?-
	VLT 111	AEC	Routemaster	RM111	Park Royal	L3297	H36/28R	11/59	London Transport RM111	London Bus Company, Northfleet (KT)
	VLT 116	AEC	Routemaster	RM116	Park Royal	L3419	H36/28R	11/59	London Transport RM116	Nicholson, Cippenham
	VLT 140	AEC	Routemaster	RM140	Park Royal	L3434	H36/28R	2/60	London Transport RM140	Duplock, Worcester Park
	VLT 158	AEC	Routemaster	RM158	Park Royal	L3699	H36/28R	2/60	London Transport RM158	Davis, Chingford
	VLT 180	→ see XVS 830								
	VLT 188	AEC	Routemaster	RM188	Park Royal	L3848	H36/28R	2/60	London Transport RM188	Fuller, Rushden
	VLT 196	AEC	Routemaster	RM196	Park Royal	L3438	H36/28R	2/60	London Transport RM196	Hunt, Fleetwood
	VLT 216	AEC	Routemaster	RM216	Park Royal	L3861	H36/28R	2/60	London Transport RM216	Clarke, Dorking (SR)
	VLT 238	AEC	Routemaster	RM238	Park Royal	L3409	PO12/26RD	3/60	London Transport RM238	Dobbing, Stibbington (CM)
	VLT 244	→ see VLT 250								
	VLT 250	AEC	Routemaster	RM244	Park Royal	L3965	H36/28R	4/60	London Transport RM244	Taylor, Pencoed
			(ex XVS 839, VLT 244)							
	VLT 254	AEC	Routemaster	RM254	Park Royal	L3994	H36/28R	4/60	London Transport RM254	Rixon, East Moseley
	VLT 268	AEC	Routemaster	RM268	Park Royal	L3769	H36/28R	3/60	London Transport RM268	London Bus Company, Northfleet (KT)
	VLT 275	AEC	Routemaster	RM275	Park Royal	L3393	H36/28R	3/60	London Transport RM275	Edmonds, London
			(ex 859 UXC, VLT 275)							
	VLT 291	AEC	Routemaster	RM291	Park Royal	L3580	H36/28R	4/60	London Transport RM291	Ward, Northampton
	VLT 298	AEC	Routemaster	RM298	Park Royal	L3441	H36/28R	4/60	London Transport RM298	London Bus Company, Northfleet (KT)
			(ex WTS 245A, VLT 298)							
	VNO 857	Bristol	KSW5G	94036	ECW	5873	L27/28R	3/53	Eastern National 4187	Henson, Northampton
	VNO 859	Bristol	KSW5G	94049	ECW	5875	L27/28RD	5/53	Eastern National 1407	Eastern National 1407 Pres.Gp., Hadleigh
	VNO 868	Bristol	KSW5G	94080	ECW	5884	L27/28R	6/53	Westcliff-on-Sea Motor Services	Ledger, Northampton
	VOI 182	→ see UCZ 1781								
	VOI 187	→ see LKZ 6715								
	VOI 8415	Bristol	RELL6G	RELL-3-2546	Alexander (Belfast)	562/18	B43D	10/80	Citybus 2415	Irish Transport Heritage
	VRF 372	Foden	PVRF6	30664	Harrington	921	C41C	6/51	Bassett, Tittensor	Webster, Lower Southrepps
	VSC 86	Leyland	Tiger Cub PSUC1/3	605772	Weymann	M9465	B47F	1/61	Edinburgh 86	Lothian Bus Consortium
	VSL 528	Bedford	CALV	214660	Kenex		M10	1/62	private owner	Clarke, Sunderland
	VSU 717	Morris	J2VM	67616	Kenex		M--	9/60	Graves, Hertford	-?-, North London
			(ex 1339 NK)							
	VTU 76	Daimler	CVG6DD	18855	Northern Counties	5001	H35/23C	2/56	SHMD 76	Jones, Burnley
(r)	VTX 444	AEC	Regent V	LD3RA372	Weymann	M7527	H37/33F	1/58	Rhondda 444	Quantock, Bishops Lydeard (SO)
	VUP 328	Leyland	Tiger Cub PSUC1/1	553579	Crossley		B44F	9/57	Economic, Whitburn 2	Hawden, Waddingham
	VUP 442	AEC	Reliance	MU3RV1562	*chassis only*			-/57	Gardiner,Spennymoor	Friends of the Pump House Museum,Walthamstow
	VVF 543	Bristol	SC4LK	113100	ECW	8960	B--F	3/57	Eastern Counties LC543	Ward, Ipswich
	VVO 735	Leyland	Tiger PS1/B	B481970	Willowbrook	56933	L--/--RD	11/48	Barton 735	-?-, -?-
			(ex KAL 380)		*(rebodied 1/57)*					

Registration	Chassis make	Model	Chassis no	Body make	Body no	Layout	Date	First owner	Current owner
VVP 911	Bedford	SB3	60102	Duple	1090/120	C41F	5/58	Sandwell, Birmingham	BaMMOT, Wythall
VVS 337	AEC	Regent V	LD2LA493	UTIC	907	H36/31F	11/61	Lisbon Electric Tramways 426	Carris AEC Preservation Group, Croydon
		(ex HH-97-96 *Portugal*)							
VVS 913	Austin	CXB	109792	Barnard	CX3	B28F	7/48	Guernsey Motors 44	Lucas, Hugh Town (IS)
		(ex 4510, 2725, 4510)							
VWG 376	→ see 404 RIU *Ireland*								
VWG 392	Leyland	Tiger Cub PSUC1/2	626922	Alexander	Y/19/10/63	C41F	5/63	Alexander Midland MPD253	Wotherspoon, Alva
VWK 239	Daimler	CVG6DD	19483	Metro-Cammell		H33/27R	7/58	Coventry 239	de Courcey, Coventry (WM)
VXI 2673	Leyland	Tiger TR2R56V16Z4	TR01130	Alexander (Belfast)	B34.09	B51F	10/91	Citybus 2673	Kells Transport Museum, Cork
VYJ 808	AEC	Routemaster	RM1361	Park Royal	L4386	H36/28R	11/62	London Transport RM1361	Bolton, -?-
		(ex 361 CLT)							
VYO 767	Bristol	MW6G	139247	ECW	11322	C--F	4/59	Tilling	Mahoney I, Brentwood
WAJ 112	Albion	Nimbus NS3AN	82058B	Plaxton	602895	C29C	4/60	Watson, Huntington	Scottish Vintage Bus Museum
WAL 782	Leyland	Tiger PS1/B	B472046	Willowbrook	56951	L31/30RD	1/48	Barton 782	Quantock, Bishops Lydeard (SO)
		(ex CWH 262)		*(rebodied 3/57)*					
WAT 164	AEC	Reliance	MU2RA1399	Weymann	M7934	B39D	9/57	Hull 64	Humberside Transport Centre
WAT 652	AEC	Regent V	LD3RA379	Roe	GO4521	H34/32RD	11/57	East Yorkshire 652	Blackman L, Halifax
WBR 246	Atkinson	Alpha PM746HL	FC9054	Marshall	B3369	B45D	12/63	Sunderland 46	Dyson, Huddersfield
WBR 248	Atkinson	Alpha PM746HL	FC9056	Marshall	B3371	B45D	1/64	Sunderland 48	North East Bus Preservation Trust
WCG 104	Leyland	Tiger Cub PSUC1/1	595155	Weymann	M9187	B45F	10/59	King Alfred, Winchester	FoKAB, Winchester
WDF 569	Leyland	Tiger Cub PSUC1/2	586799	Willowbrook	59193	DP41F	5/59	Soudley Valley, Soudley	BaMMOT, Wythall
WED 68	Bedford	CALV	141363	Martin Walter		M??	c9/59	private owner	-?-, -?-
WFN 513	AEC	Reliance	2MU3RV3307	Park Royal	B45362	DP41F	6/61	East Kent	Thompson, Kent
WFN 912	Ford	570E	510E57996	Duple	1139/150	C41F	3/61	Seath, East Studdal	Dover Transport Museum Society
WFN 980	→ see AHP 921A								
WFO 410	→ see WLT 378								
WGG 630	Bedford	C5Z1	3839	Duple	1111/24	C--F	6/59	MacBrayne 36	MacDonald, Howmore (SN)
WHL 970	Guy	Wulfrunian	FDW75191	Roe	G05694	H43/32F	10/63	West Riding 970	West Riding Wulfrunian Preservation Society
WHM 92	→ see TYJ 916								
WJY 758	Leyland	Atlantean PDR1/1	621548	Metro-Cammell		O44/33F	9/62	Plymouth 158	Furse, Plymouth
WKG 284	AEC	Reliance	2MU3RA3361	Willowbrook	60603	DP41F	8/61	Western Welsh 1284	Re-liance 1284 Preservation Group, Tredegar
WKG 287	AEC	Reliance	2MU3RA3364	Willowbrook	60606	B41F	8/61	Western Welsh 1287	Evans, Bargoed
WKJ 787	Beadle-Commer		JCB697	Beadle		C41C	11/55	Beadle demonstrator	Burdett, Corley
WLO 685	Bedford	SB3 *(diesel)*	66434	Duple	1105/34	C41F	3/59	Currie, Bexleyheath	Sidelines, Forncett St Peter (NK)
WLT 308	AEC	Routemaster	RM308	Park Royal	L3584	H36/28R	6/60	London Transport RM308	Curtis, Swansea
WLT 316	AEC	Routemaster	RM316	Park Royal	L4039	H36/28R	6/60	London Transport RM316	Murphy, Gowna
		(ex WTS 333A, WLT 316)							
WLT 329	→ see MFF 578								
WLT 349	AEC	Routemaster	RM349	Park Royal	L3562	H36/28R	7/60	London Transport RM349	Good, Croydon
WLT 357	AEC	Routemaster	RM357	Park Royal	L3633	H36/28R	7/60	London Transport RM357	Price, Gillingham (KT)
		(ex YVS 288, EDS 278A, WLT 357)							
WLT 371	AEC	Routemaster	RM371	Park Royal	L3645	O33/28RD	7/60	London Transport RM371	Ensign, Purfleet (EX)
		(ex EDS 281A, WLT 371, EDS 281A, WLT 371)							
WLT 378	AEC	Routemaster	RM378	Park Royal	L3654	H36/24R	7/60	London Transport RM378	Travelgreen, Skellow (SY)
		(ex WFO 410, WLT 378)							
WLT 436	→ see 791 UXA								

Registration	Chassis make	Model	Chassis no.	Body	Body no.	Layout	New	Original operator	Owner
WLT 446	AEC	Routemaster	RM446	Park Royal	L5069	H36/28R	8/60	London Transport RM446	RM765 Group, Nottingham
WLT 467	AEC	Routemaster	RM467	Park Royal	L3503	H36/28R	9/60	London Transport RM467	Nash, Macclesfield
		(ex XVS 851, WLT 467)							
WLT 471	→ see KVS 601								
WLT 506	AEC	Routemaster	RM506	Park Royal	L5096	H36/28R	11/60	London Transport RM506	Aston Manor Road Transport Museum
WLT 529	AEC	Routemaster	RM529	Park Royal	L3466	H36/28R	12/60	London Transport RM529	Heighway, Preston
WLT 531	AEC	Routemaster	RM531	Park Royal	L4131	H36/28R	10/60	London Transport RM531	Anderson, Wirral
		(ex 854 UXC. WLT 531)							
WLT 541	→ see 789 UXA								
WLT 560	→ see EDS 50A								
WLT 577	AEC	Routemaster	RM577	Park Royal	L3940	H36/28R	2/61	London Transport RM577	Braga, Lower Dean
WLT 597	→ see UAS 430								
WLT 606	→ see EDS 320A								
WLT 613	AEC	Routemaster	RM613	Park Royal	L3474	H36/28R	12/60	London Transport RM613	RM613 Preservation Group, Epping
		(ex TAS 419, WLT 613)							
WLT 642	AEC	Routemaster	RM642	Park Royal	L4060	H36/28R	4/61	London Transport RM642	Simmonds, Morden
WLT 646	AEC	Routemaster	RM646	Park Royal	L3512	H36/28R	1/61	London Transport RM646	London Bus Company, Northfleet (KT)
		(ex KFF 257, WLT 646)							
WLT 654	AEC	Routemaster	RM654	Park Royal	L5175	H36/28R	4/61	London Transport RM654	Cartmill & Begley, Belfast
WLT 655	AEC	Routemaster	RM655	Park Royal	L5161	H36/28R	4/61	London Transport RM655	Confidence, Leicester (LE) 15
WLT 664	→ see 860 UXC								
WLT 667	Leyland	Fleetline FE30AGR	7905424	Alexander	CB8/3677/?	H56/36D	4/80	China Motor Bus SF31	Morrison, Falkirk
		(ex VFS 542V, CE 2543 *Hong Kong*)							
WLT 675	AEC	Routemaster	RM17	Park Royal	L3823	H36/28R	3/60	London Transport RM17	Duker, Little Paxton
		(ex LDS 241A, VLT 17)							
WLT 687	→ see 205 UXJ								
WLT 719	→ see 853 UXC								
WLT 736	→ see XYJ 418								
WLT 737	AEC	Routemaster	RM737	Park Royal	L4006	H36/28R	4/61	London Transport RM737	RM737 Group, Harrow
WLT 759	AEC	Routemaster	RM759	Park Royal	L3911	H36/28R	4/61	London Transport RM759	Roulston, Glasgow
		(ex WTS 329A, WLT 759)							
WLT 765	AEC	Routemaster	RM765	Park Royal	L3975	H36/28R	4/61	London Transport RM765	RM765 Group, Nottingham
WLT 795	AEC	Routemaster	RM795	Park Royal	L4003	H10/--RD	5/61	London Transport RM795	Wealdsman Preservation Group, Headcorn
WLT 798	→ see NRH 802A *Overseas*								
WLT 822	AEC	Routemaster	RM822	Park Royal	L3523	H36/28R	7/61	London Transport RM822	Hobson, Royston
WLT 835	AEC	Routemaster	RM835	Park Royal	L3514	H36/28R	7/61	London Transport RM835	Clydemaster Preservation Group, Brentwood
WLT 848	→ see 448 UXS								
WLT 857	AEC	Routemaster	RM857	Park Royal	L5097	H36/28R	7/61	London Transport RM857	Wright, Hornchurch
WLT 882	AEC	Routemaster	RML882	Park Royal	L4235	H40/32R	8/61	London Transport RML882	Ensign, Purfleet (EX)
WLT 883	→ see TAS 466 *Overseas*								
WLT 884	AEC	Routemaster	RML884	Park Royal	L4290	H40/32R	9/61	London Transport RML884	Biddell, Woodford Bridge
WLT 885	AEC	Routemaster	RML885	Park Royal	L4205	H40/32R	9/61	London Transport RML885	Mitchell, Huddersfield
WLT 887	→ see 202 UXJ								
WLT 892	→ see 253 UXO								
WLT 893	AEC	Routemaster	RML893	Park Royal	L4215	H40/32R	10/61	London Transport RML893	London Bus Company, Northfleet (KT)
		(ex KFF 276, WLT 893)							
WLT 894	→ see 787 UXA *Overseas*								
WLT 895	→ see 252 UXO								

Reg	Make	Model	Chassis	Body	Body no	Layout	Date	Original owner	Current owner
WLT 897	→ see 254 UXO								
WLT 898	AEC	Routemaster (ex XFF 813, WLT 898)	RML898	Park Royal	L4723	H40/32R	12/61	London Transport RML898	Price, Gillingham (KT)
WLT 899	→ see 215 UXJ								
WLT 900	AEC	Routemaster	RML900	Park Royal	L4330	H40/32R	1/62	London Transport RML900	London Bus Company, Northfleet (KT)
WLT 902	AEC	Routemaster (ex ALC 464A, WLT 902)	RML902	Park Royal	L4348	H40/32R	1/62	London Transport RML902	London Bus Company, Northfleet (KT)
WLT 903	AEC	Routemaster	RML903	Park Royal	L4360	H40/32R	1/62	London Transport RML903	Metroline (LN) RML903
WLT 909	→ see WTS 418A								
WLT 910	→ see EDS 288A								
WLT 912	AEC	Routemaster	RM912	Park Royal	L4008	H36/28R	8/61	London Transport RM912	Sullivan R, Shanklin
WLT 928	AEC	Routemaster (ex 719 UXA, WLT 928)	RM928	Park Royal	L4058	H36/28R	9/61	London Transport RM928	Radnidge, Woking
WLT 938	AEC	Routemaster	RM938	Park Royal	L4066	H36/28R	11/61	London Transport RM938	Hoskin, Mitcham
WLT 960	AEC	Routemaster	RM960	Park Royal	L4179	H36/28R	11/61	London Transport RM960	Gregory, Croydon
WLT 978	→ see LDS 164A								
WLT 980	→ see USK 625								
WLT 991	AEC	Routemaster	RM991	Park Royal	L3543	H36/28R	11/61	London Transport RM991	Dickinson, Altrincham
WLT 997	→ see 839 UXC								
WLT 999	→ see WVS 423								
WLY 497	→ see BCT 899C								
WMY 709	Commer	Q25	-?-	?		B??	-/51	de Havilland, Hatfield	Evans, Chesham
WMY 886	Bedford	SB	3706	Duple	1006/253	C33F	7/51	Charing Cross Motors	Noonan, Bermondsey
WND 477	Leyland	Tiger Cub PSUC1/2	584033	Duple	1093/4	C41F	8/58	Spencer, Manchester	Hughes {Alpine}, Llandudno (CN)
WNO 478	Bristol	KSW5G	98104	ECW	6547	O33/28R	10/53	Eastern National 2380	Castle Point Transport Museum
WNO 479	Bristol	KSW5G	98140	ECW	6548	O33/28R	10/53	Eastern National 2383	Day, Pebmarsh
WNO 480	Bristol	KSW5G	98141	ECW	6549	O33/28R	11/53	Eastern National 2384	Talisman, Great Bromley (EX)
WNO 482	Bristol	KSW5G	98122	ECW	6487	O33/28R	10/53	Eastern National 2381	Salmon, South Benfleet
WNO 484	Bristol	KSW5G	98174	ECW	6489	O33/28R	9/53	Eastern National 2386	Hanford, Swansea
WOI 2211	Leyland	Leopard PSU3E/4R	8030049	Alexander (Belfast)	717/5	B53F	1/81	Ulsterbus 211	Poots, Tandragee
WOI 2235	Leyland	Leopard PSU3E/4R	8030103	Alexander (Belfast)	-?-	DP--F	3/81	Ulsterbus 235	Thompson, Newtownards
WOI 2440	Bristol	RELL6G	RELL-3-2597	Alexander (Belfast)	563/19	B52F	2/81	Ulsterbus 2440	Hart et al, Basingstoke
WOI 2444	Bristol	RELL6G	RELL-3-2601	Alexander (Belfast)	563/23	B52F	3/81	Ulsterbus 2444	Connolly, Armagh
WOI 2446	Bristol	RELL6G	RELL-3-2603	Alexander (Belfast)	563/14	B52F	12/80	Ulsterbus 2446	Simpson, Newtonabbey
WOI 2449	Bristol	RELL6G	RELL-3-2606	Alexander (Belfast)	563/26	B52F	7/81	Ulsterbus 2449	Kells Transport Museum, Cork
WPT 738	Bedford	SB3	55447	Duple	1074/318	C41F	1/58	Iveson, Esh	Rees, Sebastopol
WRA 12	AEC	Monocoach	MC3RV056	Park Royal	B37332	B45F	1/55	Booth & Fisher, Halfway	South Yorkshire Transport Museum
WRJ 179	Leyland	Titan PD2/40	623366	Metro-Cammell		H36/28F	4/63	Salford 179	Heaton, Bolton
WRL 16	Rowe	Hillmaster	C/H100	Reading	7704	B42F	6/56	Millbrook Steamboat & Trading	Glover, Instow
WSD 827	Leyland	Titan PD3/2 (ex BHN 601B, TSD 285)	591512	Alexander	6841	H41/31F	3/62	A1, Ardrossan	Hamilton, Tait & Wrae, Irvine
WSK 177	→ see LYF 21								
WSK 509	Leyland	Tiger Cub PSUC1/2 (ex YTS 723A, OMS 253)	604197	Alexander	6093	C41F	9/60	Alexander PD177	Booth/West of Scotland Bus Group, Glasgow
WSL 115	→ see KEL 94								
WSV 980	→ see TCO 537								
WTY 906	Bedford	SB5	90842	Duple Midland	CF472	B42F	11/62	Armstrong, Westerhope	Moseley (PCV), South Elmsall
WUA 832	AEC	Regent V	MD2RA138	Roe	GO4152	H33/27R	11/56	Leeds 832	Williams, York

	Reg	Make	Model	Chassis No	Body	Body No	Layout	New	First owner	Current owner
	WUS 248	AEC	Reliance	2MU3RA2466	Plaxton	592600	C37F	5/59	Cotter, Glasgow	Roulston, Glasgow
	WUU 553	Bedford	SB8	70247	Duple	1105/415	C41F	-/59	Cream, Hackney	Brenson J Jnr, Little Waltham
	WVS 423	AEC	Routemaster	RM999	Park Royal	L4256	H36/28R	1/62	London Transport RM999	Russell, Reading (BE)
			(ex WLT 999)							
	WWN 191	AEC	Reliance	2MU3RV3083	Harrington	2309	C41F	7/60	Neath & Cardiff	Hier, Swansea
(r)	WWX 48	Bedford	SB3	66872	Yeates	726	DP43F	3/59	Hargreaves, Morley	Richards, Guist (NK)
	WXI 1400	→ see DFZ 8200								
	WXI 4431	Leyland	Tiger TR2R62V16Z4	TR01191	Wright	N177	B57F	8/92	Ulsterbus 1431	Irish Transport Heritage
(r)	WXR 121	Commer	Avenger IV	94Y8023	Duple	1106/42	C41F	4/59	Davis, Notting Hill	Herefordshire Transport Collection
	WYL 137	Bristol	LH6L	LH-1291	ECW	21904	B39F	8/76	London Transport BL49	Green, Edmonton
			(ex ULO 524R, OJD 49R)							
	XAL 784	AEC	Regent V	LD3RA455	Northern Counties	5230	L35/32RD	9/57	Barton 784	Baker, Hail Weston
	XAT 368	Commer	Commando	17A0196	Park Royal	B31578	RC18C	4/47	Royal Air Force	Yorkshire Air Museum, Elvington
			(ex 08 AC 67, RAF 138076)							
(r)	XAZ 1362	Leyland	Atlantean AN68C/1R	8003583	Roe	GO8489	H43/31F	1/82	Hull 371	Griffiths, Hull
			(ex WAG 371X)							
	XAZ 1399	Leyland	Lynx LX2R11C15Z4S	LX2064	Leyland		B49F	4/91	Lothian 188	Melrose, Edinburgh
			(ex H188 OSG)							
	XBW 242	→ see AJH 163A								
	XCV 326	Bedford	SBG	50753	Duple Midland	480/24	B42F	1/57	Harper & Kellow, St Agnes	Lloyd, Wigan
(r)	XDV 851	AEC	Reliance	MU3RV2076	Willowbrook	58108	C41F	6/58	Devon General TCR851	Gibbons, Maidstone
	XFM 203	→ see ACA 603A								
	XHA 482	BMMO	D7	4482	Metro-Cammell		H37/26RD	3/56	BMMO 4482	BaMMOT, Wythall
(r)	XHA 494	BMMO	D7	4494	Metro-Cammell		RV	-/56	BMMO 4494	Tucker, Birmingham
	XHA 496	BMMO	D7	4496	Metro-Cammell		RV	-/56	BMMO 4496	BaMMOT, Wythall
	XHO 370	AEC	Reliance	2MU3RV2802	Weymann	M9284	B40F	1/60	Aldershot & District 370	Aldershot & District 370 Group, Camberley
	XHW 426	Bristol	LS5G	119088	ECW	8761	B45F	6/57	Bath Tramways 2910	Ellis, Cambridge (Gloucs)
	XKT 992	AEC	Reliance	MU3RV1302	Weymann	M7721	B42F	1/57	Maidstone & District S0215	Crouch & Carr, Maidstone
	XLG 477	Atkinson	Alpha PL745H	FC4127	Northern Counties	5002	B34C	5/56	SHMD 77	Dyson, Huddersfield
	XMR 956	Bristol	MW5G	195099	ECW	12699	B43F	9/62	Wilts & Dorest 809	Wigley, Basingstoke
	XNY 416	Guy	Arab LUF	LUF73642	Longwell Green		B44F	3/58	Aberdare 17	Cardiff Transport Preservation Group
	XOI 792	Mercedes-Benz	L608D	31032720609723	Reeve Burgess	14835	C19F	5/84	Broadmoor Hospital	Naughton, Spiddal (EI)
			(ex A 714 CRD)							
	XOI 2258	Leyland	Leopard PSU3E/4R	8030808	Wright	B146	DP53F	5/82	Ulsterbus 2258	Carson, Airdrie
	XOI 2481	Bristol	RELL6G	RELL-3-2638	Alexander (Belfast)	715/25	B45F	8/81	Citybus 2481	Shannon, Newtownards
	XOI 2520	Bristol	RELL6G	RELL-3-2677	Alexander (Belfast)	716/19	B45F	2/82	Citybus 2520	Curry, Pinxton
	XOI 2525	→ see 84-DL-2354 *Ireland*								
	XOI 2526	Bristol	RELL6G	RELL-3-2683	Alexander (Belfast)	716/27	B45F	4/82	Citybus 2526	Bean, Dymchurch
	XOI 2527	Bristol	RELL6G	RELL-3-2684	Alexander (Belfast)	716/29	B45F	4/82	Citybus 2527	Judd, Manea (CM)
	XSA 620	AEC	Reliance	2MU3RA4753	Plaxton	632608	B47F	4/63	Burnett, Mintlaw 7	XSA620 Group, Stonehaven
	XSJ 941	Bedford	CALV	214559	Martin Walter	-?-	M??	12/61	unknown	Edwards, Llanon
	XTA 839	Albion	Nimbus NS3N	82050H	Willowbrook	58006	B31F	9/58	Devon General 839	Hulme, Yatton
	XTB 91	Bedford	SBG	44311	Duple	1060/87	C41F	3/56	Robinson, Great Harwood	Blue Motors, Blackpool (LA)
	XTC 684	Leyland	Lowloader LFDD	542209	Metro-Cammell		H37/24RD	11/55	Leyland demonstrator	Thomas, Huyton
	XTO 266	AEC	Regent V	D3RV243	Park Royal	B39373	H34/28R	12/56	Nottingham 266	Scott, West Bridgford
	XUF 141	Leyland	Tiger Cub PSUC1/2	596709	Weymann	M9035	C41F	3/60	Southdown 1141	Southdown 1141 Group, Worthing

	Reg	Make	Model	Chassis no	Body	Body no	Layout	Date	First owner	Owner
	XUH 368	Leyland	Titan PD2A/30	611523	Metro-Cammell		H36/28R	11/61	Cardiff 368	Cardiff Transport Preservation Group
	XUO 721	Bristol	MW6G	135126	ECW	10047	DP41F	6/58	Western National 2902	Thorogood, Briantspuddle
	XUO 722	Bristol	MW6G	135132	ECW	10048	C39F	6/58	Western National 2239	Thorogood, Briantspuddle
	XUP 692	Albion	Aberdonian MR11L	82508D	Plaxton	2192	C41F	1/58	Gardiner, Spennymoor	Birch, Walsall
	XVC 290	Daimler	CVG6DD	19670	Metro-Cammell		RV	11/59	West Midlands 290Y	Burdett, Corley
	XVS 765	Renault	TN6A	567-670	STCRP		B33R	-/34	RATP, Paris	Moseley (PCV), South Elmsall
			(ex 26 MB 10 *Netherlands*)							
	XVS 830	AEC	Routemaster	RM180	Park Royal	L3840	H36/28R	12/59	London Transport RM180	Comer, Kingswood (GL)
			(ex VLT 180)							
	XVS 851	→ see WLT 467								
	XVX 19	Bristol	Lodekka LD5G	100021	ECW	6609	H33/25R	3/54	Eastern National 2400	Richardson, Wellow
	XWO 911	Leyland	Leopard L1	592767	Burlingham	6803	B45F	6/60	Hills, Tredegar	Rees & Roberts, Pontypool
	XWX 795	AEC	Reliance	2MU3RV2510	Roe	GO4936	C--F	5/59	Felix, Harfield 40	Felix Preservation Group / Sheffield Transport Group
			(ex DSU 457, XWX 795)							
	XYJ 418	AEC	Routemaster	RM736	Park Royal	L3461	H36/28R	4/61	London Transport RM736	Keighley Bus Museum Trust (WY)
			(ex WLT 736)							
	XYJ 717	Bristol	MW5G	139194	ECW	10436	B45F	3/59	United BU529	Bulmer, North Stainley (NY)
			(ex 929 JHN)							
(r)	XYJ 890	AEC	Reliance	2MU3RV1905	Alexander	5458	DP41F	5/58	Alexander AC140	Wallace, Broxburn
			(ex KWG 564)							
	YAZ 6393	→ see FCX 576W								
	YAZ 6412	Leyland	Leopard PSU3E/4R	7800811	Alexander (Belfast)	360/11	RV	6/78	Ulsterbus 4717	Kells Transport Museum, Cork
			(ex ROI 117)							
	YBD 201	Bristol	MW6G	184038	ECW	12230	C34F	6/61	United Counties 201	Serpell-Morris, Luton
	YBK 132	→ see AKG 219A								
	YDK 590	AEC	Reliance	2MU3RA3566	Harrington	2429	C37F	5/61	Yelloway, Rochdale	Museum of Transport, Manchester
	YDK 795	Ford	570E	510E59647	Plaxton	612503	C41F	5/61	Roberts, Rochdale	Johnson, Worksop (NG)
	YDL 315	Bristol	Lodekka FS6G	196030	ECW	12968	H33/27RD	7/62	Southern Vectis 570	Priddle, Farnham
	YDL 318	Bristol	Lodekka FS6G	196033	ECW	12971	H33/27RD	7/62	Southern Vectis 573	Pratt {Crosville}, Weston super Mare (SO)
	YEZ 2452	Leyland	Lynx LX5636LXBFR	LX1002	Alexander (Belfast)	580/3	B43F	7/86	Citybus 3007	Shannon, Newtownards
			(ex HXI 3007)							
	YFF 660	→ see AY 81 *Alderney*								
	YFO 127	Albion	Victor FT39KAN	73840H	Reading	2366	B35F	2/58	Guernsey Motors 77	Davies, Farnham
			(ex JPA 83V, 8227)							
	YFR 351	Leyland	Titan PD3/1	620516	Metro-Cammell		FH--/--R	6/62	Blackpool 351	Lancastrian Transport Trust
	YHE 240	Leyland	Tiger PS2/5	493003Y	Northern Counties	5771	H35/28F	-/50	Yorkshire Traction 1240	Berry, Radley & Wadsworth, Doncaster
			(ex HD 8555)		*(rebuilt & rebodied 4/63)*					
	YHT 929	Bristol	Lodekka LD6B	134038	ECW	9618	H33/25R	10/57	Bristol LC8436	Burt, Shaftesbury
	YHT 958	Bristol	Lodekka LD6B	138126	ECW	9272	O--/--RD	8/58	Bristol L8462	Ellis, Cambridge (Gloucs)
	YHY 78	Bristol	LS5G	119136	ECW	9666	DP41F	9/57	Bristol 2920	2920 Bus Group, Stroud
	YHY 80	Bristol	LS6G	119141	ECW	9668	B43F	11/57	Bristol 3004	Neale, Bristol
	YJG 807	AEC	Bridgemaster	2B3RA144	Park Royal	B47024	H43/29F	6/62	East Kent	East Kent Heritage, Dover
	YJI 9932	Albion	Viking VK41L	53192H	Alexander (Belfast)	-?-	B53F	9/74	WELB, Northern Ireland	Graham, Kesh
			(ex BIL 763)							
	YKR 224	AEC	Reliance	MU3RV1460	Beadle	B269	B42F	5/57	Maidstone & District SO224	Yarnell, St Leonards
	YLJ 147	Leyland	Titan PD3/1	590397	Weymann	M8586	H37/25D	6/59	Bournemouth 147	Shears D, Winkleigh

	Reg	Make	Model	Chassis no.	Body	Body no.	Layout	Date	First operator	Owner
	YNX 478	AEC	Reliance	MU3RA2010	Duple Midland	411/2	B44F	6/58	Chiltern Queens, Woodcote	Brocklehurst, Upton-upon-Severn
					(rebodied 3/73, with body new 10/56)					
	YOI 2260	Leyland	Leopard PSU3E/4R	8030059	Alexander (Belfast)	750/1	DP49F	6/82	Ulsterbus 260	Cusick, Armoy
	YOI 2274	Leyland	Leopard PSU3E/4R	8030145	Alexander (Belfast)	750/15	DP49F	5/82	Ulsterbus 274	Thompson, Newtownards
	YOI 2275	Leyland	Leopard PSU3E/4R	8030148	Alexander (Belfast)	750/16	DP49F	6/82	Ulsterbus 275	Lawton, Kircubbin
	YPT 289	Leyland	Titan PD3/4	573978	Burlingham	6581	H41/32RD	7/58	Sunderland District 289	Sunderland District Omnibus Preservation Group
	YPT 796	AEC	Reliance	MU3RV1559	Roe	GO4717	C41C	5/58	Economic, Whitburn 3	Purvis, Seaburn
	YRC 189	→ see YTS 743A								
	YRC 191	Leyland	Tiger Cub PSUC1/1	617720	Alexander	6829	DP41F	6/62	Trent 191	Trent (DE) 191
	YRC 194	Leyland	Tiger Cub PSUC1/1	617649	Alexander	6832	DP41F	6/62	Trent 194	Welshpool Town Council
			(ex OWJ 170A,YRC 194)							*(operates as Morris, Llanrhaeadr ym Mochnant (CW))*
	YRC 420	AEC	Reliance	6U3ZR36963	Plaxton	7811ACM022	C48FL	9/78	Howlett, Quorn	Matthews, Bexleyheath
			(ex ANR 900T)							
	YRV 303	Bedford	SB5	89546	*chassis on;y*			-/62	Byng, Portsmouth	Adkins, Upper Boddington
	YSG 101	Leyland	Leopard PSU3/2R	612694	Alexander	6842	B33T	12/61	Edinburgh 101	Scoular, Edinburgh
	YSK 763	Ford	ET6	7235576	Scottish Aviation		C29F	1/51	Ganson, Lerwick	Maiden, Wellington
			(ex BJT 190A, PS 2001)							
	YSU 898	Ford	532E	530E6419	Harrington	F01041	C--F	-/58	Boots, Nottingham	Carless, Wells
			(ex 958 BTO)							
	YSV 610	→ see EMW 284								
	YTG 304	Leyland	Titan PD3/4	571786	Massey	2309	H??/??F	7/58	Llynfi, Maesteg 72	Pearce, Worthing
	YTH 815	Guy	Arab IV	FD74812	Massey	2459	L31/28RD	1/62	Rees & Williams,Tycroes	South Wales Transport Preservation Trust
	YUP 6	Leyland	Titan PD2/10C	497119	Roe	GO4657	H37/28RD	-/49	Stanhope Motor Services L11	Weardale, Stanhope (DM)
			(ex AEF 680A, YUP 6, KUP 435)				*(rebodied 5/58)*			
	YVA 683	Commer	Avenger IV	94A0401	Duple	1134/1	C41F	2/61	Bell, Cumbernauld	Ronald, Paisley
	YVS 288	→ see WLT 357								
	YWF 528	Austin	J2VA	53349	Kenex		M12	12/59	Sisson, Cranswick	Teal, Cranswick
	YWS 611	Leyland	Titan PD2A/30	612861	Alexander	6752	H37/29R	1/62	Edinburgh 611	Melrose, Edinburgh
	YYB 118	Dennis	Lancet UF	160LU2	Harrington	1935	B42F	8/57	Hutchings & Cornelius, South Petherton	Webster, Lower Southrepps
	YYJ 555	Renault	TN4H	825-043	STCRP		B41R	-/37	RATP (Paris) 3996	Hyde, Southend-on-Sea
			(ex BW 2057, GGG 773N , unregistered)							
	YYJ 914	Leyland	Tiger Cub PSUC1/2	615569	Alexander	6731	C--F	7/61	Stark, Dunbar L17	Campbell, Edinburgh
			(ex ESS 989)							
(r)	YYK 765	Bedford	SB8	81225	Duple	1120/422	C41F	6/60	Cream, Islington	West of England Transport Collection
	YYS 174	Bedford	C5Z1	4668	Duple	1127/19	C21FM	5/60	MacBrayne 54	Walker, Lenzie
	YYV 912	Morris	J2BM	62820	Morris		M11	5/60	private owner	Hinson, Goldington
	3003 AH	→ see FRE 699A								
	3014 AH	Bristol	MW5G	139227	ECW	10380	B45F	3/59	Eastern Counties LL452	Burnside, Norwich
	5200 AH	Bedford	SB1	68350	Yeates	741	C41F	3/59	Smith, Wood Norton	Richards, Guist (NK)
	5789 AH	Bristol	MW5G	139276	ECW	11290	C39F	5/59	Eastern Counties LS789	Eastern Transport Collection
	9725 AT	→ see TSJ 272								
	8746 BH	Commer	Avenger IV	94A0574	Plaxton	632596	C41F	4/63	Wesley, Stoke Goldington 100	Smith, Welford-on-Avon
	2703 CD	Leyland	Leopard L2	610011	Harrington	2473	C28F	3/61	Southdown 1703	Robins, Halnaker
	2722 CD	Leyland	Leopard L2	610431	Harrington	2492	C37F	6/61	Southdown 1722	Baker, West Hoathly
										(operates as Southcoast, Chichester (WS))
	2724 CD	Leyland	Leopard L2	610430	Harrington	2496	C41F	7/61	Southdown 1724	Burtenshaw, Chichester
	2726 CD	Leyland	Leopard L2	610514	Harrington	2495	C41F	7/61	Southdown 1726	Watts, Crowborough

	5010 CD	→ see PSK 389								
	386 DD	Bedford	J2SZ2	71126	Plaxton	612512	C18F	5/61	Talbott, Moreton-in-Marsh	Price, Shobdon
	6775 DD	Leyland	Leopard PSU3/1R	620229	Plaxton	622991	C47F	4/62	Black & White L225	Black & White, Penton Mewsey (HA)
(r)	8321 DD	Bedford	SB5	90317	Duple	1145/315	C41F	5/62	Pulham, Bourton-on-the-Water	Meir, Stone
	6733 DK	→ see EDS 584B								
	7074 DK	→ see EAX 214B								
	1699 DP	Bedford	SB3	88814	Duple	1145/62	C41F	7/62	Smith, Reading	Stone & Bradbury, Reading
	5148 DP	→ see JTF 920B								
	9797 DP	Bedford	VAL14	1369	Duple	1172/56	C52F	3/64	Smith, Reading	Price, Shobdon
	6491 ED	Volvo	B58-61 (ex CCS 243T)	13163	Duple	948/6080	C51F	5/79	Docherty, Irvine	Docherty, Irvine
	5675 EL	Bristol	Lodekka FS6G	166018	ECW	11614	H33/27RD	9/60	Hants & Dorset 1448	Edwards & Tilley, Woking
	5677 EL	Bristol	Lodekka FS6G	166026	ECW	11616	H33/27RD	2/61	Hants & Dorset 1450	Three Counties Bus Preservation, Southampton
	8154 EL	Leyland	Titan PD3/1	601758	Weymann	M9529	H37/25D	10/60	Bournemouth 154	Shears D, Winkleigh
	8156 EL	Leyland	Titan PD3/1	601788	Weymann	M9528	O37/25D	10/60	Bournemouth 156	Bournemouth Heritage Transport Collection
	8159 EL	Leyland	Titan PD3/1	601971	Weymann	M9535	H35/25D	11/60	Bournemouth 159	Hawkins, Kingswear *(on loan to McAllister, Paignton (DN))*
	1252 EV	Bristol	MW5G	152067	ECW	11138	DP41F	9/59	Eastern National 488	West, Cambridge
	815 EZ	Leyland	Titan PD3/4	621372	UTA/Metro-Cammell		FH39/30F	2/63	UTA R815	Begley, Lisburn
	6234 EZ	AEC	Reliance	2MU3RA4595	UTA/Alexander		DP41F	4/63	UTA S234	Ulsterbus (NI) S234
	9579 F	→ see ILI 98 *Ireland*								
	4227 FM	Bristol	Lodekka FS6G	214133	ECW	13767	H33/27RD	5/64	Crosville DFG157	DFG157 Preservation Society, Warrington
	8518 FM	Leyland	Royal Tiger RT (ex NIL 2467, LHJ 736, A567 UTC, A677 LBV)	B50-024	Roe	GO4531	C49FT	1/84	Mercer, Longridge	Vals, Chase Terrace (ST)
	521 FN	→ see DSL 856								
	6783 FN	→ see 938 WZJ *Ireland*								
	6801 FN	AEC	Regent V	2D3RA1314	Park Royal	B49034	H40/32F	4/63	East Kent	Burlingham & Fagg, Ewell Minnis
	3016 HA	BMMO	D9	5016	BMMO		O40/32RD	11/62	Marshall, London OM5	BaMMOT, Wythall
	3035 HA	BMMO	D9	5035	BMMO		O40/32RD	1/63	Marshall, London OM6	Aston Manor Road Transport Museum
	5056 HA	BMMO	S15	5056	BMMO		B40F	3/62	BMMO 5056	Burdett, Corley
	5073 HA	BMMO	S15	5073	BMMO		B40F	-/62	BMMO 5073	BaMMOT, Wythall (WO)
	5212 HA	Leyland	Leopard PSU3/4R	622464	Willowbrook	CF381	B--F	12/62	BMMO 5212	BaMMOT, Wythall
	6314 HA	BMMO	D9	5314	BMMO		H40/32RD	-/63	BMMO 5314	Hudd, Eltham
(z)	6341 HA	BMMO	D9	5341	BMMO		H40/32RD	8/63	BMMO 5341	BaMMOT, Wythall
	6342 HA	BMMO	D9	5342	BMMO	BB5334	H40/32RD	9/63	BMMO 5342	Black Country Museum Transport Group
(z)	6360 HA	BMMO	D9	5360	BMMO		H40/32RD	12/63	BMMO 5360	BaMMOT, Wythall
	6370 HA	BMMO	D9	5370	BMMO		H40/32RD	2/64	BMMO 5370	Gray, Birmingham
	6479 HA	BMMO	S17	5479	BMMO/Willowbrook	CF738	B52F	1/64	BMMO 5479	Aston Manor Road Transport Museum
	6545 HA	BMMO	S16	5545	BMMO	BB5537	B52F	7/64	BMMO 5545	BaMMOT, Wythall (WO)
	7017 HK	Bristol	MW6G	139011	ECW	10145	C39F	7/58	Eastern National 458	Rainé, Fareham
	8943 HN	Karrier	BFD3023	D98A9893	Plaxton	612858	C14F	1/63	Harker, Reeth	Chambers, Newthorpe
	5711 HZ	Albion	Viking VK41L	53037F	Potter		B44F	-/66	Armagh Education Committee	Grimley, Dungannon
	5712 HZ	Albion	Viking VK41L	53039L	Potter		B44F	9/66	Tyrone Education Committee	Graham, Kesh
	135 KD	AEC	Reliance	2MU3RV4030	Burlingham	7457	C41F	7/62	Willow, Liverpool	Falmouth Coaches, Falmouth (CO)
	501 KD	Leyland	Atlantean PDR1/1	621346	Metro-Cammell		H43/34F	11/62	Liverpool L501	Merseyside Transport Trust
	6342 KH	→ see BAS 287								
	6689 KH	Leyland	Tiger Cub PSUC1/1	596584	Metro-Cammell		B41F	11/60	East Yorkshire 689	Ireland, Hull
	6692 KH	Leyland	Tiger Cub PSUC1/2	596316	Harrington	2220	C41F	5/60	East Yorkshire 692	Pearson, Doncaster

	6203 KW	AEC	Regent V	2D3RA1428	Metro-Cammell		H40/30F	3/64	Bradford 203	Keighley Bus Museum Trust
	6220 KW	AEC	Regent V	2D3RA1445	Metro-Cammell		H40/30F	4/64	Bradford 220	Keighley Bus Museum Trust
	9682 MT	→ see JAS 715								
	1013 MW	Leyland	Atlantean PDR1/1	612176	Weymann	M358	L39/34F	2/62	Silver Star, Porton Down 42	Silver Star 42 Group, Hampshire
	3136 MX	Ford	570E	510E77291	Duple	1151/69	C—F	6/62	Hall, Twickenham	Hunt, Halesowen
(r)	7552 MX	AEC	Renown	U204544	Park Royal	B48757	H--/--F	11/62	AEC demonstrator	FoKAB, Winchester
	6499 MZ	Mercedes Benz	O303/15R (ex B295 YOD)	300365230431 3	Mercedes Benz		C49FT	4/85	Terraneau, South Molton	Webb, Armscote (WK)
	3655 NE	Leyland	Tiger Cub PSUC1/12	625073	Park Royal	B48717	DP38D	12/62	Manchester 55	Museum of Transport, Manchester
	1339 NK	→ see VSU 717								
	7128 NK	Ford	570E	510E58303	Duple	1139/140	C41F	3/61	North Star, Stevenage	Nesbit, Somerby (LE)
	8488 NU	Bedford	VAL14	1362	Plaxton	642063	C52F	4/64	Branson, Brampton	Johnson, Worksop (NG)
	5228 NW	Leyland	Titan PD3/5	582052	Roe	GO4769	H38/32R	3/59	Leeds 228	Heaps, Bradford
	5280 NW	Leyland	Titan PD3/5	583255	Roe	GO4830	H38/32R	3/59	Leeds 280	Ensign, Purfleet (EX)
	5226 PH	→ see RIB 4407								
	2351 PO	Trojan	19	0908989	Trojan		B12F	6/59	Simmonds, Petworth	Trojan Museum Trust, Fyfield
	8031 PT	→ see WNL 259A								
	3809 PW	Bristol	MW6G	184226	ECW	12803	C39F	6/62	Eastern Counties LS809	Mahoney I, Brentwood
	7209 PW	Bedford	J2SZ2	141397	Plaxton	622924	C18F	6/62	Jarvis, Downham Market	Kelly, Middleton
	1291 RE	→ see IBI 975 *Ireland*								
	1292 RE	→ see JBI 337 *Ireland*								
	1293 RE	Guy	Arab LUF	LUF74291	Burlingham	6940	C41F	7/59	Harper, Heath Hayes 59	Rogers, Kidderminster (WO)
	1294 RE	Guy	Arab LUF	LUF74292	Burlingham	6941	C41F	7/59	Harper, Heath Hayes 60	Taylor, Lichfield
	3747 RH	AEC	Bridgemaster	2B3RA174	Park Royal	B48986	H43/29F	4/63	East Yorkshire 747	Blackman, Halifax (WY)
	6091 RK	→ see XKP 444A								
	5188 RU	Bedford	VAL14	1096	Plaxton	632541	C52F	5/63	Excelsior, Bournemouth	Johnson, Worksop (NG)
	6162 RU	Leyland	Titan PD3A/1 (ex LMN 73, 6162 RU)	L01323	Weymann	M725	O??/??F	9/63	Bournemouth 162	Shears D, Winkleigh
	6167 RU	Leyland	Titan PD3A/1 (ex LMN 78, 6167 RU)	L01408	Weymann	M728	H39/30F	9/63	Bournemouth 167	Shears D, Winkleigh
	7424 SP	AEC	Reliance	2MU3RV4246	Alexander	6879	C41F	5/62	Alexander Fife FAC4	FAC4 Preservation Group, Rosyth
	561 TD	Daimler	Fleetline CRG6LX	60021	Northern Counties	5692	H43/33F	6/62	Lancashire United 97	Lancastrian Transport Trust
	574 TD	Guy	Arab IV	FD75112	Northern Counties	5697	H41/32R	6/62	Lancashire United 110	North West Museum of Transport
	6216 TF	Guy	Arab IV	FD75355	Northern Counties	5861	H41/32R	9/63	Lancashire United 132	Norris & Bradley, Bolton
	6219 TF	Guy	Arab IV	FD75365	Northern Counties	5859	H41/32R	9/63	Lancashire United 135	LUT Society
	1975 TJ	AEC	Renown	3B3RA023	East Lancs	6010	H41/31R	10/63	Leigh 28	Finch, Higher Ince (GM)
	6666 U	→ see OSK 831								
	8332 U	AEC	Reliance	MU3RA1951	Plaxton	2291	C41C	5/58	Wallace Arnold Tours	Millington, Horsforth
	8340 U	Leyland	Tiger Cub PSUC1/2	584568	Burlingham	6569	C41F	5/58	Wallace Arnold Tours	Millington, Horsforth
	7514 UA	Daimler	CVG6LX-30DD	30057	Roe	GO4964	H38/32R	11/59	Leeds 514	Keighley Bus Museum Trust
	3916 UB	AEC	Regent V	2D3RA737	Metro-Cammell		H38/32R	6/60	Leeds 916	Berry, Milnsbridge
	3945 UE	Leyland	Tiger Cub PSUC1/1	606329	Park Royal	B45196	B--F	11/60	Stratford Blue 45	Bedford, Celbridge
	3190 UN	Commer	Avenger IV	94A0506	Plaxton	622131	C41F	6/62	Wright, Penycae	Price, Shobdon
	6249 UP	Leyland	Leopard PSU3/3R	L02125	Alexander	63/25Y3/3	DP51F	6/63	Venture 249	Herron & Noble, Blackhall Mill
	9058 UZ	Bristol	RELL6L	RELL-3-588	Alexander	PU/1768/8	B44D	5/69	Ulsterbus 1058	Begley, Lisburn
(r)	1376 VC	Ford	570E	510E77476	Duple	1151/39	C41F	6/62	RHMS, Coventry	Hunt, Halesowen
	3706 VM	Leyland	Titan PD2/37	L02706	Metro-Cammell		H37/28R	4/64	Manchester 3706	Duffy, Macclesfield
	4632 VM	Daimler	CVG6DD	19972	Metro-Cammell		H37/28R	9/63	Manchester 4632	Talbot, Leicester

8859 VR	AEC	Regent V	2D3RA1513	Neepsend		H41/32R	1/64	Mayne, Manchester	Hawkins, Findon (WS)
8860 VR	AEC	Regent V	2D3RA1514	Neepsend		H41/32R	1/64	Mayne, Manchester	Lomas, Manchester
2730 VX	Bristol	MW5G	164106	ECW	11835	B45F	11/60	Eastern National 519	McKeever, Ely
1322 WA	AEC	Reliance	2MU3RA3505	Plaxton	612604	C36F	5/61	Sheffield United 322	South Yorkshire Transport Museum
1925 WA	AEC	Bridgemaster	2B3RA104	Park Royal	B45431	H43/29F	4/61	Sheffield 525	Blackman, Halifax (WY)
3156 WE	Leyland	Titan PD2/30	582738	Roe	GO4892	H33/26RD	11/58	Sheffield 1156	South Yorkshire Transport Museum (SY)
3904 WE	Leyland	Titan PD3/1	583140	Roe	GO4877	H39/30R	6/59	Sheffield 904	South Yorkshire Transport Museum (SY)
3913 WE	→ see OWJ 357A								
4475 WE	→ see OWJ 388A								
4092 WJ	Karrier	BF3023	98A4264	Plaxton	592698	C14F	10/59	Blood Transfusion Service	Ryland, Gloucester
6330 WJ	AEC	Regent V	2D3RA698	Roe	G05121	H39/30RD	1/60	Sheffield 1330	South Yorkshire Transport Museum
7874 WJ	AEC	Regent V	2D3RA686	Alexander	5895	H37/32R	4/60	Sheffield 874	AEC Alexander Group, Sheffield
9629 WU	AEC	Reliance	2MU3RV2955	Roe	GO5160	DP41F	4/60	Felix, Hatfield 41	Felix Preservation Group, Doncaster
8124 WX	Bristol	MW6G	184034	ECW	12243	C39F	5/61	West Yorkshire CUG27	North East Bus Preservation Trust
8176 WY	AEC	Regent V	2D3RA1018	Roe	GO5337	H41/32RD	8/61	Felix, Hatfield 42	Grealy, Doncaster
675 AAM	→ see PFO 256								
20 AAX	→ see AKG 307A								
889 AAX	Leyland	Tiger Cub OPSUC1/3	586876	Weymann	M8812	DP44F	-/59	Jones, Aberbeeg 98	
		(new -/59 but not licensed until 2/61)							Cardiff Transport Preservation Group &Coleman, Abertillery
850 ABK	AEC	Reliance	2MU3RA3984	Duple	1149/3	C43F	6/62	Don, Southsea	Bayliss, Oxford
21 ACD	→ see BSR 168B								
23 ACD	Leyland	Titan PD2/37	621922	Weymann	M563	H37/27F	1/63	Brighton 23	Richardson, Ropley
137 ACY	Bristol	MW6G	184088	ECW	12687	B45F	7/61	United Welsh 127	Lines, Bristol
890 ADV	AEC	Reliance	2MU3RV2349	Willowbrook	59366	C41F	5/59	Devon General TCR890	Cotton, Saltash (CO)
692 AEH	AEC	Reliance	MU3RV1725	Weymann	M7897	B39F	7/57	Pottreies SN7692	-?-, Hampshire
		(ex DSV 335, "MKR 1", 692 AEH)							
701 AEH	Leyland	Titan PD3/4	570875	Metro-Cammell		O37/31F	8/57	Potteries H701	Quantock, Bishops Lydeard (SO)
11 AFC	→ see YTT 178S								
974 AFJ	Guy	Arab IV	FD74590	Massey	2383	H31/26R	6/60	Exeter 74	Blood, North Tawton
833 AFM	Bristol	Lodekka LD6G	120079	ECW	8493	O33/27RD	5/57	Crosville MG876	Gilroy, Alnwick (ND) 1
838 AFM	Bristol	Lodekka LD6G	120098	ECW	8498	H33/27RD	5/57	Crosville MG881	Heginbotham, Stockport
924 AHY	Bristol	MW5G	135022	ECW	9680	B45F	3/58	Bristol 2934	Walker, Wells
929 AHY	Bristol	MW5G	139063	ECW	9865	B45F	10/58	Bristol 2939	Ellis, Cambridge (Gloucs)
239 AJB	→ see YAF 151A								
240 AJB	AEC	Regent V	2D3RA1109	Park Royal	B48707	H41/32F	3/62	AERE, Harwell 106	Thomas, Huyton
241 AJB	→ see RFO 361								
243 AJB	AEC	Regent V	2D3RA1112	Park Royal	B48710	H41/32F	3/62	AERE, Harwell 109	Priest, Letcombe Regis
217 AJF	AEC	Bridgemaster	B3RA137	Park Royal	B45717	H45/31R	9/61	Leicester 217	Leicester Bridgemaster Group, Leicester
956 AJO	AEC	Regent V	MD3RV438	Park Royal	B40642	H33/28R	4/57	City of Oxford H956	Freeman, Oxford
(r) 407 ALC	Commer	Avenger IV	94A0368	Duple	1106/49	C41F	-/60	Wootten, Lewisham	Herefordshire Transport Collection
496 ALH	AEC	Reliance	2MU2RA3100	Willowbrook	60564	B42D	9/60	London Transport RW2	Hunt, Chatham
497 ALH	AEC	Reliance	2MU2RA3101	Willowbrook	60565	B42D	9/60	London Transport RW3	Smith & Cole, Epping
972 ANK	Bedford	SBG	50330	Duple	1074/100	C41F	6/57	Albanian, St Albans	Little, Ilkeston (DE)
477 AOP	AEC	Reliance	2MU3RA2884	Harrington	2213	C29F	3/60	Flights, Birmingham	Millington, Horsforth
318 AOW	AEC	Regent V	2D3RA1056	Park Royal	B47016	H--/--RD	4/62	Southampton 318	Southampton & District Transport Heritage Trust
335 AOW	Leyland	Titan PD2A/27	621727	Park Royal	B47003	H37/29R	2/63	Southampton 335	Southampton & District Transport Heritage Trust

	337 AOW	Leyland	Titan PD2A/27	621754	Park Royal	B47005	H37/29R	2/63	Southampton 337	Blair, Upham
	200 APB	AEC	Reliance	MU3RV1007	Burlingham	6244	B44F	3/56	Safeguard, Guildford	Safeguard, Guildford (SR)
	747 ATA	→ see Unregistered Vehicles								
	872 ATA	Leyland	Atlantean PDR1/1	590593	Metro-Cammell	HO51196/1	H44/32F	7/59	Devon General DL872	Hulme, Yatton
	60 AUF	→see WTS 429A								
	70 AUF	Commer	Avenger IV	94A0572	Harrington	2679	C--F	11/62	Southdown 70	Southdown 70 Group, Worthing
	273 AUF	Leyland	Leopard PSU3/1R	623838	Marshall	B3116	B49F	3/63	Southdown 673	Cooper Drake & Ferguson, Shadoxhurst
	191 AWL	AEC	Regent V	MD3RV233	Weymann	M7531	L30/26RD	10/56	City of Oxford L191	Bridges, Enstone
	71 AWN	→ see 397 CLT								
	372 BBH	Commer	Avenger IV	94A0067	Duple	1076/29	C41F	4/57	Wesley, Stoke Goldington 52	Herefordshire Transport Collection
	932 BCE	AEC	Reliance	2U3RA4026	Plaxton	622153	DP47F	6/62	Burwell & District	Burwell Museum of Fen Edge Village Life
	194 BFC	AEC	Regent V	MD3RV305	Weymann	M8001	L30/28RD	-/57	City of Oxford L194	Bridges, Enstone
(r)	750 BHA	BMMO	D7	4750	Metro-Cammell		RV	-/57	BMMO 4750	BaMMOT, Wythall
(r)	761 BHA	BMMO	D7	4761	Metro-Cammell		RV	-/57	BMMO 4761	Tucker, Birmingham
	767 BHA	BMMO	D7	4767	Metro-Cammell		RV	9/57	BMMO 4767	Powick, Tenbury Wells
	371 BKA	AEC	Regent V	LD2RA374	Park Royal	B43178	FH40/32F	8/59	Liverpool E1	Merseyside Transport Trust / Forrest, Walton
	372 BKA	Leyland	Atlantean PDR1/1	590501	Metro-Cammell		H--/--F	12/59	Liverpool E2	Merseyside Transport Trust
	647 BKL	Guy	Warrior	WUF2169	Mulliner		B45F	11/57	Leybourne Grange Hospital	-?-, Alton
(r)	252 BKM	AEC	Reliance	MU3RV1844	*chassis only*			2/58	Maidstone & District SO252	Platt, Dawlish Warren
	253 BKM	AEC	Reliance	MU3RV1845	Harrington	1967	B42F	2/58	Maidstone & District SO253	SO253 Preservation Group, Swanscombe
	381 BKM	AEC	Reliance	MU3RV1681	Harrington	1941	C--F	10/57	Maidstone & District CO381	Tkaczyk, Coleford
	557 BNG	Bristol	Lodekka FL6G	198002	ECW	13120	H37/33RD	12/62	Eastern Counties LFL57	East Anglia Transport Museum
	670 BNN	Leyland	Titan PD3/3	582749	Weymann	M8338	L35/32R	1/59	South Notts, Gotham 70	Quantock, Bishops Lydeard (SO)
	157 BRP	Bristol	MW6G	195113	ECW	13299	B45F	11/62	United Counties 157	Allin, Rushden
	519 BTA	Bristol	Lodekka FS6G	155042	ECW	11087	H33/27RD	5/60	Western National 1967	Billington, Maidenhead
	434 BTE	Crossley	Regent V	D3RV373	East Lancs	5364	H31/28RD	8/57	Darwen 17	White & Pryer, Bradnop
	958 BTO	→ see YSU 898								
	881 BTF	Leyland	Titan PD2/41	570982	East Lancs	5345	H35/28R	7/57	Lancaster 881	Ribble Vehicle Preservation Trust
	148 BTP	Leyland	Leopard L1	623280	Weymann	M673	B41D	4/63	Portsmouth 148	Howe, Portsmouth
	548 BUF	Leyland	Leopard L2	L00388	Harrington	2804	C--F	5/63	Southdown 1748	Elliott & Burtenshaw, Chichester
	654 BUP	Leyland	Tiger Cub PSUC1/2	587022	Plaxton	582479	C37F	12/58	Wilkinson, Sedgefield 54	Hughes {Alpine}, Llandudno (CN)
	352 BWB	Bedford	SB8	89884	Plaxton	622884	C41F	1/62	Kirkby, Harthill	Abbott, Leeming (NY)
	657 BWB	Leyland	Atlantean PDR1/1	613323	Park Royal	B56016	H44/33F	4/62	Sheffield 1357	Sheffield Transport Group, Doncaster
					(rebodied 8/68)					
	11 BWN	AEC	Regent V	2D3RA1079	Willowbrook	CF229	H39/32F	4/62	South Wales 571	571 Bus Preservation Group, Swansea
	824 BWN	AEC	Reliance	2MU3RA4103	Harrington	2604	C--F	4/62	South Wales 1047	South Wales Transport Preservation Trust
	811 BWR	Bristol	SUL4A	190056	ECW	13486	B36F	11/62	West Yorkshire SMA5	Leach, Keighley
	571 BWT	AEC	Reliance	2MU3RA4007	Duple	1149/6	C41F	6/62	Fearn, Dodworth	MacEwan, Amisfield (SW)
	827 BWY	Bristol	MW6G	195200	ECW	13465	B45F	5/63	West Yorkshire SMG19	Halliday, Shipley
	100 BXL	AEC	Routemaster	RM1000	Park Royal	L4882	H36/28R	3/62	London Transport RM1000	RM1000 Group, Croydon
	326 CAA	Bedford	SB3	88245	Harrington	2504	C41F	8/61	King Alfred, Winchester	FoKAB, Winchester
	422 CAX	AEC	Regent V	MD3RV565	Massey	2460	L31/28R	12/61	Bedwas & Machen 5	B&M Bus Project, Hyde
	878 CDH	Bedford	SB3	63057	Duple	1090/329	C--F	5/58	Hayes, Walsall	Jenkins, Wells
	522 CER	→ see TVS 337								
	479 CFJ	Leyland	Titan PD2A/30	610091	Massey	2422	H--/--R	4/61	Exeter 79	Ribbs & Lynne, Dulverton
	650 CHN	→ see WTS 708A								

Reg	Chassis	Model	Fleet no	Body	Body no	Layout	Date	First operator	Owner
1 CLT	AEC	Routemaster	RM1001	Park Royal	L4307	H36/28R	1/62	London Transport RM1001	Smith, Billericay
2 CLT	→ see OYM 368A								
5 CLT	AEC	Routemaster (ex ALC 290A, 5 CLT)	RM1005	Park Royal	L3430	H36/28R	3/62	London Transport RM1005	Hendy, Bath
9 CLT	AEC	Routemaster	RM1009	Park Royal	L4353	H36/28R	3/62	London Transport RM1009	London Bus Company, Northfleet (KT)
33 CLT	→ see DSL 540								
58 CLT	→ see 204 UXJ								
62 CLT	AEC	Routemaster (ex 794 UXA, 62 CLT)	RM1062	Park Royal	L4015	H36/28R	1/62	London Transport RM1062	Western Greyhound, Summercourt (CO)
63 CLT	AEC	Routemaster	RM1063	Park Royal	L4430	H36/28R	1/62	London Transport RM1063	Hughes, Swanley
69 CLT	AEC	Routemaster	RM1069	Park Royal	L4267	H36/28R	1/62	London Transport RM1069	Sullivan, Potters Bar (HT)
87 CLT	AEC	Routemaster (ex GZI 93Z *US Califormia registration*, 87 CLT)	RM1087	Park Royal	L4454	O36/28R	5/62	London Transport RM1087	Traditional, Bromley Common (LN)
97 CLT	→ see 201 UXJ								
138 CLT	AEC	Routemaster	RM1138	Park Royal	L5429	H36/28R	5/62	London Transport RM1138	Miles, South Benfleet
152 CLT	AEC	Routemaster	RM1152	Park Royal	L4311	H36/28R	5/62	London Transport RM1152	Pryer, Bradnop
164 CLT	→ see NSG 636A *Overseas*								
168 CLT	→ see 798 UXA								
174 CLT	→ see JSJ 797								
214 CLT	AEC	Routemaster	RM1214	Park Royal	L4390	H36/28R	5/62	London Transport RM1214	Blackman, Halifax (WY)
224 CLT	→ see UYJ 654								
254 CLT	AEC	Routemaster	RMF1254	Park Royal	L4601	H41/31F	10/62	London Transport RMF1254	Biddell, Woodford Bridge *(operates as Imperial Bus, Romford (LN))*
274 CLT	→ see LDS 67A								
305 CLT	→ see 799 UXA								
312 CLT	→ see MFF 509 *Overseas*								
324 CLT	→ see 852 UXC								
357 CLT	AEC	Routemaster	RM1357	Park Royal	L4604	H36/28R	12/62	London Transport RM1357	Detheridge, Raglan (CS)
361 CLT	→ see VYJ 808								
363 CLT	AEC	Routemaster	RM1363	Park Royal	L4970	H36/28R	12/62	London Transport RM1363	Knight, Hawkesbury Upton
368 CLT	AEC	Routemaster	RM1368	Park Royal	L4634	B--RD	12/62	London Transport RM1368	Morgan, St Albans
371 CLT	AEC	Routemaster	RM1371	Park Royal	L4930	H36/28R	12/62	London Transport RM1371	London Bus Company, Northfleet (KT)
380 CLT	→ see KGW 489A								
394 CLT	AEC	Routemaster	RM1394	Park Royal	L4614	H36/28R	1/63	London Transport RM1394	Humphries, Dagenham
397 CLT	AEC	Routemaster (ex LXU 397, 71 AWN, OWJ 871A, 397 CLT)	RM1397	Park Royal	L4415	H36/28R	1/63	London Transport RM1397	Lennox-Kay, Aldington
403 CLT	AEC	Routemaster (ex BHK 106A, 403 CLT)	RM1403	Park Royal	L4640	O36/20R	2/63	London Transport RM1403	Cooper, Towcester (NO)
414 CLT	AEC	Routemaster	RM1414	Park Royal	L4650	H36/28R	2/63	London Transport RM1414	Museum of Transport, Manchester
449 CLT	AEC	Routemaster (ex LDS 190A, 449 CLT)	RM1449	Park Royal	L4529	H36/28R	4/63	London Transport RM1449	Forrest, Walton
456 CLT	→ see LFF 875								
461 CLT	AEC	Routemaster	RMC1461	Park Royal	L4531	H32/25RD	7/62	London Transport RMC1461	London Bus Preservation Trust
462 CLT	AEC	Routemaster	RMC1462	Park Royal	L4676	H32/25RD	8/62	London Transport RMC1462	London Bus Company, Northfleet (KT)
469 CLT	AEC	Routemaster	RMC1469	Park Royal	L4637	H32/25RD	8/62	London Transport RMC1469	-?-, -?-
476 CLT	AEC	Routemaster	RMC1476	Park Royal	L4567	H32/25RD	10/62	London Transport RMC1476	Warneford & Knight, Gillingham
485 CLT	AEC	Routemaster (ex TAS 417, 485 CLT, TAS 417, 485 CLT)	RMC1485	Park Royal	L4736	H32/25RD	10/62	London Transport RMC1485	Ensign, Purfleet (EX)

486 CLT	AEC	Routemaster	RMC1500	Park Royal	L4639	H36/25RD	11/62	London Transport RMC1500	Lennox-Kay et al, Aldington
		(ex ALC 368A, 500 CLT)							
487 CLT	AEC	Routemaster	RMC1487	Park Royal	L4611	H32/25RD	10/62	London Transport RMC1487	Sullivan, Potters Bar (HT)
490 CLT	AEC	Routemaster	RMC1490	Park Royal	L4730	H32/25RD	11/62	London Transport RMC1490	Haywood, Kooper & Newton, Baschurch
									(on loan to Meadows, Crewe (CH))
497 CLT	AEC	Routemaster	RMC1497	Park Royal	L4619	H32/25RD	11/62	London Transport RMC1497	Gale, Avonwick
500 CLT	→ see 486 CLT								
507 CLT	AEC	Routemaster	RMC1507	Park Royal	L4727	H32/25RD	1/63	London Transport RMC1507	Humphries, Dagenham
516 CLT	AEC	Routemaster	RMC1516	Park Royal	L4734	H32/25RD	1/63	London Transport RMC1516	Almeroth, Wendling
528 CLT	→ see KGJ 117A								
543 CLT	AEC	Routemaster	RM1543	Park Royal	L4801	H36/28R	4/63	London Transport RM1543	Watson, Cheam
563 CLT	AEC	Routemaster	RM1563	Park Royal	L4830	H36/28R	4/63	London Transport RM1563	Townsend, Chiswick
568 CLT	→ see BNK 324A								
583 CLT	AEC	Routemaster	RM1583	Park Royal	L4677	H36/28R	5/63	London Transport RM1583	Lancastrian Transport Trust
									(operates as Totally Transport, Blackpool (LA))
134 CMR	AEC	Reliance	2MU3RA5099	Willowbrook	CF680	B--D	12/63	Swindon 134	Sanders, -?-
574 CNW	Daimler	CVG6LX-30DD	30143	Roe	GO5498	H39/31F	5/62	Leeds 574	Lawson, Baildon
672 COD	Bristol	SUS4A	157004	ECW	11391	B30F	2/60	Western National 600	Billington, Maidenhead
675 COD	Bristol	SUS4A	157007	ECW	11394	B30F	2/60	Western National 603	Ede, Stroud
715 COM	Ford	570E	510E59442	Duple	1139/146	C41F	2/61	Allenways, Birmingham	Hunt, Halesowen
959 CPT	Leyland	Tiger Cub PSUC1/1	594153	Duple Midland	493/44/TC/3	B45F	7/59	Summerson, West Auckland	Johnson, Brandesburton
54 CPW	Bristol	Lodekka FS5G	205064	ECW	12939	H--/--F	763	Eastern Counties LFS54	Carter, Wherstead
333 CRW	Daimler	CVG6DD	20044	Metro-Cammell		H34/29R	11/63	Coventry 333	Coventry Transport Museum
334 CRW	Daimler	CVG6DD	20045	Metro-Cammell		H34/29R	11/63	Coventry 334	Aston Manor Road Transport Museum
759 CTD	Leyland	Titab PD2/20	570980	*chassis only*			8/57	Lytham St Annes 60	1685 Group, Birmingham
760 CTD	Leyland	Titan PD2/20	570981	Northern Counties	5112	H33/28R	8/57	Lytham St Annes 61	Lancastrian Transport Trust
521 CTF	Leyland	Olympian LW1	576695	Weymann	LW47	B44F	11/57	Fishwick, Leyland 7	Hayes, Little Hoole
528 CTF	Leyland	Titan PD2/40	573884	Weymann	M7831	L30/28RD	2/58	Fishwick, Leyland 5	Ashcroft, Lostock Hall
713 CTM	Bedford	SB1	87142	Duple	1133/265	C41F	1/61	Cook, Biggleswade	Brenson J Snr, Little Waltham
445 CTT	Bedford	SB3	72068	Duple	1105/504	C41F	7/59	Hill, Stibb Cross	Hamilton, Bow (DN)
954 CUF	Leyland	Titan PD3/4	L02484	Northern Counties	6001	FH39/30F	6/64	Southdown 954	Elliott & Burtenshaw, Chichester
									(operates as Southcoast, Chichester (WS))
972 CUF	Leyland	Titan PD3/4	L02598	Northern Counties	5997	FH39/30F	6/64	Southdown 972	Pope, Pulborough
974 CUF	→ see FPH 135B								
198 CUS	AEC	Reliance	2MU3RA3687	Duple Midland	CF89	C41F	5/61	MacBrayne 63	Hunter, Fordoun
975 CWL	AEC	Regent V	LD3RA432	Park Royal	B41264	H37/28R	3/58	City of Oxford 975	Wareham, Kidlington
603 CYS	Bedford	C5C1	5068	Duple	1140/1	C29F	5/61	MacBrayne 179	McPherson & MacDonald, Howmore
605 CYS	Bedford	C5C1	5070	Duple	1140/5	C--F	6/61	MacBrayne 181	MacDonald, Howmore (SN)
980 DAE	Bristol	MW5G	139196	ECW	10361	B45F	2/59	Bristol 2960	Staniforth, Stroud
58 DAF	Scania	K112TRS	1811341	Jonckheere	20900	CH55/18CT	5/88	Mercer, Grimsargh	Gallagher, Cottenham
		(ex E839 JHJ, A20 APT, NJI 8869, E216 GNV)							*(operates as Young, Haddenham (CM))*
408 DBO	AEC	Regent V	2D3RA1451	East Lancs	6030	H35/28R	12/63	Cardiff 408	Cardiff Regent V Group
151 DBX	Albion	Nimbus NS3AN	82068K	Harrington	2816	B31F	7/63	Davies, Pencader 67	Newman, Chipping Norton
401 DCD	Leyland	Titan PD3/4	L02939	Northern Counties	6013	FCO39/30F	5/64	Southdown 401	Roadmark, Storrington (WS)
		(ex PRX 206B, 401 DCD)							
403 DCD	→ see WRU 734B								

404 DCD	→ see PRX 191B								
406 DCD	Leyland	Titan PD3/4	L03147	Northern Counties	6024	FCO39/30F	6/64	Southdown 406	Elliott & Baker, Chichester
		(ex WRU 702B, 406 DCD)							*(operates as Southcoast Motor, Chichester (WS))*
409 DCD	Leyland	Titan PD3/4	L03225	Northern Counties	6025	FCO39/30F	6/64	Southdown 409	Southdown (WS) 19909
410 DCD	Leyland	Titan PD3/4	L03226	Northern Counties	6018	FCO39/30F	5/64	Southdown 410	Stobart, Wimbledon
		(ex DHJ 301B, BHM 288, PRX 207B, 410 DCD)							
412 DCD	Leyland	Titan PD3/4	L03366	Northern Counties	6007	FCO39/30F	3/64	Southdown 412	Pearce, Worthing
		(ex AOR 158B, 412 DCD)							*(operates as Southdown Historic, Worthing (WS))*
415 DCD	→ see ZV 1461 *Ireland*								
416 DCD	Leyland	Titan PD3/4	L03398	Northern Counties	6003	FCO39/30F	3/64	Southdown 416	Pearce, Worthing
		(ex PRX 190B, 416 DCD)							*(operates as Southdown Historic, Worthing (WS))*
417 DCD	→ see PRX 189B								
419 DCD	Leyland	Titan PD3/4	L03504	Northern Counties	6005	FCO39/30F	3/64	Southdown 419	Pearce, Worthing
		(ex DRR 153B, YRC 182, PRX 186B, 419 DCD)							*(operates as Southdown Historic, Worthing (WS))*
421 DCD	→ see PRX 458B								
422 DCD	Leyland	Titan PD3/4	L03591	Northern Counties	6004	FCO39/30F	3/64	Southdown 422	Stobart, Wimbledon
		(ex AOR 157B, 422 DCD)							
423 DCD	→ see WOW 993T								
424 DCD	Leyland	Titan PD3/4	L03593	Northern Counties	6011	FCO39/30F	5/64	Southdown 424	Stephenson, Rochford (EX)
		(ex AOR 156B, 424 DCD)							
749 DCD	Leyland	Leopard L2	L02114	Harrington	2840	C39F	10/63	Southdown 1749	Burtenshaw, Chichester
750 DCD	Leyland	Leopard L2	L02115	Harrington	2841	C28F	10/63	Southdown 1750	Kenzie, Shepreth (CM)
617 DDV	Bristol	MW6G	164034	ECW	11945	C39F	6/60	Southern National 2250	Bluestone National Park Resort, Narberth
625 DDV	Bristol	MW6G	164009	ECW	11962	C39F	5/60	Western National 2246	Thorogood, Briantspuddle
395 DEL	Albion	Victor FT39AN	73791L	Heaver		B35F	12/55	Guernsey Motors 71	White, Harston
		(ex 2027)							
811 DFM	→ see TFF 251								
466 DHN	Guy	Arab IV	FD73670	Roe	G04488	H33/28R	8/57	Darlington 66	Quantock, Bishops Lydeard (SO)
390 DKK	AEC	Reliance	2MU3RV2035	Harrington	2024	DP40F	10/58	Maidstone & District CO390	Catchpole, Halling
277 DKT	AEC	Reliance	2MU3RV2067	Park Royal	B42639	DP40F	6/59	Maidstone & District SO277	Gibbons, Maidstone
403 DLD	Bedford	SB8	89645	Harrington	2569	C41F	4/62	Fallowfield & Britten	Adkins, Upper Boddington
774 DNU	Commer	Avenger III	T85A0330	Duple	1062/54	C41F	2/57	Slack, Tansley	Coach Hire, Freckleton (LA)
999 DNV	Leyland	Leopard L1	611161	Plaxton	632644	C43F	5/63	Basford, Greens Norton	Adkins, Upper Boddington
129 DPT	AEC	Reliance	2MU3RA1860	Plaxton	592595	C41F	5/59	OK (Howe), Spennymoor	Boston, Newbury
109 DRM	Bristol	Lodekka FS6G	166045	ECW	12333	H33/27RD	4/61	Cumberland 550	550 Group, Workington
		(ex AAO 547A, 109 DRM)							
3 DRP	Bedford	SB5	92130	Duple	1159/279	C41F	4/63	KW, Daventry	Wilkinson, Kettlewell (NY)
875 DTB	Guy	Arab IV	FD73815	Northern Counties	5129	H41/32R	1/58	Lancashire United 608	Larkin, Peterborough
539 DTE	AEC	Reliance	MU3RV828	Duple	1094/1	C39C	2/58	Holmeswood Coaches	Holmeswood, Holmeswood (LA)
964 DTJ	Leyland	Tiger Cub PSUC1/1	577519	Weymann	M8461	B44F	2/58	Merthyr Tydfil 100	Parfitt, Rhymney Bridge
913 DTT	Leyland	Atlantean PDR1/1	592608	Roe	GO5063	H44/31F	5/60	Devon General DL913	Bennett, Sherborne
480 DUF	Leyland	Leopard PSU3/3R	L03406	Plaxton	642799	C49F	2/64	Southdown 1180	Soul, Monkwood
509 DVT	Bedford	SB3	60922	Duple	1090/228	C41F	4/58	Williamson, Sneyd Green	Renown, Bexhill-on-Sea (ES)
282 DWN	AEC	Regent V	2D3RA1158	Roe	GO5581	B37F	-/63	South Wales 38	South Wales Transport Preservation Trust
532 DWW	Bedford	SB5	92138	Plaxton	632600	C41F	4/63	Barnsley British Co-op	Wood, Bridestowe
607 DYE	→ see LDS 201A								
620 DYE	AEC	Routemaster	RM1620	Park Royal	L4287	H36/28R	6/63	London Transport RM1620	London Bus Company, Northfleet (KT)
621 DYE	→ see KGJ 187A								

	Reg	Make	Model	Chassis no	Body	Body no	Layout	Date	First owner	Current owner
	641 DYE	AEC	Routemaster	RM1641	Park Royal	L4795	H36/28R	7/63	London Transport RM1641	Biddell, Woodford Bridge
										(operates as Imperial Bus, Romford (LN))
	654 DYE	AEC	Routemaster	RM1654	Park Royal	L4546	H36/28R	7/63	London Transport RM1654	Shaftesbury & District, Shaftesbury (DT)
	666 DYE	→ see KGJ 341A								
	691 DYE	AEC	Routemaster	RM1691	Park Royal	L4207	H36/28R	10/63	London Transport RM1691	London Bus Company, Northfleet (KT)
			(ex WTS 87A, 691 DYE)							
	699 DYE	AEC	Routemaster	RM1699	Park Royal	L4314	H36/28R	10/63	London Transport RM1699	Wood & McQueen, Hertford
	737 DYE	AEC	Routemaster	RM1737	Park Royal	L5050	H36/28R	11/63	London Transport RM1737	London Transport Museum
	772 DYE	AEC	Routemaster	RM1797	Park Royal	L5086	H36/28R	12/63	London Transport RM1797	Duker, Little Paxton
			(ex DGW 130B, 797 DYE)							
	783 DYE	AEC	Routemaster	RM1783	Park Royal	L4948	O36/26R	12/63	London Transport RM1783	Western Greyhound, Summercourt (CO)
	791 DYE	AEC	Routemaster	RM1791	Park Royal	L4979	H--/--R	1/64	London Transport RM1791	-?-, -?-
	797 DYE	→ see 772 DYE								
	804 DYE	AEC	Routemaster	RM1804	Park Royal	L5001	H36/28R	1/64	London Transport RM1804	Smith & Watson, Billericay
			(ex EYY 327B, 804 DYE)							
	822 DYE	→ see OWJ 112								
	840 DYE	AEC	Routemaster	RM1840	Park Royal	L5028	H36/28R	2/64	London Transport RM1840	Bruce et al, Haddenham (BK)
	859 DYE	AEC	Routemaster	RM1859	Park Royal	L5150	H36/28R	3/64	London Transport RM1859	Belcher, Caversham (BE)
	999 EAE	Leyland	Tiger Cub PSUC1/2	587857	Burlingham	6746	C41F	5/59	Munden, Bristol	Herefordshire Transport Collection
										(on loan from Munden, Bristol)
	651 EBD	Bristol	Lodekka FS6B	214124	ECW	13846	H33/27RD	2/64	United Counties 651	Rushden Historical Transport Society
(r)	444 EBE	AEC	Reliance	2MU3RA4648	Plaxton	632666	C41F	5/63	Johnson, Claxby	-?-, -?-
	8 EBF	→ see DFH 480A								
	85 EBK	→ see KMN 504 *Isle of Man*								
	504 EBL	Bedford	VAL14	1059	Duple	1158/44	C52F	6/63	Reliance, Newbury 87	Science Museum, Wroughton
	181 ECV	Bedford	SB1	69981	Duple	1105/440	C41F	6/59	Jennings, Bude	Greet, Broadhempston
	336 EDV	Bristol	SUL4A	157019	ECW	12065	DP33F	5/61	Western National 402	Partridge, Exeter
	338 EDV	Bristol	SUL4A	157025	ECW	12028	B36F	10/60	Western National 624	Cainey, Thornbury (GL)
	484 EFJ	Leyland	Titan PD2A/30	620425	Massey	2467	H31/26R	4/62	Exeter 84	Shorland, Exeter
	570 EFJ	AEC	Reliance	2MU4RA4277	Harrington	2634	C40F	5/62	Greenslades Tours	Tresham, Leighton Buzzard
	782 EFM	Bristol	SC4LK	141008	ECW	9710	B35F	12/57	Crosville SC12	Roberts, Sheffield
	783 EFM	Bristol	SC4LK	141013	ECW	9711	B35F	12/57	Crosville SC13	Burkinshaw, Retford
(r)	397 EFW	AEC	Reliance	6U2R33994	Plaxton	7712ACM020	C57F	3/77	Howlett, Quorn	-?-, -?-
			(ex RJU 406R)							
	969 EHW	Bristol	Lodekka LD6G	150188	ECW	10887	H33/25RD	7/59	Bath Tramways L8515	Walker & Peters, Wells
	972 EHW	Bristol	Lodekka LD6B	150192	ECW	11408	H33/25R	7/59	Bristol LC8518	Walker, Wells
	981 EHY	Bristol	MW5G	152037	ECW	11104	B45F	8/59	Bristol 2969	Walker, Wells
	990 EHY	Bristol	MW5G	152113	ECW	11113	B45F	11/59	Bath Tramways 2978	Walker, Wells
	76 EMP	Bedford	SBG	37465	Plaxton	2655	C38F	-/55	PTS, Maida Vale	Price, Shobdon
	462 EOT	Dennis	Loline III	1100L3AF1A1	Alexander	6726	H39/29F	12/62	Aldershot & District 462	Aldershot & District Omnibuses Rescue & Restoration Society
	600 ERA	→ see CSL 469								
	264 ERY	Leyland	Titan PD3A/1	622661	Park Royal	B49004	O41/33R	1/63	Leicester 264	Leicester Transport Heritage Trust
	399 ETB	Bedford	SB3	60893	Duple	1090/247	C41F	4/58	Robinson, Great Harwood	Coastal & Country, Whitby (NY)
	859 ETW	Bristol	LS5G	111037	ECW	8149	B45F	1/56	Eastern National 417	Salmon, South Benfleet
	766 EVT	Leyland	Atlantean PDR1/1	590628	Weymann	M9046	L39/34F	8/59	Potteries L9766	Potteries Omnibus Preservation Society

	805 EVT	AEC	Reliance	2MU3RV2665	Weymann	M9234	B41F	5/60	Potteries SL805	Quantock, Bishops Lydeard (SO)
	558 FBF	Bedford	SB3	88850	Duple	1145/80	C—F	7/62	Happy Times, Wednesfield	private owner, Essex
	370 FCR	AEC	Regent V	2D3RA1408	East Lancs	6021	H37/29R	11/63	Southampton 350	Turner et al, Southampton
	373 FCR	AEC	Regent V	2D3RA1411	East Lancs	6020	H37/29R	11/63	Southampton 353	Blair, Upham
	154 FCY	AEC	Regent V	2D3RA1259	Willowbrook	CF471	H39/32F	7/63	South Wales 586	Hier, Swansea
	746 FEW	Bedford	SB5	90756	Yeates	999	C44F	12/62	Whippet, Hilton	Whippet, Swavesey (CM)
	380 FGB	Bedford	VAS1	1279	Duple Northern	132/5	B29F	6/63	MacBrayne 93	MacBrayne Circle, Inverness
			(ex YTS 540A, 846 HUS)							
	773 FHA	BMMO	D9	4773	BMMO		H40/32RD	1/59	BMMO 4773	Kimberley, Brierley Hill
	519 FHN	Bristol	MW5G	139091	ECW	9834	B45F	3/59	United BU519	Mills & Thorogood, Bournemouth
	529 FJJ	Ford	570E	L8OB830982	Strachan	52056	FH33/0F	11/63	London Transport TT4	Daniels, Essex
	410 FKL	AEC	Reliance	2MU3RV2524	Harrington	2114	C41F	7/59	Maidstone & District CO410	Gibbons, Maidstone
	417 FKL	AEC	Reliance	2MU3RV2531	Harrington	2121	C--F	8/59	Maidstone & District CO417	-?-, -?-
	419 FKL	AEC	Reliance	2MU3RV2533	Harrington	2123	C41F	8/59	Maidstone & District CO419	Valentine, York
	851 FNN	AEC	Regent V	2D3RA915	Northern Counties	5483	FL37/33F	10/60	Barton 851	Quantock, Bishops Lydeard (SO)
	854 FNN	→ see AAL 522A								
	564 FTF	Leyland	Titan PD3/4	581727	Metro-Cammell		H41/32RD	9/58	Lancashire United 647	Bradshaw, Skelmersdale
	466 FTJ	Leyland	Tiger Cub PSUC1/5	584768	East Lancs	5498	B43F	9/58	Rawtenstall 58	East Lancs Transport Preservation Group
	466 FTT	Bristol	Lodekka FLF6G	169049	ECW	11750	H??/??F	6/61	Southern National 1978	Halliday, Shipley
	468 FTT	Bristol	Lodekka FLF6G	169015	ECW	11752	H38/30F	12/60	Western National 1969	Billington, Maidenhead
	804 FUF	Albion	Victor FT39AN	73737C	Reading	3220	B35F	6/54	JMT 10	Payne, Great Sampford
			(ex JPF 869N, J 15213)							
(r)	842 FUF	Albion	Victor FT39KAN	73779D	Heaver	2465	B--F	4/55	Guernsey Motors 66	Greet, Broadhempston
			(ex 6768)							
	898 FUF	Albion	Victor FT39AN	73737B	Reading	5176	B36F	6/54	Watson, St Martins	Greet, Broadhempston
			(ex 1787, 898 FUF, 1787)							
	650 FYO	Bedford	VAS2	1400	Duple Northern	132/16	B27F	10/63	Metropolitan Police	Jones, Doncaster
	103 GAA	Bedford	SB5	90678	Plaxton	632202	C41F	1/63	Barfoot, West End	Collins, Wilmington
	86 GFJ	Leyland	Titan PD2A/30	L00491	Massey	2527	H31/26R	5/63	Exeter 86	West Country Historic Omnibus & Transport Trust
	477 GFR	AEC	Reliance	2U3RA5204	Harrington	2900	C51F	2/64	Abbott, Blackpool	Kidswheels, Liverpool (XMY)
	487 GFR	AEC	Reliance	2U3RA5205	Harrington	2901	C45F	2/64	Abbott, Blackpool	Webster, Lower Southrepps
	780 GHA	BMMO	C5	4780	BMMO		C37F	3/59	BMMO 4780	Burdett, Corley
	304 GHN	Bristol	LS6B *(now LS6G)*	119204	ECW	10659	C39F	6/58	United BUC4	Aycliffe & District Bus Preservation Society
	8 GMK	Beadle-Commer		JCB705	Beadle		C41C	3/56	Valliant, Ealing	Hunt, Rookley
	123 GMO	International Harvester	?	3478	?		B??	12/09	-?-, USA	Passey, Newbury
	925 GTA	→ see MSJ 499								
	927 GTA	→ see 724 XUW								
	928 GTA	Leyland	Atlantean PDR1/1	602664	Metro-Cammell	HO52698/4	CO44/31F	5/61	Devon General DL928	Bennett, Sherborne
			(ex AFE 387A, 928 GTA)							
	931 GTA	Leyland	Atlantean PDR1/1	602728	Metro-Cammell	HO52698/7	O44/31F	6/61	Devon General DL931	Hulme, Yatton *(operates as Rubicon Classic, Bristol (GL))*
			(ex NAT 747A, 931 GTA)							
	932 GTA	Leyland	Atlantean PDR1/1	602729	Metro-Cammell	HO52698/8	O44/31F	6/61	Devon General DL932	Follwell, Stableford
	935 GTA	AEC	Reliance	2MU3RV3091	Willowbrook	60670	C41F	6/61	Devon General TCR935	Wright, Egmanton
	55 GUO	→ see JVS 293								
	56 GUO	Bristol	MW6G	184046	ECW	12240	C39F	6/61	Western National 2267	Burdett, Corley
	57 GUO	Bristol	MW6G	184074	ECW	12241	C39F	6/61	Western National 2268	Ellis, Cambridge (Gloucs)

	Reg	Make	Model	Chassis No	Body	Body No	Layout	New	First owner	Current owner
	63 GUO	Bristol	MW6G	184061	ECW	12211	DP41F	6/61	Western National 2921	Bissett, Westbury
	375 GWN	Bristol	RELH6G	212027	ECW	13739	C47F	1/64	United Welsh 18	South Wales Transport Preservation Trust
	107 GYC	Bedford	SB3	75174	Duple	1120/206	C41F	3/60	Bowerman, Taunton	Chambers, Bristol
	108 GYC	Bedford	SB3	75170	Duple	1120/207	C41F	3/60	Bowerman, Taunton	Redwoods Travel, Hemyock (DN)
	600 GYC	Karrier	BF3023	98A5742	Reading	8065	C14F	5/60	Safeway, South Petherton	Falkner, Church Hanborough
	643 HAA	Bedford	J2SZ10	168967	Plaxton	632475	C16F	5/63	Cooke, Stoughton 10	Dealtop, Plymouth (DN)
	644 HAA	Bedford	J2SZ10	168974	Plaxton	632476	C18F	6/63	Cooke, Stoughton 18	Wilkinson, Kettlewell (NY)
	861 HAL	Dennis	Loline II	101YF11	Northern Counties	5556	FL37/31F	4/61	Barton 861	Barton Cherished Vehicle Collection
	866 HAL	AEC	Reliance	2MU3RV3059	Plaxton	602322	C41F	2/61	Barton 866	Powell, Clifton
	90 HBC	Leyland	Titan PD3A/1	L02941	East Lancs	6046	H41/33R	2/64	Leicester 90	Gill, Rugeley
	104 HBU	Leyland	Titan PD3/5	L20238	Roe	GO5851	H41/32F	5/64	Oldham 104	Pryce, Rochdale
	423 HCY	AEC	Regent V	2D3RA1562	Weymann	M1467	H39/32F	10/64	South Wales 590	West, Swansea
	431 HCY	AEC	Regent V	2D3RA1573	Park Royal	B50645	H39/32F	5/64	South Wales 598	South Wales Transport Preservation Trust
	475 HDT	→ see OWJ 353A								
	476 HDT	→ see OWJ 354A								
	286 HFM	Bristol	Lodekka LD6G	138182	ECW	10224	PO33/27RD	11/58	Crosville DLG950	Plevin & Foster, Neston
	627 HFM	Bristol	Lodekka LD6B *Now LD6G)*	150068	ECW	10260	CO33/27RD	7/59	Crosville DLB978	Hamer & Morriss, Ravenstonedale (CA)
	819 HHA	BMMO	C5	4819	BMMO		C37F	-/59	BMMO 4819	Parry, Bearwood
	551 HHW	Bedford	SB3	73484	Duple	1120/172	C41F	4/60	Feltham, Bristol	Gretton, Peterborough (CM)
	247 HKX	Trojan	20	1009009	Trojan		B8F	5/59	non-PSV	Evans, Maes-y-Cwmmer
	278 HLC	→ see 535 XPJ								
	591 HNM	Bedford	CFL	KY603520	Plaxton	80C027CF	C17F	10/82	Herbert, Shefford	Golynia & Warnack, Long Melford (SK)
			(first licensed 1/85)							
(r)	201 HOU	Bedford	VAS1	1411	Plaxton	632677	C24F	7/63	Cooke, Stoughton 7	West of England Transport Collection
	387 HRR	Leyland	Leopard L1	610017	Willowbrook	60636	B45F	5/61	East Midland R387	Mason, Edinburgh
(q)	606 HTC	Bedford	SB3	66765	Plaxton	582383	C35F	2/59	Rothwell, Heywood	Greet, Broadhempston
	960 HTT	AEC	Reliance	2MU3RV3934	Willowbrook	61764	C41F	5/62	Devon General TCR960	Wren, Beddau
(r)	224 HUM	Bedford	VAL14	1285	Plaxton	632862	C49F	3/64	Wallace Arnold Tours	Johnson, Worksop (NG)
	743 HUP	Trojan	19	1509555	Trojan		B13F	5/60	Village Lane Garage, Washington	Scott, Stanley (DM)
	780 HUP	AEC	Reliance	2MU3RV3136	Park Royal	B44699	B--F	9/60	Venture 215	Gamblin, Durham
	846 HUS	→ see 380 FGB								
	800 HYD	Bedford	SB3	80549	Duple	1120/541	C41F	7/60	Bryant & Clarke, Williton	Owen, Knighton (CW)
	566 JFM	Bristol	SC4LK	147006	ECW	10489	B35F	2/59	Crosville SSG626	Chelveston Preservation Society
	780 JGY	Leyland	Titan PD2/31	590188	Reading	5116	H31/28R	6/59	JMT 27	Birks, Eastbourne
			(ex J 8588)							
	929 JHN	→ see XYJ 717								
	536 JHU	Bristol	MW5G	164189	ECW	11805	B45F	3/61	Bristol 2514	Cole, Bristol
	528 JKC	→ see KMN 519 *Isle of Man*								
	630 JNY	Leyland	Tiger Cub PSUC1/2	606204	Burlingham	7063	DP41F	1/61	John, Coity	Humphries, Datchet
	604 JPU	Bristol	SC4LK	113097	ECW	8974	B35F	6/57	Eastern National 427	Brown, Worthen
	120 JRB	Daimler	Freeline D650HS	25709	Burlingham	6753	C37F	6/59	Blue Bus, Willington DR18	Boden, Harlaston
	116 JTD	Guy	Arab IV	FD74272	Northern Counties	5369	H41/32R	5/59	Lancashire United 21	Wallwork, Bolton
	122 JTD	Guy	Arab IV	FD74305	Northern Counties	5375	H41/32R	8/59	Lancashire United 27	Museum of Transport, Manchester
	765 JTU	Bedford	SB1	77852	Plaxton	592709	C41F	2/60	Bostock, Congleton	Duffy, Macclesfield

	Reg	Make	Model	Chassis No	Body	Body No	Layout	Date	New to	Owner
	952 JUB	AEC	Regent V	2D2RA1579	Roe	GO5902	H39/31R	7/64	Leeds 952	Milner & Lintoff, Lincoln
	221 JVK	Leyland	Atlantean PDR1/1	612126	Alexander	6738	H44/34F	1/62	Newcastle 221	Slater, Wideopen
	401 JVO	Morris	JB	-?-	?		B7F	4/61	ice cream van	Graham, Leicester
	388 KDT	Leyland	Titan PD2/40	LO2173	Roe	GO4071	H34/28R	10/63	Doncaster 188	South Yorkshire Transport Museum (SY)
					(new with 9/55 body)					
	815 KDV	Bristol	Lodekka FLF6B	208023	ECW	13253	H38/30F	1/63	Western National 2010	Hoare, Chepstow (CS)
	824 KDV	Bristol	Lodekka FLF6G	210064	ECW	13262	H38/30F	5/63	Western National 2019	Stevens, Sheffield
	304 KFC	Dennis	Loline II	104YF7	East Lancs	5713	H35/28F	6/61	City of Oxford 304	Oxford Bus Museum Trust
	305 KFC	Dennis	Loline II	105YF7	East Lancs	5714	H35/28F	6/61	City of Oxford 305	Oxford Bus Museum Trust
					(sectioned for display)					
	756 KFC	AEC	Reliance	2MU3RV3107	Park Royal	B45184	B44F	10/60	City of Oxford 756	Tidbury, Kidlington
	871 KHA	BMMO	D9	4871	BMMO	BB4864	H40/32RD	7/60	BMMO 4871	BaMMOT, Wythall
	943 KHA	BMMO	D10	4943	BMMO		H43/35F	1/61	BMMO 4943	BaMMOT, Wythall
	569 KKK	AEC	Reliance	2MU3RA2894	Duple	1122/12	C41C	5/60	Ayers, Dover	Dover Transport Museum Society
(r)	246 KOT	Bedford	VAL14	1310	Duple	1172/23	C52F	3/64	Budden, Romsey	Webb, Armscote (WK)
	488 KOT	Dennis	Loline III	1121L3AF1A1	Weymann	M1361	H39/29F	12/64	Aldershot & District 488	Aldershot & District Omnibus Rescue & Restoration Society
	436 KOV	Daimler	Fleetline CRG6LX	60885	Park Royal	B49195	H43/33F	9/64	Birmingham 3436	Birmingham City Transport Society
	618 KRA	Bedford	SB1	70056	Yeates	749	C41F	5/59	Frost, Stanley	Fowler, Holbeach Drove (LI)
	253 KTA	Bristol	MW6G	184213	ECW	12850	C39F	4/62	Western National 2270	White, Gaydon
	270 KTA	Bristol	SUL4A	190033	ECW	12884	B37F	7/62	Western National 420	Sheppard, Plymouth
	271 KTA	Bristol	SUL4A	190036	ECW	12885	C33F	7/62	Western National 421	Helliker, Stroud
			(ex 10558, 31918, 271 KTA)							
	274 KTA	Bristol	SUL4A	190041	ECW	12888	DP33F	7/62	Western National 424	Tormey, Gosport
	275 KTA	Bristol	SUL4A	190042	ECW	12889	C33F	7/62	Western National 425	Sheppard, Ruscombe
	280 KTA	Bristol	SUL4A	190047	ECW	12894	DP33F	7/62	Western National 430	Webb, Bedford
			(ex 31920, 280 KTA)							
	286 KTA	Bristol	SUL4A	190037	ECW	12877	C37F	7/62	Southern National 434	Billington, Maidenhead
			(ex 31916, 286 KTA)							
	457 KTG	AEC	Regent V	2D3RA979	Metro-Cammell		H39/31F	6/61	Rhondda 457	Rhondda Heritage Park, Trehafod
	595 LCG	AEC	Renown	3B2RA083	Park Royal	B50636	H44/31F	6/64	King Alfred, Winchester	FoKAB, Winchester
	596 LCG	AEC	Renown	3B2RA084	Park Royal	B50637	H44/31F	6/64	King Alfred, Winchester	FoKAB, Winchester
	14 LFC	Morris-Commercial	FF	COA/1433/110984	Wadham		RC27F	3/61	Morris Motors Band	Oxford Bus Museum Trust
	404 LHT	→ see Q507 VHR								
	406 LHT	Bristol	MW6G	184050	ECW	12176	RV	5/61	Bristol W147	Mahoney I, Brentwood
			(ex VSV 444, 406 LHT)							
	407 LHT	Bristol	MW6G	184051	ECW	12177	RV	5/61	Bristol W144	Bissett, Westbury
	432 LKE	AEC	Reliance	2MU3RV3123	Harrington	2318	C41F	10/60	Maidstone & District CO432	Gibbons, Maidstone
	308 LKK	Albion	Nimbus NS3AN	82060B	Harrington	2349	B30F	11/60	Maidstone & District SO308	Clarke, Harpenden
	315 LKK	Albion	Nimbus NS3AN	82061B	Harrington	2356	B30F	11/60	Maidstone & District SO315	Yarnell, St Leonards
	558 LKP	Leyland	Atlantean PDR1/1	601504	Metro-Cammell	H052531/8	H44/33F	12/60	Maidstone & District DH558	Chatham Historic Dockyard Trust (KT)
	236 LNO	Bristol	Lodekka LDL6G	LDLX004	ECW	EX4	H37/33R	8/58	Eastern National 1541	Mara, Canvey
	225 LRB	Leyland	Titan PD2/30	591853	Weymann	M9173	H33/28R	1/60	Chesterfield 225	Chesterfield Borough Council

	433 MDT	Leyland	Tiger Cub PSUC1/11	626934	Roe	GO5744	B45F	10/63	Doncaster 33	Doncaster Omnibus & Light Railway Society
	434 MDT	→ see NWR 421A								
	759 MDV	Bristol	MW6G	204036	ECW	13665	C41F	4/63	Southern National 1410	Delaney, Wargrave
	766 MDV	Bristol	MW6G	204091	ECW	13672	C39F	5/63	Southern National 2278	Bodger, Portchester
(r)	991 MDV	AEC	Reliance	2MU3RV4424	Marshall	B3062	B41F	4/63	Devon General 991	Shears & Platt, Winkleigh
	312 MFC	AEC	Bridgemaster	2B3RA127	Park Royal	B45707	H43/29F	12/61	City of Oxford 312	Wareham, Kidlington
	217 MHK	Bristol	MW5G	152012	ECW	10403	DP41F	7/59	Eastern National 480	Miles, South Benfleet
	357 MHU	Bristol	MW5G	184151	ECW	12581	B45F	11/61	Bristol 2522	Everitt & Southam, Leicester
	802 MHW	Bristol	Lodekka FSF6G	179023	ECW	12285	H34/26F	10/61	Cheltenham District 6037	BaMMOT, Wythall (WO)
	601 MMA	→ see JSL 317								
	884 MMB	→ see NTU 946C								
	6 MPT	→ see ACU 304B								
	248 NEA	Daimler	CVG6-30DD	30216	Metro-Cammell		H41/33R	10/63	West Bromwich 248	BaMMOT, Wythall (WO)
	284 NHK	Bristol	MW6G	139254	ECW	11297	C41F	4/59	Eastern National 485	Williams, Bournemouth
	866 NHT	→ see XSL 228A								
	868 NHT	Bristol	Lodekka FS6G	178003	ECW	12288	CO33/27R	11/61	Bristol 8578	Smith, Newport
	869 NHT	Bristol	Lodekka FS6G (ex FAS 962, 869 NHT)	178004	ECW	12289	CO33/27R	11/61	Bristol 8579	Walker & Curtis, Wells
	324 NJO	AEC	Bridgemaster	2B3RA155	Park Royal	B48819	H40/25F	1/63	City of Oxford 324	Blackman L, Halifax
	334 NKT	AEC	Reliance	2MU3RV3824	Weymann	M26	B41F	9/61	Maidstone & District S334	Rother Valley RTS, Killamarsh
	340 NKT	AEC	Reliance	2MU3RV3830	Weymann	M5	B41F	8/61	Maidstone & District S340	Rother Valley RTS, Killamarsh
	136 NOU	Renault	TN4F	674-568	STCRP		B33R	-/35	RATP, Paris 3267	Jowitt, Niton
	918 NRT	AEC	Regent V	MD3RV593	Massey	2519	H--/--RD	1/63	Lowestoft 8	East Anglia Transport Museum
	80 NVO	Leyland	Titan PD3/4	620171	Northern Counties	5766	L33/32F	10/62	South Notts, Gotham 80	Nottingham Heritage Vehicles
	675 OCV	Bedford	SB3	88799	Duple	1145/55	C41F	8/62	Crimson, St. Ives	Wright, New Costessey
	904 OFM	Bristol	SC4LK	158016	ECW	12050	C33F	5/60	Crosville CSG655	Taylor, Bristol
	911 OFM	Bristol	SC4LK	158023	ECW	12057	C33F	6/60	Crosville CSG662	Wilson, Preston
	507 OHU	Bristol	Lodekka FLF6B	199127	ECW	13077	H38/32F	9/62	Bristol 7062	Staniforth, Stroud
	511 OHU	→ see LAS 948								
	192 OTB	Leyland	Titan PD2/40	600663	East Lancs	5647	H31/28R	6/60	Haslingden 14	Duffy, Macclesfield
	302 PFM	→ see TYJ 424								
	314 PFM	Bristol	Lodekka FS6G	166006	ECW	11582	H33/27RD	9/60	Crosville DFG33	Carters, Wherstead (SK)
	319 PFM	→ see AFM 402A								
	14 PKR	Karrier	BFD3023	D98A8306	Plaxton	612509	C14F	7/61	Davis, Sevenoaks	Golcar Transport Museum, Huddersfield
	510 PML	Bedford	SB3	60952	Plaxton	2218	C41F	3/58	Universal, Edmonton	Holt, Halifax
	751 PMU	Bedford	CAV	108192	Martin Walter	-?-	M10	9/58		Harris, Surrey
	999 PPL	Bedford	J4LZ3	58033	Plaxton	602020	C29F	6/60	Comfy, Farnham	Gudge, Farnham
	862 RAE	Bristol	SUS4A	190050	ECW	13480	B30F	11/62	Bristol 301	Ellis, Cambridge (Gloucs)
	931 RAE	Bristol	MW6G	213029	ECW	13325	B45F	7/63	Bristol 2572	Parton, Crewe
	706 RDH	Bedford	SB8	89053	Duple	1145/185	C41F	1/62	Central, Walsall	Adkins, Upper Boddington
	1 RDV	AEC	Reliance	2MU3RA4971	Harrington	2850	C41F	4/64	Devon General 1	Platt, Dawlish Warren
(r)	2 RDV	AEC	Reliance	2MU3RA4972	Harrington	2851	C41F	4/64	Devon General 2	Greet, Broadhempston

	4 RDV	AEC	Reliance	2MU3RA4974	Harrington	2853	C40F	4/64	Devon General 4	Greet, Broadhempston
			(ex TSV 850, 4 RDV)							
	7 RDV	AEC	Reliance	2MU3RA4977	Harrington	2856	C41F	4/64	Devon General 7	Warren, Martock
	9 RDV	AEC	Reliance	2U3RA4967	Marshall	B3249	B49F	6/64	Devon General 9	Platt, Dawlish Warren
	332 RJO	AEC	Renown	3B3RA050	Park Royal	B49774	H38/27F	12/63	City of Oxford 332	Wrist, Abingdon
	572 RKJ	→ see XKO 72A								
	699 RPA	AEC	Reliance	2MU3RA3074	Harrington	2302	C41F	7/60	Surrey, Sutton 43	Hurley & Belton, Worthing
	534 RTB	Guy	Arab IV	FD74544	Metro-Cammell		H41/32R	1/61	Lancashire United 43	-?-, -?-
	562 RTF	Leyland	Titan PD2/40	602768	East Lancs	5706	H35/28R	1/61	Widnes 31	North West Museum of Transport
	503 RUO	AEC	Regent V	2D3RA1465	Willowbrook	CF642	H39/30F	4/64	Devon General 503	Platt, Dawlish Warren
	507 RUO	AEC	Regent V	2D3RA1469	Willowbrook	CF646	O36/22FT	4/64	Devon General 507	Hoare, Chepstow (CS)
	966 RVO	Bedford	VAL14	1115	Yeates	0013	C50D	7/63	Barton 966	Fowler, Holbeach Drove (LI)
	900 SAF	AEC	Reliance	2U3RA4315	Harrington	2806	C47F	5/63	Hawkey, Newquay	Graves & Godlement, Sevenoaks
	482 SBJ	Commer	Avenger IV	94A0583	Plaxton	632690	C41F	9/63	Simonds, Botesdale	Simonds, Diss (NK)
	839 SEV	Leyland	National 1151/2R/0403	00263	Leyland National		B5F	12/72	Bristol C1403	Stanton & Brown, Gloucester
			(ex JHU 844L)							
	241 SFM	Bristol	SC4LK	172010	ECW	11985	B35F	1/61	Crosville SSG668	Carter, Wherstead
	256 SFM	Bristol	Lodekka FLF6B	169022	ECW	11710	H38/32F	3/61	Crosville DFB43	Merseyside Transport Trust
	841 SHW	Bristol	Lodekka FLF6B	224008	ECW	13920	O38/32F	8/64	Bristol 7900	Hoare, Chepstow (CS)
	519 SLG	Bedford	SB3	88247	Plaxton	612704	C41F	4/61	Thornley, Woodley	Cook, Wroxall
	837 SUO	Bristol	RELH6G	212061	ECW	14496	C45F	5/64	Western National 2351	Graham, Runcorn
			(ex ARU 99A, 837 SUO)							
	82 SVO	Albion	Lowlander LR3	62112F	Northern Counties	5868	H41/30F	9/63	South Notts, Gotham 82	Rimmer, Market Harborough
	213 SYB	Bedford	J1	-?-	-?-		B--F	1/63	-?-, -?-	Ball, Suffolk
(r)	345 TJO	AEC	Renown	3B3RA091	Park Royal	B50633	H--/--F	11/64	City of Oxford 345	Wareham, Kidlington
	25 TKR	AEC	Reliance	2MU3RV4412	Harrington	2657	C41F	10/62	Maidstone & District C25	Dennison, Bacup
	28 TKR	AEC	Reliance	2MU3RV4415	Harrington	2660	C37F	9/62	Maidstone & District C28	Pack, Crayford
	116 TMD	AEC	Bridgemaster	B3RA006	Park Royal	B41885	H45/31R	12/58	Liverpool E3	O'Brien, Liverpool
	597 UKM	Leyland	Atlantean PDR1/1	622369	Weymann	M540	H44/33F	4/63	Maidstone & District DH597	Brown, Wateringbury
	105 UTU	Leyland	Titan PD2/37	613076	Northern Counties	5650	H36/28F	3/62	SHMD 5	Lomax & Kenworthy, Tameside
	910 UVT	Leyland	Atlantean PDR1/1	620650	Weymann	M263	L--/--F	10/62	Potteries L910	Smith, Meir & Brundrit, Stafford
	951 UVT	Bedford	SB5	89325	Yeates	953	DP45F	3/62	Beckett, Bucknall	Smith, Meir & Brundrit, Stafford
	573 UVX	Bristol	MW5G	184057	ECW	12199	C39F	6/61	Eastern National 350	Bluestone National Park Resort, Narberth
	789 UXA	AEC	Routemaster	RM541	Park Royal	L3869	H36/28R	10/60	London Transport RM541	Heaps, Bradford
			(ex WLT 541)							
	791 UXA	AEC	Routemaster	RM436	Park Royal	L3634	H36/28R	8/60	London Transport RM436	Clifford, Tunbridge Wells
			(ex WLT 436)							
	798 UXA	AEC	Routemaster	RM1168	Park Royal	L4279	H36/28R	3/62	London Transport RM1168	Midland Classic, Burton-upon-Trent (ST)
			(e 168 CLT)							
	799 UXA	AEC	Routemaster	RM1305	Park Royal	L4413	H36/28R	9/62	London Transport RM1305	Mason, Bristol
			(ex 305 CLT)							
	839 UXC	AEC	Routemaster	RM997	Park Royal	L3763	H36/28R	10/61	London Transport RM997	Jeff, Hayes
			(ex WLT 997)							
	852 UXC	AEC	Routemaster	RM1324	Park Royal	L4500	H36/28R	10/62	London Transport RM1324	Cooper, Worthing
			(ex 324 CLT, VYJ 807, 324 CLT)							

	Reg	Make	Model	Chassis	Body	Body no	Layout	Date	New to	Owner
	853 UXC	AEC	Routemaster	RM719	Park Royal	L4070	H36/28R	3/61	London Transport RM719	Redman, Nantwich
			(ex WLT 719)							
	854 UXC	→ see WLT 531								
	859 UXC	→ see VLT 275								
	860 UXC	AEC	Routemaster	RM664	Park Royal	L4491	H36/28R	6/61	London Transport RM664	-?-, -?-
			(ex WLT 664)							
	201 UXJ	AEC	Routemaster	RM1097	Park Royal	L4136	H36/28R	1/62	London Transport RM1097	Unsworth, Culceth
			(ex 97 CLT)							
	202 UXJ	AEC	Routemaster	RML887	Park Royal	L4135	H40/32R	9/61	London Transport RML887	Oliver, Eastbourne
			(ex WLT 887)							*operated by Totally Transport, Blackpool (LA))*
	204 UXJ	AEC	Routemaster	RM1058	Park Royal	L3875	H36/28R	12/61	London Transport RM1058	Kell, Durham
			(ex 58 CLT)							
	205 UXJ	AEC	Routemaster	RM687	Park Royal	L4014	H36/28R	2/61	London Transport RM687	Wells, Nottingham
			(ex WLT 687)							
	215 UXJ	AEC	Routemaster	RML899	Park Royal	L4250	H40/32R	12/61	London Transport RML899	London Bus Company, Northfleet (KT)
			(ex WLT 899)							
	210 UXO	Albion	Nimbus NS3N	82052F	Reading	7116	B36F	6/60	Watson, St Martins	Tidley, Wick
			(ex 31235, 1309)							
	252 UXO	AEC	Routemaster	RML895	Park Royal	L4185	H40/32R	11/61	London Transport RML895	Corcoran & Mercer, Bristol
			(ex WLT 895)							
	253 UXO	AEC	Routemaster	RML892	Park Royal	L4225	H40/32R	10/61	London Transport RML892	Mann, London
			(ex WLT 892)							
	254 UXO	AEC	Routemaster	RML897	Park Royal	L4240	H40/32R	11/61	London Transport RML897	London Bus Company, Northfleet (KT)
			(ex WLT 897)							
	696 UXO	Bedford	SB3	60169	Duple	1090/145	C41F	1/58	Shadwell, Warrington	Thornes, Hemingbrough (NY)
			(ex SED 232)							
	878 UXO	Bedford	SBG	36179	Duple	1055/206	C36F	3/55	Bowyer, Northwich	Sullivan & Dawson, Consett
			(ex UMB 2)							
	448 UXS	AEC	Routemaster	RM848	Park Royal	L4123	H36/28R	6/61	London Transport RM848	Paskell, Hazlemere (BK)
			(ex WLT 848)							
(q)	870 VAR	Bedford	SB3	93623	Plaxton	632906	C41F	1/64	Don, Bishops Stortford	Greet, Broadhempston
	875 VFM	Bristol	Lodekka FSF6G	179042	ECW	12312	H34/26F	1/62	Crosville DFG65	O'Brien & Channerley, Liverpool
	882 VFM	Bristol	Lodekka FSF6G	179061	ECW	12319	O34/26F	4/62	Crosville DFG72	Lloyd-Williams, Fyfield
	891 VFM	Bristol	Lodekka FSF6G	197025	ECW	12330	O34/26F	6/62	Crosville DFG81	Pratt {Crosville}, Weston super Mare (SO)
	304 VHN	Daimler	CCG5DD	20064	Roe	GO5857	H33/28R	3/64	Darlington 4	Wilfreda-Beehive, Adwick-le-Street (SY)
	100 VRL	AEC	Reliance	2MU4RA5466	Harrington	2970	C43F	5/64	Hawkey, Newquay	Thomas R, St Austell
	824 VTD	Bedford	J4LZ2	111620	Plaxton	612735	C29F	7/61	UKAEA, Salwick	Heaton, Abram
	553 VVW	Trojan	19	1509810	Trojan	7894	C13F	4/61	Super, Upminster	Trojan Museum Trust, Fyfield
	969 VVX	Austin	566A	128403	Marshall	MMO237	B33F	4/61	Barking Borough Council	Clarke, Hinckley
	415 VYA	Leyland	Tiger TRCTL11/3RH	8700006	Alexander	31TC/2886/1	C55F	7/87	Strathtay ST18	McCombie, Monifieth
			(ex D718 FES)							
	946 WAE	Bedford	SB5	94421	Farrar		O18/16RO	4/64	London General (replica)	Chester Heritage, Saltney (CN)
					(rebodied 6/90 as replica of 1910 AEC B / LGOC)					
	504 WLG	Leyland	Royal Tiger PSU1/15	511072LG	Plaxton	622161	C45F	11/51	Florence, Morecambe	Kidswheels, Liverpool (XMY)
			(ex JP 9379)		*(rebodied 8/62)*					
	998 WNN	Bedford	VAS1	1523	Plaxton	632974	C33F	4/64	Smith, Beeston	Shaw & Duffelen, Maxey (CM)

	373 WPU	Guy	Arab IV	FD74911	Massey	2431	L34/33R	5/61	Moore, Kelvedon	Brown, Basildon
	84 WRR	Albion	Lowlander LR3	62124F	Northern Counties	6092	H41/30F	5/64	South Notts, Gotham 84	Hutt, Loughborough
	618 WTE	AEC	Reliance	2MU3RV3905	Plaxton	612853	DP41F	2/62	Lancashire United 94	Duffy, Macclesfield
	815 XFM	Bristol	MW6G	195040	ECW	12795	C39F	7/62	Crosville CMG434	Mobbs, Corby
	941 XMT	Morris	JB	JB/MR46043	Wadham		B7	-/60	non-PSV	Wilton, Crowborough
	535 XPJ	AEC	Reliance	2U3RA5316	Duple Northern	152/4	C39F	4/64	Global, London	Forsyth, Braidwood
			(ex SKH 201B, 278 HLC)							
	839 XUJ	Leyland	Tiger PS1	500332	Guernseybus		DP31F	5/51	Guernseybus 17	Ensign, Purfleet (EX)
			(ex OAS 624, 28231, 9439, J5660) *(rebodied -/92)*							
	840 XUJ	Leyland	Tiger PS1	500330	Guersneytbus		OB34F	5/51	Guernseybus 16	Ensign, Purfleet (EX)
			(ex YSL 334, 12523, 2493, J5567) *(rebodied -/89)*							
	344 XUK	AEC	Reliance	MU3RV188	Roe	GO3957	C41C	9/54	Roe demonstrator	Mulpeter, Seaford
			(ex TUG 20)							
	819 XUP	→ see VHK 177L								
	522 XUT	Ford	ET7	7272665	Barbara		B37F	5/53	Malta route bus	Ramsay, Glasgow
			(ex DBY 001, DBY 333, Y-0333, Y-1034, A-0711, 711, 674 - *all Maltese registrations*)							
	724 XUW	Leyland	Atlantean PDR1/1	602644	Metro-Cammell	H052698/3	O44/31F	6/61	Devon General DL927	Anderson, London
			(ex ABV 669A, 927 GTA)							
	831 XUW	Guy	Arab III	FD33315	Guy		B33R	-/49	Accrington 10	Blackman, Halifax (WY)
			(ex KTC 615)							
	830 XUX	Rolls Royce	25/30hp	GXM59	-?-		C10	c-/36	unknown	-?-, -?-
			(probably ex TW 6966)							
	26 YKO	Leyland	Titan PD2A/30	L01579	Massey	2555	H33/28R	10/63	Maidstone 26	Carr, Pluckley (KT)
	78 YKT	Daimer	Fleetline	60556	Northern Counties	5956	H44/33F	2/64	Maidstone & District DL78	Mee, Northfleet
	43 YPK	→ see 82-TN-266 *Ireland*								
(r)	696 YTD	Ford	570E	510E77169	Duple	1151/37	C--F	4/62	Silver Gray, Morecambe	Hunt, Halesowen
	976 YTD	Bristol	LHS6L	LHS-336	Plaxton	788BC029	C33F	9/78	Taylor, Meppershall 33	York Pullman, York (NY)
			(ex CNK 633T)							
	201 YTE	Leyland	Titan PD2/37	623778	East Lancs	5958	O37/28F	4/63	Lancaster 201	North West Museum of Transport
	202 YTE	Leyland	Titan PD2/37	623779	East Lancs	5959	O37/28F	4/63	Lancaster 202	East Yorkshire (EY) 202
	878 YTE	Commer	Avenger IV	94A0504	Plaxton	622130	C41F	5/62	Fairclough, Lostock	Slack, Matlock (DE)
	124 YTW	Volvo	B58-61	15955	Plaxton	8012VC111	C8F	8/80	Lancashire United 616	LUT Society
			(ex DEN 247W)							
	208 YVX	Bristol	MW5G	184184	ECW	12620	B45F	1/62	Eastern National 548	Bulmer, North Stainley (NY)
	AAL 522A	AEC	Regent V	2D3RA918	Northern Counties	5481	FL37/33F	10/60	Barton 854	Quantock, Bishops Lydeard (SO)
			(ex 854 FNN)							
	AAO 547A	→ see 109 DRM								
	AAO 771A	Leyland	Titan PD3/5	L00036	Metro-Cammell		FH41/31F	5/63	Ribble 1841	Reilly, Bootle
			(ex TCK 841)							
	AAX 305A	Leyland	Tiger TRCTL11/3R	8300138	Duple	435/5618	C46FT	4/84	National Welsh XC1256	Cardiff Transport Preservation Group
			(ex A256 VWO)							
	ABD 812A	→ see PSL 234								
	ABV 33A	Leyland	Titan PD2/12	562584	Metro-Cammell		H--/--RD	2/57	Trent 1012	Ellery, Cellardyke
			(ex KCH 112)							
	ABV 669A	→ see 724 XUW								

	ABV 784A	Leyland	Titan PD2/13	550784	Metro-Cammell		H33/28RD	9/55	Ribble 1392	Dodd, Dromara
			(ex 927 GTA, TRN 597A, HRN 32)							
	ACA 603A	Bristol	Lodekka LD6G	108150	ECW	7934	H--/--R	5/56	Crosville MG792	Edwards & Tilley, Woking
			(ex XFM 203)							
	ADV 854A	Leyland	Titan PD2/12	532065	Leyland		H30/26R	11/53	Plymouth 397	Quantock, Bishops Lydeard (SO)
			(ex HJY 297)							
(r)	AEF 366A	Leyland	Leopard PSU3B/4R	7200758	Plaxton	729593	C51F	9/72	Cottrell, Mitcheldean	Heslop, Hexham
			(ex EAD 861L)							
	AFM 402A	Bristol	Lodekka FS6G	166079	ECW	11587	H33/27RD	7/61	Crosville DFG38	Richards, Greasby
			(ex 319 PFM)							
	AHP 921A	Ford	570E	510E61269	Duple	1139/201	C—F	-/61	Horncastle, Deal	Hunt, Halesowen
	AJH 163A	AEC	Reliance	4MU3RA4528	Plaxton	632581	C51F	4/63	Chiltern Queens, Woodcote	Greet,, Broadhempston
			(ex XBW 242)							
	AJH 241A	AEC	Reliance	4MU3RA4261	Plaxton	622083	C51F	6/62	Chiltern Queens, Woodcote	Broadhurst, Staines
			(ex VBW 581)							
	AJM 26A	→ see WX 2658								
	AKG 219A	Leyland	Leopard L1	611692	Weymann	M9738	B44F	12/61	Portsmouth 132	Winter, Darton
			(ex YBK 132)							
	AKG 307A	Bristol	Lodekka FL6G	168025	ECW	11015	H37/33RD	10/60	Red & White L2060	Brundrit, Cotes Heath
			(ex AKG 296A, AKG 282A, AKG 232A, AKG 197A, AKG 162A, AKG 134A, AAX 630A, AAX 600A, AAX 589A, AAX 562A, AAX 529A, AAX 516A, AAX 488A, AAX 466A, AAX 451A, AAX 312A, 20 AAX							
	ALC 290A	→ see 5CLT								
	ALC 368A	→ see 486 CLT								
	AMM 56A	Bedford	J2SZ10	154966	Plaxton	622404	C14F	3/63	Bailey, Wembley	-?-, Bristol
	AMX 8A	AEC	Reliance	2U3RA4798	Harrington	2790	C51F	7/63	Valliant, Ealing	Geminiani & Hattersley, East Ham
	ANC 578A	Ailsa	B55-10	75096	Alexander	AV9/275/23	H--/--F	3/76	West Midlands PTE 4760	-?-, -?-
			(ex JOV 760P)							
	AOR 631A	Bristol	LHS6L	LHS-177	Duple	566/6700	C35F	1/75	Davies, Tredegar	Preston, Kington
			(ex HAX 399N)							
(r)	APR 167A	Leyland	Titan PD2/12	531948	*chassis only*			6/54	Barton 732	Quantock, Bishops Lydeard (SO)
			(ex RAL 334)							
	ARU 99A	→ see 837 SUO								
	BHK 106A	→ see 403 CLT								
	BHT 677A	Leyland	Atlantean PDR1/1	591768	Metro-Cammell		H43/33F	3/60	Wallasey 15	Foulkes, Ellesmere Port
			(ex HHF 15)							
	BJT 190A	→ see YSK 763								
	BLV 755A	Leyland	Leopard L1	623521	East Lancs	5945	B42D	4/63	Barrow 72	Jarvis, Coppull
			(ex JEO 772)							
	BNK 324A	AEC	Routemaster	RM1568	Park Royal	L4846	H36/28R	4/63	London Transport RM1568	Totally Transport, Blackpool (LA)
			(ex 568 CLT)							
	BVH 157A	→ see OSK 831								
(r)	DFH 480A	Bedford	SB8	88950	Duple	1145/118	C41F	6/62	Harper, Heath Hayes 69	Herefordshire Transport Collection
			(ex 8 EBF)							
	DRS 122A	Leyland	Tiger PS1	494847	Alexander	3978	C35F	7/50	Alexander PA181	McAlpine, -?-
			(ex CWG 283)							
(r)	DRS 198A	Leyland	Royal Tiger PSU1/15	520200	Alexander	4206	C41C	5/52	Alexander PC5	Bluebird Buses (SN)
			(ex CMS 371)							

Registration	Chassis	Model	Chassis no.	Body	Body no.	Layout	Date	First owner	Current owner
EDS 50A	AEC	Routemaster (ex WLT 560)	RM560	Park Royal	L5157	H36/28R	12/60	London Transport RM560	Western Buses (SW) 19971
EDS 288A	AEC	Routemaster (ex WLT 910)	RM910	Park Royal	L4138	H36/28R	8/61	London Transport RM910	Conn & Gurr, Cumbernauld
EDS 320A	AEC	Routemaster (ex WLT 606)	RM606	Park Royal	L3304	H36/28R	2/61	London Transport RM606	Lydiate, Dunfermline
EDS 486A	Leyland	Leopard PSU3/3R (ex VCS 391)	L00624	Alexander	62/Y13/1	RV	6/63	Western SMT 1065	MacDonald, Condorrat
FRE 699A	Bristol	SC4LK (ex 3003 AH)	147004	ECW	10131	B35F	1/59	Eastern Counties LC556	Burnside, Norwich
KGJ 83A	AEC	Routemaster (ex VLT 13)	RM13	Park Royal	L3525	H36/28R	11/59	London Transport RM13	Duker, Little Paxton
KGJ 117A	AEC	Routemaster (ex 528 CLT)	RM1528	Park Royal	L5269	H36/28R	3/63	London Transport RM1528	School Bus Company, Kingston Bagpuize (OX)
KGJ 187A	AEC	Routemaster (ex 621 DYE)	RM1621	Park Royal	L5003	H36/28R	6/63	London Transport RM1621	Sullivan, Guildford
KGJ 341A	AEC	Routemaster (ex 666 DYE)	RM1666	Park Royal	L5025	H36/28R	7/63	London Transport RM1666	Bramhall, Cumbria
KGW 489A	AEC	Routemaster (ex 380 CLT)	RM1380	Park Royal	L4521	H36/28R	12/62	London Transport RM1380	Campbell, Otterbourne
LAH 817A	→ see DSL 856								
LDS 67A	AEC	Routemaster (ex 274 CLT)	RM1274	Park Royal	L4394	H--/--R	12/62	London Transport RM1274	McGregor, Hassocks
LDS 164A	AEC	Routemaster (ex WLT 978)	RM978	Park Royal	L4237	O--/--R	11/61	London Transport RM978	Brown & Harlott, Romford
LDS 201A	AEC	Routemaster (ex 607 DYE)	RM1607	Park Royal	L5189	H36/28R	12/62	London Transport RM1607	Stagecoach Scotland (SE) 12107
LDS 279A	AEC	Routemaster (ex VLT 54)	RM54	Park Royal	L3307	H36/28R	9/59	London Transport RM54	Ensign, Purfleet (EX)
LDS 388A	→ see FYS 8								
NAT 747A	→ see 931 GTA								
NAT 766A	Daimler	CVG6-30DD (ex TJV 100)	30189	Roe	GO5529	H39/31F	7/62	Grimsby Cleethorpes 57	Rhodes, Lincoln
NWR 421A	Leyland	Tiger Cub PSUC1/11 (ex 434 MDT)	626935	Roe	GO5746	B??F	10/63	Doncaster 34	Winter, Darton
OWJ 170A	→ see YRC 194								
OWJ 339A	→ see RFE 482								
OWJ 340A	Saurer	L4CT1D (ex KWJ 25, JB-42-51 *Netherlands*)	1365	Saurer		B23D	9/48	Swiss Postal Service	Spiers, Henley-on-Thames
OWJ 353A	Leyland	Titan PD3/4 (ex 475 HDT)	621017	Roe	GO5549	RV	12/62	South Yorkshire PTE M3	Penney, Blackpool
OWJ 354A	Leyland	Titan PD3/4 (ex 476 HDT)	621018	Roe	GO5548	RV	12/62	South Yorkshire PTE M4	Penney, Blackpool
OWJ 357A	Leyland	Titan PD3/1 (ex 3913 WE)	583365	Roe	GO4883	RV	7/59	South Yorkshire PTE M10	Sentance, Sheffield
OWJ 388A	Leyland	Titan PD3/1 (ex 4475 WE)	583121	Roe	GO4869	RV	3/59	South Yorkshire PTE M52	Sentance, Sheffield
OWJ 871A	→ see 397 CLT								

	Reg	Chassis	Model	Chassis No	Body	Body No	Layout	Date	First operator	Owner
	OYM 368A	AEC	Routemaster (ex 2 CLT)	RM1002	Park Royal	L3987	H36/28R	11/61	London Transport RM1002	Vaughan, Channel Islands
	OYM 424A	AEC	Routemaster (ex VLT 14)	RM14	Park Royal	L3299	H36/28R	6/59	London Transport RM14	Dale, Mitcham
	TRN 851A	Leyland	Titan PD2A/24 (ex PCB 24)	621948	East Lancs	5877	H35/28R	11/62	Blackburn 24	Holmes, Blackburn
	TRN 618A	→ see ACC 629								
	WNL 66A	Volvo	B58-61 (ex AWJ 134M)	4875	Plaxton	7412VC001	C57F	6/74	Carnell, Sheffield	Naughton, Spiddal (EI)
	WNL 259A	AEC	Reliance (ex 8031 PT)	4MU3RA4138	Plaxton	622094	B55F	6/62	Economic, Whitburn 5	Hawden, Waddingham
	WTS 87A	→ see 691 DYE								
	WTS 418A	AEC	Routemaster (ex WLT 909)	RM909	Park Royal	L4167	H36/28R	11/61	London Transport RM909	London Bus Company, Northfleet (KT)
(r)	WTS 429A	Commer	Avenger IV (ex 60 AUF)	94A0516	Harrington	2669	C35C	11/62	Southdown 60	Southdown 70 Group, Worthing
	WTS 708A	Bristol	LS5G (ex 650 CHN)	119079	ECW	8888	B45F	6/57	United BU250	Dolan M, Crook
	WTS 937A	Daimler	CVG6DD (ex DRS 360)	16180	Alexander *(rebodied -/60)*	6375	H37/29R	3/51	Aberdeen 160	Mills, Aberdeen
	XKR 164A	→ see MLL 528								
	XKO 72A	Leyland	Atlantean PDR1/1 (ex 572 RKJ)	611618	Metro-Cammell	H053440/2	O44/33F	11/61	Maidstone & District DH572	Gibbons, Maidstone
	XKP 444A	Bedford	CALV (ex 6091 RK)	218688	Martin Walter	UW77415	M??	4/62	non-PSV	-?-, -?-
	XMD 47A	Leyland	Titan PD2/12 (ex KCH 106)	562711	Metro-Cammell		O32/26RD	2/57	Trent 763	Amberley Museum *(on loan from Big Bus (LN))*
	XSL 228A	Bristol	Lodekka FS6G (ex 866 NHT)	178001	ECW	12286	CO33/27R	12/61	Bristol 8576	Gilroy, Alnwick (ND) 3
	XSL 945A	Bristol	MW6G (ex OCS 712)	152190	Alexander	6018	C41F	5/60	Western SMT 1590	Roulston, Glasgow
	XSN 25A	Bristol	MW6G (ex RCS 338, OCS 713)	152191	Alexander	6021	C41F	5/60	Western SMT 1591	Roulston, Glasgow
	XWV 416A	→ see KHC 345								
	YAF 151A	AEC	Regent V (ex 239 AJB)	2D3RA1108	Park Royal	B48706	H41/32F	3/62	AERE, Harwell 105	Harpurs, Derby (DE)
	YTS 723A	→ see WSK 509								
(r)	YTS 743A	Leyland	Tiger Cub PSUC1/1 (ex YRC 189)	617556	Alexander	6827	DP41F	4/62	Trent 189	Museum of Transport, Manchester
	YTS 916A	AEC	Reliance (ex JWG 682)	MU3RV1354	Alexander	5201	C41F	6/57	Alexander AC102	Booth, Glasgow
	AAO 34B	Bristol	MW6G	213105	ECW	14172	B45F	4/64	Cumberland 231	Cumbria Omnibus Group
	ABD 252B	Bristol	RELH6G	212052	ECW	14160	C47F	3/64	United Counties 252	Gilroy, Alnwick (ND)
	ABD 253B	Bristol	RELH6G	212058	ECW	14161	C--F	3/64	United Counties 253	Sinclair et al, Eastleigh
	ABO 145B	AEC	Reliance	2MU3RA5070	Harrington	2904	C36F	2/64	Western Welsh 145	Willson, Sidcup
	ABO 147B	AEC	Reliance	2MU3RA5072	Harrington	2906	C40F	3/64	Western Welsh 147	Smith, Cwmbran
	ABO 424B	Guy	Arab V	FD75679	Neepsend		O38/32R	7/64	Cardiff 424	Reynolds, Cardiff

Reg	Make	Model	Chassis no	Body	Body no	Layout	New	First operator	Owner
ABO 434B	Guy	Arab V	FD75732	Neepsend		O37/28R	12/64	Cardiff 434	Cardiff Transport Preservation Group
ABV 33B	Leyland	Titan PD2A/24	L04326	East Lancs	6092	H35/28R	5/64	Blackburn 33	Blackburn Historical Vehicle Group
ABV 43B	Leyland	Titan PD2A/24	L20344	East Lancs	6099	H35/28R	6/64	Blackburn 43	Quantock, Bishops Lydeard (SO)
ACU 304B	Leyland	Leopard PSU3/3R	L04175	Plaxton	642052	B55F	3/64	Stanhope Motor Services	Dolan A, Crook
		(ex 6 MPT)							
ADL 459B	Bedford	SB3	94425	Duple	1170/262	C41F	4/64	Paul, Ryde 9	Isle of Wight Bus Museum
ADX 63B	AEC	Regent V	2D2RA1606	Massey	2584	H37/28R	11/64	Ipswich 63	Ipswich Transport Museum
AEL 2B	Bristol	MW6G	213154	ECW	14465	C39F	4/64	Hants & Dorset 894	Mills, Netheravon
AEL 170B	Leyland	Atlantean PDR1/1	L21162	Weymann	M1528	H43/31F	11/64	Bournemouth 170	Shears D, Winkleigh
AEX 85B	AEC	Reliance	2MU3RA5509	Pennine		B39F	11/64	Great Yarmouth 85	East Anglia Transport Museum
AFJ 77B	AEC	Reliance	2MU4RA5077	Harrington	2964	C41F	6/64	Greenslades Tours	Falmouth Coaches, Falmouth (CO)
		(ex 8229, J 16554, AFJ 77B)							
AFJ 86B	AEC	Reliance	2MU4RA5076	Harrington	2963	C41F	6/64	Greenslades Tours	Joseph, Ilford
		(ex 8230, J 16706, AFJ 86B)							
AFM 105B	Bristol	RELH6G	222004	ECW	15136	C47F	8/64	Crosville CRG530	Roberts, Sheffield
AFN 488B	AEC	Reliance	2MU4RA5111	Duple	1181/1	C34F	5/64	East Kent	Smith, Dover
AFN 775B	AEC	Regent V	2D3RA1548	Park Royal	B50044	H40/32F	2/64	East Kent	Hamilton, East Peckham
AFN 778B	AEC	Regent V	2D3RA1551	Park Royal	B50047	H36/30F	2/64	East Kent	Cooper, Shadoxhurst
AFN 780B	AEC	Regent V	2D3RA1553	Park Royal	B50049	H40/30F	2/64	East Kent	Friends of the East Kent, Dover
AFS 91B	AEC	Reliance	4MU3RA5255	Alexander	27/Y4/2563/49	B53F	9/64	Scottish Omnibuses B91	McConnell, -?-
AGE 545B	→ see 683 SIU *Ireland*								
AHN 451B	Daimler	CCG5DD	20140	Roe	GO5992	H33/28R	12/64	Darlington 7	Aycliffe & District Bus Preservation Society
AHN 455B	Daimler	CCG5DD	20144	Roe	GO5994	H33/28R	12/64	Darlington 11	Quantock, Bishops Lydeard (SO)
AJA 133B	Bedford	VAL14	1513	Strachan	52133	B52F	8/64	North Western 133	Cochrane, Christchurch
AJA 139B	Bedford	VAL14	1523	Strachan	52139	B52F	9/64	North Western 139	Hughes M, Warrington
AJA 144B	Leyland	Leopard PSU3/3R	L02726	Alexander	26Y/563/5	RV	2/64	Crosville L322	Elkin, Fareham
ALD 872B	AEC	Routemaster	RM1872	Park Royal	L5148	H36/28R	3/64	London Transport RM1872	South Devon Railway, Buckfastleigh
									(operates as Nostalgic Transport, Broadhemspton (DN))
ALD 936B	AEC	Routemaster	RM1936	Park Royal	L5214	H36/28R	7/64	London Transport RM1936	London Bus Company, Northfleet (KT)
ALD 955B	AEC	Routemaster	RM1955	Park Royal	L5367	H36/28R	6/64	London Transport RM1955	Cunningham, Camberley
ALD 962B	AEC	Routemaster	RM1962	Park Royal	L5266	H36/28R	7/64	London Transport RM1962	Ross & Taylor, Gerrards Cross
ALD 966B	AEC	Routemaster	RM1966	Park Royal	L5253	H36/28R	7/64	London Transport RM1966	Almeroth, Wendling
ALD 977B	AEC	Routemaster	RM1977	Park Royal	L5392	H36/28R	7/64	London Transport RM1977	Pratt {Crosville}, Weston super Mare (SO)
ALD 980B	AEC	Routemaster	RM1980	Park Royal	L5276	H36/28R	7/64	London Transport RM1980	Epton, Denton (LI)
ALD 989B	AEC	Routemaster	RM1989	Park Royal	L5245	H36/28R	7/64	London Transport RM1989	London Heritage Travel, Grays (EX)
ALD 990B	AEC	Routemaster	RM1990	Park Royal	L5306	H36/28R	7/64	London Transport RM1990	RM1990 Group, Reading
ALD 993B	AEC	Routemaster	RM1993	Park Royal	L5243	H36/28R	9/64	London Transport RM1993	Durrant, West Ham
ALJ 340B	Daimler	Fleetline CRG6LX	60929	MH Coachworks		H44/33F	6/64	Bournemouth 40	Shears D, Winkleigh
ALM 21B	AEC	Routemaster	RM2021	Park Royal	L5309	H36/28R	9/64	London Transport RM2021	Holmes, Blackburn
ALM 23B	AEC	Routemaster	RM2023	Park Royal	L5308	H36/28R	9/64	London Transport RM2023	Barrington, Hounslow
ALM 37B	AEC	Routemaster	RM2037	Park Royal	L5257	H36/28R	10/64	London Transport RM2037	Gay, Southampton
ALM 59B	AEC	Routemaster	RM2059	Park Royal	L5207	H36/28R	11/64	London Transport RM2059	Hayward, Baschurch
									(operates as Meadows, Crewe (CH))
ALM 78B	AEC	Routemaster	RM2078	Park Royal	L5321	H36/28R	11/64	London Transport RM2078	Eames & Hayes, Hampton
ALM 97B	AEC	Routemaster	RM2097	Park Royal	L5361	H36/28R	12/64	London Transport RM2097	Barrington, Hounslow
ALM 200B	AEC	Routemaster	RM2000	Park Royal	L5249	H36/28R	9/64	London Transport RM2000	Hurley, Goole
ALR 388B	Bedford	VAS2	1760	Duple Midland	CF841	B30F	8/64	London County Council 3151	Church, Cranleigh
AMS 295B	Leyland	Leopard PSU3/3R	L20196	Alexander	38/Y3/3063/38	RV	10/64	Alexander Midland ML301	Wotherspoon, Alva

	ANL 807B	AEC	Reliance	2MU3RA5393	Plaxton	642991	C41F	2/64	Armstrong, Westerhope 137	Graveling, Bourne
	AOR 156B	→ see 424 DCD								
	AOR 157B	→ see 422 DCD								
	AOR 158B	→ see 412 DCD								
(r)	APA 46B	AEC	Reliance	2U3RA5187	Willowbrook	CF814	B53F	1/64	Safeguard, Guildford	Powell, Kings Norton
	APT 416B	→ see DHJ 255B								
	APW 829B	Bristol	MW6G	213160	ECW	14455	C39F	5/64	Eastern Counties LS829	Ipswich Transport Museum
	ARG 17B	AEC	Reliance	2MU3RA5291	Alexander	41/Y2/2963/6	C41F	6/64	Alexander Northern NAC246	Gascoine, Blackridge
	ASC 665B	Leyland	Titan PD3/6	L21145	Alexander	E1/3463/15	H41/29F	7/64	Edinburgh 665	City of Edinburgh Council
										(on loan to Lothian Bus Consortium)
	ASC 690B	Leyland	Titan PD3/6	L21753	Alexander	E1/3463/40	H41/29F	9/64	Edinburgh 690	Mason, Edinburgh
	AUK 760B	Ford	402E	-?-	Martin Walter	U12592 4 803	M11	-/64	private owner	Sankey, Walsall
	AWA 124B	Bedford	SB13	93332	Plaxton	632917	C41F	1/64	Andrews, Sheffield	Bluebird Buses (SN)
	AYA 448B	Bedford	CASV	350012	?		M??	8/64	private owner	Yeo, Chippenham
	AYS 732B	Bedford	VAS1	1463	Duple	1171/8	C—F	5/64	MacBrayne 16	Knighton, Wellingborough
	BBK 236B	Leyland	Atlantean PDR1/1	L21233	Metro-Cammell		H43/33F	9/64	Portsmouth 236	Portsmouth 236 Group, Portsmouth
	BCH 156B	Daimler	CVG6DD	20074	Roe	GO5880	H37/28R	10/64	Derby 156	Derby Museums
	BCJ 710B	Leyland	Tiger Cub PSUC1/12	L30271	Harrington	2992	C45F	6/64	Wye Valley, Hereford	Hughes, Llandudno (CN) 29
	BDL 583B	Bristol	Lodekka FLF6G	224057	ECW	14609	H38/32F	10/64	Southern Vectis 607	Priddle, Farnham
	BKG 713B	AEC	Renown	3B3RA068	Northern Counties	6135	H38/29F	10/64	Western Welsh 713	Cwmbran Bus Preservation Group
	BKH 172B	Leyland	Panther PSUR1/1R	L22373	Roe	GO5977	B45D	12/64	Hull 172	Hull Museums Department
	BLH 123B	→ see Unregistered vehicles								
	BSR 168B	Leyland	Tiger PD2/37	621920	Weymann	M561	H37/27F	1/63	Brighton 21	McPherson, Walworth
			(ex 21 ACD)							
	BTR 361B	AEC	Regent V	2D3RA1594	Neepsend		H37/29R	10/64	Southampton 361	Southampton & District Transport Heritage Trust
	BTR 367B	AEC	Regent V	2D3RA1600	Neepsend		H37/29R	10/64	Southampton 367	Blair, Upham
	BWO 585B	AEC	Regent V	2MD3RA609	Massey	2586	L31/28R	9/64	Bedwas & Machen 8	Lomax & Kenworthy, Tameside
	BWW 654B	Leyland	Titan PD3/4	L20075	Roe	GO5890	RV	7/64	South Yorkshire PTE M18	Penney, Blackpool
	BXA 452B	Bristol	Lodekka FS6G	214135	ECW	14377	H33/27RD	3/64	Alexander Fife FRD187	Alexander's Fife Bus Preservation Society
	BXA 464B	Bristol	Lodekka FS6G	214188	ECW	14389	H33/27RD	6/64	Alexander Fife FRD199	Fife Bus Group
	CSF 25B	Bedford	VAL14	1413	Plaxton	642244	C—F	4/64	Watson, Dundee	Davidson & Coventry, Truro
			(ex RTS 463)							
	CTB 739B	Albion	Victor VT21L	78112E	Duple Northern	143/29	C41F	1/64	Albion Motors, Scotstoun	Houston, Windygates
	CTF 625B	Leyland	Titan PD2A/27	L03681	Massey	2563	H--/--F	5/64	Lytham St Annes 68	Quantock, Bishops Lydeard (SO)
	CTF 627B	Leyland	Titan PD2A/27	L03683	Massey	2562	H37/27F	5/64	Lytham St Annes 70	Lancastrian Transport Trust
	DGW 130B	→ see 772 DYE								
	DHJ 255B	Bedford	J2SZ10	198816	Plaxton	642352	C20F	6/64	Rennison, Hartburn	Mathews,West Kingsdown
			(ex APT 416B)							
	DHJ 301B	→ see 410 DCD								
	DTJ 139B	Leyland	Titan PD2/40	L04302	Roe	GO5861	H37/28R	3/64	Ashton 39	Wilson, Lytham St Annes
	DRR 153B	→ see 419 DCD								
	EAX 214B	AEC	Reliance	4U3RA5209	Plaxton	7511AC013S	C51F	4/64	Foster & Oxford, Golborne	Webb, Stevenage
			(ex 7074 DK)		*(rebodied 5/75)*					
	EBW 112B	Albion	Nimbus NS3AN	82069H	Reading	7739	B35F	5/64	Guernsey Railway 73	Longdon, Sandown
			(ex 14651)							
	EDS 508B	→ see PCN 762								
	EDS 584B	Leyland	Leopard PSU3/3R	L04217	Harrington	2912	C49F	3/64	Ellen Smith, Rochdale	Norman, Hull
			(ex 6733 DK)							

	Reg	Make	Model	Chassis No	Body	Body No	Layout	New	First operator	Current owner
	ERF 602B	Bedford	J2SZ10	193023	Plaxton	642886	C20F	2/64	Hodson, Penkridge	Champion, Berwick (Sussex)
	ETC 760B	Bedford	VAS2	1684	Plaxton	642328	C29F	4/64	Entwistle, Morecambe	Go-Goodwins, Eccles (GM)
	EUP 405B	AEC	Routemaster	3R2RH2538	Park Royal	B51611	H41/31F	12/64	Northern General 2105	Northern Routemaster Gp, Newcastle upon Tyne
	EYY 327B	→ see 804 DYE								
	FPH 135B	Leyland	Titan PD3/4 (ex 974 CUF)	L02622	Northern Counties	5987	FH--/--F	4/64	Southdown 974	Elliott & Burtenshaw, Chichester
	FTF 732B	Leyland	Leopard L1	L04362	East Lancs	6109	B44F	7/64	Haslingden 17	Beeby, Huddersfield
	HHK 369B	Bedford	VAS1	1571	Duple	1171/18	C29F	11/64	Girt, Tilbury	Graveling, Bourne
	HTF 644B	Leyland	Titan PD2/40	L22615	East Lancs	6249	H37/28R	12/64	Widnes 38	North West Museum of Transport
	HTJ 521B	Guy	Arab V	FD75635	Northern Counties	6054	H41/32F	11/64	Lancashire United 165	Leigh, Warrington
	HTJ 522B	Guy	Arab V	FD75646	Northern Counties	6057	H41/32F	11/64	Lancashire United 167	Blackman, Halifax (WY)
	JTD 300B	Guy	Arab V	FD75641	Northern Counties	6059	H--/--F	12/64	Lancashire United 166	Leigh, Warrington
(z)	JTF 920B	AEC	Reliance (ex 5148 DP)	2MU3RV4932	Neepsend		B--D	4/64	Reading 48	Rampton, Reading
	LVG 50B	Mercedes-Benz	O319D	A3191702000324	Mercedes-Benz		B14F	-/61	-?-, Finland	Yorkshire Car Collection, Keighley
	PRX 187B	→ see ZV 1461 *Ireland*								
	PRX 189B	Leyland	Titan PD3/4 (ex 417 DCD)	L03502	Northern Counties	6009	FCO39/30F	4/64	Southdown 417	-?-, Haywards Heath
	PRX 190B	→ see 416 DCD								
	PRX 191B	Leyland	Titan PD3/4 (ex 404 DCD)	L02998	Northern Counties	6023	FO39/30F	5/64	Southdown 404	-?-, -?-
	PRX 206B	→ see 401 DCD								
(r)	PRX 458B	Leyland	Titan PD3/4 (ex 421 DCD)	L03590	Northern Counties	6026	FCO39/30F	6/64	Southdown 421	Pearce, Worthing
	SKH 201B	→ see 535 XPJ								
	WRU 702B	→ see 406 DCD								
(r)	WRU 734B	Leyland	Titan PD3/4 (ex 403 DCD)	L02997	Northern Counties	6016	FCO39/30F	5/64	Southdown 403	Elliott & Baker, Chichester
	YKT 959B	AEC	Regal (ex DKT 20)	O6622253			RV	6/37	Maidstone & District P32	Howe, Polegate

	Reg	Make	Model	Chassis No	Body	Body No	Layout	New	First operator	Current owner
	AAA 503C	Dennis	Loline III	1136L3AF1A1	Weymann	M1375	H39/29F	1/65	Aldershot & District 503	Tutty, Guildford
	AAA 506C	Dennis	Loline III	1139L3AF1A1	Weymann	M1378	H39/29F	2/65	Aldershot & District 506	Jacob, Aldershot
	AAA 508C	Dennis	Loline III	1141L3AF1A1	Weymann	M1380	H39/29F	2/65	Aldershot & District 508	Aldershot & District Omnibuses Rescue & Restoration Society
	AEH 143C	AEC	Reliance	2MU4RA5524	Plaxton	652881	C41F	4/65	Potteries C1043	Potteries Omnibus Preservation Society
	ANW 710C	AEC	Reliance	2MU2RA5504	Roe	GO5990	C37F	2/65	Leeds 10	Crowther, Booker
	ARN 811C	Leyland	Leopard PSU3/3R	L24610	Weymann	M1751	DP49F	4/65	Ribble 811	Butler, Gosforth *(on loan to Ribble Vehicle Preservation Trust)*
	BCK 367C	Leyland-PCT	PD3/6	PC65/7	Leyland-PCT		H38/32F	3/65	Preston 61	North West Museum of Transport
	BCS 256C	Albion	Lowlander LR7	62125H	Northern Counties	6155	H39/30F	2/65	Highland AL41	Reid, -?-
	BCT 899C	AEC	Reliance (ex WLY 497)	2MU3RA2417	Plaxton *(rebodied 4/65)*	652580	C43F	-/59	Wing, Sleaford	Thompson, Leeds
	BDV 252C	Bristol	SUL4A	226022	ECW	14720	B36F	3/65	Western National 671	-?-, Wigan
	BED 729C	Leyland	Titan PD2/40	L40312	East Lancs	6269	H34/30F	4/65	Warrington 48	Warrington (CH) 148
	BED 731C	Leyland	Titan PD2/40	L40430	East Lancs	6271	H34/30F	5/65	Warrington 50	North West Museum of Transport
	BED 732C	Leyland	Titan PD2/40	L40523	East Lancs	6273	H34/30F	5/65	Warrington 51	Brown, Wood Green

BEF 28C	Leyland	Titan PD2/40	L40532	Roe	GO6030	H37/28RD	6/65	West Hartlepool 28	Larkin, Peterborough
BHA 399C	BMMO	D9	5399	BMMO	BB5391	H40/32RD	7/65	BMMO 5399	BaMMOT, Wythall (WO)
BHA 656C	BMMO	CM6T	5656	BMMO	C493	C44FT	9/65	BMMO 5656	BaMMOT, Wythall
BHO 543C	Bedford	CALZ30	20368805	Martin Walter	-?-	B12F	5/65	Richmond, Epsom	FOKAB, Winchester
BHU 92C	Bristol	MW6G	225002	ECW	14703	DP39F	2/65	Bristol 2138	Walker, Wells
BJX 848C	Bedford	VAS1	2043	Duple	1184/45	C29F	5/65	Abbeyways, Halifax	MacBrayne Circle
BKT 821C	AEC	Reliance	2U3RA5538	Marshall	B3437	B53F	3/65	Maidstone & District S6	Broyden, Smarden
BND 874C	Leyland	Panther Cub	L30674	Park Royal	B50015	B43D	5/65	Manchester 74	Lonergan, Stockport
BNH 246C	Daimler	CVG6DD	20125	Roe	GO6009	H33/26R	3/65	Northampton 246	Edmunds, Brighouse
BNH 250C	Daimler	CVG6DD	20129	Roe	GO6010	H33/26R	3/65	Northampton 250	Rushden Historical Transport Society
BNM 182C	Ford	570E	L80D439285T	Duple	1186/105	C41F	7/65	Keen, Witley	Adkins, Upper Boddington
BOD 25C	Bristol	Lodekka FLF6B	229185	ECW	14994	H38/32F	9/65	Southern National 2065	Billington, Maidenhead
BON 472C	Daimler	Fleetline CRG6LXSD	61097	Marshall	B3478	B37F	9/65	Birmingham 3472	Yardley Wood Bus Club
BON 474C	Daimler	Fleetline CRG6LXSD	61114	Marshall	B3480	B37F	9/65	Birmingham 3474	BaMMOT, Wythall
BOW 503C	AEC	Regent V	2D3RA1599	Neepsend		H37/29R	1/65	Southampton 366	Blackman, Halifax (WY)
BOW 507C	AEC	Regent V	2D3RA1604	Neepsend		H37/29R	3/65	Southampton 371	Southampton City Council
									(*in care of Southampton & District Transport Heritage Trust*)
BUF 122C	Leyland	Leopard PSU3/1R	L24806	Marshall	B3419	B45F	5/65	Southdown 122	Southdown 122 Group, Worthing
		(ex 6896 NI, BUF 122C)							
BUF 260C	Leyland	Titan PD3/4	L23678	Northern Counties	6206	FH39/30F	6/65	Southdown 260	Pearce, Worthing
BUF 267C	Leyland	Titan PD3/4	L23796	Northern Counties	6201	FH39/30F	5/65	Southdown 267	Lawson, Baildon (WY)
BUF 272C	Leyland	Titan PD3/4	L23974	Northern Counties	6194	FH39/30F	4/65	Southdown 272	Mulpeter, Seaford (WS)
BUF 277C	Leyland	Titan PD3/4	L24481	Northern Counties	6189	FH39/30F	4/65	Southdown 277	Porrell, Eastbourne
BUF 278C	Leyland	Titan PD3/4	L24482	Northern Counties	6190	FH39/30F	4/65	Southdown 278	Jones, Llandeilo (CW)
		(ex 217 UKL, BUF 278C)							
BUF 279C	Leyland	Titan PD3/4	L24493	Northern Counties	6191	FH39/30F	4/65	Southdown 279	Blair, Upham
BUF 425C	Leyland	Titan PD3/4	L24206	Northern Counties	6170	FCO39/30F	6/65	Southdown 425	Andybus, Dauntsey (WI)
BUF 426C	Leyland	Titan PD3/4	L24027	Northern Counties	6169	FCO39/30F	6/65	Southdown 426	Lawrance, Colchester
BUF 530C	Leyland	Titan PD2/37	L20886	Weymann	M568	H37/27F	2/65	Brighton 30	McPherson & Metcalfe, Walworth
BVL 47C	Bristol	RELL6G	222096	ECW	15223	B54F	8/65	Lincolnshire 1208	Lincolnshire 1208 Group, Waddington
BVO 9C	AEC	Reliance	4U3RA5863	Harrington	3158	C51F	7/65	Barton 1009	Barlow, Nottingham
CAG 438C	Leyland	Leopard PSU3/3R	L42394	Alexander	54/Y3/2164/7	RV	9/65	Western SMT 1045	Western SMT Preservation Society, Greenock
CAG 440C	Leyland	Leopard PSU3/3R	L42607	Alexander	54/Y3/2164/15	C--F	10/65	Western SMT L2025	-?-, Glasgow
CCG 704C	Bedford	VAL14	1819	Plaxton	672478	C49F	7/65	King Alfred, Winchester	FoKAB, Winchester
				(*rebodied 3/01 with body ex LAL 547E*)					
CCP 523C	Leyland	Titan PD2/37	L21002	Roe	GO6145	H37/28F	9/65	Halifax 278	-?-, Paignton
CCP 524C	Leyland	Titan PD2/37	L21003	Roe	GO6146	H37/28F	9/65	Halifax 279	Hoare, Chepstow (CS)
CDK 409C	Bedford	VAL14	1681	Harrington	3104	C52F	4/65	Yelloway, Rochdale	Legionnaire Group, Strood
CDK 448C	Leyland	Leopard PSU3/3R	L24371	Harrington	3120	C49F	5/65	Ellen Smith, Rochdale	Rogers, Kidderminster (WO)
CDK 853C	AEC	Reliance	4U3RA5733	Harrington	3140	C45F	6/65	Yelloway, Rochdale	Elliott, Golborne (GM)
CDL 479C	Bristol	Lodekka FLF6G	229068	ECW	14999	H38/32F	6/65	Southern Vectis 611	Isle of Wight Bus Museum
CDL 551C	Bedford	SB3	96549	Duple	1183/273	C41F	3/65	Paul, Ryde 10	Evans, Tregaron (CW)
CDR 506C	Bedford	SB13	96096	Plaxton	652673	C41F	4/65	Embankment, Plymouth	Jacobs, Axminster (DN)
CFE 231C	Bristol	Lodekka FLF6G	229208	ECW	14968	H38/32F	12/65	Lincolnshire 2532	Gallagher, Waddington
		(ex BE-20-05 *Netherlands*, CFE 231C)							
CFR 590C	Leyland	Titan PD3A/1	L24799	Metro-Cammell		H41/30R	6/65	Blackpool 390	Dickinson, Altrincham
CFR 592C	Leyland	Titan PD3A/1	L24901	Metro-Cammell		H--/--R	6/65	Blackpool 392	Manahan, Dublin
CHE 297C	Leyland	Leopard PSU3/1R	L23937/YTC3	Willowbrook	CF982	B53F	4/65	Yorkshire Traction 386	Taylor, Barnsley

	Reg	Chassis make	Chassis model	Chassis no	Body make	Body no	Layout	New	First owner	Current owner
			(ex EWB 386V, CHE 297C)							
(r)	CHL 131C	Bedford	J2SZ10	222660	Plaxton	652613	C20F	4/65	Dewhirst, Bradford	Cannon, March
	CHY 419C	Bristol	Lodekka FLF6B	229111	ECW	18456	H--/--F	7/65	Bristol C7201	Curtis, Bath
(r)	CJF 68C	Leyland	Titan PD3A/1	L20856	East Lancs	6247	H41/33R	3/65	Leicester 68	-?-, Essex
	CJF 69C	Leyland	Titan PD3A/1	L20857	East Lancs	6240	H41/33R	2/65	Leicester 69	Armstrong, Winlaton
	CJN 434C	Leyland	Titan PD3/6	L23712	Massey	2602	H38/32R	1/65	Southend 334	Salmon, South Benfleet
	CJN 436C	Leyland	Titan PD3/6	L23729	Massey	2604	H--/--R	3/65	Southend 336	Ensign, Purfleet (EX)
	CJN 441C	Leyland	Titan PD3/6	L23883	Massey	2605	H38/32R	3/65	Southend 341	Fowler, Holbeach Drove (LI)
	CKF 728C	→ see C 57 MAN *Isle of Man*								
	CKH 777C	AEC	Renown	3B3RA170	Park Royal	B52306	H40/30F	3/65	East Yorkshire 777	Blackman L&S, Halifax
	CKH 782C	AEC	Renown	3B3RA175	Park Royal	B52311	H40/30F	4/65	East Yorkshire 782	Ireland, Hull
	CNW 155C	Bedford	VAL14	1694	Harrington	3114	C44F	5/65	Heaps, Leeds 104	Kenzie, Shepreth (CM)
	CRD 152C	AEC	Reliance	2MU3RA5664	Neepsend		B34D	8/65	Reading 252	Rampton, Reading
	CRG 325C	Daimler	CVG6DD	20153	Alexander	WA/161/1364/1	H37/29R	3/65	Aberdeen 325	Aberdeen & Distrcit Transport Preservation Trust
	CRU 103C	Leyland	Leopard PSU3/2R	L21620	Weymann	M1597	DP45F	4/65	Bournemouth 103	Shears D, Winkleigh
	CRU 180C	Daimler	Fleetline CRG6LX	60938	Weymann	M1917	CO43/31F	7/65	Bournemouth 180	Shears D, Winkleigh
	CRU 184C	Daimler	Fleetline CRG6LX	60942	Weymann	M1921	O43/31F	7/65	Bournemouth 184	Ensign, Purfleet (EX)
	CRU 187C	Daimler	Fleetline CRG6LX	60945	Weymann	M1924	CO43/31F	8/65	Bournemouth 187	Totally Transport, Blackpool (LA)
	CRU 197C	Daimler	Fleetline CRG6LX	61029	Weymann	M1555	H43/31F	9/65	Bournemouth 197	Bournemouth Heritage Transport Collection
	CSG 29C	Bristol	Lodekka FLF6G	229037	ECW	15345	RV	4/65	Scottish Omnibuses E6	Devlin & Brooksbank, Currie
	CSG 43C	Bristol	Lodekka FLF6G	229093	ECW	15359	H38/32F	6/65	Scottish Omnibuses AA43	Devlin & Brooksbank, Currie
	CTT 23C	AEC	Reliance	2MU3RA5516	Park Royal	B51696	B39F	5/65	Devon General 23	Follwell, Stableford
	CTT 510C	AEC	Regent V	2D3RA1649	Park Royal	B51594	H--/--F	5/65	Devon General 510	Whitfield, Leintwardine
	CTT 513C	AEC	Regent V	2D3RA1652	Park Royal	B51597	H40/29F	5/65	Devon General 513	Platt, Dawlish Warren
	CTT 518C	AEC	Regent V	2MD3RA613	Willowbrook	CF936	H33/26F	5/65	Devon General 518	Bennett, Sherborne
	CTT 773C	Bedford	SB5	97023	Duple Northern	160/26	C41F	4/65	Heard, Hartland	Atkin, North Owersby
	CTT 774C	Bedford	VAS1	1966	Duple	1184/21	C29F	6/65	Heard, Hartland	Price, Shobdon
	CUB 331C	Leyland	Atlantean PDR1/1	L20375	Weymann	M1509	H41/29F	7/65	Leeds 331	McMullan, Tingley
	CUV 51C	Daimler	Fleetline CRG6LX	61208	Park Royal	B52960	H41/31F	9/65	London Transport XF1	Nash, Ockley
	CUV 53C	Daimler	Fleetline CRG6LX	61207	Park Royal	B52962	H41/31F	9/65	London Transport XF3	Wood & Coupe, Tonbridge
	CUV 106C	AEC	Routemaster	RM2106	Park Royal	L5343	H36/28R	12/64	London Transport RM2106	Tamkin, Leighton Buzzard (*operates as Alpha, Soulbury (BK)*)
	CUV 116C	AEC	Routemaster	RM2116	Park Royal	L5395	H36/28R	1/65	London Transport RM2116	Legg & Dyer, Chatham
	CUV 121C	AEC	Routemaster	RM2121	Park Royal	L5372	H36/28R	1/65	London Transport RM2121	Turner, Bridge of Weir
	CUV 128C	AEC	Routemaster	RM2128	Park Royal	L5465	H36/28R	1/65	London Transport RM2128	Epton, Denton (LI)
	CUV 154C	AEC	Routemaster	RM2154	Park Royal	L5475	H36/28R	3/65	London Transport RM2154	Gowdy, Ballyclare
	CUV 173C	AEC	Routemaster	RM2173	Park Royal	L5424	H36/28R	3/65	London Transport RM2173	Walsh, Dunstable
	CUV 179C	AEC	Routemaster	RM2179	Park Royal	L5411	H36/28R	3/65	London Transport RM2179	Osman, -?-
	CUV 180C	AEC	Routemaster	RM2180	Park Royal	L5453	H36/24R	4/65	London Transport RM2180	Tennant, Neston
	CUV 186C	AEC	Routemaster	RM2186	Park Royal	L5410	H36/24R	4/65	London Transport RM2186	-?-, Croydon
	CUV 208C	AEC	Routemaster	RM2208	Park Royal	L5408	H36/28R	5/65	London Transport RM2208	King, Leeds
	CUV 213C	AEC	Routemaster	RM2213	Park Royal	L5414	H36/28R	5/65	London Transport RM2213	Dobbing, Stibbington (CM)
(a)	CUV 218C	AEC	Routemaster	RCL2218	Park Royal	L5496	H--/--R	5/65	London Transport RCL2218	Nottingham Transport Heritage Centre
	CUV 219C	AEC	Routemaster	RCL2219	Park Royal	L5488	H36/29RD	6/65	London Transport RCL2219	BaMMOT, Wythall (WO)
	CUV 220C	AEC	Routemaster	RCL2220	Park Royal	L5498	CO40/27RD	5/65	London Transport RCL2220	Ensign, Purfleet (EX)
	CUV 226C	AEC	Routemaster	RCL2226	Park Royal	L5504	H--/--RD	6/65	London Transport RCL2226	RCL2226 Group, Purfleet
	CUV 229C	AEC	Routemaster	RCL2229	Park Royal	L5507	H36/29RD	6/65	London Transport RCL2229	London Transport Museum
	CUV 233C	AEC	Routemaster	RCL2233	Park Royal	L5511	H36/29RD	6/65	London Transport RCL2233	Narduzzo & Puddephatt, Marsworth

	Reg	Chassis make	Model	Chassis no.	Body make	Body no.	Layout	Date	First owner	Current owner
	CUV 239C	AEC	Routemaster	RCL2239	Park Royal	L5517	H36/29RD	6/65	London Transport RCL2239	Biddell, Woodford Bridge *(operates as Imperial Bus, Romford (LN))*
	CUV 243C	AEC	Routemaster	RCL2243	Park Royal	L5521	CO36/27RD	6/65	London Transport RCL2243	Bone, Swindon *(on loan to Meadows, Crewe (CH))*
	CUV 250C	AEC	Routemaster	RCL2250	Park Royal	L5528	CO36/27RD	6/65	London Transport RCL2250	Rowson, Truro
	CUV 254C	AEC	Routemaster	RCL2254	Park Royal	L5532	H--/--RD	7/65	London Transport RCL2254	Hart, Harrow
	CUV 260C	AEC	Routemaster	RCL2260	Park Royal	L5538	H36/29RD	6/65	London Transport RCL2260	London Bus Company, Northfleet (KT)
	CUV 261C	AEC	Routemaster	RML2261	Park Royal	L5669	H40/32R	7/65	London Transport RML2261	Bruce et al, Haddenham (BK)
	CUV 266C	AEC	Routemaster	RML2266	Park Royal	L5671	H40/32R	7/65	London Transport RML2266	Hutt, Finstock (OX)
	CUV 267C	AEC	Routemaster	RML2267	Park Royal	L5977	H40/32R	7/65	London Transport RML2267	Maslin, Swansea
	CUV 270C	AEC	Routemaster	RML2270	Park Royal	L5799	H40/32R	7/65	London Transport RML2270	Traditional, Bromley Common (LN)
	CUV 271C	AEC	Routemaster	RML2271	Park Royal	L5960	H40/32R	7/65	London Transport RML2271	Cooper, Towcester (NO)
	CUV 272C	AEC	Routemaster	RML2272	Park Royal	L5966	H40/32R	7/65	London Transport RML2272	Sullivan, Potters Bar (HT)
	CUV 273C	AEC	Routemaster	RML2273	Park Royal	L5822	H40/32R	7/65	London Transport RML2273	Sinclair, Chingford
	CUV 275C	AEC	Routemaster	RML2275	Park Royal	L5831	H40/32R	7/65	London Transport RML2275	Coastal Liner, Willenhall (WM)
	CUV 276C	AEC	Routemaster	RML2276	Park Royal	L5581	H40/32R	8/65	London Transport RML2276	Colin, Chesterfield
	CUV 277C	AEC	Routemaster	RML2277	Park Royal	L5673	H40/32R	8/65	London Transport RML2277	Weston, Chalfont St Giles
	CUV 278C	AEC	Routemaster	RML2278	Park Royal	L5642	H40/32R	8/65	London Transport RML2278	Rogers, Wallington
	CUV 280C	AEC	Routemaster	RML2280	Park Royal	L5635	H40/32R	8/65	London Transport RML2280	Wilfreda-Beehive, Adwick-le-Street (SY)
(a)	CUV 284C	AEC	Routemaster	RML2284	Park Royal	L5999	B8C	8/65	London Transport RML2284	Coulsdon Old Vehicle & Engineering Society
	CUV 290C	AEC	Routemaster	RML2290	Park Royal	L5655	H40/32R	9/65	London Transport RML2290	Oliver, Eastbourne *(operates as Totally Transport, Blackpool (LA))*
	CUV 291C	AEC	Routemaster	RML2291	Park Royal	L5988	H--/--RD	8/65	London Transport RML2291	Webb, Acton (Suffolk)
	CUV 299C	AEC	Routemaster	RML2299	Park Royal	L5649	H40/32R	10/65	London Transport RML2299	London Heritage Travel, Grays (EX)
	CUV 301C	AEC	Routemaster	RML2301	Park Royal	L5677	H40/32R	8/65	London Transport RML2301	Traditional, Bromley Common (LN)
	CUV 302C	AEC	Routemaster	RML2302	Park Royal	L5644	H40/32R	9/65	London Transport RML2302	Jennings, Northallerton
	CUV 306C	AEC	Routemaster	RML2306	Park Royal	L5584	H40/32R	10/65	London Transport RML2306	Lawford, Clacton-on-Sea
	CUV 313C	AEC	Routemaster	RML2313	Park Royal	L5591	H40/32R	9/65	London Transport RML2313	Jordan, Mattersey *(operates as Sly, Retford (NG))*
	CUV 317C	AEC	Routemaster	RML2317	Park Royal	L5595	H40/32R	9/65	London Transport RML2317	Brighton & Hove (ES) RML2317
	CUV 323C	AEC	Routemaster	RML2323	Park Royal	L5601	H40/32R	10/65	London Transport RML2323	Group 2323, Brixton
	CUV 325C	AEC	Routemaster	RML2325	Park Royal	L5603	H40/32R	10/65	London Transport RML2325	Widderkop, Sidcup
	CUV 330C	AEC	Routemaster	RML2330	Park Royal	L5608	H40/32R	10/65	London Transport RML2330	EK Bus Group, -?-
	CUV 331C	AEC	Routemaster	RML2331	Park Royal	L5609	H40/32R	10/65	London Transport RML2331	London Bus Company, Northfleet (KT)
	CUV 334C	AEC	Routemaster	RML2334	Park Royal	L5612	H40/32R	10/65	London Transport RML2334	Dunlop, Basingstoke
	CUV 335C	AEC	Routemaster	RML2335	Park Royal	L5613	H40/32R	10/65	London Transport RML2335	Rowson, Truro
	CUV 338C	AEC	Routemaster	RML2338	Park Royal	L5616	H40/32R	10/65	London Transport RML2338	Welsh Museum of Public Road Transport
	CUV 344C	AEC	Routemaster	RML2344	Park Royal	L5622	H40/32R	10/65	London Transport RML2344	Wyatt & Curtis, Bristol
	CUV 345C	AEC	Routemaster	RML2345	Park Royal	L5623	H40/32R	10/65	London Transport RML2345	Abel, Swanley
	CUV 346C	AEC	Routemaster	RML2346	Park Royal	L5624	H40/32R	10/65	London Transport RML2346	Small, Maida Vale
	CUV 350C	AEC	Routemaster	RML2350	Park Royal	L5628	O40/32R	11/65	London Transport RML2350	Fuller, Rushden *(on loan from Walker, Leicester (XLE))*
	CUV 352C	AEC	Routemaster	RML2352	Park Royal	L5563	H40/32R	11/65	London Transport RML2352	Clarke, Cirencester
(r)	CUV 357C	AEC	Routemaster	RML2357	Park Royal *(partially dismantled)*	L5654	H--/--	11/65	London Transport RML2357	Duker, Little Paxton
	CUV 359C	AEC	Routemaster	RML2359	Park Royal	L5551	H40/32R	11/65	London Transport RML2359	Bailey, Norwich
	CUV 360C	AEC	Routemaster	RML2360	Park Royal	L5610	H40/32R	11/65	London Transport RML2360	London Transport Museum
	CWM 151C	Leyland	Titan PD2/40	L20575	Weymann	M1016	O37/27F	7/65	Southport 51	Hunter, Tarleton

	Reg	Make	Model	Chassis no	Body	Body no	Layout	Date	New to	Owner
	CWM 154C	Leyland	Titan PD2/40	L20578	Weymann	M1015	O37/27F	6/65	Southport 54	Ace, Aintree (MY)
										(on loan from Merseyside PTE)
	CWN 629C	Bristol	MW6G	225024	ECW	15219	B45F	5/65	United Welsh 134	Neale, Bristol
	CYD 724C	AEC	Reliance	2MU4RA5997	Harrington	3184	C41F	7/65	Hutchings & Cornelius, South Petherton	Mosedale, Bridgwater
	CYU 90C	Bedford	J2SZ2	216076	Duple Midland	-?-	DP19F	-/65	Post Office 19621	Smith, Brentwood
(r)	DAL 616C	Bedford	VAS1	1832	*chassis only*			5/65	Gash, Newark B23	Knighton, Wellingborough
	DAX 610C	Bristol	MW6G	225042	ECW	15185	B45F	5/65	Red & White U765	Potts, Birmingham
	DBA 214C	Leyland	Atlantean PDR1/1	L23091	Metro-Cammell		H43/33F	2/65	Salford 214	Talbot & Stubbins, Leicester
	DBA 227C	Leyland	Atlantean PDR1/1	L23661	Metro-Cammell		O43/33F	3/65	Lancaster 227	Roulston, Glasgow
	DBA 228C	Leyland	Atlantean PDR1/1	L23662	Metro-Cammell		O43/33F	3/65	Lancaster 228	Hoare, Chepstow (CS)
	DBC 190C	AEC	Renown	3B3RA104	East Lancs	6312	H44/31F	8/65	Leicester 190	190 Renown Group, Leicester
	DDB 174C	Daimler	Fleetline CRG6LX	61178	Alexander	13/D/2264/10	H44/31F	8/65	North Western 174	Museum of Transport, Manchester
	DDR 201C	Leyland	Atlantean PDR1/1	L43383	Metro-Cammell		H43/34F	12/65	Plymouth 201	Ruby, Plymouth
	DEL 893C	Bristol	Lodekka FLF6B *(now 6G)*	229087	ECW	14790	H38/32F	6/65	Hants & Dorset 1523	Pratt {Crosville}, Weston super Mare (SO)
	DFM 208C	Bristol	MW6G	225025	ECW	15121	RV	5/65	Crosville SMG539	Thorogood, Briantspuddle
	DHA 962C	BMMO	CM6T	5662	BMMO		C--F	12/65	BMMO 5662	Duffill, Hatton & Mould, Chase Terrace
	DJG 618C	→ see PNW 179C *Preserved commercial vehicles on PSV chassis*								
	DJG 619C	AEC	Reliance	2U3RA5688	Park Royal	B52380	C--F	5/65	East Kent	Friends of the East Kent, Dover
	DMS 325C	Leyland	Leopard PSU3/3R	L40205	Alexander	52/Y3/1964/10	RV	5/65	Alexander Northern NTV2	Moore, Falkirk
	DMS 330C	Leyland	Leopard PSU3/3R	L40434	Alexander	52/Y3/1964/15	RV	5/65	Alexander Midland ML302	City of Edinburgh Preservation Group
	DMS 348C	Leyland	Leopard PSU3/3R	L40610	Alexander	52/Y3/1964/32	RV	6/65	Alexander Midland ML305	Bryce & Moore, Falkirk
	DMS 359C	Leyland	Leopard PSU3/3R	L42145	Alexander	53/Y3/2064/2	RV	7/65	Alexander Midland ML309	Devlin, Currie
	DMS 368C	Leyland	Leopard PSU3/3R	L42509	Alexander	53/Y3/2064/4	RV	9/65	Alexander Midland ML310	Clark, Dunipace
			(ex Q739 PES, DMS 368C)							
	DNF 708C	Daimler	Fleetline CRG6LX	61373	Metro-Cammell		O43/29C	12/65	Manchester 4708	SELNEC Preservation Society
	DNU 20C	Bristol	MW6G	213234	ECW	14710	DP43F	5/65	Midland General 296	Pestell, Ilkeston
	DRG 955C	Albion	Viking VK43L	53404C	Alexander	58Y5/766/29	C—F	12/65	Alexander Northern NNV15	Williams, Merthyr Tydfil
	DRP 86C	→ see RHN 888R								
(r)	DRP 87C	AEC	Reliance	2U3RA5751	Duple Northern	157/7	C51F	4/65	York, Northampton	Forsyth, Braidwood
	DUG 167C	Leyland	Titan PD3A/1	L41706	Roe	GO6155	RV	11/65	South Yorkshire PTE M1	SYT Preservation Group, Sheffield
	EDD 685C	Bedford	SB13	97481	Duple	1183/431	C41F	6/65	Wiltshire, Staple Hill	Fowler, Holbeach Drove (LI)
	EDL 236C	Bristol	MW6G	225127	ECW	15208	B43F	11/65	Southern Vectis 803	Britishbus Preservation Group
	EFM 631C	Bristol	Lodekka FS6G	228001	ECW	14737	H33/27RD	7/65	Crosville DFG182	Barlow, Penarth
	EHT 108C	Bristol	Lodekka FLF6G	229172	ECW	14865	H--/--F	11/65	Bristol C7219	Halliday, Shipley
	EKP 234C	Leyland	Atlantean PDR1/1	L42269	Massey	2634	H--/--F	12/65	Maidstone 34	Gibbons, Maidstone
	ESF 801C	Leyland	Atlantean PDR1/1	L42615	Alexander	A/25/2365/1	H43/31F	2/66	Edinburgh 801	City of Edinburgh Council
										(on loan to Lothian Bus Consortium)
	ETG 373C	AEC	Regent V	2MD3RA607	Weymann	M1565	RV	6/65	Wilfreda-Beehive, Adwick-le-Street	-?-, Swansea
	ETO 452C	Leyland	Atlantean PDR1/2	L40453	Metro-Cammell		H45/27D	10/65	Nottingham 452	Nottingham Heritage Vehicles
	EWT 386C	Bristol	SUL6P	226012	ECW	14549	B36F	1/65	West Yorkshire SMA17	Thornes, Hemingbrough (NY)
	FAY 597C	Bedford	CALV	381550	Martin Walter		B6	9/65	private owner	Bartlett, Gerrards Cross
	FBN 232C	Leyland	Atlantean PDR1/1	L42693	East Lancs	6301	H45/33F	10/65	Bolton 232	Bolton Bus Preservation Group
	FDB 328C	Leyland	Titan PD2/40	L43036	East Lancs	6329	H36/28R	11/65	Stockport 28	-?-, -?-
	FDB 331C	Leyland	Titan PD2/40	L43279	East Lancs	6330	H36/28R	11/65	Stockport 31	Begley, Lisburn
	FDB 334C	Leyland	Titan PD2/40	L43496	East Lancs	6332	H36/28R	12/65	Stockport 34	Steele, Crewe
	FDB 340C	Leyland	Titan PD2/40	L43932	East Lancs	6336	H36/28R	12/65	Stockport 40	Wakelin, Brinklow
										(operates as Wheels, Brinklow (WK))
	FDT 43C	Leyland	Royal Tiger Cub RTC1/1	L24407	Roe	GO6043	B45D	9/65	Doncaster 43	Callaghan, Barnsley

FFM 135C	Guy	Arab V	FD76148	Massey	2645	H41/32F	7/65 Chester 35	Davies & Dennis, Chester
FFM 136C	Guy	Arab V	FD76128	Massey	2644	H41/32F	7/65 Chester 36	Dickinson, Altrincham
FJB 739C	Bristol	Lodekka FLF6G	229151	ECW	15010	H38/32F	8/65 Thames Valley D23	School Bus Company, Kingston Bagpuize (OX)
FPT 590C	AEC	Routemaster	3R2RH2542	Park Royal	B51621	H41/31F	1/65 Northern General 2120	Ensign, Purfleet (EX)
FUU 84C	AEC	Reliance	4U3RA5831	Harrington	3125	C--F	5/65 Motorways, London	Gilkes, West Kingsdown (KT) 84
FVF 423C	Bristol	Lodekka FS5G	228050	ECW	14778	H--/--RD	11/65 Eastern Counties LFS123	Larking, Leigh-on-Sea
GAX 2C	Bristol	RELL6G	222114	ECW	15225	B54F	9/65 Red & White R265	Brown, Worthen
GFM 180C	Bristol	Lodekka FS6B	228036	ECW	14741	H33/27RD	10/65 Crosville DFB180	Rusk, Liverpool
GMB 200C	Bedford	VAL14	1569	Duple	1185/25	C—F	1/65 Bullock, Cheadle	Price, Shobdon
GNG 125C	Bristol	Lodekka FS5G	228056	ECW	14780	H33/27RD	11/65 Eastern Counties LFS125	Ipswich Transport Museum
GNU 266C	Daimler	CCG6DD	20088	Weymann	M1527	H37/28F	11/65 Chesterfield 266	Hegedus, Chesterfield
GNY 432C	Leyland	Titan PD3/4	L42817	Massey	2647	L35/33RD	10/65 Caerphilly 32	Taylor, Ystrad Mynach
GUP 743C	Bedford	VAL14	1698	Plaxton	653006	C52F	4/65 Carr, New Silksworth	Kenzie, Shepreth (CM)
HLP 10C	AEC	Reliance	2U3RA5945	Harrington	3138	C51F	7/65 Surrey, Sutton 52	Pack & Cullum, Crayford
HRC 102C	Leyland	Tiger Cub PSUC1/11	L52220	Alexander	61Y1/1165/8	C41F	12/65 Trent 102	Stanton, Nottingham
JNK 681C	Ford	676E	L80D431993D	Harrington	3019	C52F	5/65 Capital, London	Legionnaire Group, Strood
JNP 590C	Albion	Nimbus NS3AN (ex 16216)	82071D	Reading	0503B	B35F	5/65 Guernsey Railway 75	Dixon (Andrew), Annfield Plain
KAR 20C	Morris-Commercial	CV11/30 (ex FYP 702)	CV4	Stocker *(rebodied ex van 9/65)*		C16F	12/39 Stocker, St Margarets	Bennett, Pilgrims Hatch
KTC 330C	AEC	Reliance	2MU4RA5591	Harrington	3020	C41F	1/65 Warburton, Bury	-?-, -?-
KTJ 204C	Leyland	Titan PD2/37	L25039	East Lancs	6256	H37/28F	4/65 Lancaster 204	Ensign, Purfleet (EX)
MMY 991C	AEC	Reliance	2U3RA5848	Harrington	3167	C51F	7/65 Valliant, Ealing	Green Triangle, Atherton (GM)
MVX 878C	Bristol	Lodekka FLF6B *(now 6G)*	229177	ECW	14951	H38/32F	9/65 Eastern National 2841	Gilroy, Alnwick (ND) 7
NLG 946C	Bedford	SB3 (ex 884 MMB)	85895	Duple	1133/72	C41F	10/60 Meredith, Malpas	Meredith, Malpas (CH)
NTW 942C	Bristol	Lodekka FLF6G	229224	ECW	14959	H38/32F	11/65 Eastern National 2849	-?-, -?-
PTC 114C	AEC	Renown	3B3RA201	East Lancs	6316	H41/31F	9/65 Leigh 15	Museum of Transport, Manchester
PTE 944C	Leyland	Titan PD2/37	L40928	Roe	GO6076	H37/28F	11/65 Ashton 44	Museum of Transport, Manchester

ABW 225D	AEC	Regent V (ex AD 7156 *Hong Kong*)	2D2RA1769	Metal Sections		H50/32D	4/66 Kowloon Motor Bus A165	Shearman, Tunbridge Wells
BFT 740D	Bedford	VAM5	6829171	Plaxton	669244	C45F	3/66 Priory, North Shields 41	Dent, Market Rasen
BJK 672D	Leyland	Titan PD2A/30	L44480	East Lancs	6358	H--/--RD	3/66 Eastbourne 72	Porrell, Eastbourne
BJK 673D	Leyland	Titan PD2A/30	L44596	East Lancs	6359	H32/28R	3/66 Eastbourne 73	Hankin, Giltbrook
BJK 674D	Leyland	Titan PD2A/30	L44597	East Lancs	6361	H32/28R	3/66 Eastbourne 74	Pearce, Worthing
CHB 407D	Leyland	Titan PD3/4	L60635	East Lancs	6372	H41/29F	6/66 Merthyr Tydfil 142	Phillips, Rhymney
CVL 850D	Bristol	RELH6G	232127	ECW	15923	C47F	5/66 Lincolnshire 1431	Colley Hawkin & Lait, Lincoln
DEK 2D	Leyland	Titan PD2/37	L62941	Massey	2684	H37/27F	12/66 Wigan 139	Smith, Wrightington
DEK 3D	Leyland	Titan PD2/37	L62942	Massey	2685	H37/27F	12/66 Wigan 140	Millington, -?-
DET 720D	Bedford	VAM14	6821687	Farrar *(rebodied by2/90 as replica or 1910 AEC B / LGOC)*		O18/16RO	3/66 London General (replica)	North of England Open Air Museum, Beamish *(on loan from Farrar, Ivybridge (DN))*
DFB 704D	Bedford	VAM5	6828127	Farrar *(rebodied 5/86 as replica of 1910 AEC B / LGOC)*		O18/16RO	5/66 London General (replica)	Hearson, Nuthall (NG)
DFE 963D	Bristol	Lodekka FS5G	230046	ECW	15420	H33/27RD	7/66 Lincolnshire 2537	Gallagher & Stopper, Waddington
DJL 126D	Bedford	VAM5	1023	Duple	1205/45	C—F	4/66 Fowler, Holbeach Drove	Fowler, Holbeach Drove (LI)
DPV 65D	AEC	Regent V	2D2RA1808	Neepsend		H37/28R	2/66 Ipswich 65	Quantock, Bishops Lydeard (SO)

	DPV 68D	AEC	Regent V	2D2RA1811	Neepsend		H37/28R	2/66	Ipswich 68	Ipswich Transport Museum
	DRN 665D	→ see MAN 665D *Isle of Man*								
	DRN 671D	→ see F809 MAN *Isle of Man*								
	DRN 672D	→ see E156 MAN *Isle of Man*								
	DTL 489D	Leyland	Atlantean PDR1/2	L43723	Willowbrook	CF1235	H44/32F	2/66	Delaine, Bourne 60	Johnson, Derby
	EDV 502D	Bristol	MW6G	225134	ECW	15763	C39F	5/66	Western National 1420	Handford & Rymill, Solihull
	EDV 505D	Bristol	MW6G	233009	ECW	15765	C39F	5/66	Western National 1423	Johnson, Cardiff
	EDV 506D	Bristol	MW6G	233010	ECW	15766	C39F	5/66	Western National 1424	Wigley, Basingstoke
(r)	EDV 546D	Bristol	MW6G	233013	ECW	15751	C39F	5/66	Southern National 1416	Handford & Rymill, Solihull
	EDV 555D	Bristol	SUL4A	234018	ECW	15986	B36F	5/66	Southern National 692	Billington, Maidenhead
	EDW 68D	Leyland	Atlantean PDR1/1	L44013	Alexander	A/23/1865/2	H43/31F	3/66	Newport 68	Cardiff Transport Preservation Group
	EHA 415D	BMMO	D9	5415	BMMO/Willowbrook	CF1190	H40/32RD	2/66	BMMO 5415	Wakelin, Brinklow
										(operates as Wheels, Brinklow (WK))
	EHA 424D	BMMO	D9	5424	BMMO/Willowbrook	CF1199	H40/32RD	4/66	BMMO 5424	Burdett, Corley
	EHA 767D	BMMO	S17	5767	BMMO/Plaxton	669966	B52F	9/66	BMMO 5767	BaMMOT, Wythall
	EHL 472D	Bedford	VAL14	6819997	Plaxton	669346	C52F	3/66	West Riding 3	Vals, Chase Terrace (ST)
	END 832D	Leyland	Atlantean PDR1/2	L60832	MCW		H43/32F	8/66	Manchester 3832	SELNEC Preservation Society
	ENW 980D	AEC	Regent V	2D2RA1669	Roe	GO6117	H39/31R	1/66	Leeds 980	Keighley Bus Museum Trust
	EOD 524D	AEC	Regent V	2D3RA1805	MCW	HO51941/4	H34/25F	7/66	Devon General 524	Chick & Morgan, Solihull
	ERV 250D	Leyland	Atlantean PDR1/1	L44640	MCW		O43/33F	7/66	Portsmouth 9	Hampshire Bus & Coach Preservation Group
	ERV 251D	Leyland	Atlantean PDR1/1	L44728	MCW		O43/33F	7/66	Porstmouth 11	Blair, Upham
	ERV 254D	Leyland	Atlantean PDR1/1	L43749	MCW		O43/33F	7/66	Portsmouth 7	Bird, Burgess Hill (WS)
	EWS 130D	AEC	Reliance	2U3RA6100	Alexander	70/Y4/3065/24	C--F	6/66	Scottish Omnibuses ZB130	Gascoine, Blackridge
	EWS 168D	Bristol	RELH6G	232056	Alexander	67/Y/2565/27	C38FT	2/66	Scottish Omnibuses XA168	Gascoine,Thomas & Fraser, Edinburgh
	EWS 812D	Leyland	Atlantean PDR1/1	L62733	Alexander	A/25/2365/11	H43/31F	10/66	Edinburgh 812	Warren & Robertson, Edinburgh
	EWS 833D	Leyland	Titan PD3/2	L60982	Alexander	E/2/2265/14	H41/29F	7/66	Edinburgh 833	Mason, Edinburgh
	FBR 53D	Leyland	Panther PSUR1/1R	L61207	Strachan	52312	B47D	7/66	Sunderland 53	Thornton & Oliver, Annfield Plain
	FCD 286D	Leyland	Titan PD3/4	L45032	Northern Counties	6378	FH39/30F	3/66	Southdown 286	Fowler, Holbeach Drove (LI)
	FCD 292D	Leyland	Titan PD3/4	L45151	Northern Counties	6379	FH--/--F	4/66	Southdown 292	Cole, Hastings
	FCD 294D	Leyland	Titan PD3/4	L60164	Northern Counties	6375	FH39/30F	3/66	Southdown 294	Fippard, Shoreham
	FDL 927D	Bristol	MW6G	233076	ECW	15853	B45F	7/66	Southern Vectis 806	Isle of Wight Bus Museum
	FEL 751D	Bristol	MW6G	225143	ECW	15740	C39F	2/66	Hants & Dorset 904	Chick & Morgan, Solihull
	FEL 752D	Bristol	MW6G	225144	ECW	15741	C—F	2/66	Hants & Dorset 905	White, Gaydon
	FFV 447D	AEC	Reliance	2U3RA6157	Plaxton	669694	C45F	6/66	Abbott, Blackpool	Thomas, -?-
	FGS 59D	Bedford	SB	11887	Mulliner		B36F	-/52	Royal Navy	McLennan Preservation Group
			(ex 51 51 RN)							
	FHU 59D	Bristol	Lodekka FLF6B	231024	ECW	15485	H38/32F	2/66	Bristol C7246	Walker, Wells
	FHW 154D	Bristol	MW6G	233006	ECW	15718	C39F	4/66	Bristol 2148	Mahoney I, Brentwood
	FHW 156D	Bristol	MW6G	233021	ECW	15720	C39F	5/66	Bristol 2150	Walker & Curtis, Wells
	FHW 158D	Bristol	Lodekka FLF6B	231065	ECW	15488	H38/32F	3/66	Bristol C7253	M Shed, Bristol
	FJE 982D	Bedford	VAM5	6832077	Duple	1205/324	C45F	11/66	Loates, Bassingbourn	Myall, Bassingbourn (CM)
	FJF 40D	AEC	Renown	3B3RA227	East Lancs	6354	H43/31R	2/66	Leicester 40	Tucker, Whetstone
	FKF 801D	Leyland	Atlantean PDR1/1	L45028	MCW		H43/35F	6/66	Liverpool L801	Merseyside Transport Trust
	FKL 129D	AEC	Reliance	2U3RA6016	Harrington	3194	C47F	10/65	Maidstone & District C66	Cornford, Bexhill
	FNT 230D	→ see GNB 845D								
	FRJ 243D	Leyland	Titan PD2/40	L44378	MCW		H??/??F	4/66	Salford 243	Bressingham Steam Collection
	FRJ 254D	Leyland	Titan PD2/40	L44632	MCW		H36/28F	3/66	Salford 254	Museum of Transport, Manchester
	FRR 87D	Albion	Lowlander LR3	62126K	Northern Counties	6414	H41/30F	2/66	South Notts, Gotham 87	Catchpole, Halling

FUH 370D	Leyland	Tiger Cub PSUC1/11	L51796	Park Royal	B51737	B43F	1/66	Western Welsh 1370	Cardiff Regent V Group
FVA 462D	Ford	R192	BC04EA16300	Duple	1203/18	C45F	2/66	Hutchison, Overtown	White, Sheffield
FXA 715D	Albion	Viking VK43L	53408E	Alexander/Potter	677/9	C--F	10/66	Alexander Fife FNV15	Douglas & Wotherspoon, Alva
GAT 180D	Leyland	Panther PSUR1/1R	L41723	Roe	GO6141	B44D	6/66	Hull 180	Hull Bus Restorers, Hull
GCJ 333D	→ see NAB 846D								
GEE 418D	Daimler	Fleetline SRG6LW	61692	Willowbrook	CF1427	B42D	11/66	Grimsby Cleethorpes 35	Rhodes, Lincoln
GHA 327D	→ see Q340 GVC								
GHA 338D	→ see Q125 VOE								
GHA 415D	Daimler	Fleetline CRG6LX	61566	Alexander	A/26/2765/24	H44/33F	11/66	BMMO 6015	BaMMOT, Wythall
GJG 738D	AEC	Regent V	2D3RA1817	Park Royal	B54156	H40/32F	1/66	East Kent	Smith, Welford-on-Avon
GJG 739D	AEC	Regent V	2D3RA1818	Park Royal	B54157	H40/32F	1/66	East Kent	Baxter, Hawkinge
GJG 742D	AEC	Regent V	2D3RA1821	Park Royal	B54160	H40/32F	1/66	East Kent	Baxter & Newins, Hawkinge
		(ex NWJ 116D, GJG 742D)							
GJG 747D	AEC	Regent V	2D3RA1826	Park Royal	B54165	H40/32F	1/66	East Kent	Love & Richardson, St Albans
GJG 750D	AEC	Regent V	2D3RA1829	Park Royal	B54168	H40/32F	2/66	East Kent	Morgan & Vinall, Brighton
GJG 751D	AEC	Regent V	2D3RA1830	Park Royal	B54169	PO40/32F	2/66	East Kent	Dover Transport Museum Society
GJN 509D	Leyland	Leopard PSU3/1R	L44963	Marshall	B3657	B49D	3/66	Southend 209	Claydon, Corringham
GKH 661D	Bedford	VAM5	6803660	Plaxton	669147	C45F	3/66	Danby, Hull 17	-?-, -?-
GLJ 748D	Bristol	Lodekka FLF6G	231160	ECW	15614	H38/32F	6/66	Hants & Dorset 1540	Sheppard, Ruscombe
GNB 518D	Bedford	VAL14	7806015	Plaxton	672515	C52F	12/66	Manchester 205	SELNEC Preservation Society
GNB 845D	Bedford	SB3	6819892	Duple	1207/9	C41F	5/66	Salopia, Whitchurch	Howard, Ramsbottom
		(ex J 9132, FNT 230D)							
GNV 88D	AEC	Reliance	2U3RA6297	*chassis only*			4/65	York, Northampton 88	Adkins, Upper Boddington
GRD 576D	Dennis	Loline III	1170L3CF2G2	East Lancs	-?-	H38/30F	12/66	Reading 76	Rampton, Reading
GRP 260D	Bristol	MW6G	233001	ECW	15759	C39F	3/66	United Counties 260	Buckland, Hacheston (SK)
GRX 140D	Bristol	Lodekka FLF6G	231233	ECW	15658	H38/32F	9/66	Thames Valley D40	Rampton, Reading
GRY 48D	Leyland	Titan PD3A/1	L45042	MCW		H41/33R	5/66	Leicester 48	Brisco, Aldridge
GRY 60D	Leyland	Titan PD3A/1	L61395	Park Royal	B54661	H41/33R	7/66	Leicester 60	BaMMOT, Wythall
GWN 864D	AEC	Regent V	2D3RA1960	Willowbrook	CF1254	H37/27F	11/66	South Wales 636	South Wales Transport Preservation Trust
GYS 896D	Leyland	Atlantean PDR1/1	L43846	Alexander	A1/364/118	H44/34F	9/66	Glasgow LA320	Evans, London
HAC 628D	Leyland	Leopard L2	L60880	Marshall	B3651	DP41F	6/66	Stratford Blue 62	Clifford, Shoreham
HAD 915D	Bedford	VAM5	1001	Plaxton	669102	C45F	5/66	Wiltshire, Staple Hill	Renown, Bexhill-on-Sea (ES)
HBF 679D	Leyland	Titan PD2A/27	L42136	MCW		H36/28RD	1/66	Harper, Heath Hayes 27	BaMMOT, Wythall
HFM 561D	Bristol	MW6G	225150	ECW	15726	C39F	4/66	Crosville CMG561	Mobbs, Corby
HFM 573D	Bristol	RELH6G	232007	ECW	15887	C47F	5/66	Crosville CRG573	Channerley, Runcorn
HFM 594D	Bristol	RELL6G	238017	ECW	15951	DP50F	10/66	Crosville ERG594	Roberts, Sheffield
HGA 983D	Bedford	VAS1	6843959	Willowbrook	CF1307	B24FM	5/66	MacBrayne 210	MacBrayne Circle (Glasgow Group)
HHW 452D	Bristol	MW5G	233090	ECW	15794	B45F	10/66	Bristol 2636	Furness, Frampton Cotterell
HHY 186D	Bristol	Lodekka FLF6G	231286	ECW	15525	H38/32F	11/66	Bristol 7283	Richards & White, Greasby
HNW 131D	Daimler	Fleetline CRG6LX	61979	Roe	GO6294	H45/33F	11/66	Leeds 131	Keighley Bus Museum Trust
HPN 79D	Bristol	Lodekka FLF6G	231146	ECW	15478	H12/16F	5/66	Brighton Hove & District 79	Brown, Worthen
HPN 487D	Bedford	J2SZ10	225937	Plaxton	652960	C20F	5/66	Bletchley Self Drive	Johnson, Worksop (NG)
HPW 447D	Bristol	Lodekka FLF6G	231109	ECW	15547	H38/32F	5/66	Eastern Counties FLF447	Grant, Romford
HVH 472D	Daimler	CVG6LX-30DD	30411	East Lancs	6381	H41/29F	7/66	Huddersfield 472	Sidaway, Gomersal
JAH 552D	Bristol	Lodekka FLF6G	231158	ECW	15552	O38/32F	7/66	Eastern Counties FLF452	Stagecoach East (NO/CM) 19952
JAH 553D	Bristol	Lodekka FLF6G	231159	ECW	15553	H38/32F	7/66	Eastern Counties FLF453	Stagecoach East (NO/CM) 19953
JBW 527D	Bedford	VAM3	6833797	Duple	1205/272	C45F	6/66	Hambridge, Kidlington	Elmes, Pontesbury
JFM 238D	Bristol	Lodekka FS6G	230071	ECW	15415	H33/27RD	12/66	Crosville DFG238	Aberdeen & District Transport Preservation Trust

(on loan from Grampian Transport Museum)

JJD 364D	AEC	Routemaster	RML2364	Park Royal	L6037	H40/32R	11/65	London Transport RML2364	Sorrell, Maldon
JJD 368D	AEC	Routemaster	RML2368	Park Royal	L5544	H40/32R	12/65	London Transport RML2368	Small, Harpenden
JJD 371D	AEC	Routemaster	RML2371	Park Royal	L5636	H40/32R	12/65	London Transport RML2371	Beckinridge, Brighton
JJD 372D	AEC	Routemaster	RML2372	Park Royal	L6026	H40/32R	12/65	London Transport RML2372	Ponsford, Tunbridge Wells
JJD 374D	AEC	Routemaster	RML2374	Park Royal	L5687	H40/32R	12/65	London Transport RML2374	Routemaster Hire, Knebworth (HT)
JJD 380D	AEC	Routemaster	RML2380	Park Royal	L5566	H40/32R	12/65	London Transport RML2380	Traditional, Bromley Common (LN)
JJD 382D	AEC	Routemaster	RML2382	Park Royal	L6019	H40/32R	1/66	London Transport RML2382	Floyd, Bromley
JJD 388D	AEC	Routemaster	RML2388	Park Royal	L5562	H40/32R	12/65	London Transport RML2388	Barrington, Hounslow
JJD 390D	AEC	Routemaster	RML2390	Park Royal	L5599	H40/32R	1/66	London Transport RML2390	Routemaster Hire, Knebworth (HT)
JJD 391D	AEC	Routemaster	RML2391	Park Royal	L5647	H40/32R	12/65	London Transport RML2391	Allin, Rushden
JJD 393D	AEC	Routemaster	RML2393	Park Royal	L6015	H40/32R	1/66	London Transport RML2393	Hamilton. Wallington
JJD 394D	AEC	Routemaster	RML2394	Park Royal	L5542	H40/32R	1/66	London Transport RML2394	Broadcasters Bus Consortium, London
									(operates as Bruce et al, Haddenham (BK))
JJD 396D	AEC	Routemaster	RML2396	Park Royal	L5739	H40/32R	1/66	London Transport RML2396	Ricketts, Andover
JJD 400D	AEC	Routemaster	RML2400	Park Royal	L5667	H40/32R	1/66	London Transport RML2400	Platt, Pendlebury
JJD 401D	AEC	Routemaster	RML2401	Park Royal	L6025	H40/32R	1/66	London Transport RML2401	Coach Services, Thetford (NK)
JJD 405D	AEC	Routemaster	RML2405	Park Royal	L5643	H40/32R	1/66	London Transport RML2405	Ensign, Purfleet (EX)
JJD 407D	AEC	Routemaster	RML2407	Park Royal	L5674	H40/32R	1/66	London Transport RML2407	Pitt, Doncaster
JJD 408D	AEC	Routemaster	RML2408	Park Royal	L5579	H40/32R	1/66	London Transport RML2408	Bruce et al. Haddenham (BK)
JJD 411D	AEC	Routemaster	RML2411	Park Royal	L5689	H40/32R	1/66	London Transport RML2411	London Heritage Travel, Grays (EX)
JJD 412D	AEC	Routemaster	RML2412	Park Royal	L5690	H40/32R	1/66	London Transport RML2412	James, Aylesbury
JJD 413D	AEC	Routemaster	RML2413	Park Royal	L5691	H40/32R	3/66	London Transport RML2413	London Bus Company, Northfleet (KT)
JJD 414D	AEC	Routemaster	RML2414	Park Royal	L5692	H40/32R	2/66	London Transport RML2414	RML2414 Preservation Group, Cobham
JJD 416D	AEC	Routemaster	RML2416	Park Royal	L5694	H40/32R	2/66	London Transport RML2416	Robson, Horncliffe (ND)
JJD 418D	AEC	Routemaster	RML2418	Park Royal	L5696	H40/32R	1/66	London Transport RML2418	Morris, Shrewsbury
									(operates as RML2418, Wem (SH))
JJD 419D	AEC	Routemaster	RML2419	Park Royal	L5697	H40/32R	2/66	London Transport RML2419	Hood, Northwold
JJD 422D	AEC	Routemaster	RML2422	Park Royal	L5700	H40/32R	2/66	London Transport RML2422	Jenkinson, Richmond (N.Yorks)
JJD 424D	AEC	Routemaster	RML2424	Park Royal	L5702	H40/32R	3/66	London Transport RML2424	Merryweather, Peterborough
JJD 430D	AEC	Routemaster	RML2430	Park Roya;	L5708	H40/32R	3/66	London Transport RML2430	School Bus Company, Kingston Bagpuize (OX)
JJD 434D	AEC	Routemaster	RML2434	Park Royal	L5712	H40/32R	3/66	London Transport RML2434	Bennett, Dublin
JJD 440D	AEC	Routemaster	RML2440	Park Royal	L5718	H40/32R	3/66	London Transport RML2440	Cartwright, High Wycombe
JJD 443D	AEC	Routemaster	RML2443	Park Royal	L5662	H40/32R	3/66	London Transport RML2443	Walker, Bishop Auckland
JJD 446D	AEC	Routemaster	RML2446	Park Royal	L5724	H40/32R	4/66	London Transport RML2446	Mercer, Deiniolen
JJD 452D	AEC	Routemaster	RML2452	Park Royal	L5730	H40/32R	4/66	London Transport RML2452	Thrower, Warrington
JJD 453D	AEC	Routemaster	RML2453	Park Royal	L5731	H40/32R	4/66	London Transport RML2453	2453 Group, Dublin
JJD 455D	AEC	Routemaster	RML2455	Park Royal	L5733	H40/32R	4/66	London Transport RML2455	Sullivan C, Shanklin
JJD 456D	AEC	Routemaster	RML2456	Park Royal	L5734	H40/32R	4/66	London Transport RML2456	Clydemaster Preservation Group, Brentwood
JJD 460D	AEC	Routemaster	RML2460	Park Royal	L5738	H40/32R	5/66	London Transport RML2460	Veares, Plaistow
JJD 463D	AEC	Routemaster	RML2463	Park Royal	L5740	H40/32R	4/66	London Transport RML2463	Veares, Plaistow
JJD 469D	AEC	Routemaster	RML2469	Park Royal	L6006	H40/32R	4/66	London Transport RML2469	Goddard, West Ewell
JJD 474D	AEC	Routemaster	RML2474	Park Royal	L5744	H40/32R	5/66	London Transport RML2474	Moseley (PCV), South Elmsall
JJD 475D	AEC	Routemaster	RML2475	Park Royal	L5660	H40/32R	5/66	London Transport RML2475	Matthews, Keighley (WY)
JJD 477D	AEC	Routemaster	RML2477	Park Royal	L5747	H40/32R	5/66	London Transport RML2477	Day, Bromley
JJD 478D	AEC	Routemaster	RML2478	Park Royal	L5661	H40/32R	5/66	London Transport RML2478	Smith, Broadway
JJD 483D	AEC	Routemaster	RML2483	Park Royal	L5680	H40/32R	5/66	London Transport RML2486	Traditional, Bromley Common (LN)
JJD 484D	AEC	Routemaster	RML2484	Park Royal	L5768	H40/32R	5/66	London Transport RML2484	Scallion, Aberdeen

JJD 492D	AEC	Routemaster	RML2492	Park Royal	L5788	H40/32R	5/66	London Transport RML2492	Button, Colchester
JJD 499D	AEC	Routemaster	RML2499	Park Royal	L5754	H40/32R	6/66	London Transport RML2499	Dexter, Erith
JJD 504D	AEC	Routemaster	RML2504	Park Royal	L5772	H40/32R	6/66	London Transport RML2504	Kendry, West Molesey
JJD 508D	AEC	Routemaster	RML2508	Park Royal	L5808	H40/32R	6/66	London Transport RML2508	Black & White, Penton Mewsey (HA)
JJD 512D	AEC	Routemaster	RML2512	Park Royal	L5837	H40/32R	6/66	London Transport RML2512	Platt, Pendlebury
JJD 514D	AEC	Routemaster	RML2514	Park Royal	L5630	H40/32R	6/66	London Transport RML2514	Platt, Pendlebury
JJD 515D	AEC	Routemaster	RML2515	Park Royal	L5776	H40/32R	6/66	London Transport RML2515	Meadows, Crewe (CH)
JJD 517D	AEC	Routemasrer	RML2517	Park Royal	L5568	H40/32R	6/66	London Transport RML2517	Armstrong, Haywards Heath
JJD 518D	AEC	Routemaster	RML2518	Park Royal	L5797	H40/32R	6/66	London Transport RML2518	Follwell, Stableford
JJD 521D	AEC	Routemaster	RML2521	Park Royal	L5812	H40/32R	6/66	London Transport RML2521	Geffin, Hove
JJD 523D	AEC	Routemaster	RML2523	Park Royal	L5752	H40/32R	6/66	London Transport RML2523	Witcutt, Pelsall (WM)
JJD 524D	AEC	Routemaster	RML2524	Park Royal	L5802	H40/32R	6/66	London Transport RML2524	King, Leeds
JJD 526D	AEC	Routemaster	RML2526	Park Royal	L5804	H40/32R	6/66	London Transport RML2526	Bailey, Norwich
JJD 528D	AEC	Routemaster	RML2528	Park Royal	L5745	H40/32R	6/66	London Transport RML2528	Gilroy, Alnwick (ND) 5
JJD 535D	AEC	Routemaster	RML2535	Park Royal	L5821	H40/32R	7/66	London Transport RML2535	Talisman, Great Bromley (EX)
JJD 539D	AEC	Routemaster	RML2539	Park Royal	L5757	H40/32R	7/66	London Transport RML2539	Thear, Manningtree
JJD 544D	AEC	Routemaster	RML2544	Park Royal	L5848	H40/32R	7/66	London Transport RML2544	Kilby, Buntingford
JJD 546D	AEC	Routemaster	RML2546	Park Royal	L5819	H40/32R	7/66	London Transport RML2546	Stratton, Hendon (TW)
JJD 547D	AEC	Routemaster	RML2547	Park Royal	L6023	H40/32R	7/66	London Transport RML2547	Sanders, Kington
JJD 548D	AEC	Routemaster	RML2548	Park Royal	L5828	H40/32R	8/66	London Transport RML2548	Routemaster Hire, Knebworth (HT)
JJD 551D	AEC	Routemaster	RML2551	Park Royal	L5787	H40/32R	7/66	London Transport RML2551	Griffin, Newcastle upon Tyne
JJD 554D	AEC	Routemaster	RML2554	Park Royal	L5773	H40/32R	8/66	London Transport RML2554	Robson, Horncliffe (ND)
JJD 561D	AEC	Routemaster	RML2561	Park Royal	L5849	H40/32R	8/66	London Transport RML2561	Stevenson, Wokingham
JJD 562D	AEC	Routemaster	RML2562	Park Royal	L5855	H40/32R	8/66	London Transport RML2562	Brown, Gislingham
JJD 569D	AEC	Routemaster	RML2569	Park Royal	L5863	H40/32R	9/66	London Transport RML2569	Perry & Holtby, Malton (NY)
JJD 571D	AEC	Routemaster	RML2571	Park Royal	L5909	H40/32R	9/66	London Transport RML2571	Jolly, Chigwell
JJD 575D	AEC	Routemaster	RML2575	Park Royal	L5857	H40/32R	9/66	London Transport RML2575	RML2575 Group, Dublin
JJD 579D	AEC	Routemaster	RML2579	Park Royal	L5814	H40/32R	9/66	London Transport RML2579	Owen, London
JJD 583D	AEC	Routemaster	RML2583	Park Royal	L5856	H40/32R	9/66	London Transport RML2583	Detheridge, Raglan (CS)
JJD 584D	AEC	Routemaster	RML2584	Park Royal	L5846	H40/32R	9/66	London Transport RML2584	Field, Poole
JJD 586D	AEC	Routemaster	RML2586	Park Royal	L5864	H40/32R	10/66	London Transport RML2586	Webster, Wolverhampton
JJD 588D	AEC	Routemaster	RML2588	Park Royal	L5862	H40/32R	10/66	London Transport RML2588	London Heritage Travel, Grays (EX)
JJD 589D	AEC	Routemaster	RML2589	Park Royal	L5843	H40/32R	10/66	London Transport RML2589	Wright & Cole, Hornchurch
JJD 590D	AEC	Routemaster	RML2590	Park Royal	L5841	H40/32R	10/66	London Transport RML2590	Rose, Poole
JJD 591D	AEC	Routemaster	RML2591	Park Royal	L5867	H40/32R	10/66	London Transport RML2591	Routemaster Hire, Knebworth (HT)
JJD 592D	AEC	Routemaster	RML2592	Park Royal	L5847	H40/32R	10/66	London Transport RML2592	Canfield, Horsham
KBB 118D	→ see ZV 1510 *Ireland*								
KBD 712D	Bristol	Lodekka FS6G	230060	ECW	15435	H33/27RD	11/66	United Counties 712	712 Preservation Group, Luton
KBD 714D	Bristol	Lodekka FS6G	230062	ECW	15437	H33/27RD	11/66	United Counties 714	Bluebird Buses (SN)
KDT 206D	Daimler	CVG6DD	20175	Roe	GO6219	H34/28F	5/66	Doncaster 206	Doncaster Omnibus & Light Railway Society
KGJ 601D	AEC	Routemaster	R2RH/2/2807	Park Royal	B54293	H32/24F	10/66	British European Airways 8208	Duker, Little Paxton
KGJ 602D	AEC	Routemaster	R2RH/2/2808	Park Royal	B54294	H32/24F	10/66	British European Airways 8209	Boxall & Welch, Beckenham
KGJ 621D	AEC	Routemaster	R2RH/2/2827	Park Royal	B54313	H32/24F	12/66	British European Airways 8228	Cunningham, Barnet
KGY 4D	AEC	Routemaster	FR2R001	Park Royal	B53296	H41/31F	7/66	London Transport FRM1	London Transport Museum
KLP 1D	→ see PYY 28D								
KNY 495D	AEC	Regent V	2MD3RA634	Northern Counties	6373	H37/28F	11/66	Rhondda 495	Doe, Cardiff
KWE 374D	AEC	Reliance	2U3RA6273	Plaxton	669716	C49F	5/66	Sheffield United Tours 374	Jordan, Sheffield
KWT 642D	Bristol	Lodekka FS6B	228083	ECW	15446	H33/27RD	3/66	West Yorkshire DX210	Halliday, Shipley

	LDM 16D	Bedford	VAM14	6846989	Duple Northern	167/110	C45F	7/66	Phillips, Holywell	Roberts, Bagillt
	LNY 536D	Leyland	Titan PD2/37	L62869	Massey	2682	L31/29RD	10/66	Caerphilly 36	Rhymney Valley Transport Preservation Society
	LYF 307D	Leyland	Atlantean PDR1/1	L60484	MCW		CH38/12F	11/66	BOAC, Heathrow	Brooklands Museum Trust
	MRO 146D	Bedford	VAS2	6811265	Plaxton	669051	C--F	2/66	Frames, London 146	Greet, Broadhempston
	MWW 114D	Bristol	Lodekka FS6B	230037	ECW	15463	H33/27RD	8/66	York-West Yorkshire YDX233	Escrick Bus & Coach Preservation Group
	NAB 846D	Bedford	VAM5	6825974	Plaxton	669282	C--F	5/66	Wye Valley, Hereford	Price & Perry, Shobdon
			(ex GCJ 333D)							
	NMA 328D	Daimler	Fleetline CRG6LX	61356	Northern Counties	6293	H--/--F	1/66	SHMD 28	Taylor, Milnrow
	NWJ 116D	→ see GJG 742D								
	NWU 265D	Bristol	Lodekka FS6B	230055	ECW	15468	H33/27RD	12/66	York-West Yorkshire YDX221	Renshaw , Baildon
	OVX 143D	Leyland	Titan PD2A/30	L43643	Massey	2652	H33/24RD	2/66	Colchester 43	Larkin, Peterborough
	OWC 182D	Bristol	MW6G	225148	ECW	15756	C39F	2/66	Tilling T312	Moss et al, Essex
	PYY 28D	Bedford	J2SZ2	6835224	Duple Midland	CFJ2/366	C10F	7/66	Royal Household	Holland, Matlock
			(ex KLP 1D)							
	RAR 267D	Bedford	VAL14	6846478	Marshall	B3906	B40C	11/66	Interline, London	Webb, Armscote (WK)
	TTE 282D	Leyland	Titan PD2/40	L60636	East Lancs	6345	H37/28R	4/66	Widnes 42	Hayes, Little Hoole
	UTC 768D	Leyland	Leopard L2	L44877	Plaxton	669749	C43F	4/66	Lancashire United 216	Crankshaw, Meltham
	WTE 155D	Guy	Arab V	FD76611	Northern Counties	6350	H41/32F	7/66	Lancashire United 232	Dickinson, Altrincham
	XTF 98D	Leyland	Titan PD3/4	L62201	East Lancs	6377	H41/32F	9/66	Haslingden 1	Quantock, Bishops Lydeard (SO)
	YTJ 628D	AEC	Renown	3B3RA257	East Lancs	6470	H41/31F	12/66	Leigh 32	-?-, Wigan
	DEK 7E	Leyland	Titan PD2/37	L63879	Northern Counties	6455	H37/27F	2/67	Wigan 113	Wigan Transport Trust
	DFT 776E	Bedford	J2SZ10	7816006	Plaxton	672016	C20F	7/67	Priory, North Shields	Wilkinson. Scarborough
	DHC 782E	Leyland	Titan PD2A/30	700952	East Lancs	6535	H32/28R	6/67	Eastbourne 82	Eastbourne (ES) 19978
	DHC 784E	Leyland	Titan PD2A/30	701081	East Lancs	6531	O32/28R	6/67	Eastbourne 84	Pearce, Worthing
	DJP 468E	Leyland	Panther Cub	L72703	Massey	2692	B42D	8/67	Wigan 20	Edwards & Brindle, Wigan
			(ex M-1526-M *Malta*, DJP 468E)							
(r)	ECK 865E	Leyland	Lepoard PSU3/4R	L64292	Plaxton	8011LC011/S	C49F	4/67	Holmeswood, Rufford	Sutherland, Bishopbriggs
					(rebodied 12/80)					
	ECU 201E	Bristol	RESL6L	RESL-1-137	ECW	16654	B45D	4/67	South Shields 1	North East RE Group, North Shields
	EDY 565E	Bedford	VAM14	7803610	Duple	1208/225	C45F	4/67	Rowland, St Leonards 1	Rambler, Hastings (ES)
			(ex JUF 244E, EDY 565E)							
	EFB 776E	Bedford	VAS5	7852425	Duple	1211/53	C29F	6/67	Fale, Combe Down	Adkins, Upper Boddington
	EVL 549E	Leyland	Panther PSUR1/1R	701345	Roe	GO6430	DP45F	6/67	Lincoln 41	Cooke, Lincoln
	FEN 587E	Leyland	Titan PD2/37	700852	East Lancs	6452	H37/28F	6/67	Bury 187	Boughton, Brightwell
	FEN 588E	Leyland	Titan PD2/37	700853	East Lancs	6451	H37/28F	6/67	Bury 188	Bury Transport Museum
(r)	FEN 590E	Leyland	Titan PD2/37	700988	*chassis only*			6/67	Bury 190	-?-, Brighton
	FHG 573E	Leyland	Tiger Cub PSUC1/11	L72779	East Lancs	6508	B43F	3/67	Burnley Colne & Nelson 73	Heaps, Bradford
	FJY 914E	Leyland	Atlantean PDR1/1	L64849	MCW		H43/32F	4/67	Plymouth 214	Furse, Plymouth
	FKF 835E	Leyland	Atlantean PDR1/1	L64076	MCW		H43/28D	1/67	Liverpool L835	Merseyside Transport Trust
	FPR 705E	Bedford	VAS5	7837544	Duple	1211/26	C29F	5/67	Rendell, Parkstone	Hunt, Rookley
	FTH 950E	Leyland	Tiger Cub PSUC1/12	L71909	Plaxton	673226	C45F	2/67	Davies, Pencader 77	Evans, Pencader
	FWL 371E	AEC	Renown	3B3RA262	Northern Counties	6553	H38/27F	8/67	City of Oxford 371	Oxford Bus Museum Trust
	GCM 147E	Leyland	Titan PD2/37	701235	Massey	2713	RV	6/67	Birkenhead 147	Barker, Ellesmere Port
	GCM 152E	Leyland	Titan PD2/37	701399	Massey	2718	H36/30R	9/67	Birkenhead 152	Wirral Borough Council
										(*operates as Tennant, Birkenhead (MY)*)
	GFY 58E	Leyland	Titan PD2/40	L61093	MCW		PO--/--F	1/67	Southport 58	Forrest, Walton

	GRS 10E	Leyland	Tiger Cub PSUC1/13	750651	Alexander	72/Y1/1566/4	B43D	6/67 Aberdeen 10	Murray, Mills & Macduff, Aberdeen
	GRS 334E	Albion	Viking VK43AL	53413K	Alexander	88Y/1966/11	C40F	6/67 Alexander Northern NNV34	Walker, Renfrew
	GRS 343E	Albion	Viking VK43AL	53414K	Alexander	88Y/1966/20	C40F	4/67 Alexander Northern NNV43	Bluebird Buses (SN) 59943
	GWN 867E	AEC	Regent V	2D3RA1963	Willowbrook	CF1258	H37/27F	1/67 South Wales 639	Clements, Pontardawe
	HCD 347E	Leyland	Titan PD3/4	L63881	Northern Counties	6467	FH39/30F	3/67 Southdown 347	Stobart, Wimbledon
	HCD 350E	Leyland	Titan PD3/4	L63987	Northern Counties	6484	FH39/30F	7/67 Southdown 350	Elliott & Burtenshaw, Chichester
									(operates as Southcoast Motor, Chichester (WS))
(r)	HCD 363E	Leyland	Titan PD3/4	L64687	Northern Counties	6461	FH30/30F	2/67 Southdown 363	Elliott & Burtenshaw, Chichester
	HDL 23E	Bristol	RESL6G	RESL-1-121	ECW	16383	B43F	2/67 Southern Vectis 808	Greenwood, Fleur de Lys (CS)
	HDL 25E	Bristol	RESL6G	RESL-1-123	ECW	16385	B43F	2/67 Southern Vectis 810	Sinclair, Eastleigh
	HDL 255E	Bedford	VAM3	6833758	Duple	1205/302	C45F	3/67 Paul, Ryde 11	Gange, Cowes (IW)
	HDV 624E	Bristol	RELH6G	238044	ECW	16623	C45F	3/67 Western National 2365	Billington, Maidenhead
	HDV 626E	Bristol	RELL6G	RELL-3-112	ECW	16502	B53F	5/67 Western National 2700	Hembry, Sturminster Newton
(r)	HDV 634E	Bristol	MW6G	233150	ECW	16319	C--F	1/67 Western National 1429	Bluebird Buses (SN)
	HDV 638E	Bristol	MW6G	233160	ECW	16323	C39F	1/67 Western National 1433	Wheatley, Trowell
	HDV 639E	Bristol	MW6G	233161	ECW	16324	C39F	1/67 Western National 1434	Stagecoach Scotland (SE) 59939
	HDV 641E	Bristol	MW6G	233165	ECW	16326	C39F	1/67 Western National 1436	Adams, Wellingborough
	HFR 501E	Leyland	Titan PD3A/1	L64673	MCW		H41/30R	6/67 Blackpool 501	Conn Gurr & Thomson, Cumbernauld
	HFR 506E	Leyland	Titan PD3A/1	700134	MCW		H--/--R	6/67 Blackpool 506	Penney, Blackpool
	HFR 512E	Leyland	Titan PD3A/1	700322	MCW		H41/30R	6/67 Blackpool 512	Lancastrian Transport Trust
(r)	HFR 515E	Leyland	Titan PD3A/1	700490	MCW		H41/30R	6/67 Blackpool 515	Lancastrian Transport Trust
	HFR 516E	Leyland	Titan PD3A/1	700491	MCW		H41/30R	6/67 Blackpool 516	Oliver, Eastbourne
	HFR 518E	Leyland	Titan PD3A/1	700589	MCW		H41/30R	5/67 Blackpool 518	Hoare, Chepstow (CS)
	HGM 335E	Bristol	Lodekka FLF6G	236108	ECW	16672	H44/34F	3/67 Central SMT BL335	Stagecoach Scotland (SE) 19935
	HGM 346E	Bristol	Lodekka FLF6G	236119	ECW	16683	H44/34F	4/67 Central SMT BL346	Forbes, Barrhead
(r)	HGM 351E	Bristol	Lodekka FLF6G	236127	ECW	16688	H44/34F	5/67 Central SMT BL351	Forbes, Barrhead
	HJA 965E	Leyland	Titan PD2/40	700228	Neepsend		H36/28R	7/67 Stockport 65	Quantock, Bishops Lydeard (SO)
	HOR 590E	Leyland	Atlantean PDR1/2	L63329	Roe	GO6391	O43/31F	4/67 King Alfred, Winchester	FoKAB, Winchester
	HOR 592E	Leyland	Atlantean PDR1/2	L63349	Roe	GO6393	H43/33F	4/67 King Alfred, Winchester	FoKAB, Winchester
			(ex REU 52E, VCL 461, HOR 592E)						
	JAM 145E	Daimler	CVG6-30DD	30448	Northern Counties	6499	H40/30F	6/67 Swindon 145	Thamesdown (WI) 145
	JAX 117E	Bristol	MW6G	233140	ECW	15850	B45F	1/67 Red & White U1766	Bateman, Chelmsford
(r)	JCR 383E	AEC	Regent V	3D2RA1852	*chassis only*			1/67 Southampton 383	Keighley Bus Museum Trust
	JHA 868E	BMMO	S21	5868	BMMO	C606	DP49F	7/67 BMMO 5868	BaMMOT, Wythall
	JHW 68E	Bristol	Lodekka FLF6B	231303	ECW	16103	H38/32F	2/67 Bristol C7300	Hewgill, Cashe's Green
	JKE 338E	Leyland	Atlantean PDR1/1	L64010	Massey	2704	H43/31F	3/67 Maidstone 38	Gibbons, Maidstone
	JKK 188E	→ see 7064 ID *Ireland*							
	JKT 112E	Bedford	J2SZ10	7832748	Plaxton	672011	C20F	5/67 Cox, Maidstone	Sayles, Dunnet
	JMS 452E	Albion	Viking VK43AL	53415J	Alexander	89Y/1966/39	C40F	5/67 Alexander Midland MNV37	Albion Vehicle Preservation Trust
	JOW 499E	AEC	Swift	MP2R010	Strachan	40214	B47D	4/67 Southampton 1	Southampton & District Transport Heritage Trust
	JRJ 281E	Leyland	Titan PD2/40	L65351	MCW		H36/28F	4/67 Salford 281	Cotton, Manchester
(r)	JSC 854E	Leyand	Atlantean PDR1/1	700201	Alexander	A45/866/2	H43/31F	7/67 Edinburgh 854	-?-, -?-
	JSC 867E	Leyland	Atlantean PDR1/1	700547	Alexander	A37/866/17	H43/31F	8/67 Edinburgh 867	Robertson, Airth
	JSC 869E	Leyland	Atlantean PDR1/1	700549	Alexander	A37/866/20	H43/27F	8/67 Edinburgh 869	Farqhar Groundwater Hope & Thomson, Edinburgh
	JSC 883E	Leyland	Atlantean PDR1/1	701204	Alexander	A37/866/33	H43/31F	9/67 Edinburgh 883	Smith, Great Bromley
	JSC 900E	Leyland	Atlantean PDR2/1	700950	Alexander	J/5/866/50	O47/35F	4/67 Edinburgh 900	Lothian Bus Consortium
	JUF 244E	→ see EDY 565E							
	JVN 40E	Leyland	Titan PD2A/27	700229	Roe	GO6360	H33/28R	5/67 Teesside 40	500 Group, Stockton-on-Tees

	Reg	Make	Model	Chassis no	Body	Body no	Layout	Date	First operator	Owner
	KHW 306E	Bristol	RELL6L	RELL-3-122	ECW	16462	B53F	6/67	Cheltenham District 1000	BaMMOT, Wythall (WO)
	KHW 309E	Bristol	RELL6L	RELL-3-125	ECW	16465	B44D	6/67	Cheltenham District 1003	1003 Western Pioneer Group, Gloucester
	KJU 456E	Bedford	CALZ30	7304768	Martin Walter	UB28781	C11F	3/67	Smith, Braunston	-?-, -?-
	KPM 87E	Bristol	Lodekka FLF6G	236069	ECW	16090	H--/--F	1/67	Brighton Hove & District 87	Mulpeter, Seaford
	KPM 91E	Bristol	Lodekka FLF6G	236079	ECW	16094	O28/26F	3/67	Scottish Omnibuses OT2	Manning & Thomas, Gloucester
	KUS 607E	Leyland	Atlantean PDR1/1	L65246	Alexander	A1/364/150	H44/34F	5/67	Glasgow LA352	Hoskins, Westhoughton
			(ex MUS 281F, KUS 607E)							
	KVF 658E	Bristol	RESL6G	RESL-1-118	ECW	16350	B46F	6/67	Eastern Counties RS658	Eastern Transport Collection
	KVH 473E	Daimler	Fleetline CRG6LX	62222	Roe	GO6396	H44/31F	7/67	Huddersfield 473	Keighley Bus Museum Trust
	LAX 101E	Bristol	RESL6L	RESL-1-125	ECW	16353	B46F	3/67	Red & White RS167	Re-liance 1284 Preservation Group, Tredegar
	LBU 159E	Leyland	Atlantean PDR1/1	L64097	Roe	GO6370	H43/34F	3/67	Oldham 159	-?-, Manchester area
	LUS 524E	AEC	Reliance	2U3RA6628	Willowbrook	CF1506	C49F	6/67	MacBrayne 150	Macduff & Murray, Kilmarnock
	MDJ 554E	Leyland	Titan PD2A/27	L63230	East Lancs	6518	H37/28R	5/67	St Helens 54	North West Museum of Transport
	MDJ 555E	Leyland	Titan PD2A/27	L63239	East Lancs	6519	H37/28R	5/67	St Helens 55	North West Museum of Transport
	MDJ 918E	AEC	Regent V	2D3RA1975	MCW		H37/28R	7/67	St Helens 58	Blackman, Halifax (WY)
	MGB 286E	Bedford	SB5	7832521	Plaxton	673562	C41F	6/67	MacBrayne 168	MacBrayne Circle, Inverness
	NDM 950E	Bedford	VAM14	7834932	Duple Midland	CF1507	DP45F	6/67	Phillips, Holywell	Lloyd, Wigan
	NJW 719E	Daimler	Roadliner SRC6	36082	Strachan	40207	B54D	6/67	Wolverhampton 719	BaMMOT, Wythall
	NML 600E	AEC	Routemaster	RML2600	Park Royal	L5933	H40/32R	3/67	London Transport RML2600	Scott, -?-
	NML 613E	AEC	Routemaster	RML2613	Park Royal	L5859	H40/32R	4/67	London Transport RML2613	RML2613 Group, Royston
	NML 616E	AEC	Routemaster	RML2616	Park Royal	L5894	H40/32R	5/67	London Transport RML2616	Thompson, Retford
										(operates as Sly, Retford (NG))
	NML 617E	AEC	Routemaster	RML2617	Park Royal	L5912	H40/32R	5/67	London Transport RML2617	Packham, Braintree
	NML 619E	AEC	Routemaster	RML2619	Park Royal	L5880	H40/32R	4/67	London Transport RML2619	Blackmore, Nottingham (NG)
	NML 620E	AEC	Routemaster	RML2620	Park Royal	L5883	H40/32R	5/67	London Transport RML2620	Good, Croydon
	NML 625E	AEC	Routemaster	RML2625	Park Royal	L5879	H40/32R	5/67	London Transport RML2625	Collett, Colchester
	NML 626E	AEC	Routemaster	RML2626	Park Royal	L5840	H40/32R	5/67	London Transport RML2626	Kennedy, London
	NML 634E	AEC	Routemaster	RML2634	Park Royal	L5917	H40/32R	5/67	London Transport RML2634	Bruce at al, Haddenham (BK)
	NML 644E	AEC	Routemaster	RML2644	Park Royal	L5892	H40/32R	6/67	London Transport RML2644	Tucker, Northolt
	NML 645E	AEC	Routemaster	RML2645	Park Royal	L5842	H40/32R	6/67	London Transport RML2645	Staves & Broadwith, Northallerton (NY)
	NMX 586E	AEC	Reliance	6MU4R6570	Plaxton	672984	C41F	4/67	Timpson	Millard, Flexford
	NMY 630E	AEC	Routemaster	R2RH/2/2836	Park Royal	B54322	H32/24F	1/67	British European Airways 8237	Higgins, Christchurch
	NMY 631E	AEC	Routemaster	R2RH/2/2837	Park Royal	B54323	H32/24F	1/67	British European Airways 8238	London Bus Company, Northfleet (KT)
	NMY 632E	AEC	Routemaster	R2RH/2/2838	Park Royal	B54324	H32/24F	1/67	British European Airways 8239	Biddell, Woodford Bridge
										(operates as Imperial Bus, Romford (LN))
	NMY 634E	AEC	Routemaster	R2RH/2/2840	Park Royal	B54326	H32/24F	2/67	British European Airways 8241	Ensign, Purfleet (EX)
	NMY 638E	AEC	Routemaster	R2RH/2/2844	Park Royal	B54330	H32/24F	1/67	British European Airways 8245	Higgins, Christchurch
	NMY 648E	AEC	Routemaster	R2RH/2/2854	Park Royal	B54340	H32/24F	2/67	British European Airways 8255	Western Greyhound, Summercourt (CO)
	NMY 654E	AEC	Routemaster	R2RH/2/2860	Park Royal	B54346	H32/24F	3/67	British European Airways 8261	Morant, Croydon
(r)	NNY 762E	AEC	Regent V	2MD3RA640	MCW		O34/26F	6/67	Pontypridd 5	Barlow et al, Penarth
	NWW 89E	Leyland	Leopard L1	L62969	Willowbrook	CF1312	B45F	2/67	Todmorden 9	Flowers, Ossett
	OFM 3E	Bristol	RESL6G	RESL-5-103	ECW	16332	DP42F	7/67	Crosville ERG3	Roberts, Sheffield
	RUW 990E	→ see KBD 453Y								
	TUP 198E	Bedford	VAS1	6868568	Plaxton	672027	C29F	4/67	Wilson, Blaydon	Mould, Chase Terrace
	BKX 94F	Bedford	J2SZ10	7T103856	Plaxton	688012	C20F	3/68	Bletchley Self Drive	Tyler, Worcester
	DJH 731F	Bedford	VAL70	7T457715	Plaxton	688638	C52F	6/68	Fox, Hayes	Maghull Coaches, Bootle (MY)
	EJK 887F	Leyland	Panther PSUR1/1R	801747	East Lancs	6627	B45D	6/68	Eastbourne 87	Bennett, Peterborough

	EXS 569F	Bedford	J2SZ10	7830461	Plaxton	688001	C20F	12/67	Pattinson, Paisley	Bradshaw, St Annes (LA)
	FCK 942F	Leyland	Leopard PSU3/4R	800003	Plaxton	689209	C49F	4/68	Scout S942	Hurst, Lydiate
	FJC 736F	Dennis	Pax V	9395-2328	Dennis		B33F	9/68	Llandudno	Seddon, Bushbury
	FJM 311F	Ford	Transit	BCO5HA57738	Martin Walter	UB57125.8668	M12	6/68	Jackson, Kirkby Stephen	Davison, Ryhope
	FKF 918F	Leyland	Panther PSUR1A/1R	703401	MCW		B47F	9/68	Liverpool 1039	Reilly, Bootle
	FTF 702F	Leyland	Titan PD3/4	702350	East Lancs	6607	H41/32F	11/67	Ramsbotton 8	Dew, Somersham (CM)
	GEX 740F	Leyland	Atlantean PDR1/1	L65573	Marshall	B3654	B39F	3/68	Great Yarmouth 40	Wilkins, Gorleston
	GEX 741F	Leyland	Atlantean PDR1/1	L65476	Marshall	B3653	B--F	3/68	Great Yarmouth 41	Cook, Swanscombe
	GNH 258F	Daimler	CVG6DD	20186	Roe	GO6436	H33/26R	11/67	Northampton 258	Quantock, Bishops Lydeard (SO)
	GNH 261F	Daimler	CVG6DD	20189	Roe	GO6435	H33/26R	11/67	Northampton 261	Roderick, Norwich
	GTP 175F	Leyland	Panther Cub	L73708	MCW		B42D	8/67	Portsmouth 175	City of Portsmouth Preserved Transport Depot
	HCB 576F	Bedford	CALV	7305521	Martin Walter	-?-	C--F	10/67	Aspden, Blackburn	Atkin, North Owersby
	HTJ 131F	Leyland	Leopard PSU4/2R	800347	East Lancs	6620	B43F	4/68	Leigh 20	Prescott, Cheadle Hulme
	HVM 901F	Leyland	Atlantean PDR1/1	701997	Park Royal	B55359	H45/28D	3/68	Manchester 1001	Museum of Transport, Manchester
	JCP 60F	Leyland	Lion LSC1 (ex J 4601)	47464	Leyland		B31F	5/28	Jersey Railways	Science Museum, Wroughton
	JKG 497F	Daimler	CRG6LX-30	62173	Park Royal	B55735	H42/33F	1/68	Cardiff 497	Cardiff Transport Preservation Group
	JRS 22F	AEC	Swift	MP2R182	Alexander	3W/13/2366/8	B--D	6/68	Aberdeen 22	Scallion, Aberdeen
	JTF 217F	Leyland	Titan PD2A/47	800605	East Lancs	6626	H37/28F	4/68	Darwen 39	Darwen Transport Museum Trust
	JTF 218F	Leyland	Titan PD2A/47	800744	East Lancs	6625	O36/28F	4/68	Kelvin Scottish 1999	Stanton, Cheadle
	JTH 100F	Bedford	VAM14	6865784	Duple Northern	172/41	C45F	5/68	Davies, Pencader 80	Price, Shobdon
	KDB 408F	Leyland	Leopard PSU4/1R	703998	East Lancs	6599	B43D	2/68	Stockport 408	Prescott, Cheadle Hulme
	KDL 885F	Bristol	RESH6G	RESH-2-107	Duple Northern	191/5	C45F	2/68	Southern Vectis 301	Isle of Wight Bus Museum
	KED 546F	Leyland	Panther Cub	751013	East Lancs	6571	B41D	12/67	Warrington 92	Amos, Nailsea
	KGM 664F	Leyland	Leopard PSU3/1R	801332	Alexander	106/Y/2567/19	B53F	6/68	Central SMT T64	Carson, Airdrie
	KJA 871F	Leyland	Titan PD3/14	702825	East Lancs	6585	H38/32R	2/68	Stockport 71	Museum of Transport, Manchester
	KKG 215F	AEC	Reliance	6MU3R6484	Marshall	B3867	DP41F	9/67	Western Welsh 215	215 Revival Group, Swansea
	KOW 901F	AEC	Regent V	3D2RA1862	Neepsend		H--/--RD	10/67	Southampton 393	393 Group, Southampton
	KOW 902F	AEC	Regent V	3D2RA1863	Neepsend		H40/30R	9/67	Southampton 394	Blackman, Halifax (WY)
(r)	KOW 903F	AEC	Regent V	3D2RA1864	*chassis/cab*			9/67	Southampton 395	Turner, Southampton
(r)	KOW 907F	AEC	Regent V	3D2RA1868	*chassis/cab*			10/67	Southampton 399	Turner, Southampton
	KOW 909F	AEC	Regent V	3D2RA1870	Neepsend		H40/30R	11/67	Southampton 401	Blair, Upham
	KOW 910F	AEC	Regent V	3D2RA1871	Neepsend		H40/30R	12/67	Southampton 402	Southampton & District Transport Heritage Trust
	KOX 663F	AEC	Swift	MP2R077	MCW		DP44F	9/67	Birmingham 3663	Thomas, Kidderminster
	KOX 780F	Daimler	Fleetline CRG6LX	62495	Park Royal	B55210	H43/33F	4/68	Birmingham 3780	BaMMOT, Wythall
	KRD 258F	Bristol	RELL6G	RELL-6-104	Strachan	52543	B34D	12/67	Reading 258	Rampton et al, Reading
	KRU 55F	Daimler	Roadliner SRC6	36173	Willowbrook	CF1478	B49F	8/67	Bournemouth 55	Shears D, Winkleigh
	KRU 224F	Bristol	Lodekka FLF6B	236149	ECW	16168	H38/32F	7/67	Hants & Dorset 1557	Cummings et al, Bournemouth
	KTB 748F	Leyland	Leopard PSU4/1R	801392	East Lancs	6636	B42D	4/68	Widnes 48	-?-, -?-
	KUF 199F	Leyland	Leopard PSU3/1R	703017	Willowbrook	CF1603	B45F	1/68	Southdown 199	Southdown 199 Group, Worthing
	KWK 23F	Daimler	Fleetline CRG6LX	62633	ECW	16728	H??/??D	3/68	Coventry 23	23 Group, Coventry
	LDV 467F	Bristol	RELH6G	RELH-4-132	ECW	17057	C45F	3/68	Southern National 1457	Stroud RE Group
	LDV 847F	Bristol	RELH6G	RELH-4-159	ECW	17058	C45F	3/68	Southern National 2375	Duffy, Macclesfield
(r)	LFR 527F	Leyland	Titan PD3/11	800479	MCW		H--/--R	6/68	Blackpool 527	Manahan, Dublin
	LFR 529F	Leyland	Titan PD3/11	800592	MCW		H41/30R	7/68	Blackpool 529	Lancastrian Transport Trust (*operates as Totally Transport, Blackpool (LA)*)
	LFS 288F	Bristol	VRT/LL6G	VRT/LL/109	ECW	17327	O43/31F	12/68	Scottish Omnibuses AA288	Wallace, Edinburgh
	LFS 294F	Bristol	VRT/LL6G	VRT/LL/115	ECW	17333	H47/36F	12/68	Scottish Omnibuses AA294	Telfer, Oldham

LFS 296F	Bristol	VRT/LL6G	VRT/LL/117	ECW	17335	O43/31F	12/68	Scottish Omnibuses AA296	Foundry, Middlewood (SY)
		(ex 68-G-811, LFS 296F)							
LFS 303F	Bristol	VRT/LL6G	VRT/LL/124	ECW	17342	H47/36F	12/68	Scottish Omnibuses AA303	Patterson, Kings Lynn
LHA 870F	BMMO	S21	5870	BMMO	BB5758	DP49F	8/67	BMMO 5870	Gray, Birmingham
LHA 878F	BMMO	S21	5878	BMMO		DP49F	11/67	BMMO 5878	Waldron, Bromsgrove
LHL 164F	Leyland	Panther PSUR1/1R	702506	Roe	GO6454	B51F	11/67	West Riding 164	West Riding Omnibus Preservation Society
LJF 30F	Leyland	Titan PD3A/12	701890	MCW		H--/--R	12/67	Leicester 30	Leicester 30 Preservation Group, Leicester
LKT 132F	Leyland	Panther PSUR1/1R	703807	Strachan	52602	B48F	5/68	Maidstone & District 3132	Brown, Wateringbury
LLJ 443F	Bristol	Lodekka FLF6L	236252	ECW	16188	H38/32F	12/67	Hants & Dorset 1577	Geisler, Hadley Wood
LTF 842F	Bedford	J2SZ10	107965	Plaxton	688009	C—F	7/68	Henthorne, Chadderton	Cannon, March
LWG 892F	Albion	Viking VK43AL	53425D	Alexander	103Y/2167/4	C40F	-/68	Alexander Midland MNV49	Rentoul, Doune
MAA 260F	Bedford	VAL70	7T451297	Plaxton	688601	C52F	3/68	Cresta, Wimbledon	Greet, Broadhempston
MAT 848F	Leyland	Panther PSUR1/2R	701380	Marshall	B3676	DP--F	1/68	East Yorkshire 848	Ireland, Hull
MBO 1F	→ see PKH 228F								
MBO 512F	AEC	Swift	MP2R190	Alexander	4/W10/2266/7	B47D	6/68	Cardiff 512	Cardiff Transport Preservation Group
		(ex EDL 249F, WFC 365, MBO 512F)							
MFN 946F	AEC	Regent V	3D3RA2015	Park Royal	B55517	H40/32F	11/67	East Kent	East Kent (KT) 19946
MHA 901F	BMMO	S22	5901	BMMO	BB5789	DP45F	7/68	BMMO 5901	Price Penfold et al, Birmingham
MHJ 347F	Leyland	Titan PD3/4	702665	East Lancs	6611	H41/32R	12/67	Southend 347	Western Greyhound, Summercourt (CO)
MNW 343F	Leyland	Leopard PSU4/4R	801394	Plaxton	689153	C43F	6/68	Wallace Arnold Tours	Carroll, Drogheda
		(may carry incorrect registration IBI 789)							
MUO 328F	Bristol	LH6L	LH-133	ECW	17395	B41F	7/68	Western National 716	Cornwall Bus Preservation Society
MUS 274F	Leyland	Atlantean PDR1/1	701671	Alexander	A40/1166/25	H--/--F	11/67	Glasgow LA389	Delman, Glasgow
NAC 416F	Leyland	Atlantean PDR1/1	700023	Northern Counties	6557	H44/31F	12/67	Stratford Blue 10	Oxford Bus Museum Trust
NBD 311F	Bristol	RELL6G	RELL-3-218	ECW	16525	B53F	1/68	United Counties 311	Cleaveley, Gloucestershire
NEA 101F	Daimler	Fleetline CRG6LX	62576	MCW		H42/31F	1/68	West Bromwich 101	BaMMOT, Wythall
NHA 589F	Bedford	VAM70	7T452478	Plaxton	688265	C45F	4/68	Gliderways, Bearwood	Warren, Hawkhurst
NRL 101F	Bedford	VAS5	7T453743	Duple	1217/58	C29F	5/68	Jennings, Bude	Thomas C, St Austell
NTY 416F	AEC	Reliance	6MU3R7068	Plaxton	688943	C45F	2/68	Rowell, Prudhoe	Tennant, Livingston
OAX 9F	Bristol	RELH6L	RELH-4-111	ECW	17053	C47F	2/68	Red & White RC968	James, Rogerstone
OBU 163F	Leyland	Atlantean PDR1/1	702807	Roe	GO6466	H43/34F	12/67	Oldham 163	Kilroy, Stockport
OFN 709F	AEC	Reliance	6U3ZR6955	Marshall	B4113	B53F	4/68	East Kent	Cooper, Shadoxhurst
OFN 721F	AEC	Reliance	6U3ZR6967	Marshall	B4122	B--F	5/68	East Kent	East Kent Heritage, Dover
OHU 208F	Bedford	CALV	808238	Martin Walter	U36319.8581	M11	4/68	WRVS, Bristol	Lucas M, Warminster
OHU 770F	Bristol	RELL6L	RELL-3-429	ECW	16776	B53F	6/68	Bristol 1071	Hudd, Yate
ORP 273F	Bristol	RELH6G	RELH-4-179	ECW	17093	C47F	5/68	United Counties 273	Rushden Historical Transport Society
ORX 771F	Bedford	CALV30	803979	Martin Walter	-?-	M??	1/68	private owner	Knighton, Wellingborough
PAX 466F	Leyland	Titan PD3/4	703981	Massey	2751	L35/33RD	6/68	Bedwas & Machen 6	Peddle, Uttoxeter
PBJ 1F	Leyland	Titan PD2/47	701792	Massey	2722	H--/--R	8/67	Lowestoft 11	Smith, Carlton Colville
PBJ 2F	Leyland	Titan PD2/47	701793	Massey	2721	H34/28R	8/67	Lowestoft 12	Betterton, Tivetshall
PGD 216F	Bedford	SB5	7T454743	Plaxton	689470	C--F	5/68	MacBrayne 159	MacEwan, Amisfield (SW)
PGD 220F	Bedford	SB5	7T454639	Plaxton	689475	C--F	6/68	MacBrayne 164	MacEwan, Amisfield (SW)
PHT 227F	BMC	550FG	315668	Longwell Green		B22F	8/68	United Bristol Hospitals	Martin, Stenton
PKH 228F	Bristol	LHS6L	LHX003	Weymann	M9636	B30F	4/68	Western Welsh 1	Thornes, Hemingbrough (NY)
		(ex MBO 1F)		*(new with second-hand body built 5/61)*					
PTX 830F	AEC	Reliance	6MU4R6678	Plaxton	688926	C41F	2/68	Neath & Cardiff	Phillips, Neath
PYM 106F	AEC	Reliance	6MU3R7003	Plaxton	688940	C30C	7/68	Glenton, London	Hearson, Chesterton
PYM 108F	AEC	Reliance	6MU3R7070	Plaxton	688942	C30C	7/68	Glenton, London	Meadows, Crewe (CH)

RAH 681F	Bristol	RELL6G	RELL-3-446	ECW	16850	B53F	6/68	Eastern Counties RL681	Hussey & Thorogood, Basingstoke
RCH 518F	Daimler	Fleetline CRG6LX	62243	Alexander	A/43/1766/6	H44/33F	2/68	Trent 518	Robertson, Ilkeston
RFM 453F	Leyland	Tiger Cub PSUC1/11	751014	Massey	2725	B40D	9/67	Chester 53	Dennis, Chester
SMK 658F	AEC	Routemaster	RML2658	Park Royal	L5901	H40/32R	6/67	London Transport RML2658	Hobbs, Lymington
SMK 660F	AEC	Routemaster	RML2660	Park Royal	L5891	H40/32R	6/67	London Transport RML2660	Bird, Burgess Hill (WS)
SMK 666F	AEC	Routemaster	RML2666	Park Royal	L5944	H40/32R	7/67	London Transport RML2666	Tamkin, Leighton Buzzard
									(operates as Alpha, Soulbury (BK))
SMK 676F	AEC	Routemaster	RML2676	Park Royal	L5961	H40/32R	8/67	London Transport RML2676	Legge, Rickmansworth
SMK 678F	AEC	Routemaster	RML2678	Park Royal	L5958	H40/32R	7/67	London Transport RML2678	Staves & Broadwith, Northallerton (NY)
SMK 679F	AEC	Routemaster	RML2679	Park Royal	L5950	H40/32R	8/67	London Transport RML2679	Blair, Upham
									(operates as Xelabus, Colden Common (HA))
SMK 680F	AEC	Routemaster	RML2680	Park Royal	L5578	H40/32R	7/67	London Transport RML2680	Rose, Poole
SMK 683F	AEC	Routemaster	RML2683	Park Royal	L6033	H40/32R	8/67	London Transport RML2683	Ensign, Purfleet (EX)
SMK 685F	AEC	Routemaster	RML2685	Park Royal	L5589	H40/32R	8/67	London Transport RML2685	Kuhnke, Ventnor
SMK 686F	AEC	Routemaster	RML2686	Park Royal	L5611	H40/32R	8/67	London Transport RML2686	Jones, Bedlington
SMK 692F	AEC	Routemaster	RML2692	Park Royal	L6018	H40/32R	9/67	London Transport RML2692	-?-, Cheshire
SMK 700F	AEC	Routemaster	RML2700	Park Royal	L5942	H40/32R	9/67	London Transport RML2700	Tamkin, Leighton Buzzard
									(operates as Alpha, Soulbury (BK))
SMK 701F	AEC	Routemaster	RML2701	Park Royal	L5947	H40/32R	9/67	London Transport RML2701	Dawber & Hughes, Wigan
SMK 704F	AEC	Routemaster	RML2704	Park Royal	L5968	H40/32R	9/67	London Transport RML2704	Godfrey-Faussett, Selkirk
SMK 708F	AEC	Routemaster	RML2708	Park Royal	L5952	H40/32R	9/67	London Transport RML2708	Gregory, Croydon
SMK 711F	AEC	Routemaster	RML2711	Park Royal	L5989	H40/32R	9/67	London Transport RML2711	Tamkin, Leighton Buzzard
									(operates as Alpha, Soulbury (BK))
SMK 714F	AEC	Routemaster	RML2714	Park Royal	L5951	H40/32R	9/67	London Transport RML2714	London Heritage Travel, Grays (EX)
SMK 716F	AEC	Routemaster	RML2716	Park Royal	L5959	H40/32R	10/67	London Transport RML2716	RML2716 Group, Chorley
SMK 719F	AEC	Routemaster	RML2719	Park Royal	L6000	H40/32R	10/67	London Transport RML2719	Arnold, Somerton
SMK 731F	AEC	Routemaster	RML2731	Park Royal	L5975	H40/32R	10/67	London Transport RML2731	Watts, Coulsdon
SMK 732F	AEC	Routemaster	RML2732	Park Royal	L6010	H40/32R	11/67	London Transport RML2732	Gilroy, Alnwick (ND) 6
SMK 734F	AEC	Routemaster	RML2734	Park Royal	L5980	H40/32R	11/67	London Transport RML2734	Oliver, Eastbourne
									(operates as Totally Transport, Blackpool (LA))
SMK 737F	AEC	Routemaster	RML2737	Park Royal	L5626	H40/32R	11/67	London Transport RML2737	Western Greyhound, Summercourt (CO)
SMK 740F	AEC	Routemaster	RML2740	Park Royal	L5985	H40/32R	11/67	London Transport RML2740	Talbot-Jenkins, Oakham
SMK 742F	AEC	Routemaster	RML2742	Park Royal	L5993	H40/32R	11/67	London Transport RML2742	Bird, Burgess Hill (WS)
SMK 746F	AEC	Routemaster	RML2746	Park Royal	L5546	H40/32R	12/67	London Transport RML2746	Cornish, Hendon
SMK 747F	AEC	Routemaster	RML2747	Park Royal	L6004	H40/32R	12/67	London Transport RML2747	Brown, Hertford
SMK 750F	AEC	Routemaster	RML2750	Park Royal	L5656	H40/32R	12/67	London Transport RML2750	Muirhead, Hythe
SMK 751F	AEC	Routemaster	RML2751	Park Royal	L6009	H40/32R	1/68	London Transport RML2751	Lidsey & Spratt, Bromley
SMK 755F	AEC	Routemaster	RML2755	Park Royal	L5981	H40/32R	2/68	London Transport RML2755	Doyle, -?-
SMK 759F	AEC	Routemaster	RML2759	Park Royal	L5922	H40/32R	1/68	London Transport RML2759	Briscoe, Highgate
SMK 760F	AEC	Routemaster	RML2760	Park Royal	L6038	H40/32R	2/68	London Transport RML2760	East London (LN) RML2760
SMM 90F	AEC	Merlin	3P2R090	MCW		B45D	1/68	London Transport MB90	Comfort, Basingstoke
SWU 222F	→ see DMN 650 *Isle of Man*								
THN 263F	Bristol	Lodekka FLF6G	236290	ECW	17032	H38/32F	6/68	United Auto L163	North East Bus Preservation Trust
TMC 509F	Austin	250JU	3131	Austin		M12	7/68	British Red Cross	Morgan, Trelewis
TRB 589F	Bristol	Lodkekka FLF6G	236296	ECW	16989	H--/--F	6/68	Mansfield District 694	Mulpeter, Seaford
TWW 766F	Bristol	RELH6G	RELH-4-150	ECW	17064	C47F	1/68	West Yorkshire 2508	2508 Group, Keighley
UDT 455F	Leyland	Royal Tiger Cub RTC1/2	800311	Roe	GO6552	B45D	1/69	Doncaster 55	Felix Preservation Group, Doncaster
UFM 52F	Bristol	RELL6G	RELL-3-380	ECW	16791	DP50F	6/68	Crosville ERG52	Johnson, Heswall

	UFM 53F	Bristol	RELL6G	RELL-3-381	ECW	16792	DP50F	6/68	Crosville ERG53	Ashman, Romford
	ULC 88F	Renault	TN6A	590-212	STCRP		B33R	11/33	RATP, Paris 2679	Jowitt, Niton
	UPK 78F	Bedford	J2SZ10	108086	Plaxton	688014	C20F	6/68	Bicknell, Godalming	Tyler, Worcester
	UUL 651F	AEC	Reliance	6U3ZR6890	Plaxton	689043	C44F	4/68	Surrey, Sutton	Plumley, Hexham
	UUL 652F	AEC	Reliance	6U3ZR6892	Plaxton	689061	C44F	5/68	Surrey, Sutton	Plumley, Hexham
	UUL 653F	AEC	Reliance	6U3ZR7096	Plaxton	688949	C44F	5/68	Surrey, Sutton	Hurley C, Worthing
	UWX 981F	Bedford	VAL70	7T454133	Plaxton	688614	C52F	6/68	Mosley, Barugh Green	Centurion, Welton (SO)
(r)	UYO 91F	BMC	250JU	7776	BMC		M12	5/68	non-PSV	Shears C, Winkleigh
(r)	VRB 283F	Bedford	J2SZ10	103679	Plaxton	688016	C20F	3/68	Stone, Church Gresley 12	Greet, Broadhempston
	VXC 547F	Bedford	J2SZ2	164944/C1	Plaxton	688006	C20F	11/67	Cave, Shirley	Noble, Fraserburgh
	XPT 454F	Bedford	CALZ	7801413	Martin Walter	UB34087 8 573	C10F	2/68	Sinclair, South Hetton	Cope, Weston super Mare
	YLG 717F	Bristol	RESL6G	RESL-1-163	Northern Counties	6564	B43F	8/67	SHMD 117	Jones, Burnley
	AFM 103G	Bristol	RELH6G	RELH-4-196	ECW	17479	C47F	2/69	Crosville CRG103	Berry, Wootton-under-Edge
	AFM 106G	Bristol	RELH6G	RELH-4-218	ECW	17482	C47F	3/69	Crosville CRG106	Graham, Runcorn
	AFM 111G	Bristol	RELH6G	RELH-4-223	ECW	17487	C47F	5/69	Crosville CRG111	Downs, Chester
	AFM 113G	Bristol	RELL6G	RELL-3-660	ECW	17531	B53F	4/69	Crosville SRG113	Roberts, Sheffield
	AVX 975G	Bristol	Lodekka FLF6G	236337	ECW	16984	CH37/18F	8/68	Eastern National 2946	Harrison, Chelmsford
	BNU 679G	Bristol	VRT/SL6G	VRT/SL198	ECW	17781	H--/--F	5/69	Midland General 315	Waterhouse & Thurman, Ripley
	BWA 429G	→ see 410 LMN *Isle of Man*								
	CPU 979G	Bristol	VRT/SL6G	VRT/SL101	ECW	17264	H39/31F	2/69	Eastern National 3000	3000 Group, Canvey
	FKF 933G	Leyland	Panther PSUR1A/1R	703722	MCW		B47D	9/68	Liverpool 1054	Merseyside Transport Trust
	FPT 6G	Leyland	Leopard PSU3/3R	900445	Plaxton	693381	C51F	6/69	Stanhope Motor Services	Severn, Bolton
	GYJ 495G	Daimler	Fleetline CRG6LX	62565	Alexander	J/4/367/15	H44/34F	8/68	Dundee 295	Fraser, Dundee
	HCK 204G	Leyland	Panther PSUR1A/1R	702226	MCW		B47D	12/68	Preston 204	Johnstone, Burtonwood
	HCK 214G	Leyland	Panther PSUR1A/1R	801883	MI	B4158	B47D	12/68	Preston 214	Brown, Wateringbury
	HEK 88G	Bedford	J2SZ10	125792	Plaxton	692021	C20F	7/69	Eavesway, Ashton-in-Makerfield	Walls, Higher Ince (GM)
	HNK 157G	Bedford	J2SZ10	9T124765	Plaxton	692010	C15F	3/69	Armchair, Kensington	Webster, Upper Largo
	HRN 249G	Bristol	RELL6G	RELL-3-670	ECW	17455	B--D	5/69	Ribble 249	Scott, Southport
	JVV 267G	Daimler	CVG6DD	20198	Roe	GO6622	H33/26R	10/68	Northampton 267	154 Preservation Society, Northampton
	KJA 299G	Bristol	RESL6G	RESL-1-246	Marshall	B4063	B43F	9/68	North Western 299	North West Museum of Transport
	KJH 230G	AEC	Reliance	6U3ZR6998	Plaxton	692923	C53F	6/69	Don, Bishops Stortford	Falmouth Coaches, Falmouth (CO)
	LAK 309G	Leyland	Titan PD3A/12	703299	Alexander	E3/2968/12	H41/29F	4/69	Bradford 309	Keighley Bus Museum Trust
	LAK 313G	Leyland	Titan PD3A/12	703502	Alexander	E3/2968/9	H41/29F	4/69	Bradford 313	Bates & Holian, Elland
	LCB 55G	Leyland	Tiger Cub PSUC1A/13	950966	East Lancs	6762	B45F	6/69	Blackburn 55	Sharpe, Willington
	LCM 159G	Leyland	Atlantean PDR1/1	800833	Northern Counties	6792	H--/--F	10/68	Birkenhead 159	Merseyside Transport Trust
	LDX 75G	Leyland	Atlantean PDR1/1	802809	ECW	17200	O43/31F	11/68	Eastbourne 65	Hoare, Chepstow (CS)
	LDX 76G	Leylland	Atlantean PDR1/1	802810	ECW	17201	O43/31F	11/68	Eastbourne 66	Morgan, Brighton
	LMJ 653G	Fiat	52B	3260	?		B??	-/13	-?-, Yugoslavia	Science Museum, Wroughton
	LNA 166G	Leyland	Atlantean PDR2/1	801126	Park Royal	B56355	H--/--D	12/68	Manchester 1066	SELNEC Preservation Society
	LRG 14G	AEC	Reliance	6MU2R7045	Alexander	111/Y/368/2	B45F	9/68	Aberdeen 14	Macduff, Kilmarnock
	MFA 703G	Daimler	Fleetline SRG6LW	63134	Willowbrook	CF1805	B44F	4/69	Burton 103	Anthony, Burton-upon-Trent
	MJA 891G	Leyland	Titan PD3/14	804003	East Lancs	6716	H38/32R	1/69	Stockport 91	Museum of Transport, Manchester
	MJA 893G	Leyland	Titan PD3/14	804345	East Lancs	6723	H38/32F	2/69	Stockport 93	Finch, Higher Ince (GM)
	MJA 895G	Leyland	Titan PD3/14	804347	East Lancs	6720	H38/32F	2/69	Stockport 95	Marfleet & Bampfylde, Southsea
	MJA 897G	Leyland	Titan PD3/14	804371	East Lancs	6725	O38/32F	2/69	Stockport 97	Museum of Transport, Manchester
	MMW 354G	Bristol	RELL6G	RELL-3-549	ECW	17166	B44D	5/69	Wilts & Dorset 824	Holtby, Battersea
	MSD 114G	Ford	R226	BCO4HD45422	Plaxton	692751	C53F	1/69	Paterson & Brown, Kilbirnie	-?-, -?-

	MVU 947G	→ see TAO 179G								
	MWH 277G	Leyland	Atlantean PDR1A/1	802759	East Lancs	6713	H--/--F	11/68	Bolton 277	Amarnani & Neville, Bolton
	NAG 120G	Bristol	REMH6G	REMH-7-117	Alexander	M1/2767/17	C42FT	6/69	Western SMT 2214	Nicholson, Livingston
	NDK 169G	→ see RCD 108G								
	NDL 375G	Bedford	VAM70	7T456499	Duple	1221/3	C45F	3/69	Paul, Ryde 12	Duffy, Macclesfield
	NDL 490G	Bristol	VRT/SL6G	VRT/SL216	ECW	17787	H--/--F	5/69	Southern Vectis 622	622 Splinter Group, Shaftesbury
	NDL 769G	Bristol	LHS6L	LHS-105	Marshall	MM0824	B35F	7/69	Southern Vectis 833	Aycliffe & District Bus Preservation Society
	NDP 275G	Bristol	RELL6G	RELL-6-121	Pennine	433	B41D	9/68	Reading 275	King, Woodley
	NDV 537G	Leyland	Atlantean PDR1/1	703872	Metro-Cammell	HO52675/6	H43/32F	11/68	Devon General 537	Follwell, Stableford
	NLJ 821G	Bristol	RELL6G	RELL-3-514	ECW	17140	B44D	10/68	Hants & Dorset 832	Brown, Nailsea
	NLJ 825G	Bristol	RELL6G	RELL-3-521	ECW	17144	B--D	10/68	Hants & Dorset 836	Hewlett & Brown, Newport
	NOV 796G	Daimler	Fleetline CRG6LX	62952	Park Royal	B55227	H43/28D	12/68	Birmingham 3796	3796 Group, Birmingham
(r)	NOV 802G	Daimler	Fleetline CRG6LX	62958	Park Royal	B55233	H43/28D	12/68	Birmingham 3802	West Midlands Bus Preservation Society
	NOV 880G	Daimler	Fleetline CRG6LX	63036	Park Royal	B56714	H43/28D	5/69	Birmingham 3880	Smith, Walsall
	NTJ 943G	Bedford	J2SZ10	7T107710	Plaxton	688042	C20F	12/68	Battersby, Morecambe	Male, Daventry
	OCD 768G	Bristol	VRT/SL6G	VRT/SL161	ECW	17756	H--/--F	3/69	Southdown 2098	Barley, Terrill & Start, Brighton
	OFV 467G	AEC	Reliance	6U3ZR7280	Plaxton	692919	C57F	7/69	Abbott, Blackpool	Kidswheels, Liverpool (XMY)
	OHH 977G	Bedford	J2SZ10	7T108049	Plaxton	692008	C20F	9/68	Irving, Carlisle	Irving, Carlisle (CA)
	OKO 816G	Leyland	Leopard PSU3A/4R	802110	Willowbrook	CF1744	DP49F	11/68	Maidstone & District 2816	2816 Society, Gravesend
	OOR 320G	Bedford	VAL70	7T450828	Plaxton	688604	C52F	11/68	Gale, Haslemere	Webb, Armscote (WK)
	OOU 856G	Bedford	VAL70	7T459544	Duple Northern	200/2	C53F	9/68	Skinner & Harvey, Oxted	Pearce, Berinsfield (OX)
	ORU 230G	Leyland	Atlantean PDR1A/1	802640	Alexander	A55/3068/11	H43/31F	4/69	Bournemouth 230	Shears D, Winkleigh
	OSF 307G	Bristol	VRT/SL6G	VRT/SL239	ECW	18094	H43/31F	6/69	Scottish Omnibuses AA305	Priddle, Farnham
	OTA 290G	Bristol	VRT/SL6G	VRT/SL122	ECW	17315	H39/31F	5/69	Western National 1056	Billington, Maidenhead
	OTA 632G	Bristol	RELH6G	RELH-4-201	ECW	17490	C45F	3/69	Southern National 1460	West Country Historic Omnibus & Transport Trust
	OTA 640G	Bristol	RELH6G	RELH-4-208	ECW	17493	C45F	3/69	Southern National 2380	Burdett, Corley
	OTA 645G	Bristol	RELH6G	RELH-4-205	ECW	17498	C38F	3/69	Western National 2385	Wakelin, Brinklow (*operates as Wheels, Brinklow (WK)*)
	OTT 253G	Bedford	SB5	9T464692	Plaxton	692118	C41F	2/69	Trathen, Yelverton	Deeble, Darley Ford (CO)
	OUH 177G	Leyland	Leopard PSU3A/4R	900597	Plaxton	693263	C49F	4/69	Western Welsh 177	Cardiff Transport Preservation Group
	OUX 533G	Ford	R192	BC04HS52922	Duple	1227/39	C45F	5/69	Scoltock, Much Wenlock	Heartlands, Tamworth (ST)
	PBC 98G	Leyland	Atlantean PDR1A/1	803283	ECW	17183	H43/31F	12/68	Leicester 98	Countryman, Ibstock (LE)
	PBC 113G	Leyland	Atlantean PDR1A/1	803390	Park Royal	B56143	H43/31F	4/69	Leicester 113	Leicester Transport Heritage Trust
	PCG 888G	AEC	Reliance	6U3ZR7089	Plaxton	692916	C55F	10/68	Coliseum, Southampton	Millard, Flexford
	PCG 889G	AEC	Reliance	6MU3R7097	Plaxton	692855	C45F	12/68	Coliseum, Southampton	Southampton & District Transport Heritage Trust
	PHA 505G	BMMO	S22	5905	BMMO	BB5793	DP45F	8/68	BMMO 5905	Hodgekins, -?-
	PPM 206G	Bristol	RESL6G	RESL-5-162	ECW	17102	B35D	7/68	Brighton Hove & District 206	Henson, Northampton
	PPM 210G	Bristol	RESL6G	RESL-5-166	ECW	17106	B41D	7/68	Brighton Hove & District 210	BH&D 210 Preservation Group, Brighton
	PRH 255G	Leyland	Atlantean PDR1A/1	802824	Roe	GO6636	H44/31F	1/69	Hull 255	Hull Bus Restorers, Hull
	PRJ 323G	Leyland	Atlantean PDR1A/1	901211	Park Royal	B56841	H43/29D	7/69	Salford 323	Platt, Salford
	PTF 410G	Leyland	Titan PD2A/47	900873	East Lancs	6769	H--/--F	4/69	Darwen 44	Darwen Transport Museum Trust
	PTF 863G	Bedford	SB5	9T466063	Plaxton	692132	C41F	3/69	Fairclough, Lostock	Robinson, Hay-on-Wye
	RAT 872G	Daimler	Fleetline CRG6LX	63109	Park Royal	B56721	H39/29F	5/69	East Yorkshire 872	Ireland, Hull
	RBC 345G	Bedford	VAL70	7T455192	Duple Northern	182/80	C--F	4/69	Cook, Dunstable	Price, Shobdon
	RBC 999G	AEC	Reliance	6MU4R6776	Plaxton	692871	C41F	3/69	Straw, Leicester	Smith, Coalville
	RBD 319G	Bristol	RELL6G	RELL-3-497	ECW	16905	B53F	9/68	United Counties 319	Robertson, Biggleswade
	RCD 108G	AEC	Reliance (ex ARU 100A, NDK 169G)	6U3ZR6759	Plaxton	692960	C49F	5/69	Yelloway, Rochdale	Friends of the Pump House Museum, Walthamstow

	Registration	Chassis	Model	Chassis No	Body	Body No	Layout	Date	First Operator	Current Owner
	RDG 304G	Daimler	Roadliner SRP8	36298	Plaxton	693355	C47F	5/69	Black & White D304	Black & White, Penton Mewsey (HA)
	RFN 953G	Daimler	Fleetline CRG6LX	63061	Park Royal	B56543	H39/33F	5/69	East Kent	Drake & Ferguson, Deal
	RHA 919G	BMMO	S23	5919	BMMO	BB5807	B51F	12/68	BMMO 5919	Woodock, Weymouth
(r)	RKA 955G	Leyland	Panther PSUR1A/1R	802121	MCW		B20F	12/68	Liverpool 1076	Merseyside Transport Trust
	RKM 616G	Leyland	Leopard PSU3A/4R	901889	Duple Northern	204/11	C48F	7/69	Maidstone & District 4616	Walton, Woore
	ROT 353G	Bedford	VAL70	9T464417	Duple Northern	200/22	C--F	4/69	Martin, West End	Evans, Pentrefoelas (CN)
	RUB 379G	Leyland	Leopard PSU3A/4R	900996	Plaxton	693293	C53F	5/69	Wallace Arnold Tours	Brown, Aboyne (SN)
	SAX 1G	Bristol	RELH6L	RELH-4-184	ECW	17467	C47F	11/68	Red & White RC169	Brown, Worthen
	SHA 645G	Leyland	Leopard PSU4A/4R	900587	Plaxton	693166	C40F	5/69	BMMO 6145	BaMMOT, Wythall
	SKB 695G	Bristol	RELL6G	RELL-3-564	Park Royal	B55984	B45D	4/69	Liverpool 2025	Merseyside Transport Trust
	SVF 896G	Bristol	RELH6G	RELH-4-213	ECW	17737	C47F	2/69	Eastern Counties RE896	White, Harston
	SVK 616G	Leyland	Atlantean PDR1/1	803156	Alexander	J6/666/15	H45/30D	11/68	Newcastle 616	Buckley, Newcastle-upon-Tyne
	SVK 627G	Leyland	Atlantean PDR1/1	803274	Alexander	J10/666/26	O44/30F	4/69	Newcastle 627	Hoare, Chepstow (CS)
	TAO 179G	Bedford	SB5	9T466652	Duple	1224/23	C41F	4/69	Hamilton, Workington	Harrod, Bexwell (NK)
			(ex MVU 947G, J 5958, TAO 179G)							
	TBD 278G	Bristol	RELH6G	RELH-4-244	ECW	17728	DP49F	6/69	United Counties 278	Jones, Penygroes (CN)
	TBU 30G	AEC	Reliance	6MU3R6807	Plaxton	692945	C51F	4/69	Schofield, Ashton	Crowther, Booker
	THU 354G	Bristol	RESL6L	RESL-5-249	ECW	17847	B43F	7/69	Bristol 508	Hodgson, Bolton (nr Appleby)
	TVT 127G	Leyland	Leopard PSU4A/4R	802875	Marshall	B4102	B38FL	11/68	Potteries SN1127	Plant, Newcastle-under-Lyme
	TVT 128G	Leyland	Leopard PSU4A/4R	802876	Marshall	B4100	B43F	11/68	Potteries SN1128	128 Group, Stone
	TYC 250G	AEC	Reliance	6MU3R7100	Willowbrook	CF1770	B45F	12/68	Hutchings & Cornelius, South Petherton	Lartey, Peterborough
	TYD 122G	AEC	Reliance	6MU3R6774	Willowbrook	CF1978	B45F	3/69	Hutchings & Cornelius, South Petherton	Clarke, Dorking (SR)
	URR 198G	Bedford	VAS5	9T466951	Plaxton	692075	C29F	4/69	Moxon, Oldcotes	Moxon, Oldcotes (NG)
	UTG 312G	AEC	Regent V	2MD3RA643	Willowbrook	CF1824	H34/26F	3/69	Pontypridd 7	Larkin, Peterborough
	UTG 313G	AEC	Regent V	2MD3RA644	Willowbrook	CF1825	H34/26F	3/69	Pontypridd 8	Cardiff Transport Preservation Group
	UXD 129G	Bristol	RELL6L	RELL-3-620	ECW	17195	B48D	1/70	United Counties 389	Adams & McClure, Luton
	VAL 466G	Bedford	VAL70	2T471384	Plaxton	728388	C53F	4/72	Smith, Birmingham	Fosker, Denham (SK)
			(ex SCK 56K, DOE 111K)							
	VHN 527G	Daimler	Fleetline SRG6LW-33	63040	Roe	GO6539	B43D	11/68	Darlington 27	Yates, Arnold
	VLW 444G	AEC	Merlin	4P2R503	MCW		B--D	12/68	London Transport MBS444	Boxall & Daniels, Beckenham
	VLW 539G	AEC	Merlin	4P2R596	MCW		B25D	6/69	London Transport MBS539	Sibbons, Billericay
	VMP 8G	Albion	Viking VK43AL	53431F	Alexander	103Y/2167/30	C20F	10/68	Road Transport Industry Training Board 16	Forbes, Barrhead
	VMP 10G	AEC	Reliance	6U3ZR7106	Alexander	122Y/2868/1	DP57F	6/69	Road Transport Industry Training Board 24	Carson, Airdrie
	VVK 53G	Austin Morris	250JU	1786	Austin Morris		M6	-/69	Royal Navy	Johnson, Darlington
			(ex Q248 WNL, 04 RN 62)							
	WHN 411G	Bristol	VRT/SL6G	VRT/SL164	ECW	17800	H39/31F	3/69	United 601	Dolan M, Crook
	WWY 115G	Bedford	VAL70	9T464196	Plaxton	692426	C53F	1/69	Abbey, Selby	Greatholder, Rugeley
	WYP 202G	AEC	Reliance	6MU3R7271	Plaxton	692864	C45F	7/69	Surrey, Sutton	Soul, Monkwood
	WYP 203G	AEC	Reliance	6MU3R7270	Plaxton	7410AC009S	C41F	7/69	Thomas, West Ewell	Prout, Roche
						(rebodied 11/74)				
	XCH 425G	Daimler	Fleetline CRG6LX	63556	Roe	GO6722	H44/34F	7/69	Derby 225	Derby Museums
	XDH 56G	Daimler	Fleetline CRC6-36	62852	Northern Counties	6769	H51/34D	12/68	Walsall 56	Taylor, Lichfield
	XDH 516G	Daimler	Fleetline CRG6LX	62920	Northern Counties	6779	H41/27D	2/69	Walsall 116	Taylor, Lichfield
	XDH 519G	Daimler	Fleetline CRG6LX	62923	Northern Counties	6780	H41/27D	2/69	Walsall 119	Cox & Bodley, Cannock
	XFM 42G	Guy	Arab V	FD77081	Northern Counties	6814	H41/32F	3/69	Chester 42	Armour, Derby
	XWW 474G	Bristol	VRT/SL6G	VRT/SL107	ECW	17279	H39/31F	1/69	West Yorkshire VR4	Halliday, Shipley
	XWX 162G	BMC	550FG	319548	Wadham		B20F	2/69	Rolls Royce, Barnoldswick	Carter, -?-
	XYE 101G	AEC	Reliance	6MU4R7209	Plaxton	692875	C41F	4/69	Essex County, Stratford	Black & White, Penton Mewsey (HA)

	Reg	Make	Model	Chassis	Body	Body no	Seating	Date	First operator	Current owner
	YNU 351G	Bristol	Lodekka FLF6G	236326	ECW	17002	H38/32F	9/68	Midland General 313	Webb, Sutton-in-Ashfield
	AML 1H	AEC	Swift	4MP2R285	Marshall	B4461	B42F	1/70	London Transport SM1	London Bus Company, Northfleet (KT)
	AML 3H	AEC	Swift	4MP2R333	Marshall	B4464	B46F	1/70	London Transport SM3	Harlott, Ipswich
	AML 30H	AEC	Swift	4MP2R361	Marshall	B4490	B46F	4/70	London Transport SM30	Emsworth & District, Southbourne (WS)
	AML 32H	AEC	Swift	4MP2R363	Marshall	B4489	B—F	4/70	London Transport SM32	-?-, -?-
	AML 88H	AEC	Swift	4MP2R417	Park Royal	B57091	B42D	6/70	London Transport SMS88	London Bus Company, Northfleet (KT)
	AML 91H	AEC	Swift	4MP2R420	Park Royal	B57094	B--D	6/70	London Transport SMS91	Pump House Steam & Transport Trust,
										Walthamstow
	AML 97H	AEC	Swift	4MP2R426	Park Royal	B57100	B32D	5/70	London Transport SMS97	Parr, -?-
	AML 581H	AEC	Merlin	4P2R637	MCW		B--C	5/69	London Transport MBA581	Biddell, Woodford Bridge
	AML 582H	AEC	Merlin	4P2R638	MCW		B25D	5/69	London Transport MBA582	London Transport Museum
	AML 588H	AEC	Merlin	4P2R645	MCW		B--D	5/69	London Transport MBA588	Clayton, Birmingham
	AML 641H	AEC	Merlin	4P2R763	MCW		B50F	8/69	London Transport MB641	Wright, Hitchin
	BEH 147H	Daimler	Fleetline SRG6LX-36	63859	Alexander	11W/5368/9	B39D	5/70	Potteries 147	Plant, Newscastle-under-Lyme
	BPH 106H	AEC	Swift	4MP2R435	Park Royal	B57109	B38D	5/70	London Country SM106	Wilkins, Anglesey
	BPH 114H	AEC	Swift	4MP2R443	Park Royal	B57117	B38D	6/70	London Country SM114	Country Bus Rallies, East Grinstead
	BWB 148H	Leyland	Atlantean PDR2/1	901382	Park Royal	B59621	H--/--D	9/69	Sheffield 748	748 Group, Sheffield
	BWP 727H	Bedford	VAM70	0T477587	Plaxton	708197	C37F	3/70	Regent, Redditch	Price, Shobdon
	BWU 691H	Leyland	Leopard PSU4A/2R	903541	Pennine	569	B43F	11/69	Todmorden 19	Beeby, Huddersfield
	DFM 347H	Guy	Arab V	FD77108	Northern Counties	6818	H41/32F	10/69	Chester 47	North West Museum of Transport
	DWB 54H	AEC	Swift	5P2R737	Park Royal	B56117	B50F	7/70	Sheffield 54	Hatton, Sheffield
	DWU 839H	Bristol	VRT/SL6G	VRT/SL2/142	ECW	18244	O39/30F	8/70	York-West Yorkshire YVR52	Halliday, Shipley
	EFM 163H	Bristol	RELH6G	RELH-4-258	ECW	18140	C47F	3/70	Crosville CRG163	Jones, Porthmadog
	EFM 181H	Bristol	RELL6G	RELL-3-1065	ECW	18410	B53F	5/70	Crosville SRG181	SRG Group, Widnes
	ENU 93H	Leyland	Panther PSUR1A/1R	803293	Northern Counties	6720	B49D	9/69	Chesterfield 93	Corroy, Chesterfield
	FRB 208H	Bristol	RELL6G	RELL-3-1083	ECW	18522	B44D	7/70	Midland General 146	Schofield, Derby
	FRB 211H	Bristol	VRT/SL6G	VRT/SL2/126	ECW	18206	H39/31F	6/70	Midland General 322	BaMMOT, Wythall
	FWC 439H	Bristol	RELL6G	RELL-3-919	ECW	17606	B47F	12/69	Eastern National 1516	Edwards, Witham
	GUP 647H	AEC	Reliance	6MU3R7330	Plaxton	703565	B55F	12/69	OK, Bishop Auckland	Duffy, Macclesfield
	JVL 619H	Bristol	VRT/SL6G	VRT/SL/264	ECW	17779	H39/31F	8/69	Lincolnshire 1904	Belton, Scunthorpe
	JVL 928H	Bristol	LHS6P	LHS-113	ECW	17993	B--F	11/69	Lincolnshire 1809	Belton, Scunthorpe
	KCK 381H	Leyland	Leopard PSU4A/4R	903893	Plaxton	709076	C41F	4/70	Ribble 1000	Beattie, Reading
			(ex LIL 7077, NIJ 6060, JEP 609, KCK 381H)							
	KNK 369H	→ see UIA 884								
(r)	KNK 371H	Bedford	J2SZ10	9T134811	Plaxton	692035	C15F	9/69	Rickards, Brentford 26	Sloan, Tunbridge Wells
	KNK 373H	Bedford	J2SZ10	9T143933	Plaxton	702037	C15F	9/69	Rickards, Brentford 28	Kenzie, Shepreth (CM)
(r)	KNK 379H	Bedford	VAL70	9T471508	Plaxton	708357	C53F	4/70	Thompson, Edmonton	Johnson, Worksop (NG)
	LEF 60H	Bristol	RELL6L	RELL-3-1120	ECW	18656	B46D	9/70	Hartlepool 60	Larkin, Peterborough
	LFE 832H	Bristol	RELL6G	RELL-3-1092	ECW	18515	B--F	8/70	Lincolnshire 1216	Gallagher, Waddington
			(ex XKH 293H, 897 EYX, LFE 832H)							
	LVV 455H	Ford	Transit	-?-	Strachan		B16F	9/69	-?-, -?-	-?-, Barry
	LWR 229H	International Harvester	Loadstar 1600	-?-	Superior		B28F	-/71	United States Air Force	-?-, Leeds
	MPR 534H	Bedford	VAL70	0T473288	Plaxton	708381	C53F	5/70	Rendell, Parkstone	Cooper, Killamarsh (DE)
	MUR 200H	Bedford	J2SZ10	9T146270	Plaxton	702041	C16F	10/69	Rickards, Brentford 29	Sloan, Tunbridge Wells
	MUR 202H	Bedford	J2SZ10	9T146625	Plaxton	702042	C20F	11/69	Rickards, Brentford 31	Rasey, Penton Grafton
	MVE 400H	Bedford	J2SZ2	9T143502	Plaxton	692023	C20F	10/69	Ely Hospital	Newby, Mirfield
	NEB 506H	Bedford	J2SZ2	0T151335	Plaxton	708001	C20F	2/70	Blood Transfusion Service	Mathews, West Kingsdown

	Reg	Make	Model	Chassis No	Body	Body No	Layout	Date	First Owner	Current Owner
	NNB 547H	Leyland	Atlantean PDR2/1	902857	East Lancs	6803	H47/32F	11/69	SELNEC PTE 1142	SELNEC Preservation Society
	NNB 589H	Daimler	Fleetline CRG6LXB	63355	Park Royal	B56648	H47/28D	2/70	SELNEC PTE 2130	SELNEC Preservation Society
	NNB 598H	Daimler	Fleetline CRG6LXB	63364	Park Royal	B56657	H47/35F	2/70	SELNEC PTE 2139	Hycote, Royton
	NRG 26H	AEC	Swift	2MP2R317	Alexander	9W13/3468/2	B--D	9/69	Aberdeen 26	Aberdeen & District Transport Preservation Trust
	NRG 69H	Albion	Viking VK43AL	53435L	Alexander	124Y/3768/6	C40F	4/70	Alexander Northern NNV69	Scotmech Trucks, Dundee
	OAG 535H	Leyland	Leopard PSU3/3R	901476	Alexander	125Y/4268/13	RV	4/70	Western SMT 1075	Taybus Vintage Vehicle Society
	OBK 602H	AEC	Reliance	6MU4RE6865	Plaxton	708885	C26FT	4/70	Byng, Portsmouth	Richardson, Tilehurst
	OBN 300H	Leyland	Atlantean PDR1A/1	901656	East Lancs	6818	H43/27D	10/69	SELNEC PTE 6800	Neville et al, Bolton
	OFC 902H	Bristol	VRT/SL6G	VRT/SL2/102	ECW	18208	H39/31F	4/70	City of Oxford 902	Clements, Oxford
	OMB 1H	Ford	R226	BCO4JG57905	Plaxton	708743	C53F	1/70	Bullock, Cheadle	Adkins, Upper Boddington
	ONF 865H	Leyland	Atlantean PDR2/1	7001694	Park Royal	B57224	H--/--D	7/70	SELNEC PTE 1177	SELNEC Preservation Society
	OSD 720H	Ford	R192	BC04JB46346	Plaxton	708558	C45F	12/69	Paterson & Brown, Kilbirnie	-?-, -?-
	PAG 318H	Leyland	Leopard PSU3A/4R	7000005	Plaxton	709139	C51F	1/70	A1, Ardrossan	Docherty, Irvine
	PDL 491H	Bristol	LH6L	LH-447	ECW	18733	B10F	5/70	Southern Vectis 829	Nash & Hussey, Ockley
	PFR 554H	AEC	Swift	MP2R259	Marshall	B4459	B47D	4/70	Blackpool 554	Lancastrian Transport Trust
	PKG 532H	Daimler	Fleetline CRG6LX	63532	Willowbrook	CF1912	H44/30D	11/69	Cardiff 532	Cardiff Transport Preservation Group
	POD 829H	Bristol	RELL6G	RELL-3-817	ECW	17641	B53F	9/69	Southern National 2730	Harris, Newport (Isle of Wight)
	POD 830H	Bristol	RELL6G	RELL-3-818	ECW	17642	B53F	9/69	Southern National 2731	Sinclair, Eastleigh
	PSD 281H	Bedford	VAS5	0T478670	Plaxton	708089	C29F	4/70	Conway, Irvine	Liddell, Auchinleck (SW)
	PUF 161H	Leyland	Leopard PSU3/1R	804462	Northern Counties	6868	DP49F	11/69	Southdown 461	Elliott & Burtenshaw, Chichester
	PUF 165H	Leyland	Leopard PSU3/1R	804606	Northern Counties	6865	DP49F	9/69	Southdown 465	Southdown 465 Group, Worthing
			(ex SZY 587, PUF 165H)							
	RDV 419H	Bristol	RELH6G	RELH-4-266	ECW	18154	C45F	2/70	Western National 1468	Sharpe, Derby
	RDV 423H	Bristol	RELH6G	RELH-4-274	ECW	18158	C45F	3/70	Western National 1472	Smart, Chippenham
	RDV 433H	Bristol	RELH6G	RELH-4-290	ECW	18173	C45F	5/70	Western National 1482	Fowler, Burntwood
	RLJ 341H	Bristol	RELL6G	RELL-3-823	ECW	17615	B45D	9/69	Hants & Dorset 3016	Robinson, Swindon
	RLJ 793H	Bristol	LH6L	LH-381	ECW	17899	B39D	2/70	Hants & Dorset 3033	Mills & Hursthouse, Netheravon
	SEL 247H	Leyland	Atlantean PDR1A/1R	903002	Alexander	J14/3268/8	H43/31F	12/69	Bournemouth 247	Lang, Rathcoole
	SNT 925H	Bedford	VAL70	0T477080	Plaxton	708407	C53F	6/70	Foxall, Bridgnorth	Ingall, Rand
	SOE 913H	Daimler	Fleetline CRG6LX	63258	Park Royal	B56755	H47/33D	10/69	West Midlands 3913	Bristol Road Group, Norwich
(r)	SOE 937H	Daimler	Fleetline CRG6LX	63282	*chassis only*			11/69	West Midlands 3937	3997 Group, Wolverhampton
	SRJ 328H	Leyland	Atlantean PDR2/1	7000088	MCW		H47/31D	6/70	SELNEC PTE 1205	Museum of Transport, Manchester
	SSF 237H	Bedford	VAL70	0T474940	Duple	213/139	C53F	6/70	Edinburgh 237	Wallace, Edinburgh
	SSF 359H	Leyland	Atlantean PDR1A/1	7001729	Alexander	J23/969/4	H--/--D	6/70	Edinburgh 359	Melrose, Edinburgh
	STO 526H	Leyland	Atlantean PDR1A/1	7000372	Northern Counties	6999	H47/30D	7/70	Nottingham 526	Nottingham Heritage Vehicles
	THL 261H	Bristol	RELL6G	RELL-3-1105	ECW	18643	B53F	7/70	West Riding 261	Keel, Selby
	TKH 270H	Leyland	Atlantean PDR1A/1	902581	Roe	GO6784	H43/28D	12/69	Hull 270	Green, Hull
	TMS 585H	Leyland	Leopard PSU3/1R	7000907	Alexander	138Y/769/1	C49F	5/70	Road Transport Industry Training Board 84	Carson, Airdrie
(a)	TOB 986H	Daimler	Fleetline CRG6LX	63695	Park Royal	B56848	H--/--D	3/70	West Midlands 3986	3997 Group, Wolverhampton
	TOB 997H	Daimler	Fleetline CRG6LX	63707	Park Royal	B56859	H47/33D	4/70	West Midlands 3997	3997 Group, Wolverhampton
	TRY 118H	Bristol	RELL6L	RELL-3-924	ECW	18104	B48F	12/69	Leicester 118	Hussey, Basingstoke
	TRY 122H	Bristol	RELL6L	RELL-3-935	ECW	18108	B47D	12/69	Leicester 122	Worman, Keighley
	TTA 400H	Bedford	SB5	0T477185	Duple	216/55	C41F	6/70	Down, Ottery St Mary	Greet, Broadhempston
	TTD 386H	Leyland	Titan PD3/4	902844	East Lancs	6640	H41/32F	11/69	Ramsbottom 11	Museum of Transport, Manchester
	TTR 167H	Leyland	Atlantean PDR1A/1	903814	East Lancs	6840	H45/31F	2/70	Southampton 133	Southampton & District Transport Heritage Trust
	TUT 888H	Bedford	VAL70	0T473933	Plaxton	708390	C53F	2/70	Weston, Leicester	Rosleyn Coaches, Par (CO)
	UAD 316H	Daimler	Roadliner SRP8	36340	Plaxton	709457	C47F	4/70	Black & White D316	Ementon, Nantwich
	UBD 757H	Bristol	VRT/SL6G	VRT/SL/269	ECW	17823	H39/31F	10/69	United Counties 757	Robertson, Biggleswade

ABH 358 is a 1933 Leyland Cub with Duple body from Gerald & Simon Emerton's Bounty Collection; its is seen at the Potteries rally at Wedgwood Pottery in May 2010. (Peter Bates)

UT 7836 is a 1930 Willowbrook bodied Gilford AS6. It is currently owned by Nick Sargent but at the time of this August 1981 view in Dunbar it was with previous owner Ted Heslop. (Peter Bates)

Since this view taken in Nottingham in June 1980, ex-Bedwas & Machen AEC Regal III / Bruce 7 (JWO 355) had emigrated to South Africa, and is nowadays a resident at the Sandstone Heritage Foundation. (Peter Bates)

John Smith & Sons of Dalton have owned Leyland Tiger PS1 / Plaxton DPY 335 since it was new in 1947. In October 2007 it attended the Aire Valley Running Day and is pictured in Otley. (Peter Bates)

DUX 655 is a 1947 Daimler CVD6 with 1948 Metalcraft coachwork. Owned by the DUX 655 Group, it is seen at Exeter Services in July 1986. (Peter Bates)

For the launch in April 1986 on his book on the Bedford OB, John Woodhams' CCF 648 was posed for photos in Bushey Park. It operates as part of his vintage tours business based in the Isle of Wight. (Peter Bates)

LVO 530 is a 1951 Austin K8CVC with Kenex coachwork owned by Terry Leach and seen at Wedgwood Pottery in May 2010. (Peter Bates)

Roger Burdett's vehicles make welcome regular appearances at running days; here Foden PVRF6 / Metalcraft NTU 125 is arriving at the Potteries running day at Wedgwood Pottery in May 2009. (Peter Bates)

Still with the successor to its original operator is Plymouth Citybus 358 (MCO 658), a 1956 Metro-Cammell bodied Leyland Titan PD2/12 opentopper. In this October 1993 view it was visiting the West of England Transport Collection open day at Winkleigh. (Peter Bates)

David and Ewan Pring of Timebus Travel have four examples of the London Transport RLH class of provincial specification Weymann-bodied AEC Regent IIIs. RLH23 (MXX 223) was entered in the Historic Commercial Vehicles Society's London to Brighton Run in May 1985 and is seen at the break point in Crawley. (Peter Bates)

In addition to its comprehensive collections of trams, the National Tramway Museum also has this 1937 ex-Sheffield AEC Regent CWJ 410 converted to a tower wagon for tramway overhead maintenance. Although seen here at Crich in August 1981, it is not currently on public display. (Peter Bates)

Jones of Flint acquired this ex-Ribble Leyland Tiger Cub / Burlingham in 1975 and subsequently retained it for preservation. It is seen on Bodafon Fields, Llandudno in May 2009. (Peter Bates)

Phil Platt's Grey Cars liveried ex Devon General 1 (1 RDV) is a Harrington-bodied AEC Reliance, pictured at Exeter Services in July 1986. (Peter Bates)

Chris Bulmer, North Stainley operates Bristol MWs on leisure services in the Yorkshire Dales. Former Eastern National 208 YVX is seen here leaving Hawes for Redmire in September 2009. (Peter Bates)

Irish Transport Heritage's ex Ulsterbus 343 (DXI 3343) is pictured on Bodafon Fields, Llandudno in May 2009. It is a Leyland Tiger TRBTL11/2RP with Alexander (Belfast) body. (Peter Bates)

The majority of vehicles from the Bournemouth Heritage Transport Collection have been re-housed by Dan Shears at the West of England Transport Collection. This is an earlier view taken at Sandtoft in July 1986. (Peter Bates)

In the rain at Showbus 2010 is BHA 656C, a BMMO CM6T motorway coach which is part of the BaMMOT collection at the Transport Museum, Wythall. (Peter Bates)

Ex-Lincolnshire Road Car Bristol RELH6G / ECW 1431 (CVL 850D) is owned by three members of the Lincolnshire Vintage Vehicle Society and is seen visiting the Trolleybus Museum, Sandtoft in July 2011. (Peter Bates)

New as Alexander Northern NNV43, GRS 343E is an Albion Viking VK43L with Alexander body preserved by Stagecoach subsidiary Bluebird Buses; it is pictured at Showbus 2006. (Peter Bates)

VMP 10G, an Alexander bodied AEC Reliance, was new to the Road Transport Industry Training Board but is preserved in a livery based on that of Baxters of Airdire. It is a working preserved bus in the fleet of John Carson, Chapelhall and is seen in April 2010 in Glasgow. (Peter Bates)

George Atkin has restored his Plaxton bodied Bedford SB5 SHO 628P in his own livery. It was new to the government research establishment at Porton Down and later served as a driver trainer with First Cymru. In September 2010 it attended the Meadowhall rally. (Peter Bates)

At Showbus 2010 is former United Counties 59 (OVV 59R), a Duple bus bodied Ford R1014 owned by Tim and Martin Roberts, collectively the 59 Group. (Peter Bates)

A September 2009 visitor to Heaton Park in Manchester, Highland L25 (CAS 519W) is an Alexander-bodied Leyland Leopard preserved by Les Scott. (Peter Bates)

Seen at Meadowhall in September 2010 is Mick Jessop's ex Yorkshire Traction Leyland National 245 (NKU 245X). It is based at Keighley Bus Museum where it forms part of the class VI fleet, (Peter Bates)

UTN 501Y is a 1983 ex-Northern General MCW Metrobus owned by Lee Garrett; it is seen visiting the Trolleybus Museum, Sandtoft in July 2011. (Peter Bates)

This ex Midland Red North ECW bodied Leyland Olympian is seen at Chatsworth House in June 2009; at that time it was with Vals Classic Coaches, Chase Terrace but has since passed to a new owner. (Peter Bates)

MAS, Anston imported this 1980 Crown School Bus from the USA in 2008. Seen here at Meadowhall in September 2008 with Californian registration 5W 13180, it has since been allocated UK registration GHL 212V. (Peter Bates)

The National Tramway Museum's 902 was built by CKD Tatra in 1975 for Halle, near Leipzig in Germany. It arrived at Crich and is seen here in July 2008. (Peter Bates)

	Reg	Make	Model	Chassis No	Body	Body No	Layout	Date	New to	Owner
	UGB 138H	Bedford	SB5	9T469083	Willowbrook	CF1947	B40F	8/69	MacBrayne 35	MacBrayne Circle
	UHA 225H	Daimler	Fleetline CRG6LXB	63213	Alexander	J12/1868/70	H45/30D	11/69	BMMO 6225	Harper, Stourbridge
	UHA 941H	BMMO	S23	5941	BMMO	BB5829	B51F	1/70	BMMO 5941	BaMMOT, Wythall
	UHA 956H	BMMO	S23	5956	BMMO/Plaxton	BB5844/692355	B51F	11/69	BMMO 5956	BaMMOT, Wythall (WO)
	UHA 963H	BMMO	S23	5963	BMMO/Plaxton	BB5851/692363	B51F	12/69	BMMO 5963	Wakelin, Brinklow
										(operates as Wheels, Brinklow (WK))
(r)	UHA 969H	BMMO	S23	5969	BMMO/Plaxton	BB5857/692369	B51F	12/69	BMMO 5969	Wakelin, Brinklow
	UHA 977H	BMMO	S23	5977	BMMO/Plaxton	BB5865/692386	B51F	2/70	BMMO 5977	Davies, Catshill
	UHA 981H	BMMO	S23	5981	BMMO/Plaxton	BB5869/692390	B51F	3/70	BMMO 5981	BaMMOT, Wythall
	UKA 562H	Leyland	Atlantean PDR2/1	902924	Alexander	2L1/2268/1	H47/32D	12/69	Merseyside PTE 1111	Merseyside Transport Trust
	UKE 403H	Leyland	Leopard PSU4A/4R	902023	Marshall	B4391	B45F	4/70	Maidstone & District 3403	Mee, Northfleet
	UOU 417H	Leyland	Panther PSUR1A/1R	903247	Plaxton	709511	B52F	1/70	King Alfred, Winchester	FoKAB, Winchester
	UOU 419H	Leyland	Panther PSUR1A/1R	903249	Plaxton	709513	B52F	1/70	King Alfred, Winchester	FoKAB, Winchester
	UTD 298H	→ see EIB 8234								
	VBD 310H	Bedford	VAL70	0T476066	Plaxton	708400	C48F	4/70	Coales, Wollaston 50	Barker, Roydon (EX)
	VKF 894H	Bedford	J2SZ10	0T161567	Plaxton	708021	C20F	7/70	Middleton, Liverpool	Morton, Owermoigne
	VMO 228H	Bristol	LH6L	LH-314	ECW	17932	B41F	9/69	Thames Valley 211	Rampton, Reading
	VMO 234H	Bristol	LH6L	LH-357	ECW	17935	B41F	11/69	Thames Valley 214	Robertson, Biggleswade
	VRY 562H	→ see VUB 396H								
	VTD 441H	Leyland	Tiger Cub PSUC1/12	950120	Fowler		B44F	3/70	Fishwick, Leyland 12	Hayes, Little Hoole
	VUB 396H	Leyland	Leopard PSU3A/4R	7000732	Plaxton	709185	C53F	4/70	Wallace Arnold Tours	Dodsworth, Boroughbridge (NY)
			(ex VRY 562H TIB 8792, VRY 562H, OO 1908, VUB 396H)							
	VUD 348H	Leyland	Leopard PSU3A/4R	7000112	Plaxton	709116	C51F	3/70	Heyfordian, Upper Heyford	-?-, -?-
			(ex FIL 7662, VUD 348H)							
	WHA 237H	Leyland	Leopard PSU3A/4R	7002000	Plaxton	709161	RV	7/70	BMMO 6237	Dolan A & Purvis, Crook
	WHW 374H	Bristol	RELH6L	RELH-4-306	ECW	18766	DP49F	6/70	Bristol 2062	Stroud RE Group
	WNG 864H	Bristol	RELL6G	RELL-3-995	ECW	18457	B50F	3/70	Eastern Counties RLE864	Patterson, Kings Lynn
	WPW 869H	Bristol	RELL6G	RELL-3-1038	ECW	18462	DP50F	4/70	Eastern Counties RLE869	Stanton, Gloucester
	XNX 136H	Leyland	Leopard PSU3A/4R	7001612	Alexander	135Y/2869/1	C49F	5/70	Stratford Blue 36	Aston Manor Road Transport Museum
	YNN 650H	Leyland	Leopard PSU3A/4R	901225	Willowbrook	CF2074	DP51F	12/69	Gash, Newark LO7	Hines, Barnsley
	YYX 997H	→ see PZR 990 *Ireland*								
	YRT 898H	AEC	Swift	2MP2R481	ECW	18063	B45D	10/69	Lowestoft 4	East Anglia Transport Museum
	AHA 451J	Leyland	Leopard PSU4B/4R	7101365	Plaxton	713057	C40F	5/71	Midland Red 6451	Potts, Birmingham
	AHT 206J	Bristol	RELL6L	RELL-3-1312	ECW	18383	B50F	3/71	Bristol C1222	Gould, Bristol
	ANV 775J	Bristol	VRT/SL6G	VRT/SL2/200	ECW	18895	H39/31F	7/71	United Counties 775	Robertson, Biggleswade
	AOT 21J	Renault	TN4H	745-572	STCRP		B41R	-/36	RATP, Paris 3380	Jowitt, Niton
	ATD 281J	Leyland	Atlantean PDR1A/1	903736	Northern Counties	7062	H44/33F	11/70	Lytham St Annes 77	Lancastrian Transport Trust
	AUB 170J	AEC	Swift	5P2R965	Roe	GO7002	B--D	7/71	Leeds 1070	Harrogate Coach, Green Hammerton (NY)
	AUD 310J	Leyland	Leopard PSU3B/4R	7100629	Plaxton	713194	C51F	3/71	Slatters, Long Hanborough	Clements et al, Oxford
			(ex FIL 7661, AUD 310J)							
	AUM 915J	Ford	R226	BC04KG53758	Duple	230/28	C53F	4/71	Wallace Arnold Tours	Hughes, Cleckheaton
	BHH 83J	→ see UUF 335J								
	BHO 670J	Bedford	VAL70	1T489281	Duple Northern	229/16	C53F	8/71	Castle, Waterlooville	Redgate & Howdle, Stoke-on-Trent
	BTX 332J	Leyland	Leopard PSU4A/2R	7001429	Willowbrook	CF2110	B--F	4/71	Western Welsh 2332	Friends of Rhondda Heritage Park
	CBU 636J	→ see SAB 784								
	CRR 537J	Bristol	RELL6L	RELL-3-1006	Marshall	B4698	B--F	9/70	East Midland 0537	Curry, Pinxton
	CYA 181J	AEC	Reliance	6MU3R7511	Plaxton	719539	B47F	12/70	Hutchings & Cornelius, South Petherton	Hearson, Chesterton

DAL 771J	AEC	Reliance	6U2R7520	Plaxton	718983	C53F	12/70	Barton 1146	Wheatley & Brown, Trowell
DRC 550J	→ see DIV 83 *Ireland*								
DTD 776J	Ford	R192	BC04KG50613	Duple	228/32	C45F	4/71	Mitton, Colne	Brown, Aboyne (SN)
DVT 167J	AEC	Reliance	6U2R7341	Alexander	132Y/5468/7	C49F	10/70	Potteries 167	Hearson, Chesterton
EDJ 244J	AEC	Swift	2MP2R849	Marshall	B4804	B44D	3/71	St Helens 244	Hearson & Machin, Chesterton
EDJ 248J	AEC	Swift	2MP2R853	Marshall	B4808	B44D	5/71	St Helens 248	Fenech, Farnham
EGN 369J	AEC	Swift	4MP2R773	Park Royal	B57408	B33D	1/71	London Transport SMS369	London Bus Preservation Trust
EGP 1J	Daimler	Fleetline CRG6LXB	63804	Park Royal	B57488	H44/24D	1/71	London Transport DMS1	London Transport Museum
EGP 33J	Daimler	Fleetline CRG6LXB	64113	Park Royal	B57520	O45/23F	11/70	London Transport DMS33	Ensign, Purfleet (EX)
EGP 115J	Daimler	Fleetline CRG6LXB	64194	Park Royal	B57602	H--/--D	7/71	London Transport DMS115	McLeod, Bromley
EGP 132J	Daimler	Fleetline CRL6-30	65122	Park Royal	B57794	H44/24D	7/71	London Transport DMS132	Simmonds, Morden
FEH 169J	→ see 3044 MI *Ireland*								
FLY 755J	Seddon	Pennine 4	48336	Plaxton	713563	C51F	3/71	Essex Coachways, Stratford	Keeber, Leicester (LE)
FRR 194J	Leyland	Leopard PSU3B/4R	7100172	Plaxton	713247	C53F	4/71	Moxon, Oldcotes	Moxon, Oldcotes (NG)
FWW 188J	→ see SVS 281								
FYG 663J	Bedford	VAL70	0T480197	Willowbrook	CF2364	B56F	10/70	Wigmore, Dinnington	Price, Shobdon
GAN 744J	Leyland	Leopard PSU5/4R	7101290	Plaxton	713282	C57F	9/71	Banfield, Peckham	Heslop, Hexham
GAN 745J	Leyland	Leopard PSU5/4R	7101646	Plaxton	713283	C57F	9/71	Banfield, Peckham	Heslop, Hexham
GPA 112J	AEC	Reliance	6MU4R7783	Plaxton	712838	C45F	6/71	Safeguard, Guildford	Atkin, North Owersby
GPF 875J	→ see UUF 329J								
HFM 196J	Bristol	RELL6G	RELL-3-1218	ECW	18425	B48D	11/70	Crosville SRG196	SRG Group, Widnes
HNP 898J	Leyland	Atlantean PDR1A/1	7003162	East Lancs	6950	O45/31F	3/71	Southampton 139	Foster, Bournemouth
		(ex WOW 529J)							
JFM 650J	Daimler	Fleetline CRG6LX	64650	Northern Counties	7149	H43/29F	12/70	Chester 50	Davies, Chester
JHD 333J	Daimler	Fleetline CRG6LX	64407	Alexander	J29/1569/8	H--/--F	5/71	Yorkshire Woollen 33	-?-, St Albans
JWU 335J	Bristol	RELL6G	RELL-3-1486	ECW	19084	B52F	5/71	West Yorkshire SRG144	Pinnington, Blackburn
LRN 60J	Bristol	VRL/LH6L	VRL/LH2/136	ECW	18312	CH42/18CT	3/71	Standerwick 60	Scott, Southport
		(ex ARU 199A, ARU 500A, IJI 5367, LRN 60J)							
LRN 321J	→ see IZS 677 *Ireland*								
MCK 229J	Leyland	Panther PSUR1B/1R	7003888	Pennine	765	B47D	6/71	Preston 229	Blair, Wakefield
		(ex MAN 1836, MCK 229J)							
MJX 222J	→ see SV 6107								
NCK 106J	→ see 411 LIP *Ireland*								
NCK 338J	Bristol	RESL6L	RESL-8-242	ECW	19453	B47F	7/71	Ribble 338	Smith & Gardner, Chorley *(on loan to Ribble Vehicle Preservation Trust)*
NNU 447J	Bristol	RELL6G	RELL-3-1483	ECW	19194	B44D	6/71	Midland General 148	Bennett, Derby
NNU 449J	Bristol	RELL6G	RELL-3-1485	ECW	19196	B44D	6/71	Midland General 150	Challands, Selston
ONK 649J	Leyland	Leopard PSU3A/4R	7000628	Plaxton	709148	C53F	8/70	World Wide, London	Williams, Scorrier
PCW 203J	Bristol	RESL6L	RESL-8-178	Pennine	1090	B46F	7/71	Burnley, Colne & Nelson 103	North East RE Group, North Shields
PFY 72J	Leyland	Panther PSUR1B/1R	7004190	Marshall	B4787	B--D	8/71	Southport 72	-?-, -?-
PJE 999J	Bedford	YRQ	1T484779	Plaxton	712354	C45F	4/71	Kenzie, Shepreth	Kenzie, Shepreth (CM)
PNF 941J	Leyland	Atlantean PDR1A/1	7003009	Northern Counties	7063	H43/32F	3/71	SELNEC PTE EX1	SELNEC Preservation Society
PRG 40J	AEC	Reliance	6MU2R7515	Alexander	148Y/3969/1	B--F	9/70	Aberdeen 40	Macduff & Murray, Kilmarnock
PRG 124J	Daimler	Fleetline CRG6LX	64525	Alexander	1L4/669/3	H48/37F	2/71	Aberdeen 124	Aberdeen & District Transport Preservation Trust
PVV 888J	Bedford	J2SZ10	0T162152	Plaxton	712003	C20F	6/71	Country Lion, Northampton	Alton, Belper
RAR 690J	Bedford	VAL70	9T461819	Van Hool	4465	C49F	1/71	All Seasons, London	Maghull Coaches, Bootle (MY)
RFA 406J	Daimler	Fleetline CRG6LX	63783	Northern Counties	7147	H--/--F	11/70	Burton 106	Meredith, Merton Park
RNA 220J	Daimler	Fleetline CRG6LXB	65023	Park Royal	B57728	H47/29D	5/71	SELNEC PTE 2220	SELNEC Preservation Society

	Reg	Make	Model	Chassis no	Body	Body no	Layout	New	First operator	Owner
	RNA 236J	Daimler	Fleetline CRG6LXB	65039	Park Royal	B57745	H47/29D	6/71	SELNEC PTE 2236	Ellis, Pelsall
	RSD 732J	Leyland	Leopard PSU3/3R	7003130	Alexander	54AYS/1273/34	B53F	4/71	Western SMT 2341	Stainburn, Allerton Bywater (WY)
			(ex TNA 161J, SPR 35, RSD 732J - *rebodied 7/75*)							
	RSX 84J	Daimler	Fleetline CRG6LXB	64673	Alexander	AD3/4169/3	O44/31F	5/71	Alexander Fife FRF51	Galloway, Glasgow
			(ex PSU 314 , RXA 51J)							
	RXA 51J	→ see RSX 84J								
	SDL 636J	Bristol	VRT/SL6G	VRT/SL2/173	ECW	18918	H--/--F	3/71	Southern Vectis 626	Grant, Polegate
	SDL 638J	Bristol	VRT/SL6G	VRT/SL2/175	ECW	18920	H39/31F	3/71	Southern Vectis 628	Roberts, Birkin & Newman, Bembridge
	SFR 127J	AEC	Reliance	6U3ZR7480	Plaxton	708958	C53F	8/70	Abbott, Blackpool	Garbutt, Holbeach
	STL 725J	Bedford	YRQ	1T483655	Willowbrook	70933	DP43F	2/71	Simmons, Great Gonerby	Lloyd, Wigan
	SWV 155J	Daimler	Fleetline CRG6LX	64316	Northern Counties	7092	H--/--D	9/70	Swindon 155	Dolan, Crook
	TCD 374J	Daimler	Fleetline CRG6LX-30	63923	Northern Counties	7071	H40/31F	9/70	Southdown 374	Southdown 374 Group, Worthing
	TCD 383J	Daimler	Fleetline CRG6LX-30	63932	Northern Counties	7076	H35/0F	10/70	Southdown 383	Pearce, Worthing
	TCD 481J	Bristol	RESL6L	RESL-8-101	Marshall	B4620	B45F	10/70	Southdown 481	Croombs, Fareham
	TCD 490J	Bristol	RESL6L	RESL-8-119	Marshall	B4622	B45F	10/70	Southdown 490	Wilcox, Rayleigh
	TDV 217J	Leyland	Panther PSUR1B/1R	7001594	Marshall	B4537	B--D	9/70	Devon General 217	West Country Historic Omnibus & Transport Trust
	TFV 117J	AEC	Reliance	6U3ZR7481	Plaxton	708959	C44F	8/70	Abbott, Blackpool	Evans, Blackpool
			(ex 500 SZO, TFV 117J)							
	TFV 127J	AEC	Reliance	6U3ZR7482	Plaxton	708960	C44F	4/71	Abbott, Blackpool	Kidswheels, Liverpool (XMY)
	TFV 475J	Bedford	VAL70	1T487259	Duple Northern	229/32	C53F	5/71	Murray, Blackpool	Evans, Pentrefoelas (CN)
	TGM 214J	Daimler	Fleetline CRG6LX	64696	ECW	18248	H43/34F	5/71	Central SMT D14	Wallace, Edinburgh
	TKG 518J	Leyland	Leopard PSU4A/2R	7001392	Willowbrook	CF2088	RV	3/71	Western Welsh 1518	Cardiff Transport Preservation Group
	TNA 161J	→ see RSD 732J								
	TRU 947J	Bristol	RELL6G	RELL-3-1303	ECW	18608	DP50F	1/71	Wilts & Dorset 846	Holtby, Battersea
	TUF 81J	Leyland	Atlantean PDR1A/1	7002152	Willowbrook	CF1951/69275	H44/29D	2/71	Brighton 81	Mulpeter, Seaford
	TUJ 921J	Bedford	YRQ	0T482126	Willowbrook	CF2357	DP45F	10/70	Salopia, Whitchurch	-?-, Gwynedd
	TUO 74J	AEC	Reliance	6MU3R7296	Willowbrook	CF2055	B41F	2/71	Devon General 74	Hulme, Yatton
	TUO 255J	Bristol	RELL6G	RELL-3-1181	ECW	18526	B53F	11/70	Western National 2743	Thorpe, Willenhall
	TUX 906J	Bedford	YRQ	1T482619	Duple	227/52	C45F	3/71	Corvedale, Ludlow 6	Price, Shobdon
	UEL 562J	Bristol	RELL6G	RELL-3-1292	ECW	18509	DP50F	12/70	Hants & Dorset 3046	Frampton, Southampton
	UEL 564J	Bristol	RELL6G	RELL-3-1343	ECW	18511	DP50F	1/71	Hants & Dorset 3048	Hyland & Warwick, Prestwood
	UFJ 229J	→ see IJI 5367								
	UTU 596J	Guy	Otter	NLLODP47252	Mulliner		B26F	11/57	Douglas 9	BaMMOT, Wythall
			(ex WMN 485)							
	UTU 597J	→ see WMN 487 *Isle of Man*								
	UUF 110J	Bristol	VRT/SL6G	VRT/SL2/177	ECW	18932	H39/31F	4/71	Southdown 510	Stobart, Wimbledon
	UUF 116J	Bristol	VRT/SL6G	VRT/SL2/183	ECW	18938	H39/31F	4/71	Southdown 516	Jenkins, Horsham
	UUF 328J	Leyland	Leopard PSU3B/4R	7100503	Plaxton	713163	C47F	9/71	Southdown 1828	Duffy, Macclesfield
			(ex TJI 6310, XYC 561, UUF 328J)							
	UUF 329J	Leyland	Leopard PSU3B/4R	7100269	Plaxton	713139	C28FT	4/71	Southdown 1829	Smith R, Churchdown
			(ex GPF 875J, 408 DCD, UUF 329J)							
	UUF 335J	Leyland	Leopard PSU3B/4R	7100472	Plaxton	713158	C53F	5/71	Southdown 1835	SRARMA, Reading
			(ex BHH 83J, LOI 5726, UUF 335J)							
	VFU 864J	Bedford	J2SZ10	0T161925	Plaxton	718018	C--F	1/71	Sheffield, Cleethorpes	Mackley, Earl Shilton
	VJG 187J	AEC	Swift	5P2R933	Marshall	B4710	B48F	11/70	East Kent	East Kent Heritage, Dover
(r)	VNK 911J	Bedford	VAL70	1T484662	Duple Northern	229/8	C—F	5/71	Plaskow & Margo, Edgware	Webb, Armscote (WK)
	VRU 124J	Daimler	Fleetline CRG6LXB	64656	Roe	GO7026	H43/31F	6/71	Hants & Dorset 1901	Blair, Upham
	VTY 543J	Leyland	Leopard PSU3A/4R	7001153	Plaxton	709244	C53F	8/70	Tyne Valley, Acomb	Shears D, Winkleigh

	WHE 352J	Leyland	Leopard PSU3A/4R	903464	Willowbrook	CF2026	B53F	11/70	Yorkshire Traction 352	Taylor, Barnsley
	WJG 470J	AEC	Reliance	6U3ZR7722	Plaxton	713009	C53F	5/71	East Kent	Coulter, Horsham
	WJH 129J	Bedford	VAL70	1T483751	Duple Northern	229/15	C--F	6/71	Gilbert, Bovingdon	Greet, Broadhempston
	WNK 563J	Bedford	J2SZ2	1T180985	Willowbrook	69295	C20F	5/71	Hertfordshire County Council	Sweeney, Muthill (SE)
	WOW 529J	→ see HNP 898J								
	WOW 531J	Leyland	Atlantean PDR1A/1	7003230	East Lancs	6936	H--/--F	1/71	Southampton 141	Cook & Burden, Southampton
	WRP 767J	Bristol	VRT/SL6G	VRT/SL2/152	ECW	18234	H39/31F	9/70	United Counties 767	Robertson, Biggleswade
(r)	XGA 8J	Leyland	Atlantean PDR1A/1	7002216	Alexander	J20/5268/10	H--/--F	9/70	Glasgow LA510	Roulston, Glasgow
	XGA 15J	Leyland	Atlantean PDR1A/1	7002529	Alexander	J20/5268/17	H45/29F	9/70	Glasgow LA517	517 Gtoup, Glasgow
	XJF 130J	Seddon	Pennine 4	48335	Plaxton	713570	C53F	1/71	Watts, Leicester	Keeber, Leicester (LE)
	XKC 789J	Leyland	Atlantean PDR2/1	7003506	Alexander	2L2/2269/12	H47/32D	5/71	Merseyside PTE 1162	-?-, Liverpool
			(ex MAN 1378, XKC 789J)							
	XON 41J	Daimler	Fleetline CRG6LX	64813	Park Royal	B58066	H43/33F	7/71	West Midlands 4041	Aston Manor Road Transport Museum
	XUS 484J	Bedford	J2SZ10	0T166369	Plaxton	702006	C--F	12/70	Hamilton, Glasgow	Tyler, Worcester
	YAX 474J	Leyland	Tiger Cub PSUC1/2	554629	Willowbrook	CF2078	DP45F	-/56	Davies, Tredegar	Williams, Merthyr Tydfil
			(ex SJJ 304)		*(rebodied 4/71)*					
	YHA 283J	Daimler	Fleetline CRG6LXB	64302	Alexander	J26/1269/23	H--/--D	1/71	BMMO 6283	6283 Group, Stafford
	YHA 361J	Ford	R192	BC04KR59195	Plaxton	719868	DP21F	2/71	BMMO 6361	-?-, Exeter
	YHE 237J	Leyland	Leopard PSU4B/4R	7101086	Alexander	8AY/2470/4	RV	5/71	Yorkshire Traction L10	Taylor, Barnsley
	YHT 802J	Bristol	RESL6L	RESL-8-123	ECW	18665	B43F	9/70	Bristol 516	Ferris, Yate
	YHU 502J	Bristol	RELL6L	RELL-3-1139	ECW	18363	B--F	10/70	Bristol C1182	Gould, Bristol
	YHY 592J	Bristol	RELL6L	RELL-3-1284	ECW	18333	B50F	1/71	Bristol 1212	Fricker {North Somerset}, Nailsea (SO)
	YUE 718J	Ford	R226	BCO4JK48789	Plaxton	708728	C53F	8/70	Wainfleet, Nuneaton	Adkins, Upper Boddington
	YWO 445J	Bedford	SB5	1T484461	Duple	232/28	C41F	5/71	Evans, New Tredegar 27	Evans, New Tredegar
	ABC 330K	Bedford	J2SZ10	0T163717	Plaxton	712004	C20F	9/71	Lett, Leicester	Dew, Somersham (CM)
	AKM 425K	Leyland	Leopard PSU4A/2R	7003114	Willowbrook	69371	B52F	10/71	Maidstone & District 3425	Grant, Polegate
	ARY 225K	Scania	BR111MH	541814	MCW		B46D	7/72	Leicester 225	Webster, Leicester
	BCR 379K	Seddon	Pennine RU	48483	Seddon	1034	B44F	3/72	Southampton 15	Southampton & District Transport Heritage Trust
	BKC 236K	Leyland	Atlantean PDR1A/1	7103944	Alexander	AL1/971/1	H43/32F	3/72	Merseyside PTE 1236	Merseyside Transport Trust
	BKC 263K	Leyland	Atlantean PDR1A/1	7105249	Alexander	AL1/971/28	H43/32F	5/72	Merseyside PTE 1263	Rimmer, Litherland
	BKC 276K	Leyland	Atlantean PDR1A/1	7200377	Alexander	AL1/971/41	H43/32F	6/72	Merseyside PTE 1276	-?-, -?-
	BNT 79K	→ see 415 ZD *Ireland*								
	CBD 778K	Bristol	VRT/SL6G	VRT/SL2/246	ECW	18898	H39/31F	1/72	United Counties 778	Lewis, Dudley
	CCG 296K	Bristol	RESL6G	RESL-8-269	ECW	19551	B19D	10/71	Aldershot & District 651	Grant, Romford
	CDC 166K	Seddon	Pennine 6	48449	Plaxton	729377	C45F	1/72	Bob's, Middlesbrough 26	Price, Shobdon
(r)	CDC 167K	Seddon	Pennine 6	50571	Plaxton	729378	C--F	3/72	Bob's, Middlesbrough 27	Price, Shobdon
	CDC 168K	Seddon	Pennine 6	50572	Plaxton	729379	C41F	3/72	Bob's, Middlesbrough 28	Price, Shobdon
	CDD 235K	Bedford	VAL70	2T472097	Plaxton	728384	C53F	5/72	Grindle, Cinderford	Grindle, Drybrook
	CHA 460K	Leyland	Leopard PSU4B/4R	7101849	Plaxton	713066	C47F	12/71	BMMO 6460	Smith, -?-
	CNG 525K	Bristol	LH6P	LH-576	ECW	19619	B45F	8/71	Eastern Counties LH525	Bristol Road Group, Norwich
	DAE 511K	Bristol	RELL6L	RELL-3-1579	ECW	19401	B50F	1/72	Bristol C1257	Strange, Verwood
	DAO 293K	Bristol	RELL6L	RELL-3-1655	ECW	19132	B53F	1/72	Cumberland 293	Frampton, Southampton
	DAO 295K	Bristol	RELL6L	RELL-3-1657	ECW	19134	B53F	1/72	Cumberland 295	295 Group, Workington
	DHW 293K	Bristol	LH6L	LH-591	ECW	19634	B42F	1/72	Bristol 353	Walker, Wells
	DOE 111K	→ see VAL 466G								
	DRM 950K	Bedford	YRQ	2T470845	Duple	257/4	C45F	5/72	Titterington, Blencow	Elmes, Pontesbury
	DRX 631K	Bristol	RELL6G	RELL-3-1767	ECW	19363	B49F	6/72	Thames Valley & Aldershot 492	Rampton, Reading

Reg	Make	Model	Chassis no	Body	Body no	Layout	New	First owner	Current owner
EAH 44K	Bedford	YRQ	2T470531	Duple	244/72	C45F	2/72	Chenery, Dickleburgh	Prentice, West Calder
ECG 112K	Bristol	RELL6G	RELL-3-1730	ECW	19020	B44D	4/72	Gosport & Fareham 12	Lawson & O'Grady, Gosport
EHU 373K	Bristol	RELL6L	RELL-3-1650	ECW	19277	B50F	2/72	Cheltenham District 1272	Smart, Chippenham
EHU 386K	Bristol	RELL6L	RELL-3-1760	ECW	19290	B50F	6/72	Bristol 1292	Gould, Bristol
EHY 111K	→ see PJY 2								
EKJ 448K	Leyland	Leopard PSU4B/2R	7200105	Marshall	34873	B52F	7/72	Maidstone & District 3448	Chatham Historic Dockyard Trust (KT)
EKL 456K	Leyland	Leopard PSU4B/2R	7200351	Marshall	34881	B52F	7/72	Maidstone & District 3456	Simpson, Whittlesey
EPW 516K	Bristol	RELL6G	RELL-3-1716	ECW	19220	B53F	4/72	Eastern Counties RL516	Patterson, Kings Lynn
EUD 256K	AEC	Reliance	6MU4R7371	Plaxton	729868	B47F	3/72	Chiltern Queens, Woodcote	Oxford Bus Museum Trust
EUR 358K	→ see UKE 609X								
EWO 460K	Leyland	Leopard PSU3B/4R	7200484	Plaxton	729766	C51F	7/72	Hill, Tredegar	Sherratt, Derby
FAR 724K	Bedford	VAL70	2T473072	Duple	241/29	C53F	6/72	Langley Coach Co, Slough	Ellis, Pelsall
FRF 762K	Seddon	Pennine 4	50599	Seddon	1105	B42F	1/72	Green Bus, Rugeley 22	Evans, Rugeley
GBB 516K	Leyland	Atlantean PDR2/1	7103170	Alexander	J40/2369/9	H48/30D	6/72	Tyneside PTE 680	McKale, Gateshead
		(ex N875 MAN, GBB 516K)							
GBB 524K	Leyland	Atlantean PDR2/1	7103550	Alexander	J40/2369/17	H48/29D	6/72	Tyneside PTE 688	Bowe, Newcastle upon Tyne
GHY 135K	Bristol	RELH6L	RELH-4-453	ECW	19806	DP49F	7/72	Bristol 2073	Smart, Chippenham
GTJ 781K	Bedford	J2SZ2	1T178977	Plaxton	??8029	C17FL	10/71	Lancashire Social Services	Mathews,West Kingsdown
GYC 160K	Bristol	LH6L	LH-605	ECW	19689	B--F	1/72	Hutchings & Cornelius, South Petherton	Hitchens, Bristol
HAL 513K	Bedford	YRQ	1T487561	Duple	227/206	RV	8/71	Hylton, Glenfield	Kingston Bus Preservation Society
HHB 183K	Leyland	Leopard PSU3B/4R	7104563	East Lancs	7060	B51F	1/72	Merthyr Tydfil 183	Norman, Aberbargoed
HLG 812K	Bedford	VAL70	2T470731	Plaxton	738398	C53F	6/72	Naylor, Stockton Heath	Price, Newcastle
JDJ 260K	AEC	Swift	3MP2R1351	Marshall	34971	B44D	2/72	St Helens 260	McGarry, Widnes
JEH 198K	Bristol	RESL6L	RESL-8-343	ECW	19510	B43F	6/72	Potteries 198	Buttery, Stoke-on-Trent
JGF 753K	AEC	Swift	4MP2R1231	MCW		B33D	9/71	London Transport SMS753	Brophy, Rotherhithe
JGY 964K	Bedford	VAS2	1T489614	Willowbrook	70686	B18F	9/71	Metropolitan Police 3367G	Hoyles, Bilborough
JMC 121K	AEC	Reliance	6MU4R7927	Plaxton	728796	C34C	3/72	Glenton, London	Cooper, Killamarsh (DE)
JMC 123K	AEC	Reliance	6MU4R8023	Plaxton	728798	C41C	2/72	Glenton, London	Woods, Standish
JMF 243K	Renault	TN6A	590-087	STCRP		B33R	-/33	RATP, Paris 2481	Williams, Canterbury
JPA 121K	AEC	Reliance	6U2R7616	Park Royal	B58265	DP45F	1/72	London Country RP21	Brophy, Rotherhithe
JPA 125K	AEC	Reliance	6U2R7620	Park Royal	B58269	DP45F	1/72	London Country RP25	Graves, Watford
JPA 190K	AEC	Reliance	6U2R7685	Park Royal	B58334	DP45F	4/72	London Country RP90	Morris, Carshalton
JPF 108K	AEC	Swift	3MP2R1001	Alexander	17W/571/8	DP45F	3/72	London Country SMA8	London Bus Company, Northfleet (KT)
JPF 113K	AEC	Swift	3MP2R1006	Alexander	17W/571/13	DP45F	3/72	London Country SMA13	Mann, Stockton
JPL 153K	Leyland	Atlantean PDR1A/1	7200886	Park Royal	B58387	H43/29D	7/72	London Country AN53	Clitheroe Parr & Boxall, Bromley
JPL 179K	Leyland	Atlantean PDR1A/1	7201482	Park Royal	B58413	H43/29D	10/72	London Country AN79	Trew & Douch, Stevenage
JRT 82K	AEC	Swift	2MP2R505	Willowbrook	69215	B40D	12/71	Ipswich 82	Ipswich Transport Museum
KHC 814K	Leyland	Atlantean PDR1A/1	7104423	East Lancs	7050	O45/31F	2/72	Eastbourne 14	Bennett, Peterborough
KHC 815K	Leyland	Atlantean PDR1A/1	7104424	East Lancs	7049	O45/31F	2/72	Eastbourne 15	Bennett, Peterborough
KHD 921K	Leyland	Leopard PSU3B/4R	7200208	Marshall	34956	B53F	6/72	Yorkshire Woollen 341	Williams, Merthyr Tydfil
LDT 627K	Bedford	J2SZ10	1T184553	Plaxton	728011	C20F	1/72	Thistle, Doncaster	-?-, -?-
LLH 889K	AEC	Swift	5P2R1136	Sparshatt	3778	B36D	3/72	BOAC, Heathrow	Brooklands Museum Trust
LXE 275K	Bedford	SB5	2T470881	Plaxton	728171	C41F	4/72	Costin, Dunstable	Kinloch, London
MCN 30K	Leyland-NGT	Tynesider	NGT3000	Metro-Cammell/NGT		H39/29F	4/72	Northern General 3000	Thornton & Kell, Durham
MJP 59K	AEC	Reliance	6MU4R7971	Plaxton	728874	C28F	3/72	Eavesway, Ashton-in-Makerfield	Tomlinson, Tewkesbury
MRR 811K	AEC	Reliance	6U2R8034	Plaxton	729687	DP64F	7/72	Barton 1229	Brown, Wateringbury
MSE 693K	Bedford	YRQ	2T473719	Duple	257/66	C45F	6/72	Paterson, Dufftown	Paterson, Dufftown
		(ex DRS 85K, WAV 397, MSE 693K)							

(r)	NEC 237K	Bedford	VAL70	2T472884	Plaxton	728386	C53F	4/72	Brown, Ambleside	Johnson, Worksop (NG)
	NEK 9K	Leyland	Atlantean AN68/2R	7201098	Northern Counties	7430	H48/31D	7/72	Wigan 9	Project Group, Wigan
	NEK 31K	Seddon	Pennine 6	51935	Plaxton	729453	C53F	4/72	Smith, Wigan	-?-, Wigan
	NHN 250K	Daimler	Fleetline SRG6LX-36	64444	Roe	GO7164	B48D	8/72	Darlington 50	North East Bus Preservation Trust
	NHN 260K	Daimler	Fleetline SRG6LX-36	64454	Roe	GO7172	B48D	8/72	Darlington 60	Naisbett, Luton
	NWA 257K	Daimler	Fleetline CRG6LXB	64513	Alexander	AL3/3869/11	H43/31F	4/72	Sheffield 257	Darwin, Middleton
	NWW 163K	Bristol	LH6L	LH-620	Plaxton	729251	C45F	3/72	Robinson, Great Harwood 163	Blue Motors, Blackpool (LA)
	OCK 366K	Bristol	RESL6L	RESL-8-351	ECW	19481	B47F	7/72	Ribble 366	Lancastrian Transport Trust
										(operates as Totally, Blackpool (LA))
	OCK 367K	Bristol	RESL6L	RESL-8-352	ECW	19482	B47F	7/72	Ribble 367	Pinnington, Blackburn
	OCK 985K	Bristol	VRT/SL6G	VRT/SL2/234	ECW	18849	H39/31F	2/72	Ribble 1985	East Anglia Transport Museum
	OCK 988K	Bristol	VRT/SL6G	VRT/SL2/237	ECW	18852	H39/31F	2/72	Ribble 1988	Eastern Transport Collection
	OCK 995K	Bristol	VRT/SL6G	VRT/SL2/267	ECW	18859	O39/31F	4/72	Ribble 1995	Patterson, Kings Lynn
	OCK 997K	Bristol	VRT/SL6G	VRT/SL2/284	ECW	18861	H39/31F	5/72	Ribble 1997	Lancastrian Transport Trust
										(operates as Totally, Blackpool (LA))
	OEF 74K	Bristol	RELL6L	RELL-3-1789	ECW	19781	B46D	7/72	Hartlepool 74	Hull & Country Bus Preservation Group
	OFM 957K	Daimler	Fleetline CRG6LXB	64653	Northern Counties	2701	O43/29F	2/72	Chester 57	North West Museum of Transport
					(rebodied 1/85)					
	OTD 593K	→ see LCB 925P								
	OTW 116K	Kassbohrer	S130	158670	Kassbohrer		C51F	8/71	Kirby, Rayleigh	Kirby, Rayleigh (EX)
	OWE 271K	Bristol	VRT/SL6G	VRT/SL2/322	East Lancs	7203	H43/30F	8/72	Sheffield 271	Ireland, Solihull
	OWT 820K	Ford	R226	BC04LE45875	Plaxton	728663	C53F	3/72	Pepper, Thurnscoe 39	Walsh, Nelson
	OWY 197K	Leyland	Leopard PSU3B/4R	7200891	Plaxton	729736	C53F	4/72	Laycock, Barnoldswick	Simpson {Pennine}, Skipton (NY)
	OWY 750K	Bristol	RESL6G	RESL-8-348	ECW	20244	B33D	6/72	Keighley-WestYorkshire 2109	Halliday, Shipley
	PEX 174K	AEC	Swift	3MP2R1378	Willowbrook	70723	B43D	1/72	Great Yarmouth 74	Kear, Quedgeley
	PFX 571K	→ see 355 SZB *Ireland*								
	PFX 572K	Bedford	YRQ	1T489389	Plaxton	712430	C45F	10/71	Rendell, Parkstone	Greet, Broadhempston
	PNU 114K	Leyland	Atlantean PDR1A/1	7103713	Northern Counties	7259	H--/--D	12/71	Chesterfield 114	Hopkinson & Collis, Chesterfield
	RCP 274K	Daimler	Fleetline CRG6LX	66121	Northern Counties	7385	H--/--F	5/72	Halifax 84	Wigan Transport Trust
	RPR 738K	Bedford	VAL70	1T488607	Plaxton	712418	C53F	4/72	Rendell, Parkstone	Andybus, Dauntsey (WI)
	SCK 56K	→ see VAL 466G								
	SJA 352K	Bristol	RELL6L	RELL-3-1299	Marshall	B4774	B49F	8/71	North Western 352	Thorpe et al, Willenhall
	SJA 382K	Bristol	RELL6L	RELL-3-1546	ECW	19142	B49F	10/71	North Western 382	Downs, Chester
	SJO 271K	Renault	TN4H	749-443	STCRP		B41R	-/36	RATP, Paris 3489	Jowitt, Niton
	SRS 56K	AEC	Swift	2MP2R495	Alexander	18W13/471/9	B43D	1/72	Aberdeen 56	Aberdeen & Distrtict Transport Preservation Trust
	SVW 274K	Bristol	RELL6G	RELL-3-1743	ECW	19243	B53F	4/72	Eastern National 1546	Carters, Wherstead (SK)
	SWC 24K	Bristol	RELL6L	RELL-3-1738	ECW	19787	B53F	5/72	Colchester 24	Gilroy, Alnwick (ND) 4
	SWC 25K	Bristol	RELL6L	RELL-3-1739	ECW	19788	B53F	5/72	Colchester 25	Britishbus Preservation Group
	SWC 26K	Bristol	RELL6L	RELL-3-1740	ECW	19789	B49F	5/72	Colchester 26	Frampton, Southampton
	SXA 63K	Daimler	Fleetline CRG6LXB	65364	Alexander	AD8/1670/3	H44/31F	10/71	Alexander Fife FRF63	Douglas & Wotherspoon, Alva
	TBK 190K	Leyland	Atlantean PDR2/1	7004607	Seddon	768	B40D	8/71	Portsmouth 190	Portsmouth 190 Group
	TBK 191K	Leyland	Atlantean PDR2/1	7004608	Seddon	769	B40D	9/71	Portsmouth 191	Brown, Leigh Park
	TBK 196K	Leyland	Atlantean PDR2/1	7100168	Seddon	774	B40D	1/72	Portsmouth 196	Newing-Davis, Bankfoot
	TDL 563K	Bristol	RELL6G	RELL-3-1527	ECW	19347	DP48F	7/71	Southern Vectis 863	McCririck, Littlehampton
	TDL 564K	Bristol	RELL6G	RELL-3-1528	ECW	19348	OB53F	7/71	Southern Vectis 864	Village Bus Co, Wellow
	TDL 566K	Bristol	RELL6G	RELL-3-1628	ECW	19350	B53F	1/72	Southern Vectis 866	Blair, Upham
	TDL 567K	Bristol	RELL6G	RELL-3-1629	ECW	19351	B53F	1/72	Southern Vectis 867	-?-, Lincolnshire
	TFM 267K	Bristol	RELH6L	RELH-4-467	ECW	19889	C47F	7/72	Crosville CRL267	Sharpe, Derby

	TJO 56K	AEC	Reliance	6MU4R7749	Marshall	B4909	DP49F	12/71	City of Oxford 56	Bridges, Enstone
	TKU 462K	→ see KUI 2269								
	TKU 467K	Leyland	Atlantean PDR2/1	7101751	Alexander	1L3/2769/65	H--/--D	8/71	Bradford 467	Shepherd, Bradford
	TKU 469K	→ see UIB 3987								
	TNB 759K	Daimler	Fleetline CRG6LXB	64804	Northern Counties	7323	H45/27D	2/72	SELNEC PTE EX19	SELNEC Preservation Society
	TNE 14K	Bedford	SB5	2T471747	Plaxton	728144	C41F	4/72	Fingland, Rusholme	Higgins R, Tarvin
	TPT 6K	Leyland	Leopard PSU5/4R	7200767	Plaxton	729802	DP68F	5/72	Weardale, Frosterley	Dolan M, Crook
(r)	TSP 939K	Leyland	Leopard PSU4B/4R	7202566	Plaxton	728979	C45F	7/72	Rennie, Dunfermline	Butler, Gosforth
			(ex JBZ 8646, HHR 37K, 8 EBF, TSP 939K)							
(r)	TWH 807K	Leyland	Atlantean PDR2/1	7103647	East Lancs	7032	H--F	12/71	SELNEC PTE 6807	Bolton Bus Preservation Group
	TWH 809K	Leyland	Atlantean PDR2/1	7103649	East Lancs	7030	H49/37F	12/71	SELNEC PTE 6809	Bolton Bus Preservation Group
	TXJ 507K	Leyland	National 1151/2R/0202	00101	Leyland National		B46D	3/72	SELNEC PTE EX30	Museum of Transport, Manchester
	UFC 430K	Daimler	Fleetline CRL6	65452	Northern Counties	7230	H43/27D	1/72	City of Oxford 430	Oxford Bus Museum Trust
	UVE 593K	Bedford	J2SZ2	2T127309	Plaxton	728015	C20F	7/72	Blood Transfusion Service	Whiteside, Wimborne
	VDL 264K	Bedford	YRQ	2T471267	Plaxton	729849	B49F	3/72	Seaview Services 4	Hunt, Rookley
(r)	VDX 115K	Bedford	VAL70	2T473089	Duple Northern	241/33	C53F	5/72	Classic, Lowestoft	Evans, Pentrefoelas (CN)
	VOD 88K	Bristol	LHS6L	LHS-120	Marshall	30851	B33F	2/72	Western National 88	Bennett, Sherborne
			(ex 12728, VOD 88K)							
	VOD 101K	Bristol	RELL6G	RELL-3-1532	ECW	19306	B53F	8/71	Western National 2758	Gamblin & Rodham, Durham
	VOD 123K	Bristol	LHS6L	LHS-129	Marshall	30861	B33F	2/72	Western National 1253	Ricketts, Rhos-on-Sea
	VOD 124K	Bristol	LHS6L	LHS-130	Marshall	30860	B33F	2/72	Western National 1254	Derrick, Plymstock
	VOD 125K	Bristol	LHS6L	LHS-131	Marshall	30862	B33F	2/72	Western National 1255	Western National Preservation Group
(r)	VOD 542K	Bristol	VRT/SL6G	VRT/SL2/202	ECW	18907	H--/--F	8/71	Western National 542	Thorogood, Briantspuddle
	VOD 545K	Bristol	VRT/SL6G	VRT/SL2/205	ECW	18910	H39/31F	8/71	Western National 545	Gilkes, West Kingsdown (KT)
	VOD 550K	Bristol	VRT/SL6G	VRT/SL2/210	ECW	18915	H43/31F	8/71	Western National 550	Thorogood, Briantspuddle
	VVJ 675K	→ see JAX 354								
	WBN 900K	Bedford	J2SZ10	2T125686	Plaxton	728017	C20F	6/72	Bolton Round Table	-?-, -?-
	WFM 801K	Leyland	National 1151/2R/0403	00102	Leyland National		B44D	5/72	Crosville SNL801	Martin, Leeds
	WFR 147K	AEC	Reliance	6U3ZR7923	Plaxton	728850	C45F	3/72	Blackhurst, Blackpool	Stokes, Holbeach Drove
	WFS 300K	Leyland	Atlantean PDR1A/1	7104831	Alexander	J35/4069/50	H45/30D	4/72	Edinburgh 300	Hunt, Fleetwood
	WNU 430K	Bedford	YRQ	2T473160	Plaxton	728364	C45F	7/72	Bull, Tideswell	Warren, Martock
	WSD 756K	Leyland	Leopard PSU3/3R	7200960	Alexander	18AY/2670/4	RV	6/72	Western SMT 2366	Glasgow Vintage Vehicle Trust
	WUF 537K	Bristol	VRT/SL6G	VRT/SL2/292	ECW	18959	H43/27D	7/72	Southdown 537	Terrill, Lewes
	WUH 570K	→ see 72-D-27 *Ireland*								
	WUH 584K	Daimler	Fleetline CRL6	65486	MCW		H43/31F	1/72	Cardiff 584	Brewer, Cardiff
	WUH 585K	Daimler	Fleetline CRL6	65487	MCW		H43/31F	1/72	Cardiff 585	Brewer, Cardiff
(r)	WUO 439K	Austin-Morris	250JU	-?-	Austin-Morris		M??	10/71	Taw & Torridge, Merton	Shears, Winkleigh
	XEL 826K	Bristol	LH6L	LH-584	ECW	19653	B43F	12/71	Hants & Dorset 1540	Hussey, Basingstoke
	XKC 808K	→ see MAN 1379 *Isle of Man*								
	XKC 862K	Leyland	Atlantean PDR2/1	7003943	Alexander	2L3/2269/85	H49/31D	4/72	Merseyside PTE 1235	-?-, Isle of Man
			(ex MAN 3432, XKC 862K)							
	XLJ 726K	Bristol	RELL6G	RELL-3-1734	ECW	19338	DP50F	6/72	Hants & Dorset 1651	Hussey et al, Basingstoke
	XRD 23K	Bristol	VRT/LL6G	VRT/LL2/105	Northern Counties	7177	H47/30D	8/71	Reading 23	Rampton, Reading
(r)	XRD 24K	Bristol	VRT/LL6G	VRT/LL2/106	Northern Counties	7179	H--/--D	8/71	Reading 24	Rampton, Reading
	XRU 277K	Leyland	Atlantean PDR1A/1	7104828	Alexander	J14/3268/32	H43/31F	3/72	Bournemouth 277	Shears D, Winkleigh
	XUJ 489K	Bedford	YRQ	2T492742	Duple	257/9	C45F	5/72	Jones, Market Drayton 133	Elmes, Pontesbury
	XUR 290K	Bedford	VAL70	2T471136	Plaxton	728379	C53F	1/72	Morgan, Bognor Regis	Maxwell, Brandesburton

	Registration	Make	Model	Chassis no	Body	Body no	Layout	Date	First owner	Current owner
	XWS 165K	Bedford	J2SZ2	0T160195	Plaxton	702032	C20F	5/70	Drambuie, Edinburgh	Allan, Dunfermline
					(first licensed 2/72)					
	YDW 756K	Scania	BR111MH	541824	MCW		B40D	7/72	Newport 56	Newport Scania Group, Newport
	YDW 758K	Scania	BR111MH	541836	MCW		B40D	7/72	Newport 58	Harley, Newport
	YJG 587K	AEC	Swift	5P2R1092	Alexander	16W/3370/7	B51F	12/71	East Kent	Brown, Wateringbury
	YKV 161K	Leyland	Leopard PSU3B/4R	7201257	Plaxton	729035	C51F	6/72	Red House, Coventry	Roberts, Stockport
	YOX 130K	→ see ZS 8621 *Ireland*								
	YOX 133K	Daimler	Fleetline CRG6LX	64948	Park Royal	B58158	H43/33F	12/71	West Midlands PTE 4133	Emery, -?-
(z)	YOX 235K	Daimler	Fleetline CRG6LX	65013	MCW		H--/--F	7/72	West Midlands PTE 4235	BaMMOT, Wythall
	YWL 134K	Leyland	Leopard PSU3B/4R	7201105	Plaxton	729759	C53F	1/73	Jarvis, Middle Barton	Clements et al, Oxford
			(ex FIL 7663, YWL 134K)							
	ACT 540L	Leyland	Atlantean AN68/2R	7203700	Northern Counties	7534	H47/35F	3/73	Delaine, Bourne 72	Delaine, Bourne (LI) 72
			(ex YCT 3, ACT 540L)							
	AJA 408L	Bristol	VRT/SL6G	VRT/SL2/439	ECW	20009	H43/32F	5/73	SELNEC PTE 408	SELNEC Preservation Society
	ATA 563L	Bristol	VRT/SL6G	VRT/SL2/543	ECW	20082	H43/32F	8/73	Western National 563	Bennett, Sherborne
	AUP 651L	Bedford	VAS5	CW453015	Plaxton	732059	C29F	7/73	Weardale, Frosterley	Blue Motors, Blackpool (LA)
	BCD 820L	Leyland	National 1151/1R/0102	00601	Leyland National		B49F	6/73	Southdown 20	Science Museum, Wroughton
	BDV 318L	Bristol	LH6L	LH-755	Marshall	35108	C39F	11/73	Western National 1318	Cocks, Carnmenellis
	BFJ 175L	Bristol	VRT/SL6G	VRT/SL2/483	ECW	20067	H43/32F	7/73	Western National 1075	Thorogood, Briantspuddle
	BFS 1L	Leyland	Atlantean AN68/1R	7201863	Alexander	AL8/3171/2	H45/30D	12/72	Edinburgh 1	Lothian Bus Consortium
(r)	BFS 463L	Bedford	YRQ	2T472338	Alexander	24AY/1571/5	C45F	10/72	Scottish Omnibuses ZC463	Gascoine, Blackridge
	BFS 471L	Bedford	YRQ	2T472455	Alexander	24AY/1571/9	C45F	10/72	Scottish Omnibuses ZC471	Gascoine, Blackridge
	BFS 476L	Leyland	Leopard PSU3/3R	7203832	Alexander	30AY/1671/1	C49F	1/73	Scottish Omnibuses ZH476	Wallace Gascoine & Fraser, Edinburgh
	BPT 672L	→ see 4217 IN *Ireland*								
	BSG 537L	Leyland	Leopard PSU3/3R	7301390	Alexander	40AY/1072/11	C49F	7/73	Scottish Omnibuses ZH537	Robertson, Rosyth
	BUP 736L	Leyland	Leopard PSU5/4R	7301534	Plaxton	733133	DP57F	6/73	Weardale, Frosterley	Gibson et al, Stanley
(r)	BWG 833L	Leyland	Leopard PSU3/3R	7203674	Alexander	25AYS/1071/9	B--F	10/72	Alexander Midland MPE133	McKerracher, Stirling
	BWS 105L	Seddon	Pennine 4-236	53098	Pennine	1178	B25F	1/73	Edinburgh 105	Lothian Bus Consortium
	CDK 171L	AEC	Reliance	6U3ZR23652	Plaxton	732852	C45F	5/73	Yelloway, Rochdale	Roberts, Stockport
	CDK 172L	AEC	Reliance	6U3ZR23654	Plaxton	732851	C45F	5/73	Yelloway, Rochdale	Buckley, Darwen
	CFS 111L	Seddon	Pennine 4-236	54643	Pennine	1194	B25F	5/73	Edinburgh 111	Hartley, -?-
	CKC 308L	Daimler	Fleetline CRG6LXB	66598	MCW		H--/--F	12/72	Merseyside PTE 3008	Morris, Wallasey
	CRU 301L	Bristol	VRT/SL6G	VRT/SL2/362	ECW	19989	H44/33F	1/73	Hants & Dorset 3301	Cumming, Blandford Forum / H&DW&D
	DKC 300L	Leyland	Atlantean AN68/1R	7201847	Alexander	AL5/4070/5	H43/32F	9/72	Merseyside PTE 1300	Wigan Transport Trust
	DKC 301L	Leyland	Atlantean AN68/1R	7201965	Alexander	AL5/4070/6	H43/32F	9/72	Merseyside PTE 1301	Smith, Rainford
	DKC 305L	Leyland	Atlantean AN68/1R	7201848	Alexander	AL5/4070/10	H43/32F	9/72	Merseyside PTE 1305	Wilson, Warrington
	DKC 330L	Leyland	Atlantean AN68/1R	7203153	Alexander	AL5/4070/35	H43/32F	12/72	Merseyside PTE 1330	Merseyside Transport Trust
	DKC 365L	Leyland	Atlantean AN68/1R	7204613	Alexander	AL5/4070/70	H43/32F	3/73	Merseyside PTE 1365	Morris, Wallasey
	DLJ 116L	Daimler	Fleetline CRL6-30	66079	Alexander	AL10/4870/7	H43/31F	2/73	Bournemouth 116	Bournemouth Heritage Transport Collection
	DNT 174L	Bedford	YRQ	CW451172	Plaxton	733475	C45F	7/73	Price, Newcastle	Price, Shobdon
	DSF 751L	Commer	2000LB	160929	Rootes		M--	7/73	Royal Mail 375009	Cott, Winfarthing
	EAD 861L	→ AEF 366A								
	EFK 530L	Austin	250JU	46082	Austin		M??	5/73	-?-, -?-	Chambers, Moneymore
	EFN 178L	Leyland	National 1151/1R/0402	00560	Leyland National		B25DL	5/73	East Kent	Sealy, Hythe
	ETY 91L	Daimler	Fleetline CRL6	65430	ECW	19708	H--/--D	8/72	Tyneside 91L	Tyne & Wear Bus Preservation Group
	EUF 738L	Bedford	VAL70	2T473290	Plaxton	732085	C53F	5/73	Chivers, Elstead	Evans, Pentrefoelas (CN)
			(ex 1924 RH, RPB 222L)							

	EWG 22L	Leyland	Leopard PSU3/3R	7301395	Alexander	38AY/1672/1	C49F	5/73	Alexander Midland MPE152	Forbes, Angus
(r)	FCV 258L	Bedford	YRQ	2T475255	Duple	257/95	C45F	9/72	Prout, Port Isaac	Thomas C&R, St Austell
	FDG 468L	AEC	Reliance	6MU4R7788	Plaxton	739674	C45F	2/73	Cottrell, Mitcheldean	Smith R, Churchdown
	FEL 105L	Leyland	Leopard PSU3B/4R	7300038	Plaxton	733594	C47F	6/73	Bournemouth 105	Bournemouth Heritage Transport Collection
	FKM 708L	Leyland	Atlantean PDR1A/1	7104560	MCW		H45/33F	12/72	Maidstone & District 5708	Bennett, Gillingham
	FKM 713L	Leyland	Atlantean PDR1A/1	7200169	MCW		O--/--F	11/72	Maidstone & District 5713	Bennett, Gillingham
	FKM 719L	Leyland	Atlantean PDR1A/1	7200884	MCW		CH40/29F	12/72	Maidstone & District 5719	Bennett, Gillingham
	FRA 521L	AEC	Reliance	6U3ZR24011	Plaxton	732813	C51F	4/73	Littlewood, Sheffield	Fowler, Holbeach Drive (LI)
			(ex 20 VWC, VWA 290L)							
	FSN 224L	→ see HIL 8785								
(a)	GAU 728L	Leyland	National 1051/2R/0101	00812	Leyland National		B--D	7/73	Nottingham 728	Nottingham Heritage Vehicles
	GDF 650L	AEC	Reliance	6U3ZR22594	Plaxton	733668	C53F	4/73	Marchants, Cheltenham	Berry, Bristol
	GRM 353L	Leyland	National 1151/1R/0401	00357	Leyland National		B52F	2/73	Cumberland 353	Workington Transport Heritage Trust
	GRP 794L	Bristol	VRT/SL6G	VRT/SL2/387	ECW	20051	H39/31F	2/73	United Counties 794	794 Preservation Group, Kettering
	HAH 537L	Bristol	LH6P	LH-651	ECW	19631	B45F	9/72	Eastern Counties LH537	Appleton, Higham Ferrers
	HFN 57L	→ see A204 TAR								
	HFN 58L	→ see A200 TAR								
	HFN 59L	→ see A590 JGU								
	HGD 903L	Leyland	Atlantean AN68/1R	7301503	Alexander	AL25/4570/47	H45/30D	6/73	Glasgow LA697	Carroll, Bristol
	HHA 101L	Leyland	National 1151/1R/2501	00230	Leyland National		B51F	12/72	BMMO 101	West Midlands Bus Preservation Society
	HHA 183L	Leyland	Leopard PSU4B/4R	7300131	Plaxton	732940	C40F	4/73	BMMO 183	-?-, Crewe
	HHA 188L	Leyland	Leopard PSU4B/4R	7300198	Plaxton	732945	C45F	2/73	BMMO 188	Sargeant & Reekie, Wem
	HHW 920L	Bristol	RELL6G	RELL-3-1831	ECW	19269	B44D	1/73	Bristol C1307	Hudd, Yate
	HKE 680L	Bristol	VRT/SL6G	VRT/SL2/379	ECW	20106	H43/29F	1/73	Maidstone & District 680	Law, Brentwood
	HKE 690L	Bristol	VRT/SL6G	VRT/SL2/425	ECW	20116	O43/34F	3/73	Maidstone & District 690	Mulpeter, Seaford
	HOR 413L	Leyland	National 1151/2R/0403	00211	Leyland National		B44D	10/72	Gosport & Fareham 13	Jackson, Portsmouth
	HVF 455L	Saurer	CRD	20312/16	?		C12F	-/40	GFM, Switzerland 52	Science Museum, Wroughton
			(ex FR 1347 *Switzerland*; on display as FR 1347)							
	JDC 544L	Daimler	Fleetline CRL6	66736	Northern Counties	7358	H43/27D	4/73	Teesside L544	500 Group, Stockton-on-Tees
	JHA 227L	Leyland	Leopard PSU3B/2R	7300499	Marshall	35043	DP49F	4/73	BMMO 227	Evans, Rugeley
	JHA 234L	Leyland	Leopard PSU3B/2R	7300588	Marshall	35050	DP49F	5/73	BMMO 234	Midland Red S27 Preservation Group
	JHA 246L	Leyland	Leopard PSU3B/2R	7300696	Marshall	35062	DP49F	7/73	BMMO 246	de Courcey, Coventry (WM)
	JHU 844L	→ see 839 SEV								
	JMA 413L	Bristol	RELH6L	RELH-4-480	ECW	19859	C49F	10/72	North Western 413	Wita, Ammanford
	KCG 627L	Leyland	National 1151/1R/0402	00676	Leyland National		B49F	7/73	Thames Valley & Aldershot 127	Freeman & Mathieson, Abingdon
	KNR 328L	→ see PIB 3673								
	KUM 514L	Bedford	YRQ	CW455336	Plaxton	732295	C45F	6/73	Wallace Arnold Tours	Beech, Leicester
	KUM 533L	Leyland	Leopard PSU3B/4R	7300039	Plaxton	733027	C53F	3/73	Wallace Arnold Tours	Smart, Chippenham
			(ex 9210 AD, KUM 533L)							
	KUM 542L	Bedford	SB5	CW453776	Plaxton	732130	C25FL	5/73	Leeds Wounded Warriors	Heaps, Bradford
	LHT 171L	Bristol	RELL6L	RELL-3-1911	ECW	20146	B50F	6/73	Bristol 1317	Bristol RE1317 Preservation Group
	LOU 776L	Bedford	VAL70	2T473189	Plaxton	732403	C53F	3/73	Castle, Horndean	Soul, Monkwood
	LUR 510L	Bedford	VAL70	2T473363	Plaxton	732402	C53F	5/73	Brunt, Potters Bar	Brown, Builth Wells (CW)
	MGP 226L	Bristol	VRT/SL6G	VRT/SL2/481	ECW	20846	H43/34F	6/73	Department of Transport	Kirk, Lincoln
	MGX 593L	Ford	Transit	BC05MY65871	Ford		M10	1/73	non-PSV	Asbury, Smethwick
	MHW 285L	Bristol	RELL6L	RELL-3-1932	ECW	20134	B53F	7/73	Bristol C1325	Brown, Nailsea
	MJH 280L	Seddon	Pennine 4	53809	Plaxton	733302	C44F	5/73	Armchair, Brentford	Hamilton, Bow (DN)
	MLH 426L	Daimler	Fleetline CRL6	66320	MCW		H44/24D	11/72	London Transport DMS1426	Wright & Cole, Hornchurch

	MLK 550L	Daimler	Fleetline CRL6	66286	Park Royal	B58637	H--/--D	3/73	London Transport DMS550	Bamford, Ramsgate
	MLK 708L	Ford	Transit	BC05MG66031	Strachan	15671	B16F	9/72	London Transport FS8	Emsworth & District, Southbourne (WS)
	MLK 716L	Ford	Transit	BC05MG56621	Strachan	-?-	B16F	10/72	London Transport FS16	Bullions, Romford
	MLK 719L	Ford	Transit	BD05NJ54446	Strachan	16973	B16F	12/73	London Transport FS19	Bullions, Romford
	MRO 200L	Bedford	VAL70	2T473280	Plaxton	732885	C53F	7/73	McIntyre, Roydon	Smith, Pylle (SO)
	MTX 947L	AEC	Reliance	6MU4R23428	Plaxton	732819	C49F	1/73	Edwards, Beddau	Selmes, Gosport
	NDM 69L	Bedford	YRQ	2T475369	Duple	257/82	C45F	12/72	Phillips, Holywell	Elmes, Pontesbury
	NNY 817L	Bedford	YRT	CW451843	Plaxton	732156	C53F	1/73	Davies, Penygraig	Norman, Aberbargoed
	NPD 108L	Leyland	National 1151/2R/0402	00216	Leyland National		B18D	10/72	London Country LN8	Holden, Bude
	NPD 142L	→ see JIL 2157								
	NPD 145L	Leyland	National 1151/1R/0402	00368	Leyland National		B30D	3/73	London Country LNC45	Moore, Smarden
	NPP 71L	→ see RNE 192W								
(z)	NRT 565L	AEC	Swift	3MP2R22543	ECW	20318	B45D	1/73	Lowestoft 18	Eastern Transport Collection
	NSD 423L	→ see UZY 705 *Ireland*								
	NUD 105L	Bristol	VRT/SL6G	VRT/SL2/427	ECW	19936	CH38/30F	3/73	City of Oxford 105	Clements, Oxford
	OCH 261L	Daimler	Fleetline CRG6LX	66580	Roe	GO7238	H44/34F	4/73	Derby 261	Varty, Mickleover
(r)	OCH 263L	Daimler	Fleetline CRG6LX	66582	Roe	GO7232	H--/--F	3/73	Derby 263	Varty, Mickleover
	OHO 2L	Ford	K1110	BC02MT62187	Mitchell		O18/16RO	7/73	London General B340 (replica)	National Motor Museum, Beaulieu
			(replica of 1911 AEC B / LGOC)							
	PDJ 269L	AEC	Swift	3MP2R22661	Marshall	34982	B42D	12/72	St Helens 269	Vivyan, St Helens
	PGC 204L	Scania	BR111MH	542162	MCW		B41D	8/73	London Transport MS4	Newport Scania Group, Newport
	PTF 714L	Bristol	RELH6L	RELH-4-476	ECW	19871	C49F	10/72	Ribble 1019	Ribble Vehicle Preservation Trust
	PTF 718L	→ see FIB 1763								
(a)	PTF 727L	Leyland	National 1151/2R/0401	00206	Leyland National		B4C	11/72	Ribble 381	Ribble Vehicle Preservation Trust
	PTF 728L	Leyland	National 1151/2R/0401	00207	Leyland National		B--D	11/72	Ribble 382	Smith & Fitton, Chorley
										(on loan to Ribble Vehicle Preservation Trust)
	PVT 207L	Bristol	RESL6L	RESL-8-374	ECW	19686	B44F	10/72	Potteries 207	Buttery, Stoke-on-Trent
	PYJ 125L	Austin Morris	250JU	41581	Austin Morris		M12	8/72	Ministry of Defence	-?-, -?-
	PYJ 461L	Daimler	Fleetline CRG6LXB	66154	Alexander	AL7/4970/20	H--/--D	12/72	Dundee 161	Fordyce, Dundee
	RBY 43L	Bedford	VAL70	2T473197	Plaxton	732397	C53F	4/73	Exclusive, Hounslow	Hurst, Standish
	RCH 629L	Bristol	VRT/SL6G	VRT/SL2/414	ECW	20036	H43/34F	12/72	Trent 767	Robertson, Ilkeston
	RPB 222L	→ see EUF 738L								
	RTC 645L	Leyland	National 1151/1R/0101	00155	Leyland National		B52F	9/72	Widnes 1	North West Museum of Transport
	RVO 657L	Leyland	Leopard PSU3B/4R	7300005	Plaxton	733735	C53F	2/73	Barton 1235	Rennie & Baker, Melton Mowbray
	RVO 668L	Leyland	Leopard PSU3B/4R	7300314	Plaxton	733747	C53F	7/73	Barton 1246	Clark, Derby
	RUY 999L	AEC	Reliance	6U3ZR22466	Plaxton	733662	C49F	12/72	Harris, Catshill	Harris, Catshill (WO)
(r)	SAN 913L	Bedford	VAL70	2T473235	Plaxton	732401	C53F	2/73	Drewery, Woodford Bridge	Price & Perry, Shobdon
	SGF 483L	Bristol	RELH6L	RELH-4-327	Plaxton	713372	C51F	5/71	Isle of Man Road Services 40	Talisman, Great Bromley (EX)
			(ex 40 WMN)							
	SGT 360L	→ see SHH 85M								
	SHN 80L	Bristol	RELH6G	RELH-4-622	ECW	20364	DP49F	7/73	United 6080	Waterhouse, Ripley
	STJ 847L	Seddon	Pennine RU	52538	Seddon	1100	B51F	10/72	Lytham St Annes 47	Lancastrian Transport Trust
	TCH 274L	Bristol	RELH6G	RELH-4-596	ECW	20337	DP49F	6/73	Midland General 274	Monk et al, Derby
	UFX 360L	Bedford	VAL70	2T473507	Plaxton	732399	C53F	2/73	Seaview, Parkstone	Dew, Somersham (CM)
	UOA 322L	Leyland	National 1151/1R/0401	00337	Leyland National		B49F	2/73	Eastern National 1702	Cooper, Bolsover
			(ex NAT 555A, WNO 551L)							
	USS 416L	Bedford	VAS5	CW453420	Plaxton	732082	C29F	7/73	Glass, Haddington	Moore, Barnsley
	UWA 296L	Leyland	Atlantean AN68/1R	7301024	Alexander	AL13/2270/22	H43/31F	4/73	Sheffield 296	296 Group, Sheffield

	VER 262L	AEC	Reliance	6U3ZR21968	Alexander	31/AY/871/2	C53F	9/72	Premier, Cambridge 262	Tidbury, Kidlington
			(ex 558 BWL , VER 262L)							
	VHK 177L	Bristol	RELH6G	RELH-4-493	ECW	19857	C49F	10/72	Tilling 9441	East Anglia Transport Museum
			(ex 819 XUP, VHK 177L, 929 CVJ, VHK 177L)							
	VJT 307L	Bedford	SB5	CW453762	Plaxton	732129	C41F	6/73	House, Hilton	Lewis, Henstridge (SO)
			(ex VHR 828, VJT 307L)							
	VNB 101L	Leyland	Atlantean AN68/1R	7201491	Park Royal	B59723	H43/32F	5/72	SELNEC PTE 7001	Museum of Transport, Manchester
	VNB 108L	Leyland	Atlantean AN68/1R	7201851	Park Royal	B59737	O43/32F	9/72	SELNEC PTE 7008	Burge, Chatham
			(ex CYC 658A, VNB 101L)							
	VNB 132L	Leyland	Atlantean AN68/1R	7203542	Park Royal	B59787	O43/32F	11/72	SELNEC PTE 7032	SELNEC Preservation Society
	VNB 170L	→ see YNE 87L								
	VNB 173L	Leyland	Atlantean AN68/1R	7202178	Northern Counties	7456	H43/32F	10/72	SELNEC PTE 7147	SELNEC Preservation Society
	VNB 177L	Daimler	Fleetline CRG6LXB	65659	Northern Counties	7433	H45/27D	10/72	SELNEC PTE 7206	SELNEC Preservation Society
	VNB 203L	Daimler	Fleetline CRG6LXB	65752	Northern Counties	7466	H--/--D	1/73	SELNEC PTE 7232	SELNEC Preservation Society
	VTP 262L	Leyland	Atlantean AN68/1R	7202084	Alexander	AL6/970/8	H45/30D	8/72	Portsmouth 262	Shilton, Burton-upon-Trent
	VWA 290L	→ see FRA 521L								
	VWM 82L	Leyland	Atlantean AN68/1R	7204199	Alexander	AL14/2070/2	H45/29D	5/73	Southport 82	Rimmer, Litherland
	VWM 83L	Leyland	Atlantean AN68/1R	7204290	Alexander	AL14/2070/3	H45/29D	5/73	Southport 83	Weatherby, Southport
	VWM 88L	Leyland	Atlantean AN68/1R	7204234	Alexander	AL14/2070/8	H--/--D	6/73	Southport 88	Weatherby, Southport
	WBN 955L	Leyland	Atlantean AN68/1R	7201857	Park Royal	B59742	O43/32F	9/72	SELNEC PTE 7077	SELNEC Preservation Society
	WFM 808L	Leyland	National 1151/2R/0403	00141	Leyland National		B??D	9/72	Crosville SNL808	Bryan, Chester
	WFM 823L	Leyland	National 1151/2R/0403	00182	Leyland National		B21D	10/72	Crosville SNL823	Meeham, Saltburn
			(ex CAP 10, WFM 823L)							
	WNO 537L	Bristol	RELL6G	RELL-3-1823	ECW	19245	B53F	10/72	Eastern National 1548	Salmon, South Benfleet
	WNO 551L	→ see UOA 322L								
	WNO 556L	Leyland	National 1151/1R/0401	00458	Leyland National		B50F	2/73	Eastern National 1707	Wilson, Bishops Stortford
	WWH 43L	Daimler	Fleetline CRG6LXB	65803	Park Royal	B59917	H43/32F	7/73	SELNEC PTE 7185	SELNEC Preservation Society
	XAK 355L	Daimler	Fleetline CRL6	65658	Alexander	AL4/5370/20	H43/31F	8/72	Bradford 355	Bates & Holian, Elland
	XDL 122L	Bristol	RELH6G	RELH-4-479	ECW	19874	C49F	9/72	Southern Vectis 302	Hewlett, Newport
			(ex WWE 35L, 222 WFM, XDL 122L)							
	XGM 450L	Leyland	Leopard PSU3/3R	7201645	Alexander	19AYS/1771/15	B53F	9/72	Central SMT T150	Crichton & Ferguson, Glasgow
	XJA 534L	Leyland	Atlantean AN68/1R	7204472	Park Royal	B59853	H43/32F	1/73	SELNEC PTE 7143	SELNEC Preservation Society
	XRB 415L	Leyland	National 1151/2R/0403	00184	Leyland National		B44D	12/72	Midland Generlal 415	Stanton, Nottingham
	XTM 122L	Ford	R226	BC04LM44934	Plaxton	729548	C53F	8/72	Currie, Bexleyheath	Ingram, Whitby
	XTP 287L	Leyland	Atlantean AN68/1R	7300676	Alexander	AL23/3070/15	H45/30D	6/73	Portsmouth 287	Chandler, Worcester
	YDB 453L	Seddon	Pennine 4-236	52567	Seddon	1152	B25F	12/72	SELNEC PTE EX56	SELNEC Preservation Society
	YFM 280L	Bristol	RELL6G	RELL-3-1889	ECW	20171	DP50F	1/73	Crosville ERG280	Channerley, Runcorn
(r)	YNE 87L	Leyland	Atlantean AN68/1R	7300450	Park Royal	B59866	H--/--F	2/73	SELNEC PTE 7070	SELNEC Preservation Society
			(ex VNB 170L)							
	YSD 350L	Leyland	Leopard PSU3/3R	7202568	Alexander	23AY/2771/14	B41F	4/73	Western SMT 2390	Western Buses (SW) 59950
	YTA 415L	Bedford	J2SZ2	2T134213	Willowbrook	72316	B19F	12/72	Royal Navy	Denham, Kingston
			(ex 04 RN 02 - previously *carried FS 8000 for display purposes*)							
	YVC 20L	Bedford	VAL70	1T492952	Plaxton	728407	C53F	8/72	Shaw, Coventry	Dekkaman, Blaydon (TW)
	AHN 611M	Bristol	LH6L	LH-965	ECW	21262	B43F	7/74	United 1611	Bulmer, North Stainley (NY)
	AWJ 134M	→ see WNL 66A								
	NAT 349M	Leyland	Atlantean AN68/1R	7400467	Roe	GO7431	H43/29F	7/74	Hull 349	Hull & Country Bus Preservation Group
	NAT 354M	Leyland	Atlantean AN68/1R	7400659	Roe	GO7427	H43/32F	7/74	Hull 354	Green, Hull

	Reg	Make	Model	Chassis no	Body	Body no	Layout	New	First owner	Owner
(r)	NCD 559M	Bristol	VRT/SL6G	VRT/SL2/616	ECW	20551	H43/31F	11/73	Southdown 559	Cardiff Transport Preservation Group
	NCH 768M	Bristol	RELH6L	RELH-4-691	ECW	21409	DP49F	7/74	Trent 285	Henson, Northampton
	NDL 637M	Bristol	VRT/SL6G	VRT/SL2/598	ECW	20579	H39/31F	10/73	Southern Vectis 637	Newman & Harris, Ryde
	NDP 70M	Bristol	RELH6G	RELH-4-642	Plaxton	733876	C49F	10/73	Thames Valley & Aldershot 70	Thorpe et al, Willenhall
	NEL 845M	Bristol	LH6L	LH-724	ECW	20258	B43F	8/73	Hants & Dorset 3512	Mills, Hursthouse & Holtby, Netheravon
	NFA 12M	Daimler	Fleetline CRG6LX	67586	Willowbrook	70906	H44/33F	8/73	Burton 12	Meredith, Merton Park
	NFJ 590M	Bristol	LH6L	LH-845	ECW	20423	B43F	10/73	Western National 1590	Bradley, Harrogate
	NFJ 592M	Bristol	LH6L	LH-847	ECW	20425	B43F	12/73	Western National 1592	Delbridge, Ivybridge
(r)	NFM 292M	Bristol	RELL6G	RELL-3-1981	ECW	20183	DP36F	10/73	Crosville ERL292	Rampton, Reading
	NFR 497M	AEC	Reliance	6U3ZR25026	Plaxton	723850	C53F	8/73	Abbott, Blackpool	-?-, Edinburgh
	NHB 190M	Bristol	RESL6G	RESL-8-402	ECW	20827	B47F	11/73	Merthyr Tydfil 190	Henson, Northampton
	NHR 156M	Daimler	Fleetline CRG6LX	67643	*chassis only*			10/73	Swindon 156	BaMMOT, Wythall
	NMS 576M	Leyland	Leopard PSU3/3R	7302114	Alexander	41AYS/1572/18	B53F	9/73	Alexander Midland MPE176	Booth, Glasgow
	NNN 7M	Bristol	RELH6L	RELH-4-686	ECW	21404	DP47F	7/74	Mansfield District MC7	Sharpe, Derby
	NNU 123M	Daimler	Fleetline CRL6	67438	Roe	GO7351	H42/29D	8/73	Chesterfield 123	123 Group, Chesterfield
	NNU 124M	Daimler	Fleetline CRL6	67439	Roe	GO7349	H42/29D	8/73	Chesterfield 124	123 Group, Chesterfield
	NOB 413M	Bristol	VRT/SL6G	VRT/SL2/691	MCW		H43/33F	4/74	West Midlands PTE 4413	Hill. Redditch
	NPT 672M	Bedford	YRT	CW453681	Plaxton	732409	C53F	8/73	Roberts, Wingate	Roberts, Wingate (DM)
	NRG 154M	Leyland	Atlantean AN68/1R	7320669	Alexander	AL26/2671/13	H45/29D	11/73	Aberdeen 154	Grampian Transport Museum
	NTT 319M	Bristol	LH6L	LH-757	Marshall	B35109	C37F	11/73	Western National 1319	Cocks, Carnmenellis
	NUD 78M	Bristol	RELH6L	RELH-4-632	ECW	20346	DP5F	9/73	City of Oxford 78	Thorpe et al, Willenhall
	NYG 802M	Bristol	RELH6L	RELH-4-625	Plaxton	733861	C49F	9/73	West Yorkshire 1042	Webb et al, Guildford
			(ex 5735 UA, NYG 802M)							
	OAE 954M	Bristol	RELL6L	RELL-3-1954	ECW	20151	B50F	10/73	Bristol 1332	Abus, Bristol (GL)
(r)	OAE 957M	Bristol	RELL6L	RELL-3-1958	ECW	20154	B--F	11/73	Bristol 1335	Hoare, Chepstow (CS)
	OAX 500M	AEC	Reliance	6MU4R23355	Plaxton	733958	B47F	11/73	Henley, Abertillery	-?-, -?-
	OBT 693M	→ see RRH 335M								
	OCT 990M	Bedford	YRQ	1T493192	Duple	415/2040	C45F	1/74	Wing, Sleaford	Tomlinson, Gunnislake
	OEB 498M	Austin	250JU	51216F	Austin		M12	3/74	-?-, -?-	Chambers, Moneymore
	OEH 604M	Bristol	VRT/SL6G	VRT/SL2/685	ECW	20667	H43/31F	1/74	Potteries 604	Potteries Omnibus Preservation Society
	OFR 970M	AEC	Swift	3MP2R26972	Marshall	35071	B47D	4/74	Blackpool 570	Lancastrian Transport Trust
	OFR 989M	AEC	Swift	3MP2R28209	Marshall	35090	B47D	5/74	Blackpool 589	-?-, -?-
	OHU 38M	Bristol	RELL6L	RELL-3-1942	ECW	20139	B44D	10/73	Bristol C1330	Hewlett, Newport
	OLV 551M	Leyland	Atlantean AN68/1R	7401462	Alexander	AL29/872/6	O43/32F	5/74	Merseyside PTE 1551	CAPS, Liverpool
	ONN 294M	Leyland	Leopard PSU3B/4R	7403073	Plaxton	7411LX560	C53F	6/74	Barton 1411	Barton 1411 Group, Clifton
	ORU 532M	Bristol	LH6L	LH-945	ECW	21324	treelopper	5/74	Hants & Dorset 3532	Mills, Hursthouse & Holtby, Netheravon
	OTO 540M	Leyland	Atlantean AN68/1R	7302378	East Lancs	2501	H47/30D	12/73	Nottingham 540	Nottingham Heritage Vehicles
	OTO 555M	→ see RAU 804M								
	OTO 570M	Leyland	Atlantean AN68/1R	7302376	East Lancs	2531	H47/30D	3/74	Nottingham 570	Nottingham Heritage Vehicles
	OTO 571M	→ see 74-KE-527 *Ireland*								
	OWC 720M	Bristol	RELL6L	RELL-3-2011	ECW	20818	B53F	12/73	Colchester 20	Buckley & Minto, Newcastle upon Tyne
	OWC 722M	Bristol	RELL6L	RELL-3-2013	ECW	20820	B49F	12/73	Colchester 22	Hussey et al, Basingstoke
	OWC 723M	Bristol	RELL6L	RELL-3-2014	ECW	20821	B49F	12/73	Colchester 23	-?-, Shrewsbury
	OWT 776M	Bristol	RELL6G	RELL-3-1984	ECW	20242	B53F	5/74	West Yorkshire 1403	Lawson, Littleborough
(a)	PDU 125M	Daimler	Fleetline CRG6LX	67447	East Lancs	7247	O??/??F	9/73	Coventry 125	Museum of British Road Transport, Coventry
	PDU 135M	Daimler	Fleetline CRG6LX	67457	East Lancs	7246	H44/30F	9/73	Coventry 135	Hodkinson, Coventry
	PFW 419M	Bedford	SB5	CW451186	Plaxton	74SB009	C41F	5/74	Appleby, Conisholme	Stones, North Somercotes
	PHA 319M	Leyland	Leopard PSU3B/2R	7400376	Marshall	35136	DP49F	5/74	BMMO 319	Evans & Wood, Rugeley

	Registration	Make	Model	Chassis No	Body	Body No	Layout	Date	Original Operator	Current Owner
	PHA 370M	Ford	R1014	BC04NC69443	Plaxton	7410FB802	DP23F	5/74	Midland Red 370	BaMMOT, Wythall
	PHA 371M	Ford	R1014	BC04NC69755	Plaxton	7410FB803	B27F	4/74	Midland Red 371	-?-, Exeter
	PKE 809M	Bristol	VRT/SL6G	VRT/SL2/657	ECW	20642	H43/34F	12/73	Maidstone & District 5809	Hamilton, East Peckham
	PKG 587M	Bristol	VRT/SL6G	VRT/SL2/631	ECW	20793	H43/31F	3/74	Cardiff 587	Cardiff Transport Preservation Group
	PKH 600M	Bedford	VAS5	DW451453	Plaxton	74VAS029	C29F	4/74	Xanthine, Hull	Lambert, St Helens
	PNM 757M	Bedford	YRQ	CW452611	Plaxton	7410QC024	C45F	3/74	Eayrs, Goldington	Bedford, Staines
	PPY 650M	Bedford	YRT	DW452039	Duple	417/3038	C53F	3/74	Abbott, Leeming	Abbott, Leeming (NY)
	PRW 137M	Leyland	Leopard PSU3B/4R	7301159	Plaxton	732998	C51F	4/74	Red House, Coventry	Bristol RE1317 Preservation Group
	PUF 249M	Ford	R1114	BC04PS61836	Duple	423/4426	C49F	5/74	Southdown 1409	Maynes, Buckie (SN)
(r)	PUO 328M	Bristol	LH6L	LH-908	Plaxton	7410BC006	C39F	6/74	Western National 1328	Cockram, Bristol
	PUO 331M	Bristol	LH6L	LH-912	Plaxton	7410BC002	C39F	6/74	Western National 1331	Bristol RE1317 Preservation Group
	PWC 515M	Bristol	VRT/SL6G	VRT/SL2/710	ECW	20500	H39/31F	3/74	Eastern National 3040	Salmon, South Benfleet
	RAD 777M	Bedford	YRQ	DW454207	Placton	7410QX529	C45F	5/74	Cottrell, Mitcheldean	Ward, Drybrook
	RAG 393M	Leyland	Leopard PSU3/3R	7303209	Alexander	44AY/2072/11	RV	4/74	Ulsterbus 4890	Geary, Paisley
	RAU 804M	Leyland	Atlantean AN68/1R	7304429	East Lancs	B5201	B45F	1/74	Nottingham 555	Clinton, Birmingham
			(ex OTO 555M)		*(rebodied 3/94)*					
	RBD 111M	Bedford	YRT	DW455578	Willowbrook	73893	B53F	7/74	United Counties 111	Robertson, Biggleswade
	RBT 172M	AEC	Reliance	6MU4R24617	Plaxton	732857	C51F	5/74	Boddy, Bridlington	-?-, North West
	RBW 87M	Bristol	RELH6L	RELH-4-676	ECW	21437	DP49F	7/74	City of Oxford 87	Clements, Oxford
			(ex PIX 390, RBW 87M)							
	RCJ 211M	Bedford	VAS5	DW453748	Plaxton	74VAS042	C29F	7/74	Bengry, Leominster	Payne, Great Sampford
	RFM 61M	Daimler	Fleetline CRG6LX	66772	Northern Counties	7549	H43/29F	3/74	Chester 61	Dennis, Chester
	ROK 459M	Daimler	Fleetline CRG6LX	67731	East Lancs	2703	H44/30F	7/74	West Midlands PTE 4459	23 Group, Coventry
	RPU 869M	Bristol	RELH6G	RELH-4-658	ECW	21448	DP49F	5/74	National Travel South East	Dicker, Hastings
			(ex MHE 213M, 223 FWW, RPU 869M)							
	RRH 335M	Leyland	Leopard PSU3B/4R	7303992	Plaxton	743555	C53F	12/73	Connor & Graham, Easington	Hull 245 Group, Hull
			(ex UYH 375, OBT 693M)							
	RRM 148M	Leyland	National 1151/1R/2308	00943	Leyland National		B51F	10/73	Leyland National demonstrator	Royle, Osoyoos, Canada *(in the care of the Suburban Express Group, Norwich)*
	RRM 915M	Bedford	YRQ	DW454101	Plaxton	7410QX530	C45F	7/74	Wright, Nenthead	Wright, Nenthead (CA)
	RTB 809M	Bristol	RESL6L	RESL-8-396	East Lancs	3303	B47F	11/73	Darwen 7	Darwen Transport Museum Trust
	SAH 851M	Bristol	RELH6G	RELH-4-724	Plaxton	7411BXR510	C49F	6/74	Eastern Counties RE851	Bissett, Westbury
	SCS 333M	Leyland	Leopard PSU3/3R	7401476	Alexander	65AY/3873/7	DP49F	7/74	Western SMT 2464	Handley, Stoneville, W.Australia (kept in UK)
	SCS 335M	Leyland	Leopard PSU3/3R	7401595	Alexander	65AY/3873/9	DP49F	7/74	Western SMT 2466	McGowan, Falkirk
	SCS 365M	Leyland	Leopard PSU3/3R	7403053	Alexander	65AY/3873/39	C49F	3/75	Western SMT 2496	Duffy, Macclesfield
	SCS 366M	Leyland	Leopard PSU3/3R	7403054	Alexander	65AY/3873/40	B53F	3/75	Western SMT 2497	Ward, Reading
			(ex 74-TN-505, SCS 366M)							
	SEO 209M	Leyland	National 11351/1R	01348	Leyland National		B48F	6/74	Barrow 9	Barrow Transport Museum
(r)	SFM 304M	Bristol	RELH6L	RELH-4-680	ECW	21450	DP51F	5/74	Crosville CRL304	Ribble Vehicle Preservation Trust
	SHH 85M	AEC	Reliance	6MU4R7791	Plaxton	732766	C41F	4/73	Essex County, Stratford	Everett, Lincoln
			(ex SGT 360L)							
	SHY 707M	Leyland	Leopard PSU5/4R	7102534	Van Hool	4027	C57F	4/74	Turner, Bristol	Judd, Manea (CM)
	SPK 203M	AEC	Reliance	6U3ZR25043	Plaxton	732840	C49F	11/73	London Country P3	Lawrance & Walker, Colchester
	SUG 591M	Leyland	Atlantean AN68/2R	7400950	Roe	GO7442	H--/--D	4/74	West Yorkshire PTE 591	Fairchild & McClintoch, Leeds
	TGY 102M	Leyland	National 1051/2R/3001	00775	Leyland National		B24D	11/73	London Transport LS2	Kells Transport Museum, Cork
	TGY 105M	Leyland	National 1051/2R/3001	00818	Leyland National		B24D	11/73	London Transport LS5	Norris, Colchester
	TGY 106M	→ see 73-C-22 *Ireland*								
	THM 515M	Daimler	Fleetline CRL6	66993	*promotional vehicle*			11/73	London Transport DMS1515	London Bus Company, Northfleet (KT)

	Registration	Chassis make	Chassis model	Chassis no	Body make	Body no	Layout	Date	First owner	Current owner
	THM 601M	Daimler	Fleetline CRL6	67182	MCW		H47/32F	2/74	London Transport DMS1601	O'Connor, Beckenham
	THM 684M	Daimler	Fleetline CRL6	67430	MCW		O44/28D	7/74	London Transport DMS1684	London Bus Company, Northfleet (KT)
	TME 134M	AEC	Reliance	6MU4R25741	Plaxton	7410ACCE004	C38C	4/74	Glenton, London	Dolan A&M, Crook
	TTC 517M	→ see MAN 1935 *Isle of Man*								
	UJX 920M	Leyland	Leopard PSU4B/2R	7303491	Plaxton	743999	B45F	12/73	Halifax 10	Stoneywood Motors, Sowerby Bridge
	UMT 903M	→ see IIW 670								
	UNW 30M	→ see 9393 AI *Ireland*								
	UPE 203M	Leyland	National 1051/1R/0402	01192	Leyland National		B--F	5/74	London Country SNB103	Knorn, Ruabon
	UTF 732M	Leyland	Leopard PSU3B/4R	7403737	Duple	433/5150	C49F	8/74	Ribble 1052	Butler, Gosforth *(on loan to Ribble Vehicle Preservation Trust)*
	UTJ 595M	Leyland	National 1151/1R/2811	00498	Leyland National		C22F	5/73	Leyland Research Department	-?-., Derby
	UVL 873M	Bristol	RELL6L	RELL-3-1965	Alexander	148Y/2571/8	B48F	11/73	Lincoln 73	Lincolnshire Vintage Vehicle Society
	VNK 771M	Bedford	VAS5	DW452006	Duple	412/1222	C—F	2/74	Comex, London	-?-, -?-
	VPB 121M	Leyland	Atlantean AN68/1R	7401466	Park Royal	B60655	H43/28D	5/74	London Country AN121	Wall, Stevenage
	VSB 164M	Bedford	YRT	CW458857	Plaxton	7411TB804	B60F	4/74	Craig, Campbeltown	Ryan, Glasgow
	VSS 158M	Ford	R1014	BC04MY66268	Plaxton	7410FX502	C45F	1/74	Wiles, Port Seton	Winter, Darton
	WEX 685M	AEC	Swift	3MP2R24503	ECW	20835	B43D	10/73	Great Yarmouth 85	Blair, Wakefield
	WEX 687M	AEC	Swift	3MP2R24628	ECW	20838	B43D	11/73	Great Yarmouth 87	Naisbett, Luton
	WPG 217M	Leyland	National 10351/1R/SC	01351	Leyland National		DP39F	8/74	London Country SNC117	Knorn, Ruabon
	WWJ 754M	Daimler	Fleetline CRG6LXB	67602	Park Royal	B58428	H43/27D	11/73	Sheffield 754	Sheffield Transport Group, Doncaster
	XRR 615M	Leyland	Leopard PSU3B/4R	7300599	Plaxton	733757	C53F	8/73	Barton 1286	Stanton, Nottingham
	XVU 341M	Seddon	Pennine 4-236	54679	Seddon	1231	B23F	11/73	SELNEC PTE 1711	SELNEC Preservation Society
	XVU 352M	Seddon	Pennine 4-236	56075	Pennine	1271	B19F	6/74	Greater Manchester PTE 1722	Museum of Transport, Manchester
	XVU 363M	Seddon	Pennine 4-236	56098	Pennine	1282	B19F	7/74	Greater Manchester PTE 1733	SELNEC Preservation Society
	XXA 854M	Leyland	Leopard PSU3/3R	7400506	Alexander	63AYS/1873/4	RV	4/74	Alexander Fife 1054	Gifford Transport Group
	XXA 859M	→ see HDZ 5488								
	YCH 890M	Bristol	RELH6L	RELH-4-647	ECW	21439	C49F	5/74	Trent 150	Pearsall et al, Runcorn
	YFY 4M	Leyland	National 1151/2R/0402	01143	Leyland National		B49F	1/74	Southport 4	Foster S, Darlington
	YNA 321M	Daimler	Fleetline CRG6LXB	65886	Northern Counties	7646	H43/32F	2/74	SELNEC PTE 7366	SELNEC Preservation Society
	YRC 125M	Bristol	VRT/SL6G	VRT/SL2/737	ECW	20534	H43/34F	5/74	Trent 780	Waterhouse & Thurman, Ripley
	YWB 494M	International	Harvester 1853FC	64/9044	Superior(Ohio)		B44F	-/64	United States Air Force	Bentwaters Aviation Society, Bentwaters
			(ex 64 B 2428 *USAF*)							

	Registration	Chassis make	Chassis model	Chassis no	Body make	Body no	Layout	Date	First owner	Current owner
	BHN 693N	Bristol	RELH6L	RELH-4-745	ECW	21421	DP49F	9/74	United 6093	Lane, Woking
	BNE 729N	Seddon	Pennine 4-236	57090	Pennine	1284	B19F	8/74	Greater Manchester PTE 1735	SELNEC Preservation Society
	BNE 751N	Leyland	Atlantean AN68/1R	7403313	Northern Counties	7847	H43/32F	8/74	Greater Manchester PTE 7501	SELNEC Preservation Society
	BNE 764N	Bristol	LH6L	LH-922	ECW	21485	B43F	11/74	Greater Manchester PTE 1321	SELNEC Preservation Society
	CST 703N	Ford	R1114	BC04PT62571	Alexander	48AYS/973/4	B53F	8/74	Highland T93	Park, Seghill
	GBF 78N	Bristol	VRT/SL6G	VRT/SL2/889	ECW	20685	O43/31F	12/74	Potteries 622	Pearson, Stoke-on-Trent
			(ex 507 EXA, GBF 78N)							
	GBV 102N	Leyland	Atlantean AN68/2R	7403897	Alexander	AL34/873/2	H49/33D	12/74	Preston 102	Rimmer, Litherland
	GCL 349N	Bristol	RELH6G	RELH-4-750	ECW	21426	DP49F	12/74	Eastern Counties RLE747	Bristol Road Group, Norwich
	GCN 2N	→ see NDS 658N								
(r)	GDR 207N	Leyland	Atlantean AN68/1R	7500011	Park Royal	B60828	H--/--D	4/75	Plymouth 82	-?-, Reading
	GEF 191N	Bristol	RELL6L	RELL-3-2021	ECW	21496	DP48F	1/75	Hartlepool 91	Larkin, Peterborough
	GEU 371N	Leyland	National 10351/1R	01729	Leyland National		B44F	12/74	Bristol 1459	Brown, Nailsea
	GGG 300N	Ailsa	B55-10	74004	Alexander	AV4/274/1	H44/35F	3/75	Greater Glasgow PTE AV1	Transport Preservation Trust, Beith

	GGG 773N	→ see YYJ 555								
	GGR 103N	Leyland	Atlantean AN68/2R	7403051	Northern Counties	7956	H47/36F	10/74	OK, Bishop Auckland	Slater Trotter & Cook, Wideopen
	GHB 148N	Bristol	RESL6L	RESL-8-413	ECW	21477	B44F	11/74	Cynon Valley 15	Carroll, Cardiff
(a)	GHM 818N	Daimler	Fleetline CRL6	68212	MCW		H--/--D	4/75	London Transport DM1818	Yeldham Transport Museum
	GHM 868N	Daimler	Fleetline CRL6	68347	MCW		H44/24D	6/75	London Transport DMS1868	Parr, Huseyin & Bexley, Croydon
	GHV 2N	Daimler	Fleetline CRL6	68174	Park Royal	B59089	H44/27D	11/74	London Transport DM1002	Brown, Romford
	GHV 51N	Daimler	Fleetline CRL6	68265	Park Royal	B59138	H44/32F	1/75	London Transport DM1051	Sibbons & Collett, Billericay
	GHV 52N	Daimler	Fleetline CRL6	68264	Park Royal	B59139	H44/27D	3/75	London Transport DM1052	London Bus Company, Northfleet (KT)
	GHV 69N	Daimler	Fleetline CRL6	68295	Park Royal	B59156	H45/28D	3/75	London Transport DM1069	Hinson, Potterspury
	GHV 504N	Bristol	LHS6L	LHS-236	ECW	21752	B29F	6/75	London Transport BS4	Adams, Goudhurst
	GHV 505N	Bristol	LHS6L	LHS-237	ECW	21753	B26F	7/75	London Transport BS5	-?-, Maidstone
	GHV 999N	Daimler	Fleetline CRL6	68167	Park Royal	B59086	H44/27D	12/74	London Transport DM999	Ricketts, Andover
	GJD 194N	→ see JEU 509N								
	GJD 196N	→ see MIB 4194								
(r)	GJF 274N	Scania	BR111DH	542619	MCW		H45/31F	1/75	Leicester 274	BORIS Owners Group, Reading
	GJF 301N	Scania	BR111DH	542755	MCW		H45/28D	3/75	Leicester 301	Harris, Leicester
	GJW 43N	Leyland	Leopard PSU3B/2R	7402272	Marshall	35160	DP49F	10/74	Midland Red 343	Reekie, Wem
	GKA 74N	Bristol	VRT/SL6G	VRT/SL2/911	East Lancs	2827	H--/--F	2/75	Merseyside PTE 2122	Merseyside Transport Trust
	GLJ 467N	Bristol	VRT/SL6G	VRT/SL2/865	ECW	20531	H43/31F	11/74	Hants & Dorset 3315	Black & White, Penton Mewsey (HA)
	GLJ 681N	Leyland	National 11351/1R/SC	01879	Leyland National		DP48F	1/75	Hants & Dorset 3645	Johnson, -?-
	GLS 280N	Leyland	Leopard PSU3/3R	7404506	Alexander	60AYS/2573/22	B--F	11/74	Alexander Midland MPE210	Scott, Cumbernauld
	GNC 276N	Seddon-Lucas		56081	Pennine	1309	B19F	3/75	Greater Manchester PTE EX62	Museum of Transport, Manchester
	GND 505N	Daimler	Fleetline CRG6LXB	65952	Northern Counties	7719	H43/32F	11/74	Greater Manchester PTE 7439	Neville, Bolton
	GNG 710N	Bristol	VRT/SL6G	VRT/SL2/933	ECW	20480	H43/31F	1/75	Eastern Counties VR144	Denny, Worlingham
	GNJ 570N	Bristol	VRT/SL6G	VRT/SL2/905	ECW	20568	PO??/??F	12/74	Southdown 570	Edwards & Tilley, Woking
	GNJ 573N	Bristol	VRT/SL6G	VRT/SL2/908	ECW	20571	H43/31F	12/74	Southdown 573	Terrill, Lewes
			(ex IUI 2138, GNJ 573N)							
	GNJ 583N	Bristol	VRT/SL3/510	VRT/SL3/108	ECW	20561	H--/--F	5/75	Southdown 583	Mulpeter, Seaford
	GNM 232N	Bristol	LHS6L	LHS-192	Plaxton	758BC003M	C33F	4/75	Richmond, Epsom	Brenchley, Canvey
			(ex TIW 2107, GNM 232N)							
	GNM 235N	Bristol	LHL6L	LHL-222	Plaxton	7511BC002	C51F	3/75	Richardson, East Sheen 74	Mayle, Holsworthy
	GNU 568N	Leyland	National 11351/1R	01753	Leyland National		B49F	12/74	Trent 421	Barrett & Fairbrother, Guildford
	GNU 569N	Leyland	National 11351/1R	01754	Leyland National		B49F	12/74	Trent 422	Stanton, Gloucester
	GOG 535N	Daimler	Fleetline CRL6	68638	Park Royal	B60229	H43/33F	5/75	West Midlands PTE 4535	-?-, -?-
	GOG 578N	Daimler	Fleetline CRL6	68669	Park Royal	B60272	H43/33F	6/75	West Midlands PTE 4578	Brewer, Cardiff
	GOG 653N	Bristol	VRT/SL6G	VRT/SL2/975	MCW		H43/33F	3/75	West Midlands PTE 4653	Vals, Chase Terrace (ST)
(r)	GOG 684N	Bristol	VRT/SL6G	VRT/SL2/1114	MCW		H43/33F	7/75	West Midlands PTE 4684	Davies, Wolverhampton
	GOH 357N	Leyland	Leopard PSU3B/2R	7403067	Marshall	35174	DP49F	11/74	Midland Red 357	Yarsley, Stourbridge
	GPC 731N	Leyland	National 11351/1R	01739	Leyland National		B49F	11/74	Thames Valley & Aldershot 182	Rampton, Reading
			(fitted with a Volvo engine)							
	GPD 301N	Bristol	LHS6L	LHS-166	ECW	21381	B35F	9/74	London Country BN33	Treacy, Newtownards
	GPD 310N	Bristol	LHS6L	LHS-175	ECW	21390	B35F	11/74	London Country BN42	Britishbus Preservation Group
	GPD 313N	Bristol	LHS6L	LHS-180	ECW	21393	B--F	11/74	London Country BN45	Three Counties Bus & Commercial Vehicle Society
	GPD 318N	Bristol	LHS6L	LHS-185	ECW	21398	B35F	2/75	London Country BN50	Prescott, Rettendon
	GRC 889N	→ see 74-KE-528 *Ireland*								
	GRX 1N	Scania	BR111DH	542765	MCW		H45/28D	4/75	Reading 1	BORIS Owners Group, Reading
	GSL 908N	Daimler	Fleetline CRG6LXB	67792	Alexander	AL31/1372/13	H49/34D	4/75	Dundee 120	Taybus Vintage Vehicle Society
	GSX 121N	Bedford	YRT	EW453879	Alexander	70AY/1974/10	B53F	5/75	Edinburgh 121	Docherty, Edinburgh

GUG 547N	Leyland	Atlantean AN68/1R	7403409	Roe	GO7496	PO8/11F	10/74	West Yorkshire PTE 6020	West Yorkshire PTE Preservation Gp, Shipley
GUP 907N	Bristol	LH6L	LH-998	ECW	21274	B43F	2/75	United 1623	Dolan, Willington
GVN 914N	Bedford	YRT	EW450649	Duple	517/2317	C53F	1/75	Abbott, Leeming	Abbott, Leeming (NY)
GWA 836N	Daimler	Fleetline CRG6LXB	68948	ECW	21498	H43/27D	4/75	South Yorkshire PTE 836	Gregory, Sheffield
GWY 690N	Leyland	Leopard PSU4B/4R	7405237	Plaxton	7410LX501	C45F	2/75	West Yorkshire PTE 64	Craven, Keighley
GYB 727N	Bedford	YRQ	DW456462	Plaxton	7410QX517	C45F	12/74	Smith, Pylle	Smith, Pylle (SO)
HAX 399N	→ see AOR 631A								
HCS 351N	Bedford	YRQ	EW450153	Plaxton	7510QB802	DP45F	5/75	Arran Transport, Brodick	Lighthouse & Transport Museum, Arran
HCS 792N	Leyland	Leopard PSU3/3R	7405668	Alexander	54AYS/1273/7	B53F	3/75	Western SMT 2507	Hines, Barnsley
HCS 793N	Leyland	Leopard PSU3/3R	7405880	Alexander	54AYS/1273/8	B53F	3/75	Western SMT 2508	Renfrewshire Bus Preservation Group
HEJ 337N	→ see 75-KK-539 *Ireland*								
HEN 868N	Leyland	Leopard PSU4C/2R	7501434	Northern Counties	7974	B47F	5/75	Chester 68	Dennis, Chester
HFL 950N	Bedford	YRT	EW452254	Plaxton	7511TC096M	C53F	4/75	Shaw, Maxey	-?-, Spalding
HFM 186N	Leyland	National 11351/1R/SC	01943	Leyland National		DP48F	2/75	Crosville ENL930	ENL Consortium, Colwyn Bay
HHH 272N	Bristol	VRT/SL6G	VRT/SL2/991	ECW	21215	PO43/34F	3/75	Cumberland 401	Cumbria Omnibus Group
HJA 121N	Seddon	Pennine 4-236	57581	Pennine	1314	B--F	4/75	Greater Manchester PTE 1737	SELNEC Preservation Society
HNB 24N	Leyland	National 10351/1R	01987	Leyland National		B41F	3/75	Greater Manchester PTE 105	SELNEC Preservation Society
HNE 641N	Leyland	Leopard PSU3B/4R	7500131	ECW	21499	C49F	4/75	Greater Manchester PTE 81	Amis, Manchester
HNT 945N	Bedford	VAS5	EW452904	Duple	511/1001	C29F	3/75	Corvedale, Ludlow 42	Price, Shobdon
HNY 938N	Mercedes-Benz	LPO608D	31408620898733	Plaxton	757.5MC001M	C29F	6/75	Davies, Tredegar	Thornes, Hemingbrough (NY)
HOR 305N	Leyland	Atlantean AN68/1R	7501065	Alexander	AL40/3773/4	H45/30D	5/75	Portsmouth 305	Hampshire Bus & Coach Preservation Group
HOR 306N	Leyland	Atlantean AN68/1R	7501198	Alexander	AL40/3773/5	H45/30D	5/75	Portsmouth 306	Blair, Upham
HPF 310N	→ see SIB 6711								
HPF 318N	Leyland	National 10351/1R/SC	02169	Leyland National		DP39F	4/75	London Country SNC168	Knight, Flitwick
		(ex AVS 238N, HIL 9374, HPF 318N)							
HRN 99N	Leyland	Atlantean AN68/1R	7402766	Northern Counties	7962	H43/31F	3/75	Fylde 79	Lancastrian Transport Trust
				(completed by Willowbrook 73582)					
HSO 61N	Leyland	Leopard PSU4C/4R	7501072	Alexander	99AY/575/1	C45F	6/75	Grampian 61	Aberdeen & District Transport Preservation Trust
HTA 844N	Leyland	National 11351/1R	02401	Leyland National		B49F	7/75	Western National 2813	Snell, Penzance
		(fitted with a DAF engine)							
HTG 354N	Bristol	RESL6L	RESL-8-450	ECW	21512	B44F	5/75	Cynon Valley 43	Smith, Cwmbran
HTU 155N	Bristol	VRT/SL6G	VRT/SL2/959	ECW	21148	H43/31F	3/75	Crosville DVG266	Barnes, Penketh
HTU 159N	Bristol	VRT/SL6G	VRT/SL2/996	ECW	21152	H43/31F	3/75	Crosville DVG270	Sharpe, Derby
HUM 951N	AEC	Reliance	6U3ZR29311	Plaxton	7411AB801	B66F	1/75	Clayforth, Guiseley	Thornes, Hemingbrough (NY)
		(ex LBT 380N, HUM 951N)							
HVU 243N	→ see LRN 418N								
HVU 244N	AEC	Reliance	6U3ZR29791	Plaxton	7412AC014	C49F	3/75	Yelloway, Rochdale	Museum of Transport, Manchester
HVU 248N	AEC	Reliance	6U3ZR30501	Plaxton	7511AC022	C45F	4/75	Yelloway, Rochdale	Duffy, Macclesfield
HWN 978N	Leyland	Leopard PSU3C/4R	7501669	Plaxton	7511LX507M	C53F	6/75	Evans, Brynamman	-?-, Cheltenham
HWU 57N	→ see LRN 480N								
JAJ 293N	Bristol	RELL6L	RELL-3-2041	ECW	21530	B46D	5/75	Hartlepool 93	Nielsen, Hartlepool
JAJ 296N	Bristol	RELL6L	RELL-3-2044	ECW	21533	B46D	5/75	Hartlepool 96	Hart et al, York
JBF 169N	Daimler	Fleetline CRL6	67908	Northern Counties	7580	H44/33F	3/75	Turner, Brown Edge 19	Hearson, Chesterton
JEU 509N	Bristol	RELH6L	RELH-4-764	Plaxton	7411BCR003	C49F	3/75	National Travel South East	Bissett, Westbury
		(ex CSV 524, GJD 194N)							
JFG 354N	Leyland	Atlantean AN68/1R	7500000	East Lancs	4609	O44/29D	7/75	Brighton 54	Mulpeter, Seaford
JFJ 500N	→ see 31917 *Guernsey*								

	JFJ 506N	Bristol	LH6L	LH-1119	Plaxton	7510BC016S	C45F	7/75	Greenslade 326	Heginbotham, Irthlingborough
			(ex 31913, JFJ 506N)							
	JFJ 507N	Bristol	LH6L	LH-1120	Plaxton	7510BC017S	C45F	7/75	Greenslade 327	Stafford, Bedford
			(ex 31914, 12723, JFJ 507N)							
	JFJ 508N	→ see 31915 *Guernsey*								
	JFT 228N	Leyland	Atlantean AN68/1R	7403507	Park Royal	B60722	O43/31F	8/74	Gateshead & District 211M	North East Bus Preservation Trust
			(ex KKH 372N, RCN 111N)							
	JFV 295N	Leyland	Leopard PSU3B/4R	7401305	East Lancs	A3407	B52F	4/75	Halton 9	Darwen Transport Museum Trust
					(rebodied 1/83)					
	JGA 189N	Leyland	Atlantean AN68/1R	7500623	Alexander	AL38/1174/7	H43/31F	5/75	Greater Glasgow PTE LA907	Park & Tennant, Seghill
(r)	JGA 199N	Leyland	Atlantean AN68/1R	7501294	Alexander	AL38/1174/17	H--/--F	5/75	Greater Glasgow PTE LA917	Roulston, Glasgow
	JGV 332N	Bedford	YRT	EW451890	Plaxton	7511TB802	B64F	5/75	Squirrel. Hitcham	Emsworth & District, Southbourne (WS)
	JHB 165N	Bedford	YRT	EW450478	Duple	517/2350	C53F	6/75	Evans, New Tredegar	Evans, New Tredegar
			(ex MIL 3729, JHB 165N)							
	JJT 437N	Bristol	VRT/SL6G	VRT/SL2/1091	ECW	20957	H43/31F	6/75	Hants & Dorset 3325	Cole, Frinton-on-Sea
	JJT 446N	Bristol	VRT/SL6G	VRT/SL2/1100	ECW	20966	H43/31F	6/75	Hants & Dorset 3334	Mills, Hursthouse & Holtby, Landford
	JMY 120N	Leyland	National 11351/1R/EXC	01487	Leyland National		C??FT	c6/74	Leyland National demonstrator	Bellinger, Penge
	JNG 50N	Bristol	VRT/SL6G	VRT/SL2/1077	ECW	21058	O43/31F	5/75	Eastern Counties VR152	Carters, Wherstead (SK)
	JPF 869N	→ see 804 FUF								
	JUG 356N	Bristol	LHS6L	LHS-221	ECW	21580	B29F	7/75	West Yorkshire PTE 40	Pearce, Worthing
			(ex 12723, 31914, JUG 356N)							
(r)	JUG 357N	Bristol	LHS6L	LHS-222	ECW	21581	B29F	7/75	West Yorkshire PTE 41	Staniforth, Stroud
			(ex 12727, 31915, JUG 357N)							
	JUS 774N	Leyland	Atlantean AN68/1R	7501431	Alexander	AL38/1174/27	H45/31F	6/75	Greater Glasgow PTE LA927	Budd, Glasgow
	JWE 400N	Bedford	YRQ	EW451208	Plaxton	7510QC051	C45F	6/75	Whitehead, Conisbrough	Andrew, Rhewl (CN)
	JWU 244N	Leyland	Leopard PSU4C/4R	7501070	Plaxton	7510LB803	DP43F	6/75	West Yorkshire PTE 8501	
										Huddersfield Passenger Transport Enthusiasts Society
	JWW 227N	Bristol	VRT/SL6G	VRT/SL2/1067	ECW	21034	H43/31F	5/75	York-West Yorkshire 3968	West Yorkshire Road Car Co Pres. Group
			(ex RIL 1680, JWW 227N)							
	KBR 252N	Volvo	B58-61	6658	Plaxton	7512VC016	DP68F	5/75	Stanhope Motor Services	Renton, Silksworth
	KBW 118N	→ see MBW 612N								
	KGR 491N	Bristol	LHS6L	LHS-204	Duple	566/6704	C35F	6/75	Scotts Grey, Darlington	Humphries, Thatcham
	KLE 80N	→ see GFO 641								
	KSF 1N	Ailsa	B55-10	75/011	Alexander	AV6/2574/1	H44/35F	5/75	Alexander Fife FRA1	Fife Bus Club, Methil
	KVY 789N	Bedford	YRQ	EW450844	Duple	516/2214	C45F	5/75	Gorwood, East Cottingwith	Thornes, Hemingbrough (NY)
	LBT 380N	Bristol	LHS6L	LHS-202	Plaxton	758BC013M	C35F	5/75	Thornes, Bubwith 74	Thornes, Hemingbrough (NY)
			(ex JCV 385N, WRL 270, KKH 101N, LBT 380N)							
	LRN 418N	AEC	Reliance	6U3ZR29872	Plaxton	7512AC011	C53F	3/75	Yelloway, Rochdale	Roberts, Stockport
			(ex 163 PPB, HVU 243N)							
	LRN 480N	Leyland	Leopard PSU3C/4R	7501741	Plaxton	7511LC007M	C53F	7/75	Wallace Arnold Tours	Batchelor, Darwen (LA)
			(ex WHA 712, HWU 57N)							
(r)	MBW 612N	Leyland	Leopard PSU5/4R	7405041	Plaxton	7512LC001	C50F	5/75	Heyfordian, Upper Heyford	Kick, Oxford
			(ex 2110 UK, KBW 118N)							
	NDS 658N	Ailsa	B55-10	74006	Alexander	AV3/374/2	H44/35F	6/75	Tyne & Wear PTE 402	Tyne & Wear Bus Preservation Group
			(ex MJI 7419, NDS 658N, GCN 2N)							
	ORC 417N	Bristol	RELH6G	RELH-4-736	ECW	21412	B53F	8/74	Midland General 288	Phillips, Rhymney
	RCN 111N	→ see JFT 228N								
	RGV 284N	Leyland	Leopard PSU3B/4R	7402287	Willowbrook	73767	B55F	9/74	Hedingham & District L84	Hedingham & District (EX) L84

	RRU 594N	→ see 3460 ZW *Ireland*								
	RRU 822N	Ford	R1014	BC04PJ54882	Plaxton	7410FC043	C45F	2/75	AC Tours, Bournemouth	Walters, Talke
	SCD 731N	Leyland	Atlantean AN68/1R	7403882	Park Royal	B60727	H43/30F	9/74	Southdown 731	Blair, Upham
	SHR 780N	→ see CAZ 3693								
(z)	SRP 817N	Bristol	VRT/SL6G	VRT/SL2/808	ECW	20607	H43/31F	9/74	United Counties 817	Robertson, Biggleswade
	TEC 599N	AEC	Reliance	6MU4R28177	Plaxton	7410AX501	C45F	8/74	Jackson, Kirkby Stephen	Emerton, Nantwich
	TNX 901N	Bedford	YRT	DW455415	Plaxton	7411TC068	C53F	8/74	Cotton, Bilton	Peters, Mundesley
	TOE 527N	Ailsa	B55-10	74001	Alexander	AV2/574/1	H44/35F	9/74	West Midlands 4527	4738 Preservation Group, Birmingham
	UMO 180N	Leyland	National 11351/1R	01545	Leyland National		B49F	8/74	Thames Valley & Aldershot 180	Nash, Ockley
	XTB 728N	Leyland	Atlantean AN68/1R	7402342	East Lancs	2901	H43/31F	8/74	Fishwick, Leyland 18	Hayes, Little Hoole
	XTB 729N	Leyland	Atlantean AN68/1R	7402386	East Lancs	2902	H43/31F	8/74	Fishwick, Leyland 19	Hayes, Little Hoole
	HTR 557P	Leyland	Atlantean AN68/1R	7503329	East Lancs	4902	H45/31F	10/75	Southampton 195	Southampton & District Transport Heritage Trust
	JDK 914P	Bristol	RESL6L	RESL-8-446	East Lancs	5104	B45F	10/75	Rossendale 14	Darwen Transport Museum Trust
	JHW 103P	Leyland	National 11351/1R	02382	Leyland National		B52F	8/75	Bristol 3015	Gardiner, Gloucester
	JHW 108P	Bristol	VRT/SL3/501	VRT/SL3/131	ECW	20931	O43/29F	12/75	Bristol C5034	Powell, Weston super Mare
	JHW 118P	Bristol	LH6L	LH-1109	ECW	21717	B43F	10/75	Bristol 358	Jenkins, Faversham
	JJG 1P	Leyland	Atlantean AN68/1R	7502670	ECW	21989	H43/30F	3/76	East Kent 7001	London Bus Company, Northfleet (KT)
	JMW 168P	Bristol	RESL6G	RESL-8-464	ECW	21508	B43F	8/75	Thamesdown 168	Swindon Vintage Omnibus Society
	JMW 169P	Bristol	RESL6G	RESL-8-465	ECW	21509	B43F	8/75	Thamesdown 169	1820 Group, Doncaster
	JOU 160P	Bristol	VRT/SL3/501	VRT/SL3/122	ECW	20924	H43/28F	10/75	Cheltenham District 5030	Hampshire Bus (HA) 15760
			(fitted with a Gardner 6LXB engine)							
	JOU 161P	Bristol	VRT/SL3/501	VRT/SL3/123	ECW	20925	H43/27D	10/75	Cheltenham District 5031	Sly, Tewkesbury
	JOV 613P	Daimler	Fleetline CRG6LX	68718	Park Royal	B60307	H43/33F	8/75	West Midlands PTE 4613	Munro et al, Kings Heath
	JOV 714P	Bristol	VRT/SL6G	VRT/SL2/1154	MCW		H43/33F	11/75	West Midlands PTE 4714	Aston Manor Road Transport Museum
	JOV 738P	Ailsa	B55-10	75075	Alexander	AV9/275/1	H44/35F	1/76	West Midlands PTE 4738	4738 Preservation Group, Birmingham
	JOV 749P	Ailsa	B55-10	75086	Alexander	AV9/275/12	H44/35F	2/76	West Midlands PTE 4749	Darwin & Patrickson, Middleton
	JOV 760P	→ see ANC 578A								
	JOV 761P	Ailsa	B55-10	75089	Alexander	AV9/275/24	H44/35F	3/76	West Midlands PTE 4761	-?-, -?-
	JOX 506P	Leyland	National 11351A/1R	03340	Leyland National		B45F	7/76	Midland Red 506	Follwell & Owen, Newcastle-under-Lyme
	JPO 55P	Leyland	Leopard PSU3C/4R	7503831	Duple	633/5100	C53F	10/75	Easson, Southampton	-?-, -?-
	JTH 756P	Leyland	National 11351/1R	02621	Leyland National		B52F	9/75	South Wales 756	Evans, Swansea
	JWM 689P	Leyland	Atlantean AN68A/1R	7601150	East Lancs	6004	H43/32F	4/76	Merseyside PTE 1689	-?-, -?-
	KCR 108P	Leyland	National 10351/2R	03250	Leyland National		B40D	3/76	Portsmouth 108	Sheffield Joint Omnibus Club
			(ex 2704 MN, KCR 108P)							
	KDT 281P	Bedford	YRQ	EW455155	Plaxton	7410QC074	C45F	10/75	Mawby Crowcroft & Fell, Barnsley	Kenward, Bromsgrove (WO)
	KEW 785P	Bedford	YRT	EW456287	Plaxton	7511TC155M	C53F	9/75	Robinson, Kimbolton	Murphy, Huddersfield
			(ex RBZ 2566, KEW 785P)							
	KFF 586P	AEC	Reliance	6U3ZR32740	Plaxton	7611AC009	C53F	6/76	Parry, Blaenau Ffestiniog	Graham, Kilwinning
	KHT 122P	Leyland	National 11351/1R	03278	Leyland National		B52F	6/76	Bristol G3024	Stanton, Gloucester
	KHU 318P	→ see 685 DID *Ireland*								
	KHU 326P	Bristol	LH6L	LH-1190	ECW	21735	B43F	2/76	Bristol 376	Staniforth, Stroud
	KJD 260P	Scania	BR111DH	543821	MCW		H43/29D	7/76	London Transport MD60	Almeroth, Wendling
	KJD 401P	Bristol	LH6L	LH-1166	ECW	21856	B39F	2/76	London Transport BL1	London Transport Museum
	KJD 402P	Bristol	LH6L	LH-1235	ECW	21857	B39F	3/76	London Transport BL2	Wells, Ipswich
	KJD 413P	Bristol	LH6L	LH-1246	ECW	21868	B43F	3/76	London Transport BL13	Pinder & Alger, Loddiswell
	KJD 419P	Bristol	LH6L	LH-1252	ECW	21874	B—F	6/76	London Transport BL19	Pinder & Alger, Loddiswell
	KJD 431P	Bristol	LH6L	LH-1271	ECW	21886	B39F	6/76	London Transport BL31	Green, Edmonton

Registration	Chassis make	Chassis model	Chassis no	Body make	Body no	Layout	New	First operator	Current owner
KJD 434P	Bristol	LH6L	LH-1274	ECW	21889	B39F	7/76	London Transport BL34	Bird, Burgess Hill (WS)
KJD 507P	Leyland	National 10351A/2R	03485	Leyland National		DP36D	5/76	London Transport LS7	Nash, Ockley
KJD 524P	Leyland	National 10351A/2R	03559	Leyland National		B36D	8/76	London Transport LS24	Bowyer, London
KJD 535P	Leyland	National 10351A/2R	03594	Leyland National		DP35D	8/76	London Transport LS35	Davey & Tomms, Luton
KJD 557P	→ see 76-C-248 *Ireland*								
KMW 175P	Daimler	Fleetline CRG6LX	68733	ECW	20850	O43/31F	2/76	Thamesdown 175	Pearce, Worthing
									(due to be operated as Southdown Historic, Worthing (WS)
KON 306P	→ see 76-LK-541 *Ireland*								
KON 311P	Leyland	Fleetline FE30ALR	7505030	MCW		H43/33F	2/76	West Midlands PTE 6311	BaMMOT, Wythall (WO)
KON 323P	Leyland	Fleetline FE30ALR	7504846	MCW		H43/33F	3/76	West Midlands PTE 6323	-?-, Staffordshire
KOU 791P	Bristol	VRT/SL3/6LXB	VRT/SL3/244	ECW	20913	H39/31F	5/76	Bristol 5505	Williams, Bristol
KPA 369P	Leyland	National 11351/1R	02724	Leyland National		B49F	9/75	Thames Valley & Aldershot 218	Morton, Little London (HA)
KPC 204P	Bedford	YRQ	EW454064	Plaxton	7510QC089	C45F	10/75	Harding, Betchworth	Evans & Wood, Rugeley
KPC 211P	Bedford	YRT	EW453622	Duple	517/2427	C53F	9/75	Warner, Milford	Centurion, Welton (SO)
		(ex RIB 8809, KPC 211P)							
KRE 279P	Leyland	National 11351/1R	02563	Leyland National		B52F	9/75	Potteries 279	Wright, Fenton
KRH 411P	Scania	BR111DH	543244	MCW		H44/29F	9/75	Hull 411	Almeroth, Wending
KSO 74P	Leyland	National 10351/2R	02975	Leyland National		B40D	3/76	Grampian 74	Macduff, Kilmarnock
		(ex 4294 MAN, KSO 74P)							
KTT 38P	Bristol	LH6L	LH-1135	ECW	21655	B43F	9/75	Western National 108	Partridge, Exeter
KTT 42P	Bristol	LH6L	LH-1139	ECW	21659	B43F	8/75	Western National 112	Nelson, Bedlington
KTT 43P	Bristol	LH6L	LH-1140	ECW	21660	B43F	8/75	Western National 113	Greet, Broadhempston
KTT 316P	→ see ODV 287P								
KUC 911P	Daimler	Fleetline CRL6	68447	MCW		H--/--D	9/75	London Transport DMS1911	Clitheroe, Bromley
KUX 321P	Ford	R1114	BC04PA65627	Willowbrook	75135	B54F	9/75	Valley, Bishops Castle	Eyles, Tibberton
KVD 444P	Leyland	Leopard PSU3C/4R	7503098	Plaxton	7511LC054M	C51F	9/75	Guards, London	-?-, -?-
		(ex IIL 3985, KVD 444P)							
KVO 429P	Leyland	National 11351/2R	02584	Leyland National		B50F	9/75	Trent 429	429 Group, Ruddington
LBN 201P	Leyland	Leopard PSU3C/4R	7601179	Plaxton	7511LX546M	C51F	2/76	Southend 201	Hatton, Chase Terrace
LBN 202P	Leyland	Leopard PSU3C/4R	7601180	Plaxton	7511LX547M	C51F	2/76	Southend 202	Chapman, Stevenage
LCB 925P	Bedford	J2SZ2 *(now J2SZ10)*	2T128006	Plaxton	728016	C20F	-/72	Prestwich Hospital	Sutton, Redgrave
		(ex OTD 593K)							
LED 70P	Bristol	RESL6G	RESL-8-467	East Lancs	5302	B44F	1/76	Warrington 70	Lawrenson, Ince
LED 71P	Bristol	RESL6G	RESL-8-468	East Lancs	5303	B44F	1/76	Warrington 71	Lynas, Runcorn
LED 73P	Bristol	RESL6G	RESL-8-470	East Lancs	5301	B44F	1/76	Warrington 73	Arnold, Warrington
LER 666P	Bedford	YLQ	FW453742	Duple	615/2055	C41F	4/76	Kenzie, Shepreth	Fuller, Rushden
LEU 263P	Bristol	VRT/SL3/6LXB	VRT/SL3/267	ECW	20949	O43/27D	7/76	Bristol C5055	Pratt {Crosville}, Weston super Mare (SO)
		(ex 68523, AY 586, LEU 263P)							
LEU 269P	Bristol	VRT/SL3/6LXB	VRT/SL3/256	ECW	20927	O43/27D	4/76	Cheltenham District 5044	Brown, Nailsea
LHW 504P	Bedford	YMT	FW454666	Plaxton	7611TC115	C53F	7/76	Wessex, Bristol 504	Hamilton, Bow (DN)
LKP 385P	Ailsa	B55-10	75071	Alexander	AV7/2774/5	H44/35F	12/75	Maidstone & District 5385	Tucker & Pinnock, Chatham
LPB 218P	Leyland	National 10351/1R	03139	Leyland National		B41F	2/76	London Country SNB218	Simister & Skinner, Chelmsford
LRA 801P	Bristol	VRT/SL3/501	VRT/SL3/168	ECW	21007	H43/34F	11/75	Midland General 801	Waterhouse, Ripley
		(fitted with a Gardner engine)							
LSX 16P	Ailsa	B55-10	75033	Alexander	AV6/2574/16	H44/35F	9/75	Alexander Fife FRA16	Nicholson, Fife
LTE 489P	Leyland	Leopard PSU3D/2R	7602203	Plaxton	7611LB807	B48F	7/76	Lancashire United 438	Orrell, Warrington
LTE 491P	Leyland	Leopard PSU3D/2R	7602204	Plaxton	7611LB809	B48F	7/76	Lancashire United 440	LUT Society
LTG 798P	Leyland	Leopard PSU3C/2R	7504211	East Lancs	5402	B51F	2/76	Rhymney Valley 8	Evans, Bargoed

	Registration	Chassis	Model	Chassis No	Body	Body No	Layout	New	First Owner	Current Owner
	LUG 523P	Leyland	Leopard PSU4C/4R	7504472	Plaxton	7610LB803	DP43F	4/76	West Yorkshire PTE 8523	-?-, -?-
(r)	LUH 104P	Bristol	LHS6L	LHS-245	ECW	21983	B—F	6/76	Cardiff 106	Taylor, Ystrad Mynach
	LUH 105P	Bristol	LHS6L	LHS-246	ECW	21984	DP27F	5/76	Cardiff 105	Taylor, Ystrad Mynach
	LUX 523P	Bedford	YLQ	FW453694	Duple	615/2023	C45F	5/76	Whittle, Highley	Price & Perry, Shobdon
	LWB 377P	Ailsa	B55-10	75134	Van Hool McArdle	04/0008	H44/31D	6/76	South Yorkshire PTE 377	Heaton, Dinnington
	LWB 388P	Ailsa	B55-10	75149	Van Hool McArdle	04/0019	H44/31D	7/76	South Yorkshire PTE 388	388 Group, Sheffield
	LYH 147P	AEC	Reliance	6MU4R32139	Plaxton	7610ACCE004AM	C45C	6/76	Glenton, London	Bamford, Southowram
	LYH 148P	AEC	Reliance	6MU4R30902	Plaxton	7610ACCE003AM	C34C	3/76	Glenton, London	Cooper, Killamarsh (DE)
	MAE 959P	Leyland	LVB668	7505399	den Oudsten	5874	B32D	8/76	Nefkens, Netherlands 42	Kells Transport Museum, Cork
			(ex 31-15-PB *Netherlands*)							
	MAE 962P	Leyland	LVB668	7505405	den Oudsten	5889	B32D	8/76	Nefkens, Netherlands 48	Kells Transport Museum, Cork
			(ex 89-19-NG *Netherlands*)							
	MAU 612P	→ see 75-KE-527 *Ireland*								
	MAU 616P	→ see 75-KE-526 *Ireland*								
	MCA 620P	Bristol	LH6L	LH-1133	ECW	21695	B43F	10/75	Crosville SLL620	Hull & Country Bus Preservation Group
	MEL 560P	Bristol	VRT/SL3/6LX	VRT/SL3/225	ECW	20971	H43/31F	3/76	Hants & Dorset 3359	Ennis, Pembrokeshire
	MFR 306P	Leyland	Leopard PSU3C/2R	7504518	Alexander	95AYS/5374/6	B53F	2/76	Lancaster 306	Smith & Gardner, Chorley
	MFS 444P	Bedford	YLQ	EW454413	Plaxton	7510QC105M	C45F	10/75	Reid & Mackay, Edinburgh	Prentice, Haddington (SS)
			(ex IIL 4595, MFS 444P)							
	MGE 183P	Ailsa	B55-10	75056	Alexander	AV8/5074/8	H44/35F	12/75	Glasgow AV8	Transport Preservation Trust, Beith
	MHS 21P	Leyland	Leopard PSU3C/4R	7600177	Alexander	86AYS/4174/18	RV	3/76	Ulsterbus 4882	Shannon, Newtownards
	MOD 820P	Leyland	National 11351/1R	03237	Leyland National		B50F	3/76	Western National 2820	Byrne, Okehampton
	MOD 823P	Leyland	National 11351A/1R	03352	Leyland National		B50F	7/76	Western National 2823	Billington, Maidenhead
	MPT 299P	→ see ORC 545P								
	MRT 6P	Leyland	Atlantean AN68A/1R	7600015	Roe	GO7701	H43/29D	5/76	Ipswich 6	Ipswich Transport Museum
	MSF 122P	Leyland	Leopard PSU3C/4R	7503288	Alexander	100AY/5774/1	C49F	11/75	Lothian 122	Hunt, Fleetwood
	MSF 467P	Leyland	Atlantean AN68A/1R	7505328	Alexander	AL36/773/67	H45/30D	2/76	Lothian 467	Kells Transport Museum, Cork
	MSF 468P	Leyland	Atlantean AN68A/1R	7505329	Alexander	AL36/773/68	H45/30D	2/76	Lothian 468	Coyle & Fox, Livingston
	MSF 469P	→ see 76-C-1026 *Ireland*								
	MSF 750P	Seddon	Pennine 7	59649	Alexander	M9/3274/4	C42FT	6/76	Scottish Omnibuses XS750	Booth et al, Glasgow
	MSJ 385P	Seddon	Pennine 7	59997	Alexander	5AT/4974/21	C24FL	7/76	Western SMT 2579	Kennedy, Glasgow
	MTV 755P	Leyland	Leopard PSU3C/4R	7505575	Duple	634/5174	DP53F	3/76	Nottingham 755	Stanton, Nottingham
	MUA 45P	Bristol	LHS6L	LHS-242	ECW	21585	DP27F	7/76	West Yorkshire PTE 45	Merseyside Transport Trust
	MUA 865P	Leyland	Atlantean AN68/1R	7503334	Roe	GO8485	H43/30F	1/76	Yorkshire Woollen 768	Goldthorpe, Dewsbury
					(*rebodied 6/81*)					
	MUL 688P	→ see Unregistered Vehicles								
(z)	MVC 12P	Bedford	YRT	EW456391	Plaxton	7611TX537	C53F	1/76	Chapel End, Nuneaton	Lang, Rathcoole
			(ex LCC 589P, MVC 12P)							
	MWG 499P	Leyland	Leopard PSU5A/4R	7601745	Duple	635/5203	C53F	7/76	National Travel (North East)	-?-, Nuneaton
			(ex CEO 952, MWG 499P)							
	NAH 135P	Bristol	VRT/SL3/501	VRT/SL3/287	ECW	21072	H43/31F	4/76	Eastern Counties VR172	Patterson, Kings Lynn
	NBR 665P	Bristol	LH6L	LH-1168	ECW	21613	B43F	11/75	United 1665	Bulmer, North Stainley (NY)
	NCS 10P	Leyland	Fleetline FE30AGR	7603686	Alexander	AL48/974/3	H43/31F	7/76	A1 (Murray), Ardrossan	Evans, Blackpool
	NCS 16P	Leyland	Fleetline FE30AGR	7603490	Alexander	AL48/974/2	H43/31F	7/76	A1 (Hill), Ardrossan	Scottish Vintage Bus Museum
	NCS 25P	Ailsa	B55-10	75127	Alexander	AV13/3975/1	H44/35F	8/76	A1 (Docherty), Ardrossan	Groves Hamilton & Miller, Symington
	NEH 917P	→ see YIY 685 *Ireland*								
	NFX 132P	Daimler	Fleetline CRL6	66095	Alexander	AL46/4870/23	CO43/31F	6/76	Bournemouth 132	Morris, Shrewsbury
	NFX 133P	Daimler	Fleetline CRL6	66096	Alexander	AL46/4870/24	CO43/31F	6/76	Bournemouth 133	Davies & Bradley, Oswestry

	Reg	Make	Model	Chassis no	Body	Body no	Layout	Date	New to	Owner
	NFX 137P	Daimler	Fleetline CRL6	66100	Alexander	AL46/4870/28	CO43/31F	6/76	Bournemouth 137	-?-, Bournemouth
	NHG 732P	→ see UJI 6314								
(a)	NKJ 849P	Commer	KC6055	352790	Rootes		B--F	4/76	Enham Village Centre	FoKAB, Winchester
	NJT 831P	→ see OIX 179 *Ireland*								
	NNC 855P	AEC	Reliance	6U3ZR33482	Duple	645/5764	C8F	4/76	Yelloway, Rochdale	Haddock, Altrincham
	NNK 817P	→ see DAD 798Y								
	NNO 66P	Leyland	Atlantean AN68A/1R	7600249	ECW	21537	H43/31F	5/76	Colchester 66	-?-, -?-
	NPE 218P	Bedford	J2SZ2	DW113188	Caetano	75/26	C20F	7/76	Heron, Horley	Jenkins, Wells
	NRN 397P	Leyland	Atlantean AN68/1R	7502389	Park Royal	B61756	H43/30F	3/76	Ribble 1397	Butler, Gosforth
										(on loan to Ribble Vehicle Preservation Trust)
	ODV 287P	Volvo	B58-56	7304	Duple	573/7013	C53F	9/75	Trathen, Yelverton	Parsons, Margate
			(ex 676 GDV, KTT 316P)							
	OLN 65P	Bedford	J2SZ2	DW112455	Caetano	75/27	C20F	6/76	Chapman, Feltham	Silverman, Ely
	ONN 571P	Leyland	Atlantean AN68/1R	7601555	Willowbrook		H43/31F	7/76	Trent 571	Towle & Campbell, Awsworth
					(rebodied 11/77)					
	OPP 222P	Seddon	Atkinson Pennine 7	60705	Plaxton	7612SC002AM	C57F	6/76	Sworder, Walkern 3	Sworder, Molesworth
	ORC 545P	Leyland	Atlantean AN68/1R	7503703	ECW	21954	O35/12F	10/75	Northern General 3299	Nottingham Transport Heritage Centre
			(ex YRC 194, MPT 299P)							
	OUM 727P	Bedford	J2SZ10	DW112068	Caetano	75/23	C20F	4/76	Anderton, Keighley	Howlett, Shepshed
	OWW 905P	Bristol	VRT/SL3/6LX	VRT/SL3/346	ECW	21026	H43/31F	5/76	West Riding 757	Halliday, Shipley
	PPT 446P	Leyland	Leopard PSU3C/4R	7601748	Plaxton	7611LB803	B55F	7/76	Eden, West Auckland L14	Scarlett, Shildon
	PYA 646P	AEC	Reliance	6U3ZR33167	Plaxton	7611AC046	C51F	5/76	Berry, Taunton	Howlett, Shepshed
	RFR 177P	Leyland	Leopard PSU3C/4R	7503729	Duple	533/5724	C51F	4/76	Robinson, Great Harwood 177	Meir, Stone
	RFR 424P	Leyland	Atlantean AN68/1R	7505314	ECW	22018	H43/31F	5/76	Ribble 1424	Burke, West Auckland
	RGF 231P	Bristol	LHS6L	LHS-251	Plaxton	768BC003	C33F	6/76	Richmond, Epsom	Burke, West Auckland
	SHO 628P	Bedford	SB5	EW456264	Plaxton	75NJM010	C37F	4/76	CDE, Porton Down	Atkin, North Owersby
	SMS 120P	Daimler	Fleetline CRG6LXB	67476	Alexander	AD14/1972/12	H44/31F	7/76	Alexander Midland MRF120	Booth, Glasgow
(z)	ACW 919R	Leyland	National 11351A/1R	04361	Leyland National		B52F	5/77	Halton 19	Ribble Vehicle Preservation Trust
	BCK 706R	Leyland	Titan B15	7705689	Park Royal	B60770	H44/33F	6/77	Leyland demonstrator	Hayes, Little Hoole
			(ex TMX 535R, VLT 240, BCK 706R)							
	LTK 100R	Leyland	Atlantean AN68A/1R	7601073	Roe	GO7768	H--/--D	2/77	Plymouth 100	-?-, -?-
	LTR 336R	→ see LSU 857								
	MBE 612R	→ see 77-LK-536 *Ireland*								
	MBE 613R	Leyland	Fleetline FE30AGR	7605667	Roe	GO7774	O45/29D	12/76	Grimsby Cleethorpes 113	East Midland (DE) 15513
	MDL 880R	Leyland	National 11351/1R	03550	Leyland National		B49F	8/76	Southern Vectis 880	Watts, Beccles
	MFN 41R	Bristol	VRT/SL3/6LXB	VRT/SL3/456	ECW	22052	H--/--F	9/76	East Kent 7641	Bamford, Ramsgate
	MOU 739R	Bristol	VRT/SL3/6LXB	VRT/SL3/394	ECW	21791	H43/28F	10/76	Bristol G5065	Ball, Inkpen
	MPX 945R	Ford	Transit	BDO5ST63237	Dormobile	6985 901 4 8 77	C--F	4/77	Angela, Bursledon	Shears C, Winkleigh
			(ex 6768, MPX 945R)							
	MVK 538R	Leyland	Atlantean AN68A/2R	7601728	Alexander	AL51/3875/39	H38/34F	12/76	Tyne & Wear PTE 538	Buckley Minto & McHaddan, Newcastle-upon-Tyne
	NDE 916R	Bristol	LH6L	LH-1309	ECW	22384	B45F	2/77	Jones, Carmarthen 12	Britishbus Preservation Group
	NDL 652R	Bristol	VRT/SL3/6LXB	VRT/SL3/467	ECW	22193	H43/31F	11/76	Southern Vectis 652	Stewart, Shenfield
	NDL 656R	Bristol	VRT/SL3/6LXB	VRT/SL3/644	ECW	22197	H43/31F	1/77	Southern Vectis 656	Shepherd, Edinburgh
	NDP 31R	Bristol	VRT/LL3/6LXB	VRT/LL3/103	Northern Counties	7817	H--/--D	9/76	Reading 31	Ball, Inkpen
	NDP 38R	Bristol	VRT/LL3/6LXB	VRT/LL3/110	Northern Counties	7823	H47/29D	10/76	Reading 38	Ball, Inkpen
(z)	NEN 965R	Leyland	National 11351A/1R	04146	Leyland National		B49F	2/77	Lancashire United 478	BaMMOT, Wythall
	NFN 84R	Leyland	National 11351A/1R	04435	Leyland National		DP48F	7/77	East Kent 1184	Baxter, Hawkinge

	Reg	Make	Model	Chassis no	Body	Body no	Layout	New	First operator	Owner
	NOC 600R	Leyland	Fleetline FE30AGR	7602519	Park Royal	B61940	H43/33F	11/76	West Midlands PTE 6600	West Midlands Bus Preservation Society
	NOE 544R	Leyland	National 11351A/1R	03548	Leyland National		B49F	9/76	Midland Red 544	BaMMOT, Wythall
	NOE 600R	Leyland	National 11351A/1R	04113	Leyland National		B49F	3/77	Midland Red 600	Owen, Wolverhampton
			(fitted with a Cummins engine)							
	NOE 602R	Leyland	National 11351A/1R	04115	Leyland National		B49F	3/77	Midland Red 602	Peters, Kings Norton
	NPJ 472R	Leyland	National 11351A/1R	03647	Leyland National		B49F	9/76	Thames Valley & Aldershot 251	Barrett & Fairbrother. Guildford
	NPK 250R	Leyland	National 10351A/1R	03977	Leyland National		B41F	11/76	London Country SNB250	-?-, -?-
	NPK 257R	Leyland	National 10351A/1R	04011	Leyland National		B41F	12/76	London Country SNB257	Davey & Tomms, Luton
	NSP 326R	Ailsa	B55-10	76054	Alexander	AV11/2575/20	H44/33F	9/76	Tayside 126	Taybus Vintage Vehicle Society
(r)	NTC 573R	Bristol	VRT/SL3/6LXB	VRT/SL3/620	ECW	22110	H43/31F	5/77	Bristol C5097	Billington, Maidenhead
	NWO 491R	→ see 76-C-1007 *Ireland*								
	OAS 287R	Leyland	National 11351A/1R	04384	Leyland National		DP45F	7/77	West Midlands PTE 6825	Aston Manor Road Transport Museum
			(ex MIL 9755, OOX 825R) *(fitted with a Volvo engine)*							
	OBN 502R	Leyland	Fleetline FE30AGR	7605413	Northern Counties	8278	H43/31F	4/77	Lancashire United 485	SELNEC Preservation Society
	OCN 913R	→ see UKV 362R								
	OCU 769R	Scania	BR111DH	544264	MCW		H45/29F	4/77	Tyne & Wear PTE 769	Buckley & Minto, Newcastle upon Tyne
	OCU 772R	Scania	BR111DH	544267	MCW		H45/29D	4/77	Tyne & Wear PTE 772	Rampton & Williams, Reading
(r)	OCU 773R	Scania	BR111DH	544268	MCW		H45/29D	4/77	Tyne & Wear PTE 773	BORIS Owners Group, Reading
	OCU 807R	Leyland	Fleetline FE30AGR	7605811	Alexander	AL58/578/8	H44/30F	6/77	Tyne & Wear PTE 807	Buckley & Minto, Newcastle-upon-Tyne
	ODL 666R	Bristol	VRT/SL3/6LXB	VRT/SL3/757	ECW	22628	H43/31F	4/77	Southern Vectis 666	Bartram & Budden, Shanklin
	OFB 968R	Bristol	LH6L	LH-1360	ECW	22335	B43F	6/77	Bristol 395	-?-, Dursley
	OJD 45R	Bristol	LH6L	LH-1287	ECW	21900	B41F	9/76	London Transport BL45	Taylor, Ystrad Mynach
	OJD 47R	Bristol	LH6L	LH-1289	ECW	21902	B--F	9/76	London Transport BL47	McDonald, Hampshire
			(ex 14857, OJD 47R)							
	OJD 49R	→ see WYL 137								
	OJD 54R	Bristol	LH6L	LH-1296	ECW	21909	B43F	11/76	London Transport BL54	Reynolds, Cardiff
	OJD 55R	Bristol	LH6L	LH-1297	ECW	21910	B39F	10/76	London Transport BL55	Tanner, London
	OJD 66R	Bristol	LH6L	LH-1308	ECW	21921	B45F	11/76	London Transport BL66	-?-, -?-
(r)	OJD 77R	Bristol	LH6L	LH-1332	ECW	21932	B—F	1/77	London Transport BL77	Pinder & Alger, Loddiswell
	OJD 81R	Bristol	LH6L	LH-1336	ECW	21936	DP40F	12/76	London Transport BL81	Green, Edmonton
	OJD 85R	Bristol	LH6L	LH-1340	ECW	21940	B39F	1/77	London Transport BL77	Wallis, Swanley
	OJD 87R	Bristol	LH6L	LH-1350	ECW	21942	B39F	4/77	London Transport BL87	Britishbus Preservation Group
	OJD 88R	→ see OJD 93R								
	OJD 93R	Bristol	LH6L	LH-1351	ECW	21943	B39F	4/77	London Transport BL88	Bird, Burgess Hill (WS)
			(ex OJD 88R)							
	OJD 95R	Bristol	LH6L	LH-1368	ECW	21950	B33F	5/77	London Transport BL95	Mitchell, Eastleigh
	OJD 127R	Leyland	Fleetline FE30AGR	7505350	Park Royal	B60906	O45/29F	8/76	London Transport DMS2127	Boxall, Beckenham *(on loan to Meadows, Crewe (CH))*
	OJD 172R	Leyland	Fleetline FE30AGR	7602739	*chassis only*			11/76	London Transport DMS2172	London Bus Preservation Trust
	OJD 216R	Leyland	Fleetline FE30AGR	7603766	MCW		H44/24D	2/77	London Transport DMS2216	O'Connor, Beckenham
	OJD 357R	Leyland	Fleetline FE30ALR	7605195	Park Royal	B60956	H44/24D	1/77	London Transport DMS2357	Turne, Edmonton
	OJD 375R	Leyland	Fleetline FE30ALR	7605074	Park Royal	B60974	H44/24D	1/77	London Transport DMS2375	Huseyin, London
	OJD 456R	Leyland	Fleetline FE30ALR	7607680	Park Royal	B61055	H41/23D	6/77	London Transport DMS2456	Boxall, Beckenham
	OJD 858R	Leyland	National 10351A/2R	04283	Leyland National		B44F	3/77	London Transport LS58	Hatton, Chase Terrace
	OJD 868R	Leyland	National 10351A/2R	04329	Leyland National		B44F	3/77	London Transport LS68	Ashton. Hadfield
	OJD 879R	Leyland	National 10351A/2R	04388	Leyland National		DP42F	6/77	London Transport LS79	Cole, Hornchurch
			(ex JIL 2793, OJD 879R)							
	OJD 891R	→ see 77-C-292 *Ireland*								

	OJD 898R	Leyland	National 10351A/2R	04474	Leyland National		B36D	5/77	London Transport LS98	Kriesler, Wallington
	OJD 903R	Leyland	National 10351A/2R	04497	Leyland National		B36D	8/77	London Transport LS103	McGregor, Bathgate
	OKW 515R	Leyland	Fleetline FE30AGR	7606299	MCW		H46/27F	4/77	South Yorkshire PTE 1515	South Yorkshire Transport Trust
	OKY 89R	AEC	Reliance	6U3ZR35492	Plaxton	7712ACM043	C55F	7/77	National Travel (East)	Plant, Newcastle-under-Lyme
	OOX 825R	→ see OAS 287R								
	OPC 26R	Leyland	Leopard PSU3C/4R	7602212	Duple	718/5455	B53F	12/76	Safeguard, Guildford	Kirwin, Guildford
			(ex XIL 8033, OPC 26R)							
(r)	ORD 105R	Scania	BR111DH	544240	MCW		H45/28D	3/77	Reading 105	Rampton & Williams, Reading
	ORD 106R	Scania	BR111DH	544241	MCW		H45/28D	3/77	Reading 106	Williams, Merthyr Tydfil
	ORS 60R	Leyland	Leopard PSU4C/4R	7600055	Alexander	103AY/3275/1	C45F	4/77	Grampian 60	Hearson & Machin, Chesterton
	ORS 209R	Leyland	Atlantean AN68A/1R	7603702	Alexander	AL54/2074/12	H45/29D	2/77	Grampian 209	Aberdeen & District Transport Preservation Trust
	OSJ 606R	Leyland	Leopard PSU3C/3R	7601738	Alexander	94AY/5274/2	RV	12/76	Ulsterbus 4891	Kells Transport Museum, Cork
	OSJ 607R	Leyland	Leopard PSU3C/3R	7601740	Alexander	94AY/5274/3	B53F	12/76	Western SMT 2607	McLaughlin, Port Glasgow
	OSJ 609R	Leyland	Leopard PSU3C/3R	7602956	Alexander	94AY/5274/5	B16F	12/76	Western SMT 2609	Dixon, Waringstown
	OSJ 620R	Leyland	Leopard PSU3C/3R	7603026	Alexander	94AY/5274/16	B53F	12/76	Western SMT 2620	Dixon, Waringstown
	OSJ 629R	Leyland	Leopard PSU3C/3R	7603087	Alexander	94AY/5274/25	DP49F	1/77	Western SMT 2629	Hamilton, Glasgow
	OSR 204R	Bristol	VRT/LL3/6LXB	VRT/LL3/138	Alexander	AL52/6374/16	H49/34D	3/77	Tayside 205	Taybus Vintage Vehicle Society
	OTG 44R	AEC	Reliance	6MU4R31952	Duple	641/5551	C41F	11/76	Crookes, Cardiff	Platt, Dawlish Warren
	OTN 457R	Scania	BR111DH	544374	MCW		H46/30F	7/77	Tyne & Wear PTE 457	Buckley & Minto, Newcaste-upon-Tyne
	OUC 45R	Leyland	Fleetline FE30AGR	7602359	MCW		H44/32F	11/76	London Transport DMS2045	Emsworth & District, Southbourne (WS)
	OUC 99R	Scania	BR111DH	543948	MCW		H43/29D	10/76	London Transport MD99	Almeroth, Wendling
	OUC 100R	Scania	BR111DH	543949	MCW		H43/29D	9/76	London Transport MD100	BORIS Owners Group, Reading
	OVV 59R	Ford	R1014	BC04RP67315	Duple	625/4784	B43F	9/76	United Counties 59	59 Preservation Group, Corby
	OYJ 64R	Leyland	Atlantean AN68A/1R	7605610	East Lancs	6604	H44/29D	1/77	Brighton 64	Mulpeter, Seaford
	OYV 777R	Bedford	VAS3	GW450129	Dormobile	5224 77 1361	B--F	1/77	Greater London Council A1826	Jagoutz, Shanklin
	PCD 80R	Leyland	National 11351A/1R	04100	Leyland National		B49F	1/77	Southdown 34	Llewellyn, Crowborough
	PEB 2R	Bedford	YMT	GW453214	Plaxton	7711TC181	C45F	4/77	Kenzie, Shepreth	Kenzie, Shepreth (CM)
	PHB 309R	Leyland	Leopard PSU3D/2R	7603926	Duple	638/5407	B53F	3/77	Rhymney Valley 9	Norman, Aberbargoed
	PHL 454R	Bristol	LHS6L	LHS-262	Plaxton	778BC017	C35F	4/77	Ulph, Brecks	York Pullman, York (NY)
	PJP 798R	Ford	Transit	BD05TJ63838	Deansgate		M12	4/77	Granway, Knutsford	Cossey, Worthing
	PKP 548R	→ see 76-C-999 *Ireland*								
	PPH 439R	AEC	Reliance	6U2R35428	Plaxton	7711AX524	C49F	6/77	London Country RS9	Howard, Hoddesdon
	PPH 462R	Bristol	VRT/SL3/501	VRT/SL3/750	ECW	22059	H43/31F	6/77	London Country BT2	Smith M, Bristol
	PPH 470R	Bristol	VRT/SL3/501	VRT/SL3/774	ECW	22067	H43/31F	7/77	London Country BT10	-?-, Bristol
			(fitted with a Gardner 6LXB engine)							
	PPH 471R	Bristol	VRT/SL3/501	VRT/SL3/775	ECW	22068	H43/31F	4/77	London Country BT11	Smith M, Bristol
			(fitted with a Gardner 6LXB engine)							
	PRA 109R	Leyland	Leopard PSU3C/4R	7603060	Alexander	8AT/1275/3	C49F	11/76	Trent 109	123 Group, Chesterfield
	PRA 113R	Leyland	Leopard PSU3C/4R	7603534	Alexander	6AT/1075/1	RV	11/76	Trent 113	Scottish Vintage Bus Museum
	PRR 454R	Leyland	National 11351A/1R	03884	Leyland National		B49F	12/76	Midland General 454	Barrett & Fairbrother, Guildford
	PSJ 825R	Ailsa	B55-10	76115	Van Hool McArdle	06/0001	H44/31F	3/77	A1, Ardrossan	Hannan, North Berwick
(z)	PTT 75R	Leyland	National 11351A/1R	04071	Leyland National		B52F	2/77	Western National 2852	BaMMOT, Wythall
	PUF 586R	Bristol	VRT/SL3/6LXB	VRT/SL3/609	ECW	22185	H34/31F	1/77	Southdown 586	Elkin, Fareham
	PWE 534R	Leyland	Fleetline FE30AGR	7605753	Alexander	AL55/2272/5	H45/29D	5/77	South Yorkshire PTE 1534	Allen, Sheffield
	RAP 126R	Willys-Overland		C101	replica		B??F	-/30	lorry chassis, Zimbabwe	Roe, Burgess Hill
					(replica body built ??/??)					
	RAU 624R	Bedford	YLQ	FW453537	Plaxton	7710QC013	C45F	11/76	Gash, Newark B30	Marshall, Sutton-on-Trent (NG)
	RBJ 460R	Bedford	YLQ	FW454365	Plaxton	7710QC009AM	C45F	11/76	Braybrooke, Mendlesham	Millard, Flexford

	Reg	Make	Model	Chassis No	Body	Body No	Type	Date	First Owner	Current Owner
	RDC 106R	Bristol	VRT/SL3/6LXB	VRT/SL3/628	Northern Counties	8153	H43/31F	9/77	Cleveland Transit 106	500 Group, Stockton
	RDX 19R	Leyland	Atlantean AN68A/1R	7603623	Roe	GO7786	H43/29D	9/76	Ipswich 19	-?-, Ipswich
	REK 921R	→ see TJI 1691								
	RGS 598R	Bedford	YMT	FW454711	Duple	679/7300	C57F	4/77	Tricentrol, Dunstable	Dasey, Carbrooke
	RHE 987R	Bristol	LHS6L	LHS-304	Plaxton	778BC010	C33F	7/77	Thistle, Doncaster	Gilmore, Plymouth
	RHN 888R	AEC	Reliance	2U3RA5741	Plaxton	7711AC037/S	C53F	3/65	Begg, Middlesbrough	Bowman, Burthwaite (CA)
			(ex DRP 86C)		*(rebodied 5/77)*					
	RJU 406R	→ see 397 EFW								
	ROC 300R	Foden	NC	94510	Northern Counties	8173	H43/33F	8/77	West Midlands PTE 6300	Cherry, Bootle (MY)
	RRB 119R	Leyland	Leopard PSU3D/4R	7605810	Duple	734/5325	C49F	3/77	Trent 119	Crosby, Nottingham
	RRR 517R	Bedford	YMT	FW454547	Plaxton	7611TX521	C53F	12/76	Barton 517	Cochrane, Peterlee (DM)
	RRS 46R	Leyland	Leopard PSU3E/4R	7606373	Duple	734/5350	C49F	4/77	Alexander Northern NPE46	Roulston, Glasgow
	RSD 973R	Seddon	Pennine 7	60965	Alexander	110AY/376/7	B53F	6/77	Western SMT 2670	McGowan, Falkirk
	RSD 978R	Seddon	Pennine 7	60855	Alexander	110AY/376/12	B53F	6/77	Western SMT 2675	Judd, Manea (CM)
	RUF 37R	Leyland	National 11351A/2R	04258	Leyland National		B44D	2/77	Southdown 37	McKenzie, East Grinstead
	RWU 534R	Leyland	Leopard PSU4D/4R	7603784	Plaxton	7610LB815	DP43F	12/76	West Yorkshire PTE 8534	Rawnsley, Keighley
	SDD 146R	Leyland	Leopard PSU3E/4R	7608412	Plaxton	7711LC096	C53F	5/77	National Travel (South West) 146	Lloyd-Owen, Churchdown
			(ex HIL 8027, SDD 146R)							
	SDX 35R	Leyland	Atlantean AN68A/1R	7606392	Roe	GO7811	H43/29D	3/77	Ipswich 35	-?-, Bury St Edmunds
	SFJ 106R	Bristol	VRT/SL3/6LXB	VRT/SL3/823	ECW	22749	H43/31F	6/77	Western National 1106	1106 Society, Petworth
	SKR 556R	Leyland	National 11351A/1R	04414	Leyland National		B49F	5/77	Maidstone & District 3556	Bellinger & Hamilton, Penge
(r)	SRJ 734R	Leyland	Atlantean AN68A/1R	7604786	Northern Counties	8230	H41/32F	5/77	Greater Manchester PTE 7734	SELNEC Preservation Society
	SRY 759R	AEC	Reliance	6U2R33609	Plaxton	7711AC033	C53F	6/77	Cleverly, Pontypool	Parsons, Margate
	SVL 830R	Bristol	LH6L	LH-1342	ECW	22369	B43F	2/77	Lincolnshire 1045	Wilkinson, Lincoln
	TMB 880R	Leyland	Leopard PSU4D/2R	7603913	Duple	637/5307	B47F	12/76	Chester 80	Dennis, Chester
	TMX 535R	→ see BCK 706R								
	TPT 6R	AEC	Reliance	6U3ZR34102	Plaxton	7611AX514	C53F	9/76	Bond, Willington	Dolan A, Crook
	TPU 67R	Leyland	Atlantean AN68A/1R	7700165	ECW	22320	H43/31F	5/77	Colchester 67	-?-, Lowestoft
	TUB 250R	Foden	NC	93742	Northern Counties	8133	H43/31F	4/77	West Yorkshire PTE 7250	Cherry, Bootle (MY)
	UFJ 974R	Bedford	J2SZ2	7T108235	Willowbrook	CFJ2/444	B20F	c1/69	Royal Navy	Morgan, Carnoustie
			(ex 12 RN 78)							
(r)	UGR 694R	Bristol	VRT/SL3/6LXB	VRT/SL3/520	ECW	22222	H43/31F	12/76	United 694	Gardiner, Gloucester
	UHG 736R	Leyland	National 11351A/1R	03562	East Lancs	B8407	B49F	10/76	London Country 359	Aldous, Swindon
			(ex JIL 2199, UHG 736R)		*(rebodied 9/94)*					
	UKV 362R	Bedford	YLQ	GW451910	Plaxton	7710QCM028	C25FL	3/77	Moor-Dale, Newcastle	Brown, Warrington
			(ex LUY 742, OCN 913R)							
	ULO 524R	→ see WYL 137								
	UWP 96R	Ford	R1114	BC04SB69173	Plaxton	7611FX518	C53F	9/76	Dudley, Radford	Dudley, Radford (WO)
	VGJ 317R	Leyland	Leopard PSU5A/4R	7604689	Plaxton	7712LCM038	C55F	4/77	Richmond, Epsom	Holder, Charlton (OX)
	VPT 598R	Leyland	National 11351A/1R	04191	Leyland National		B49F	2/77	Northern General 4598	Northern General Preservation Group, Hetton-le-Hole
	XCW 955R	Leyland	National 11351A/1R	04118	Leyland National		B49F	1/77	Fishwick, Leyland 24	Ashcroft, Lostock Hall
	XMS 245R	Leyland	Leopard PSU3C/3R	7601583	Alexander	94AY/5274/44	B53F	3/77	Alexander Midland MPE245	-?-, -?-
	XMS 252R	Leyland	Leopard PSU3C/3R	7602325	Alexander	94AY/5274/51	B53F	3/77	Alexander Midland MPE252	McKerracher, Stirling
	BDS 827S	Bedford	YLQ	HW453112	Pilcher-Greene		C28DLT	3/78	Argyll & Clyde Health Board	Walker, Glasgow
	CFM 86S	Leyland	Fleetline FE30AGR	7703263	Northern Counties	8313	H43/29F	2/78	Chester 86	Davies, Chester
(r)	CFM 353S	Leyland	National 11351A/1R	05244	Leyland National		B--F	5/78	Crosville SNL353	Kells Transport Museum, Cork

	Reg	Make	Model	Chassis No	Body	Body No	Layout	New	First operator	Current owner
	CGF 312S	Leyland	Leopard PSU5C/4R	7705895	Plaxton	7812LCM041	C55F	7/78	Richmond, Epsom	Rushden Historical Transport Society
	CSG 773S	Ailsa	B55-10	76089	Alexander	AV16/2376/22	H44/35F	2/78	Scottish Omnibuses VV773	Lothian Bus Consortium
	CSG 792S	Seddon	Pennine 7	63899	Plaxton	7811SXM510	C49F	4/78	Scottish Omnibuses YS792	Wallace, Edinburgh
	DDM 11S	→ see FCA 234S								
	EBV 85S	→ see OJI 4371								
	EFS 228S	Leyland	Leopard PSU3E/4R	7801227	Alexander	13AT/3877/1	C49F	6/78	Lothian 228	Sharp, Edinburgh
	EFS 229S	Leyland	Leopard PSU3E/4R	7801424	Alexander	13AT/3877/2	C49F	7/78	Lothian 229	Robertson, Rosyth
	EFS 230S	Leyland	Leopard PSU3E/4R	7801654	Alexander	13AT/3877/3	DP53F	7/78	Lothian 230	Docherty & McClelland, Edinburgh
	ESC 847S	Seddon	Pennine 7	61882	Alexander	118AY/966/16	B51F	6/78	Scottish Omnibuses S847	Carlyle, Dalkeith
	FCA 234S	Ford	R1114	BC04TD59503	Plaxton	7811FXMT525	C53F	3/78	Huxley, Malpas	Beardsmore, Threapwood
			(ex HIL 3931, DDM 11S)							
	GCK 279S	Bedford	YLQ	FW455017	Plaxton	7810QCM008	C45F	3/78	Florence, Morecambe	Battersby, Luton
			(ex A111 MAN, GCK 279S)							
	GLS 265S	Leyland	Leopard PSU3D/4R	7608380	Alexander	11AT/1376/4	C49F	1/78	Alexander Midland MPE265	Grant & Gray, Cumbernauld
	GMS 297S	Leyland	Leopard PSU3E/4R	7704479	Alexander	117AYS/1476/21	B53F	4/78	Alexander Midland MPE297	-?-, -?-
	GMS 305S	Leyland	Leopard PSU3E/4R	7704788	Alexander	117AYS/1476/24	B53F	4/78	Alexander Midland MPE305	Caledonian Bus Preservation Group, Glasgow
	HNP 154S	Leyland	Atlantean AN68A/1R	7701955	East Lancs	7603	O43/31F	4/78	Brighton 3	Pearce, Worthing
			(ex TYJ 3S)							
	HUD 476S	Bristol	VRT/SL3/6LXB	VRT/SL3/1122	ECW	22805	H43/27D	1/78	City of Oxford 476	Oxford Bus Museum Trust
	HUD 479S	Bristol	VRT/SL3/6LXB	VRT/SL3/1136	ECW	22808	H43/27D	1/78	City of Oxford 479	Hopkins, Maidstone
	MTJ 771S	Leyland	National 11351A/1R	04611	Leyland National		B--F	8/77	Merseyside PTE 1771	Merseyside Transport Trust
	OEM 788S	Leyland	Atlantean AN68A/1R	7800322	MCW		H43/32F	6/78	Merseyside PTE 1788	Morris, Wallasey
	OHF 858S	Leyland	National 11351A/1R	05226	Leyland National		DP45F	5/78	Merseyside PTE 1000	Cherry, Bootle (MY)
	OHF 968S	→ see 78-C-152 *Ireland*								
	PJC 630S	Ford	R1114	BC04TD59500	Duple	823/4461	C53F	5/78	Creams, Porthmadog	Evans, Llangefni
	PTD 640S	Leyland	Fleetline FE30AGR	7700314	Northern Counties	2426	H43/32F	8/77	Greater Manchester PTE 6912	SELNEC Preservation Society
					(rebodied 1/83)					
	PTD 655S	Leyland	Fleetline FE30AGR	7701954	Northern Counties	8336	H43/32F	4/78	Lancashire United 511	LUT Society
	PTD 673S	Leyland	National 11351A/1R	05229	Leyland National		B49F	5/78	Lancashire United 536	Moss T, Bolton
(r)	PUN 100S	Ford	R1114	BC04ST56921	Plaxton	7711FCM246	C53F	8/77	Lovering, Combe Martin	-?-, Newqiuay
	PWS 492S	Leyland	Leopard PSU3E/4R	7701523	Plaxton	8311LLP1X01R	DP49F	8/77	Bristol 2098	Amos, Nailsea
			(ex VJT 738, PWS 492S)		*(rebodied 9/83)*					
	RCU 588S	Leyland	Atlantean AN68A/2R	7603506	Willowbrook	76518	H--/--D	2/78	Tyne & Wear PTE 588	Foster, West Auckland
	RCU 838S	Leyland	Fleetline FE30AGR	7604789	Alexander	AL58/578/39	H44/30F	10/77	Tyne & Wear PTE 838	North East Bus Preservation Trust
	REU 326S	Bristol	LH6L	LH-1471	ECW	22857	B43F	2/78	Bristol 415	Arkell, Nailsworth
	RHC 51S	AEC	Reliance	6U2R33884	Plaxton	7711AC007	C53F	8/77	Killick & Vincent, Dallington	Atkin, North Owersby
	RHT 503S	Bristol	VRT/SL3/6LXB	VRT/SL3/1070	ECW	22451	H43/31F	1/78	Bristol C5109	Powell, Weston super Mare
	RRL 375S	Leyland	Leopard PSU3C/4R	7604314	Plaxton	7711LX519	C53F	8/77	Oates, Lelant	Byrne, Okehampton
	RTH 931S	Bristol	VRT/SL3/501	VRT/SL3/1011	ECW	22425	CO43/31F	10/77	South Wales 931	Morgans, Swansea
			(fitted with aGardner 6LXB engibe)							
	RVB 977S	Bristol	VRT/SL3/6LXB	VRT/SL3/1494	Willowbrook	77683	O43/31F	8/78	East Kent 7977	Houselander, Ashford
	SAE 755S	Leyland	National 11351A/1R	05004	Leyland National		B50F	4/78	Bristol 3052	Minnett, Stroud
	SBK 740S	Leyland	National 11351A/2R	05405	Leyland National		B44D	7/78	Gosport & Fareham 40	Aberdeen & District Transport Preservation Trust
	SCN 250S	Leyland	Atlantean AN68A/2R	7701820	Alexander	AL60/2775/6	H49/37F	2/78	Tyne & Wear PTE 250	Burn, Newcastle-upon-Tyne
	SCN 268S	Leyland	Atlantean AN68A/2R	7702964	Alexander	AL60/2775/24	H49/37F	4/78	Tyne & Wear PTE 268	North East Bus Preservation Trust
	SCN 276S	→ see PIW 4791								
	SDA 757S	Leyland	Fleetline FE30AGR	7701061	East Lancs	7337	H43/33F	2/78	West Midlands 6757	Munro & Ward, Kings Heath

	SDA 832S	MCW	Metrobus DR102/1	MB5007	MCW		H45/31F	5/78	West Midlands PTE 6832	WM MCW Bus Group, Birmingham
			(ex JIL 8209, SDA 832S)							
	SHE 557S	Leyland	Fleetline FE30AGR	7702865	Alexander	AL55/2272/28	H45/33F	3/78	South Yorkshire PTE 1557	South Yorkshire Transport Trust
	SKG 901S	Bristol	VRT/SL3/501	VRT/SL3/941	ECW	22573	H43/31F	8/77	Red & White HR2277	Start & Bacon, Worthing
	SOA 658S	Leyland	National 11351A/1R	04584	Leyland National		B49F	10/77	Midland Red 658	Peters, Kings Norton
	SOA 674S	Leyland	Leopard PSU3E/4R	7703142	Plaxton	7711LX505	C49F	1/78	Midland Red 674	Garnham, Kingstanding
	SOP 405S	Dodge	2000LB	431597	Rootes		M11	2/78	Royal Mail 7780002	-?-, Scotland
	SSN 243S	Ailsa	B55-10	77008	Alexander	AV17/2876/8	H44/31D	11/77	Tayside 243	-?-, -?-
	SSN 248S	Ailsa	B55-10	77013	Alexander	AV17/2876/13	H44/31D	11/77	Tayside 248	Brown & Cumming, Edinburgh
	SWS 774S	Bristol	LH6L	LH-1499	ECW	23489	B43F	7/78	Bristol 428	Jamieson et al, Donemana
	TCE 131S	→ see NIL 5377								
	TET 745S	Leyland	Fleetline FE30AGR	7608100	Roe	GO7897	H43/33F	12/77	Morgan, Armthorpe	Sheffield Joint Omnibus Club
	THX 101S	MCW	Metrobus DR101/3	MB5010	MCW		H43/28D	4/78	London Transport M1	Ensign, Purfleet (EX)
	THX 102S	MCW	Metrobus DR101/3	MB5011	MCW		H43/28D	6/78	London Transport M2	Sullivan, Potters Bar (HT)
	THX 105S	MCW	Metrobus DR101/3	MB5014	MCW		H43/28D	7/78	London Transport M5	Small-Brown-Figg Preservation Group
	THX 112S	→ see Unregistered Vehicles								
	THX 118S	→ see 78-C-313 *Ireland*								
	THX 129S	→ see 78-C-325 *Ireland*								
	THX 130S	→ see VIB 8319								
(r)	THX 188S	Leyland	National 10351A/2R	05026	Leyland National		B36D	5/78	London Transport LS188	Gardiner, Usk
	THX 217S	Leyland	National 10351A/2R	05166	Leyland National		B24D	4/78	London Transport LS217	Attwood, Hay-on-Wye
			(ex CAP 7, THX 217S)							
	THX 220S	Leyland	National 10351A/2R	05173	Leyland National		B36D	9/78	London Transport LS220	Brown, Greenhithe
	THX 266S	Leyland	National 10351A/2R	05350	Leyland National		B44F	7/78	London Transport LS266	Lear, Ashbury Station
	THX 271S	Leyland	Fleetline FE30ALR	7607057	MCW		O44/24D	8/77	London Transport DMS2271	London Bus Company, Northfleet (KT)
(r)	THX 333S	Leyland	Fleetline FE30ALR	7703445	MCW		H--/--D	1/78	London Transport DMS2333	Boxall & Clitheroe, Bromley
	THX 401S	Leyland	Titan TNLXB2RRSp	T1	Park Royal		H44/22D	8/78	London Transport T1	London Bus Company, Northfleet (KT)
	THX 402S	Leyland	Titan TNLXB2RRSp	T2	Park Royal		H44/22D	9/78	London Transport T2	London Bus Company, Northfleet (KT)
	THX 646S	Leyland	Fleetline FE30ALR	7705464	Park Royal	B61245	H44/28D	7/78	London Transport DM2646	Ensign, Purfleet (EX)
	TNY 849S	AEC	Reliance	6U3ZR35088	Plaxton	7811AC001	C53F	2/78	Humphreys, Pontypridd	Staples, Aberdare
	TOF 702S	Leyland	National 11351A/1R	05137	Leyland National		B49F	5/78	Midland Red 702	Wigmore, Hereford
	TPE 159S	Leyland	National 11351A/1R	05029	Leyland National		B49F	2/78	Thames Valley & Aldershot 283	
			(fitted with a Gardner 6HLXB engine)							Vale of Glamorgan Bus Preservation Group
	TPE 163S	Leyland	National 11351A/1R	05059	Leyland National		B49F	2/78	Thames Valley & Aldershot 287	Hier, Swansea
			(fitted with a Gardner 6HLXB engine)							
	TPE 164S	Leykand	National 11351A/1R	05060	Leyland National		B—F	3/78	Thames Valley & Aldershot 288	Wigmore & Wild, Hereford
	TPJ 61S	Bristol	LHS6L	LHS-271	ECW	22914	B35F	11/77	London Country BN61	London Transport Museum
	TPN 103S	Bristol	VRT/SL3/6LXB	VRT/SL3/797	ECW	22403	CO43/27D	9/77	Southdown 603	603 Preservation Group, Hove
	TSJ 64S	Leyland	Leopard PSU3D/4R	7604292	Alexander	116AY/476/1	B53F	12/77	Western SMT 2704	-?-, Stranraer
	TSJ 71S	Leyland	Leopard PSU3D/4R	7604515	Alexander	116AY/476/8	B53F	12/77	Western SMT 2711	Thompson & McAlinney, Newtownards
	TSJ 79S	Leyland	Leopard PSU3D/4R	7605179	Alexander	116AY/476/16	B53F	1/78	Western SMT 2732	McLaughlin, Port Glasgow
	TSL 94S	Ford	R1014	BC04SR53776	Duple	821/4004	C45F	1/78	McLaughlan, Perth	Crowe, Dundee
	TVP 849S	Leyland	National 11351A/1R	05126	Leyland National		B22DL	8/78	West Midlands PTE 6849	Pedley, Wolverhampton
			(fitted with s DAF engine)							
	TVP 889S	→ see 78-D-1015 *Ireland*								
	TWN 933S	Bristol	VRT/SL3/501	VRT/SL3/1363	ECW	23233	H--/--F	5/78	South Wales 933	Hayward, Haverfordwest
	TYJ 3S	→ see HNP 154S								
	TYJ 5S	Leyland	Atlantean AN68A/1R	7702102	East Lancs	7605	H43/31F	5/78	Brighton 5	Mulpeter, Seaford

	TYJ 12S	→ see 76-KE-566 *Ireland*								
	UDL 669S	Bristol	VRT/SL3/6LXB	VRT/SL3/1295	ECW	23264	H43/31F	3/78	Southern Vectis 669	Henson, Northampton
	UDL 673S	Bristol	VRT/SL3/6LXB	VRT/SL3/1299	ECW	23268	H43/31F	4/78	Southern Vectis 673	Isle of Wight Bus Museum
	UDT 181S	Leyland	Atlantean AN68A/1R	7705335	East Lancs	7808	H45/29D	7/78	South Yorkshire PTE 1581	South Yorkshire Transport Trust
	UDT 189S	Leyland	Atlantean AN68A/1R	7705942	East Lancs	7813	H45/29D	7/78	South Yorkshire PTE 1589	Sheffield 1589 Group, Sheffield
	UFG 625S	Bristol	VRT/SL3/6LXB	VRT/SL3/1014	ECW	22597	H43/27D	10/77	Southdown 625	Lane & Mulpeter, Brighton
	UFP 175S	Scania	BR111DH	544627	MCW		H44/31F	11/77	Leicester 175	Baxter, -?-
	UFP 233S	Dennis	Dominator	DD101/102	East Lancs	7401	H43/31F	10/77	Leicester 233	Leicester Transport Heritage Trust
	UFX 858S	Bristol	VRT/SL3/6LXB	VRT/SL3/969	ECW	22391	CO43/31F	10/77	Hants & Dorset 3377	Mills Hursthouse Holtby & Cook, Netheravon
	UFX 860S	Bristol	VRT/SL3/6LXB	VRT/SL3/975	ECW	22393	CO43/31F	11/77	Hants & Dorset 3379	Upton, Gosport
(r)	UNA 848S	Leyland	Atlantean AN68A/1R	7701237	Park Royal	B61631	H43/32F	12/77	Greater Manchester PTE 7848	SELNEC Preservation Society
	UPB 312S	Leyland	National 10351A/1R	04767	Leyland National		B41F	10/77	London Country SNB312	Berg & Bedford, New Haw
	UPB 331S	Leyland	National 10351A/1R	04835	Leyland National		B41F	11/77	London Country SNB331	SNB340 Preservation Group, Godstone
			(fitted with a Volvo engine)							
	UPB 340S	Leyland	National 10351A/1R	04858	Leyland National		B41F	11/77	London Country SNB340	SNB340 Preservation Group, Godstone
	URF 677S	Bristol	VRT/SL3/501	VRT/SL3/1194	ECW	22830	H43/31F	2/78	Potteries 677	Parry, Stoke-on-Trent
	UVX 7S	Bristol	LH6L	LH-1409	ECW	22362	B43F	9/77	Eastern National 1103	Hartwell, Chelmsford
	UWA 150S	Leyland	Fleetline FE30AGR	7704521	Roe	GO7928	H44/29D	7/78	Chesterfield 150	Spire Fleetline Preservation Group, Chesterfield
	UWA 154S	Leyland	Fleetline FE30AGR	7704855	Roe	GO7931	H44/29D	7/78	Chesterfield 154	Spire Fleetline Preservation Group, Chesterfield
(r)	UWA 159S	Leyland	Fleetline FE30AGR	7705214	Roe	GO7936	H44/29D	7/78	Chesterfield 159	Spire Fleetline Preservation Group, Chesterfield
	UWO 240S	AEC	Reliance	6U3ZR36356	Duple	842/5767	C51F	3/78	Henley, Abertillery	Pack, Crayford
	UWV 611S	Bristol	VRT/SL3/6LXB	VRT/SL3/1130	ECW	22411	CO43/31F	1/78	Southdown 611	Bluebird Buses (SN) 15711
	UWV 623S	Bristol	VRT/SL3/6LXB	VRT/SL3/1213	ECW	22423	CO43/31F	3/79	Southdown 623	Morton, Little London (HA)
	VAR 899S	Leyland	National 11351A/1R	04911	Leyland National		B49F	12/77	Eastern National 1833	Simister, Chelmsford
	VBA 151S	Leyland	Atlantean AN68A/1R	7703379	Northern Counties	8362	H43/32F	1/78	Greater Manchester PTE 8151	GM Buses Group
	VDV 121S	Bristol	VRT/SL3/6LXB	VRT/SL3/1223	ECW	22764	H43/31F	3/78	Western National 1121	Barley, Brighton
	VDV 122S	Bristol	VRT/SL3/6LXB	VRT/SL3/1224	ECW	22765	H43/31F	3/78	Western National 1122	Partridge, Exeter
	VDV 123S	Bristol	VRT/SL3/6LXB	VRT/SL3/1395	ECW	23393	H43/33F	7/78	Western National 584	Inner Circle Group, Exeter
	VDV 134S	Bristol	VRT/SL3/6LXB	VRT/SL3/1023	ECW	22427	CO43/31F	11/77	Western National 934	Partridge, Exeter
(r)	VDV 136S	Bristol	VRT/SL3/6LXB	VRT/SL3/1025	ECW	22429	O43/31F	10/77	Western National 936	Hull Bus Restorers, Hull
	VDV 137S	Bristol	VRT/SL3/6LXB	VRT/SL3/1026	ECW	22436	CO43/31F	3/78	Western National 937	West Country Historic Omnibus & Transport Trust
	VDV 141S	Bristol	VRT/SL3/6LXB	VRT/SL3/1154	ECW	22434	CO43/31F	2/78	Western National 941	Williams, Goldsithney
	VHB 678S	Bristol	VRT/SL3/501	VRT/SL3/1430	ECW	23208	O43/31F	7/78	National Welsh LR4378	Barlow Stanley & Carroll, Cardiff
	VKE 566S	Leyland	National 11351A/1R	04713	Leyland National		B41F	9/77	Maidstone & District 3566	Lane, Eastbourne
			(fitted with a Volvo engine)							
	VNO 740S	Leyland	National 11351A/1R	04674	Leyland National		B49F	8/77	Eastern National 1817	Blackwater Preservation, Essex
(r)	VPA 153S	Leyland	Atlantean AN68A/1R	7704691	Park Royal	B62553	H43/30F	6/78	London Country AN153	Butler, Gosforth
	VPF 285S	Bristol	VRT/SL3/6LXB	VRT/SL3/1359	ECW	23276	H43/31F	5/78	Thames Valley & Aldershot 955	Williams, Merthyr Tydfil
	VPW 85S	Bristol	VRT/SL3/6LXB	VRT/SL3/563	ECW	22270	H43/31F	9/77	Eastern Counties VR190	Patterson, Kings Lynn
	VRC 480S	Leyland	Fleetline FE30ALR	7603322	Northern Counties	8277	H44/31F	1/78	South Notts, Gotham 111	Kingston Bus Preservation Society
	WAD 640S	Ford	R1114	BCRSUL58010	Plaxton	7811FXMT502	C53F	4/78	Ladvale, Dursley	Dasey, Carbrooke
	WAH 587S	Leyland	National 11351A/1R	04759	East Lancs	B15006	B52F	9/77	Eastern Counties LG587	Carters, Wherstead (SK)
			(ex NIL 3956, WAH 587S)		*(rebodied 12/95)*					
	WED 992S	AEC	Reliance	6U3ZR36837	Duple	843/5809	C57F	7/78	Smith, Wigan	-?-, Tewkesbury
	WFX 257S	Leyland	National 11351A/1R	05188	Leyland National		DP48F	5/78	Hants & Dorset 3732	Robinson. Aldershot
	WGY 598S	→ see EGT 458T								
	WHH 556S	Leyland	National 11351A/2R	05034	Leyland National		B52F	4/78	Leyland Research Dept REV01	Workington Transport Heritage Trust
			(ex DIL 4942, WHH 556S)							

	WKO 132S	Bristol	VRT/SL3/6LXB	VRT/SL3/1413	ECW	22931	H43/31F	6/78	Maidstone & District 5132	Broadhurst, Byfleet
	WKO 137S	Bristol	VRT/SL3/6LXB	VRT/SL3/1472	ECW	22936	H43/31F	7/78	Maidstone & District 5137	Sealy, Hythe
	WKO 138S	Bristol	VRT/SL3/6LXB	VRT/SL3/1473	ECW	22937	H43/31F	7/78	Maidstone & District 5138	Dicker, Hastings
	WNW 159S	Leyland	Atlantean AN68A/1R	7607697	Roe	GO7852	H43/32F	9/77	West Yorkshire PTE 6159	Harrogate Coach, Green Hammerton (NY)
(r)	WPH 358S	AEC	Regent III	O9612068	Northern Counties	4262	H--/--RD	6/48	Douglas 61	Lord, Rochdale
			(ex JMN 725)							
(r)	WYJ 171S	Leyland	National 11351A/2R	05386	Leyland National		B30D	6/78	Southdown 71	Simister, Chelmsford
	XAP 642S	Bristol	VRT/SL3/6LXB	VRT/SL3/1467	ECW	23222	H43/31F	7/78	Southdown 642	Hussey & Marwick, Basingstoke
	XBU 1S	Leyland	Fleetline FE30AGR	7801420	Northern Counties	8630	H43/32F	6/78	Greater Manchester PTE 8001	SELNEC Preservation Society
	XBU 17S	Leyland	Fleetline FE30AGR	7801473	Northern Counties	8646	H43/32F	7/78	Greater Manchester PTE 8017	McAllister, Peterborough
	XDV 608S	Bristol	VRT/SL3/6LXB	VRT/SL3/1406	ECW	23400	H43/31F	7/78	Western National 1128	Powell, Weston super Mare
	XFW 951S	Bristol	LH6L	LH-1449	ECW	22889	B43F	12/77	Lincolnshire 1056	Lincolnshire 1056 Group, Waddington
	XNG 770S	Leyland	National 11351A/1R	05408	Leyland National		B52F	7/78	Eastern National LN770	Patterson, Kings Lynn
										(long term loan from Ipswich Transport Museum)
	XNM 820S	Bedford	YMT	GW456448	Duple	817/2445	C53F	3/78	Armchair, Brentford	Reid, Livingston
	XNN 622S	78-KE-547 *Ireland*								
	XNV 882S	Bristol	VRT/SL3/6LXB	VRT/SL3/1214	ECW	22705	H43/31F	2/78	United Counties 882	Pain, Milton Keynes
	XRR 831S	Ford	R1114	BC04TK59982	Plaxton	7811FCMT195	C53F	5/78	Slack, Tansley	Slack, Matlock (DE)
	XUS 575S	Leyland	Atlantean AN68A/1R	7700878	Alexander	AL59/3775/104	H--/--F	10/77	Greater Glasgow PTE LA1204	Hay & Grant, Glasgow
	YEV 307S	Leyland	National 11351A/1R	05165	Leyland National		B49F	4/78	Eastern National 1849	Hughes S, Colchester
			(fitted with a Volvo engine)							*(on loan from Panther, Parkeston (EX))*
	YEV 308S	Leyland	National 11351A/1R	05177	Leyland National		B49F	4/78	Eastern National 1850	Norris, Colchester
	YJN 455S	DAF	MB200DKL600	150776	Plaxton	7812DCM005	C50F	5/78	Staines, Clacton	Talisman, Great Bromley (EX)
	YMJ 554S	→ see BUR 438T								
	YMJ 555S	Bedford	YMT	HW453262	Duple	817/2555	C53F	6/78	Lodge, High Easter	Lodge, High Easter (EX)
	YMJ 561S	AEC	Reliance	6U3ZR37063	Plaxton	7812ACM015	C57F	6/78	Randall, London	Roberts, Stockport
	YSF 88S	Leyland	Leopard PSU3E/4R	7701832	Alexander	114AYS/1276/22	B53F	9/77	Alexander Fife FPE88	Ross, St Andrews
	YSF 89S	Leyland	Leopard PSU3E/4R	7700993	Alexander	114AYS/1276/23	B53F	9/77	Alexander Fife FPE89	Hines, Barnsley
	YTT 178S	Bedford	YMT	GW454928	Plaxton	7811TCM039	C42FT	4/78	Rossmore, Parkstone	Renown, Bexhill (ES)
			(ex 407 JWO, XLJ 426S, 11 AFC)							
	YVL 837S	Bristol	LH6L	LH-1487	ECW	22896	B43F	4/78	Lincolnshire 1063	Wilkinson, Lincoln
	AAK 111T	Leyland	National 10351B/1R	05926	Leyland National		B44F	2/79	South Yorkshire PTE 11	South Yorkshire Transport Trust
(r)	AAP 648T	Bristol	VRT/SL3/6LXB	VRT/SL3/1659	ECW	23228	H43/31F	12/78	Southdown 648	Terrill, Lewes
	AAP 651T	Bristol	VRT/SL3/6LXB	VRT/SL3/1662	ECW	23231	H43/31F	12/78	Southdown 651	Brighton VR Group, Woodingdean
	AFH 186T	Leyland	Leopard PSU5C/4R	7801179	Duple	835/5435	C57F	8/78	National Travel (South West) 186	
			(ex 29 DRH, AFH 186T)	*(fitted with a Volvo engine)*						Emery, Wednesfield
	AFJ 692T	Bristol	LH6L	LH-1519	Plaxton	7810BXM508	C41F	11/78	Western National 3131	Derrick, Plymstock
	AFJ 697T	Bristol	VRT/SL3/6LXB	VRT/SL3/1577	ECW	23404	H43/31F	12/78	Western National 1132	1132 Group, Lincoln
	AFJ 706T	Bristol	VRT/SL3/6LXB	VRT/SL3/1595	ECW	23413	H43/31F	12/78	Western National 1141	Williams, Goldsithney
	AFJ 707T	Leyland	National 11351A/1R	05524	Leyland National		B52F	10/78	Western National 2868	Delbridge, Ivybridge
	AFJ 708T	Leyland	National 11351A/1R	05526	Leyland National		B21D	9/78	Western National 2869	Billington, Maidenhead
	AFJ 727T	Bristol	LH6L	LH-1549	Plaxton	7910BXM502/S	C41F	4/79	Western National 3307	West Country Historic Omnibus & Transport Trust
	AFJ 729T	Bristol	LH6L	LH-1551	Plaxton	7910BXM504/S	C41F	4/79	Western National 3309	Billington, Maidenhead
	AFJ 736T	→ see 31921 *Guernsey*								
	AFJ 740T	Bristol	LH6L	LH-1560	Plaxton	7910BXM508/S	C43F	5/79	Western National 3320	Caldicott, Bournemouth
	AFJ 747T	Bristol	VRT/SL3/6LXB	VRT/SL3/1822	ECW	23417	H43/31F	6/79	Western National 1145	Western Greyhound, Summercourt (CO)
	AFJ 749T	Bristol	VRT/SL3/6LXB	VRT/SL3/1830	ECW	23419	H43/31F	6/79	Western National 1147	Williams, Goldsithney

	AFJ 760T	Bristol	VRT/SL3/6LXB	VRT/SL3/1956	ECW	24113	H43/31F	9/79	Western National 1153	Harris, Crediton
	AFJ 764T	Bristol	VRT/SL3/6LXB	VRT/SL3/1974	ECW	24117	H43/31F	11/79	Western National 1157	West Country Historic Omnibus & Transport Trust
	AFJ 766T	Bristol	VRT/SL3/6LXB	VRT/SL3/1976	ECW	24119	H43/31F	11/79	Western National 1159	Bennett, Sherborne
	AHH 206T	→ see NIL 7242								
	AJD 166T	→ see 79-KY-600 *Ireland*								
	AJT 143T	Leyland	Fleetline FE30ALR	7800002	Alexander	AL65/1674/1	H43/31F	11/78	Bournemouth 143	Bournemouth Passenger Transport Association
	AKK 172T	→ see UEY 441T								
	ANE 2T	Leyland	Titan TNLXB1RF	T48	Park Royal		H47/26F	4/79	Greater Manchester PTE 4002	SELNEC Preservation Society
	ANJ 306T	Leyland	Leopard PSU3E/4R	7803610	Plaxton	7811LXM587	C53F	11/78	Southdown 1306	Pullen, Shoreham
	ANR 900T	→ see YRC 420								
	ARC 645T	→ see 78-KE-560 *Ireland*								
	ARC 666T	Leyland	Atlantean AN68A/1R	7802434	Northern Counties	8442	H47/31D	11/78	Nottingham 666	Nottingham Transport Heritage Centre
	ASD 844T	Seddon	Pennine 7	66903	Alexander	125AY/3177/20	B53F	3/79	Western SMT 544	Western SMT Pres. Society, Greenock
	ATV 672T	Leyland	Atlantean AN68A/1R	7704071	Northern Counties	7950	H47/31D	10/78	Nottingham 672	Kells Transport Museum, Cork
	AUJ 745T	Bedford	YLQ	JW452256	Duple	915/2113	C45F	2/79	Corvedale, Ludlow	Worsdell. Torfaen
	AYJ 97T	Leyland	National 11351A/1R	06040	Leyland National		B52F	3/79	Southdown 97	Davey & Tomms, Luton
(r)	AYJ 100T	Leyland	National 11351A/1R	06103	Leyland National		B52F	4/79	Southdown 100	Minnett, Stroud
	AYR 339T	Leyland	National 10351A/2R	06302	Leyland National		B40D	8/79	London Transport LS339	Pedley & Barnard, Wolverhampton
	AYR 343T	Leyland	National 10351A/2R	06313	Leyland National		B44F	8/79	London Transport LS343	Pierce, Buntingford
	BCS 867T	Leyland	Fleetline FE30AGR	7801555	Northern Counties	8607	H44/41F	5/79	Western SMT 2867	Roulston, Glasgow
	BFX 570T	Bristol	VRT/SL3/6LXB	VRT/SL3/1790	ECW	23179	H43/31F	3/79	Hants & Dorest 3402	Wilkins, Cowbridge
	BFX 666T	Bristol	VRT/SL3/6LXB	VRT/SL3/1803	ECW	23190	H43/31F	3/79	Hants & Dorset 3413	Wilts & Dorset (DT) 4413
	BJU 13T	Bedford	YMT (ex NIW 1639, BJU 13T)	HW456493	Plaxton	7911TX516	C53F	1/79	Theobald, Long Melford	Atherton, Leighton Buzzard
	BKE 832T	Bristol	VRT/SL3/6LXB	VRT/SL3/1754	ECW	22940	H43/31F	2/79	Maidstone & District 5832	Veitch & Raine, Faversham
	BKE 847T	Bristol	VRT/SL3/6LXB	VRT/SL3/1731	ECW	22962	H43/31F	1/79	Maidstone & District 5847	Thomas & Warren, Hawkhurst
	BKE 848T	Bristol	VRT/SL3/6LXB	VRT/SL3/1732	ECW	22963	H43/31F	1/79	Maidstone & District 5848	Warren, Hawkhurst
	BKE 849T	Bristol	VRT/SL3/6LXB	VRT/SL3/1814	ECW	22964	H43/31F	3/79	Maidstone & District 5849	Thomas & Warren, Hawkhurst
	BNC 960T	Leyland	Atlantean AN68A/1R	7806190	Park Royal	B62508	H43/32F	7/79	Greater Manchester PTE 7960	SELNEC Preservation Society
	BPL 469T	Leyland	National 10351B/1R	06160	Leyland National		B41F	5/79	London Country SNB469	Simister & Berg, Chelmsford
	BRC 837T	Bristol	VRT/SL3/6LXB	VRT/SL3/1738	ECW	23304	H43/31F	2/79	Trent 837	Todd, Stanmore
	BSD 859T	Seddon	Pennine 7	67617	Alexander	128AY/3077/15	C49F	5/79	Western SMT 559	Duffy, Macclesfield
	BSJ 904T	→ see 79-DL-630 *Ireland*								
	BSJ 917T	Leyland	Leopard PSU3E/4R	7901148	Alexander	129AY/3277/28	B53F	6/79	Western SMT L2917	-?-, -?-
	BTB 689T	AEC	Reliance	6U3ZR38216	Duple	943/5805	C53F	5/79	Smith, Wigan	-?-, St Helens
	BTB 690T	AEC	Reliance	6U3ZR38390	Duple	943/5806	C57F	6/79	Smith, Wigan	Taylor, -?-
	BTX 206T	Leyland	Titan TNLXB1RF (ex WDA 1T)	T25	Park Royal		H43/29F	10/78	West Midlands PTE 7001	Parker, Bristol
	BUR 438T	AEC	Reliance (ex YMJ 554S)	6U3ZR35728	Plaxton	7812ACM016	C42FT	6/78	Best, Ealing	Dolan, Crook
	BYJ 920T	→ see USV 424								
	CCS 243T	→ see 6491 ED								
	CHH 210T	Leykand	National 10351B/1R	06111	Leyland National		B44F	3/79	Cumberland 210	Workington Transport Heritage Trust
	CJU 998T	→ see LIL 9929								
	CNK 633T	→ see 976 YTD								
	CNR 274T	Bedford	CFL	JY605226	Plaxton	78C003CF	C15F	3/79	Cresswell, Church Gresley	Flack, Hardwick (Cambs)
	CRM 927T	Leyland-DAB	LG17575-690/4	7834057	Leyland National		AB--D	5/79	Leyland demonstrator	Chambers, Exeter
	CRS 63T	Leyland	Leopard PSU3E/4R	7805146	Alexander	15AT/2777/4	C49F	3/79	Alexander Northern NPE63	Judge, Birmingham

	CRS 66T	Leyland	Leopard PSU3E/4R	7805263	Alexander	15AT/2777/6	DP49F	3/79	Alexander Northern NPE66	Bloomfield, Ponyclun
			(ex JFW 915T, 565 BNX, CRS 66T)							*(on loan to Price, Aberfan (CS))*
	CTM 405T	→ see 476 ZY *Ireland*								
	CUT 402T	AEC	Reliance	6U3ZR33400	Plaxton	7912AC008/S	C53F	3/79	Reliant, Ibstock	Wickens, Williton
	CVF 29T	Bristol	VRT/SL3/6LXB	VRT/SL3/1691	ECW	23456	H43/31F	1/79	Great Yarmouth 29	Peters, Mundesley
	CVF 31T	Bristol	VRT/SL3/6LXB	VRT/SL3/1693	ECW	23458	H43/31F	3/79	Great Yarmouth 31	Eastern Transport Collection
	CWU 140T	Leyland	Fleetline FE30AGR	7801303	Roe	GO7959	H43/33F	9/78	West Yorkshire PTE 7140	Transport Yorkshire Preservation Group
	DAR 120T	Leyland	National 11351A/1R	05923	Leyland National		B49F	2/78	Eastern National 1898	Wilson, Bishops Stortford
	DJF 631T	→ see HIL 7081								
	DNW 840T	Leyland	National 10351B/1R	05607	Leyland National		B44F	9/78	West Yorkshire Road Car 1002	Boocock, Keighley
	DSE 980T	Bedford	YLQ	HW457380	Plaxton	7910QX504	C33F	1/79	Low, Tomintoul	Western Isles Transport Preservation Group
	DWU 37T	Bedford	VAS5	HW456203	Plaxton	78PJK040	C29F	10/78	National Coal Board	Liddell, Auchinleck (SW)
	DWY 659T	Leyland	Leopard PSU3E/4R	7803513	Plaxton	7811LXM560	C49F	10/78	West Yorkshire Road Car 2557	-?-, Sherburn
	EBC 567T	Bedford	YMT	JW451712	Unicar	BD22	C53F	7/79	Moon, Shepshed	Winson, Loughborough (LE)
			(ex ACY 854 *Malta*, Y-0854 *Malta*, EBC 567T)							
	EBM 459T	→ see JIW 4045								
	EFP 521T	Mercedes-Benz	O317	31720710002729	Ludewig	27098	RB52T	8/66	Krefeld 5561	Mills, Aberdeen
			(ex KR-ZD 61 *Germany*)							
	EGB 62T	Leyland	Leopard PSU3E/3R	7802446	Alexander (Belfast)	519/18	B53F	2/79	Central SMT T330	Vale of Glamorgan Bus Preservation Gp
(r)	EGB 70T	Leyland	Leopard PSU3E/3R	7802989	Alexander	120AYS/677/26	B53F	1/79	Central SMT T338	Assiph, Dundee
(r)	EGT 458T	Leyland	National 11351A/3R	05150	Leyland National		B—F	9/78	British Airways BU051	McGregor, Bathgate
			(ex UIB 3076, EGT 458T, WGY 598S)							
	EGV 101T	Ford	R1114	BC04TE57935	Plaxton	7911FC007	C53F	2/79	Forget Me Not, Otley	-?-, -?-
	ERB 534T	→ see 79-WX-628 *Ireland*								
	EWW 205T	→ see 79-MN-522 *Ireland*								
	EWW 207T	Leyland	Leopard PSU3E/4R	7807291	Plaxton	7911LC067	C49F	4/79	Wallace Arnold (Devon)	Freeman & Norton, Huntingdon
	FWR 218T	Bristol	VRT/SL3/6LXB	VRT/SL3/1893	ECW	23435	H43/31F	6/79	York-West Yorkshire 3721	Lear, Ashbury Station
	GFM 333T	Bedord	YLQ	HW453815	Duple	815/2163	C45F	9/78	Wiiliams, Ponciau	Price & Perry, Shobdon
	GGE 156T	Leyland	National 10351A/1R	05940	Leyland National		B41F	2/79	Greater Glasgow PTE LN1	Roulston, Glasgow
	GGE 173T	Leyland	National 10351A/1R	06053	Leyland National		B41F	3/79	Greater Glasgow PTE LN18	Glasgow Vintage Vehicle Trust
	GMB 375T	→ see 78-C-1139 *Ireland*								
	GMB 390T	Leyland	National 11351A/1R	05772	Leyland National		B49F	12/78	Crosville SNL390	Lloyd, Machynlleth (CW)
			(*fitted with a Gardner engine*)							
	GSU 832T	Leyland	Leopard PSU3E/3R	7804369	Alexander	126AYS/4177/18	B53F	3/79	Central SMT T350	Cox & Hamer, Burnley
	GSU 866T	Leyland	Leopard PSU3E/3R	7801755	Alexander (Belfast)	519/32	B53F	7/79	Central SMT T384	McCormick, Dumbarton
	HBD 919T	Bristol	VRT/SL3/6LXB	VRT/SL3/1954	ECW	24077	CH40/28F	7/79	United Counties 919	Three Counties Bus & Commercial Vehicle Society
	HGB 438T	Bedford	CFL	HY626424	Reeve Burgess	11592	C17F	4/79	Kelly, Blantyre	Savage, Rotherham
	HLG 360T	Bedford	YLQ	HW453477	Plaxton	7810QCM050	C45F	9/78	Coppenhall, Sandbach	Herefordshire Transport Collection
	JPT 901T	Bristol	VRT/SL3/501	VRT/SL3/1629	ECW	22999	H43/31F	12/78	Northern General 3401	3401 Preservation Society, Durham
	JPT 906T	Bristol	VRT/SL3/501	VRT/SL3/1642	ECW	23004	H41/31F	12/78	Northern General 3406	Ruddick, Consett
			(ex LDS 190A, LHT 728P, LDS 190A, 449 CLT, JPT 906T)							
	JSF 928T	Seddon	Pennine 7	66727	Alexander	14AT/2277/27	C49F	2/79	Eastern Scottish ZS928	Wallace, Edinburgh
	JSF 929T	Seddon	Pennine 7	66728	Alexander	14AT/2277/28	C49F	2/79	Eastern Scottish ZS929	Rathbone, Edinburgh
	JSX 595T	Leyland	Atlantean AN68A/1R	7804532	Alexander	AL74/2676/20	H45/30D	3/79	Lothian 595	Lothian Bus Consortium
	JTU 588T	Leyland	National 10351B/1R	05947	Leyland National		B--D	2/79	Crosville SNL588	McGregor, Bathgate
	KRN 117T	Leyland	Leopard PSU3E/4R	7806171	Duple	834/5334	C47F	5/79	Ribble 1117	Ribble Vehicle Preservation Trust
	LHG 438T	Bristol	VRT/SL3/501	VRT/SL3/1571	ECW	23034	H43/31F	12/78	Ribble 1438	Duffy, Macclesfield
	MBR 439T	Leyland	Atlantean AN68A/1R	7806737	ECW	23683	H43/31F	4/79	Northern General 3539	-?-, Co Durham

	MFV 34T	Leyland	Leopard PSU4E/4R	7804076	East Lancs	5705	B47F	2/79	Burnley & Pendle 34	Hall, Buckie
	MUP 712T	Bristol	LH6L	LH-1552	ECW	23509	B43F	5/79	United 1712	Britishbus Preservation Group
	OGR 625T	Leyland	Leopard PSU3E/3R	7800660	Plaxton	7811LCM076	C53F	4/79	Weardale, Stanhope	Weardale, Stanhope (DM)
	RLS 469T	Ford	R1014	BC04TD60972	Alexander	124AYS/2877/5	B45F	1/79	Alexander Midland MT69	Webster & Scott, Inverkeilor
	SAS 859T	Leyland	Fleeltine FE30AGR	7803340	ECW	23504	H43/32F	11/78	Highland Omnibuses D17	Farquhar, Livingston
	STK 125T	Leyland	Atlantean AN68A/1R	7805329	Roe	GO8077	O43/31F	4/79	Plymouth 125	Paske, Chelmsford
	STK 129T	→ see GZJ 9575								
	STK 131T	Leyland	Atlantean AN68A/1R	7804975	Roe	GO8075	H43/31F	5/79	Plymouth 131	Byrne, Okehampton
	STK 133T	Leyland	Atlantean AN68A/1R	7805261	Roe	GO8074	H43/31F	4/79	Plymouth 133	Delbridge, Ivybridge
	TCC 2T	Ford	R1114	BCRSUY36172	Duple	923/4508	C53F	4/79	Creams, Porthmadog	Evans, Pentrefoelas (CN)
	TFN 980T	Bristol	VRT/SL3/6LXB	VRT/SL3/1520	Willowbrook	77686	H43/31F	8/78	East Kent 7980	Sealy, Hythe
	TOU 637T	→ see PJI 3534								
(r)	TTC 540T	Leyland	National 11351A/1R	05547	Leyland National		B52F	1/79	Bristol 3072	McGregor, Bathgate
	TWH 689T	Leyland	Leopard PSU3E/4R	7802776	Plaxton	7811LXM614	C53F	10/78	Lancashire United 541	LUT Society
	TWH 690T	Leyland	Fleetline FE30AGR	7801177	Northern Counties	8655	H43/32F	8/78	Lancashire United 515	Edwards & Brindle, Wigan
	TWS 910T	Bristol	VRT/SL3/6LXB	VRT/SL3/1677	ECW	23063	H43/27D	3/79	Bristol 5129	Bristol Aero Collection
	UEY 441T	Bedford	YMT	FW455496	Duple	820/2960	B63F	10/78	Maidstone 72	Kells Transport Museum, Cork
			(ex PJI 3044, AKK 172T)							
	ULS 330T	Leyland	Leopard PSU3E/4R	7805929	Alexander	127AYS/2977/14	B53F	4/79	Alexander Midland MPE330	Fisher, Dundee
	ULS 653T	Leyland	Leopard PSU3E/4R	7806732	Duple	934/5312	C--F	5/79	Alexander Midland MPE346	Callaghan, Barnsley
	ULS 658T	Leyland	Fleetline FE30AGR	7806212	ECW	23582	H43/32F	6/79	Alexander Midland MRF133	Carson, Airdrie
	UMR 199T	Leyland	Fleetline FE30AGR	7802476	ECW	23480	H43/31F	10/78	Thamesdown 199	Thamesdown (WI) 299
	UOR 320T	→ see CMN 34C *Isle of Man*								
	UOR 321T	→ see CMN 35C *Isle of Man*								
	UOR 330T	→ see CMN 44C *Isle of Man*								
	UVK 290T	Leyland	Atlantean AN68A/2R	7704091	Alexander	AL60/2775/47	H49/27F	8/78	Tyne & Wear PTE 290	Buckley, Newcastle-upon-Tyne
	VAE 499T	Leyland	National 10351B/1R	05803	Leyland National		B44F	1/79	Bristol 700	Frost Arkell & Screen, Hardwicke
	VTH 941T	Bristol	VRT/SL3/501	VRT/SL3/1456	ECW	23241	H43/31F	8/78	South Wales 941	Stewart & Law, Essex
	VTH 942T	Bristol	VRT/SL3/501	VRT/SL3/1457	ECW	23242	H43/31F	8/78	South Wales 942	Hier, Swansea
(r)	WAE 294T	Bristol	LH6L	LH-1577	ECW	23520	B—F	8/79	Bristol 442	Bulmer, North Stainley (NY)
	WCE 95T	Bedford	YMT	HW455457	Plaxton	7911TX539	C53F	4/79	Cambridgeshire Police	Prentice, Carstairs
	WDA 1T	→ see BTX 206T								
	WDA 4T	Leyland	Titan TNLXB1RF	T28	Park Royal		H47/29F	1/79	West Midlands PTE 7004	Smith & Lowrey, Swadlincote
	WDA 700T	Leyland	Fleetline FE30AGR	7804344	MCW		H43/33F	1/79	West Midlands PTE 7000	Aston Manor Road Transport Museum
	WDA 835T	MCW	Metrobus DR102/1	MB5059	MCW		H43/30F	10/78	West Midlands PTE 6835	BaMMOT, Wythall
	WDA 918T	→ see 78-LK-578 *Ireland*								
	WDA 919T	→ see 78-LK-579 *Ireland*								
	WDA 956T	Leyland	Fleetline FE30AGR	7803289	MCW		B37F	10/78	West Midlands PTE 6956	Munro & Ward, Kings Heath
	WDA 965T	→ see 78-D-997 *Ireland*								
	WDA 985T	→ see 78-LK-580 *Ireland*								
	WDA 986T	Leyland	Fleetline FE30AGR	7804125	MCW		H43/33F	12/78	West Midlands PTE 6986	Holland, Shetland
	WDK 562T	AEC	Reliance	6U3ZR38212	Plaxton	7912AC016	C49F	4/79	Yelloway, Rochdale	Quantock, Bishops Lydeard (SO)
	WEB 410T	→ see IUI 6410								
	WEB 411T	→ see IUI 6411								
	WJM 807T	→ see 79-TS-93 *Ireland*								
	WOW 993T	Leyland	Titan PD3/4	L03592	Northern Counties	6027	FCO39/30F	6/64	Southdown 423	Nicholas, Portsmouth
			(ex 423 DCD)							
	WRD 162T	MCW	Metrobus DR102/8	MB5191	MCW		H43/27D	7/79	Reading 162	Rampton & Williams, Reading

	Registration	Make	Model	Chassis No	Body	Body No	Layout	Date	First Operator	Owner
	WTG 348T	Bristol	VRT/SL3/6LXB	VRT/SL3/1535	Alexander	AL57/1776/22	H44/31F	11/78	Cardiff 348	Cardiff Transport Preservation Group
	WTG 375T	Bristol	VRT/SL3/6LXB	VRT/SL3/1781	Alexander	AL78/4077/18	H44/31F	6/79	Cardiff 375	Carroll & Barlow, Penarth
	WTG 902T	Leyland	Leopard PSU3E/4R	7802118	Plaxton	7811LXM649	C51F	8/78	Cardiff 2	Taylor, Ystrad Mynach
	WTH 957T	Bristol	VRT/SL3/501	VRT/SL3/1844	ECW	23257	H43/31F	3/79	South Wales 957	Hier, Swansea
	WTH 961T	Bristol	VRT/SL3/501	VRT/SL3/1855	ECW	23261	H43/31F	3/79	South Wales 961	Evans, Swansea
	WTS 263T	Ailsa	B55-10	77032	Alexander	AV22/3977/8	H44/31D	2/79	Tayside 263	Assiph & Wemyss, Dundee
	WTS 266T	Ailsa	B55-10	77035	Alexander	AV22/3977/11	H44/31D	2/79	Tayside 266	Watt & Payne, Dundee
	WTS 271T	Ailsa	B55-10	78008	Alexander	AV23/3977/16	H44/31D	2/79	Tayside 271	Fordyce, Dundee
	WTS 272T	Ailsa	B55-10	78009	Alexander	AV23/3977/17	O44/31D	2/79	Tayside 272	Taybus Vintage Vehicle Society
	WTS 273T	Ailsa	B55-10	78010	Alexander	AV23/3977/18	H44/31D	2/79	Tayside 273	Sinclair, Dundee
	WTS 276T	Ailsa	B55-10	78007	Alexander	AV22/3977/21	H44/31D	3/79	Tayside 276	Assiph, Dundee
	WVJ 181T	Bedford	VAS5	HW453313	Plaxton	78PJK009	C29F	1/79	Evans, New Tredegar	Evans, New Tredegar
	WYV 4T	Leyland	Titan TNLXB2RRsp	T4	Park Royal		H44/26D	10/78	London Transport T4	London Bus Company, Northfleet (KT)
	WYV 6T	Leyland	Titan TNLXB2RRsp	T6	Park Royal		H44/26D	11/78	London Transport T6	Cole, Hornchurch
	WYV 13T	Leyland	Titan TNLXB2RRsp	T13	Park Royal		H44/34F	3/79	London Transport T13	Dawber, Wigan
	WYV 21T	Leyland	Titan TNLXB2RRsp	T21	Park Royal		H44/24D	3/79	London Transport T21	Dawber, Wigan
	WYV 23T	Leyland	Titan TNLXB2RRsp	T24	Park Royal		H44/22D	3/79	London Transport T23	London Bus Preservation Trust
	WYV 40T	Leyland	Titan TNLXB2RRsp	T53	Park Royal		H44/26D	7/79	London Transport T40	Mercer, Romford
	WYV 56T	Leyland	Titan TNLXB2RRsp	T80	Park Royal		H44/26D	8/79	London Transport T56	Bolton, Hull
	WYV 820T	Bedford	YLQ	JW453604	Duple	915/2150	C45F	9/79	Russian Embassy	Andybus, Dauntsey (WI)
			(ex 248 D 193)							
	WYW 6T	MCW	Metrobus DR101/8	MB5065	MCW		H43/28D	9/78	London Transport M6	London Bus Preservation Trust
	WYW 28T	MCW	Metrobus DR101/8	MB5087	MCW		H43/28D	2/79	London Transport M28	London Bus Company, Northfleet (KT)
	XER 134T	→ see ESU 912								
	XOU 396T	Bristol	RELL6L	RELL-3-2308	NZMB / Hawke		B47D	2/79	Christchurch 531	Walker, Wells
			(ex JD 4954 *New Zealand)*							
	XPK 51T	AEC	Reliance	6U2R36593	Duple	842/5757	C53F	11/78	London Country RB51	Wills, Stevenage
			(ex YOI 2517, XPK 51T)							
	XWG 647T	→ see 78-D-921 *Ireland*								
	XWG 655T	Leyland	Atlantean AN68A/1R	7803199	Roe	GO8029	H45/29D	12/78	South Yorkshire PTE 1655	Sheffield Joint Omnibus Club
	YBL 69T	Leyland	Titan TNLXB2RRsp	T39	Park Royal		H44/30F	3/79	Reading 69	Rampton, Reading
	YBO 16T	Leyland	Leopard PSU3E/2R	7803327	East Lancs	5801	B51F	4/79	Rhymney Valley 16	Evans, New Tredegar
	YCD 75T	Leyland	National 11351A/2R	05477	Leyland National		B28DL	8/78	Southdown 75	Southdown National Heritage Group, Hove
	YDL 135T	Ford	R1014	BCRSUB262590	Duple	925/4755	B47F	5/79	Isle of Wight County Council	Watts, Beccles
	YDW 566T	Leyland	Leopard PSU4E/2R	7803938	Marshall	270101	B45F	2/79	Islwyn 27	Williams, Merthyr Tydfil
	YJB 69T	Leyland	Titan TNLXB2RRsp	T39	Park Royal		H44/30F	3/79	Reading 69	Rampton, Reading
	YKG 961T	Leyland	Titan PD2/1	500146	Leyland		H30/26R	6/50	Isle of Man Road Services 13	Freeman, Hampshire
			(ex MMN 11)							
	YKU 227T	Ford	R1114	BCRSUL58390	Caetano	78029	C53F	1/79	Shaw, Barnsley	Stanton, Cheadle
			(ex USV 331, YKU 227T)							
	YPL 84T	AEC	Reliance	6U2R37878	Duple	942/5748	C53F	4/79	London Country RB84	Knorn, Ruabon
			(ex 7845 LJ, YPL 84T)							
	YPL 407T	Leyland	National 10351B/1R	05688	Leyland National		B41F	12/78	London Country SNB407	Thurston, Sheffield
(r)	YPL 433T	Leyland	National 10351B/1R	05744	Leyland National		B--F	1/79	London Country SNB433	Berg & Bedford, New Haw
	YPL 448T	Leyland	National 10351B/1R	05840	Leyland National		B41F	1/79	London Country SNB448	Byrne, Okehampton
	YPL 449T	Leyland	National 10351B/1R	05931	Leyland National		B41F	3/79	London Country SNB449	Berg & Bedford, New Haw
	YVN 518T	→ see SJI 6568								
	YVN 521T	→ see MCZ 8545								

Registration	Chassis	Chassis No	Body	Body No	Layout	New	First Operator	Current Owner
YYE 297T	Leyland National 10351A/2R	05882	Leyland National		B38F	2/79	London Transport LS297	East London Traction Society
AAE 647V	Leyland National NL116L11/1R	06680	Leyland National		B52F	5/80	Bristol 3503	Gardiner, Gloucester
AAE 650V	Leyland National NL116L11/1R	06732	Leyland National		B52F	4/80	Bristol 3506	Gardiner, Gloucester
AAE 658V	Leyland National NL116L11/1R	06909	Leyland National		B52F	7/80	Bristol 3514	Gardiner, Gloucester
AFB 585V	Bristol LH6L	LH-1593	ECW	23536	B43F	2/80	Bristol 454	Cox, Burnley
AFB 592V	Bristol LH6L	LH-1600	ECW	23543	B43F	5/80	Bristol 461	Walker & Peters, Wells
AFB 593V	Bristol LH6L	LH-1601	ECW	23544	B43F	5/80	Bristol 462	Lane, Woking
AFB 597V	Bristol LH6L	LH-1605	ECW	23548	B43F	6/80	Bristol 466	Green Triangle, Atherton (GM)
AHG 334V	Leyland Atlantean AN68A/2R	7904783	East Lancs	9704	H50/36F	7/80	Blackpool 334	Lancastrian Transport Trust *(operates as Totally Transport, Blackpool (LA))*
AHU 518V	Bristol VRT/SL3/6LXB	VRT/SL3/2293	ECW	24183	H--/--F	5/80	Bristol 5141	Willmott, Bristol
AHW 201V	Bristol VRT/SL3/6LXB	VRT/SL3/2352	ECW	24192	H43/27D	6/80	Bristol 5150	Curtis, Bath
AVK 134V	Leyland Atlantean AN68A/2R	7900361	Alexander	AL79/1979/1	H--/--F	7/80	Tyne & Wear PTE 134	McHaddan, Newcastle-upon-Tyne
AVK 160V	Leyland Atlantean AN68A/2R	7901428	Alexander	AL79/1979/27	H49/37F	7/80	Tyne & Wear PTE 160	Welford, Burnhope
AVK 176V	Leyland Atlantean AN68A/2R	7901358	Alexander	AL79/1979/43	H49/37F	8/80	Tyne & Wear PTE 176	Atkinson et al, Pittington
AWN 815V	Leyland National 11351A/1R	06603	Leyland National		B52F	11/79	South Wales 815	Hier, Swansea
BBT 310V	→ see 80-KK-239 *Ireland*							
BBW 21V	Leyland Leopard PSU3E/4R	7902785	Duple	934/5336	C49F	11/79	Oxford 21	Oxford Bus Museum Trust
BCB 613V	Leyland Fleetline FE30AGR	7900091	Northern Counties	8895	H43/32F	3/80	Greater Manchester PTE 6960	Holden, Bolton
BEP 978V	Bristol VRT/SL3/501	VRT/SL3/2299	ECW	23881	H43/31F	4/80	South Wales 978	Adams & Bemmer, Caversham
BHY 998V	Leyland National NL116L11/1R	07015	Leyland National		B52F	7/80	Bristol 3524	Gardiner, Gloucester
BMR 202V	Leyland Fleetline FE30AGR	7902609	ECW	24200	H43/31F	2/80	Thamesdown 202	Larkin, Peterborough
BMR 204V	Leyland Fleetline FE30AGR	7902667	ECW	24203	H43/31F	2/80	Thamesdown 204	Robinson, Swindon
BOK 1V	MCW Metrobus DR102/12	MB5228	MCW		H43/30F	12/79	West Midlands PTE 2001	Vals. Chase Terrace (ST)
(r) BOK 35V	MCW Metrobus DR102/12	MB5362	MCW		H43/30F	2/80	West Midlands PTE 2035	West Midlands Bus Preservation Society
BOM 7V	MCW Metrobus DR104/4	MB5197	MCW		H43/30F	11/79	West Midlands PTE 7007	WM MCW Bus Group, Birmingham
BOU 6V	Leyland National NL116L11/1R	07027	Leyland National		B52F	10/80	Bristol 3531	Vick, Dursley
	(ex JNJ 815V, BOU 6V)							
BTE 206V	→ see 80-LK-469 *Ireland*							
BUH 239V	Leyland National NL106L11/1R	06954	Leyland National		B44F	5/80	National Welsh NS8011	Gardiner, Usk
BUH 240V	Leyland National NL106L11/1R	06955	Leyland National		B44F	5/80	National Welsh NS8012	Gardiner, Usk
BVP 765V	Leyland National 11351A/1R	06426	Leyland National		B49F	11/79	Midland Red 765	Vale of Glamorgan Bus Preservation Group
BVP 767V	Leyland National 11351A/1R	06430	Leyland National		B49F	11/79	Midland Red 767	Vale of Glamorgan Bus Preservation Group
BVP 784V	Leyland Leopard PSU3E/4R	7930116	Plaxton	7911LX667	C53F	6/80	Midland Red 784	Riley, Tamworth
BVP 794V	→ see HIL 8436							
BVP 808V	Leyland National NL116L11/1R	06675	Leyland National		B49F	1/80	Midland Red 808	Follwell & Owen, Newcastle-under-Lyme
BVP 811V	Leyland National NL116L11/1R	06710	Leyland National		B49F	3/80	Midland Red 811	Follwell & Owen, Newcastle-under-Lyme
BYW 363V	Leyland National 10351A/2R	06365	Leyland National		B36D	9/79	London Transport LS363	Norris, Colchester
BYW 418V	Leyland National 10351A/2R	06522	Leyland National		B42F	1/80	London Transport LS418	Macey, Luton
	(ex MRP 5V, BYW 418V) *(fitted with a Leyland O680 engine)*							
BYW 431V	Leyland National 10351A/2R	06556	Leyland National		B38F	11/79	London Transport LS431	Rose, London Colney
BYW 432V	Leyland National 10351A/2R	06561	Leyland National		B44F	11/79	London Transport LS432	Moody, Keighley
	(fitted with a Volvo engine)							
BYX 193V	→ see BMN 193V *Isle of Man*							
BYX 278V	MCW Metrobus DR101/12	MB5571	MCW		H43/28D	6/80	London Transport M278	Hart, Heathrow
CCY 820V	Leyland National NL116L11/R	06673	Leyland National		B52F	1/80	South Wales 820	-?-, -?-
CJH 123V	Bristol VRT/SL3/6LXB	VRT/SL3/2187	ECW	24156	CH41/25F	2/80	Thames Valley & Aldershot 983	King, Woodley

	CJH 141V	Bristol	VRT/SL3/6LXB	VRT/SL3/2439	ECW	24560	H43/31F	7/80	Thames Valley & Aldershot 601	Kennedy, Hayling Island
	CUL 96V	Leyland	Titan TNLXB2RRsp	T126	Park Royal		H44/26D	10/79	London Transport T96	-?-, -?-
	CUL 122V	Leyland	Titan TNLXB2RRsp	T152	Park Royal		H39/32F	12/79	London Transport T122	Rowlands & Wilton, Liverpool
	CUL 127V	Leyland	Titan TNLXB2RRsp	T127	Park Royal		H??/??D	1/80	London Transport T127	Dawber, Wigan
	CUL 197V	Leyland	Titan TNLXB2RRsp	T277	Park Royal		PO44/26D	4/80	London Transport T197	Lochhead, -?-
	CVE 7V	→ see FFL 164V								
	CWG 696V	Leyland	Atlantean AN68A/1R	7902554	Alexander	AL76/1874/16	H45/33F	9/79	South Yorkshire PTE 1696	North West Museum of Transport
	CWG 720V	Leyland	Atlantean AN68A/1R	7903393	Alexander	AL76/1874/40	H45/29D	3/80	South Yorkshire PTE 1720	Reid, Canada (kept in UK)
	CWG 756V	Leyland	Atlantean AN68A/1R	7902847	Roe	GO8124	H45/29D	9/79	South Yorkshire PTE 1756	Parkinson, Rotherham
	CYT 24V	Ford	Transit	BDVPUR253460	Dormobile	2947 ??? ??	B--F	11/79	London Transport FS24	Austin, Sudcup
	DDL 667V	Bedford	YMT	JW456672	Duple	017/2412	C53F	11/79	Paul, Sandown	Roselyn Coaches, Par (CO)
			(ex BAZ 6532, DDL 667V)							
	DDW 65V	Leyland	Leopard PSU4E/2R	7902228	East Lancs	5806	B45F	10/79	Rhymney Valley 65	Evans, Bargoed
	DNY 534V	Leyland	Leopard PSU4E/2R	7903244	Marshall	270220	B45F	12/79	Islwyn 34	Barnett, Blackwood
	DOC 26V	Leyland	National NL116L11/1R	06785	Leyland National		B50F	3/80	West Midlands PTE 7026	1026 Group, Birmingham
			(*fitted with a DAF engine*)							
	DOC 37V	Leyland	National NL116L11/1R	06801	Leyland National		B50F	5/80	West Midlands PTE 7037	Pedley, Burntwood
(r)	DOC 51V	Leyland	National NL106L11/1R	06824	Leyland National		B40F	5/80	West Midlands PTE 7051	Gardiner, Gloucester
	DOC 52V	Leyland	National NL106L11/1R	06825	Leyland National		B40F	5/80	West Midlands PTE 7052	7052 Preservation Group, Birmingham
	DSD 936V	Seddon	Pennine 7	68553	Alexander	17AT/978/4	C49F	9/79	Western SMT 2936	Scottish Vintage Bus Museum
	DSD 974V	Seddon	Pennine 7	69687	Alexander	17AT/978/30	C49F	12/79	Western SMT 2974	-?-, -?-
	DSD 983V	Seddon	Pennine 7	68841	Alexander	133AYS/479/1	B60F	3/80	Western SMT 2983	Devine, Kirkfieldbank
	DSP 928V	Volvo	B55-10	80008	Alexander	AV30/2577/8	H44/34F	6/80	Tayside 28	-?-, -?-
	EAP 937V	Leyland	Leopard PSU5C/4R	7902845	Duple	935/5470	C55F	12/79	Southdown 1337	Spencer, Fakenham
			(ex KIB 7027, EAP 937V)							
	ECS 57V	Ailsa	B55-10	79015	Alexander	AV27/3078/1	H44/35F	9/79	A1 (T Hunter), Ardrossan	-?-, -?-
	ECS 883V	Leyland	Fleetline FE30AGR	7802070	Northern Counties	8623	H44/31F	11/79	Western SMT 2883	McLaughlin, Port Glasgow
	ECS 885V	Leyland	Fleetline FE30AGR	7801598	Northern Counties	8625	H44/31F	11/79	Western SMT 2885	McLaughlin, Port Glasgow
	EDT 205V	Leyland	National NL116L11/1R	06703	Leyland National		B52F	1/80	Yorkshire Traction 205	Clarke, Brampton Bierlow
(r)	EDT 208V	Leyland	National NL116L11/1R	06707	Leyland National		B52F	2/80	Yorkshire Traction 208	Clarke, Brampton Bierlow
(r)	EDT 216V	Leyland	National NL116L11/1R	06758	Leyland National		B52F	3/80	Yorkshire Traction 216	Clarke, Brampton Bierlow
	ELJ 214V	Bristol	VRT/SL3/6LXB	VRT/SL3/2096	ECW	24090	H43/31F	11/79	Hants & Dorset 3422	Allen, Poole
	ELJ 220V	Bristol	VRT/SL3/6LXB	VRT/SL3/2102	ECW	24096	H43/31F	1/80	Hants & Dorset 3428	Steele, Chippenham
	EMS 362V	Leyland	Leopard PSU3E/4R	7902336	Alexander	18AT/1678/4	C49F	2/80	Alexander Midland MPE362	Turner, Bridge of Weir
	EMS 366V	Leyland	Leopard PSU3E/4R	7902533	Alexander	18AT/1678/8	C49F	2/80	Alexander Midland MPE366	McKerracher, Stirling
(r)	EON 823V	Leyland	National NL116L11/1R	06916	Leyland National		B49F	9/80	Midland Red 823	Gardiner, Gloucester
	EPC 898V	→ see 79-WW-61 *Ireland*								
	EPD 511V	Leyland	National 10351B/1R	06446	Leyland National		B41F	9/79	London Country SNB511	Chantler, Headcorn
(r)	EPD 538V	Leyland	National 10351B/1R	06553	Leyland National		B41F	10/79	London Country SNB538	McGregor, Bathgate
	EPD 543V	Leyland	National 10351B/1R	06579	Leyland National		B41F	12/79	London Country SNB543	Nash, Ockley
	EPH 229V	Leyland	Atlantean AN68A/1R	7903298	Roe	GO8269	H43/30F	2/80	London Country AN229	Graham, Carlisle
(r)	EPM 126V	AEC	Reliance	6U2R38577	Duple	042/5733	C53F	11/79	London Country RB126	Wills, Stevenage
	EPM 134V	AEC	Reliance	6U2R38695	Duple	042/5736	C49F	11/79	London Country RB134	Knorn, Ruabon
	EPM 136V	→ see UFX 718								
	EPM 137V	AEC	Reliance	6U2R38581	Plaxton	8011AX502/S	C53F	11/79	London Country RS137	Assiph, Dundee
	ERU 159V	Leyland	Fleetline FE30ALR	7805338	Alexander	AL80/1774/9	H43/31F	11/79	Bournemouth 159	Hulks, Doncaster
	EWB 386V	→ see CHE 297C								
	EWF 456V	MCW	Metrobus DR102/13	MB5399	MCW		PO46/27D	1/80	South Yorkshire PTE 456	Frith, Sheffield

	EYP 29V	Bedford	YMQ	LW450709	Plaxton	8111QC002	C45F	4/81	Smith, Tring	Webb, Armscote (WK)
			(ex TRO 420W, 688 UYB, TRO 420W)							
	FDV 780V	Bristol	VRT/SL3/6LXB	VRT/SL3/2038	ECW	24128	H43/31F	12/79	Western National 1168	Ellis, Cambridge (Gloucs)
	FDV 787V	Bristol	LHS6L	LHS-350	ECW	23609	B35F	10/70	Western National 1557	Pope, Pulborough
	FDV 790V	Bristol	LHS6L	LHS-353	ECW	23612	B35F	10/79	Western National 1560	Billington, Maidenhead
			(ex 14531, FDV 790V)							
	FDV 793V	Bristol	LHS6L	LHS-356	ECW	23615	B27F	12/79	Western National 1563	Sinclair, Eastleigh
	FDV 803V	Leyland	Leopard PSU3E/4R	7903743	Plaxton	7911LX532	C45FT	12/79	Western National 3547	Billington, Maidenhead
			(ex KTA 986V, 925 GTA, FDV 803V)							
(r)	FDV 819V	Bristol	VRT/SL3/6LXB	VRT/SL3/2365	ECW	24147	H--/--F	5/80	Western National 1187	Dolan M, Crook
	FDV 827V	Leyland	Leopard PSU3E/4R	8030081	Willowbrook	79838	C49F	8/80	Western National 3536	Garnham, Coventry
	FDV 829V	Leyland	National NL116L11/1R	06654	Leyland National		B52F	3/80	Western National 2883	Selway, Haywards Heath
	FFL 164V	Bedford	YLQ	JW457838	Duple	015/2129	C45F	3/80	Kenzie, Shepreth	Fowler, Holbeach Drove (LI)
			(ex CVE 7V)							
	FKM 304V	Dennis	Dominator	DD129/194	Willowbrook	791913	H44/31F	6/80	Maidstone & District 5304	Mee, Northfleet
	FKP 112V	Dodge	2500LB	443578	Rootes		M12	9/79	Parker, Nottingham	Williams, Birmingham
	FRA 534V	Leyland	National 11351A/1R	06624	Leyland National		B52F	12/79	Trent 534	Beard, Manningtree
	FTO 538V	→ see 79-KE-545 *Ireland*								
	FUT 240V	Dennis	Dominator	DDA120/176	East Lancs	9412	H--/16F	6/80	Leicester 240	Fowkes, Southampton
	FUU 977V	Bedford	VAS5	JW457235	Lex		B25F	7/80	Metropolitan Police	Mould, Reading
	FVM 191V	Bedford	CFL	JY621159	Plaxton	79C012CF	C17F	8/79	Shearings, Altrincham	Parsons, Margate
	FWA 450V	Leyland-DAB	LG17575-690/4	7934122	Leyland National		AB--C	2/80	South Yorkshire PTE 2007	Chambers, Exeter
	FWA 475V	Leyland	National NL106L11/1R	06869	Leyland National		B44F	4/80	South Yorkshire PTE 1075	South Yorkshire Transport Trust
	GAW 593V	Ford	Transit	BDVZWM351560	Ford		M11	1/80	Priory School, Shrewsbury	Burden, Wolverhampton
	GBU 1V	MCW	Metrobus DR101/6	MB5021	MCW		H43/30F	9/79	Greater Manchester PTE 5001	SELNEC Preservation Society
			(ex OPP 741V, GBU 1V)							
	GCS 35V	Leyland	Leopard PSU3E/4R	7903680	Alexander	138AY/2078/6	B53F	3/80	Western SMT L35	-?-, -?-
	GCS 50V	Leyland	Leopard PSU3E/4R	7903545	Alexander	137AY/2078/21	B53F	4/80	Western SMT L50	Barclay, Irvine
	GCS 56V	→ see 80-DL-729 *Ireland*								
	GCS 57V	Leyland	Leopard PSU3E/4R	7904373	Alexander	137AY/2078/28	B53F	5/80	Western SMT L57	-?-, -?-
	GCS 60V	→ see 80-CE-427 *Ireland*								
	GCS 69V	Leyland	Leopard PSU3E/4R	7904175	Alexander	137AY/2078/40	B53F	6/80	Western SMT L69	Campbell Devine & Duncan, Paisley
	GEK 14V	Leyland	Atlantean AN68A/1R	7902662	East Lancs	9504	H45/31F	3/80	Warrington 14	Arnold, Warrington
(r)	GEL 683V	Bristol	VRT/SL3/6LXB	VRT/SL3/2206	*chassis only*			2/80	Hants & Dorset 3433	Burt & Hembry, Shaftesbury
	GEL 686V	Bristol	VRT/SL3/6LXB	VRT/SL3/2266	ECW	24104	H43/31F	4/80	Hants & Dorest 3436	5070 Group, Blandford
	GHL 212V	Crown	School Bus	39132	Crown		B53F	-/80	school bus, USA	MAS, Anston (SY)
			(ex 5W 13180 *USA*)							
	GNF 10V	Leyland	Titan TNLXB/1RF	T68	Park Royal		H47/26F	12/79	Greater Manchester PTE 4010	Rogers, Swindon
	GNF 15V	Leyland	Titan TNTL11/1RF	T73	Park Royal		H47/26F	5/80	Greater Manchester PTE 4015	SELNEC Preservation Society
	GNF 16V	Leyland	Fleetline FE30AGR	7805150	Northern Counties	8902	H43/32F	7/80	Greater Manchester PTE 8141	SELNEC Preservation Society
	GRF 709V	Bristol	VRT/SL3/501	VRT/SL3/2268	ECW	23812	H43/31F	4/80	Potteries 709	Pearson, Stoke-on-Trent
	GRU 162V	Leyland	Fleetline FE30AGR	7902234	Alexander	AL84/2978/2	H43/31F	3/80	Bournemouth 162	Bournemouth Aviation Museum
	GRU 168V	Leyland	Fleetline FE30AGR	7902436	Alexander	AL84/2978/8	H43/31F	2/80	Bournemouth 168	Reynolds, Mangotsfield
	GSO 5V	→ see KRS 539V								
	GSO 80V	Leyland	Leopard PSU3E/4R	7902780	Alexander	136AYS/1878/4	DP49F	1/80	Alexander Northern NPE80	Greenhill, -?-
	GSO 86V	Leyland	Leopard PSU3E/4R	7903146	Alexander	136AYS/1878/10	B53F	2/80	Alexander Northern NPE86	Taybus Vintage Vehicle Society
	GSO 90V	Leyland	Leopard PSU3E/4R	7903528	Alexander	136AYS/1878/14	DP49F	2/80	Alexander Northern NPE90	Duffy, Macclesfield
(q)	GSO 91V	Leyland	Leopard PSU3E/4R	7903499	Alexander	136AYS/1878/15	DP49F	2/80	Alexander Northern NPE91	Duffy, Macclesfield

	Reg	Make	Model	Chassis no	Body	Body no	Layout	New	First operator	Current owner
	GSO 92V	Leyland	Leopard PSU3E/4R	7903500	Alexander	136AYS/1878/16	B53F	2/80	Alexander Northern NPE92	Forbes, Angus
	GSO 94V	Leyland	Leopard PSU3E/4R	7903659	Alexander	136AYS/1878/18	B53F	2/80	Alexander Northern NPE94	Sharp, Newmilns
	GTO 47V	→ see 80-D-1163 *Ireland*								
	GTO 301V	Leyland	Fleetline FE30AGR	7803808	Northern Counties	8703	H43/30F	2/80	Derby 301	Daimler Benz Preservation Group
	HDB 101V	Leyland	Fleetline FE30AGR	7806029	Northern Counties	8745	H43/32F	12/79	Greater Manchester PTE 8101	Lindley, Farnborough
	HDB 116V	Leyland	Fleetline FE30AGR	7804943	Northern Counties	8826	H43/32F	4/80	Greater Manchester PTE 8116	SELNEC Preservation Society
(r)	HDB 124V	Leyland	Fleetline FE30AGR	7805656	Northern Counties	8834	H43/32F	5/80	Greater Manchester PTE 8124	SELNEC Preservation Society
	HFG 923V	Leyland	National NL116L11/1R	07001	Leyland National		B52F	6/80	Southdown 123	Vine, Yeovil
	HFX 423V	→ see 80-MO-151 *Ireland*								
	HHH 372V	Leyland	National NL116L11/1R	06921	Leyland National		B??F	5/80	Cumberland 372	Nairn, Godalming
	HKX 553V	Bedford	JJL	JW800101	Marshall	260253	C13FT	-/78	Marshall demonstrator	Jagger, St Annes
					(first licensed 9/79)					
(r)	HNE 251V	Leyland	Leopard PSU5C/4R	7904127	Duple	935/5425	C53F	1/80	National Travel (West) 1251	Spencer, Fakenham
	HNN 114V	Leyland	Fleetline FE30ALR	7901900	Northern Counties	8786	H44/31F	2/80	South Notts, Gotham 114	Kingston Bus Preservation Society
	HRS 265V	Leyland	Atlantean AN68A/1R	7903831	Alexander	AL86/1677/5	O45/29D	4/80	Grampian 265	Roulston, Glasgow
	HRS 270V	Leyland	Atlantean AN68A/1R	7903861	Alexander	AL86/1677/10	H45/29D	4/80	Grampian 270	Andrew, Aberdeen
	HRS 271V	Leyland	Atlantean AN68A/1R	7903642	Alexander	AL86/1677/11	O45/29D	5/80	Grampian 271	Roulston, Glasgow *(operates as Roulston, Beith (SW))*
	HRS 278V	→ see 80-G-704 *Ireland*								
	HRY 698V	Bedford	YMT	JW456493	Plaxton	8011TC076	C53F	1/80	King of the Road, Worthing	Simmonds, Sandhurst
			(ex 6691 PH, HRY 698V)							
	HSD 71V	→ see WDS 115V								
	HSD 73V	Leyland	Fleetline FE30AGR	7905633	Alexander	AD19/779/4	H44/31F	7/80	Western SMT R73	Barclay, Irvine
			(ex WDS 112V, 705 DYE, HSD 73V)							
	HSD 86V	Leyland	Fleetline FE30AGR	8000646	Alexander	AD19/779/17	H44/31F	7/80	Western SMT R86	Roulston, Glasgow
	HTO 980V	Bedford	YMT	JW457472	Plaxton	8011TC123	C53F	3/80	Leah, Huthwaite	Crosby, Nottingham
			(ex JIL 6903, HTO 980V)							
	JAW 84V	→ see JUX 103V								
	JDU 901V	DAF	MB200DKTL550	191919	Plaxton	8011DC008	B65F	7/80	Bonas, Coventry	Middleton, Rugeley
			(ex NSE 25V, GSU 315, JDU 901V)							
	JKH 194V	→ see OAT 536V								
	JKM 165V	→ see MWV 840								
(r)	JMJ 633V	Bedford	YMT	JW454187	Plaxton	7911TX581	C53F	1/80	Moore, Windsor	Repton, Little Bookham (SR)
	JNJ 815V	→ see BOU 6V								
	JPA 81V	→ see LSV 748								
	JPA 82V	Albion	Victor FT39KAN	73821E	Heaver		B35F	1/57	Guernsey Motors 72	Ritchie & Walker, Glasgow
			(ex 4022)							
	JPA 83V	→ see YFO 127								
	JPA 84V	→ see TFO 249								
	JRE 354V	Leyland	Leopard PSU3E/4R	7902391	Plaxton	7911LX649	C53F	10/79	Middleton, Rugeley 56	Stanton, Cheadle
	JSA 102V	Leyland	Leopard PSU3F/4R	7904941	Alexander	19AT/679/5	C49F	6/80	Alexander Northern NPE102	Forbes, Angus
	JTM 109V	AEC	Reliance	6U2R38504	Duple	944/5904	B53F	11/79	Tillingbourne (Sussex), Gomshall	Larking, Bromley
	JUM 214V	Leyland	Atlantean AN68A/1R	7901280	Roe	GO8162	H43/32F	3/80	West Yorkshire PTE 6214	West Yorkshire PTE Preservation Gp, Shipley
	JUM 505V	MCW	Metrobus DR101/7	MB5047	MCW		H46/31F	3/80	West Yorkshire PTE 7505	Keighley Bus Museum Trust
	JUX 103V	Ford	R1114	BCRSAB272680	Plaxton	8011FC144	C53F	8/80	Price, Wrockwardine Wood	Price, Telford
			(ex JAW 84V)							
	JWT 757V	Bristol	VRT/SL3/6LXB	VRT/SL3/2008	ECW	23898	H43/31F	10/79	West Yorkshire Road Car 1724	Peters, Farnborough
	KAD 359V	Leyland	Leopard PSU5C/4R	7904874	Plaxton	8012LC022	C57F	3/80	National Travel South West 359	Lloyd-Owen, Churchdown

	KAU 564V	Leyland	Leopard PSU3E/4R	7930029	Plaxton	8011LX539	C53F	7/80	Barton 1564	Towle & Campbell, Awsworth
	KOO 790V	Bristol	VRT/SL3/6LXB	VRT/SL3/2270	ECW	23793	H39/31F	3/80	Eastern National 3072	Deal, Marks Tey
	KRS 539V	Leyland	National NL106L11/1R	06777	Leyland National		B44F	4/80	Alexander Northern NPN5	Wade, Godstone
			(ex GSO 5V)							
	KUB 544V	Leyland	Leopard PSU3E/4R	7903807	Plaxton	7911LX539	C49F	12/79	West Yorkshire Road Car 2570	Escrick Bus & Coach Preservation Group
	KVF 247V	Bristol	VRT/SL3/6LXB	VRT/SL3/2252	ECW	24064	H43/31F	4/80	Eastern Counties VR247	Lewis, Dudley
	KWY 228V	Leyland	Atlantean AN68A/1R	7901863	Roe	GO8176	H43/32F	5/80	West Yorkshire PTE 6228	West Yorkshire PTE Preservation Gp, Shipley
	LAG 188V	Leyland	National NL116L11/1R	06652	Leyland National		B52F	1/80	East Yorkshire 188	Hull Bus Restorers, Hull
	LBD 923V	Bristol	VRT/SL3/6LXB	VRT/SL3/2137	ECW	24081	H43/31F	1/80	United Counties 923	-?-, Oxfordshire
	LBU 875V	Leyland	Fleetline FE30AGR	7905531	Northern Counties	8825	H44/33F	4/80	Turner, Brown Edge 8	Cherry, Bootle
			(ex JIL 8213, LVT 699V)							
	LFH 719V	Leyland	Leopard PSU3E/4R	7930098	Plaxton	8011LX576	C49F	6/80	Castleways, Winchcombe	Lear, Ashbury Station
	LHS 747V	Ailsa	B55-10	79027	Alexander	AV28/2478/13	H44/35F	11/79	Central SMT AH23	Gilmour & Gray, Glasgow
	LSU 381V	Leyland	Atlantean AN68A/1R	7900297	Alexander	AL82/2276/74	H45/33F	12/79	Greater Glasgow PTE LA1324	McCormick, Dumbarton
	LUA 282V	Leyland	Leopard PSU5D/4R	8030026	Plaxton	8012LC032	C53F	5/80	Wallace Arnold Tours	Western Greyhound, Summercourt (CO)
	LUA 714V	Bristol	VRT/SL3/6LXB	VRT/SL3/2200	ECW	23905	H43/31F	2/80	West Yorkshire Road Car 1731	Longley, London
	LVT 699V	→ see LBU 875V								
	MMJ 528V	Ford	R1114	BCRSWJ457550	Duple	023/4501	C53F	2/80	FHW, Willenhall	Lavin, Langley Park
	MNK 429V	Leyland	Leopard PSU3E/4R	7903233	Duple	033/5174	C53F	5/80	Fox, Hayes 58	Macey, Luton
	NAT 198V	Leyland	National NL116L11/1R	06975	Leyland National		B49F	6/80	East Yorkshire 198	Foster S, Darlington
	NFW 36V	Bristol	VRT/LL3/6LXB	VRT/LL3/146	East Lancs	602	H50/36F	8/80	Lincoln 36	Lincolnshire Vintage Vehicle Society
	NLP 389V	Leyland	National NL116L11/3R	07054	Leyland National		B49F	7/80	British Airways, Heathrow C280	Woods, Topham
(z)	NRO 229V	DAF	MB200DKL600	181255	Plaxton	7912DC013	C53F	5/80	Seamarks, Westoning 121	East Anglia Transport Museum
			(ex 1440 PP, 7476 PP, NRO 229V)							
	NUB 93V	AEC	Reliance	6U2R38781	Plaxton	8011AC001/S	C53F	5/80	Compass, Wakefield	Hearson, Chesterton
	OAT 536V	Leyland	Leopard PSU3E/4R	7902319	Plaxton	7911LX567	C49F	10/79	East Yorkshire 194	Hull, Newcastle upon Tyne
			(ex WLT 694, JKH 194V)							
	OLG 601V	Bedford	YMT	JW452967	Plaxton	7911TX536	C53F	8/79	Phillips, Holywell 9	Phillips, Holywell (CN)
	OSC 62V	Ailsa	B55-10	79011	Alexander	AV25/2178/16	H44/35F	10/79	Alexander Fife FRA62	Gray et al, Glasgow
	OSC 602V	Leyland	Atantean AN68A/1R	7805427	Alexander	AL74/2676/25	H45/30D	8/79	Lothian 602	Lea, Dunstable
	OSG 74V	Leyland	Fleetline FE30AGR	7900009	ECW	23566	H--/--F	10/79	Scottish Omnibuses DD74	Farquhar, Livingston
	OTL 633V	Bedford	YMT	KW452210	Plaxton	8011TX561	C53F	5/80	Everett, Atterby	Everett, Atterby
	PFE 542V	Bristol	VRT/SL3/6LXB	VRT/SL3/2446	ECW	24330	H43/31F	7/80	Lincolnshire 1958	Lincolnshire Vintage Vehicle Society
	RMA 435V	Bristol	VRT/SL3/501	VRT/SL3/2278	ECW	23846	H43/31F	4/80	Crosville DVL435	Crosville VR Group, St Helens
	RMA 442V	Bristol	VRT/SL3/501	VRT/SL3/2310	ECW	23853	H43/31F	5/80	Crosville DVL442	DVL442 Group, Wirral
	RSG 824V	Leyland	National NL116L11/1R	06683	Leyland National		B52F	2/80	Alexander Fife FPN24	Williams, Merthyr Tydfil
(r)	RSG 825V	Leyland	National NL116L11/1R	06684	Leyland National		B52F	2/80	Alexander Fife FPN25	McGregor, Bathgate
	SDM 94V	Leyland	Fleetline FE30AGR	7900367	Northern Counties	8792	H43/29F	2/80	Chester 94	Davies, Chester
	SDM 96V	Leyland	Fleetline FE30AGR	7900423	Northern Counties	8789	PO43/29F	2/80	Chester 96	Bohemia Classic Buses, Czech Republic (*care of Rhymney Valley Transport Preservation Society*)
	SGR 935V	Bristol	VRT/SL3/501	VRT/SL3/1960	ECW	23758	H--/--F	10/79	Northern General 3435	Buckley & Minto, Newcastle-upon-Tyne
	SPT 963V	Leyland	Leopard PSU3E/4R	7901258	Plaxton	8011LX501	C53F	3/80	OK, Bishop Auckland	Cook, Musselburgh
	SSX 602V	Seddon	Pennine 7	70088	Alexander	132AYS/2278/12	B8F	3/80	Scottish Omnibuses S602	Wallace, Edinburgh
	TBR 527V	Leyland	Leopard PSU3E/4R	7900741	Duple	939/5630	B55F	10/79	Trimdon Motor Services	-?-, -?-
	TRN 481V	Leyland	Atlantean AN68A/1R	7901813	ECW	23724	H43/31F	1/80	Ribble 1481	Ribble Vehicle Preservation Trust
	TRN 808V	Leyland	National 10351B/1R	06395	Leyland National		B42F	8/79	Ribble 808	Premiere, Nottingham (NG)
			(ex FSV 428, TRN 808V)							

	Registration	Chassis	Chassis No	Body	Body No	Layout	New	Original operator	Current owner
	TRN 810V	Leyland National 10351B/1R	06415	Leyland National		B44F	8/79	Ribble 810	Moss T & D, Bolton
									(on loan to Ribble Vehicle Preservation Trust)
	TWM 220V	Leyland Atlantean AN68A/1R	7804391	East Lancs	9317	H45/33F	10/79	Merseyside PTE 1836	Pendleton, Litherland
	UEM 36V	Leyland National NL116L11/1R	06692	Leyland National		B49F	1/80	Merseyside PTE 6036	Naylor, Billinge
	UHG 141V	Leyland Atlantean AN68A/2R	7902378	Alexander	AL83/1777/9	H49/36F	3/80	Preston 141	Hunt, Fleetwood
	UKA 23V	MCW Metrobus DR103/2	MB5202	MCW		H43/30F	2/80	Merseyside PTE 0023	Pendleton, Litherland
	UPT 681V	Leyland National NL116L11/1R	06930	Leyland National		B49F	4/80	Northern General 4681	Smith & Perryman, Chester-le-Street
		(fitted with a Volvo engine)							
	VFS 542V	→ see WLT 667							
	VHF 57V	Bedford YMT	KW450875	Plaxton	8011TC141	C53F	5/80	Topping, Liverpool	O'Brien, Liverpool
	VJY 141V	Leyland Atlantean AN68A/1R	7902112	East Lancs	207	H43/28D	1/80	Plymouth 141	Hearn, Barnstaple
	WDS 112V	→ see HSD 73V							
	WDS 115V	Leyland Fleetline FE30AGR	7905453	Alexander	AD19/779/2	H44/31F	7/80	Western SMT R71	Western SMT Preservation Society, Greenock
		(ex WLT 364, HSD 71V)							
	WFU 707V	→ see 4050 ZW *Ireland*							
	WUP 961V	Leyland Leopard PSU3F/5R	7904935	Duple	034/5359	C53F	5/80	Burrell, Newsham	Burrell, Newsham (NY)
	XHG 96V	Leyland Atlantean AN68A/1R	7900859	Northern Counties	8785	H??/31F	5/80	Fylde 96	Mitchell, Blackpool
	XJJ 663V	Bristol VRT/SL3/6LXB	VRT/SL3/2394	ECW	24023	H43/31F	6/80	East Kent 7663	Hull & Country Bus Preservation Group
	XJJ 669V	Bristol VRT/SL3/6LXB	VRT/SL3/2454	ECW	24583	H43/31F	6/80	East Kent 7669	Hull & Country Bus Preservation Group
	YAE 518V	Bristol LH6L	LH-1586	ECW	23529	B43F	11/79	Bristol 451	Hawksworth, Sudbrooke
	YJK 934V	Leyland Atlantean AN68A/2R	7900426	East Lancs	8609	H47/35F	9/79	Eastbourne 34	Bennett, Peterborough
(r)	YTE 587V	Leyland Fleetline FE30AGR	7806718	Northern Counties	8738	H43/32F	11/79	Lancashire United 573	SELNEC Preservation Society
	ADR 192W	→ see TJI 4036							
	AFM 2W	→ see PIL 7013							
(r)	APT 117W	Leyland National NL116L11/1R	07095	Leyland National		B49F	8/80	United Automobile 3117	Smith, Chester-le-Street
	APT 808W	Bristol VRT/SL3/6LXB	VRT/SL3/2520	ECW	24315	H43/31F	8/80	United Automobile 808	Isaacs, Alne
	AUP 369W	Leyland Atlantean AN68B/1R	7905760	Roe	GO8325	H43/30F	10/80	Northern General 3469	Wightman, Silksworth
	AUP 377W	Leyland Atlantean AN68B/1R	8000106	Roe	GO8343	H43/30F	11/80	Northern General 3477	-?-, -?-
	BCA 126W	Leyland Tiger TRCTL11/3R	8100332	Duple	135/5489	C57F	4/81	Bostock, Congleton 36	Stainthorpe, Skelton (CD)
	BFW 428W	→ see FRN 816W							
	BGR 684W	Bedford YMT	KW452384	Duple	020/2959	B53F	8/80	Jolly, South Hylton	Parker-Dix, Hetton-le-Hole
	BMA 521W	Bristol VRT/SL3/6LXB	VRT/SL3/3009	ECW	24808	H43./31F	7/81	Crosville DVG521	Barnes, Penketh
	BTU 914W	Leyland National NL116AL11/3R	07417	Leyland National		B30T	4/81	Manchester Airport N5	Davies, West Kirby
		(ex Unregistered)							
	CAB 2W	Bedford VAS5	DT109435	Plaxton	838PJS4C11A	C29FL	12/83	Hereford & Worcester CC	Acorn, Trelewis (CS)
		(ex A763 YAB)							
	CAS 516W	Leyland Leopard PSU3G/4R	8130028	Alexander	147AY/2480/6	C49F	6/81	Highland Omnibuses L22	-?-, -?-
	CAS 519W	Leyland Leopard PSU3G/4R	8130036	Alexander	147AY/2480/9	C49F	6/81	Highland Omnibuses L25	Scott, Southport
	CAS 520W	Leyland Leopard PSU3G/4R	8130041	Alexander	147AY/2480/10	C49F	6/81	Highland Omnibuses L26	McCormick, Oban
	CEO 720W	Leyland National NL116L11/1R	07180	Leyland National		B45F	9/80	Barrow 20	Barrow Transport Museum
	CEO 723W	Leyland National NL116L11/1R	07183	Leyland National		B49F	9/80	Barrow 23	Barrow Transport Museum
	CSF 157W	Leyland Leopard PSU3F/4R	8130151	Alexander	146AYS/1780/3	B53F	6/81	Alexander Fife FPE157	Drury, Stranraer
	CSF 158W	Leyland Leopard PSU3F/4R	8130153	Alexander	146AYS/1780/4	B53F	6/81	Alexander Fife FPE158	Kells Transport Museum, Cork
	CSF 160W	Leyland Leopard PSU3G/4R	8130291	Alexander	146AYS/1780/6	B53F	6/81	Alexander Fife FPE160	Rojay, Wigan (GM)
	CSF 166W	Leyland Leopard PSU3F/4R	8130395	Alexander	146AYS/1780/12	B53F	7/81	Alexander Fife FPE166	Kells Transportt Museum, Cork
	DAE 510W	MCW Metrobus DR103/4	MB5708	MCW		H15/17F	10/80	Bristol 6000	Williams, Bristol

Reg	Make	Model	Chassis no	Body	Body no	Layout	Date	First owner	Owner
DBV 26W	Bristol	VRT/SL3/6LXB	VRT/SL3/2616	ECW	24409	H43/31F	11/80	Ribble 2026	Kells Transport Museum, Cork
DBV 42W	Leyland	Leopard PSU4E/4R	7902238	East Lancs	5713	B47F	9/80	Burnley & Pendle 42	Goode & Harris, Penarth
DBV 43W	Leyland	Leopard PSU4E/4R	7902252	East Lancs	5712	B47F	9/80	Burnley & Pendle 43	Shears C, Winkleigh
DBV 100W	Leyland	Olympian B45	B45-02	ECW	EX15	H45/33F	8/80	Ribble 2100	Ribble Vehicle Preservation Trust
DBV 831W	Leyland	National NL106L11/1R	07093	Leyland National		B44F	8/80	Ribble 831	McCall, Widnes *(on loan to Ribble Vehicle Preservation Trust)*
DBV 845W	→ see 81-C-1657 *Ireland*								
DEN 247W	→ see 124 YTW								
DFV 641W	Leyland	National 10951/2R *(first registered 8/80)*	00432	ECW	EX13	B—C	c4/73	ECW development vehicle	Nash, Ockley
DHW 351W	Bristol	VRT/SL3/680 *(fitted with a Gardner 6LXB engine)*	VRT/SL3/2917	ECW	24436	H43/31F	7/81	Bristol 5529	Stanley, Bristol
DWH 706W	Leyland	Fleetline FE30AGR	7901069	Northern Counties	8926	H43/32F	12/80	Lancashire United 613	SELNEC Preservation Society
EJR 110W	Leyland	Atlantean AN68C/2R	8000197	Alexander	AL91/2079/7	H49/37F	12/80	Tyne & Wear PTE 110	group, Sunderland
EJR 111W	Leyland	Atlantean AN68C/2R	8000085	Alexander	AL91/2079/8	H49/37F	12/80	Tyne & Wear PTE 111	Treble One Preservation Gp, Newcastle upon Tyne
EJR 129W	Leyland	Atlantean AN68C/2R	8000895	Alexander	AL91/2079/26	CH45/33F	1/81	Northern General 3529	Ward McKale & McKenzie, Felling
ERV 115W	Leyland	National NL106AL11/1R	07516	Leyland National		B41F	7/81	Portsmouth 115	Bruton, Nailsworth
ESF 647W	Leyland	Victory 2 (ex CH 9399 *Hong Kong*)	JVTB800619	Alexander		H60/42D	10/80	China Motor Bus LV36	Scottish Vintage Bus Museum
ESF 678W	Volvo	B58-61 (ex GSV 351, TIB 8575, VOI 4611, RVM 958W)	16508	Plaxton	8112VC015	C53F	6/81	O'Brien, Farnworth	Montgomery, Musselburgh
ETP 61W	Leyland	Tiger TRCTL11/3R (ex PJI 8325, ETP 61W)	8100464	Plaxton	8112LC040	C53F	6/81	Easson, Southampton	Botley, Lee-on-Solent
EWN 995W	Bristol	VRT/SL3/510	VRT/SL3/2551	ECW	24293	H43/31F	9/80	South Wales 995	Hanford, Swansea
EWS 739W	Bristol	VRT/SL3/0680 *(fitted with a Gardner 6LXB engine)*	VRT/SL3/2925	ECW	24438	H43/31F	7/81	Bristol 5531	Willetts, Bristol
EWS 746W	Bristol	VRT/SL3/680 *(fitted with a Gardner 6LXB engine)*	VRT/SL3/2943	ECW	24445	H--/--F	7/81	Bristol 5538	Pullen, Stroud
EWS 748W	Bristol	VRT/SL3/680 *(fitted with a Gardner 6LXB engine)*	VRT/SL3/2953	ECW	24447	H43/31F	7/81	Bristol 5540	Stroud RE Group
EWS 751W	Bristol	VRT/SL3/680 *(fitted with a Gardner 6LXB engine)*	VRT/SL3/2956	ECW	24450	H43/31F	6/81	Bristol 5543	Robinson, Swindon
EWS 753W	Bristol	VRT/SL3/680	VRT/SL3/2958	ECW	24452	H44/31F	10/81	Bristol 5545	Ellis, Cambridge (Glos)
FBV 271W	Bristol	LHS6L	LHS-374	ECW	24718	B35F	10/80	Ribble 271	Puttock, Esher
FCX 576W	AEC	Reliance (ex YAZ 6393, FCX 576W)	6U2R38768	Plaxton	8011AC006/S	C53F	8/80	Traject {Abbeyways}, Huddersfield	Romer, Bear Cross (DT)
FES 831W	Volvo	B58-61	16712	Duple	149/8055	B59F	2/81	Gloagtrotter, Perth	Bluebird Buses (SN) 59931
FRN 816W	Leyland	Tiger TRCTL11/3R (ex BFW 428W, NCT 833, BFW 428W, MSV 927, BFW 233W, MSV 927, FRN 816W)	8003589	Van Hool	9685	C51F	2/81	Leyland demonstrator	Kelly, Brimington
FSL 62W	Leyland	Leopard PSU3E/4R (ex 6689 DP, GSL 306W)	8030697	Plaxton	8011LX548	C53F	12/80	Tayside 306	Taybus Vintage Vehicle Society
FSL 615W	Bedford	YMQ	KW453227	Plaxton	8010QC030	C45F	7/80	Henderson, Markinch	Short , Glasgow
FTH 991W	Volvo	B58-61 (ex OUF 359W, 789 CLC, FTH 991W)	16710	Plaxton	8112VC045	C57F	6/81	Morris, Swansea	-?-, Swansea
FTH 992W	Volvo	B58-61 (ex LFX 602, FTH 992W)	15857	Plaxton	8112VC019	C53F	4/81	Morris, Swansea	-?-, Swansea
(r) FTH 995W	Volvo	B58-61	16466	Plaxton	8112VC007	C53F	5/81	Morris, Swansea	-?-, Swansea
FTN 708W	Leyland	National NL116AL11/1R	07509	Leyland National		B49F	7/81	Northern General 4708	Ruddick, Consett

	Reg.	Make	Model	Chassis No.	Body	Body No.	Layout	New	First owner	Current owner
	FTN 710W	Leyland	National NL116AL11/1R	07511	Leyland National		B49F	7/81	Northern General 4710	North East Bus Preservbation Trust
			(fitted with a Volvo engine)							
	FYX 817W	Leyland	Leopard PSU3E/4R	7930158	Duple	034/5339	C49F	8/80	Grey Green, Stamford Hill	Freeman & Norton, Huntingdon
			(ex VIB 5069, FYX 817W)							
	GAX 137W	Leyland	Leopard PSU4F/2R	8031166	Marshall	270320	B45F	3/81	Islwyn 37	Evans, New Tredegar
	GBO 304W	→ see 81-KE-398 *Ireland*								
	GCK 428W	Leyland	National NL116AL11/1R	07343	Leyland National		B49F	2/81	Fishwick, Leyland 7	-?-, Lancashire
	GCK 429W	Leyland	National NL116AL11/1R	07344	Leyland National		B49F	2/81	Fishwick, Leyland 8	Hayes, Little Hoole
	GFR 101W	Leyland	Olympian ONLXB/1R	ON1	ECW	EX17/24948	H45/32F	2/81	Ribble 2101	Fearnley & Wilde, Harrogate
(r)	GGM 84W	Bristol	VRT/SL3/6LXB	VRT/SL3/2724	ECW	24573	PO--/--F	11/80	Thames Valley & Aldershot 614	Denny, Worlingham
	GHG 343W	Leyland	Atlantean AN68C/2R	8003243	East Lancs	703	H50/36F	6/81	Blackpool 343	Hughes, Colchester
	GRN 896W	→ see 643 MIP *Ireland*								
	GSL 306W	→ see FSL 62W								
	GTX 761W	Bristol	LHS6L	LHS-380	ECW	24709	DP27F	2/81	National Welsh MD8026	Hill, Stroud
	GTX 762W	Bristol	LHS6L	LHS-381	ECW	24710	DP27F	1/81	National Welsh MD8027	Smith Townsend & Cross, Cwmbran
	GUW 443W	Leyland	National NL106AL11/2R	07325	East Lancs	B5639	B24D	1/81	London Transport LS443	Brown, Greenhithe
			(ex PMY 178W, WLT 843, GUW 443W)		*(rebodied 4/94)*					
	GUW 444W	Leyland	National NL106AL11/2R	07326	Leyland National		B24D	2/81	London Transport LS444	Wright, Hitchin
			(fitted with a Volvo engine)							
	GUW 485W	Leyland	National NL106AL11/2R	07371	Leyland National		B36D	5/81	London Transoort LS485	London Bus Company, Northfleet (KT)
	GYE 252W	Leyland	Titan TNLXB2RR	0301	Park Royal / Leyland		H44/28D	2/81	London Transport T252	Delaney, -?-
	GYE 273W	Leyland	Titan TNLXB2RR	0322	Leyland		PO44/27D	7/81	London Transport T273	Roulston, Glasgow
	GYE 394W	MCW	Metrobus DR101/12	MB5766	MCW		H43/28D	9/80	London Transport M394	Rose, London Colney
	GYE 605W	MCW	Metrobus DR101/14	MB6377	MCW		H43/--F	8/81	London Transport M605	-?-, -?-
	HJB 455W	Bristol	VRT/SL3/6LXB	VRT/SL3/2658	ECW	24604	H43/31F	11/80	Thames Valley & Aldershot 635	Denny, Worlingham
	HRL 626W	→ see 81-KE-329 *Ireland*								
	JCK 852W	Leyland	National NL106AL11/1R	07504	East Lancs	B1301	B41F	6/81	London & Country 252	Nash, Ockley
			(fitted with a Gardner engine)		*(rebodied 12/91)*					
	JDO 241W	Bedford	YMT	KW451477	Plaxton	8011TX564	C53F	3/81	Fowler, Holbeach Drove	Fowler, Holbeach Drove (LI)
	JHE 161W	MCW	Metrobus DR104/6	MB5959	MCW		H46/31F	2/81	South Yorkshire PTE 1861	South Yorkshire Transport Trust
	JJD 47W	→ see KUI 6566								
	JKW 281W	Leyland	Atlantean AN68B/1R	7905614	Alexander	AL94/1280/5	H43/32F	2/81	South Yorkshire PTE 1781	Parkinson, Rotherham
	JKW 290W	Leyland	Atlantean AN68B/1R	7905721	Alexander	AL94/1280/14	H45/29D	2/81	South Yorkshire PTE 1790	Griffiths, Chesterfield
	JKW 331W	Leyland	Atlantean AN68B/1R	7905616	Marshall	270354	H45/29D	3/81	South Yorkshire PTE 1831	Griffiths, Chesterfield
	JUD 597W	Ford	R1014	BCRSAB235620	Plaxton	8010FX501	C45F	10/80	House, Watlington	Oxford Bus Museum Trust
	JUH 228W	Leyland	Leopard PSU4F/2R	8031193	Duple	138/5601	B47F	5/81	Merthyr Tydfil 228	Williams, Merthyr Tydfil
(r)	JWE 247W	Leyland	Leopard PSU5D/4R	8030551	Plaxton	8012LC058	C50F	10/80	National Travel East	Norman, Aberbargoed
	JWV 126W	→ see 80-C-1528 *Ireland*								
	JWV 259W	Bristol	VRT/SL3/6LXB	VRT/SL3/2757	ECW	24661	H43/31F	2/81	Southdown 259	Western Greyhound, Summercourt (CO)
	JWV 266W	→ see IUI 5036								
	JWV 270W	Bristol	VRT/SL3/680	VRT/SL3/2872	ECW	24672	H43/31F	4/81	Southdown 270	270 Group, Brighton
			(fitted with aGardner 6LXB engine)							
	JWV 272W	Bristol	VRT/SL3/680	VRT/SL3/2886	ECW	24674	H43/33F	4/81	Southdown 272	School Bus Company, Kingston Bagpuize (OX)
			(ex HSV 673, JWV 272W) *(fitted with a Gardner 6LXB engine)*							
	JWV 273W	Bristol	VRT/SL3/680	VRT/SL3/2887	ECW	24675	H43/31F	4/81	Southdown 273	Aldous, Swindon
			(ex WJI 2849, JWV 273W) *(fitted with a Gardner 6LXB engine)*							
	JWV 275W	Bristol	VRT/SL3/680	VRT/SL3/2897	ECW	24677	H43/31F	4/81	Southdown 275	Hampshire Bus & Coach Preservation Group

Reg	Make	Model	Chassis no	Body	Body no	Layout	Date	First owner	Current owner
JWV 976W	Bristol	VRT/SL3/680	VRT/SL3/2898	ECW	24678	H43/31F	4/81	Southdown 276	Stobart, Wimbledon
		(fitted with a Gardner 6LXB engine)							
KDL 202W	Bristol	LHS6L	LHS-368	ECW	24715	DP31F	11/80	Southern Vectis 202	Hampshire Bus & Coach Preservation Group
KDL 203W	Bristol	LHS6L	LHS-369	ECW	24716	DP31F	11/80	Southern Vectis 203	Budden, Shanklin
KHG 184W	→ see LCW 411W								
KHH 378W	Leyland	National NL116L11/1R	07186	Leyland National		B52F	10/80	Cumberland 378	Workington Transport Heritage Trust
KKG 109W	Leyland	National NL116AL11/1R	07490	Leyland National		B52F	5/81	Gwent Health Authority	Gardiner, Usk
		(ex NIB 2796, KKG 109W)							
KKU 111W	Dennis	Dominator	DDA133/284	Alexander	RH1/3179/11	H46/32F	5/81	South Yorkshire PTE 2111	-?-, -?-
KKU 120W	Dennis	Dominator	DDA133/294	Alexander	RH1/3179/20	H46/32F	6/81	South Yorkshire PTE 2120	Sentance, Sheffield
KNT 815W	Bedford	CFL	JY631667	Plaxton	80C020CF	C17F	10/80	Price, Wrockwardine Wood	Greet, Broadhempston
		(ex BBT 380V, KNT 815W)							
KPJ 240W	Leyland	Atlantean AN68B/1R	7905417	Roe	GO8309	H--/--F	10/80	London Country AN240	Luff, Rougham
KPJ 264W	Leyland	Atlantean AN68B/1R	8000440	Roe	GO8378	H43/30F	2/81	London Country AN264	Paske, Chelmsford
KRM 431W	→ see PHH 149W								
KRU 848W	Bristol	VRT/SL3/6LXB	VRT/SL3/2654	ECW	24426	H43/31F	11/80	Hants & Dorset 3448	Cole, Frinton-on-Sea
KRU 850W	Bristol	VRT/SL3/6LXB	VRT/SL3/2656	ECW	24428	H43/31F	1/81	Hants & Dorset 3450	Wilts & Dorset 4450 Pres Group, Sandtoft
KRU 851W	Bristol	VRT/SL3/6LXB	VRT/SL3/2701	ECW	24429	H43/31F	12/80	Hants & Dorset 3451	Sargent, Kibworth
KRU 855W	Bristol	VRT/SL3/6LXB	VRT/SL3/2705	ECW	24433	H43/31F	12/80	Hants & Dorset 3455	Reynolds, Mangotsfield
KSD 103W	Volvo	B55-10	80030	Alexander	AV31/1179/4	H44/35F	10/80	Western SMT A103	Carson & Gilmour, Airdrie
KWA 22W	Leyland	National NL116L11/1R	07250	Leyland National		B49F	12/80	South Yorkshire PTE 22	Griffiths, Chesterfield
KWG 131W	→ see EXI 6301								
LCW 411W	Leyland	Tiger TRCTL11/3RH	8100558	Duple	135/5480	C57F	6/81	Premier, Preston	-?-, -?-
		(ex 1958 PH, KHG 184W)							
LFJ 844W	Bristol	VRT/SL3/6LXB	VRT/SL3/2528	ECW	24466	H43/31F	10/80	Western National 1200	Western National Preservation Group
LFJ 847W	Bristol	VRT/SL3/6LXB	VRT/SL3/2540	ECW	24469	H43/31F	10/80	Western National 1203	Billington, Maidenhead
LFJ 855W	Bristol	VRT/SL3/6LXB	VRT/SL3/2627	ECW	24474	H43/31F	10/80	Western National 1208	Courtnage, Saltash
LFJ 858W	Bristol	VRT/SL3/6LXB	VRT/SL3/2674	ECW	24477	H43/31F	12/80	Western National 1211	Western Greyhound, Summercourt (CO)
LFJ 873W	Bristol	VRT/SL3/6LXC	VRT/SL3/2802	ECW	24492	H43/31F	4/81	Western National 1226	Cornwall Bus Preservation Society
LHE 601W	Volvo	B58-56	16759	Plaxton	8111VC006	C53F	5/81	Johnson, Hodthorpe	Johnson, Worksop (NG)
LMS 168W	Leyland	Fleetline FE30AGR	8001187	Alexander	AD20/979/17	H44/31F	9/80	Alexander Midland MRF168	Conn & Gurr, Cumbernauld
LMS 374W	Leyland	Leopard PSU3F/4R	7930144	Alexander	140AYS/1279/11	B53F	8/80	Alexander Midland MPE374	Bryce Moore & Thomson, Falkirk
LMS 385W	Leyland	Leopard PSU3F/4R	8030105	Alexander	140AYS/1279/14	DP49F	8/80	Alexander Midland MPE385	Assiph, Dundee
LMS 985W	Dodge	2090P	619887	Rootes		M11	8/80	Royal Mail 9750055	Harrop, Stockport
LNU 571W	Leyland	Leopard PSU3E/4R	7930050	Plaxton	8011LX543	C53F	8/80	Barton 571	Harpurs, Derby (DE)
LPN 356W	→ see JUI 4233								
LPY 721W	Bedford	VAS5	LW450993	Duple	112/1052	C29F	5/81	OK, Bishop Auckland	Moore, Carlteon Forehoe
LRB 214W	Leyland	National NL116AL11/1R	07439	Leyland National		B52F	5/81	Trent 214	Vale of Glamorgan Bus Preservation Group
MAP 340W	Leyland	Leopard PSU3F/4R	8030960	Plaxton	8111LX512	C53F	3/81	Southdown 1340	-?-, Ashford
MCH 351W	Bedford	YMT	KW452132	Duple	020/2962	B55F	8/80	National Coal Board	Kells Transport Museum, Cork
MEK 22W	→ see 80-D-1371 *Ireland*								
MEW 148W	Volvo	B10M-61	000624	Plaxton	8112VCV913	C51F	6/81	Miller, Foxton	Jarvis, Aberdeen
MFX 174W	Leyland	Fleetline FE30AGR	8001329	Alexander	AL93/2779/6	H43/31F	2/81	Bournemouth 174	Dorset Heritage/Brown, Holton Heath (DT)
MHN 131W	Leyland	National NL116L11/1R	07494	Leyland National		B49F	5/80	United 3733	Aycliffe & District Bus Preservation Society
MNC 513W	Leyland	Atlantean AN68A/1R	7905886	Northern Counties	8874	H43/32F	9/80	Greater Manchester PTE 8313	-?-, Manchester
MNC 525W	Leyland	Atlantean AN68A/1R	8000289	Northern Counties	8886	H43/32F	10/80	Greater Manchester PTE 8325	SELNEC Preservation Society
MNU 695W	→ see 80-C-1459 *Ireland*								
MPL 136W	→ see 81-D-1380 *Ireland*								

	Reg	Make	Model	Chassis No	Body	Body No	Layout	New	First Owner	Current Owner
	MRJ 8W	Bristol	VRT/SL3/6LXB	VRT/SL3/2449	ECW	24207	H43/31F	8/80	Mayne, Manchester 8	Legget-Bond {The Chocolate Box}, Bungay
	MRJ 100W	Leyland	Leopard PSU5D/5R	8030612	Plaxton	8112LC035	C57F	3/81	Yelloway, Rochdale	Tepper, Rochdale
			(ex NBZ 1670, MRJ 100W)							
	MRJ 232W	→ see PIB 5891								
	MRJ 233W	Leyland	Fleetline FE33ALR	8001789	Northern Counties	2010	H49/33F	6/81	Southend 233	Stephenson, Rochford (EX)
	MRU 551W	→ see PJI 7756								
	MSD 724W	Volvo	B10M-61	000626	Plaxton	8112VCV902	C49FT	4/81	Docherty, Irvine	Docherty, Irvine
			(ex 4151 D, MSD 724W)							
	MUT 253W	Dennis	Dominator	DD120/237	East Lancs	411	H46/33F	2/81	Leicester 253	Fowkes, Southampton
	NAU 292W	Volvo	B58-61	14309	Duple	049/7045	C57F	1/81	Wright, Newark	Townsend, Newark
	NEH 731W	Bristol	VRT/SL3/501	VRT/SL3/2546	ECW	24283	H43/31F	8/80	Potteries 731	Pearson, Stoke-on-Trent
	NJA 568W	Leyland	Olympian B45/TL11/1R	B45-05	Northern Counties	8901	H43/30F	10/80	Greater Manchester PTE 1451	SELNEC Preservation Society
	NNN 479W	Leyland	Atlantean AN68A/1R	8001154	Roe	GO8571	H46/34F	2/81	Nottingham 479	Stanton, Nottingham
	NNU 71W	Leyland	Leopard PSU3E/4R	8030046	Duple	133/5182	C53F	1/81	Glover, Ashbourne	-?-, Lincoln
	OHA 517W	Ford	R1114	BCRSAB284150	Duple	023/4531	C53F	9/80	Caney, Birmingham	Sanders, -?-
	ORJ 83W	MCW	Metrobus DR102/21	MB6220	MCW		H43/30F	6/81	Greater Manchester PTE 5083	Museum of Transport, Manchester
	OTB 24W	Leyland	Atlantean AN68C/1R	8003482	East Lancs	1503	H45/33F	6/81	Warrington 24	Vale of Glamorgan Bus Preservation Group
(r)	OTB 27W	Leyland	Atlantean AN68C/1R	8003510	East Lancs	1504	H45/33F	6/81	Warrington 27	-?-, -?-
	OUF 933W	→ see 80-C-1528 *Ireland*								
	PAG 515W	Bristol	VRT/SL3/6LXB	VRT/SL3/2540	ECW	24298	H43/32F	8/80	East Yorkshire 515	Griffiths, Hull
	PEX 620W	Leyland	National NL116AL11/1R	07445	Leyland National		B42F	4/81	Eastern Counties LN620	Cooper, Thetford
	PFC 515W	Bristol	VRT/SL3/6LXB	VRT/SL3/2999	ECW	24947	H43/30F	7/81	City of Oxford 515	-?-, Oxford
	PFH 90W	Bedford	YMT	KW452070	Duple	017/2628	C53F	3/81	Cathedral, Gloucester	Price & Perry, Shobdon
	PHH 149W	Bristol	VRT/SL3/6LXB	VRT/SL3/2590	ECW	24248	H43/31F	10/80	Cumberland 431	Burrow & Pritchard, Workington
			(ex KRM 431W)							
	PNB 805W	→ see 81-D-997 *Ireland*								
	PNM 682W	Bedford	YLQ	KW452892	Duple	050/1561	C35F	9/80	Ashridge College, Berkhamsted	Dennis, Okehampton
(a)	PNM 695W	Bedford	YMQ	KW453742	Duple	050/1555	C35F	3/81	Tricentrol, Dunstable	JTM's Recovery, Langley Park
	PNW 310W	→ see 83-D-4174 *Ireland*								
	PRO 439W	Bristol	LHS6L	LHS-361	Plaxton	808BC001	C33F	10/80	Skinner & Harvey, Oxted	Millington, Horsforth
	PUA 294W	Leyland	Atlantean AN68C/1R	8002016	Roe	GO8394	H43/32F	1/81	West Yorkshire PTE 6294	Harrogate Coach, Green Hammerton (NY)
	PUA 299W	Leyland	Atlantean AN68C/1R	8002128	Roe	GO8399	H43/32F	1/81	West Yorkshire PTE 6299	Beeby, Huddersfield
	PUA 300W	Leyland	Atlantean AN68C/1R	8002131	Roe	GO8400	H43/32F	1/81	West Yorkshire PTE 6300	Beeby, Huddersfield
	PUM 149W	Bristol	VRT/SL3/6LXB	VRT/SL3/2503	ECW	24304	H43/31F	8/80	West Yorkshire Road Car 1746	West Yorkshire Road Car Preservation Group, Shipley
	PWL 999W	Leyland	Olympian B45/TL11/2R	B45-07	Alexander	3078/1	H50/32D	9/80	Leyland demonstrator	Wareham, Kidlington
			(ex SBS 5396 B *Singapore*)							
	PWY 31W	→ see 81-C-1414 *Ireland*								
(r)	PWY 39W	Bristol	VRT/SL3/6LXB	VRT/SL3/2668	ECW	24349	H43/31F	11/80	West Yorkshire Road Car 1753	Mulpeter, Seaford
	RAH 260W	Bristol	VRT/SL3/6LXB	VRT/SL3/2690	ECW	24623	H43/31F	12/80	Eastern Counties VR260	Jordan, Ormesby
	RAH 268W	Bristol	VRT/SL3/6LXB	VRT/SL3/2860	ECW	24631	H43/31F	3/81	Eastern Counties VR268	Patterson, Kings Lynn
	RBJ 36W	Leyland	Atlantean AN68C/1R	8002292	East Lancs	1601	H46/30F	11/80	Ipswich 36	Vale of Glamorgan Bus Preservation Group
	RDS 589W	Leyland	Atlantean AN68A/1R	7904064	Alexander	AL88/2279/50	H45/33F	10/80	Greater Glasgow PTE LA1400	Roulston, Glasgow
	RDS 597W	Leyland	Atlantean AN68A/1R	8000292	Alexander	AL88/2279/58	H45/33F	12/80	Greater Glasgow PTE LA1408	Transport Preservation Trust, Beith
	RGV 690W	Bedford	YMT	KW453730	Duple	017/2493	C53F	4/81	Suffolk County Council	Jervis, Stoke-on-Trent
			(ex 8466 PH, RGV 690W)							
	RHS 400W	Wales & Edwards		-?-	JSP (West Bromwich)		B12F	-/80	South of Scotland Electricity	-?-, Cranleigh

(r)	RLN 237W	DAB	35-690/4	8002572	Roe	GO9706	B--D	3/81	British Airways, Heathrow C310	Chambers, Exeter
			(front section only of articulated bus)							
	RMS 400W	Leyland	Leopard PSU3G/4R	8130068	Alexander	21AT/2180/3	C49F	6/81	Alexander Midland MPE400	Short, Bearsden
	RNE 192W	Bedford	J2SZ10	2T128113	Plaxton	738006	C20F	11/72	Todd, Whitchurch	Lewis, Castle Caereinion (CW)
			(ex NPP 71L)							
	RNE 692W	Bedford	CFL	JY631781	Plaxton	80C022CF	C17F	4/81	Jackson, Altrincham	Jones, Cleeve (SO)
	RUA 450W	Bristol	VRT/SL3/6LXB	VRT/SL3/2685	ECW	24368	H43/31F	11/80	Yorkshire Woollen 450	-?-, Tunbridge Wells
	RUA 455W	Bristol	VRT/SL3/6LXB	VRT/SL3/2865	ECW	24373	H43/31F	3/81	Yorkshire Woollen 455	Wiles, Sheffield
	RVM 958W	→ see ESF 678W								
	SAG 520W	MCW	Metrobus DR102/17	MB6019	MCW		H43/30F	2/81	Hull 520	Griffiths, Hull
	SGS 503W	Bedford	YMT	KW451119	Duple	017/2635	C53F	3/81	Prairie, West Drayton	Griffiths, Morriston
	SGS 504W	Leyland	Tiger TRCTL11/3R	8100507	Plaxton	8112LC067	C53F	5/81	Ebdon, Sidcup	Vals, Chase Terrace (ST)
	SLH 3W	→ see 81-C-1619 *Ireland*								
	SNM 441W	→ see 81-LH-379 *Ireland*								
	SNV 933W	Bristol	VRT/SL3/6LXB	VRT/SL3/2465	ECW	24682	H43/31F	8/80	United Counties 933	Ward {Koncpet}, Milton Keynes (BK)
	STW 18W	Leyland	National NL116L11/1R	07210	Leyland National		B49F	10/80	Eastern National 1937	Stebbing, Weeley
			(ex MSU 433, STW 18W)							
	STW 30W	Bristol	VRT/SL3/6LXB	VRT/SL3/2797	ECW	24643	H39/31F	4/81	Eastern National 3086	Payne, Great Sampford
	SUB 793W	Bristol	VRT/SL3/6LXB	VRT/SL3/2843	ECW	24365	H43/31F	3/81	York-West Yorkshire 3769	Mathers & Hitchen, Stockport
	SVV 587W	Leyland	National NL116L11/1R	07142	Leyland National		B49F	9/80	United Counties 587	Knight, Flitwick
	SVV 588W	Leyland	National NL116L11/1R	07205	Leyland National		B49F	10/80	United Counties 588	Billingham, Wisbech
	SVV 589W	Leyland	National NL116L11/1R	07206	Leyland National		B49F	10/80	United Counties 589	Billingham, Wisbech
	TJN 974W	Bedford	YMQ	LW451830	Wadham Stringer	8664/81	DP33F	7/81	Eastern National 1051	Salmon, South Benfleet
	TRO 420W	→ see EYP 29V								
	TYD 911W	Leyland	Leopard PSU3F/5R	8030066	Duple	139/5621	B61F	11/80	Safeway, South Petherton	Woodock, Weymouth
	UAR 597W	Bristol	VRT/SL3/6LXB	VRT/SL3/3005	ECW	24846	H43/31F	7/81	Eastern National 3107	Day, Pebmarsh
	UGB 193W	Leyland	Atlantean AN68A/1R	8100010	Alexander	AL96/4080/1	H45/33F	10/81	Greater Glasgow PTE LA1440	Roulston, Glasgow *(operates as Roulston, Beith (SW))*
	UGB 196W	Leyland	Atlantean AN68A/1R	8100075	Alexander	AL96/4080/4	H45/33F	5/81	Greater Glasgow PTE LA1443	Budd, Glasgow
	UMJ 452W	Bedford	YMQ	KW453710	Plaxton	808QC017/S	C35F	6/81	Harmer, Pevensey Bay	Renown, Bexhill (ES)
	VBM 717W	→ see 81-KK-162 *Ireland*								
	VCA 455W	Bristol	VRT/SL3/6LXB	VRT/SL3/2507	ECW	24515	H43/31F	8/80	Crosville DVG455	Hembry, Sturminster Newton
	VCA 458W	Bristol	VRT/SL3/6LXB	VRT/SL3/2560	ECW	24518	H43/31F	9/80	Crosville DVG458	-?-, Essex
	VCA 463W	Bristol	VRT/SL3/6LXB	VRT/SL3/2565	ECW	24523	H43/31F	9/80	Crosville DVG463	-?-, Lincolnshire
	VVV 952W	Bristol	VRT/SL3/6LXB	VRT/SL3/2880	ECW	24701	H43/31F	4/81	United Counties 952	Fosbury, Blaenau Ffestiniog
	WCA 893W	Ford	R1114	BCRSAR355070	Plaxton	8011FC267	C53F	4/81	Meredith, Malpas	Meredith, Malpas (CH)
			(ex JED 904, WCA 893W)							
	WFS 139W	Leyland	Leopard PSU3F/4R	7930076	Alexander	141AYS/1379/5	B--F	9/80	Alexander Fife FPE139	Todd, Eaglesham
	WFS 145W	Leyland	Leopard PSU3F/4R	7930067	Alexander	141AYS/1379/11	B53F	10/80	Alexander Fife FPE145	Gray, Bearsden
	WFS 153W	→ see 80-CE-449 *Ireland*								
	WNO 115W	Kassbohrer	S215HD	1790000106341	Kassbohrer		C47F	4/81	Kirby, Rayleigh	Kirby, Rayleigh (EX)
	WTU 487W	Bristol	VRT/SL3/501	VRT/SL3/2805	ECW	24547	H43/31F	2/81	Crosville DVL487	Johnson, Hazel Grove
	WWM 904W	Dennis	Dominator	DD120B/222	Willowbrook	792178	H45/33F	7/80	Merseyside PTE 0027	Cammack, Liverpool
	WWM 922W	→ see 80-W-172 *Ireland*								
	XBG 982W	Bedford	CFL	KY625574	Plaxton	80C038CF	C13FL	10/80	Littlewoods, Liverpool	Atkin, North Owersby
	XEM 898W	Leyland	Atlantean AN68C/1R	8002654	Alexander	AL92/780/26	H43/32F	3/81	Merseyside PTE 1898	Bennett, Heswall
	XGO 225W	→ see MIL 9372								
	XLV 140W	Leyland	National NL116AL11/1R	07378	Leyland National		B49F	3/81	Merseyside PTE 6140	North West Museum of Transport

	XLV 156W	Leyland National	NL116AL11/1R	07403	Leyland National		B49F	4/81	Merseyside PTE 6156	Johnson & Hillan, St Helens
	YFS 308W	Leyland National	NL116L11/1R	07317	Leyland National		B48F	1/81	Scottish Omnibuses N308	McGregor, Bathgate
	YFS 310W	Leyland National	NL116L11/1R	07319	Leyland National		B48F	1/81	Scottish Omnibuses N310	McGregor, Bathgate
	YMA 99W	Dennis	Dominator	DD121B/255	Northern Counties	8946	H43/29F	3/81	Chester 99	North West Museum of Transport
	YMB 512W	Bristol	VRT/SL3/6LXB	VRT/SL3/2960	ECW	24799	O43/31F	5/81	Crosville DVG512	Hamer, Oxford
	YUY 94W	Ford	R1114	BCRSAR310800	Plaxton	8011FC201	C53F	8/80	Spring, Evesham	Lear, Ashbury Station
	ABW 82X	Leyland	Leopard PSU3F/5R	8030293	Plaxton	8211LLS6X501	C53F	3/82	Eaglen, Morton	Hayward, Rugeley
			(ex USU 800, DFE 361X)							
	ACL 913X	→ see 82-KE-590 *Ireland*								
	ACM 705X	Leyland	Olympian ONTL11/1R	ON39	ECW	25048	H46/31F	11/81	Merseyside PTE 0031	Sutton, Liverpool
	AFY 187X	Leyland	Atlantean AN68B/1R	7904587	Willowbrook	762201	H45/33F	12/81	Merseyside PTE 1867	Moore & Gouldbourne, Liverpool
	ARP 601X	Leyland	Olympian ONLXB/1R	ON35	ECW	24971	CH45/27F	10/81	United Counties 601	Brown, Worthen
(r)	AVL 745X	Leyland	Leopard PSU3G/4R	8130933	ECW	25085	B53F	3/82	Lincolnshire 1456	-?-, -?-
	BEV 105X	Leyland	Leopard PSU3E/4R	7930037	Plaxton	8011LX567	C53F	1/82	Hedingham & District L105	Easton et al, Brighton
	BTL 485X	→ see JIL 2426								
	CBM 13X	Leyand	Tiger TRCTL11/3R	8108536	Plaxton	8212LTS6C005	C46FT	5/82	Premier, Watford	Ferguson, Todmorden
	CKB 166X	Leyland National	NL116AL11/1R	07643	Leyland National		B49F	4/82	Merseyside PTE 6169	Foster S, Darlington
	CKC 625X	→ see DEM 269X								
	CUS 302X	Leyland	Atlantean AN68A/1R	8100077	Alexander	AL96/4080/9	H45/33F	10/81	Strathclyde PTE LA1448	Transport Preservation Trust, Beith
										(operates as Roulston, Beith (SW))
	DEM 269X	Leyland	Tiger TRCTL11/2R	8103095	Duple	234/5330	C--F	6/82	Merseyside PTE 7010	Cammack, Liverpool
			(ex VKB 708, CKC 625X)							
	DFE 361X	→ see ABW 82X								
	EFW 215X	→ see 82-C-1941 *Ireland*								
	FCA 10X	Leyland National	NL116AL11/2R	07620	Leyland National		B48D	2/82	Crosville SNL10	Howard, Great Sankey
	FGE 423X	Dennis	Dominator	DD137B/448	Alexander	RL6/581/2	H45/34F	6/82	Central SMT D23	Anderson, Airdrie
	FHS 757X	→ see 82-DL-1355 *Ireland*								
	FTR 268X	Leyland	Atlantean AN68C/1R	8100710	East Lancs	905	H40/31F	10/81	Southampton 268	Savin, Southampton
	FTR 270X	Leyland	Atlantean AN68C/1R	8100749	East Lancs	904	H40/31F	10/81	Southampton 270	Cook, Southampton
	FTR 271X	Leyland	Atlantean AN68C/1R	8100763	East Lancs	901	H40/31F	9/81	Southampton 271	393 Group, Southampton
	GCA 126X	→ see NTH 263X								
	GFM 104X	Leyland	Olympian ONLXB/1R	ON315	ECW	25246	H45/32F	9/82	Crosville DOG104	Plant, Newcastle-under-Lyme
	GSC 621X	Leyland	Atlantean AN68C/1R	8100318	Alexander	AL98/3180/1	H43/30D	9/81	Lothian 621	-?-, -?-
	GSC 637X	Leyland	Atlantean AN68C/1R	8100555	Alexander	AL98/3180/17	H45/30F	8/81	Lothian 637	-?-, -?-
	GSC 658X	Leyland	Atlantean AN68C/1R	8100750	Alexander	AL98/3180/38	H45/30D	10/81	Lothian 658	Wilson, Warrington
	GSC 659X	Leyland	Atlantean AN68C/1R	8100670	Alexander	AL98/3180/39	H45/30D	10/81	Lothian 659	Gifford Transport Group
	GSC 667X	Leyland	Olympian ONTL11/1R	ON42	Alexander	RH6/2579/2	H47/28D	4/82	Lothian 667	Lothian Bus Consortium
	HSC 166X	→ see AY 593 *Alderney*								
	HSC 173X	Leyland	Cub CU435	566476	Duple	137/5564	B31F	12/81	Lothian 173	National Museums of Scotland
										(*in the care of the Lothian Bus Consortium*)
	HSR 46X	Volvo	B55-10	81123	Alexander	RV3/2179/11	H48/36F	11/81	Tayside 46	Taybus Vintage Vehicle Society
	HUF 604X	Leyland National	NL116AL11/1R	07607	Leyland National		B49F	1/82	Southdown 135	Pearce, Worthing
			(ex 405 DCD, RUF 435X)							
	JFT 412X	Bedford	YMQ	LW451799	Duple	115/2100	C45F	8/81	Greaves, Annitsford	Dew, Somersham (CM)
	JFT 413X	Scania	BR112DH	1801922	Alexander	RH8/4380/1	H47/32F	3/82	Tyne & Wear PTE 413	Buckley & Minto, Newcastle upon Tyne
			(ex RND 882X, JIL 8211, JFT 413X)							
	JTY 403X	Leyland	Olympian ONLXB/1R	ON173	ECW	25008	H45/32F	1/82	Northern General 3603	Johnson, Tynemouth

	KEP 829X	Leyland	National NL116AL11/1R	07598	Leyland National		B44F	12/81	South Wales 829	Hier, Swansea
	KSX 102X	Leyland	National NL116AL11/2R	07650	Leyland National		B42D	3/82	Lothian 102	Lothian Bus Consortium
(z)	KSX 103X	Leyland	National NL116AL11/2R	07651	Leyland National		B42D	3/82	Lothian 103	Coyle, Livingston
	KWO 569X	Bristol	LHS6L	LHS-402	ECW	25063	DP27F	9/81	National Welsh MD8115	Britishbus Preservation Group
			(ex 19676, 19678, KWO 569X)							
	KYN 306X	Leyland	Titan TNLXB2RR	0355	Leyland		H44/24D	9/81	London Transport T306	Delaney, London
	KYV 334X	Leyland	Titan TNLXB2RR	0383	Leyland		H44/24F	10/81	London Transport T334	Bolton, Hull
	KYV 339X	Leyland	Titan TNLXB2RR	0388	Leyland		H39/30F	10/81	London Transport T339	Rishworth, Worcester
	KYV 358X	Leyland	Titan TNLXB2RR	0407	Leyland		H44/24D	11/81	London Transport T358	Merryweather Longmire & Mortock, Peterborough
	KYV 341X	→ see IUI 2142								
	KYV 424X	Leyland	Titan TNLXB2RR	0473	Leyland		H39/30F	2/82	London Transport T424	Goulbourne, Liverpool
	KYV 447X	Leyland	Titan TNLXB2RR	0497	Leyland		H44/24D	3/82	London Transport T447	Brown, Romford
	KYV 451X	→ see 82-D-2970 *Ireland*								
	KYV 506X	Leyland	Titan TNLXB2RR	0556	Leyland		H44/24D	7/82	London Transport T506	Doyle, -?-
	KYV 531X	Leyland	Titan TNLXB2RR	0581	Leyland		H44/24D	7/82	London Transport T531	Ladd, Iver
	KYV 532X	→ see 82-MH-641 *Ireland*								
	KYV 781X	MCW	Metrobus DR101/14	MB6693	MCW		H43/28D	3/82	London Transport M781	Conn & Gurr, Cumbernauld
	KYV 792X	MCW	Metrobus DR101/14	MB6704	MCW		H43/28D	3/82	London Transport M792	Cade, London
	LBO 11X	→ see MIW 5795								
	LCY 299X	→ see YLW 895X								
	LEC 197X	→ see SUX 476X								
	LEC 646X	→ see 222 VPI *Ireland*								
	LFR 855X	→ see SIB 6706								
	LFR 866X	Leyland	National NL106AL11/R	07562	Leyland National		B44F	12/81	Ribble 866	Davies, West Kirby
	LKG 19X	→ see CSV 253								
	NDW 141X	Leyland	Tiger TRCTL11/2R	8101877	Plaxton	8211LTS6X503	C53F	3/82	Hill, Tredegar	Evans, Bargoed
			(ex MIL 6897, NDW 141X)							
	NDW 146X	→ see 82-C-1636 *Ireland*								
	NDW 147X	Leyland	Tiger TRCTL11/2R	8102831	Plaxton	8211LTS6X509	C53F	3/82	Hills, Tredegar	Skinner, Tredegar
			(ex 505 AYB, NDW 147X)							
	NDW 407X	Volvo	B55-10	81175	Northern Counties	2108	H39/35F	3/82	Cardiff 407	Cardiff Transport Preservation Group
	NKU 144X	Dennis	Dominator	DDA133/368	Alexander	RH1/3179/44	H46/32F	12/81	South Yorkshire PTE 2144	Griffiths, Chesterfield
	NKU 214X	Dennis	Dominator	DDA133/488	Alexander	RH1/3179/114	H46/32F	6/82	South Yorkshire PTE 2214	Penney, Blackpool
	NKU 245X	Leyland	National NL116AL11/1R	07548	Leyland National		B52F	10/81	Yorkshire Traction 245	Jessop, Keighley
										(operates as Keighley Bus Museum, Keighley (WY))
	NOA 462X	MCW	Metrobus DR102/27	MB6793	MCW		H43/30F	7/82	West Midlands PTE 2462	Walcott, Birmingham
	NTH 263X	Leyland	Tiger TRCTL11/2R	8102613	Plaxton	8211LTV4X912	C53F	3/82	Roberts, Cefn	-?- ,-?-
			(ex 7 WTJ, SNT 808X, 6052 VT, GCA 126X)							
	OCW 8X	Leyland	Atlantean AN68C/1R	8102208	East Lancs	A2503	H43/31F	4/82	Blackburn 8	Boden, Harlaston
	ODL 525X	Bedford	YNT	LW452607	Plaxton	8111TC051	C53F	8/81	Moss, Sandown	Morgan-Huws, Whitwell
	OFV 620X	Leyland	National NL116AL11/1R	07599	Leyland National		B49F	12/81	Fishwick, Leyland 16	Fishwick, Leyland (LA) 16
	OFV 621X	Leyland	National NL116AL11/1R	07600	Leyland National		B49F	12/81	Fishwick, Leyland 26	SWI, Cullompton (XDN)
										(*rallied by Fishwick National 2 Group, Cullompton*)
	OHE 275X	→ see 83-C-2836 *Ireland*								
	OPS 550X	Bedford	YMQ	LW451538	Duple	151/1575	C35F	9/81	Mills, Baltasound	Leighfield, Grittenham
	PAJ 829X	Bristol	VRT/SL3/6LXB	VRT/SL3/3062	ECW	24868	H43/31F	9/81	United 829	Dolan M, Crook
	PEF 6X	Bedford	VAS5	LW453449	Duple	111/1000	DP31F	9/81	Stanhope Motor Services	Fowler, Holbeach Drove (LI)
	PFV 819X	→ see 3680 MN *Isle of Man*								

Registration	Chassis	Model	Chassis no.	Body	Body no.	Seating	New	First operator	Current owner
PPH 277X	Leyland	Leopard PSU5C/4R	8030338	Duple	235/5412	C57F	1/82	Cowdrey, Gosport	-?-, Bedford
PWF 514X	Ford	Transit	-?-	Dormobile	-?-	B10FL	4/82	Derbyshire Ambulance Service	Rother Valley Road Transport Society
RDL 309X	Leyland	Leopard PSU3G/4R	8131532	ECW	25355	C51F	5/82	Southern Vectis 309	Isle of Wight Bus Museum
		(ex TDL 483X, VDL 263, RDL 309X)							
RDT 121X	→ see 82-KK-487 *Ireland*								
RNU 433X	Leyland	Atlantean AN68C/1R	8100387	Northern Counties	2078	H47/31D	10/81	Nottingham 433	Nottingham Heritage Vehicles
RRM 386X	Leyland	National NL116AL11/1R	07572	Leyland National		B52F	12/81	Cumberland 386	McGregor, Bathgate
RRM 634X	Leyland	Leopard PSU3G/4R	8130752	ECW	25077	C49F	3/82	Cumberland 634	Forbes, Angus
RTV 438X	Leyland	Atlantean AN68C/1R	8100506	Northern Counties	2083	H47/33D	10/81	Nottingham 438	Combellack, Nottingham
RTV 442X	Leyland	Atlantean AN68C/1R	8100280	Northern Counties	2087	H47/33D	11/81	Nottingham 442	Nottingham Heritage Vehicles
RUF 435X	→ see HUF 604X								
SCH 116X	Leyland	Fleetline FE30ALR	8002297	ECW	25066	H44/31F	12/81	South Notts, Gotham 116	Roberts, Crewe
		(ex XAZ 1410, SCH 116X)							
SHH 389X	Leyland	National NL116AL11/1R	07626	Leyland National		B52F	2/82	Cumberland 389	Campbell & Devine, Paisley
SHH 392X	→ see 82-D-2899 *Ireland*								
SKL 681X	Bristol	VRT/SL3/6LXB	VRT/SL3/3063	ECW	24914	H41/31F	9/81	East Kent 7681	Bamford, Ramsgate
SNC 365X	Leyland	Leopard PSU3C/4R	8030044	Plaxton	8112LC075	C57F	4/82	Mayne, Manchester 65	Hughes, Widnes
		(ex MJI 5765, SNC 365X)							
SND 120X	MCW	Metrobus DR102/23	MB6257	MCW		H43/30F	10/81	Greater Manchester PTE 5120	Amis, Manchester
SND 455X	Leyland	Atlantean AN68B/1R	8101435	Northern Counties	2173	H0/21F	11/81	Greater Manchester PTE 8455	SELNEC Preservation Society
SND 460X	Leyland	Atlantean AN68B/1R	8100971	Northern Counties	2178	H43/32F	12/81	Greater Manchester PTE 8460	MacKay, Bolton
SND 501X	Leyland	Atlantean AN68B/1R	8102830	Northern Counties	2228	H43/32F	5/82	Greater Manchester PTE 8501	SELNEC Preservation Society
SND 508X	Leyland	Atlantean AN68B/1R	8102210	Northern Counties	2235	H43/32F	5/82	Greater Manchester PTE 8508	SELNEC Preservation Society
SND 550X	Bristol	LHS6L	LHS-395	East Lancs	806	B32F	6/82	Rossendale 50	Roberts, Bury
SRC 114X	→ see 82-LS-323 *Ireland*								
SSA 5X	Leyland	Olympian ONLXB/1R	ON6	Alexander	RL3/1980/4	H45/32F	10/81	Alexander Northern NLO5	Bieniowski, Edinburgh
STO 244X	Leyland	Leopard PSU3F/5R	8030220	Plaxton	8111LC017	C53F	3/82	Wilfreda, Ranskill	Leyland Leopard Group, Evesham
STT 605X	→ see 81-C-1617 *Ireland*								
SUX 476X	Leyland	Tiger TRCTL11/3R	8101282	Plaxton	8212LTS5C023	C49FT	2/82	Robinson, Great Harwood 197	Fudge Rushton & Berry, Stoke-on-Trent
		(ex OIW 7027, LEC 197X)							
TBC 50X	Dennis	Dominator	DDA142/350	East Lancs	426	H43/33F	1/82	Leicester 50	Leicester Transport Heritage Trust
TMS 403X	Leyland	Leopard PSU3G/4R	8130120	Alexander	150AYS/2280/1	DP49F	1/82	Alexander Midland MPE403	McCormick, Dumbarton
TMS 408X	Leyland	Leopard PSU3G/4R	8130188	Alexander	150AYS/2280/6	DP49F	1/82	Alexander Midland MPE408	McKerracher, Stirling
TND 128X	Volvo	B58-61	16755	Duple	249/8100	C53F	4/82	Smith, Wigan 128	-?-, -?-
		(ex GIL 6240, TND 128X)							
TPC 111X	→ see TJI 7514								
TPD 109X	Leyland	Olympian ONTL11/1R	ON215	Roe	GO8599	H43/29F	5/82	London Country LR9	Knorn, Ruabon
TPL 762X	Leyland	Tiger TRBTL11/2R	8101065	Plaxton	8211LTS5X512	C53F	4/82	Tillinbourne Bus, Cranleigh	-?-, -?-
TSO 16X	Leyland	Olympian ONLXB/1R	ON191	ECW	25268	H45/32F	2/82	Alexander Northern NLO16	Denman, Erskine
TTT 168X	Leyland	Atlantean AN68C/1R	8100972	East Lancs	A2806	H43/31F	12/81	Plymouth 168	Hudson, Plymouth
TTT 170X	Leyland	Atlantean AN68C/1R	8101066	East Lancs	A2802	H43/31F	12/81	Plymouth 170	Allen & Beverley, Plymouth
TTT 171X	Leyland	Atlantean AN68C/1R	8101074	East Lancs	A2809	H43/31F	12/81	Plymouth 171	Plymouth City Transport Preservation Group
TVH 136X	Ford	R1014	BCRSAS412500	Plaxton	828FTS5C003	C35F	4/82	Traject {Abbeyways}, Huddersfield	Hall, Buckie
		(ex 699 WAE, TVH 136X)							
UBC 644X	Ford	R1114	BCRSAL262060	Plaxton	8211FTS5C018	C53F	2/82	Allenways, Birmingham	Snaith, Otterburn (ND)
UJT 987X	Bedford	YMT	KW452432	Plaxton	8111TC047	C53F	3/82	Ellison, Ashton Keynes	Webb, Armscote (WK)
UKE 609X	Ford	R192	BC04MA48061	Duple	121/4082	C45F	8/72	Davie, Rye	Handley, Leek
		(ex EUR 358K)		*(rebodied 9/81)*					

UKK 419X	Ford	Transit	BDVPBM06757	Robin Hood		C16F	9/81	Eglinton, Sittingbourne	-?-, -?-
ULS 615X	MCW	Metrobus DR102/28	MB6719	Alexander	RL5/681/2	H45/33F	3/82	Alexander Midland MRM15	Docherty & Gray, Glasgow
ULS 640X	MCW	Metrobus DR104/10	MB6744	Alexander	RL5/681/27	H45/33F	7/82	Alexander Midland MRM40	Duncan, Cumbernauld
ULS 714X	Leyland	Leopard PSU3G/4R	8131640	Alexander	23AT/1581/2	C49F	4/82	Alexander Midland MPE414	Smith, Bearsden
ULS 716X	Leyland	Leopard PSU3G/4R	8131676	Alexander	23AT/1581/4	C49F	4/82	Alexander Midland MPE416	Bryce & Quinn, Falkirk
ULS 717X	Leyland	Leopard PSU3G/4R	8131868	Alexander	23AT/1581/5	C49F	4/82	Alexander Midland MPE417	Booth & Thomas, Glasgow
URS 318X	Leyland	Atlantean AN68C/1R	8102767	Alexander	AL99/880/3	O45/29D	5/82	Grampian 318	Aberdeen & District Transport Preservation Trust
URS 321X	Leyland	Atlantean AN68C/1R	8102956	Alexander	AL99/880/6	PO45/29F	5/82	Grampian 321	Roulston, Glasgow *(operates as Roulston, Beith (SW))*
UVT 49X	Bristol	VRT/SL3/6LXB	VRT/SL3/3101	ECW	25065	CH41/29F	10/81	Stevenson, Spath 49	Roberts, Sheffield
UWW 7X	Leyland	Olympian ONLXB/1R	ON102	Roe	GO8540	H47/29F	3/82	West Yorkshire PTE 5007	Rogers, Swindon
UWW 9X	Leyland	Olympian ONLXB/1R	ON111	Roe	GO8542	H47/29F	3/82	West Yorkshire PTE 5009	-?-, Leeds
		(ex CMN 45C *Isle of Man*, UWW 9X)							
UWW 13X	Leyland	Olympian ONLXB/1R	ON122	Roe	GO8546	H47/29F	3/82	West Yorkshire PTE 5013	Clitheroe, Bromley
VEX 291X	Bristol	VRT/SL3/6LXB	VRT/SL3/3097	ECW	24939	CH41/25F	11/81	Eastern Counties VR291	Hales & Bloomfield, Wem
VEX 294X	Bristol	VRT/SL3/6LXB	VRT/SL3/3100	ECW	24942	H43/31F	10/81	Eastern Counties VR294	Carters, Wherstead (SK)
VEX 295X	Bristol	VRT/SL3/6LXB	VRT/SL3/2976	ECW	24777	H43/31F	8/81	Eastern Counties VR295	Routespek, Earsham (NK)
VJO 201X	Leyland	Olympian ONLXB/1R	ON253	ECW	25138	H47/28D	6/82	City of Oxford 201	Wareham, Kidlington
VJT 606X	→ see 82-KE-588 *Ireland*								
VJT 621X	→ see 82-D-2091 *Ireland*								
VOY 182X	Leyland	Tiger TRCTL11/2R	8101609	Plaxton	8211LTV4X904	C49F	12/81	British Airways, Heathrow C315	TM Travel (SY)
VPR 17X	Bedford	YNT	LW452403	Plaxton	8211NTS5C018	C53F	4/82	South Dorset, Swanage	MacLean, Portnockie
VUD 30X	Leyland	Leopard PSU3G/4R	8131609	ECW	25358	C47F	4/82	City of Oxford 30	Clements et al, Oxford
VVH 1X	→ see 82-D-2571 *Ireland*								
WAG 371X	→ see XAZ 1362								
WAG 376X	Leyland	Atlantean AN68C/1R	8003600	Roe	GO8494	H43/31F	2/82	Hull 376	Griffiths, Hull
WDD 17X	Bedford	YNT	LW453085	Plaxton	8211NTS6X507	C53F	2/82	Beard, Cinderford	Andrews, Waterlooville
WKE 360X	→ see 82-C-2012 *Ireland*								
WKH 526X	Bristol	VRT/SL3/6LXB	VRT/SL3/3057	ECW	24877	H43/31F	11/81	East Yorkshire 526	Hull Bus Restorers, Hull
WRJ 448X	Volvo	B55-10	80048	Northern Counties	2162	H45/32F	5/82	Greater Manchester 1448	SELNEC Preservation Society
		(ex MIL 8338, WRJ 448X)							
WWL 209X	Leyland	Olympian ONLXB/1R	ON293	ECW	25146	H47/28D	6/82	City of Oxford 209	Hull & Country Bus Preservation Group
XAG 206X	→ see 81-TS-407 *Ireland*								
XGS 771X	Leyland	Leopard PSU3E/4R	7903636	Duple	033/5168	C53F	9/81	Goldon Boy, Roydon	Penforth-Ivany, -?-
		(ex YKP 975X, YSU 873, XGS 771X)							
XHK 221X	Bristol	VRT/SL3/6LXB	VRT/SL3/3032	ECW	24901	H43/31F	10/81	Eastern National 3116	Abus, Bristol (GL)
XHK 228X	Bristol	VRT/SL3/6LXB	VRT/SL3/3043	ECW	24908	H43/31F	11/81	Eastern National 3123	Brown, Worthen
XHK 234X	Bristol	VRT/SL3/6LXB	VRT/SL3/3088	ECW	24930	H43/31F	12/81	Eastern National 3129	Harrison, Chelmsford
XUA 73X	Leyland	National NL116AL11/1R	07629	Leyland National		B49F	1/82	West Riding 73	West Riding Omnibus Preservation Society
		(fitted with a Gardner 6HLXB engine)							
YKP 975X	→ see XGS 771X								
YLW 895X	Bedford	YMQ	LW452511	Lex	0955	B37F	11/81	South Wales 299	-?-, Swansea
		(ex RIB 7018, GGK 236X, SVO 89, LCY 299X)							
YNW 33X	Leyland	Leopard PSU3E/4R	8030027	Plaxton	8011LC024	C53F	3/82	Shilton, Leeds	-?-, -?-
AFL 534Y	→ see 82-CN-149 *Ireland*								
ALS 102Y	Leyland	Tiger TRBTL11/2R	8201429	Alexander	27AT/682/1	C49F	1/83	Alexander Midland MPT102	Moore, Falkirk
		(ex FSU 382, ALS 102Y)							

	Reg	Make	Model	Chassis no	Body	Body no	Layout	New	First owner	Current owner
	ANA 1Y	Leyland	Olympian ONTL11/1R	ON475	Northern Counties	2386	H43/30F	10/82	Greater Manchester PTE 3001	SELNEC Preservation Society
	ANA 8Y	Leyland	Olympian ONTL11/1R	ON572	Northern Counties	2393	H43/30F	7/83	Greater Manchester PTE 3008	Wilson, Warrington
(r)	ANA 9Y	Leyland	Olympian ONTL11/1R	ON595	Northern Counties	2394	H43/30F	7/83	Greater Manchester PTE 3009	SELNEC Preservation Society
	ANA 10Y	Leyland	Olympian ONTL11/1R	ON606	Northern Counties	2395	H43/30F	7/83	Greater Manchester PTE 3010	SELNEC Preservation Society
	ANA 114Y	→ see LIL 7804								
	ANA 447Y	DAF	MB200DKFL600 (ex 6185 RU, ANA 447Y)	233289	Plaxton	8312DKP1C19N	C51F	4/83	Jackson, Altrincham	Lee, Herne Bay
	ANA 551Y	Leyland	Atlantean AN68D/1R	8200488	Northern Counties	2284	H43/32F	9/82	Greater Manchester PTE 8551	Owen & Cox, Wigan
	ANA 564Y	Leyland	Atlentean AN68D/1R	8200842	Northern Counties	2297	H43/32F	10/82	Greater Manchester PTE 8564	Holmes & Clarke, Blackburn
	ANA 568Y	Leyland	Atlantean AN68D/1R	8200877	Northern Counties	2301	H43/32F	10/82	Greater Manchester PTE 8568	Graham, Carlisle
	ANA 601Y	Leyland	Atlantean AN68D/1R	8201009	Northern Counties	2334	H43/32F	12/82	Greater Manchester PTE 8601	SELNEC Preservation Society
	ANA 622Y	Leyland	Atlantean AN68D/1R	8201200	Northern Counties	2368	H43/32F	2/83	Greater Manchester PTE 8622	Worrall, Swinton
	ANA 645Y	Leyland	Atlantean AN68D/1R	8300316	Northern Counties	2433	H43/32F	6/83	Greater Manchester PTE 8645	Worrall, Swinton
	BAC 551Y	→ see FLD 447Y								
	BBW 214Y	Leyland	Olympian ONLXB/1R	ON352	ECW	25151	H47/28D	10/82	City of Oxford 214	Oxford Bus Museum Trust
	BFV 222Y	→ see RIL 9158								
	BRW 738Y	DAF	SB2005DHU605	200557	Plaxton	8212DRS4C009	C53F	8/82	Smith, Wilmcote	Smith, Welford-on-Avon
(r)	BUT 19Y	Leyland	Tiger TRCTL11/2R	8300226	Plaxton	8311LTP1X542	C49F	6/83	Leicester 19	McCombie, Monifieth
	CBV 775Y	Leyland	Royal Tiger RT (ex 544 UYD, CBV 775Y, XHG 245Y)	B50-04	Leyland		C53F	9/82	Leyland test rig	Workington Transport Heritage Trust
	CKE 170Y	→ see 82-C-2154 *Ireland*								
	CLJ 413Y	Bristol	LHS6L	LHS-408	Plaxton	828BSS5C012	C33F	3/83	Bere Regis, Dorchester	Hampshire Bus & Coach Preservation Group
	CUB 24Y	Leyland	Olympian ONLXB/1R	ON395	Roe	GO8654	H47/29F	10/82	West Yorkshire PTE 5024	Harrogate Coach, Green Hammerton (NY)
	DAD 798Y	Leyland	Leopard PSUC3C/4R (ex NNK 817P)	7504521	Plaxton	7611LC013	C53F	4/76	Frames, London	Macey, Luton
	DEM 762Y	MCW	Metrobus DR102/29	MB6756	Alexander	RH12/1881/7	H45/33F	9/82	Merseyside PTE 0062	Yeo, Merseyside
	DEM 779Y	Leyland	Atlantean AN68D/1R	8200450	Alexander	AL100/1981/12	H43/32F	8/82	Merseyside PTE 1979	-?-, St Helens
	DEM 789Y	Leyland	Atlantean AN68D/1R	8200605	Alexander	AL100/1981/22	H43/32F	9/82	Merseyside PTE 1989	-?-, -?-
	DEM 822Y	Volvo	B55-10	82201	Alexander	RV6/2081/2	H45/34F	8/82	Merseyside PTE 0055	-?-, Liverpool
	DRN 177Y	Leyland	Atlantean AN68D/2R	8300541	East Lancs	A3214	H50/36F	7/83	Preston 177	-?-, Carlisle
	EEH 902Y	Leyland	Olympian ONLXB/1R	ON712	ECW	25626	H45/32F	6/83	Midland Red North 1902	-?-, Launceston
	EEH 905Y	Leyland	Olympian ONLXB/1R	ON750	ECW	25629	H45/32F	7/83	Midland Red North 1905	Riley, Tamwoth
	EFD 923Y	Volvo	B10M-61	003764	Duple	349/7004	C57F	4/83	FHW, Willenhall	York Pullman, York (NY)
	EKA 220Y	Leyland	Tiger TRCTL11/2R	8102859	Duple	234/5339	C49F	8/82	Merseyside PTE 7020	Cammack, Liverpool
	EKA 224Y	Dennis	Lancet	SD510/118	Duple	356/5712	DP31F	3/83	Merseyside PTE 7024	Collier & Soley, Ince
	EWW 544Y	Leyland	Olympian ONLXB/1R (ex 544 WRA, EWW 544Y)	ON807	ECW	25584	H45/32F	7/83	West Riding 544	-?-, -?-
	FAH 275Y	Volvo	B10M-61	003383	Plaxton	8212VTS5C008	C57F	4/83	Smith, Wood Norton	Joplin, Tittleshall (NK)
	FKK 845Y	MCW	Metroliner CR126/2 (ex 620 UKM, FKK 845Y)	MB7229	MCW		C51F	5/83	East Kent 8845	Mackintosh, Birmingham
	FKK 846Y	→ see UIB 5303								
	FLD 447Y	Bedford	YMP (ex RIB 7002, BAC 551Y)	CT104410	Plaxton	828MQS5C001	C35F	8/82	Bonas, Coventry	Knox, Glasgow
	FNM 853Y	→ see 83-C-17 *Ireland*								
	FRU 675Y	Leyland	Tiger TRCTL11/3R (ex RIB 8744, KGS 490Y)	8200996	Plaxton	8312LTH1C922	C50F	6/83	Travellers, Hounslow	Reynolds, Mangotsfield
	FWH 461Y	Scania	BR112DH	1802093	Northern Counties	2166	H43/32F	3/83	Greater Manchester PTE 1461	SELNEC Preservation Society
	GEX 790Y	Bova	Europa EL26/581	2153	Bova		C53F	5/83	Bird, Hunstanton	Moseley (PCV), South Elmsall

	GKE 442Y	Leyland	Olympian ONTL11/2Rsp	ON758	ECW	25684	CH45/28F	6/83	Maidstone & District 5442	-?-, -?-
	GTA 528Y	Volvo	B58-56	16371	Plaxton	8011VC054	C53F	5/83	Heard, Hartland	-?-, Plymouth
	HEX 326Y	Mercedes-Benz	O305	30700013039397	Behr		B38D	-/83	Solingen 173	Ward & Pearson, Enfield
			(ex SG SW123 *Germany*)							
	HHJ 376Y	Leyland	Tiger TRCTL11/2R	8300013	Alexander	2TE/2382/5	C53F	3/83	Eastern National 1115	-?-, -?-
	JDY 888Y	Bedford	VAS5	CT104531	Plaxton	838PJS4C001	C29F	1/83	Rowland & Goodwin, St Leonards	Rambler, Hastings (ES)
	KBD 453Y	Bedford	VAL14	6875971	Plaxton	672486	C--F	5/67	Homerton Coaches, Homerton	Cochrane, Christchurch
			(ex RUW 990E)							
	KGB 361Y	Ford	R1014	BCRSAY402910	Plaxton	818FC005	C35F	8/82	Southern, Barrhead	Hearson, Chesterton
	KGS 490Y	→ see FRU 675Y								
	KOW 274Y	Leyland	Atlantean AN68C/1R	8200618	East Lancs	907	H40/31F	11/82	Southampton 274	Blair, Upham
	KTL 44Y	Leyland	Olympian ONLXB/2R	ON527	East Lancs	613	H50/35F	12/82	Lincoln 44	Hanslip, Peacehaven
	KTL 45Y	Leyland	Olympian ONLXB/2R	ON528	East Lancs	615	H50/35F	12/82	Lincoln 45	Lincolnshire Vintage Vehicle Society
	KVJ 291Y	Bedford	CFL	CV614523	Plaxton	82C041CF	C17F	2/82	Hill, Hereford	Golynia, Long Melford
	LEO 734Y	Leyland	Atlantean AN68D/1R	8201528	Northern Counties	2476	H43/32F	2/83	Barrow 104	Barrow Transport Museum
	LEO 735Y	Leyland	Atlantean AN68D/1R	8201530	Northern Counties	2477	H43/32F	2/83	Barrow 105	Barrow Transport Museum
	LHO 992Y	Leyland	Tiger TRCTL11/2R	8200546	Plaxton	8311LTP1X503	C53F	3/83	Trimdon Motor Services	Dolan A, Crook
			(ex TBC 658, LHO 992Y)							
	LUS 436Y	Leyland	Leopard PSU3G/4R	8230952	Alexander	157AYS/1181/6	B—F	1/83	Central SMT T436	Glasgow Vintage Vehicle Trust
	LWS 34Y	Leyland	Olympian ONLXB/1R	ON389	Roe	GO8639	H47/29F	9/82	Bristol 9518	Minnett, Stroud
	MDS 217Y	→ see 83-C-1899 *Ireland*								
	MEU 603Y	→ see IIL 4317								
	MNS 10Y	Leyland	Tiger TRBTL11/2R	8300001	Alexander	4TE/1282/4	C47F	4/83	Central SMT LT10	Robertson, Rosyth
	MNS 45Y	Dennis	Dominator	DD162/594	Alexander	RL7/982/4	PO45/34F	3/83	Cental SMT D45	Cooper, Ipswich
	NBD 103Y	→ see CIL 5626								
	NFS 170Y	Leyland	Leopard PSU3G/4R	8230065	Alexander	24AT/881/1	C49F	10/82	Alexander Fife FPE170	Gifford Transport Group
	NFS 175Y	Leyland	Leopard PSU3G/4R	8230168	Alexander	24AT/881/6	C49F	10/82	Alexander Fife FPE175	Davidson & Houston, Glasgow
	NFS 176Y	Leyland	Leopard PSU3G/4R	8230194	Alexander	24AT/881/7	C49F	10/82	Alexander Fife FPE176	Clark, Dunipace
	NTC 135Y	Leyland	Olympian ONLXB/1R	ON731	Roe	GO8736	H47/29F	5/83	Bristol 9536	Kells Transport Museum, Cork
	NUW 553Y	→ see HIG 5681								
	NUW 567Y	Leyland	Titan TNLXB2RR	0617	Leyland		H44/24D	11/82	London Transport T567	London Transport Museum
	NUW 636Y	Leyland	Titan TNLXB2RR	0686	Leyland		H44/26D	12/82	London Transport T636	Cornish, Hendon
	OHV 684Y	Leyland	Titan TNLXB2RR	0734	Leyland		H44/26D	2/83	London Transport T684	Griffin, Bromley
	OHV 762Y	Leyland	Titan TNLXB2RR	0822	Leyland		H44/27D	4/83	London Transport T762	Transport Preservation Trust, Beith
	OHV 806Y	Leyland	Titan TNLXB2RR	0866	Leyland		H44/26D	7/83	London Transport T806	Colin, Chesterfield
	OSN 852Y	Volvo	B55-10	82233	Northern Counties	2425	H48/36F	4/83	Tayside 52	Patrickson, Wigan
	OSN 862Y	Volvo	B55-10	82242	East Lancs	A3702	H48/36F	5/83	Tayside 62	Fisher, Dundee
(r)	OSN 875Y	Volvo	B55-10	82255	East Lancs	A3715	H48/36F	5/83	Tayside 75	Fisher & Patrickson, Dundee
	POG 516Y	MCW	Metrobus DR102/27	MB6917	MCW		H43/30F	9/82	West Midlands PTE 2516	Bolton, Hull
	PSF 316Y	Leyland	Tiger TRBTL11/2R	8200389	Alexander	25AT/2381/6	C49F	12/82	Eastern Scottish ZH316	Docherty, Edinburgh
	PSX 186Y	Leyland	Leopard PSU3G/4R	8230780	Alexander	154AYS/981/7	B53F	12/82	Alexander Fife FPE186	-?-, Edinburgh
(r)	PSX 188Y	Leyland	Leopard PSU3G/4R	8230874	Alexander	154AYS/981/9	B53F	12/82	Alexander Fife FPE188	Campbell & Todd, Glasgow
	PSX 189Y	Leyland	Leopard PSU3G/4R	8230968	Alexander	154AYS/981/10	B53F	12/82	Alexander Fife FPE189	group, Dunfermline
	PWO 87Y	Leyland	Leopard PSU4G/2R	8230937	East Lancs	-?-	B45F	11/82	Rhymney Valley 87	Edwards, Cardiff
	PUL 91Y	→ see RIW 8799								
	RBO 510Y	Leyland	Olympian ONLXB/1R	ON487	East Lancs	2904	H43/29F	2/83	Cardiff 510	Cardiff Transport Preservation Group
	RCY 119Y	→ see 83-CW-273 *Ireland*								
	RMO 76Y	Leyland	Titan TNLXC1RF	0778	Leyland		H39/27F	3/83	Reading 76	Rampton, Reading

	RMO 202Y	→ see BKZ 2460								
	RMO 203Y	Leyland	Tiger TRCTL11/2R	8201621	Plaxton	8311LTP1X517	C53F	3/83	Reading 203	Rampton, Reading
			(ex EDZ 215, RMO 203Y)							
	ROX 618Y	MCW	Metrobus DR102/27	MB7116	MCW		H43/30F	2/83	West Midlands PTE 2618	23 Group, Coventry
	RSC 190Y	Leyland	Leopard PSU3G/4R	8230969	Alexander	26AT/582/1	C49F	12/82	Alexander Fife FPE190	Aitken & Baird, Edinburgh
	RSC 192Y	Leyland	Leopard PSU3G/4R	8231121	Alexander	26AT/582/3	C49F	12/82	Alexander Fife FPE192	-?-, Kilmarnock
	RSC 194Y	Leyland	Leopard PSU3G/4R	8231150	Alexander	26AT/582/5	C49F	12/82	Alexander Fife FPE194	Robertson, Rosyth
	SBL 70Y	Leyland	Titan TNLXB2RR	0752	Leyland		H44/28F	2/83	Reading 70	Rampton, Reading
	SDT 249Y	Dennis	Dominator	DDA133/548	Alexander	RH1/3179/149	H46/32F	10/82	South Yorkshire PTE 2249	O'Reilly, Sheffield
	SDT 260Y	Dennis	Dominator	DDA133/561	Alexander	RH1/3179/160	H46/32F	11/82	South Yorkshire PTE 2260	Penney, Blackpool
	SJR 612Y	Leyland	Olympian ONLXB/1R	ON378	ECW	25125	H--/--F	12/82	Northern General 3612	Buckley Walker & Minto, Newcastle upon Tyne
	SSG 321Y	→ see 83-TS-530 *Ireland*								
(z)	TFS 106Y	Leyland	National NL116TL11/2R	07717	Leyland National		B42D	3/83	Lothian 106	Coyle, Livingston
	THL 288Y	see 83-TS-403 *Ireland*								
	UHG 353Y	Leyland	Atlantean AN68D/2R	8200555	East Lancs	A3003	H49/36F	7/82	Blackpool 353	123 Group, Chesterfield
	UTN 501Y	MCW	Metrobus DR102/37	MB7285	MCW		H46/31F	8/83	Northern General 3501	Garrett, Murton
	UWJ 288Y	Dennis	Dominator	DDA165/614	Alexander	RH14/282/14	H46/32F	5/83	South Yorkshire PTE 2288	Sanders, Sheffield
	VBV 18Y	Leyland	Atlantean AN68C/1R	8200368	East Lancs	A2513	H43/31F	9/82	Blackburn 18	-?-, -?-
	VCW 597Y	Dennis	Lancet	SD505/107	Marshall	270501	B51F	8/82	Blackpool 597	Heslop, Hexham
	VRC 612Y	Leyland	Leopard PSU3G/4R	8231069	Plaxton	8211LLS5X513	C53F	9/82	Barton 612	Allen & Bairstow, Nottingham
	VWA 34Y	Leyland	National NL116HLXB/1R	07730	Leyland National		DP47F	5/83	East Midland 34	Stevenson, Chesterfield
	WDL 310Y	→ see TJI 8780								
	WDL 692Y	Leyland	Olympian ONLXB/1R	ON620	ECW	25525	CH40/30F	5/83	Southern Vectis 692	Riley, Peterborough
	WNJ 479Y	Dodge	2090P	623266	Rootes		M11	2/83	Royal Mail 0750069	Royal Mail Archive Fleet
	WPH 118Y	Leyland	Tiger TRCTL11/2R	8200185	East Lancs	A9323	B53F	8/82	Midland Red North 1738	Owen, -?-
					(rebodied 4/92)					
	WPH 139Y	Leyland	Tiger TRCTL11/2R	8200447	East Lancs	A9308	B51F	9/82	Midland Red North 1719	Owen, -?-
					(*rebodied 12/89*)					
	XAO 135Y	→ see 83-WW-194 *Ireland*								
	XFG 25Y	Leyland	National NL116HLXB/1R	07702	Leyland National		B49F	4/83	Brighton 25	Gardiner, Gloucester
	XHG 245Y	→ see CBV 775Y								
	XSS 40Y	Leyland	Leopard PSU3G/4R	8230708	Alexander	156AYS/1481/2	B53F	12/82	Alexander Northern NPE40	-?-, -?-
(r)	XSS 41Y	Leyland	Leopard PSU3G/4R	8230947	Alexander	156AYS/1481/3	B53F	12/82	Alexander Northern NPE41	Webster & Scott, Inverkeilor
	XSS 43Y	Leyland	Leopard PSU3G/4R	8231179	Alexander	156AYS/1481/5	B53F	12/82	Alexander Northern NPE43	Webster & Scott, Inverkeilor
	XSS 335Y	Leyland	Atlantean AN68D/1R	8201451	Alexander	AL101/980/5	H45/29D	1/83	Grampian 335	Sharp, Newmilns
	XSS 345Y	Leyland	Atlantean AN68D/1R	8201555	Alexander	AL101/980/15	H45/29D	3/83	Grampian 345	Aberdeen & District Transport Preservation Trust
	YPD 101Y	Leyland	Tiger TRCTL11/2R	8201042	Duple	334/5236	C51F	3/83	London Country TD1	Bird, Burgess Hill (WS)
	YPD 105Y	Leyland	Tiger TRCTL11/2R	8201625	Duple	334/5240	C53F	3/83	London Country TD5	-?-, -?-
	A144 AMO	MCW	Metrobus DR102/44	MB7790	MCW		CH39/27F	7/84	Reading 144	Morton, Little London (HA)
	A633 BCN	MCW	Metrobus DR102/43	MB7719	MCW		H46/31F	5/84	Northern General 3633	Welford, Burnhope
	A312 BDL	→ see TJI 8782								
	A811 CCD	Leyland	Tiger TRCTL11/3R	8300694	Duple	435/5505	C50F	3/84	Southdown 1011	Stanford, Crawley
	A108 CFS	Leyland	National NL116TL11/2R	07761	Leyland National		B27D	3/84	Lothian Buses 108	McGregor, Bathgate
	A714 CRD	→ see XOI 792								
	A700 DDL	Leyland	Olympian ONLXB/1R	ON1183	ECW	25825	H45/30F	2/84	Southern Vectis 700	Isle of Wight Bus Museum
	A747 DWP	Bedford	SB5	ET101977	Duple	8301/0103	C40F	4/84	Mascot, St Helier	Payne, Great Sampford
			(ex J 91728, J 40614)							

	Reg	Chassis	Model	Chassis No	Body	Body No	Layout	Date	New to	Owner
	A126 EPA	Leyland	Tiger TRCTL11/2RH	8301004	Plaxton	8411LTP1X534	C53F	1/84	London Country TP26	-?-, Thetford
			(ex DCZ 2319, A 126 EPA)							
	A137 EPA	Leyland	Tiger TRCTL11/2RH	8301042	Plaxton	8411LTP1X545	C53F	2/84	London Country TP37	Garnham, Coventry
	A913 ERM	Bedford	YNT	ET101727	Plaxton	8411NTP1C017	C53F	4/84	Irving, Dalston	Western Isles Transport Preservation Group
	A137 FDC	→ see 83-LK-712 *Ireland*								
	A953 FHH	→ see 84-D-7523 *Ireland*								
	A506 FSS	Dennis	Lancet	SDA516/134	Alexander	2P/1583/5	B53F	3/84	Alexander Northern ND6	Machin, Stoke-on-Trent
	A319 GLV	Leyland	Olympian ONTL11/1R	ON837	Alexander	RH18/3871/4	CH40/23F	8/83	Merseyside PTE 0067	-?-, Liverpool
	A323 GLV	Leyland	Atlantean AN68D/1R	8300469	Alexander	AL102/3082/3	H43/32F	9/83	Merseyside PTE 1003	Morris,Wallasey
	A581 HDB	→ see TKZ 9780								
	A362 HHG	Leyland	Atlantean AN68D/2R	8300677	East Lancs	A3908	H49/36F	8/83	Blackpool 362	Lancastrian Transport Trust
	A111 HLV	Leyland	Atlantean AN68D/1R	8301321	Alexander	AL103/2483/16	H43/32F	2/84	Merseyside PTE 1031	Wigan Transport Trust
	A112 HLV	Leyland	Atlantean AN68D/1R	8301295	Alexander	AL103/2483/17	H43/32F	2/84	Merseyside PTE 1032	Rowlands & Collingwood, Liverpool
	A115 HLV	Leyland	Atlantean AN68D/1R	8301309	Alexander	AL103/2483/20	H43/32F	2/84	Merseyside PTE 1035	Hodge, Liverpool
	A116 HLV	Leyland	Atlantean AN68D/1R	8301370	Alexander	AL103/2483/21	H43/32F	3/84	Merseyside PTE 1036	Rimmer, Litherland
	A135 HLV	Leyland	Atlantean AN68D/1R	8301496	Alexander	AL103/2483/40	H43/32F	4/84	Merseyside PTE 1055	Rowlands, Liverpool
	A153 HLV	Volvo	B55-10	83069	Alexander	RV10/2583/3	H44/37F	6/84	Merseyaide PTE 0071	-?-, Merseyside
			(ex 5958 VT, A153 HLV)							
	A657 HNB	Leyland	Atlantean AN68D/1R	8300504	Northern Counties	2448	H43/32F	8/83	Greater Manchester PTE 8657	Brundrit, Cotes Heath
(r)	A662 HNB	Leyland	Atlantean AN68D/1R	8300545	Northern Counties	2450	H43/32F	8/83	Greater Manchester PTE 8662	SELNEC Preservation Society
	A697 HNB	Leyland	Atlantean AN68D/1R	8300664	Northern Counties	2537	H43/32F	1/84	Greater Manchester PTE 8697	Stephenson A, Bolton
	A700 HNB	Leyland	Atlantean AN68D/1R	8300676	Northern Counties	2540	H43/32F	1/84	Greater Manchester PTE 8700	SELNEC Preservation Society
	A472 HNC	Dennis	Falcon V	DD405/117	Northern Counties	2412	H--/--F	5/84	Greater Manchester PTE 1472	SELNEC Preservation Society
	A767 HPF	→ see CIW 708								
	A954 HVC	Ford	Transit	BDVZDJ19872	Ford		M12	10/83	Staffordshire Fire Brigade	Jones, Telford
	A511 HVT	Leyland	Tiger TRCTL11/3RH	8300810	Plaxton	8412LTH1C759	C53F	12/83	Midland Red North 1511	Owen, Stafford
			(ex EIL 3017, A511 HVT)							*(on loan to Cooper, Cannock (ST))*
	A706 HVT	Leyland	Tiger TRCTL11/2RH	8301165	Duple	439/5821	B51F	3/84	Midland Red North 1706	Brundrit, Cotes Heath (ST)
	A590 JGU	AEC	Reliance	6U3ZR24481	Berkhof	624	C49F	8/73	East Kent 8203	Plumley, Hexham
			(ex IIW 783, A203 TAR, HFN 59L) *(rebodied 8/84)*				(alternative chassis number EBC8408AS)			
	A 50 JLW	→ see UIL 2090								
	A747 JRE	Leyland	Olympian ONLXB/1R	ON1126	ECW	25821	H45/32F	1/84	Potteries 747	Pearson, Stoke-on-Trent
	A120 KBA	→ see KUX 774								
	A680 KDV	Leyland	Olympian ONLXB/1R	ON927	ECW	25662	H45/32F	10/83	Devon General 1804	Inner Circle Group, Exeter
			(ex MAN 54N, A680 KDV)							
	A686 KDV	Leyland	Olympian ONLXB/1R	ON995	ECW	25672	H45/32F	11/83	Devon General 1814	Billington, Maidenhead
			(ex MAN 57N, A686 KDV)							
	A301 KJT	Leyland	National NL116TL11/1R	07768	Leyland National		DP47F	5/84	Provincial 1	Sherwin & Marshall, Fareham
	A677 LBV	→ see 8518 FM								
	A451 LCK	→ see 666 XPI *Ireland*								
	A813 LEL	Quest 80	VM	4406/1/35	Plaxton	8412QVP1C10N	C53F	4/84	Excelsior, Bournemouth	Quest VM Group, Birmingham
	A150 LFR	Leyland	Tiger TRCTL11/2R	8300961	Duple	434/5200	C51F	12/83	Ribble 1150	McCall, Widnes
										(on loan to Ribble Vehicle Preservation Trust)
	A462 LFV	Leyland	Atlantean AN69/2L	7801729	ECW	25310	H47/35	-/78	Fishwick, Leyland 2	Hayes, Little Hoole
					(first bodied 1/84)					
	A701 LNC	Leyland	Atlantean AN68D/1R	8300674	Northern Counties	2541	H43/32F	2/84	Greater Manchester PTE 8701	SELNEC Preservation Society
	A706 LNC	Leyland	Atlantean AN68D/1R	8300917	Northern Counties	2552	H43/32F	2/84	Greater Manchester PTE 8706	Museum of Transport, Manchester
	A726 LNC	→ see 84-D-7221 *Ireland*								

	A126 MBA	→ see 84-D-706 *Ireland*								
	A927 MDV	Ford	Transit	BDVPDL06906	Carlyle	MC1-1	B16F	12/83	Devon General 7	West Country Historic Omnibus & Transport Trust
					(Dormobile shell 751 922 83)					
	A504 MHG	→ see 84-D-6758 *Ireland*								
	A33 MRN	Leyland	Olympian ONTL11/2R	ON1067	ECW	25762	H47/25F	2/84	Preston 33	Preston Bus Preservation Group
	A686 MWX	Leyland	Olympian ONLXB1/R	ON1137	ECW	25856	H45/32F	1/84	York-West Yorkshire 3835	Halliday, Shipley
	A758 NNA	Leyland	Atlantean AN68D/1R	8301451	Northern Counties	2604	H43/32F	6/84	Greater Manchester PTE 8758	Wilcock, Liverpool
	A762 NNA	→ see 84-D-7336 *Ireland*								
	A763 NNA	Leyland	Atlantean AN68D/1R	8301438	Northern Counties	2609	H43/32F	6/84	Greater Manchester PTE 8763	Edwards & Brindle, Wigan
	A765 NNA	Leyland	Atlantean AN68D/1R	8301450	Northern Counties	2611	H43/32F	7/84	Greater Manchester PTE 8765	SELNEC Preservation Society
	A749 NTA	Ford	Transit	BDVPDM29083	Ford		M8L	-/83	Devon Social Services	Shears C, Winkleigh
	A577 NWX	Leyland	Olympian ONLXB/1R	ON1331	ECW	25870	H45/32F	7/84	West Riding 577	Hurley Moore & Peacock, Wakefield
	A658 OCX	Leyland	Olympian ONLXB/1R	ON1348	ECW	25906	H45/32F	7/84	Yorkshire Traction 658	Law, Swinton
	A695 OHJ	Leyland	Tiger TRCTL11/2RH	8300941	Alexander	2TE/2383/5	C53F	11/83	Eastern National 1126	Wilson, Bishops Stortford
			(ex XIL 8034, A695 OHJ)							
	A201 OKJ	MCW	Metrobus DR102/42	MB7694	MCW		H46/31F	3/84	Maidstone & District 5201	Maidstone & District Bus Group, Maidstone
			(ex GIG 2694, A201 OKJ)							
	A 30 ORJ	Leyland	Olympian ONLXB/1R	ON1296	Northern Counties	2645	H43/30F	7/84	Greater Manchester PTE 3030	SELNEC Preservation Society
	A103 OUG	Leyland	Olympian ONTL11/1R	ON1068	Northern Counties	2613	H43/28F	4/84	South Yorkshire, Pontefract 103	Scott et al, -?-
	A858 OVJ	Bedford	SB5	DT104038	Wright	D237	DP40F	2/84	Myall, Bassingbourn	Myall, Bassingbourn (CM)
	A542 PCW	Leyland	National NL116HLXCT/1R	07778	Leyland National		B--F	7/84	Blackpool 542	Lancastrian Transport Trust
	A543 PCW	→ see 84-LK-1039 *Ireland*								
	A888 PKR	Leyland	Olympian ONLXB/1R	ON1269	ECW	25948	CH42/27F	5/84	Madistone & District 5888	Warren, Staplehurst
	A733 PSU	Volvo	B55-10	83026	Alexander	RV8/2982/26	H44/35F	8/83	Strathclyde PTE A107	-?-, -?-
	A735 PSU	Volvo	B55-10	83028	Alexander	RV8/2982/28	H44/35F	9/83	Strathclyde PTE A109	Tennant, Wetherby
	A198 RUR	Leyland	Tiger TRCTL11/3R	8201179	Plaxton	8312LTH1C867	C49FT	6/84	Leyland demonstrator	Hamilton, Bow (DN)
			(ex MIL 5577, A198 RUR)							
	A205 SAE	Leyland	Tiger TRCTL11/3R	8300636	Plaxton	8412LTP1X501	C53F	10/83	Bristol 2205	Williams, Bristol
			(ex 530 OHU, A205 SAE)							
	A952 SAE	Leyland	Olympian ONLXB/1R	ON938	Roe	GO8752	H47/29F	12/83	Bristol 9552	Walker, Wells
	A954 SAE	Leyland	Olympian ONLXB/1R	ON945	Roe	GO8754	H47/29F	1/84	Bristol 9554	Walker Curtis & Curtis, Wells
(r)	A945 SUL	MCW	Metrobus DR101/16	MB7426	MCW		PO43/28D	11/83	London Transport M945	-?-, -?-
	A 20 SAM	→ see J198 OSW								
	A101 SUU	Volvo	B55-10	83055	Alexander	RV16/3283/1	H43/31D	4/84	London Transport V1	V1 Preservation Group, Harlow
										(on loan to Brundrit, Cotes Heath (ST))
	A103 SUU	Volvo	B55-10	83057	Alexander	RV16/3283/3	H36/27D	6/84	London Transport V3	London Bus Company, Northfleet (KT)
	A250 SVW	Leyland	Tiger TRCTL11/3RP	8400134	Duple	8370/0299	C57F	7/84	Southend 250	Ensign, Purfleet (EX)
	A102 SYE	Leyland	Olympian ONLXB/1R	ON1116	ECW	25764	H47/28D	2/84	London Buses L2	Boxall & Wood, Beckenham
										(on loan to Meadows, Crewe (CH))
	A888 SYE	Leyland	Titan TNLXB2RR	0948	Leyland		H44/26D	11/83	London Transport T888	Colegate, Abbey Wood
	A890 SYE	Leyland	Titan TNLXB2RR	0950	Leyland		H44/26D	11/83	London Transport T890	Sullivan, Potters Bar (HT)
	A910 SYE	Leyland	Titan TNLXB2RR	0970	Leyland		H44/26D	12/83	London Transport T910	Dunkley, Coulsdon
	A961 SYE	Leyland	Titan TNLXB2RR	1021	Leyland		H44/26D	2/84	London Transpprt T916	Dunkley, Coulsdon
	A986 SYE	Leyland	Titan TNLXB2RR	1046	Leyland		H44/27D	4/84	London Transport T986	Moore, Hillsboro, Texas, USA
										(still in UK in care of Routemaster Owners & Operators Association)
	A961 SYF	MCW	Metrobus DR101/17	MB7523	MCW		H43/28D	1/84	London Transport M961	Bolton, Hull
	A200 TAR	AEC	Reliance	6U3ZR24418	Berkhof	618	C49F	7/73	East Kent 8200	Roberts, Stockport
			(ex HFN 58L)		*(rebodied 5/84)*		(alternative chassis number EBC8405AS)			

A204 TAR	AEC	Reliance	6U3ZR24380	Berkhof	625	C49F	7/73	East Kent 8204	-?-, Coventry
		(ex HFN 57L)			*(rebodied 6/84)*	(alternative chassis numer EBC8409AS)			
A630 THV	Leyland	Titan TNLXB2RR	1090	Leyland		H44/26D	7/84	London Transport T1030	T1030 Preservation Group, Dartford *(on loan to Go-Coachhire, Swanley (KT))*
A651 THV	Leyland	Titan TNLXB2RR	1111	Leyland		H44/26D	7/84	London Transport T1051	Bolton, Hull
A701 THV	MCW	Metrobus DR101/17	MB7563	MCW		H43/28D	3/84	London Transport M1001	Colin, Chesterfield
A714 THV	MCW	Metrobus DR101/18	MB7650	MCW		H41/28D	4/84	London Transport M1014	Rose, London Colney
A813 THW	Leyland	Olympian ONLXB/1R	ON1322	Roe	GO8814	CO47/29F	6/84	Bristol 8613	Brown, Nailsea
A741 TTW	Ensign	JP1 MkII	EBC/84/14/G	Ensign		CH43/22C	4/84	Londoners, Peckham	Wakelin, Brinklow
A537 TYW	Dodge	G08	ED716960	Wadham Stringer	-?-	B??	6/84	British Rail	Brown, Greenhithe
A685 UOE	MCW	Metrobus DR102/27	MB7319	MCW		H43/30F	11/83	West Midlands PTE 2685	Dodd, Wolverhampton
A686 UOE	MCW	Metrobus DR102/27	MB7320	MCW		H43/30F	10/83	West Midlands PTE 2686	-?-, -?-
A441 UUV	MCW	Metrobus DR102/45	MB7692	MCW		H43/28D	6/84	London Transport M1441	Patrickson, Wigan
A790 UYL	Leyland	Cub CU355	CE01557	Wadham Stringer	8450/84	B??FL	7/84	Greater London Council A0346	Claydon, Corringham
A849 UYM	see 84-D-4144 *Ireland*								
A 25 VDS	Leyland	Tiger TRBLXB/2RH	8400069	Alexander	15TS/1983/5	B53F	5/84	Central SMT LT25	Kennedy Budd & Anderson, Glasgow
A436 VNY	Volvo	B55-10	83044	Northern Counties	2520	H39/35F	2/84	Cardiff 436	Carroll Barlow Clausen & Morgan, Cardiff
A256 VWO	→ see AAX 305A								
A 57 WDT	→ see HIL 8418								
A503 WGF	Volvo	B10M-61	007397	Plaxton	8412VZH1C33N	C57F	4/84	Richmond, Epsom	Chancellor, Kempsey
		(ex 2290 PK, A503 WGF)							
A110 WVP	MCW	Metrobus GR133/1	MB7601	MCW		H43/30F	6/84	West Midlands PTE 8110	Aston Manor Road Transport Museum
A298 XAK	Dennis	Dominator	DDA165/625	Alexander	RH19/283/4	H46/32F	9/83	South Yorkshire PTE 2298	Sentance, Sheffield
A317 XAK	Dennis	Dominator	DDA165/666	Northern Counties	2488	H47/33F	11/83	South Yorkshire PTE 2317	Sentance, Sheffield
A325 XHE	→ see 84-C-3663 *Ireland*								
A543 XLG	→ see 84-D-7523 *Ireland*								
A118 XWE	MCW	Metrobus DR104/11	MB7384	MCW		H47/33F	10/83	South Yorkshire PTE 1918	South Yorkshire Transport Trust
		(ex JIL 8206, A118 XWE)							
A763 YAB	→ see CAB 2W								
A754 YAF	Leyland	Olympian ONLXB/1R	ON982	ECW	25665	CH44/32F	11/83	Western National 1808	Williams, Goldsithney
A414 YAK	Dennis	Dominator	DDA901/705	Alexander	RH20/383/14	H46/32F	2/84	South Yorkshire PTE 2414	Parkinson, Rotherham
A438 YAK	Dennis	Dominator	DDA901/759	Alexander	RH20/383/38	H46/32F	7/84	South Yorkshire PTE 2438	-?-, Rotherham
A417 YBO	→ see 84-C-3189 *Ireland*								
A717 YFS	→ see 83-LH-930 *Ireland*								
B136 ACK	Leyland	Tiger TRCTL11/3RZ	8401217	Duple	8572/0602	C48FT	4/85	Ribble 136	Brocken, Carnforth *(operates as Hacking, Carnforth (LA))*
B811 AOP	MCW	Metrobus DR102/27	MB7885	MCW		H43/30F	11/84	West Midlands PTE 2811	2811 Group, Birmingham
B493 CBD	→ see LKZ 9307								
B361 CDT	Dennis	Dominator	DDA901/723	East Lancs	A5007	H46/33F	9/84	South Yorkshire PTE 2361	Sheffield Joint Omnibus Club
B 24 CGA	Volvo	Citybus B10M-50	008317	Alexander	RV20/1684/1	H47/37F	3/85	A1 (Meney), Ardrossan	DJ International, Barrhead (SW)
		(ex VCS 376, B24 CGA)							
B417 CMC	Leyland	Tiger TRCTL11/3R	8201282	Plaxton	8312LTP1C104	C53F	5/85	British Airways CC8007	Griffiths, Swansea
B 11 CTB	Leyland	Olympian ONLXCT/3R	ON332	ECW	26236	CH49/22F	4/83	Citybus, Hong Kong C51	Rogers, Swindon
		(ex EUI 530, B984 YTC, DE 4281 *Hong Kong*)							
B155 DHL	Leyland	National NL116HLXCT/1R	07793	Leyland National		B52F	12/84	Chesterfield 55	Walker Cooper Stephenson & Thurston, Sheffield
B201 DTU	Leyland	Olympian ONLXB/1R	ON1859	ECW	26067	CH42/32F	7/85	Crosville EOG201	Roberts, Stockport
B 52 DWE	→ see 84-C-3721 *Ireland*								

	Reg	Make	Model	Chassis No	Body	Body No	Layout	Date	First Owner	Current Owner
	B632 DWF	Leyland	Tiger TRCTL11/2RH	8400844	Alexander	4P/1984/8	B52F	5/85	East Midland 632	Stevenson & Cooper, Chesterfield
	B976 DWG	→ see B674 GWJ								
	B42 ECV	Leyland	Tiger TRCTL11/3RZ	8400906	Van Hool	11704	C57F	4/85	Smith, Wigan 311	Watts, Chesterfield
			(ex 353 TPF, B311 UNB)							
	B177 FFS	Volvo	Citybus B10M-50	008319	Alexander	RV18/1184/1	H47/37F	2/85	Alexander Fife FRA77	977 Group, Fife
	B157 FWJ	→ see TER 840								
	B207 GNL	Ford	Transit	BDVYET76094	Alexander	AM1/2584/8	B16F	4/85	Northern General 207	Cartwright, Ryton
	B449 GUF	Dodge	2090P	619898	Rootes		M11	1/81	Royal Mail 9750066	Cott, Winfarthing
	B674 GWJ	Dennis	Dorchester	SDA805/125	Plaxton	8411DDP1C01N	C49F	3/85	South Yorkshire PTE 76	-?-, -?-
			(ex 7958 NU, B674 GWJ, 476 HDT, B976 DWG)							
	B555 HAL	Volvo	B10M-61	007744	Plaxton	8412VZH1C769	C53F	9/84	Derby 5	-?-, Stroud
			(ex XAF 759, B555 HAL)							
	B997 JTN	→ see RIL 4827								
	B105 KPF	Leyland	Tiger TRCTL11/3RH	8400611	East Lancs	A9319	B59F	12/84	Midland Red North 1725	Owen, -?-
					(rebodied 9/91)					
	B294 KPF	Leyland	Tiger TRCTL11/3RH	8401113	Plaxton	8512LTP2X519	C51F	2/85	London Country TPL94	-?-, -?-
	B638 KVO	→ see 85-WH-93 *Ireland*								
	B666 KVO	Volvo	B10M-61	007914	Plaxton	8512VZH2C757	C53F	5/85	Derby 6	-?-, Stroud
			(ex 852 YYC, B666 KVO)							
	B926 KWM	Leyland	Atlantean AN68D/1R	8400183	Alexander	AL103/2483/55	H43/32F	9/84	Merseyside PTE 1070	201 Restoration Group, Wallasey
	B624 LJU	→ see 84-KY-1195 *Ireland*								
(a)	B360 LOY	Leyland	National NL116TL11/3R	07783	Leyland National		B33T	9/84	British Airways BU396	Kinsella, Standish
										(for use as exhibition unit by North West Vehicle Restoration Trust)
	B578 LPE	Leyland	Olympian ONTL11/2R	ON1708	ECW	26189	CH45/28F	1/85	Thames Valley & Aldershot 1510	Martin, Swindon
			(ex OAZ 9330, B578 LPE)							
	B349 LSO	Leyland	Olympian ONLXB/1R	ON1619	Alexander	RL19/784/2	H45/32F	1/85	Alexander Northern NLO49	Wallace, Edinburgh
			(fitted with a Gardner 5LXCT engine)							
	B605 LSO	MCW	MetroHiliner HR131/2	MB8055	MCW		C48FT	3/85	Northern Scottish NCM5	Vals, Chase Terrace (ST)
	B717 MDC	→ see 84-C-3607 *Ireland*								
	B259 MDL	Ford	Transit	BDVYET76017	Carlyle	CBS50	B16F	5/85	Southern Vectis 259	Hemmett, Basingstoke
					(Dormobile shell 4247 925 85)					
	B121 MSO	Leyland	Olympian ONLXB/1RV	ON1716	Alexander	RH27/583/10	H47/24D	4/85	Grampian 121	Aberdeen & District Transport Preservation Trust
			(fitted with a Gardner 6LXCT engine)							
	B 88 MUT	DAF	SB2300DHS585	236085	Smit	985	C53F	4/85	Adkins, Upper Boddington	Adkins, Upper Boddington
			(ex TBZ 5873, B 88 MUT)							
	B401 NJF	Ford	Transit	SFAYXXBDVYET75415	Rootes	17620	B16F	7/85	Midland Fox M1	Leicestershire Museums
	B242 NUT	→ see 85-MH-1211 *Ireland*								
	B 31 PAJ	Dennis	Falcon HC	SDA415/157	Northern Counties	2826	B--D	9/85	Hartlepool 31	Larkin, Peterborough
	B252 PHN	Leyland	Olympian ONLXB/1R	ON1882	ECW	26138	H45/32F	5/85	United 252	Scott, Newcastle-upon-Tyne
	B 65 PJA	Leyland	Olympian ONLXB/1R	ON1382	Northern Counties	2680	H43/30F	11/84	Greater Manchester PTE 3065	Museum of Transport, Manchester
	B 97 PKS	MCW	Metrobus DR102/47	MB7924	Alexander	RL18/484/9	H45/33F	12/84	Midland Scottish MRM97	Webster & Scott, Inverkeilor
	B100 PKS	MCW	Metrobus DR132/6	MB7927	Alexander	RL18/484/12	H45/33F	2/85	Midland Scottish MRM100	Conn & Gurr, Cumbernauld
	B105 PKS	MCW	Metrobus DR132/6	MB7932	Alexander	RL18/484/17	H45/33F	4/85	Midland Scottish MRM105	Gray, Bearsden
	B144 RWY	Leyland	Olympian ONLXB/1R	ON1524	Roe	GO8857	H47/27F	8/84	West Yorkshire PTE 5504	Harrogate Coach, Green Hammerton (NY)
	B101 SJA	Leyland	Olympian ONLXB/1R	ON1658	Northern Counties	2717	H43/30F	2/85	Greater Manchester PTE 3101	SELNEC Preservation Society
	B901 TVR	Dennis	Dominator	DDA1003/819	Northern Counties	2772	H43/32F	3/85	Greater Manchester PTE 2001	SELNEC Preservation Society
	B310 UNB	→ see RXI 5598								
	B311 UNB	→ see B42 ECV								

Registration	Chassis	Model	Chassis No	Body	Body No	Layout	Date	Original Operator	Owner
B 75 URN	Leyland	Atlantean AN68D/2R	8400199	Northern Counties	2612	CH43/33F	10/84	Fylde 75	Blackpool Transport Omnibus Group
		(ex NJI 5505, B 75 URN)							
B176 VDV	Volvo	Citybus B10M-50	007356	East Lancs	A5102	H42/35F	11/84	Plymouth 176	Plymouth City Transport Preservation Group
B610 VWU	Leyland	Tiger TRCTL11/3RH	8400324	Plaxton	8512LTP2X533	C—F	6/85	West Yorkshire PTE 1610	Transport Yorkshire Preservation Group
B459 WHJ	MCW	Metroliner CR126/9	MB7753	MCW		C51F	9/84	Eastern National 1602	Mackintosh, Birmingham
		(ex SJI 9333, B459 WHJ)							
B900 WRN	Leyland	Tiger TRCTL11/2RH	8400709	Duple	8412/0503	B49F	12/84	Ribble 900	900 Group, Liverpool
									(on loan to Ribble Vehicle Preservation Trust)
B105 WUL	MCW	Metrobus DR134/1	MB7845	MCW		H43/26D	12/84	London Transport M1105	Holmes. Blackburn
B200 WUL	MCW	Metrobus DR101/17	MB8112	MCW		H43/28D	3/85	London Transport M1200	London Bus Company, Northfleet (KT)
B100 WUV	→ see NIB 5232								
B101 WUV	Leyland	Titan TNLXB2RR	1161	Leyland		H44/26D	9/84	London Transport T1101	-?-, -?-
B102 WUV	Leyland	Titan TNLXB2RR	1162	Leyland		H44/26D	9/84	London Transport T1102	Brown, Greenhithe
B232 XEU	MCW	Metroliner DR130/6	MB8061	MCW		CH??/??DT	3/85	Wessex 232	Science Museum, Wroughton
B106 XJO	Ford	Transit	BDVPEL64798	Carlyle	CBS5	B16F	3/85	South Midland SM6	Oxford Bus Museum Trust
				(Dormobile shell 2802 925 84)					
B509 YAT	Bedford	YNT	ET106889	Plaxton	8511NTP2C017	C53F	5/85	France, Market Weighton	Barclay, Irvine
B295 YOD	→ see 6499 MZ								
B949 YHS	Dodge	G08	717108	Marshall	270640	B20F	9/84	Strathclyde PTE M28	-?-, Cumbria
				(also with demountable Aitken van body)					
B818 YKR	Freight Rover	Sherpa	229466	Dormobile	0064 979 85	B20F	c4/85	Dormobile demonstrator	McClintoch, Leeds
B984 YTC	→ see B11 CTB								
B 21 YYS	Volvo	B55-10	84002	Alexander	RV17/3683/2	H44/35F	11/84	Strathclyde PTE A120	Transport Preservation Trust, Beith
C416 AHT	Ford	Transit	BDVYFP88568	Carlyle	CBS117	B16F	2/86	Bristol 7416	Williams, Bristol
				(Dormobile shell 4328 924 85)					
C612 ANW	Leyland	Olympian ONLXB/1R	ON1927	ECW	26125	CH41/30F	8/85	West Riding 612	Bennett, Wrenthorpe
C468 BHY	Ford	Transit	BDVYFG04820	Dormobile	4842 975 85	B16F	3/86	Bristol 7468	Blay, Fishponds
C332 BUV	MCW	Metrobus DR101/17	MB8353	MCW		H43/28D	9/85	London Buses M1332	Hughes, Dublin
C424 BUV	MCW	Metrobus DR101/17	MB8469	MCW		H45/30F	12/85	London Buses M1424	Blackman, Halifax (WY)
C113 CAT	Dennis	Dominator	DDA1007/869	East Lancs	A5513	CH43/28F	2/88	Hull 113	-?-, -?-
C201 CBU	Leyland	Olympian ONLXB/1R	ON2076	Northern Counties	2931	H43/30F	2/86	Greater Manchester PTE 3201	SELNEC Preservation Society
C214 CBU	Leyland	Olympian ONLXB/1R	ON2189	Northern Counties	2944	CH43/26F	3/86	Greater Manchester PTE 3214	Clegg, Eccles
C215 CBU	Leyland	Olymoian ONLXB/1R	ON2268	Northern Counties	2945	H43/30F	3/86	Greater Manchester PTE 3215	Dusntan, Middleton
C225 CBU	Leyland	Olympian ONLXB/1R	ON2182	Northern Counties	2955	H43/30F	5/86	Greater Manchester PTE 3225	SELNEC Preservation Society
C481 CBU	Volvo	Citybus B10M-50	009583	Northern Counties	2857	H46/33F	6/86	Greater Manchester PTE 1481	SELNEC Preservation Society
C807 CBU	Dodge	S56	214404	Northern Counties	2922	B22F	7/86	Greater Manchester PTE 1807	Taylor, Leeds
C823 CBU	Dodge	S56	214879	Northern Counties	2968	B18F	7/86	Greater Manchester PTE 1823	SELNEC Preservation Society
C 41 CHM	Leyland	Olympian ONLXB/1RH	ON2323	ECW	26323	H42/26D	3/86	London Buses L41	-?-, -?-
C100 CHM	Leyland	Olympian ONLXB/1RH	ON2382	ECW	26412	H42/26D	7/86	London Buses L100	Cooper, Ipswich
C762 DHX	Ford	Transit	SFAVXXBDVVFR97299	Ford		M15	4/86	Unknown	M4 Minibuses, Lyneham
C395 DML	Leyland	Olympian ONLXB/1R	ON1938	ECW	28249	H43/34F	8/85	Metrobus, Orpington	Wallis, Swanley
C862 DYD	Ford	Transit	BDVYFB92990	Robin Hood	7570	B16F	10/85	Southern National 300	Billington, Maidenhead
C869 DYD	Ford	Transit	BDVYFB93195	Robin Hood	7575	B16F	10/85	Southern National 307	Dale, Sherborne
C501 DYM	Fiat	49-10	1272	Robin Hood	9881	DP21F	6/86	Orpington Buses RH1	Gurney, Petts Wood
C526 DYT	Volkswagen	LT55	GH012708	Optare	82	B25F	7/86	London Buses OV2	London Transport Museum
C201 EKJ	Mercedes-Benz	L608D	31032720705006	Rootes	17950	B20F	2/86	Maidstone & District 1001	Brown, Wateringbury

	Reg	Chassis make	Model	Chassis no.	Body	Body no.	Layout	New	First owner	Current owner
	C233 ENE	Leyland	Olympian ONLXB/1R	ON2299	Northern Counties	2993	O43/30F	6/86	Greater Manchester PTE 3233	SELNEC Preservation Society
	C519 FFJ	Ford	Transit	BDVYFA02126	Carlyle	CBS265	B16F	2/86	Devon General 519	-?-, Lake District
					(Dormobile shell 4643 924 85)					
	C526 FFJ	Ford	Transit	BDVYFA02950	Carlyle	CBS269	DP16F	12/85	Devon General 526	Suttle, Irthlingborough
					(Dormobile shell 4700 924 85)					
	C705 FFJ	Ford	Transit	BDVYFA02346	Robin Hood	8536	B16F	1/86	Devon General 705	West Country Historic Omnibus & Transport Trust
	C748 FFJ	Ford	Transit	BDVYFC06149	Carlyle	CBS318	B16F	4/86	Devon General 748	Lacey, Broadclyst
					(Dormobile shell 4942 924 85)					
	C760 FFJ	Ford	Transit	BDVYFC06946	Carlyle	CBS337	B16F	5/86	Devon General 760	RML2418, Wem (SH)
					(Dormobile shell 5024 924 85)					
(a)	C724 FKE	Ford	Transit	BDVYFC10252	Dormobile	S5205 975 86	B16F	7/86	East Kent 24	East London Traction Society
	C759 FMC	→ see 86-MO-445 *Ireland*								
	C920 FMP	Leyland	Lynx LX1126LXCTFR1	LX1004	Leyland		B51F	6/86	Leyland demonstrator	Smith, Pontefract
	C253 FRJ	Leyland	Olympian ONLXB/1R	ON10099	Northern Counties	3046	H43/26F	7/86	Greater Manchester PTE 3253	Wigan Transport Trust
	C255 FRJ	Leyland	Olympian ONLXB/1R	ON10101	Northern Counties	3048	H43/26F	7/86	Greater Manchester PTE 3255	Prescott, Cheadle Hulme
	C801 FRL	Mercedes-Benz	L608D	31032720702091	Reeve Burgess	15476	B20F	1/86	Western National 104	Williams, Goldsithney
	C208 FVU	MCW	Metrobus DR132/8	MB8210	Northern Counties	3006	CH43/29F	7/86	Greater Manchester PTE 5208	Museum of Transport, Manchester
(r)	C949 GAF	Mercedes-Benz	L608D	31032720702284	Reeve Burgess	15480	B20F	2/86	Western National 106	West Country Historic Omnibus & Transport Trust
	C787 GGB	Volvo	B10M-61	007951	Plaxton	8512VZP2C018	C57F	8/85	Syme, Clydebank	-?-, -?-
	C454 GKE	Leyland	Olympian ONTL11/2RH	ON10120	ECW	26381	CH45/28F	6/86	Maidstone & District 5454	Rogers, Swindon
			(ex B10 MLT, C454 GKE)							
	C 41 GKG	Leyland	Tiger TRBTL11/2R	8500390	East Lancs	A6203	DP47F	12/85	Islwyn 41	Rhymney Valley Transport Preservation Society
	C 42 GKG	Leyland	Tiger TRBTL11/2R	8500391	East Lancs	A6202	DP47F	12/85	Islwyn 42	Barnett & Taylor, Blackwood
	C207 GTU	Leyland	Olympian ONLXB/1R	ON2057	ECW	26073	CH42/29F	10/85	Crosville EOG207	Hamer, Oxford
			(ex A17 ALS, C207 GTU)							
	C594 GVU	Bedford	YMP	GT104233	Plaxton	869.5MQP2C008	C35F	6/86	Angel, Tottenham	-?-, -?-
			(ex SIL 5798, C594 GVU, JIL 6316, C535 DWW, WRC 751, C337 UFP)							
	C896 GYD	Ford	Transit	BDVYFC06569	Robin Hood	8628	B16F	5/86	Southern National 334	Sharman, Bere Regis
	C923 GYD	Ford	Transit	BDVYFC08006	Robin Hood	8655	B16F	7/86	Southern National 361	Sharman, Bere Regis
(r)	C942 GYD	Ford	Transit	BDVYFC07644	Dormobile	5059 975 86	B16F	7/86	Southern National 380	Sharman, Bere Regis
	C 41 HDT	Dennis	Domino	SDA1202/102	Optare	05	B33F	8/85	South Yorkshire PTE 41	Heaton, Dinnington
	C 46 HDT	Dennis	Domino	SDA1202/107	Optare	06	B33F	8/85	South Yorkshire PTE 46	Heaton, Dinnington
	C 53 HDT	Dennis	Domino	SDA1202/125	Optare	13	B33F	9/85	South Yorkshire PTE 53	Heaton, Dinnington
	C113 HDT	→ see BBZ 6818								
	C200 HGF	Mercedes-Benz	L608D	31040420632244	Plaxton	85WO4921	C20F	9/85	Richmond, Epsom	Aberdeen & District Transport Preservation Trust
			(ex LSK 546, C200 HGF)							
	C415 HJN	Leyland	Olympian ONLXB/1RH	ON10010	ECW	26551	CH42/30F	2/86	Eastern National 4015	Cole, Frinton-on-Sea
	C418 HJN	Leyland	Olympian ONLXB/1RH	ON10013	ECW	26554	CH42/30F	2/86	Eastern National 4018	Norris, Colchester
	C101 HKG	Ford	Transit	BDVYFC06551	Robin Hood	8610	B16F	2/86	National Welsh 1	Cardiff Transport Preservation Group
	C501 HOE	Ford	Transit	BDVYET90659	Carlyle	CBS221	B16F	11/85	London Buses FS29	Pitt, Heston
					(Dormobile shell 4203 926 85)					
	C502 HOE	Ford	Transit	BDVYET75758	Carlyle	CBS103	B16F	11/85	London Buses FS27	Phillipson, Biggin Hill
					(Dormobile shell 3504 926 85)					
	C207 HTH	Mercedes-Benz	L608D	31032720705053	Robin Hood	9226	B20F	12/85	South Wales 207	Purnell, Swansea
	C724 JJO	Ford	Transit	BDVYFC10779	Carlyle	CBL379	B20F	9/86	City of Oxford 724	Oxford Bus Museum Trust
					(Dormobile shell 6134 926 85)					
	C729 JJO	Ford	Transit	BDVYFK14183	Carlyle	CBL378	DP20F	9/86	City of Oxford 729	Wareham, Kidlington
					(Dormobile shell 6137 926 85)					

C877 JWE Dennis Dominator DDA910/876 Alexander RH33/185/7 H46/32F 11/85 South Yorkshire PTE 2457 Webster, Rotherham
C882 JWE Dennis Dominator DDA910/881 Alexander RH33/185/13 H46/32F 12/85 South Yorkshire PTE 2462 Bowden, Rotherham
C147 KBT Leyland Olympian ONLXB/1R ON1945 Optare 16 O47/29F 12/85 West Yorkshire PTE 5147 Mitchell, Oakworth
(operates as Keighley Bus Museum, Keighley (WY))
C507 KBT Leyland Olympian ONTL11/1R ON1984 Optare 17 H47/27F 10/85 West Yorkshire PTE 5507 Transport Yorkshire Preservation Group
C807 KBT Leyland Cub CU435 CF00789 Optare 52 B33F 7/86 West Yorkshire PTE 1807 Transport Yorkshire Preservation Groip
C141 KFL DAF SB2300DHS585 259451 Jonckheere 19527 C53FT 8/85 Young, Rampton Young, Haddenham (CM)
(ex KUI 8329, C141 KFL)
C217 KMA MCW Metroliner DR130/27 MB8509 MCW CH55/22FT 4/86 Crosville CMC217 O'Keefe, Croydon
(ex VAV 15, C217 KMA)
C724 LCP → see PIL 5863
C655 LFT Leyland Olympian ONLXB/1R ON2155 Alexander RH35/485/55 H45/31F 3/86 Tyne & Wear PTE 655 North East Bus Preservation Trust
C656 LFT Leyland Olympian ONLXB/1R ON2156 Alexander RH35/485/56 H45/31F 3/86 Tyne & Wear PTE 656 Buckley Minto & McHaddan, Newcastle-upon-Tyne
C61 LHL Ford Transit BDVYFC10767 Carlyle CBL369 DP—F 7/86 South Yorkshire PTE 61 South Yorkshire Transport Trust
(Dormobile shell 6121 926 85)
C522 LJR Leyland Olympian ONCL10/1RV ON1894 ECW 26025 H42/30F 8/85 Northern General 3522 Ruddick, Consett
C656 LJR Leyland Olympian ONCL10/1RZ ON1936 ECW 26028 H45/32F 8/85 Northern General 3656 Garrett, Murton
C959 LWJ MCW Metrobus DR102/53 MB8674 MCW CH42/28F 8/86 South Yorkshire PTE 1959 -?-, -?-
C722 MRC Leyland National NL116TL11H/1R 07829 Leyland National B52F 8/85 Nottingham 722 Nottingham Heritage Vehicles
C723 MRC Leyland National NL116TL11H/1R 07830 Leyland National B52F 9/85 Nottingham 723 -?-,Chesterfield
C724 MRC Leyland National NL116TL11H/1R 07834 Leyland National B50F 9/85 Nottingham 724 Stanton, Nottingham
C664 NMB Scania K112CRS 1807798 Van Hool 12568 C53FT 6/86 Penniston, Melton Mowbray Romdrive, Melton Mowbray (LE)
(ex MIB 2273, RIL 8182, C664 NMB, 847 XKJ, C675 WJU, OO 1908, C158 WJU)
C 89 NNV Volvo B10M-61 007123 Caetano 185013 B57F 1/86 Wilder, Feltham Telling, -?-
C 24 NVV Ford Transit BDVYET75967 Carlyle CBS43 B16F 12/85 United Counties 24 Skevington & Adams, Wingfield
(Dormobile shell 3468 924 85)
C455 OAP → see 85-LK-1327 *Ireland*
C457 OAP → see 85-LK-1328 *Ireland*
C844 OBG Quest 80 B 4201/97 Locomotors B23F 10/85 Merseyside PTE 0087 Miller, Foxton
C 49 OCM Leyland National NL116TL11H/1R 07835 Leyland National B52F 11/85 Halton 33 Roberts, Sheffield
C455 OFL → see C369 RFE
C771 OCN MCW Metrobus DR102/55 MB8562 MCW H46/31F 5/86 Northern General 3771 Buckley & Minto, Newcastle-upon-Tyne
C989 OFR → see TIL 2878
C109 OHH → see 86-C-4486 *Ireland*
(r) C926 PFL Ford R1115 BCRSCJ19216 Plaxton 8611FDP2C004 C53F 4/86 Duncan, Sawtry Stanton, Cheadle
(ex TAZ 5542, C926 PFL)
C369 RFE Leyland Tiger TRCTL11/3R 8500499 Plaxton 8612LZH2C781 C49FT 3/86 Cambus 455 Garnham, Coventry
(ex TJI 1617, C455 OFL)
C307 SAO Duple 425 SDAK1503/003 Duple 8485/0575 C55FT 9/85 Whittle, Kidderminster Vals, Chase Terrace (ST)
(ex LIL 9812, C307 SAO, ESK 978, C326 VNP, JPY 505)
C638 SFH Ford Transit BDVYFB94625 Alexander AM2/685/25 B16F 9/85 Cheltenham & Gloucester 638 Stubbington, Banbury
C777 SFS Leyland Olympian ONTL11/2R ON2181 ECW 26259 H51/32D 12/85 Lothian 777 Lothian Bus Consortium
C164 SPB Leyland Tiger TRBTL11/2R 8500500 Duple 8512/0705 B53F 11/85 Safeguard, Guildford Kirwin, Guildford
C100 UBC Dennis Dominator DDA1010/890 East Lancs A6605 H46/33F 7/86 Leicester 100 Harris, Leicester
C101 UBC Dennis Dominator DDA1010/891 East Lancs A6606 H46/33F 7/86 Leicester 101 Arnold, Warrington
C337 UFP → see C594 GVU
C120 VBF Mercedes-Benz L608D 31032720630238 PMT 3420 B20F 9/85 Potteries MMM120 Potteries Omnibus Preservation Society
C135 VRE Mercedes-Benz L608D 31032720705005 PMT 3595 B20F 2/86 Potteries MMM135 Davies, Stoke-on-Trent

	Registration	Chassis	Model	Chassis No	Body	Body No	Layout	New	First operator	Current owner
	C161 VRE	Ford	Transit	BDVYFB91609	PMT	3432	B16F	1/86	Potteries 161	Townley, Burslem
	C177 VSF	Leyland-DAB	Lion	8500805	Alexander	RH37/1485/4	CH45/37F	6/86	Eastern Scottish ZLL177	Bienowski & Sadler, Edinburgh
	C158 WJU	→ see C664 NMB								
	C518 WBF	Leyland	Tiger TRCTL11/3RZ	8500786	Duple	8595/0045	C50FT	5/86	Midland Red North 1518	Williams, Merthyr Tydfil
			(ex GUI 6060, JIL 3253, C518 WBF)							
	C 77 XWK	→ see 86-D-8229 *Ireland*								
	C751 YBA	Dennis	Domino	SDA1201/101	Northern Counties	2752	B24F	9/85	Greater Manchester PTE 1751	SELNEC Preservation Society
	D642 ALR	→ see RIB 8742								
	D800 ALR	→ see TIL 5977								
	D428 ASF	Dodge	S56	GD215933	Alexander	AM10/1086/28	B21F	10/86	Eastern Scottish R428	Cochrane, Edinburgh
	D656 BCK	→ see 87-KK-2064 *Ireland*								
	D631 BPL	Dennis	Lancet	SDA525/155	Duple	8617/0095	B43F	10/86	Hestair Dennis demonstrator	Campbell, Paisley
	D 90 CFA	Ford	Transit	BDVYGU34187	Dormobile	7116 990 86	B16F	1/87	Midland Red North 90	Brundrit, Cotes Heath
	D463 CKV	Freight Rover	Sherpa	SEYZMBFC7AN268488	Rootes	18232	B16F	10/86	Midland Red (South) 463	Heartlands, Tamworth (ST)
	D836 CNV	Fiat	315-8-17	000212	Caetano	185195	C28F	6/87	Scancoaches, Willesden	Shaw, Warwick
	D902 CSH	Leyland	Olympian ONTL11/1RH	ON10361	Alexander	RL31/1986/2	CH43/27F	3/87	Lowland Scottish 902	Robertson, Rosyth
	D 5 CTB	Leyland	Olympian ONTL11/3R	ON1802	ECW	26242	CH55/41F	-/85	Leyland demonstrator	Rogers, Swindon
			(ex DU 5866 *Hong Kong - fitted with a Cummins L10 engine*)							
	D103 DAJ	Mercedes-Benz	L608D	31032720730689	Reeve Burgess	16191	B20F	9/86	Hartlepool 103	-?-, -?-
	D310 DSR	MCW	Metrobus DR102/52	MB8604	Alexander	RL29/2185/2	CH41/31F	8/86	Strathtay SM10	Webster, -?-
	D702 EES	Dodge	S56	HD216719	Alexander	AM22/3686/4	B23F	3/87	Tayside 202	-?-, -?-
	D819 EES	Leyland	Olympian ONLXB/1RV	ON10367	Alexander	RL32/2086/3	H43/29F	4/87	Strathtay Scottish SO19	Assiph Fisher Fraser & Macintosh, Dundee
	D583 EWS	Freigh Rover	Sherpa	AN268533	Dormobile	6870 983 86	B16F	10/86	Badgerline 4583	Fear, Somerset
	D278 FAS	Leyland	Tiger TRCTL11/3RH	8600438	Alexander	28TE/2186/3	C53F	6/87	Highland Scottish Z278	123 Group, Chesterfield
			(ex VLT 45, D278 FAS)							
	D718 FES	→ see 415 VYA								
	D904 FHN	→ see MAZ 7584								
	D138 FYM	Leyland	Olympian ONLXB/1RH	ON2421	ECW	26433	H42/26D	9/86	London Buses L138	Ipswich Bus Preservation Group
			(ex WLT 838, D138 FYM)							
	D194 FYM	Leyland	Olympian ONLXB/1RH	ON2526	ECW	26519	H42/26D	11/86	London Buses L194	O'Connor, Beckenham
	D201 FYM	Leyland	Olympian ONLXB/1RH	ON2538	ECW	26526	H42/26D	11/86	London Buses L201	Boxall & Griffin, Bromley *(on loan to Meadows, Crewe (CH))*
	D101 GHY	Volvo	B10M-56	014786	Alexander	10P/4086/2	DP53F	5/87	Badgerline 101	Fricker {North Somerset}, Nailsea (SO)
			(ex KFX 791, D101 GHY)							
	D503 GHY	Volvo	B10M-61	014806	Van Hool	13024	C48FT	5/87	Badgerline 2503	Williams, Bristol
	D708 GHY	Volvo	Citybus B10M-50	015005	Alexander	RV27/4186/9	CH47/35F	5/87	Badgerline 5708	Williams, Bristol
	D125 HML	→ see 87-C-13993 *Ireland*								
	D229 HMT	Leyland	Tiger TRCTL11/3RZ	8600279	Van Hool	12973	C57F	3/87	Travellers, Hounslow	Watts, Chesterfield
			(ex FIL 8614, D229 HMT)							
	D705 HUA	Freight Rover	Sherpa	256270	Optare	32	M16	9/86	West Yorkshire PTE 1705	Transport Yorkshire Preservation Group
	D707 HUA	Freight Rover	Sherpa	256300	Optare	36	M--	9/86	West Yorkshire PTE 1707	Transport Yorkshire Preservtaion Group
	D275 JVR	Leyland	Olympian ONLXB/1R	ON10243	Northern Counties	3071	H43/30F	4/87	Greater Manchester Buses 3275	Clegg, Eccles
	D277 JVR	Leyland	Olympian ONLXB/1R	ON10231	Northern Counties	3088	H43/26F	5/87	Greater Manchester Buses 3277	SELNEC Preservation Society
	D302 JVR	MCW	Metrobus DR102/51	MB8214	Northern Counties	3010	CH43/29F	9/86	Greater Manchester PTE 5302	SELNEC Preservation Society
	D230 LCY	Mercedes-Benz	L608D	31032720756192	Robin Hood	9744	B20F	10/86	South Wales 230	Hanford, Swansea
	D501 LNA	Leyland	Lynx LX563LXCTZR1	LX1021	Leyland		B48F	12/86	Greater Manchester Buses 501	SELNEC Preservation Society
(r)	D312 LNB	MCW	Metrobus DR102/51	MB8620	Northern Counties	3020	CH43/29F	11/86	Greater Manchester Buses 5312	SELNEC Preservation Society

	D320 LNB	MCW	Metrobus DR102/51	MB8628	Northern Counties	3028	CH43/29F	2/87	Greater Manchester Buses 5320	SELNEC Preservation Society
	D 41 MAG	Fiat	49-10	2002345	Robin Hood	10187	C16F	1/87	East Yorkshire 41	Muir, Christchurch
	D647 MDB	MCW	Metrorider MF151/3	MB8920	MCW		B23F	4/87	Greater Manchester Buses 1647	GM MR Group, Stockport
	D892 MDB	Dodge	S56	216619	Northern Counties	3143	B20F	1/87	Greater Manchester Buses 1892	Taylor, Leeds
	D509 MJA	Fiat	49-10	002876	Robin Hood	10798	B19F	2/87	Greater Manchester Buses 1509	SELNEC Preservation Society
	D901 MWR	Volkswagen	LT55	HH000074	Optare	235	DP21F	4/87	Yorkshire Rider 1700	Tindall, Huddersfield
	D536 NDA	Freigh Rover	Sherpa	266184	Carlyle	CFL464	B19F	10/86	West Midlands PTE 536	Howdle, Clayhanger
					(Dormobile shell 6324 982 86)					
	D591 NDA	Fiat	49-10	002747	Robin Hood	9948	B19F	10/86	West Midlands 591	Cole, Birmingham
	D912 NDA	MCW	Metrobus DR102/59	MB8677	MCW		CH43/26F	10/86	West Midlands PTE 2912	Gottard, Streetly
	D934 NDA	MCW	Metrobus DR102/59	MB8699	MCW		CH43/26F	10/86	West Midlands PTE 2934	-?-, Haywards Heath
	D957 NDA	MCW	Metrobus DR102/59	MB8722	MCW		CH43/26F	11/86	West Midlands 2957	WM MCW Bus Group, Birmingham
	D101 NDW	Leyland	Lynx LX112TL11Z1R	LX1045	Leyland		B49F	4/87	Merthyr Tydfil 101	Feldman, Stevenage
	D674 NNE	MCW	Metrorider MF151/3	MB8947	MCW		B23F	4/87	Greater Manchester Buses 1674	Museum of Transport, Manchester
	D676 NNE	MCW	Metrorider MF151/3	MB8949	MCW		B23F	4/87	Greater Manchester Buses 1676	Museum of Transport, Manchester
	D553 NOE	Ford	Transit	BDVYFK14179	Carlyle	CFL383	B20F	10/86	West Midlands 553	BaMMOT, Wythall
			(ex B14 TJW, D553 NOE)		(Dormobile shell 6135 926 85)					
	D554 NOE	Ford	Transit	BDVYFC10780	Carlyle	CBL384	B--F	10/86	West Midlands 554	Vals, Chase Terrace (ST)
			(ex B12 TJW, D554 NOE)		(Dormobile shell 6128 926 85)					
	D 62 NOF	Freight Rover	Sherpa	267455	Carlyle	CFL482	B20F	1/87	Manchester Minibuses 62	Museum of Transport, Manchester
					(Dormobile shell 6534 982 86)					
	D 63 NOF	Freight Rover	Sherpa	267748	Carlyle	CFL481	B18F	1/87	Manchester Minibuses 63	Museum of Transport, Manchester
					(Dormobile shell 6531 982 86)					
	D167 NON	Freight Rover	Sherpa	274311	Carlyle	CFL593	B16F	1/87	Manchester Minibuses 167	-?-, Glasgow
					(Dormobile shell 7360 982 86)					
(r)	D176 NON	Freight Rover	Sherpa	273220	Carlyle	CFL602	B16F	1/87	Manchester Minibuses 176	Taylor, Leeds
					(Dormobile shell 7292 982 86)					
	D124 NUS	Mercedes-Benz	L608D	31032720730343	Alexander	AM7/186/18	B21F	10/86	Kelvin Scottish 1124	MacKenzie Bus, Denny (SE)
	D504 NWG	Mercedes-Benz	L608D	31032720719783	Alexander	AM4/2585/4	B20F	11/86	Yorkshire Traction 504	McCafferty & Andrews, Somerset
	D275 OOJ	Freight Rover	Sherpa	801336	Carlyle	C2.002	B20F	6/87	Carlyle demonstrator	Keighley Bus Museum Trust (WY)
	D379 OSU	Leyland	Tiger TRBLXB/2RH	8600182	Alexander	25TS/2385/11	B53F	1/87	Central Scottish LT79	Davidson, Glasgow
	D472 OWE	Dennis	Dominator	DDA1011/903	Alexander	RH41/285/7	CH40/33F	10/86	South Yorkshire PTE 2472	2472 Preservation Group, -?-
	D473 OWE	Dennis	Dominator	DDA1011/904	Alexander	RH41/285/8	CH40/33F	10/86	South Yorkshire PTE 2473	2472 Preservation Group, -?-
	D474 OWE	Dennis	Dominator	DDA1011/905	Alexander	RH41/285/9	H45/33F	10/86	South Yorkshire PTE 2474	Thurston, Sheffield
	D479 OWE	Dennis	Dominator	DDA1011/911	Alexander	RH41/285/14	CH40/33F	10/86	South Yorkshire PTE 2479	2472 Preservation Group, -?-
	D489 OWE	Dennis	Dominator	DDA1013/920	Alexander	RH42/285/4	CH45/33F	11/86	South Yorkshire Transport 2489	Sheffield Joint Omnibus Club
	D511 PPU	Leyland	Olympian ONTL11/2RH	ON10077	ECW	26418	CH45/24F	7/86	Eastern National 4511	Stephenson, Rochford (EX)
	D122 PTT	Ford	Transit	BDVWHC60460	Mellor	52030	B16F	2/87	Thames Transit 122	Oxford Bus Museum Trust
	D754 PTU	Freight Rover	Sherpa	270480	Dormobile	7027 983 86	B16F	10/86	Crosville MSR754	Titterton, Blurton
	D 22 PVS	Freight Rover	Sherpa	SAZZNVPC7AN272308	Dormobile	6825 983 86	B16F	2/87	Luton & District 61	Muir, Christchurch
	D150 RAK	Dodge	S56	217207	Reeve Burgess	16519	B25F	5/87	South Yorkshire Transport 150	Davies, Oswestry
	D165 RAK	Dodge	S56	217276	Reeve Burgess	16334	B34F	7/87	South Yorkshire Transport 165	Cochrane, Edinburgh
	D782 RFM	Freight Rover	Sherpa	269850	Dormobile	6955	B16F	11/86	Crosville MSR782	-?-, -?-
	D685 SEM	Dodge	S56	216556	Alexander	AM18/3586/7	B23F	1/87	Merseyside 7685	-?-, Liverpool
	D101 TTJ	Dodge	S56	217254	Northern Counties	3426	DP20F	7/87	Warrington 101	Arnold, Warrington
	D826 UTF	→ see KBZ 7145								
	D 79 VCC	Mercedes-Benz	L608D	31032720781212	Reeve Burgess	16055	B20F	12/86	Crosville Wales MMM79	Roberts, Sheffield
	D 30 VCW	→ see 86-C-4606 *Ireland*								

D 30 VEY	→ see 87-C-14811 *Ireland*							
D 68 VJC	→ see 87-LK-3557 *Ireland*							
D133 VJK	Bedford YMP	HT101167	Plaxton	878MSP3C024	C33F	4/87	Rowland & Goodwin, St Leonards 33	Rambler, Hastings (ES)
	(ex UDY 910, D133 VJK)							
D106 VRP	Mercedes-Benz L608D	31032720762376	Robin Hood	9775	B20F	9/86	Milton Keynes 06	North Buckinghamshire Preservation Group
D112 WCC	Freight Rover Sherpa	277988	Carlyle	CFL737	B18F	5/87	Crosville Wales MSL112	Burton Bus Preservation Society
			(Dormobile shell 7787 991 86)					
D741 WRC	Ford R1014	BCRSWP408170	Plaxton	8710FTP2C001	C45F	3/87	Slack, Tansley	McCalden, Glasgow
D 35 XNV	Bedford YMP	GT104257	Plaxton	868MQP2C016	C35F	9/86	Country Lion, Northampton	Woodward, Huddersfield
D383 XRS	Leyland Olympian ONLXB/1RV	ON10364	Alexander	RL33/2286/9	H47/30F	4/87	Northern Scottish NLO83	59 Preservation Group, Corby
D384 XRS	Leyland Olympian ONLXB/1RV	ON10366	Alexander	RL33/2286/10	H47/30F	4/87	Northern Scottish NLO84	Robertson, Biggleswade
	(ex WLT 512, D384 XRS)							
D560 YCW	Volkswagen LT55	HH003029	Optare	212	B21F	5/87	Blackpool 560	Williams, Merthyr Tydfil
E100 AFW	Leyland Tiger TRCTL11/2RZ	8700072	Duple	8612/0422	B59F	8/87	Delaine, Bourne 100	-?-, -?-
E389 AYA	Sarao Jeepney	-?-	Sarao		B11	-/87	-?-, Philippines	Tomkinson, Bolton
	(ex PJS 429 *Philippines registration)*							
E211 BDV	Ford Transit	BDVWJA36644	Mellor	56676	B16F	6/88	Devon General 211	Burton Bus Preservation Society
E186 BNS	MCW Metrorider MF154/12	MB9868	MCW		B33F	6/88	Strathclyde Buses M89	Hay & Grant, Glasgow
E206 BOD	Duple 425	SDA1510/055	Duple	8785/0493	C53F	4/88	Western National 2240	Billington, Maidenhead
	(ex 550 XBV, E206 BOD)							
E640 BRS	Leyland Tiger TRCTL11/3RH	8700025	Alexander	32TC/2986/5	C57F	9/87	Northern Scottish NCT40	Forbes & Muir, Montrose
	(ex FSU 309, E640 BRS, BSK 756, E640 BRS)							
E320 BVO	Volvo Citybus B10M-50	016538	East Lancs	A8105	H47/38D	3/88	Nottingham 320	Nottingham Heritage Vehicles
E321 BVO	Volvo Citybus B10M-50	016539	East Lancs	A8110	H47/38D	5/88	Nottingham 321	Nottingham Heritage Vehicles
E522 DCU	Mercedes-Benz L307D	60236720825998	Devon Conversions	281D	M12L	12/87	Tyne & Wear Dial-a-Ride	-?-, Stanley
E903 DRG	Ford R1114	BC04RK63329	Plaxton	7511FC129M	C53F	-/75	Smith, Langley Park	Dolan, Crook
	(first licensed 1/88)							
E131 DRS	Leyland Olympian ONCL10/2RZ	ON10791	Alexander	RH54/4387/8	H49/29D	7/88	Grampian 131	Aberdeen & District Transport Preservation Trust
E832 EUT	→ see 87-MH-3474 *Ireland*							
E216 GNV	→ see 58 DAF							
E187 HSF	Volvo Citybus B10M-50	014982	Alexander	RV25/3286/1	CH45/35F	8/87	Eastern Scottish VV187	Barclay, Irvine
E114 KDX	→ see 88-D-43778 *Ireland*							
E267 KEF	→ see 87-C-14637 *Ireland*							
E941 KEU	Fiat 49-10	4758	Robin Hood	11093	B21F	8/87	Badgerline 4941	-?-, -?-
E887 KYW	Leyland Lynx LX112TL11ZR1S	LX1068	Leyland		B47F	10/87	Cowie 887	Gardner, Tunbridge Wells
E570 MAC	Talbot Pullman	420149	Talbot		B20F	6/88	Barrow 99	Barrow Transport Museum
E571 MAC	→ see VIL 8730							
E489 MEL	MCW Metrorider MF150/49	MB9432	MCW		B23F	12/87	Wilts & Dorset 2338	Wilding, Shaftesbury
E805 MOU	Mercedes-Benz 811D	67030320858963	Optare	467	B31F	5/88	Badgerline 3805	Williams, Bristol
E819 MOU	Mercedes-Benz 811D	67030320885912	Optare	570	DP27F	7/88	Badgerline 3819	Williams, Bristol
E823 MOU	Mercedes-Benz 811D	67030320887687	Optare	572	DP27F	7/88	Badgerline 3823	Williams, Bristol
E153 OMD	Leyland Olympian ON6LXB/1RH	ON10640	Optare	305	H47/29F	2/88	Maidstone 753	Boxall Griffin & Welch, Bromley
E928 PBE	→ see 88-C-16323 *Ireland*							
E204 PWY	Mercedes-Benz 811D	67030320837938	Optare	245	DP28F	11/87	Yorkshire Rider 2004	Transport Yorkshire Preservation Group
E218 PWY	→ see LIL 7960							
E347 REL	MCW Metrorider MF150/87	MB9788	MCW		B23F	5/88	Wilts & Dorset 2347	Bournemouth Passenger Transport Association

E216 RDW	→ see 88-C-16273 *Ireland*								
E 48 TYG	Leyland	Royal Tiger RT	RTC87.23	Leyland		C53F	3/88	West Riding 48	Rogers, Swindon
E446 TYG	Fiat	49-10	2003731	Robin Hood	11287	B25F	4/88	West Yorkshire Road Car 191	Halliday, Shipley
E304 VEP	Mercedes-Benz	709D	66900320882393	Reeve Burgess	17171	DP25F	6/88	South Wales 304	Hanford, Swansea
E559 VBG	Mercedes-Benz	814L	67041425358126	North West Coach Sales		C29F	7/88	Roberts, Bootle	Aaron, New Forest
E 64 WDT	Leyland	Lynx LX112TL11ZR1R	LX1085	Leyland		B49F	12/87	Chesterfield 64	Rush, Chesterfield
E178 WDV	→ see 87-C-14597 *Ireland*								
E346 WYS	Dodge	S56	JD219143	Alexander	AM39/2087/24	B25F	1/88	Clydeside Scottish 346	Stafford, Renfrew (SW)
E186 XKO	Leyland	Tiger TRCTL11/3ARH	TR00267	Plaxton	8812LUH3C772	C53F	4/88	Maidstone & District 2186	Cutler, Maidstone
		(ex YSU 870, E186 XKO)							
F100 AKB	Renault	PR100.2	100226	Northern Counties	3736	B47F	10/88	Northern Counties demonstrator	Lake, Huddersfield
		(ex WUK 155, F100 AKB)							
F 90 CBD	Volvo	B10M-60	021594	Jonckheere	21643	C51FT	5/89	Goodwin, Stockport	Go-Goodwins, Eccles (GM)
		(ex RIW 4098, 89-MN-1265 *Ireland*, F90 CBD)							
F471 CJK	MCW	Metrorider MF158/9	MB9924	MCW		C28F	8/88	Chatfield, Worthing	Cutts, Christchurch
		(ex NSU 512, F471 CJK, 419 DCD, F565 HPP)							
F238 CNY	Leyland	Lynx LX112L10ZR1R	LX1381	Leyland		DP47F	3/89	Cardiff 238	Alder Jeenes Morgan & Smith, Cardiff
F240 CNY	Leyland	Lynx LX112L10ZR1R	LX1383	Leyland		DP47F	3/79	Cardiff 240	Bates & Thomas, Barry
		(ex AIG 7821, F240 CNY)							
F279 DRJ	Leyland	Olympian ONLXB/1RZ	ON10794	Northern Counties	3612	H43/30F	9/88	Greater Manchester Buses 3279	SELNEC Preservation Society
F301 DRJ	Leyland	Olympian ONLXB/1RZ	ON10866	Northern Counties	3634	H43/30F	2/89	Greater Manchester Buses 3301	SELNEC Preservation Society
F305 DRJ	Leyland	Olympian ONLXB/1RZ	ON10868	Northern Counties	3638	H43/30F	1/89	Greater Manchester Buses 3305	SELNEC Preservation Society
F649 FGE	Mercedes-Benz	507D	66736220896060	Steedrive	D5771	B17F	10/88	Crainey, Kilsyth	Western Isles Transport Preservation Group
F242 FNE	Fiat	49-10	005124	Northern Counties	3514	DP22F	12/88	Dunstan, Middleton	Dunstan, Middleton (GM)
F444 GAT	Mercedes-Benz	709D	66900320946970	Reeve Burgess	17675	B23F	6/89	East Yorkshire 444	-?-, East Yorkshire
F267 GUA	Sarao	Jeepney	-?-	Sarao		B12	-/88	new	Yorkshire Car Collection, Keighley
				(imported new from Philipines)					
F561 HPP	MCW	Metrorider MF158/9	MB9837	MCW		B33F	8/88	Chatfield, Worthing	-?-, -?-
F565 HPP	→ see F471 CJK								
F107 HVK	Leyland	Lynx LX112L10ZR1S	LX1266	Leyland		B49F	1/89	Busways 107	North East Bus Preservation Trust
F904 JRG	Scania	N113CRB	1814828	Alexander	4PS/3888/4	B51F	3/89	Busways 904	Brennan, Sevenoaks
F915 JRG	Scania	N113CRB	1813947	Alexander	4PS/3888/15	B51F	3/89	Busways 915	Welford, Burnhope
F918 JRG	Scania	N113CRB	1815007	Alexander	4PS/3888/18	B51F	3/89	Busways 918	Buckley, Newcastle-upon-Tyne
F251 JRM	Leyland	Lynx LX112L10ZR1S	LX1310	Leyland		B51F	6/89	Cumberland 251	Workington Transport Heritage Trust
F722 LRG	→ see PIL 9243								
F724 LRG	Leyland	Lynx LX1126LXCTZR1R	LX1246	Leyland		B47F	2/89	Northern General 4724	Spire Fleetline Preservation Group, Chesterfield
F406 LTW	Leyland	Lynx LX112L10ZR1R	LX1172	Leyland		B49F	8/88	Eastern National 1406	Norris, Colchester
F409 LTW	Leyland	Lynx LX112L10ZR1R	LX1175	Leyland		B49F	8/88	Eastern National 1409	-?-, Chesterfield
F601 MSL	Leyland	Olympian ONLXB/2RZ	ON10795	Alexander	RL38/4887/1	H51/36F	8/88	Hampshire Bus 201	Hampshire Bus (HA) 14951
F110 NES	Leyland	Olympian ON6LXCT/5RZ	ON10898	Alexander	RL39/5587/1	H66/44F	4/89	Stagecoach, Perth	United Counties (NO) 14000
F292 NHJ	MCW	Metrobus DR102/71	MB9941	MCW		H46/27F	11/88	Ensign, Purfleet 292	Ensign, Purfleet (EX)
F506 NJE	Leyland	Olympian ON6LXB/1RH	ON10910	Northern Counties	3753	H45/30F	11/88	Cambus 506	Longmire Riley & Merryweather, Peterborough
F441 OFG	Dennis	Dart	9SDL3002/102	Duple	8911/1095	B--F	8/89	Hestair Duple demonstrator	Jones, Moulton
F591 OHT	Fiat	49-10	5355	Dormobile	9507 811 88	B20F	8/88	Bristol 7591	Williams, Bristol
F867 ONR	→ see 89-C-18900 *Ireland*								
F115 PHM	Volvo	Citybus B10M-50	018738	Alexander	RV35/2188/1	H46/29D	9/88	Cowie, Stamford Hill 115	London Transport Museum
F295 PTP	Dennis	Dominator	DDA1023/967	East Lancs	A9007	H45/31F	1/89	Southampton 295	Burden, Southampton

	Registration	Chassis	Model	Chassis no.	Body	Body no.	Layout	Date	First operator	Owner
	F575 RCW	Volkswagen	LT55	JH013447	Optare	531	B21F	8/88	Blackpool 575	Lancastrian Transport Trust
	F771 RHP	→ see 88-LK-3740 *Ireland*								
	F817 RJF	→ see 89-LS-1669 *Ireland*								
	F611 RTC	Leyland	Lynx LX2R11C15Z4R	LX1454	Leyland		B49F	5/89	Bristol 1611	-?-, -?-
	F622 RTC	Leyland	Lynx LX2R11C15Z4R	LX1465	Leyland		B49F	7/89	Bristol 1622	Williams, Bristol
	F98 STB	Dennis	Dominator	DDA1017/978	East Lancs	A8711	H51/37F	6/89	Warrington 98	Arnold, Warrington
	F106 UEF	Leyland	Olympian ONCL10/2RZ	ON11065	Northern Counties	3766	H47/35F	4/89	OK, Bishop Auckland	County Durham BPG, Hetton-le-Hole
	F603 VEW	Leyland	Tiger TRBTL11/2RP	TR00303	Duple	8822/0699	B59F	9/88	Delaine, Bourne 103	Jones, Moulton
	F23 XOF	MCW	Metrobus DR102/64	MB9785	MCW		H43/30F	1/89	West Midlands 3023	Aston Manor Road Transport Museum
	F53 XOF	MCW	Metrobus DR102/70	MB10236	MCW		H43/30F	2/89	West Midlands 3053	Kwok, Coventry
	F57 XOF	MCW	Metrobus DR102/70	MB10240	MCW		H43/30F	2/89	West Midlands 3057	-?-, Staffordshire
			(ex YCZ 8661, F57 XOF)							
	F63 XOF	MCW	Metrobus DR102/70	MB10246	MCW		H43/30F	3/89	West Midlands 3063	Barker, Wolverhampton
	F65 XOF	MCW	Metrobus DR102/70	MB10248	MCW		H43/30F	3/89	West Midlands 3065	23 Group, Coventry
	F80 XOF	MCW	Metrobus DR102/70	MB10263	MCW		H43/30F	4/89	West Midlands 3080	-?-. -?-
	F158 XYG	Leyland	Olympian ONCL10/1RZ	ON10922	Northern Counties	3646	H45/29F	11/88	Yorkshire Rider 5158	Transport Yorkshire Preservation Group
	F685 YOG	MCW	Metrorider MF150/113	MB10086	MCW		B23F	12/88	West Midlands 685	Aston Manor Road Transport Museum
	F238 YTJ	Leyland	Olympian ONCL10/1RZ	ON11024	Alexander	RH59/3488/8	H45/30F	4/89	Merseyside 238	Rowlands, Liverpool
	F261 YTJ	Leyland	Olympian ONCL10/1RZ	ON11026	Northern Counties	3783	H47/30F	2/89	Merseyside 261	Wright, Maghull
	F105 YVP	MCW	Metrorider MF150/116	MB10111	MCW		DP23F	10/88	London Buses MRL105	Lewis, Ilford
(a)	G571 BHP	Talbot	Freeway	446202	Talbot		M8L	2/90	Entrust Care, Coventry	Barrow Transport Museum
	G642 BPH	Volvo	Citybus B10M-50	022449	Northern Counties	3894	H45/35F	10/89	London Country Bus 642	Paske, Chelmsford
			(ex XIL 3492, G642 BPH							
	G611 CEF	Leyland	Lynx LX2R11C15Z4R	LX1413	Leyland		B49F	11/89	Cleveland Transit 11	Shaw, Brighton
	G105 EOG	Leyland	Lynx LX2R11C15Z4R	LX1528	Leyland		B49F	9/89	West Midlands 1105	-?-, -?-
	G266 EOG	Leyland	Lynx LX2R11C15Z4R	LX1754	Leyland		DP45F	4/90	West Midlands 1266	Cleaver, Coventry
	G280 EOG	→ see 90-OY-2565 *Ireland*								
	G292 EOG	Leyland	Lynx LX2R11C15Z4R	LX1831	Leyland		B49F	6/90	West Midlands 1292	Peters, Kings Norton
	G141 HNP	→ see 90-LK-5381 *Ireland*								
	G142 HNP	Leyland	Lynx LX2R11C15Z4R	LX1772	Leyland		B49F	4/90	Midlland Red West 1142	Peters, Kings Norton
	G258 HUH	Leyland	Lynx LX2R11C15Z4R	LX1442	Leyland		B49F	1/90	Cardiff 258	Cardiff Transport Preservation Group
	G259 HUH	Leyland	Lynx LX2R11C15Z4R	LX1443	Leyland		B49F	1/90	Cardiff 259	Rhymney Valley Transport Preservation Society
	G186 JHG	Leykand	Olympian ONLXB/2RZ	ON11407	Alexander	RL51/989/27	CH47/32F	10/89	Ribble 2186	McCall, Widnes
	G254 JYG	DAF	SB220LC550	335562	Optare	5051	B47F	12/89	Yorkshire Rider 1254	Transport Yorkshire Preservation Group
	G293 KWY	Leyland	Lynx LX112L10ZR1R	LX1314	Leyland		B49F	11/89	Keighley & District 201	Fearnley & Wilde, Harrogate
	G166 LWN	Volvo	B10M-60	024159	Plaxton	9012VCB1894	C51FT	4/90	South Wales 166	South Wales Transport Preservation Trust
			(ex PJI 5286, G166 LWN)							
	G101 NBV	DAF	SB220LC550	0E332308	Optare	5073	DP48F	3/90	Blackpool 101	Lloyd, -?-
	G434 NGE	Mercedes-Benz	609D	66806320879524	Scott	4744	C24F	9/89	Simpson, Inverkip	Kells Transport Museum, Cork
	G141 NPT	Leyland	Tiger TRCL10/3ARZA	TR00658	Duple	8989/1161	C53FT	11/89	Bissett, Ryton	-?-, -?-
			(ex PIL 2164, G141 NPT)							
	G 77 PKR	Mercedes-Benz	609D	6680632P009084	Reeve Burgess	17917	DP19F	12/89	Maidstone & District 1077	Pettie, Sittingbourne
	G571 PNS	Leyland	Roadrunner 9-13R	L020650	Wright	L108	B28FL	2/90	Strathclyde Regional Council	Ramsay, Glasgow
	G567 PRM	Mercedes Benz	709D	6690032P041003	Alexander	AM81/2589/90	DP21F	6/90	Ribble 567	Pringle, Bearsden
			(ex XIL 1483, G567 PRM)							
	G545 RDS	Volvo	Citybus B10M-50	024027	Alexander	RV50/189/45	H47/37F	2/90	Strathclyde Buses AH101	Kennedy, Glasgow

	G251 SRG	DAF	SB220LC550	329723	Optare	5036	B48F	11/89	Northumbria 251	Fickling & Kennan, -?-
	G 39 TGW	Dennis	Dart	8.5SDL3003/179	Carlyle	C25.083	B34F	7/90	Selkent DT39	Gurney, Petts Wood
	G806 TMX	Leyland	Olympian	ON2R50C13Z4 ON11504	Leyland	DD1105	H47/31F	5/90	Metrobus, Orpington 806	Suggett, -?-
	G909 TWS	Leyland	Olympian	ONCL10/1RZ ON11063	Leyland	DD1075	CH43/29F	10/89	Badgerline 9009	Williams, Bristol
	G709 VRY	→ see 90-MH-4542 *Ireland*								
	G504 VYE	Dennis	Dart	8.5SDL3003/142	Duple	D8901/0038	V38F	3/90	London United DT4	Sullivan, Potters Bar (HT)
	G506 VYE	Dennis	Dart	8.5SDL3003/144	Duple	D8901/0040	B28F	3/90	London United DT6	Newing-Davis, Bankfoot
			(ex RIL 9774, G506 VYE)							
	G515 VYE	Dennis	Dart	8.5SDL3003/153	Duple	D9001/0049	DP28F	1/90	London United DT15	Beardsell, Frith End
	G526 VYE	Dennis	Dart	8.5SDL3003/172	Duple	D9001/0060	B31F	4/90	London United DT26	West Wight Bus Preservation Group, Freshwater
	G645 WDV	Volkswgen	LT31	LH017630	Devon Conversions	760D	M10	6/90	Help the Aged, Crediton	Hearn, Bideford
	G183 WGX	Leyland	Olympian	ONCL10/1RZ ON11237	Alexander (Belfast)	D01.01	H47/31F	3/90	Dublin Bus RH1	Emery, Chase Terrace
			(ex 90-D-1001 *Ireland)*							
	G362 XGM	→ see 89-C-19014 *Ireland*								
	G111 XOW	Leyland	Lynx	LX2R11C15Z4R LX1391	Leyland		B47F	3/90	Southampton 111	Savin, Southampton
	G330 XRE	Mercedes-Benz	811D	67030320944250	PMT	9144	B28F	10/89	PMT 330	Brundrit, Cotes Heath (ST)
	G334 XRE	Mercedes-Benz	811D	67030320951616	PMT	9155	B28F	10/89	PMT 334	Gale, Meir
	G759 XRE	Leyland	Olympian	ONCL10/1RZ ON11276	Leyland	DD1063	CH43/29F	9/89	PMT 759	Buttery, Stoke-on-Trent
	G 38 YHJ	Leyland	Lynx	LX2R11C15Z4R LX1622	Leyland		B49F	11/89	Colchester 38	Charsley, -?-
	G168 YRE	Mercedes-Benz	709D	6690032P017478	LHE		B29F	3/90	Stevensons 168	Boddice et al, Swadlincote
	G565 YTR	Fiat	49-10	2501333	Phoenix	1171	B23F	4/90	Phoenix demonstrator	Watts, Beccles
	H810 AGX	Leyland	Olympian	ON2R50C13Z4 ON20028	Leyland	DD1142	H47/31F	2/91	Metrobus, Orpington	Boxall Griffin & Hall, Beckenham
	H 74 ANG	Dennis	Condor	DDA1810/643	Duple Metal Sections		H69/41D	12/90	China Motor Bus DM17	Moore Thornhill & Brown, Norwich
			(ex ES 997 *Hong Kong*)							
	H423 BNL	Scania	N113DRB	1818830	Alexander	RH87/2190/3	H47/29F	3/91	Busways 423	Welford, Burnhope
	H426 BNL	Scania	N113DRB	1818833	Alexander	RH87/2190/9	H47/29F	3/91	Busways 426	Buckley & Minto, Newcastle-upon-Tyne
(r)	H598 CNL	DAF	SB220LC550	329750	Optare	5129	DP48F	11/90	Northumbria 260	Transport Yorkshire Preservation Group
	H401 CJF	→ see 90-C-16424 *Ireland*								
	H523 CTR	ACE	Cougar	89015	Wadham Stringer	2829/90	B41F	12/90	Provincial 3	Provincial Society, Fareham
	H 3 FBT	DAF	SB220LC550	0H000008	Optare	5153	DP48F	4/91	Fylde 3	Lancastrian Transport Trust
	H252 GEV	→ see 90-LK-5372 *Ireland*								
	H253 GEV	→ see 90-LK-5373 *Ireland*								
	H256 GEV	→ see 90-LK-5374 *Ireland*								
	H265 GEV	Leyland	Olympian	ON2R50G13Z4 ON11580	Leyland	DD1118	CH43/29F	7/90	Southend 265	Claydon, Corringham
	H801 GRE	DAF	SB220LC550	344106	Optare	5080	DP48F	8/90	PMT SAD801	Pearson, Stoke-on-Trent
	H860 GRE	Leyland	Lynx	LX2R11C15Z4R LX1866	Leyland		DP48F	8/90	PMT 860	Plant, Newcastle-under-Lyme
	H140 GVM	Dennis	Dominator	DDA2033/1080	Northern Counties	4162	H43/29F	4/91	Greater Manchester Buses 2040	SELNEC Preservation Society
	H466 GVM	Scania	N113CRB	1818894	Northern Counties	4176	H47/28F	6/91	Greater Manchester Buses 1466	Birchall, Bury
			(ex 7195 BY, H466 GVM)							
	H467 GVM	Scania	N113CRB	1818895	Northern Counties	4177	H47/28F	6/91	Greater Manchester Buses 1467	SELNEC Preservation Society
	H 35 HBG	Leyland	Lynx	LX2R11C15Z4R LX2006	Leyland		B51F	5/91	Halton 35	1075 Group, St Helens
	H886 LOX	Dennis	Dart	9SDL3002/245	Carlyle	C26.005	B35F	12/90	Warrington 209	-?-, -?-
	H262 MFX	Dennis	Dominator	DDA1033/1088	East Lancs	B0410	H47/33F	6/91	Bournemouth 262	Hawkins, Kingswear
	H577 MOC	Dennis	Dart	8.5SDL3003/247	Carlyle	C25-128	B28F	9/90	London United DT77	Coleman, Isle of Wight
			(ex RIL 9774, H577 MOC, WLT 339, H577 MOC)							
	H373 MVT	Mercedes-Benz	811D	6703032P028377	PMT	9218	B29F	4/91	PMT 373	Gale, Meir
	H842 NOC	Dennis	Dart	9SDL3002/448	Carlyle	C26.010	B35F	3/91	Warrington 214	Arnold, Warrington

H188 OSG	→ see XAZ 1399								
H775 PTW	Leyland	Olympian ON2R50C13Z4	ON11638	Alexander (Belfast)	D02.10	H47/33F	9/90	Dublin Bus RH28	Cooper, Ipswich
		(ex 90-D-1028 *Ireland*)							
H174 RBO	Optare	MetroRider MR01	VN1082	Optare	1082	B31F	7/91	Cardiff 174	Cardiff Transport Preservation Group
H387 SET	Bedford	Midi	688518	Post Office Workshops		M11	1/91	Royal Mail 0750102	Cott, Winfarthing
H 54 VRH	→ see 90-LH-5008 *Ireland*								
H816 WKH	Scania	N113DRB	1817623	East Lancs	B0101	H47/37F	9/90	Hull 816	Hull & Country Bus Preservation Group
H904 XGA	→ see IBZ 3051								
H124 YGG	→ see IUI 9892								
H615 YTC	Leyland	Lynx LX2R11C15Z4R	LX1907	Leyland		B49F	8/90	Badgerline 3615	Gould, Bristol
H616 YTC	→ see 90-LK-5382 *Ireland*								
J216 AET	Mercedes-Benz	811D	6703032N001151	Alexander	AM90/2491/3	B31F	5/92	Chesterfield 16	Jones, Chesterfield
J377 AWT	Leyland	Lynx LX2R11C15Z4S	LX2104	Leyland		B49F	11/91	West Riding 377	Hurley, Wakefield
J217 BWU	Optare	MetroRider MR03	VN1162	Optare	1162	B26F	1/92	London Buses MRL217	Phillips, -?-
J475 FSR	DAF	400	CN910630	Post Office Workshops		M14	3/92	Royal Mail 1750066	Cott, Winfarthing
J858 FTC	Mercedes-Benz	709D	6690032P155901	Plaxton	91.7MCV0485	B23F	10/91	Badgerline 3858	Bristol Vintage Bus Group
J501 GCD	Dennis	Dart	9.8SDL3107/655	Alexander	AM88/1591/1	B41F	12/91	Hastings & District 501	Southdown (WS) 32501
J953 LKK	Ford	Transit	BDVVLY86403	Crystals	556	B20F	8/91	Kent County Council	Thornes, Hemingbrough (NY) 128
		(ex SAC 500, J953 LKK, OKP 980, J953 LKK) *(Dormobile frame 50861 997 90)*							
J329 LLK	Volvo	B10M-46	028407	Plaxton	919.8VAA0488	C43F	1/92	Marton, West Drayton	Welch, -?-
J701 NHA	Dennis	Dart	9.8SDL3004/441	East Lancs	B0702	B42F	9/91	Midland Red (North) 701	Brundrit, Cotes Heath
J710 ONF	Volvo	Citybus B10M-50	026865	Northern Counties	4172	H45/32FL	2/92	Greater Manchester Buses 7010	SELNEC Preservation Society
J198 OSW	Volvo	B10M-60	021988	Plaxton	9012VCB1700	C51FT	1/92	Paterson & Brown, Kilbirnie	-?-, -?-
		(ex A 20 SAM)							
J198 PEY	Dennis	Dart	9.8SDL3012/620	Plaxton	919.8HPN0469	B40F	1/92	Thomas, Upper Llandwrog	-?-, -?-
J135 PVC	Leyland	Olympian ON2R50C13Z4R	ON11736	Leyland	DD1138	H47/25D	4/91	Volvo-Leyland demonstrator	Boxall Griffin & Clitheroe, Bromley
J872 RPJ	MCW	Metrorider MF156	MB9699	MCW		C25F	-/91	Bova (lhd demonstrator)	Mackintosh, Birmingham
		(ex 182 SKN, J872 RPJ) *(first licensed in UK 1/92)*							
J786 TDC	→ see 00-C-35652 *Ireland*								
J801 WSF	Leyland	Olympian ON2R50C13Z4	ON20384	Alexander	RL64/792/1	H47/32F	6/92	Fife Scottish 701	Fife Scottish (SE) 14701
J317 XVX	Dennis	Dart	9SDL3011/617	Wright	N190	B35F	2/92	County DW317	Thorne, South Ockendon
		(ex 9163 AP, J317 XVX)							
J139 YRM	Leyland	Olympian ON2R50C13Z4	ON11802	Leyland	DD1159	H47/29F	10/91	Walthamstow Citybus 139	Rogers, Swindon
K514 BHN	MAN	11.190	WMA46912496082835	Optare	4014	B42F	6/93	United Auto 1514	-?-, Skelton
K888 BWU	Leyland	Olympian ON2R50C13Z4	ON20486	Northern Counties	4343	H47/30F	11/92	Capital Citybus 165	-?-, Bromley
K117 CSG	Dennis	Dart	9SDL3016/1205	Alexander	AM98/2592/6	B35F	12/92	Lothian 117	Lothian Bus Consortium
K909 CVW	Dennis	Dart	9SDL3016/979	Plaxton	929HMN0656	B35F	8/92	Thamesway 909	Blackwater Preservation, Essex
K232 DAC	Peugeot	J5	VF3290BE200363100	Peugeot		M11	2/93	Peugeot demonstrator	Coventry Transport Museum
		(prototype electric minibus)							
K521 EFL	Fiat	49-10	2054766	Marshall	C29.049	B23F	4/93	Selkent FM1	Gurney, Petts Wood
K601 ESH	Dennis	Dart	9.8SDL3017/948	Alexander	AM92/1591/84	B40F	8/92	Fife Scottish (SE) 601	Fife Scottish (SE) 32201
K409 FHJ	Dennis	Dart	9.8SDL3018/1301	Plaxton	939.8HPN1234	B40F	3/93	County DPL409	-?-, -?-
K 1 GRT	Mercedes-Benz	O405G	35721121068901	Alexander	??/692/1	AB60T	11/92	Grampian 1	Aberdeen & District Transport Preservation Trust
K601 HUG	Scania	N113CRB	1821625	Alexander	AF04/2392/1	B50F	4/93	Yorkshire Rider 8601	Stazicker, Rawdon
K101 JMV	Leyland	Lynx LX2R11C15Z4S	LX2133	Leyland		B51F	8/92	Metrobus, Orpington	Shepherd, Washington
K62 KEX	Dennis	Dart	9.8SDL3025/1449	East Lancs	6601	DP43F	5/93	Great Yarmouth 62	East Anglia Transport Museum

	Reg	Chassis	Model	Chassis no	Body	Body no	Layout	New	First operator	Owner
	K621 LAE	Leyland	Olympian ON2R50C13Z5	ON20578	Northern Counties	4368	H47/29F	1/93	Bristol 9621	Willmott, Bristol
	K361 LWS	DAF	400	CN916990	G&M	J1552	M16	9/92	Rothwell, Plymouth	Chambers, Exeter
					(converted from van 10/97)					
(r)	K852 MTJ	Leyland	Lynx LX2R11C15Z4R	LX2067	Leyland		B51F	8/92	Halton 64	-?-, -?-
	K853 MTJ	Leyland	Lynx LX2R11C15Z4R	LX2142	Leyland		B51F	8/92	Halton 57	North West Museum of Transport
	K879 ODY	Mercedes-Benz	709D	6690032N004207	Alexander (Belfast)	M0909	B25F	4/93	Stagecoach (South) 879	Turner, Bishops Waltham
	K723 PNL	Dennis	Dart	9.8SDL3035/1415	Alexander	AM101/3592/1	B40F	7/93	Busways 1723	Hines, Sunderland
	K105 SFJ	Dennis	Dart	9.8SDL3017/1024	Plaxton	929.8HPN0348	B40F	10/92	Plymouth 105	Darch, Plymouth
	K909 SKR	Leyland	Olympian ON2R50C13Z4	ON20734	Northern Counties	4395	H47/30F	2/93	Maidstone & District 5909	Weber, Gravesend
(a)	K134 SRH	Dennis	Dart	9SDL3024/1486	Plaxton	939HSN1745	B34F	9/93	East London DRL134	McHaddan, Newcastle-upon-Tyne
	K888 TKS	Leyland	Olympian ON2R50C13Z4	ON20487	Northern Counties	3901	H46/29F	4/93	Capital Citybus 166	-?-, Bromley
	K916 VDV	Fiat	59-12	2067611	Mellor	00174	B28F	5/93	Blue Admiral 2040	City of Portsmouth Preserved Transport Depot
	K625 YVN	Leyland	Lynx LX2R11V18Z4S	LX2126	Leyland		B49F	7/92	Cleveland Transit 25	Kells Transport Museum, Cork
	K626 YVN	Leyland	Lynx LX2R11V18Z4S	LX2127	Leyland		B49F	7/92	Cleveland Transit 26	Viscount (CM) 29626
(r)	K628 YVN	Leyland	Lynx LX2R11V18Z4S	LX2129	Leyland		B49F	7/92	Cleveland Transit 28	Kells Transport Museum, Cork
	L328 AUT	Mercedes-Benz	709D	669003N0196749	Leicester Carriage Builders		B25F	6/94	Midland Fox M328	Fowkes, Southampton
	L512 BOD	DAF	400	CN938940	DAF		M16	10/93	Okehampton College	Shears C, Winkleigh
	L929 CTT	Fiat	59-12	2091404	Mellor	00854	B21D	3/94	Devon General 1000	West Country Historic Omnibus & Transport Trust
	L933 CTT	Fiat	59-12	2090933	Mellor	00859	B21D	3/94	Devon General 1004	Williams, Bristol
	L247 FDV	Fiat	49-10	2083741	Mellor	01160	B13D	7/94	Iveco demonstrator	Oxford Bus Museum Trust
	L501 HCY	Dennis	Dart	9SDL3034/1543	Plaxton	939.2HWN1636	B31F	10/93	South Wales 501	South Wales Transport Preservation Trust
	L133 HVS	Volvo	B10B-58	000437	Alexander	AF07/593/1	B51F	10/93	Buffalo, Flitwick 37	-?-, -?-
	L158 JNH	Volvo	B10M-60	032073	Plaxton	9312VCM1428	C51F	8/93	United Counties 158	Rogers, Swindon
	L866 LFS	Mercedes-Benz	711D	6693032N015426	Plaxton	937MNV1854	B25F	1/94	Clydeside 2000 261	Stafford, Renfrew (SW)
	L802 MEV	Dennis	Dart	9SDL3034/1684	Plaxton	939.2HWN1886	B35F	12/93	Eastern National 802	Brown, Romford
	L668 MSF	Volvo	B6-50	005366	Alexander	AM104/993/29	DP40F	2/94	Fife Scottish 668	Morrish, Burton-in-Kendal
	L837 MWT	Optare	Metrorider MR07	VN1351	Optare	1351	B31F	9/93	Darlington 37	Hayward, Thornton
	L601 PWR	Volvo	Olympian YN2RV18Z4	025431	Northern Counties	4744	H47/29F	7/94	Yorkshire Rider 5601	-?-, Rawdon
	L639 PWR	Scania	N113CRB	1823358	Alexander	AF12/2893/4	B48F	5/94	Yorkshire Rider 8639	Stazicker, Rawdon
										(on loan to Oxfordshire Playbus, Upper Heyford (XOX))
	L648 PWR	Scania	N113CRB	1823367	Alexander	AF12/2893/13	B48F	6/94	Yorkshire Rider 8648	Transport Yorkshire Preservation Group
	L132 TFB	Dennis	Lance	11SDA3112/248	Plaxton	9311.9HYL1681	B49F	1/94	Badgerline 132	Gould, Bristol
	L227 TKA	Volvo	B6-50	005401	Plaxton	9410.2WVN2338	B38F	5/94	MTL (Manchester) 7227	Rowlands, Liverpool
	L888 TTT	Volvo	Olympian YN2RV18Z4	025001	Northern Counties	4544	H47/29F	10/93	Capital Citybus 168	Bromley Bus Preservation Group
	L201 UNS	Leyland	Olympian ON2R50C13V3	ON20846	Alexander	RL67/4692/52	H47/31F	10/93	Strathclyde Buses LO101	LO101 Preservation Group, Glasgow
	L401 VCV	Dennis	Dart	9.8SDL3035/1815	Plaxton	9410HXN2586	B40F	4/94	Western National 401	Partridge, Exeter
	L116 YOD	Dennis	Dart	9.8SDL3035/1595	Plaxton	9310HXN1730	B40F	11/93	Plymouth 116	Cooksey, Plymouth
	L888 YTT	Volvo	Olympian YN2RV16Z4	025002	Northern Counties	4539	H47/29F	10/93	Capital Citybus 167	Bromley Bus Preservation Group
	L116 YVK	Dennis	Dart	9SDL3034/1736	Northern Counties	4654	B35F	2/94	Kentish Bus 116	Thompson, Shrewsbury
	M586 ANG	Volvo	B6-50	005732	Plaxton	9410.2VZN2378	B40F	11/94	Eastern Counties VP86	Wells & Thorpe, Ipswich
	M839 ATC	Mercedes-Benz	709D	6690032N022759	Plaxton	947MHV2435	B25F	8/94	Bristol 7839	-?-, Bristol
	M739 BSJ	Volvo	B6-50	005655	Alexander	AM115/1893/74	DP40F	10/94	Western Scottish V339	Western Buses (SW) 30339
	M902 DRG	Volvo	B10B-58	000834	Alexander	AF10/3093/5	B51F	9/94	Busways 902	Tyne & Wear Bus Preservation Group
	M627 HDV	Fiat	59-12	2113205	Wadham Stringer	4594/94	B21D	9/94	Devon General 1029	West Country Historic Omnibus & Transport Trust
(a)	M52 HOD	Volvo	B6-50	005633	Plaxton	9410.2VZN2900	B40F	10/94	Plymouth 52	Plymouth City Transport Preservation Group
	M53 HOD	Volvo	B6-50	005639	Plaxton	9410.2VZN2901	B40F	10/94	Plymouth 53	Cooksey, Plymouth

Registration	Chassis make	Chassis model	Chassis no.	Body make	Body no.	Layout	New	First operator	Current owner
M350 JBO	Mercedes-Benz	709D	6690032N021591	Alexander (Belfast)	M25080894	B25F	9/94	Red & White 350	Lacey, Broadclyst
M396 KVR	Mercedes-Benz	709D	6690032N023579	Alexander(Belfast)	M3207	B27F	2/95	AA (Dodds), Troon	Transport Preservation Trust, Beith
M109 PWN	Dennis	Javelin	12SDA2153/1185	Plaxton	9512HCP3869	C53F	5/95	South Wales 109	South Wales Transport Preservation Trust
M106 RMS	Scania	L113CRL	1823652	Alexander	AF15/394/3	B51F	1/95	Clydeside 2000 506	-?-, -?-
M245 UTM	Mercedes-Benz	709D	6690032N030653	Marshall	C19.346	B21D	5/95	Devon General 1053	Lacey, Broadclyst
M670 VJN	Mercedes-Benz	709D	6690032N026130	Plaxton	957MHV3177	B23F	3/95	Eastern National 670	-?-, -?-
M736 VSC	Fiat	59-12	2112537	Mellor	01064	B16F	1/96	Royal Mail 3750014	Cott, Winfarthing
M939 XKA	Mercedes-Benz	609D	6680632N030576	Devon Conversions	550M	DP16FL	4/95	GM Accessible Transport	Museum of Transport, Manchester
N624 CDB	Dennis	Dart	9.8SDL3054/3186	Northern Counties	5295	B39F	5/96	Greater Manchester North 1124	SELNEC Preservation Society
N652 CDB	Dennis	Dart	9.8SDL3054/3058	Plaxton	9510HXN4775	B40F	5/96	Greater Manchester North 1152	SELNEC Preservation Society
N592 CKA	Volvo	B10B-58	TA002230	Wright	U191	B49F	10/95	Merseyside 6592	Rowlands, Liverpool
N811 CKA	Optare	MetroRider MR13	VN1782	Optare	1782	B31F	8/95	Fareway 7811	Woolfe & Moore, Liverpool
N299 CKB	Volvo	Olympian YN2RC16Z4	026461	Northern Counties	5285	CH39/28F	3/06	Merseyside 3299	-?-, -?-
N302 CKB	Volvo	Olympian YN2RC16Z4	026458	Northern Counties	5287	CH39/28F	3/96	Merseyside 3302	Callaghan & Wagg, Liverpool
N952 CPU	Dennis	Dart	9.8SDL3054/2820	Plaxton	9510HXN4369	B39F	10/95	Thamesway 952	Bell, -?-
N801 DNE	Volvo	B10M-55	045729	Alexander	9606/1	B49F	7/96	Greater Manchester South 801	-?-, -?-
N301 FOR	Iveco	59-12	2151637	Mellor	02285	B29F	11/95	Marchwood, Totton 263	-?-, -?-
N589 GRN	Optare	MetroRider MR37	VN1847	Optare	1847	B25F	11/95	Blackpool 589	Hayward, Thornton
N590 GRN	Optare	MetroRider MR37	VN1848	Optare	1848	B25F	11/95	Blackpool 590	Lancastrian Transport Trust
N213 HSJ	Volvo	B10M-62	044637	Van Hool	32564	C53F	5/96	Meney, Saltcoats	Docherty, Irvine
		(ex VST 915, N213 HSJ)							
N326 JTL	Volvo	B6-50	005903	East Lancs	B14506	B44F	11/95	Lincolnshire 326	Gallagher, Waddington
N243 PDL	Iveco	59-12	2164574	Marshall	C31-170	DP23F	5/96	Southern Vectis 243	Harrison, Cowes
N276 PDV	Mercedes-Benz	709D	6690032N034453	Plaxton	957.6MHV4217	B25F	10/95	Plymouth 276	Byrne, Okehampton
N143 PTG	Optare	MetroRider MR15	VN1912	Optare	1912	B31F	4/96	Cardiff 143	Cardiff Transport Preservation Group
N474 RVK	Mercedes-Benz	709D	6690032N042272	Alexander	9526/145	B23F	4/96	Busways 1474	Cartwight, Gateshead
N239 VPH	Dennis	Dart SLF	SFD112BR1TGW10195	East Lancs	B20403	B31F	7/96	Guildford & West Surrey DSL39	Weber, Gravesend
N322 WCH	Optare	MetroRider MR15	VN1853	Optare	1853	B31F	11/95	Trent 222	Heritage Collection of H&DW&D
N769 WRC	Volvo	B10M-55	043767	Alexander	9502/2	B48F	9/95	Nottingham 769	Nottingham Heritage Vehicles
N401 WVR	Mercedes-Benz	811D	6703032N027969	Alexander	9510/1	B31F	11/95	Greater Manchester South 401	SELNEC Preservation Society
P701 BTA	Volvo	B6-53	006186	Alexander	9163/51	B35F	3/97	Bayline 701	Pratt, Torquay
P329 HVX	Dennis	Dart	SFD212BR5TGD13467	Plaxton	969.2HWN5779	B34F	10/96	County DP329	Weber, Gravesend
P411 MLA	Dennis	Dart	SFD412BR5TGD13378	Plaxton	9610HXN5729	B37F	8/96	Centrewest D41	Griffin, Bromley
P920 RSC	LDV	Pilot	DN014738	LDV		M10	6/97	Royal Mail 6750039	Cott, Winfarthing
P916 RYO	Volvo	Olympian YN2RV18Z4	027745	Northern Counties	5679	H47/27D	6/97	London General NV116	Boxall & Griffin, Bromley
									(on loan to Go-Coachhire, Swanley (KT))
P190 SGV	Optare	Excelo L1150	VN9117	Optare	9117	B38F	6/97	Ipswich 190	Ipswich Bus Preservation Group
P164 TNY	Mercedes-Benz	711D	6693032N046980	Plaxton	967.6MRV5901	B27F	10/96	Rhondda Buses 164	Cardiff Transport Preservation Group
Q995 CPE	AEC	Regent III	O9617464	Park Royal	L3017	O26/26R	10/53	London Transport RT4588	Cowdery, Newton Abbot
		(ex NLP 581)							
Q644 GFV	Leyland	Titan PD3/4	611325	Metro-Cammell		RV	10/61	Preston R1	Wilkinson, South Shields (TW)
		(ex PRN 908)							
Q723 GHG	Leyland	Tiger RETL11	8500750	ECW	EX68	B51F	-/85	Leyland demonstrator	Marshall, Nuneaton
				(first registered 1/91)					
Q340 GVC	Leyland	Leopard PSU4/4R	L61081	Plaxton	669732	RV	7/66	BMMO 5827	New Generation Bus Preservation, Dudley

		(ex GHA 327D)							
Q313 KUA	Ford	TT	-?-	?		Ch12	-/26	-?-, -?-	Campbell, Harrogate
Q739 PES	→ see DMS 368C								
Q507 VHR	Bristol	MW6G	184012	ECW	12174	RV	5/61	Bristol W151	Staniforth, Stroud
		(ex 404 LHT)							
Q125 VOE	Leyland	Leopard PSU4/4R	L61643	Plaxton	669743	RV	7/66	BMMO 5838	Follwell & Owen, Newcastle-under-Lyme
		(ex GHA 338D)							
R186 DDX	Optare	Excel L1150	VN9177	Optare	9177	B37F	11/97	Ipswich 186	-?-, Ipswich
R189 DDX	Optare	Excel L1150	VN9179	Optare	9179	B27F	11/97	Ipswich 189	Ipswich Bus Preservation Group
R846 FSX	→ see 97-WH-3861 *Ireland*								
R228 SCH	Optare	MetroRider MR15	VN2206	Optare	2206	B31F	9/97	Nottingham 228	Colne Estuary Preserved Buses
R810 YUD	Dennis	Dart SLF	322BR1VGW11744	Alexander	9705/80	B37F	2/98	Thames Transit 810	Minnett, Stroud
R718 YWC	Dennis	Dart	412BR5VGD13565	Plaxton	9710HXN7335	B43F	10/97	East London PD18	Carters, Wherstead (SK)
S112 GUB	Optare	MetroRider MR35	VN2281	Optare	2281	B25F	8/98	Warrington 112	Arnold. Warrington
S412 GUB	Mercedes-Benz	O814D	6703732N075646	Plaxton	987.8MWV8953	B27F	8/98	Yorkshire Rider 2412	Derrick, Plymstock
S509 LHG	Optare	MetroRider MR37	VN2291	Optare	2291	B25F	12/98	Blackpool 509	Greensmith, Saltburn
S510 LHG	Optare	MetroRider MR37	VN2292	Optare	2292	B25F	12/98	Blackpool 510	Lloyd, -?-
S529 RWP	Mercedes-Benz	O814D	6703732N072695	Plaxton	987.8MWV8314	B27F	8/98	Midland Red West 529	Williams, Goldsithney
LK 53 MBO	Mercedes-Benz	Citaro O530	62807523602680	Mercedes-Benz		B30D	12/03	First Capital ESQ64991	Science Museum, Wroughton
LK 53 MBU	Mercedes-Benz	Citaro O530	62807523603418	Mercedes-Benz		B30D	12/03	First Capital ESQ64992	Transport Preservation Trust, Beith
LK 53 MBV	Mercedes-Benz	Citaro O530	62807523603446	Mercedes-Benz		B30D	12/03	First Capital ESQ64993	London Transport Museum

Alderney registration

AY 81	Albion	Victor FT39AN	73821D	Heaver		B35F	1/57	Guernsey Railway 60	Curtis, Alderney (CI)
		(ex YFF 660, 3338)							
AY 91	Bedford	SB3	ET102376	Duple	8301/0098	C41F	3/84	Blue Coach, St Helier 23	Myall, Bassingbourn (CM)
		(ex J26626) *(fitted with a Bedford diesel engine)*							
AY 593	Leyland	Cub CU435	566466	Duple	137/5557	B31F	11/81	Lothian 166	-?-, Norfolk
		(ex HSC 166X)							

Guernsey registrations

653	→ see DFP 496								
1309	→ see 210 UXO								
1463	→ see MSV 412								
1529	→ see RSJ 747								
1559	Albion	Victor PH115	25006L	Reading *(rebodied 2/55)*	5185	B32F	7/36	Watson, St Martins	Ridley, Orpington
1787	→ see 898 FUF								
1982	→ see KSU 288								
2027	→ see 395 DEL								
2493	→ see 840 XUJ								
2493	Bedford	J4EZ1	2T124550	Sparshatt	9666K	B35F	4/72	Guernsey Motors 112	Stevenson, Worcester
3338	→ see AY 81 *Alderney*								
3409	→ see MSJ 702								
4022	→ see JPA 82V								

	Reg	Chassis	Model	Chassis No	Body	Body No	Layout	Date	First owner	Current owner
	4029	→ see LSV 748								
	4510	→ see VVS 913								
	6436	→ see RFO 375								
	6438	Albion	Victor FT39N	73004B	Heaver	9711	B35F	3/51	Guernsey Railway 38	Wilson, Milngavie
	6768	→ see 842 FUF								
	6769	Albion	Victor FT39AN	73780C	Heaver	2466	B35F	5/55	Guernsey Railway 55	Walker, Renfrew
	8227	→ see YFO 127								
	8228	→ see TFO 249								
	8229	Albion	Victor FT39KAN	73842E	Reading	2367	B35F	3/58	Guernsey Motors 79	Heal, Sandford
	8230	→ see ESV 215								
	9439	→ see 839 XUJ								
	14651	→ see EBW 112B								
	14838	Bedford	J4EZ1	6816013	Reading	2405C	B35F	7/66	Guernsey Motors 101	Keeling, Nottingham
	14867	→ see VHO 462								
	16216	→ see JNP 590C								
	31915	Bristol	LH6L (ex 12327, JFJ 508N)	LH-1121	Plaxton	7510BC018S	C45F	8/75	Greenslade 328	Gray Andrews & Allen, South Devon
	31921	Bristol	LH6L (ex AFJ 736T)	LH-1576	Plaxton	7910BXM518/S	C45F	8/79	Western National 3316	Britishbus Preservation Group
	47638	Ford	R1015 (ex J 43063)	BCRSEA40557	Wadham Stringer	8537/84	B45F	10/84	JMT 23	Miller, Edinburgh

Jersey registrations

	Reg	Chassis	Model	Chassis No	Body	Body No	Layout	Date	First owner	Current owner
	J 1199	→ see SV 6107								
	J 1359	→ see FAS 982								
(r)	J 1681	Seddon	Pennine 4	42340	Pennine		B32F	4/68	JMT 681	Bell, St Helier
	J 4540	→ see JSU 173								
	J 4601	→ see JCP 60F								
	J 5149	→ see KEL 679								
	J 5567	→ see 840 XUJ								
	J 5660	→ see 839 XUJ								
	J 6332	Leyland	Titan TD2	1690	Leyland		H27/24R	-/32	JMT 25	Banfield, Staplehurst
	J 6986	→ see LSU 857								
	J 7247	Bedford	OB (ex JAB 661)	136245	Duple	49993	C29F	5/50	Powell, Summerfield	Tantivy Blue Coach, St Helier (CI)
	J 7682	Seddon	Pennine 4	42341	Pennine		B32F	4/68	JMT 682	Bell, St Helier
	J 8121	Dennis	Triton	173TV3	Reading	1472	B21F	7/53	JMT 43	-?-, -?-
	J 8535	→ see JAX 354								
	J 8588	→ see 780 JGY								
	J 8697	→ see UWP 154F *Overseas*								
	J 9151	→ see JWU 307								
	J 9522	Leyland	PD1A	471841	Leyland		H56R	-/47	JMT 30	Glover & Wilson, Ripon
	J 9567	Morris-Commercial	C	756C23531	Underhill/Willowbrook *(new with rebuilt secondhand body new -/29)*		B23F	5/36	Safety Coach 10	Lawson, Baildon
	J 11429	→ see OSJ 512								
	J 13540	Dennis	Pax	1110D2	Reading	6812	B21F	3/50	JMT 82	Courtnage, Four Marks
	J 15213	→ see 804 FUF								
	J 26626	→ see AY 91 *Alderney*								

	Reg									
	J 40614	→ see A747 DWP								
	J 43063	→ 47638 *Guernsey*								

Isle of Man registrations

	Reg	Make	Model	Chassis no	Body	Body no	Layout	New	First operator	Owner
	MN 765	Ford	T	-?-	Dixie (Market Bosworth)		B??	-/16	-?-, -?-	Howland, Isle of Man
			(ex -?-)							
	MN 2615	Tilling Stevens	TS3A	2826	*chassis only*			5/23	Douglas 10	London Transport Museum
	MN 5105	→ see MAN 1928 *Isle of Man*								
	MN 5454	Thornycroft	BC	16287	Hall Lewis	1916	B28D	5/28	Isle of Man Railway 13	Isle of Man Transport (IM)
			(ex MAN 1928, MN 5454)							
	DMN 650	AEC	Regent	O6615965	Northern Counties		H27/25R	4/39	Douglas 50	Jennings, Douglas
			(ex SWU 222F, DMN 650)							
	FMN 955	→ see SVS 281								
	HMN 689	→ see MAN 691D *Isle of Man*								
	HMN 787	Leyland	Tiger PS1	462354	ECW	2352	B35R	4/48	Isle of Man Road Services 34	Kneale & Hurd, Isle of Man
			(ex MAN 1947, HMN 787)							
	JMN 725	→ see WPH 358S								
	JMN 727	→ see MSL 294								
	KMN 501	Leyland	Titan PD2/1	484669	Leyland		H30/26R	2/49	Isle of Man Road Services 71	Isle of Man Transport (IM)
	KMN 502	→ see GFO 641								
	KMN 504	Leyland	Titan PD2/1	490611	Leyland		H30/26R	2/49	Isle of Man Road Services 2	Isle of Man Transport (IM)
			(ex 85 EBK, KMN 504)							
	KMN 519	Leyland	Comet CPO1	490414	Park Royal	B34279	B30F	1/50	Douglas 21	Wilson, Bootle
			(ex 528 JKC, KMN 519)							
	KMN 835	AEC	Regent III	9612E2071	Northern Counties	4265	H30/26R	6/49	Douglas 64	Isle of Man Transport (IM)
(r)	KMN 839	AEC	Regent III	9612E4491	*chassis only*			6/49	Douglas 68	72 Group, Lancaster
			(ex 113 KGC, KMN 839)							
	MAN 1379	Leyland	Atlantean PDR2/1	7101517	Alexander	2L4/2269/31	H49/31D	9/71	Merseyside PTE 1181	Craine, Douglas
			(ex XKC 808K)							
	MAN 1927	Leyland	Lion LSC1	45955	Massey	623	B28R	7/27	Manxland 27	Isle of Man Transport (IM)
			(ex MN 5105)							
	MAN 1935	Bedford	YRQ	DW453617	Duple	415/2065	C45F	6/74	Harrison, Morecambe	-?-, Isle of Man
			(ex B111 MAN, TTC 517M)							
	MAN 1968	→ see 410 LMN								
	MMN 11	→ see YKG 961T								
	MMN 57	→ see YTF 162J *Overseas*								
	MMN 302	Leyland	Olympic HR40	502364	Weymann	L15	B40F	6/51	Isle of Man Road Services 84	Davis, Isle of Man
	NMN 355	AEC	Regal IV	9821LT751	Metro-Cammell		B39F	12/52	London Transport RF382	Sharp, Onchan
			(ex APA 136A, MXX 24)							
	NMN 906	Leyland	Royal Tiger PSU1/13	520996	Leyland		B44F	5/52	Isle of Man Road Services 88	Rimmer, Onchan
	NMN 907	Leyland	Royal Tiger PSU1/13	521234	Leyland		B44F	6/52	Isle of Man Road Services 89	Merseyside Transport Trust
	WMN 6	Leyland	Tiger Cub PSUC1/1	575432	Weymann	M7988	B44F	7/57	Isle of Man Road Services 20	Pye, Preston
	WMN 485	→ see UTU 596J								
	WMN 487	Guy	Otter	NLLODP47259	Mulliner		B26F	11/57	Douglas 11	Smith, Chelford
			(ex UTU 597J, WMN 487)							
	XMN 345	→ see XMC 168A *Overseas*								
	XMN 346	Leyland	Titan PD3/3	580999	Metro-Cammell		H41/32R	6/58	Isle of Man Road Services 32	Isle of Man Transport (IM)
	1949 MN	Bedford	OB	123524	Duple	55656	C29F	1/50	Bailey, Turvey	Tours, Douglas (IM) 49

(ex BVH 319A, HTM 20)
1949 MN (previous holder) → see SS 7376
3680 MN Leyland Tiger Cub PSUC1/2 614776 Willowbrook CF146 B43F 8/61 Isle of Man Road Services 54 Crellin, Douglas
(ex PFV 819X, 3680 MN)
7 MAN → see 67 UMN *Isle of Man*
900 EMN Bedford VAS1 6847692 Duple Midland CF1336 B30F 7/66 Douglas 7 Howe, Andreas
29 HMN → see POR 428
697 HMN Leyland Leopard PSU4/1R 701014 Willowbrook CF1454 DP41F 6/67 Isle of Man Road Services 97 Davis, Kirk Michael
410 LMN AEC Regent V 3D2RA2024 Willowbrook CF1616 H37/27F 12/68 Douglas 15 Isle of Man Transport (IM)
(ex BWA 429G, MAN 1968, 410 LMN)
67 UMN Leyland Titan PD3A/1 L20654 Metro-Cammell H41/32R 7/64 Isle of Man Road Services 60 Isle of Man Transport (IM)
(ex 7 MAN)
40 WMN → see SGF 483L
CMN 34C Leyland Atlantean AN68A/1R 7705468 Alexander AL64/3575/1 H45/28D 12/78 Portsmouth 320 Denne & Faragher, Isle of Man
(ex UOR 320T)
CMN 35C Leyland Atlantean AN68A/1R 7705474 Alexander AL64/3575/11 H45/28D 2/79 Portsmouth 321 -?-, Isle of Man
(ex UOR 321T)
CMN 44C Leyland Atlantean AN68A/1R 7705799 Alexander AL64/3575/9 H45/30F 1/79 Portsmouth 330 Davis, Isle of Man
(ex UOR 330T)
MAN 665D Leyland Leopard PSU4/4R L62309 Marshall B3828 B44F 12/66 Ribble 665 Davis, Kirk Michael
(ex D440 MAN, F457 MAN, DRN 665D)
MAN 691D AEC Regent III O9612064 Northern Counties 4113 H--/--R 8/47 Douglas 58 Manx Transport Trust, Jurby
(ex HMN 689)
BMN 83G Leyland Olympian ONCL10/1RZ ON10735 Leyland DD1002 H47/31F 7/88 Isle of Man Transport 83 Manx Transport Trust, Jurby
MAN 24H Leyland National 11351/1R 03313 Leyland National B52F 4/76 Isle of Man Road Services 24 Manx Transport Museum Group
MAN 32N Leyland National 11351A/1R 04431 Leyland National B52F 5/77 Isle of Man Transport 32 Edwards, Ballasalla
DMN 16R Leyland Olympian ON2R50C13Z4 ON11692 Alexander (Belfast) D02.18 H47/31F 10/90 Dublin Bus RH36 Manx Transport Trust, Jurby
(ex 90-D-1036 *Ireland)*
DMN 25R Dennis Dart SLF 322BR1VGW10880 Marshall C39.062 B37F 9/97 Isle of Man Transport 35 Carey, Andreas
BMN 58V Leyland Olympian ON2R50C16Z4 ON11333 Northern Counties 4019 H47/30F 5/90 Isle of Man Transport 58 Denne, Port Erin
BMN 64V Leyland Olympian ON2R50C16Z4 ON11339 Northern Counties 4025 H47/30F 5/90 Isle of Man Transport 64 Denne, Port Erin
BMN 193V MCW Metrobus DR101/9 MB5335 MCW H43/26D 12/79 London Transport M193 Cannan, Ramsey
(ex BYX 193V)
C 57 MAN Leyland Atlantean PDR1/1 L41581 Metro-Cammell H43/35F 12/65 Liverpool L728 Cannan & Dodge, Onchan
(ex CKF 728C)
D440 MAN → see MAN 665D *Isle of Man*
(r?) E156 MAN Leyland Leopard PSU4/4R L62523 Marshall B3836 B44F 12/66 Ribble 672 Davis, Kirk Michael
(ex DRN 672D)
(r) F809 MAN Leyland Leopard PSU4/4R L62522 Marshall B3835 B44F 12/66 Ribble 671 Davis, Kirk Michael
(ex DRN 671D)

Republic of Ireland registrations

BI 5014 → see DB 2243
IH 408 Bedford YRQ EW454585 Alexander (Belfast) -?- B45F 6/75 Western H&SS Board McGonagle, Buncrana (EI)
(ex AUI 4122)
IY 1940 AEC Regent III 9612E4653 Park Royal B33407 O30/22RD 8/49 Morecambe & Heysham 58 Transport Museum Society of Ireland
(ex KTF 587)
(r) IY 1947 Bedford OB 94761 Duple 52351 C29F 12/48 Birmingham Police Telford, Coleraine (NI)

Reg	Chassis	Model	Chassis no	Body	Body no	Layout	New	First owner	Current owner
		(ex JOH 262)							
IY 7383	GNR		4/51/389	Park Royal/GNR		B33R	-/51	Great Northern Railway 389	Cavan & Leitrim Railway
IY 7384	GNR		5/51/390	Park Royal/GNR		DP33R	-/51	Great Northern Railway 390	Transport Museum Society Ireland
IY 8044	GNR		3/52/396	Park Royal/GNR		B--R	-/52	Great Northern Railway 396	Cavan & Leitrim Railway
SI 2001	Van Hool	T815	YE281500A01C16601	Van Hool	16601	C53F	4/86	CIE CVH1	Kells Transport Museum, Cork
SI 2003	Van Hool	T815	YE281500A01C16603	Van Hool	16603	C53F	4/86	CIE CVH3	-?-, -?-
SI 2005	Van Hool	T815	YE281500A01C16605	Van Hool	16605	C53F	4/86	CIE CVH5	-?-, -?-
SI 2010	Van Hool	T815	YE281500A01C16610	Van Hool	16610	C53F	4/86	CIE CVH6	-?-, -?-
SI 2011	Van Hool	T815	YE281500A01C16611	Van Hool	16611	C53F	4/86	CIE CVH11	Dempsey, Celbridge
SI 2012	Van Hool	T815	YE281500A01C16612	Van Hool	16612	C53F	4/86	CIE CVH12	-?-, -?-
SI 2014	Van Hool	T815	YE281500A01C16614	Van Hool	16614	C53F	4/86	CIE CVH14	Kells Transport Museum, Cork
SI 2015	Van Hool	T815	YE281500A01C16615	Van Hool	16615	C53F	4/86	CIE CVH15	Kells Transport Museum, Cork
SI 2019	Van Hool	T815	YE281500A01C16619	Van Hool	16619	C53F	5/86	CIE CVH19	Kells Transport Museum, Cork
SI 2026	Van Hool	T815	YE281500A01C16626	Van Hool	16626	C53F	5/86	CIE CVH26	-?-, -?-
SI 2029	Van Hool	T815	YE281500A01C16629	Van Hool	16629	C53F	5/86	CIE CVH29	Willis, Dublin
SI 3003	Van Hool	T815	YE281500H01C16588	Van Hool	16588	C53F	5/86	CIE EVH3	-?-, -?-
SI 3007	Van Hool	T815	YE281500H01C16592	Van Hool	16592	C51FT	6/86	CIE EVH7	-?-, -?-
SI 3008	Van Hool	T815	YE281500H01C16593	Van Hool	16593	C51FT	6/86	CIE EVH8	Kells Transport Museum, Cork
SI 3010	Van Hool	T815	YE281500H01C16595	Van Hool	16595	C51FT	6/86	CIE EVH10	Hughes, Dublin
SI 3011	Van Hool	T815	YE281500H01C16596	Van Hool	-?-	C51FT	6/86	CIE EVH11	Kells Transport Museum, Cork
				(rebodied 1/92)					
SI 3012	Van Hool	T815	YE281500H01C16597	Van Hool	16597	C51FT	6/86	CIE EVH12	Kells Transport Museum, Cork
SI 3014	Van Hool	T815	YE281500H01C16599	Van Hool	16599	C51FT	6/86	CIE EVH14	-?-, -?-
ZC 714	Leyland	Titan TD4	13664	Leyland		H32/26R	-/37	Dublin United R1	Transport Museum Society of Ireland
ZD 726	GNR		3/41/324	GNR		B35R	-/41	Great Northern Railway 324	Ulster Folk & Transport Museum
				(rebodied -/49)					
ZD 939	Leyland	Tiger TS11	306652	CIE		B35F	7/47	CIE T11	Manahan, Dublin
		(chassis built in -/40 but not bodied until 7/47)							
ZD 942	Leyland	Tiger TS11	306655	CIE		B35F	7/47	CIE T14	Glynn, Graigue
		(chassis built in -/40 but not bodied until -/47)							
ZD 950	Leyland	Tiger TS11	306665	CIE		C30F	7/47	CIE T22	Wheatley, Drogheda
		(chassis built in -/40 but not bodied until 7/47)							
ZD 7163	Leyland	Tiger OPS3	472913	*chassis only*			9/48	CIE P23	Transport Museum Society of Ireland
ZF 608	Mercedes-Benz	L608D	-?-	Mercedes-Benz		C20F	by5/85	O'Regan, Cork	Kells Transport Museum, Cork
ZH 3926	AEC	Regal III	O962231	Park Royal	B33615	C35R	6/48	Great Northern Railway 427	Transport Museum Society of Ireland
ZH 3937	AEC	Regent III	9612E3745	Park Royal	B33613	H30/26RD	7/48	Great Northern Railway 438	Transport Museum Society of Ireland
ZH 4538	Leyland	Titan PD2/3	485135	Leyland		H33/27R	-/49	CIE R389	Transport Museum Society of Ireland
ZI 9708	Dennis	Lancet	170414	DUT		B32R	-/33	Dublin United 390	Transport Museum Society of Ireland
ZJ 5904	Leyland	Tiger OPS3/1	496529	CIE		RV	-/50	CIE P164	Shannon & Bedford, Cork
ZJ 5933	Leyland	Tiger OPS3/1	501049	CIE		RV	-/51	CIE P193	Transport Museum Society of Ireland
ZJ 5960	Leyland	Tiger OPS3/1	502171	CIE		B39R	-/51	CIE P220	Manahan, Dublin
ZJ 6021	Leyland	Tiger OPS3/1	497032	CIE		RV	-/51	CIE P281	Elliott, Bray
ZJ 6024	Leyland	Tiger OPS3/1	502763	CIE		FC30F	6/51	CIE P284	Manahan, Dublin
ZL 2718	GNR		12/50/387	Park Royal/GNR		B--R	-/50	Great Northern Railway 387	Transport Museum Society of Ireland
ZL 6816	Leyland	Titan OPD2/1	520223	CIE		H37/31R	1/53	CIE R506	Transport Museum Society of Ireland
ZO 6819	Leyland	Tiger PS2/14	521697	CIE		B39R	-/53	CIE P309	Transport Museum Society of Ireland
ZO 6834	Leyland	Tiger PS2/14	530944	CIE		RV	-/53	CIE P324	Manahan, Dublin
ZO 6857	Leyland	Tiger PS2/14	531320	CIE		B39R	10/53	CIE P347	Transport Museum Society of Ireland

	Reg	Make	Model	Chassis no	Body	Body no	Layout	New	First operator	Owner
	ZO 6881	Leyland	Royal Tiger PSU1/15	532403	CIE		C34C	-/54	CIE U10	Transport Museum Society of Ireland
	ZO 6949	Leyland	Royal Tiger PSU1/15	531692	CIE		B39D	-/54	CIE U78	Transport Museum Society of Ireland
	ZO 6960	Leyland	Titan OPD2/1	530646	CIE		H37/31R	7/53	CIE R541	Bedford, Celbridge
	ZS 8621	Daimler	Fleetline CRG6LX	64945	Park Royal	B58155	H--/--F	12/71	West Midlands PTE 4130	Lang, Rathcoole
			(ex YOX 130K)							
	ZU 5000	Leyland	Royal Tiger PSU1/9	530644	Saunders-Roe		B44C	-/53	Irish Army	Cavan & Leitrim Railway
	ZU 9241	Leyland	Titan OPD2/1	541645	CIE		H37/31RD	1/55	CIE R567	Transport Museum Society of Ireland
	ZV 1460	→ see LYC 731								
	ZV 1461	Leyland	Titan PD3/4	L03397	Northern Counties	6020	FCO39/30F	5/64	Southdown 415	Pearce, Worthing
			(ex PRX 187B, 415 DCD)							
	ZV 1510	Leyland	Atlantean PDR1/1	L60703	Metro-Cammell		O44/33F	8/66	Newcastle 118	North East Bus PreservationTrust
			(ex KBB 118D)							
	ZV 2428	Leyland	Royal Tiger PSU1/15	520092	Plaxton	669913	C43F	3/52	Hunter, Seaton Delaval	Universal, Portlaoise (EI)
			(ex EJR 791)		*(rebodied 1/66)*					
	ZV 3839	→ see MSJ 606								
	ZV 9400	→ see KEL 94								
	ZV 50203	Bedford	OB	100257	Duple	52508	C29F	3/49	Fyffe, Dundee	Devereux, Dublin
			(ex 184 XUF, ATS 689)							
	ZY 79	AEC	Regal IV	9822E1543	Park Royal / GNR		B45R	2/54	Great Northern Railway 274	Transport Museum Society of Ireland
	ZY 1715	AEC	Regal IV	9822E1843	Park Royal / GNR		B40F	1/55	Great Northern Railway 345	Cavan & Leitrim Railway
					(latterly converted to a railbus for Bord na Mona, Ireland)					
	AIT 934	Mercedes-Benz	O309	30910221090418	Asco	73108	C21F	6/73	Flagline, Carrick-on-Shannon	Transport Museum Society of Ireland
	AZD 143	Leyland	Leopard L2	622441	CIE		B45F	11/62	CIE E93	Hegarty, Kilkenny
	AZD 156	Leyland	Leopard L2	623536	CIE		B45F	6/63	CIE E106	Quirke, Dungourney
	AZD 203	Leyland	Leopard L2	L02899	CIE		B45F	6/64	CIE E140	Bedford, Celbridge
	BIK 253	→ see BIK 257 *Ireland*								
(a)	BIK 257	Leyland	Titan OPD2/2	560677	CIE		RV	-/56	CIE R653	Transport Museum Society of Ireland
			(ex BIK 253)							
	BIK 286	Leyland	Titan OPD2/12	561367	CIE		H37/31R	10/56	CIE R686	Manahan, Dublin
	CYI 629	Leyland	Titan OPD2/2	582299	CIE		H37/31R	9/58	CIE R827	Kells Transport Museum, Cork
	CYI 665	Leyland	Titan PD3/2	583132	CIE		H41/33R	4/59	CIE RA30	Molloy, Blackrock
	CYI 670	Leyland	Titan PD3/2	582518	CIE		H41/33R	5/59	CIE RA35	Doherty, Dublin
	CZA 667	Leyland	Leopard L2	611141	CIE		B45F	10/61	CIE E7	Manahan, Dublin
	CZA 668	Leyland	Leopard L2	611142	CIE		B45F	10/61	CIE E8	Cavan & Leitrim Railway
	CZA 674	Leyland	Leopard L2	611252	CIE		B45F	12/61	CIE E14	Bus Eireann (EI) E14
	CZA 678	Leyland	Leopard L2	611405	CIE		B45F	12/61	CIE E18	Elliott, Bray
	CZA 718	Leyland	Leopard L2	613531	CIE		B45F	6/62	CIE E58	Shannon, Cork
	DIV 83	Daimler	Fleetline CRG6LX	64391	Alexander	J27/1369/15	H44/33F	3/71	Trent 550	Transport Museum Society of Ireland
			(ex DRC 550J)							
	EZH 17	Leyland	Leopard PSU3/4R	L24466	CIE		B43F	5/65	CIE C17	Transport Museum Society of Ireland
	EZH 26	Leyland	Leopard PSU3/4R	L24972	CIE		B45F	5/65	CIE C26	Manahan, Dublin
(a)	EZH 64	Leyland	Leopard PSU3/4R	L41357	CIE		B--F	8/65	CIE C64	Transport Museum Society of Ireland
	EZH 97	Leyland	Leopard PSU3/4R	L40994	CIE		B45F	11/65	CIE C97	Flynn, Blackrock
	EZH 145	Leyland	Leopard PSU3/4R	L43300	CIE		B45F	2/66	CIE C145	Molloy, Blackrock
	EZH 154	Leyland	Leopard PSU3/4R	L43774	CIE		B45F	2/66	CIE C154	Molloy, Blackrock
(z)	EZH 155	Leyland	Leopard PSU3/4R	L43660	CIE		B--F	2/66	CIE E155	Bedford, Celbridge
	EZH 160	Leyland	Leopard PSU3/4R	L43890	CIE		B43F	2/66	CIE C160	Kinane, Dublin

EZH 168	Leyland	Leopard PSU3/4R	L44063	CIE		B45F	4/66	CIE C168	Kinane, Dublin
EZH 170	Leyland	Leopard PSU3/4R	L44154	CIE		B45F	4/66	CIE C170	Bedford, Celbridge
EZH 173	Leyland	Leopard PSU3/4R	L44231	CIE		B45F	4/66	CIE C173	Bedford, Celbridge
EZH 176	Leyland	Leopard PSU3/4R	L44416	CIE		B45F	4/66	CIE C176	Boland, Dublin
EZH 177	Leyland	Leopard PSU3/4R	L44418	CIE		B45F	4/66	CIE C177	Flynn, Blackrock
EZH 205	Leyland	Leopard PSU3/4R	L60603	CIE		DP55F	6/66	CIE C205	Flynn, Blackrock
EZH 215	Leyland	Leopard PSU3/4R	L60948	CIE		DP55F	5/66	CIE C215	Flynn, Blackrock
EZH 231	Leyland	Leopard PSU3/4R	L45161	CIE		B55F	5/66	CIE C231	Transport Museum Society of Ireland
EZH 234	Leyland	Leopard PSU3/4R	L45085	CIE		B55F	6/66	CIE C234	Molloy, Blackrock
EZL 1	Bedford	VAS5	7860031	CIE		B33F	11/67	CIE SS1	Transport Museum Society of Ireland
EZV 9	GAC	R	RB9	GAC		B47F	6/85	CIE KR9	Kells Transport Museum, Cork
EZV 11	GAC	R	RB11	GAC		B45F	6/85	CIE KR11	Kells Transport Museum, Cork
FCI 323	Bristol	LL5G	81173	ECW	4584	B39R	10/50	Crosville KG156	Bedford, Celbridge
		(ex LFM 737)							
GSI 353	Bombadier	GMDD	DD353	Bombardier		H45/27D	6/83	CIE KD353	Transport Museum Society of Ireland
HZA 230	Leyland	Titan PD3/2	600273	CIE		H41/33R	7/60	CIE RA105	Transport Museum Society of Ireland
HZA 231	Leyland	Titan PD3/2	600725	CIE		H41/33R	9/60	CIE RA106	Grace, Dublin
HZA 279	AEC	Regent V	2D2RA813	CIE		H41/28RD	5/61	CIE AA2	Transport Museum Society of Ireland
HZD 593	Leyland	Worldmaster ERT2/1	629518	Van Hool	4808	C44F	-/63	CIE WVH13	Transport Museum Society of Ireland
				(rebodied 6/70)					
HZD 596	Leyland	Worldmaster ERT2/1	L00401	Van Hool	6002	C44F	-/63	CIE WVH22	Hendron, Arklow
				(rebodied -/71)					
IBI 789	→ see MNW 343F								
IBI 975	Guy	Arab LUF	LUF71950	Willowbrook	59199	C41F	7/59	Harper, Heath Hayes 57	O'Neill, Dublin
		(ex 1291 RE)							
ILI 98	Bristol	SC4LK	141030	ECW	9990	B35F	1/58	Eastern National 455	Bedford, Celbridge
		(ex 9579 F)							
IZS 677	Bristol	RESL6L	RESL-8-169	Marshall	B4662	B47F	3/71	Ribble 321	Smith & Gardner, Chorley
		(ex LRN 321J)							*(on loan to Ribble Vehicle Preservation Trust)*
JBI 337	Guy	Arab LUF	LUF74290	Willowbrook	59200	C41F	7/59	Harper, Heath Hayes 58	O'Neill, Dublin
		(ex 1292 RE)							
JRI 67	Leyland	Titan OPD2/1	556118	CIE		H37/31R	2/56	CIE R637	Manahan, Dublin
KID 154	Leyland	Tiger PS1	471893	NIRTB		B34R	-/47	NIRTB A8520	Bedford, Celbridge
		(ex GZ 7588)							
KZU 452	AEC	Reliance	2HMU3LA443	Verheul		C35F	-/64	Vavo Greyhound 112	O'Sullivan, Hospital (EI)
		(ex XB-51-04 *Netherlands*)							
LZS 175	GAC	C	CB175	GAC		B45F	1/85	CIE KC175	-?-, -?-
LZS 179	GAC	C	CB179	GAC		B35D	1/85	CIE KC179	Manahan, Dublin
LZS 181	GAC	C	CB181	GAC		B35D	1/85	CIE KC181	Manahan, Dublin
MZU 878	AEC	Reliance	2HMU3LA449	Verheul		C41F	-/64	Vavo Greyhound 114	O'Sullivan, Hospital (EI)
		(ex XB-62-58 *Netherlands*)							
NZE 580	Leyland	Leopard L2	L20267	CIE		B45F	8/64	CIE E152	Molloy, Blackrock
NZE 598	Leyland	Leopard L2	L21526	CIE		B45F	11/64	CIE E170	Transport Museum Society of Ireland
NZE 620	Leyland	Titan PD3A/6	1974	Park Royal/CRV		H41/33R	1/65	CIE R911	Transport Museum Society of Ireland
NZE 622	Leyland	Titan PD3A/6	1976	Park Royal/CRV		H41/33R	2/65	CIE R913	Kells Transport Museum, Cork
NZE 629	Leyland	Titan PD3A/6	1984	Park Royal/CRV		O--/--R	6/65	CIE R920	Transport Museum Society of Ireland
OIK 984	Leyland	Titan OPD2/2	573802	CIE		H37/31R	1/58	CIE R788	Manahan, Dublin

	OIX 179	Ford	R1014	BC04RM64149	Plaxton	7610FB818	B43F	5/76	Hants & Dorset 3814	Lang, Rathcoole
			(ex NJT 831P)							
	OYI 802	Leyland	Titan PD3/2	590148	CIE		H41/33R	5/59	CIE RA37	Walsh, Dublin
	OYI 838	Leyland	Titan PD3/2	591569	CIE		H41/33R	12/59	CIE RA73	Cullen, Dublin
	PZR 990	Bedford	VAL70	9T470867	Plaxton	708352	C53F	5/70	Margo, Streatham 109	Leonard, Coolgreany (EI)
			(ex YYX 997H) *(carried YYX 998H in error when new)*							
(r)	PZV 181	GAC	R	RB181	GAC		B47F	12/85	CIE KR181	Kells Transport Museum, Cork
(r)	PZV 185	GAC	R	RB185	GAC		B47F	1/86	CIE KR185	Kells Transport Museum, Cork
	UZG 100	GAC	C	CB100	GAC		B35D	6/84	CIE KC100	Transport Museum Society of Ireland
	UZG 101	GAC	C	CB101	GAC		B45F	6/84	CIE KC101	-?-, -?-
	UZG 104	GAC	C	CB104	GAC		B35D	6/84	CIE KC104	Hughes, Dublin
	UZG 106	GAC	C	CB106	GAC		B35D	6/84	CIE KC106	Manahan, Dublin
	UZG 116	GAC	C	CB116	GAC		B45F	12/85	CIE KC116	Manahan, Dublin
	UZG 118	GAC	C	CB118	GAC		B45F	5/86	CIE KC118	-?-, -?-
	UZG 129	GAC	C	CB129	GAC		B45F	7/84	CIE KC129	Kells Transport Museum, Cork
(r)	UZG 134	GAC	C	CB134	GAC		B45F	8/84	CIE KC134	Kells Transport Museum, Cork
	UZG 147	GAC	C	CB147	GAC		B45F	1/85	CIE KC147	Kells Transport Museum, Cork
	UZG 152	GAC	C	CB152	GAC		B45F	4/85	CIE KC152	Kells Transport Museum, Cork
	UZG 153	GAC	C	CB153	GAC		B45F	4/85	CIE KC153	Kells Transport Museum, Cork
(r)	UZG 155	GAC	C	CB155	GAC		B45F	8/85	CIE KC155	Kells Transport Museum, Cork
	UZG 157	GAC	C	CB157	GAC		B45F	8/85	CIE KC157	Kells Transport Museum, Cork
	UZG 159	GAC	C	CB159	GAC		B45F	4/85	CIE KC159	Kells Transport Museum, Cork
(r)	UZG 162	GAC	C	CB162	GAC		B45F	4/85	CIE KC162	Kells Transport Museum, Cork
	UZG 168	GAC	C	CB168	GAC		B45F	9/86	CIE KC168	-?-, -?-
	UZH 258	Leyland	Leopard PSU3/4R	L60517	CIE		DP55F	9/66	CIE C258	Bedford, Celbridge
	UZO 798	Mercedes-Benz	O302	3022422007013	Mercedes-Benz		C47F	2/69	ITF, Dublin	O'Sullivan, Hospital (EI)
	UZU 615	Bedford	SB5	681375	Murphy		B45F	9/71	CIE SS615	Kells Transport Museum, Cork
(r)	UZY 705	Bedford	YRQ	CW453365	Plaxton	732249	C--F	6/73	Conway, Irvine	Lang, Rathcoole
			(ex NSD 423L)							
	VZI 44	Leyland	Atlantean PDR1/1	L62487	CIE		H43/35F	3/67	CIE D44	Transport Museum Society of Ireland
	VZI 316	Leyland	Atlantean PDR1A/1	7000545	CIE		H43/31D	3/70	CIE D316	Hughes & Flynn, Dublin
	WZJ 724	Bedford	VAM14	7826702	Duffy		C45F	5/67	O'Grady, Santry	Transport Museum Society of Ireland
	YIY 685	Bedford	YRT	EW454945	Duple	517/2419	C53F	3/76	Stoddard, Cheadle	Kells Transport Museum, Cork
			(ex XAM 104A, NEH 917P)							
	YIY 927	Bedford	YRT	EW455659	Duple	517/2449	C53F	4/76	Crosson, Drogheda	Lang, Rathcoole
	ZSI 35	GAC	C	CB35	GAC		B49F	12/83	CIE KC35	Kells Transport Museum, Cork
	ZSI 48	GAC	C	CB48	GAC		B35D	12/83	CIE KC48	Phipps, Dublin
	9393 AI	Leyland	Leopard PSU3B/4R	7401298	Plaxton	7411LC105	C53F	5/74	Wallace Arnold Tours	Kells Transport Museum, Cork
			(ex UNW 30M)							
	1704 ID	Ford	R1114	BC04TJ93361	Van Hool McArdle	02/037	C49F	6/77	Jackson, Cavan	Manahan, Dublin
	7064 ID	Leyland	Panther PSUR1/1R	L63892	Willowbrook	CF1399	B49F	3/67	Maidstone & District S88	Brown, Wateringbury
			(ex JKK 188E)							
	2 IK	Leyland	Leopard PSU5/4R	7004514	CIE		DP48F	6/71	CIE M2	-?-, Achill Island
			(fitted with a DAF engine)							
	8 IK	Leyland	Leopard PSU5/4R	7004736	CIE		B49F	6/71	CIE M8	Kells Transport Museum, Cork
	19 IK	Leyland	Leopard PSU5/4R	7100071	CIE		DP48F	6/71	CIE M19	Hughes, Dublin
			(fitted with a General Motors engine)							

	Reg	Chassis	Chassis No	Body	Seating	Date	Ex	Owner
	20 IK	Leyland Leopard PSU5/4R *(fitted with a General Motors engine)*	7100072	CIE	DP49F	5/71	CIE M20	Flynn, Blackrock
	25 IK	Leyland Leopard PSU5/4R *(fitted with a DAF engine)*	7100587	CIE	B48F	5/71	CIE M25	Kells Transport Museum, Cork
	31 IK	Leyland Leopard PSU5/4R *(fitted with a DAF engine)*	7100589	CIE	DP55F	6/71	CIE M31	Connell, Motherwell
	34 IK	Leyland Leopard PSU5/4R *(fitted with a General Motors engine)*	7100588	CIE	DP55F	7/71	CIE M34	-?-, -?-
	35 IK	Leyland Leopard PSU5/4R *(fitted with a DAF engine)*	7100590	CIE	B55F	6/71	CIE M35	Kells Transport Museum, Cork
	42 IK	Leyland Leopard PSU5/4R *(fitted with a DAF engine)*	7100566	CIE	B55F	7/71	CIE M42	Kells Transport Museum, Cork
	45 IK	Leyland Leopard PSU5/4R	7003602	CIE	B55F	7/71	CIE M45	Hughes, Dublin
	50 IK	Leyland Leopard PSU5/4R *(fitted with a DAF engine)*	7004516	CIE	DP55F	9/71	CIE M50	Hughes, Dublin
	56 IK	Leyland Leopard PSU5/4R *(fitted with a General Motors engine)*	7004015	CIE	DP55F	10/71	CIE M56	Kells Transport Museum, Cork
	58 IK	Leyland Leopard PSU5/4R *(fitted with a General Motors engine)*	7004275	CIE	DP53F	9/71	CIE M58	-?-, -?-
	67 IK	Leyland Leopard PSU5/4R	7004016	CIE	B55F	10/71	CIE M67	Flynn, Blackrock
	74 IK	Leyland Leopard PSU5/4R *(fitted with a General Motors engine)*	7101075	CIE	DP55F	7/71	CIE M74	Carolan, Cavan
	76 IK	Leyland Leopard PSU5/4R *(fitted with a General Motors engine)*	7101077	CIE	B55F	7/71	CIE M76	Kells Transport Museum, Cork
	80 IK	Leyland Leopard PSU5/4R *(fitted with a DAF engine)*	7101081	CIE	B55F	7/71	CIE M80	Kells Transport Museum, Cork
	82 IK	Leyland Leopard PSU5/4R *(fitted with a DAF engine)*	7101182	CIE	DP55F	7/71	CIE M82	Kells Transport Museum, Cork
(r)	91 IK	Leyland Leopard PSU5/4R *(fitted with a DAF engine)*	7101259	CIE	B55F	9/71	CIE M91	Kells Transport Museum, Cork
	92 IK	Leyland Leopard PSU5/4R *(fitted with a General Motors engine)*	7101260	CIE	DP55F	8/71	CIE M92	Flynn, Blackrock
(r)	106 IK	Leyland Leopard PSU5/4R *(fitted with a General Motors engine)*	7100979	CIE	B55F	11/71	CIE M106	Kells Transport Museum, Cork
	112 IK	Leyland Leopard PSU5/4R *(fitted with a General Motors engine)*	7102955	CIE	DP55F	2/72	CIE M112	Flynn, Blackrock
(r)	117 IK	Leyland Leopard PSU5/4R *(fitted with a DAF engine)*	7101351	CIE	B55F	12/71	CIE M117	Kells Transport Museum, Cork
	120 IK	Leyland Leopard PSU5/4R *(fitted with a DAF engine)*	7101444	CIE	DP55F	12/71	CIE M120	Transport Museum Society of Ireland
	127 IK	Leyland Leopard PSU5/4R *(fitted with a DAF engine)*	7101608	CIE	DP55F	12/71	CIE M127	Lang, Rathcoole
	131 IK	Leyland Leopard PSU5/4R *(fitted with a DAF engine)*	7101911	CIE	DP55F	1/72	CIE M131	Manahan, Dublin
	132 IK	Leyland Leopard PSU5/4R *(fitted with a DAF engine)*	7101912	CIE	B55F	1/72	CIE M132	Kells Transport Museum, Cork
	137 IK	Leyland Leopard PSU5/4R *(fitted with a DAF engine)*	7101980	CIE	DP55F	4/72	CIE M137	Flynn, Blackrock

	143 IK	Leyland	Leopard PSU5/4R	7102042	CIE		DP55F	5/72	CIE M143	Flynn, Blackrock
			(fitted with a DAF engine)							
	146 IK	Leyland	Leopard PSU5/4R	7102167	CIE		DP55F	4/72	CIE M146	Flynn, Blackrock
			(fitted with a DAF engine)							
(r)	154 IK	Leyland	Leopard PSU5/4R	7102346	CIE		DP55F	4/72	CIE M154	Flynn, Blackrock
			(fitted with a DAF engine)							
(r)	161 IK	Leyland	Leopard PSU5/4R	7102353	CIE		DP55F	5/72	CIE M161	Flynn, Blackrock
			(fitted with a DAF engine)							
	166 IK	Leyland	Leopard PSU5/4R	7102486	CIE		DP55F	5/72	CIE M166	Carolan, Cavan
			(fitted with a General Motors engine)							
	167 IK	Leyland	Leopard PSU5/4R	7102487	CIE		DP55F	5/72	CIE M167	Manahan, Dublin
			(fitted with a Cummins engine)							
	169 IK	Leyland	Leopard PSU5/4R	7102489	CIE		DP55F	6/72	CIE M169	Manahan, Dublin
			(fitted with a DAF engine)							
	172 IK	Leyland	Leopard PSU5/4R	7102954	CIE		DP48F	5/72	CIE M172	Flynn, Blackrock
			(fitted with a General Motors engine)							
	177 IK	Leyland	Leopard PSU5/4R	7103135	CIE		DP48F	3/72	CIE M177	Hughes, Bray
			(fitted with a DAF engine)							
	182 IK	Leyland	Leopard PSU5/4R	7103253	CIE		B48F	5/72	CIE M182	Kells Transport Museum, Cork
			(fitted with a DAF engine)							
	192 IK	Leyland	Leopard PSU5/4R	7104902	CIE		DP55F	6/72	CIE M192	Kells Transport Museum, Cork
			(fitted with a DAF engine)							
	203 IK	Leyland	Leopard PSU5/4R	7104621	CIE		DP50F	7/72	CIE M203	Flynn, Blackrock
	205 IK	Leyland	Leopard PSU5/4R	7104623	CIE		DP48F	7/72	CIE M205	Flynn, Blackrock
			(fitted with a General Motors engine)							
	207 IK	Leyland	Leopard PSU5/4R	7104625	CIE		DP55F	9/72	CIE M207	Flynn, Blackrock
	209 IK	Leyland	Leopard PSU5/4R	7104627	CIE		DP50F	10/72	CIE M209	Lang, Rathcoole
			(fitted with a General Motors engine)							
	210 IK	Leyland	Leopard PSU5/4R	7104628	CIE		DP55F	3/73	CIE M210	Hendron, Arklow
			(fitted with a General Motors engine)							
(r)	212 IK	Leyland	Leopard PSU5/4R	7104630	CIE		DP55F	7/74	CIE M212	Kells Transport Museum, Cork
			(fitted with a General Motors engine)							
	376 IK	Leyland	Atlantean PDR1A/1	7002769	CIE		H43/35F	10/70	CIE D376	Transport Museum Society of Ireland
	4217 IN	Leyland	Leopard PSU3B/4R	7300687	Plaxton	733728	C53F	6/73	Trimdon Motor Services	-?-, -?-
			(ex BPT 672L)							
	3044 MI	AEC	Reliance	6U2R7727	Alexander	9AY/2370/2	C49F	5/71	Potteries 169	Hearson, Chesterton
			(ex FEH 169J)							
	415 ZD	Leyland	Atlantean PDR1A/1	7104230	CIE		H41/33D	9/72	CIE D415	Manahan, Dublin
			(ex BNT 75K, 415 ZD)							
	464 ZD	Leyland	Atlantean PDR1A/1	7203240	CIE		H43/31D	12/72	CIE D464	Hall, Dublin
	471 ZD	Leyland	Atlantean PDR1A/1	7203655	CIE		H43/31D	2/73	CIE D471	Hughes & Flynn, Dublin
(r)	4500 ZF	Leyland	Leopard PSU3E/4R	7705936	Van Hool	8069	C53F	2/79	Cronin, Cork	Manahan, Dublin
	702 ZI	Bedford	VAS5	YW727731	Van Hool McArdle	SS702	B33F	9/73	CIE SS702	Kells Transport Museum, Cork
	715 ZI	Bedford	VAS5	YW727448	Van Hool McArdle	SS715	B33F	9/73	CIE SS715	Durkan, Ballina
	736 ZI	Bedford	VAS5	YW728231	Van Hool McArdle	SS736	B33F	9/73	CIE SS736	Manahan, Dublin
	737 ZI	Bedford	VAS5	YW727356	Van Hool McArdle	SS737	B33F	9/73	CIE SS737	O'Donovan, -?-
	747 ZI	Bedford	VAS5	YW728238	Van Hool-McArdle	SS747	B33F	9/74	CIE SS747	Carolan, Cavan
	748 ZI	Bedford	VAS5	YW728229	Van Hool McArdle	SS748	B33F	9/74	CIE SS748	Durkan, Ballina

	635 ZO	Leyland	Atlantean AN68/1R	7401892	Van Hool McArdle	01/071	O--/--F	3/75	CIE D635	-?-, -?-
	665 ZO	Leyland	Atlantean AN68/1R	7403156	Van Hool McArdle	01/059	O45/33F	2/75	CIE D665	Kells Transport Museum, Cork
	694 ZO	Leyland	Atlantean AN68/1R	7404119	Van Hool McArdle	01/086	H45/29D	6/75	CIE D694	Transport Museum Society of Ireland
	711 ZO	Leyland	Atlantean AN68/1R	7404944	Van Hool McArdle	01/103	H45/29D	6/75	CIE D711	Kells Transport Museum, Cork
	592 ZU	Leyland	Atlantean PDR1A/1	7303885	Van Hool McArdle	D592	H43/31D	7/74	CIE D592	-?-, Ireland
	3460 ZW	Ford	R1014	BC04PU59046	ECW	20887	B45F	9/74	Hants & Dorset 3594	Lang, Rathcoole
			(ex RRU 594N)							
	4050 ZW	Ford	R1114	BCRSWS369920	Plaxton	8011FC067	C--F	1/80	Granville, Grimsby	Lang, Rathcoole
			(ex WFU 707V)							
	476 ZY	Bedford	YMT	JW452445	Plaxton	7911TC162	C53F	5/79	Stanley, Hersham	Repton, Little Bookham (SR)
			(ex CTM 405T)							
	71 AHI	Leyland	Tiger Cub PSUC1/2	605832	Metro-Cammell		B41F	1/61	Western Welsh 1274	Bedford, Celbridge
			(ex UKG 274)							
	685 DID	Bristol	LH6L	LH-1172	ECW	21727	B43F	2/76	Bristol 368	Lang, Rathcoole
			(ex KHU 318P)							
	70 JZL	Bombardier	GMDD	DD70	Bombardier		H45/27D	12/81	CIE KD70	Rouslton, Glasgow
	156 JZL	Bombardier	GMDD	DD156	Bombardier		H45/27D	4/82	CIE KD156	Kells Transport Museum, Cork
	184 JZL	Bombardier	GMDD	DD184	Bombardier		H45/27D	4/82	CIE KD184	Kells Transport Museum, Cork
	199 JZL	Bombardier	GMDD	DD199	Bombardier		H45/27D	6/82	CIE KD199	Manahan, Dublin
	411 LIP	Leyland	Leopard PSU4B/4R	7100688	Plaxton	729107	C--F	7/71	Ribble 1006	Butler, Gosforth
					(ex NCK 106J)		*(received body new 8/72 from GUR 484L by3/11)*			*(on loan to Ribble Vehicle Preservation Trust)*
	643 MIP	Volvo	B58-56	14126	Duple	047/6013	C--F	2/81	NW Coachlines, Kirkham	Cavan & Leitrim Railway
			(ex GRN 896W)							
	830 NIK	Leyland	Atlantean AN68/1R	7505141	Van Hool McArdle	01/227	H45/29D	9/77	CIE D839	Hughes, Dublin
	839 NIK	Leyland	Atlantean AN68/1R	7505394	Van Hool McArdle	01/231	H45/29D	1/78	CIE D839	Willis, Dublin
	221 OZU	Bombardier	GMDD	DD221	Bombardier		H45/27D	7/82	CIE KD221	Hughes, Dublin
	236 OZU	Bombardier	GMDD	DD236	Bombardier		H45/27D	7/82	CIE KD236	Geoghegan, Dublin
	241 OZU	Bombardier	GMDD	DD241	Bombardier		H45/27D	8/82	CIE KD241	Harbourne, Dublin
	404 RIU	Albion	Lowlander LR1	62117J	Alexander	63/C9/12	H40/31F	12/63	Alexander Midland MRE38	Transport Museum Society of Ireland
			(ex 405 RIU, VWG 376)							
	683 SIU	AEC	Reliance	2U3RA5370	Duple	1181/13	C43F	6/64	MacBrayne 194	MacBrayne Circle
			(ex AGE 545B)							
	355 SZB	Leyland	Leopard PSU5/4R	7101647	Plaxton	713296	C57F	8/71	Rendell, Parkstone	Motor Vehicle Preservation Society of Ireland
			(ex PFX 571K)							*(operates as Rivercourt Coaches, Dublin (EI))*
	777 TYI	Bedford	SB5	YW616105	Van Hool McArdle	05/001	B45F	8/79	CIE SS777	-?-, -?-
	782 TYI	Bedford	SB5	YW616112	Van Hool McArdle	05/???	B45F	1/79	CIE SS782	Kells Transport Museum, Cork
	788 TYI	Bedford	SB5	YW616109	Van Hool McArdle	05/026	B45F	1/79	CIE SS788	Kells Transport Museum, Cork
	793 TYI	Bedford	SB5	YW615429	Van Hool McArdle	05/012	B45F	9/79	CIE SS793	Manahan, Dublin
	120 UZD	Mercedes-Benz	O303/15R	30122521007466	Van Hool	8033	C48F	4/78	PMPA, Dublin	Martin, Limerick (EI)
(r)	222 VPI	Leyland	Tiger TRCTL11/3R	8101364	Plaxton	8212LTS5C028	C57F	3/82	Shaw, Silverdale	Kells Transport Museum, Cork
			(ex LEC 646X)							
	14 VZJ	Bombardier	GMIC	IC14	Bombardier		DP45F	3/81	CIE KE14	Harbourne, Dublin
	35 VZJ	Bombardier	GMTC	TC35	Bombardier		DP47F	5/81	CIE KE35	Manahan, Dublin
	938 WZJ	AEC	Regent V	2D3RA1296	Park Royal	B49016	H--/--F	3/63	East Kent	O'Neill, Dublin
			(ex 6783 FN)							
	666 XPI	Leyland	Tiger TRCTL11/3R	8300396	Van Hool	10847	C50F	10/83	Leyland demonstrator	Kells Transport Museum, Cork
			(ex A451 LCK)							

	Reg	Make	Model	Chassis No	Body	Body No	Layout	New	Original Operator	Owner
	53-OY-20	AEC	Regal IV (ex MXX 435)	9821LT745	Metro-Cammell		B39F	2/53	London Transport RF458	Garahy, Birr
	72-D-27	Daimler	Fleetline CRL6 (ex WUH 570K)	65471	MCW		H--/--F	1/72	Cardiff 570	Brewer, Cardiff
	73-C-22	Leyland	National 1051/2R/3001 (ex TGY 106M)	00819	Leyland National		B36D	11/73	London Transport LS6	Kells Transport Museum, Cork
	74-KE-527	Leyland	Atlantean AN68/1R (ex OTO 571M) *(carries incorrect registration 78-KE-560)*	7303178	East Lancs	2532	O47/32F	3/74	Nottingham 571	Kells Transport Museum, Cork
	74-KE-528	Leyland	Atlantean AN68/1R (ex GRC 889N)	7405027	East Lancs	4004	O47/32F	12/74	Nottingham 589	Kells Transport Museum, Cork
(r)	75-D-70	Leyland	Leopard PSU3C/4R (ex HOI 2922)	7404364	Alexander (Belfast)	-?-	B49F	2/75	Ulsterbus 1922	Kells Transport Museum, Cork
	75-D-79	Leyland	Leopard PSU3C/4R (ex HOI 2925)	7403845	Alexander (Belfast)	-?-	B49F	2/75	Ulsterbus 1925	Kells Transport Museum, Cork
(r)	75-D-101	Leyland	Leopard PSU3C/4R (ex HOI 2926)	7404301	Alexander (Belfast)	-?-	B49F	2/75	Ulsterbus 1926	Kells Transport Museum, Cork
	75-KE-526	Leyland	Atlantean AN68/1R (ex MAU 616P)	7504189	East Lancs	4031	O47/33F	12/75	Nottingham 616	Kells Transport Museum, Cork
	75-KE-527	Leyland	Atlantean AN68/1R (ex MAU 612P)	7505042	East Lancs	4027	O47/33F	12/75	Nottingham 612	Kells Transport Museum, Cork
	75-LK-539	Bristol	LHS6L (ex FAO 69N, LHH 744, FAO 61N, SMK 828, HEJ 337N)	LHS-214	Plaxton	758BX504M	C35F	6/75	James, Llangeitho	Barratt, Cappamore (EI)
	76-C-248	Leyland	National 10351A/2R (ex KJD 557P)	03630	Leyland National		B--D	10/76	London Transport LS57	Kells Transport Museum, Cork
	76-C-999	Leyland	National 11351A/1R (ex XIA 857, XIA 256, PKP 548R - *fitted with a Cummins engine*)	03947	Leyland National		B48F	12/76	Maidstone & District 3548	Kells Transport Museum, Cork
	76-C-1007	Leyland	National 11351A/1R (ex NWO 491R)	03638	Leyland National		B52F	9/76	National Welsh N4676	Kells Transport Museum, Cork
	76-C-1026	Leyland	Atlantean AN68A/1R (ex MSF 469P)	7505330	Alexander	AL36/773/69	H45/30D	2/76	Lothian 469	Kells Transport Museum, Cork
	76-D-74	Bedford	YLQ (ex LOI 1864)	FW455607	Alexander (Belfast)	-?-	B45F	11/76	Ulsterbus 1864	Kells Transport Museum, Cork
	76-D-75	Bedford	YLQ (ex LOI 1868)	FW455702	Alexander (Belfast)	-?-	B45F	11/76	Ulsterbus 1868	Lang, Rathcoole
	76-LK-541	Leyland	Fleetline FE30ALR (ex SJI 6321, KON 306P) *(fitted with a Gardner engine)*	7504847	MCW		H43/33F	1/76	West Midlands PTE 6306	Kells Transport Museum, Cork
(r)	77-C-292	Leyland	National 10351A/2R (ex OJD 891R)	04446	Leyland National		B--D	8/77	London Transport LS91	Kells Transport Museum, Cork
	77-D-213	Bristol	RELL6G (ex POI 2192)	RELL-3-2251	Alexander (Belfast)	-?-	B51F	12/77	Ulsterbus 2192	Kells Transport Museum, Cork
	77-D-214	Bristol	RELL6G (ex POI 2151)	RELL-3-2181	Alexander (Belfast)	-?-	B51F	9/77	Citybus 2151	Phipps, Dublin
	77-D-816	Bristol	RELL6G (ex MOI 2134)	RELL-3-2164	Alexander (Belfast)	183/14	B49F	2/77	Ulsterbus 2134	Shannon, Newtownards
	77-D-824	Leyland	Leopard PSU3D/4R (ex NOI 1968)	7605107	Alexander (Belfast)	-?-	B49F	5/77	Ulsterbus 1968	Kells Transport Museum, Cork
	77-D-827	Bristol	RELL6G (ex POI 2156)	RELL-3-2186	Alexander (Belfast)	-?-	B51F	9/77	Citybus 2156	Kells Transport Museum, Cork

	77-LH-519	Bristol	RELL6G	RELL-3-2246	Alexander (Belfast)	-?-	B52F	12/77	Ulsterbus 2187	Kells Transport Museum, Cork
			(ex POI 2187)							
	77-LK-536	Leyland	Fleetline FE30AGR	7605666	Roe	GO7773	H45/29D	1/77	Grimsby Cleethorpes 112	Lang, Rathcoole
			(ex MBE 612R)							
	78-C-152	Bristol	LHL6L	LHL-264	Plaxton	7811BCM010	C53F	7/78	Cox, Wallasey	Kells Transport Museum, Cork
			(ex OHF 968S)							
	78-C-313	Leyland	National 10351A/2R	04819	Leyland National		B--D	2/78	London Transport LS118	Kells Transport Museum, Cork
			(ex THX 118S)							
	78-C-325	Leyland	National 10351A/2R	04851	Leyland National		B--D	2/78	London Transport LS129	Kells Transport Museum, Cork
			(ex THX 129S)							
	78-C-1139	Leyland	National 11351A/1R	05479	Leyland National		B49F	8/78	Crosville SNL375	Kells Transport Museum, Cork
			(ex GMB 375T)							
	78-D-140	Bedford	SB5	GW455143	Marshall	280105	B40F	2/78	Royal Navy/ Bus Eireann BM15	Bedford, Celbridge
			(ex 42 RN 98)							
	78-D-191	Bedford	SB5	FW454910	Marshall	260416.7	B40F	1/78	Royal Navy/ Bus Eireann BM42	Kells Transport Museum, Cork
			(ex 60 RN 02)							
	78-D-251	Bedford	SB5	GW457358	Marshall	280120	B39F	2/78	Royal Navy/ Bus Eireann BM51	Carolan, Cork
			(ex BUR 558S, 43 RN 13)							
(r)	78-D-260	Bedford	SB5	HW454509	Marshall	280243.0	B37F	8/78	RAF/ Bus Eireann BM58	Carolan, Cavan
			(ex 47 AC 94)							
	78-D-328	Bedford	SB5	HW454515	Marshall	280233.3	B39F	8/78	RAF/ Bus Eireann BM72	Kells Transport Museum, Cork
			(ex 47 AC 84)							
	78-D-362	Bedford	SB5	GW456506	Marshall	280115	B39F	2/78	RAF/ Bus Eireann BM84	Kells Transport Museum, Cork
			(ex 43 RN 08)							
	78-D-364	Bedford	SB5	HW451275	Marshall	280204	B40F	7/78	RAF/ Bus Eireann BM86	Kells Transport Museum, Cork
			(ex 47 AC 55)							
	78-D-824	Bristol	RELL6G	RELL-3-2252	Alexander (Belfast)	-?-	B52F	12/77	Ulsterbus 2193	Kennedy, Dromod
			(ex POI 2193)							
	78-D-825	Bristol	RELL6G	RELL-3-2239	Alexander (Belfast)	-?-	B52F	12/77	Ulsterbus 2180	Kells Transport Museum, Cork
			(ex POI 2180)							
	78-D-845	Bedford	SB5	HW454119	Marshall	280220.1	B39F	7/78	RAF / Bus Eireann BM100	Kells Transport Museum, Cork
			(ex 47 AC 71)							
	78-D-921	Leyland	Atlantean AN68A/1R	7802630	Roe	GO8023	O43/29D	12/78	South Yorkshire PTE 1647	Kells Transport Museum, Cork
			(ex XWG 647T)							
	78-D-997	Leyland	Fleetline FE30AGR	7803361	MCW		O43/33F	11/78	West Midlands PTE 6965	Kells Transport Museum, Cork
			(ex WDA 965T)							
	78-D-1015	Leyland	Fleetline FE30AGR	7705508	MCW		O43/33F	7/78	West Midlands PTE 6889	Kells Transport Museum, Cork
			(ex TVP 889S)							
	78-KE-547	Leyland	Atlantean AN68A/1R	7800017	Northern Counties	7941	O47/33F	6/78	Nottingham 662	Kells Transport Museum, Cork
			(ex XNN 662S)							
	78-KE-560	Leyland	Atlantean AN68A/1R	7801915	East Lancs	9010	O47/31D	12/78	Nottingham 645	Kells Transport Museum, Cork
			(ex ARC 645T) *(carries incorrect registration 74-KE-527)*							
	78-KE-566	Leyland	Atlantean AN68A/1R	7702724	East Lancs	7612	O47/31F	3/78	Brighton 12	Kells Transport Museum, Cork
			(ex TYJ 12S)							
	78-LK-578	Leyland	Fleetline FE30AGR	7802125	MCW		H43/33F	8/78	West Midlands PTE 6918	Lang, Rathcoole
			(ex WDA 918T)							
	78-LK-579	Leyland	Fleetline FE30AGR	7802041	MCW		H43/33F	8/78	West Midlands PTE 6919	Lang, Rathcoole
			(ex WDA 919T)							

	Registration	Make	Model	Chassis No	Body	Body No	Layout	Date	First Owner	Current Owner
	78-LK-580	Leyland	Fleetline FE30AGR	7803783	MCW		H43/33F	12/78	West Midlands PTE 6985	Lang, Rathcoole
			(ex WDA 985T)							
	79-DL-630	Leyland	Leopard PSU3E/4R	7901022	Alexander	129AY/3277/15	B52F	6/79	Western SMT L2904	Devine, Glasgow
			(ex BSJ 904T)							
	79-KE-545	Leyland	Leopard PSU3E/4R	7807234	Plaxton	7911LX626	C53F	9/79	Barton 538	Kells Transport Museum, Cork
			(ex FTO 538V)							
	79-KY-600	Leyland	Leopard PSU4E/4R	7800427	Plaxton	7910LCCE003	C41F	3/79	Glenton, New Cross	McAlinney & Miller, Newtownards
			(ex AJD 166T)							
	79-MN-522	Leyland	Leopard PSU3E/4R	7806720	Plaxton	7911LC065	C53F	4/79	Wallace Arnold (Devon)	Motor Vehicle Preservation Society of Ireland
			(ex VDF 769, EWW 205T)							
	79-TS-93	Leyland	Leopard PSU3E/4R	7803475	Plaxton	7811LXM582	C53F	12/78	Thames Valley & Aldershot 87	Kells Transport Museum, Cork
			(ex WJM 807T)							
(r)	79-WW-61	Bedford	YMT	JW456329	Duple	017/2435	C53F	11/79	Fleet Coaches, Fleet	Lang, Rathcoole
			(ex EPC 898V)							
	79-WX-628	Leyland	Leopard PSU3E/4R	7806653	Plaxton	7911LX622	C53F	7/79	Barton 534	Phelan, New Ross
			(ex ERB 534T)							
	80-C-1459	Leyland	Atlantean AN68A/1R	7902204	Northern Counties	8864	H47/33D	12/80	Nottingham 695	Kells Transport Museum, Cork
			(ex MNU 695W)							
	80-C-1528	Leyland	National NL116L11/1R	07127	Leyland National		B52F	8/80	Southdown 126	Kells Transport Museum, Cork
			(ex OUF 933W, SYC 852, JWV 126W)							
	80-CE-427	Leyland	Leopard PSU3E/4R	7904267	Alexander	137AY/2078/31	B53F	5/80	Western SMT L60	-?-, Ennis
			(ex GCS 60V)							
	80-CE-449	Leyland	Leopard PSU3F/4R	7930097	Alexander	145AYS/1379/19	B62F	11/80	Alexander Fife FPE153	-?-, Ennis
			(ex WFS 153W)							
(r)	80-D-529	Bedford	SB5	JW455313	Marshall	280555.3	B39F	2/80	Army/ Bus Eireann BM63	Kells Transport Museum, Cork
			(ex 10 HF 53)							
	80-D-1163	Leyland	Fleetline FE30AGR	7803363	Northern Counties	8697	O43/29F	1/80	Derby 47	Kells Transport Museum, Cork
			(ex GTO 47V)							
	80-D-1371	Leyland	Atlantean AN68B/1R	7905683	East Lancs	501	O45/31F	12/80	Warrington 22	Kells Transport Museum, Cork
			(ex MEK 22W)							
	80-DL-729	Leyland	Leopard PSU3E/4R	7904027	Alexander	137AY/2078/27	B53F	5/80	Western SMT L56	Nash, Ockley
			(ex WDS 291V, GCS 56V)							
	80-G-704	Leyland	Atlantean AN68A/1R	7903763	Alexander	AL86/6077/70	O45/29D	4/80	Grampian 278	Kells Transport Museum, Cork
			(ex HRS 278V)							
(r)	80-KK-239	Bedford	YMT	HW455845	Duple	017/2476	C53F	3/80	Smith, Thirsk	Kells Transport Museum, Cork
			(ex BBT 310V) *(fire damaged)*							
	80-LK-469	Leyland	Leopard PSU3E/4R	7904691	Duple	034/5356	DP53F	4/80	Southend 206	Kells Transport Museum, Cork
			(ex BTE 206V)							
	80-MO-151	Ford	R1114	BCRSWU260130	Plaxton	8011FC047	C49F	4/80	Exclesior, Bournemouth	Kells Transport Museum, Cork
			(ex HFX 423V)							
	80-W-172	Leyland	Atlantean AN68B/1R	7904297	Willowbrook	792182	H45/33F	11/80	Merseyside PTE 1845	Kells Transport Museum, Cork
			(ex WWM 922W)							
	81-C-1414	Leyland	Leopard rebuild	ICL008/81	Plaxton	8111LCR001/S	C53F	5/81	Independent, Horsforth 31	Kells Transport Museum, Cork
			(ex KIW 2923, PWY 31W)							
	81-C-1617	Volvo	B10M-61	000913	Van Hool	9938	C53F	11/81	Trathen, Yelverton	Kells Transport Museum, Cork
			(ex AHZ 2044, UCW 337X, ESK 908, KJI 2572, RND 636X, FIL 2688, YRF 233X, LOI 1791, STT 605X)							
	81-C-1619	Volvo	B58-61	15396	Plaxton	8112VCV904	C51F	4/81	Albatross, Brentford	Kells Transport Museum, Cork
			(ex OUF 971W, CLC 983T, YOI 8815, SLH 3W)							

	Reg	Chassis make	Chassis model	Chassis no.	Body make	Body no.	Layout	New	First owner	Current owner
	81-C-1657	Leyland	National NL106L11/1R (ex RIL 9168, DBV 845W)	07233	Leyland National		B44F	4/81	Ribble 845	Kells Transport Museum, Cork
(r)	81-D-997	Leyland	Leopard PSU3F/4R (ex PNB 805W)	8030492	Plaxton	8111LC050	C53F	4/81	Shearing, Altrincham	Kells Transport Museum, Cork
	81-D-1380	Leyland	Leopard PSU3E/4R (ex MPL 136W)	8031231	Duple	134/5386	C53F	7/81	London Country DL16	Kells Transport Museum, Cork
	81-D-1477	Volvo	B57 (ex SBS 4718M *Singapore*)	7487	New Zealand Motor Bodies		B52F	3/81	SBS 4718/ Bus Eireann VS6	Roulston, Glasgow
	81-D-1514	Volvo	B57 (ex SBS 4791A *Singapore*)	7911	New Zealand Motor Bodies		B52F	12/81	SBS 4791/ Bus Eireann VS122	Carolan, Cavan
(r)	81-D-1586	Volvo	B57 (ex SBS 4746G *Singapore*)	7689	New Zealand Motor Bodies		B52F	7/81	SBS 4746/ Bus Eireann VS43	Kells Transport Museum, Cork
	81-D-1616	Volvo	B57 (ex SBS 3448Z *Singapore*)	7516	New Zealand Motor Bodies		B52F	4/81	SBS 3448/ Bus Eireann VS27	Carolan, Cavan
	81-D-1622	Volvo	B57 (ex SBS 3453H *Singapore*)	7712	New Zealand Motor Bodies		B52F	4/81	SBS 3453/ Bus Eireann VS63	Kells Transport Museum, Cork
	81-KE-329	Bedford	YNT (ex HRL 626W)	LW451018	Plaxton	8111TX503	C53F	1/81	Deeble, Darleyford	Hardcastle, Moyne
	81-KE-398	Ford	R1114 (ex PMU 770, GBO 304W)	BCRSAB454980	Duple	123/4566	C53F	4/81	Falconer, Cardiff	Kells Transport Museum, Cork
(r)	81-KK-162	DAF	MB200DKTL600 (ex VBM 717W)	195518	Plaxton	8012DC037	C53F	5/81	Seamarks, Luton 170	Kells Transport Museum, Cork
	81-LH-379	Bedford	YNT (ex LDA 713W, SIB 3258, OYD 424, SNM 441W)	LW450578	Duple	117/2600	C53F	2/81	Dell, Chesham	Lang, Rathcoole
(r)	81-LK-390	Leyland	Leopard PSU5E/5R (ex 50 AC 19)	8031047	Wadham Stringer	8470/81	B54F	-/81	Royal Air Force	Kells Transport Museum, Cork
	81-TS-407	Leyland	Leopard PSU3F/4R (ex SIB 6614, XAG 206X)	8030804	East Lancs (*rebodied 10/92*)	B1803	DP49F	8/81	Scarborough & District 234	Kells Transport Museum, Cork
	82-C-1636	Leyland	Tiger TRCTL11/2R (ex NDW 146X)	8102770	Plaxton	8211LTS6X508	C53F	3/82	Hills, Tredegar	Kells Transport Museum, Cork
	82-C-1941	Ford	R1114 (ex JIL 9308, EFW 215X)	BCRSAY413730	Duple	223/4573	C53F	4/82	Granville, Grimsby	Kells Transport Museum, Cork
	82-C-2012	Leyland	Leopard PSU3F/5R (ex WKE 360X, MIL 9312, WKE 360X)	8030322	Plaxton	8111LC019	C53F	2/82	Reliance, Gravesend	Kells Transport Museum, Cork
	82-C-2154	Leyland	Leopard PSU3G/4R (ex CKE 170Y)	8131903	ECW	25389	C49F	11/82	Maidstone & District 2170	Kells Transport Museum, Cork
	82-CN-149	Bedford	YNT (ex AFL 534Y)	LW452072	Plaxton	8211NTS5C003	C57F	8/82	Kiddle, St Ives	Lang, Rathcoole
(r)	82-D-2091	Ford	R1114 (ex VJT 621X)	BCRSAY287760	Plaxton	8211FTS5C006	C53F	4/82	Excelsior Group, Bournemouth	Kells Transport Museum, Cork
	82-D-2368	Volvo	B57 (ex SBS 3498D *Singapore*)	7751	New Zealand Motor Bodies		B52F	4/82	SBS 3498/ Bus Eireann VS136	Kells Tansport Museum, Cork
	82-D-2452	Volvo	B57 (ex SBS 3520Y *Singapore*)	7918	New Zealand Motor Bodies		B52F	6/82	SBS 3520/ Bus Eireann VS164	Carolan, Cork
	82-D-2457	Volvo	B57 (ex SBS 3527D *Singapore*)	7854	New Zealand Motor Bodies		B52F	8/82	SBS 3527/ Bus Eireann VS177	Kells Transport Museum, Cork
	82-D-2485	Volvo	B57 (ex SBS 3531R *Singapore*)	7913	New Zealand Motor Bodies		B52F	9/82	SBS 3531/ Bus Eireann VS180	Kells Transport Museum, Cork

	82-D-2489	Volvo	B57	7898	New Zealand Motor Bodies		B52F	9/82	SBS 3532/ Bus Eireann VS178	Kells Transport Museum, Cork
			(ex SBS 3532M *Singapore*)							
	82-D-2550	Volvo	B57	8295	New Zealand Motor Bodies		B52F	11/82	SBS 4822/ Bus Eireann VS215	Roulston, Glasgow
			(ex SBS 4822U *Singapore*)							
	82-D-2571	Ford	R1114	BCRSAA496860	Duple	123/4567	C53F	4/82	Laking, Harthill	Kells Transport Museum, Cork
			(ex FVL 331X, VVH 1X)							
	82-D-2899	Leyland	National NL116AL11/1R	07655	Leyland National		B52F	4/82	Cumberland 392	Kells Transport Museum, Cork
			(ex SHH 392X)							
	82-D-2970	Leyland	Titan TNLXB2RR	0501	Leyland		H44/24F	4/82	London Transport T451	Kells Transport Museum, Cork
			(ex KYV 451X)							
(r)	82-DL-1355	Volvo	B10M-61	003518	Duple	249/9082	C53F	4/82	Park, Hamilton	Kells Transport Museum, Cork
			(ex HUI 4742, FHS 757X)							
	82-KE-588	Ford	R1114	BCRSAT420260	Plaxton	8211FTS5C034	C53F	4/82	Excelsior Group, Bournemouth	Lang, Rathcoole
			(ex VJT 606X)							
	82-KE-590	Ford	R1114	BCRSAS375350	Duple	223/4578	C53F	2/82	Norfolk, Great Yarmouth 313	Kells Transport Museum, Cork
			(ex ACL 913X)							
(r)	82-KK-487	Leyland	Tiger TRCTL11/3R	8103035	Duple	236/5502	C53F	6/82	Roe, Stainforth	Kells Transport Museum, Cork
			(ex RDT 121X)							
	82-LK-461	Leyland	Leopard PSU5E/5R	8230988	Wadham Stringer	9683/82	B54F	3/82	Royal Air Force	Kells Transport Museum, Cork
			(ex 51 AC 01)							
	82-LS-323	Volvo	B55-10	80053	Northern Counties	2114	H38/35F	3/82	Derby 114	Kells Transport Museum, Cork
			(ex SRC 114X)							
	82-MH-541	Leyland	Titan TNLXB2RR	0582	Leyland		H44/24D	7/82	London Transport T532	Byrne, Dublin
			(ex KYV 532X)							
(r)	82-TN-266	Van Hool	T815	YE281500A02M14246	Van Hool	14246	C49FT	5/82	Blair & Palmer,Carlisle	Kells Transport Museum, Cork
			(ex 43 YPK)							
	83-C-17	Leyland	Tiger TRCTL11/3R	8200622	Plaxton	8312LTH1C901	C50F	1/83	Baxter, Isleworth	Kellls Transport Museum, Cork
			(ex FNM 853Y)							
	83-C-1899	Bova	Europa EL26/581	2118	Bova	1708	C53F	3/83	Hutchison, Overtown	Kells Transport Museum, Cork
			(ex MDS 217Y)							
	83-C-2836	Leyland	Tiger TRCTL11/3R	8200199	Duple	235/5484	C57F	6/82	National Travel East	Kells Transport Museum, Cork
			(ex OHE 275X)							
(r)	83-CW-273	Leyland	Tiger TRCTL11/3R	8201605	Duple	335/5354	C46FT	5/83	South Wales 119	Kells Transport Museum, Cork
			(ex MKH 896A, RCY 119Y)							
	83-D-3802	Volvo	B57	8403	New Zealand Motor Bodies		B52F	7/83	SBS 4867/ Bus Eireann VS243	Kells Transport Museum, Cork
			(ex SBS 4867R *Singapore*)							
	83-D-3879	Volvo	B57	8399	New Zealand Motor Bodies		B52F	11/83	SBS 4893/ Bus Eireann VS270	Carolan, Cavan
			(ex SBS 4893P *Singapore*)							
	83-D-4174	Leyland	Leopard PSU3F/4R	8031151	Plaxton	8111LC031	C49F	3/81	Wallace ArnoldTours	Kells Transport Museum, Cork
			(ex GWY 165Y, PNW 310W)							
	83-DL-1651	Bristol	RELL6G	RELL-3-2752	Alexander (Belfast)	754/16	B52F	5/83	Ulsterbus 2595	Connolly, Armagh
			(ex BXI 2595)							
	83-LH-930	Leyland	Olympian ONTL11/2R	ON932	ECW	25712	H51/32D	10/83	Lothian 717	Kells Transport Musuem, Cork
			(ex A717 YFS)							
	83-LK-712	Leyland	National NL116HLXCT/1R	07748	Leyland National		B49F	12/83	United 3137	Kells Transport Museum, Cork
			(ex A137 FDC)							
	83-TS-403	Leyland	Tiger TRCTL11/3R	8201294	Plaxton	8312LTH1C940	C50F	3/83	National Travel East	Kells Transport Museum, Cork
			(ex THL 288Y)							

Registration	Make	Model	Chassis No	Body	Body No	Layout	Date	First Owner	Current Owner
83-TS-530	Leyland	Leopard PSU5D/4R	8031239	Duple	235/5430	C46FT	1/83	Rennie, Dunfermline	Kells Transport Museum, Cork
		(ex OJL 822Y, PS 2045, SSG 321Y)							
83-WW-194	Ford	R1115	BCRSCT17990	Plaxton	8311FDP1C005	C53F	1/83	Yeowart, Whitehaven	Kells Transport Museum, Cork
		(ex XAO 135Y)							
84-C-3189	Dodge	S56	CD207335	Reeve Burgess	14842	B25F	6/84	South Wales Constabulary	Kells Transport Museum, Cork
		(ex A417 YBO)							
84-C-3607	Volvo	B10M-61	005575	Duple	349/7007	C55F	8/84	Cochrane, Shotton Colliery	Kells Transport Museum, Cork
		(ex B717 MDC, 1922 FS, B717 MDC)							
84-C-3663	Leyland	Royal Tiger	B50-041	Plaxton	8412LRH1C05N	C49FT	4/84	National Travel East	Kells Transport Museum, Cork
		(ex JUI 3085, TJI 6572, A325 XHE)							
84-C-3716	Bristol	RELL6G	RELL-3-2688	Alexander (Belfast)	753/2	B45F	4/82	Citybus 2521	Kells Transport Museum, Cork
		(ex AXI 2531)							
84-C-3721	Leyland	Tiger TRCTL11/2RH	8400633	Alexander	20TE/1884/2	C49F	11/84	East Midland 52	Kells Transport Museum, Cork
		(ex B 52 DWE)							
84-D-706	Leyland	Tiger TRCTL11/3RZ	8301367	Plaxton	8412LTH1C822	C53F	5/84	National Travel West 126	Kells Transport Museum, Cork
		(ex A126 MBA)							
84-D-4144	Leyland	Royal Tiger RT	RT1001	Plaxton	8412LRH1C12N	C53F	4/84	Grey Green, Stamford Hill	Kells Transport Museum, Cork
		(ex A868 SKK, KEL 128, A849 UYM)							
84-D-6758	Leyland	Royal Tiger RT	B50.28	Roe	GO4545	C50F	5/84	Leyland demonstrator	Kells Transport Museum, Cork
		(ex 2028 RU, A504 MHG)							
84-D-7221	Leyland	Atlantean AN68D/1R	8300985	Northern Counties	2572	H43/32F	4/84	Greater Manchester PTE 8726	Kells Transport Museum, Cork
		(ex A726 LNC)							
84-D-7336	Leyland	Atlantean AN68D/1R	8400004	Northern Counties	2608	H43/32F	7/84	Greater Manchester PTE 8762	Kells Transport Museum, Cork
		(ex A762 NNA)							
84-D-7523	Bedford	YMP	ET101997	Plaxton	848MQP1C001	C35F	6/84	Messenger, Aspatria	Kells Transport Museum, Cork
		(ex A543 XLG, FSU 804, A953 FHH)							
84-DL-2349	Bristol	RELL6G	RELL-3-2726	Alexander (Belfast)	780/10	B52F	5/84	Citybus 2569	Kells Transport Museum, Cork
		(ex BXI 2569)							
84-DL-2354	Bristol	RELL6G	RELL-3-2682	Alexander (Belfast)	716/25	B48F	2/84	Citybus 2525	Kells Transport Museum, Cork
		(ex XOI 2525)							
84-DL-2360	Bristol	RELL6G	RELL-3-2695	Alexander (Belfast)	753/9	B48F	4/84	Citybus 2538	Kells Transport Museum, Cork
		(ex AXI 2538)							
84-G-659	Ford	R1014	BC04TD65055	Wright	E155	C45F	4/84	Sureline, Lurgan	Kells Transport Museum, Cork
		(ex HIB 2138)							
84-KY-1195	Bedford	YNT	ET105372	Plaxton	8411NTP1C044	C53F	12/84	Wainfleet, Nuneaton	Kells Transport Museum, Cork
		(ex B624 LJU)							
84-LK-1039	Leyland	National NL116HLXCT/1R	07779	Leyland National		B49F	6/84	Blackpool 543	Kells Transport Museum, Cork
		(ex A543 PCW)							
85-D-2412	Bedford	SB5	HW456143	Marshall	280263	B40F	9/78	RAF/ Bus Eireann BM65	Bedford, Celbridge
		(ex 48 AC 14)							
85-LK-1327	Leyland	National NL116HLXCT/1R	07801	Leyland National		B49F	9/85	Southdown 155	Kells Transport Museum, Cork
		(ex C455 OAP, YAZ 8744, C455 OAP)							
85-LK-1328	Leyland	National NL116HLXCT/1R	07824	Leyland National		B49F	10/85	Southdown 157	Kells Transport Museum, Cork
		(ex C457 OAP, PAZ 3185, C457 OAP)							
85-MH-1211	Bedford	Venturer YNV	FT700202	Plaxton	8512NVP2C005	C57F	4/85	Rogers, Langwith	Kells Transport Museum, Cork
		(ex B942 RJF, NIB 5525, B242 NUT)							
85-TS-861	Dodge	G13	ED717817	Wadham Stringer	8865/85	B39FA	5/85	Ministry of Defence	Kells Transport Museum, Cork
		(ex 31 KC 26)							

	85-WH-93	Ford	R1114	BCRSWM515300	Plaxton	8511FTP2C001	C53F	5/85	Slack, Tansley	Kells Transport Museum, Cork
			(ex B638 KVO)							
	86-C-4486	Leyland	Tiger TRCTL11/3RH	8500655	Plaxton	8612LZH2C759	C??F	4/86	Cumberland 109	Kells Transport Museum, Cork
			(ex LIB 1380, C109 OHH, WLT 708, C109 OHH)							
	86-C-4606	Leyland	Lynx LX112TL11ZR1	LX1032	Leyland		B47F	11/86	Fishwick, Leyland 30	Kells Transport Museum, Cork
			(ex D 30 VCW)							
	86-D-8229	Leyland	Tiger TRCTL11/3RZ	8500871	Plaxton	8612LTP2C005	C51F	5/86	Midland Red South 77	Kells Transport Museum, Cork
			(ex C77 XWK)							
(r)	86-MO-445	Leyland	Royal Tiger RT	RT1021	Plaxton	8412LRH1C756	C53F	3/86	Armchair, Brentford	Kells Transport Museum, Cork
			(ex C759 FMC)							
	87-C-13993	Bedford	Venturer YNV	FT700467	Duple	8450/0568	C53F	1/87	Wheeler, Sawbridgeworth	Kells Transport Museum, Cork
			(ex A2 NPT, D125 HML)							
(r)	87-C-14597	Leyland	Tiger TRCTL11/3R	8600308	Duple	8690/0384	C--F	8/87	Nightingale, Exmouth	Kells Transport Museum, Cork
			(ex E178 WDV)							
	87-C-14637	Leyland	Tiger TRCTL11/2RP	TR00108	Plaxton	8811LTP3C002	C47F	11/87	United 1307	Kells Transport Museum, Cork
			(ex E267 KEF)							
	87-C-14811	DAF	MB200DKFL600	234314	Duple	8530/0635	C57F	2/87	Royal Red, Llandudno	Kells Transport Museum, Cork
			(ex D30 VEY)							
	87-D-2302	GAC	C	CB202	GAC		B45F	-/85	CIE KC202	-?-, -?-
			(first licensed 1/87)							
(r)	87-KK-2064	Volvo	B10M-61	013807	Duple	8693/0399	C53F	7/87	Park, Hamilton	Kells Transport Museum, Cork
			(ex D656 BCK)							
	87-LK-3557	Volvo	B10M-61	011819	Plaxton	8612VMH2C751	C53F	3/87	Jones, Pwllheli	Kells Transport Museum, Cork
			(ex 832 JYA, D68 VJC)							
	87-LS-1516	Dodge	G13	HD724710	Wadham Stringer	1597/87	B45F	10/87	Army	Kells Transport Museum, Cork
			(ex 93 KF 55)							
	87-MH-3474	Bedford	Venturer YNV	FT700415	Plaxton	8712NVP3C027	C57F	10/87	Wainfleet, Nuneaton	Kells Transport Museum, Cork
			(ex E832 EUT)							
	88-C-16273	Leyland	Tiger TRCTL11/3ARZ	TR00223	Plaxton	8812LUH3C762	C53F	3/88	Hills, Tredegar	Kells Transport Museum, Cork
			(ex E216 RDW)							
	88-C-16323	Leyland	Tiger TRBLXCT/2RH	TR00128	Alexander	11P/2187/2	DP51F	1/87	Grimsby Cleethorpes 28	Kells Transport Museum, Cork
			(ex E928 PBE)							
(r)	88-D-19015	Leyland	Tiger TRCL10/3ARZA	TR00451	Alexander	337E/5487/15	C53F	8/88	Bus Eireann TE15	Kells Transport Museum, Cork
	88-D-43778	Dennis	Falcon HC	SDA419/188	East Lancs	A8601	B44D	7/88	Ipswich 114	Kells Transport Museum, Cork
			(ex E114 KDX)							
(r)	88-LK-3740	DAF	SB2305DHS585	306594	Caetano	858036	C53F	11/88	Bonas, Coventry	Kells Transport Museum, Cork
			(ex F540 OEB, A 13 WMT, F771 RHP)							
(r)	89-C-18900	TAZ	D3200	910	TAZ		C53F	1/89	Eurobus, Harmondsworth	Kells Transport Museum, Cork
			(ex F329 NSH, A9 KRT, F867 ONR)							
	89-C-19014	Fiat	49-10	2011359	LHE		B23F	11/89	West Berkshire Health Authority	Kells Transport Museum, Cork
			(ex G362 XGM)							
	89-D-10622	GAC	C	CB160	GAC		B45F	-/85	CIE KC160	Kells Transport Museum, Cork
			(first registered 3/89)							
(r)	89-LS-1669	TAZ	D3200	1225	TAZ		C49FT	6/89	Thandi, Smethwick	Kells Transport Museum, Cork
			(ex F817 RJF)							
	89-MN-414	Mercedes-Benz	L407D	-?-	?		M16	6/89	Rice, Scotstown	Kells Transport Museum, Cork
(r)	89-TS-1159	TAZ	D3500	1123	TAZ		C49FT	5/89	Kavanagh B, Urlingford	Kells Transport Museum, Cork

	Registration	Chassis	Model	Chassis no.	Body	Body no.	Layout	Date	New to	Owner
	90-C-16424	Dennis	Javelin	12SDA1919/599	Caetano	058026	C49FT	10/90	Dent, Market Rasen	Kells Transport Museum, Cork
			(ex H401 CJF)							
	90-D-1001	→ see G183 WGX								
	90-D-1007	Leyland	Olympian ONCL10/1RZ	ON11256	Alexander (Belfast)	D01/07	H47/27D	6/90	Dublin Bus RH7	Hughes, Dublin
	90-D-1019	Leyland	Olympian ON2R50C13Z4	ON11656	Alexander (Belfast)	D02.01	H--/--D	8/90	Dublin Bus RH19	Hall, Dublin
	90-D-1028	→ see H775 PTW								
	90-D-1036	→ see DMN 16R *Isle of Man*								
	90-LH-5008	Volvo	B10M-60	025186	Plaxton	9012VCB1978	C46FT	8/90	East Yorkshire 54	Bond, Sheffield
			(ex H 54 VRH)							
	90-LK-5372	Leyland	Lynx LX2R11C15Z4S	LX1759	Leyland		B49F	7/90	County LX252	Kells Transport Museum, Cork
			(ex H252 GEV)							
	90-LK-5373	Leyland	Lynx LX2R11C15Z4S	LX1777	Leyland		B49F	7/90	County LX253	Kells Transpprt Museum, Cork
			(ex H253 GEV)							
	90-LK-5374	Leyland	Lynx LX2R11C15Z4S	LX1798	Leyland		B49F	7/90	County LX256	Kells Transport Museum, Cork
			(ex H256 GEV)							
	90-LK-5381	Leyland	Lynx LX2R11C15Z4S	LX1771	Leyland		B49F	3/90	Midland Red West 1141	Kells Transport Museum, Cork
			(ex G141 HNP)							
	90-LK-5382	Leyland	Lynx LX2R11C15Z4S	LX1908	Leyland		B49F	8/90	Badgerline 3616	Kells Transport Museum, Cork
			(ex H616 YTC)							
	90-MH-4542	TAZ	D3200	1269	TAZ		C53F	4/90	Phillips, Dagenham	Kells Transport Museum, Cork
			(ex G709 VRY)							
	90-OY-2565	Leyland	Lynx LX2R11C15Z4R	LX1819	Leyland		B49F	6/90	West Midlands 1280	Kells Transport Museum, Cork
			(ex G280 EOG)							
	91-D-1091	Leyland	Olympian ON2R50C13Z4	ON20048	Alexander (Belfast)	D04.03	H47/27D	5/91	Dublin Bus RH91	Hislip, Dublin
(r)	91-D-10032	DAF	MB230LB615	000479	Plaxton	9112DAB0199	C53F	4/91	Irish Bus PD32	Kells Transport Museum, Cork
	91-D-10125	Leyland	Olympian ON2R50C13Z4	ON20289	Alexander (Belfast)	D06.02	H47/27D	12/91	Dublin Bus RH125	McGuire, Dublin
	91-D-46988	Van Hool	A500	-?-	Van Hool	-?-	B14D	6/91	Aer Lingus, Dublin Airport	Kells Transport Museum, Cork
	91-D-46991	Van Hool	A500	YE250000N02C21520	Vah Hool	21520	B14D	6/91	Aer Lingus, Dublin Airport	Kells Transport Museum,Cork
	92-D-13731	GAC	C	CB169	GAC		B45F	-/85	CIE KC169	Kells Transport Musuem, Cork
			(*first registered 6/92*)							
	93-D-8007	Mercedes-Benz	709D	6690032N008311	Alexander (Belfast)	M07.07	B--F	12/93	Dublin Bus MA7	Willis, Dublin
	94-D-181	Volvo	Olympian YN2RC16Z4	025915	Alexander (Belfast)	D09.06	H47/27D	6/94	Dublin Bus RA181	-?-, Dublin
	94-D-33063	DAF	SB220LT550	003892	Alexander (Belfast)	B51.23	B43D	12/94	Dublin Bus AD63	-?-, -?-
	97-WH-3861	Kassbohrer	S250	WKK13400001015083	Kassbohrer		C53F	8/97	Silver Coach Lines, Edinburgh	Kells Transport Museum, Cork
			(ex TLZ 1787, R846 FSX, PSU 616, R846 FSX)							
	99-C-28703	Renault	G13	SDGG13AKKD729628	Wadham Stringer	2649/89	DP38F	11/89	United States Air Force	Kells Transport Museum, Cork
			(ex G806 YTA, 90 B 2051)							
	99-D-60020	Volvo	B6BLE	010086	Wright	B480	B35F	12/99	Dublin Bus WV20	Hughes, Dublin
			(ex V655 PHJ, WIL 9217, V655 PHJ, 99-D-60020 *Ireland*)							
	00-C-35652	Leyland	Swift ST2R44C97T5	LBM00270	Reeve Burgess	17725	C37F	8/91	Martindale, Ferryhill	Kells Transport Museum, Cork
			(ex B7 BED, J786 TDC)							

American registration

5W 13180 → see GHL 212V

Australian registration

050 OJO → see GSU 378
ANQ 778 AEC Regent III O961807 Commonwealth Engineering H--/--RD -/48 Sydney 1984 North West Museum of Transport

Cyprus registration

TCY 900 Bedford J6LZ5 6854872 Koukoulides B36D 7/66 Liatsos, Asomatos Adkins, Upper Boddington

French registration

117 QDV 75 Saviem SC10 UMR 653231 Saviem B42D -/77 RATP, Paris 7687 London Transport Museum

German registration

KL E-65 Mercedes-Benz O305 -?- Mercedes-Benz B?? -/70 Kaiserslautern Ward & Pearson, Enfield

Hong Kong registration

AD 7156 → see ABW 225D
ET 778 Leyland Olympian ON3R49C18Z4 ON11793 Alexander RH82/1390/23 CH53/41F 2/91 Citybus, Hong Kong 152 Rogers, Swindon

Malta registration

BUS 364 Bedford QL 23364 Sammut B36F -/43 Malta route bus Malta Historic Vehicle Group
(ex DBY 364, Y-0364, Y-1065, A-1242, 1242, 699 *all Malta*) *(rebodied date unknown)* *(on extended visit to UK)*
DBY 001 → see 522 XUT
EBY 565 Baileys (Malta) MP139 Gauci B40F 12/62 Malta toute bus Jurby Transport Museum, Jurby
(ex Y-0565, Y-1266, A-2590, 2590 *all Malta*)

Portuguese registration

FL-14-86 AEC Regal III 9631E548 Weymann/CCFL M3556 B16D 11/48 Lisbon 54 Wareham, Kidlington
IF-14-62 AEC Regal III O963443 CCFL B16D 10/48 Lisbon 104 Roulston, Glasgow
(*rebodied -/72*)

Swiss registration

FR 1347 → see HVF 455L

Unregistered or unknown registration

--- AEC K -?- Brush O--/--RO c-/14 -?-, -?- St Neots School, St Neots
--- Albion A16 960E ? Ch18 -/20 -?-, New Zealand Farrall, Chester
(r) --- Bedford OB 130666 Duple 55766 C29F 6/51 Williams, Waunfawr Transport Museum Society of Ireland
(ex 419 JZD, ACC 712)
--- Bedford KZ -?- Steel Bros B??T -/53 school bus, New Zealand Stefani, Doncaster (Q)
--- Bedford CAV -?- ? M?? -/58 private owner Trowsdale, Exmouth
(ex 747 ATA)
--- Bedford VAL70 -?- Duffy B40D -/71 Aer Lingus 301 Transport Museum Society of Ireland
--- Bedford VAS2 1795 Duple Midland CF878 B--F 10/64 London County Council 3159 Farrell, Dundalk
(ex BLH 123B)
--- Bristol LHS6L LHS-268 Duple 666/6700 C35F 6/76 Grey Green, Stamford Hill Lucas, Kingsley
(ex CAZ 6900, MUL 688P)
--- Delahaye 10/12 -?- -?- wagonette -/12 -?-, -?- Campbell, Harrogate
--- den Oudsten LOB 57LOB637 den Oudsten B43D -/74 VAD, Ermele 2426 -?-, -?-
(ex Z-23-44, 29-41-AB *Netherlands*)
(r) --- Dennis 3-ton 20088 *chassis only* 5/22 -?-, -?- Giles, Gamlingay
--- Dennis Dart SLF SFD1230R1RG/0101 Plaxton -?- B—F -/96 Dennis test rig -?-, -?-

	---	Ford	TT	-?-	Lund	B10	-/26	Lund, Duffield	Lund, Wistow
					(replica body -/97)				
	---	Ford	TT	-?-	replica	Ch12	-/24	chassis imported from France	Knapton, Bradford
			(ex SL 9806)		*(replica body new -/83)*				
	---	GMC	PD4501	PD4501-083	GMC	RC43F	-54	Greyhound T-902	Hall, Rainham
	---	Halley	-?-		*chassis only*		-/12	-?-, -?-	Halleys Garage, Glasgow
	---	Karrier	?	-?-	?	B??F	-/2?	-?-, -?-	Golcar Transport Museum, Huddersfield
(r)	---	Leyland	SG11	-?-	*chassis only*		-/25	-?-, -?:-	Hubbuck, Petersfield
(r)	---	Leyland	Atlantean PDR1/1	582862	Metro-Cammell	H--/--F	-/59	development vehicle	Ribble Vehicle Preservation Trust
	---	Leyland	National 10351A/2R	04812	Leyland National	B—D	2/78	London Transport LS112	Kells Transport Museum, Cork
			(ex THX 112S)						
	---	Leyland	National NL116AL11/3R	07416	Leyland National	B30T	4/81	Manchester Airport N4	Davies, West Kirby
	---	Milnes-Daimler	30hp	-?-	*chassis only*		by12/16	Sussex Motor Company	Southdown Omnibus Trust
	---	MOC		-?-	LGOC (?)	O--/--RO	-/07	-?-, -?-	Weatherhead, Woburn Sands
					(body ex LGOC new c-/11)				
	---	Morgan	?	-?-	?	B?	-/15	-?-, -?-	Williams, Fishguard
			(ex DS 7922)						
	---	Morrison	Electricar FL	A4289	?	B24	-/67	Royal Showground	BaMMOT, Wythall
	---	Moulton		MD/1970/AM1	Moulton	C23F	-/70	development vehicle	Science Museum, Wroughton
	---	Napier	2-ton	-?-	Mitchell	O??/??RO	-/13	-?-, -?-	Ward, Harrogate
					(replica body by12/79)				
	---	Optare	MetroRider		Optare	B--	-/93	new	London Transport Museum MRL242
					(built new as sectioned display)				
	---	Saviem	SC10	-?-	Saviem	B??T	-/75	Choisy-le-Roi	Wild, Leeds
						(with open rear balcony)			
	---	Straker-Squire		-?-	*chassis only*		-/??	-?-, -?-	Whitewebbs Museum, Enfield
		(also suggested chassis may be Belsize)							
	---	Thornycroft	A12	-?-	-?-	B19	-/31	-?-, -?-	Hammond, Basingstoke
	---	Tilling Stevens	TTA1	-?-	Tilling	O--/--RO	c-/12	Tilling	Weatherhead, Woburn Sands
	---	Tilling Stevens	TS3	829	?	O18/16RO	-/16	lorry chassis	Cook, Worfield
					(body ex British Autombile Traction)				
	---	Tilling Stevens	TS7	-?-	Tilling	O--/--RO	-/23	Tilling	Weatherhead, Woburn Sands
	---		*body only*		Hurst Nelson (?)	O--/--RO	-/??	National	Drewitt, Epsom
					(body from Clarkson steam bus)				
	---		*body only*		Hurst Nelson (?)	O--/--RO	-/??	National	Drewitt, Epsom
					(body from Clarkson steam bus)				
	---		*body only*		LGOC (?)	O--/--RO	-/??	-?-, -?-	Golcar Transport Museum, Huddersfield
	---		*body only*		LGOC (?)	O--/--RO	-/??	-?-, -?-	Ward, Harrogate
	---		*body only*		LGOC (?)	O--/--RO	-/??	-?-, -?-	Ward, Harrogate

PRESERVED TROLLEYBUSES

AK 9627		*body only*		Bradford City Transport		B--R	9/14	Bradford 515	Bradford Industrial Museum
CU 3593	Karrier	E4	30005	Weymann	C5083	H29/26R	5/37	South Shields 204	British Trolleybus Society
DX 3988	Railless			Short		B30D	9/23	Ipswich 2	Ipswich Transport Museum
DX 5610	Ransomes	D	1746	Ransomes	561	B31D	5/26	Ipswich 9	Ipswich Transport Museum
DX 5617	Ransomes	D	1755	*chassis only*			5/26	Ipswich 16	Ipswich Transport Museum
DX 5621	Ransomes	D	1757	Ransomes	572	B--D	6/26	Ipswich 20	Ipswich Transport Museum
DX 5629	Garrett	O	279	Strachan & Brown		B31D	7/26	Ipswich 26	Ipswich Transport Museum
DX 5631	Garrett	O	281	*chassis only*			7/26	Ipswich 29	Long Shop Museum, Leiston
DX 8871	Ransomes	D	2065	Ransomes	1217	B31D	8/30	Ipswich 44	Science Museum, Wroughton
DY 4965	Guy	BTX60	BTX22717	Dodson	7662	O26/31RO	4/28	Hastings 3	Hastings Borough Council
DY 5458	Guy	BTX	BTX23162	Ransomes	852	B32C	2/29	Hastings 45	Trolleybus Museum Company
DY 5584	Guy	BTX	BTX23363	Ransomes	969	B--C	6/29	Hastings 57	Sandtoft Transport Centre
FW 8990	AEC	661T	661T192	Park Royal	-?-	H30/26R	3/37	Cleethorpes 54	Fieldsend, Chelmsford
FZ 7883	AEC	664T	664T799	Harkness/Park Royal		H36/32R	-/43	Belfast 98	Ulster Folk & Transport Museum
FZ 7897	Guy	BTX	BTX36913	Harkness		H36/32R	4/48	Belfast 112	Ulster Folk & Transport Museum
GZ 8532	Guy	BTX	BTX36955	Harkness		H36/32R	3/49	Belfast 168	Trolleybus Museum Company
GZ 8547	Guy	BTX	BTX36970	Harkness		H36/32R	1/49	Belfast 183	Transport Museum Society of Ireland
HX 2756	AEC	663T	663T006	UCC		H32/24R	5/31	London United 1	London Transport Museum
KW 6052	English Electric		1002	English Electric		B--F	11/29	Bradford 562	Sandtoft Transport Centre
PV 817	Ransomes	D	2162	Ransomes	1520	H24/24R	12/33	Ipswich 46	Ipswich Transport Museum
PV 8270	Karrier	W	50364	Park Royal	B37214	H30/26R	2/48	Ipswich 105	Ipswich Transport Museum
RB 6614	AEC	662T	662T002	English Electric		B--F	-/32	Notts & Derby 307	Bowden & Collins, Nottingham
RC 8472	Sunbeam	W	50088	Weymann	C8014	H30/26R	8/44	Derby 172	Sandtoft Transport Centre
RC 8575	Sunbeam	W	50133	Park Royal	B29200	H30/26R	7/45	Derby 175	Sandtoft Transport Centre
RV 4649	AEC	661T	661T028	English Electric		H26/24R	8/34	Portsmouth 201	Portsmouth Museums
TV 4484	Ransomes	D6	2140	*chassis only*			11/31	Nottingham 46	Sandtoft Transport Centre
TV 9333	Karrier	E6	54072	Brush		H--/--R	8/34	Nottingham 367	Notts & Derby Preservation Society
UK 9978	Guy	BTX	BTX23732	Guy		H--/--R	5/31	Wolverhampton 78	Black Country Museum Transport Group
WT 7101	Straker-Clough			Brush		H--/--RO	-/24	Keighley 5	Bradford Industrial Museum (*in care of Keighley Bus Museum Trust*)
WT 7108	Straker-Clough		T29	Brush		B--F	-/24	Keighley 12	North of England Open Air Museum, Beamish
WW 4688	Garrett	O	O379	Garrett		B--C	2/28	Mexborough & Swinton 34	British Trolleybus Society
ADX 196	Sunbeam	F4	50680	Park Royal	B33264	H30/26R	7/50	Ipswich 126	Ipswich Transport Museum
ALJ 973	Sunbeam	MS2	12068T	Park Royal	B3636	H31/25D	3/35	Bournemouth 99	British Trolleybus Society
ALJ 986	Sunbeam	MS2	12081T	Park Royal	B3649	O40/29R	6/35	Bournemouth 202	Trolleybus Museum Company
ARC 515	Sunbeam	F4	50668	Brush		H30/26R	2/49	Derby 215	Aston Manor Road Transport Museum
ARD 676	AEC	661T	661T274	Park Royal	B5326	H30/26R	5/39	Reading 113	British Trolleybus Society
AVH 470	Karrier	E6	31048	*chassis only*			4/38	Huddersfield 470	Sandtoft Transport Centre
BDJ 87	BUT	9611T	9611T006	East Lancs	4282	H30/26R	1/51	St Helens 187	Sandtoft Transport Centre
BDY 809	Sunbeam	W	50435	Weymann	C9162	H30/26R	10/47	Hastings 34	London Trolleybus Preservation Society
CDT 636	Karrier	W	50182	Roe (*rebodied 3/55*)	GO3965	H34/28R	7/45	Doncaster 375	Doncaster Omnibus & Light Railway Society
CET 613	Sunbeam	MS2C	12253	East Lancs		B--C	2/43	Rotherham 74	Stubbs, Burton-upon-Trent
CKG 193	AEC	664T	664T862	Northern Counties		H38/32R	3/42	Cardiff 203	British Trolleybus Society
CPM 61	AEC	661T	661T343	Weymann	M2095	H28/26R	9/39	Brighton Hove & District 6340	Science Museum, Wroughton
CUL 260	AEC	664T	664T168	Metro-Cammell		H40/30R	7/36	London Transport 260	London Trolleybus Preservation Society

	Reg	Chassis	Model	Chassis no	Body	Body no	Layout	New	Original operator	Current owner
	CVH 741	Karrier	MS2	60007	Park Royal	B32189	H40/30R	7/47	Huddersfield 541	Trolleybus Museum Company
	DBO 475	BUT	9641T	9641T078	East Lancs	4190	H38/29D	-/48	Cardiff 215	National Museum of Wales
	DKY 703	Karrier	W	50170	East Lancs	5605	H37/29F	5/45	Bradford 703	Shears D, Winkleigh
					(rebodied 3/60)					
	DKY 704	Karrier	W	50171	East Lancs	5595	H37/29F	5/45	Bradford 704	Cardiff & South Wales Trolleybus Project
					(rebodied 10/59)					
	DKY 706	Karrier	W	50173	East Lancs	5601	H37/29F	5/45	Bradford 706	Oliver, Australia (*kept in UK*)
					(rebodied 1/60)					
(r)	DKY 711	Karrier	W	50178	East Lancs	5608	H37/29F	6/45	Bradford 711	Trolleybus Museum Company
					(rebodied 5/60)					
	DKY 712	Karrier	W	50179	East Lancs	5606	H37/29F	7/45	Bradford 712	Shears D, Winkleigh
					(rebodied 4/60)					
	DKY 713	Karrier	W	50180	East Lancs	5607	H37/29F	8/45	Bradford 713	-?-, Barnsley
					(rebodied 5/60)					
(r)	DKY 731	Karrier	W	50252	East Lancs	5596	H37/29F	5/46	Bradford 731	Black Country Museum Transport Group, Dudley
					(rebodied 10/59)					
	DKY 735	Karrier	W	50256	East Lancs	5594	H37/29F	3/46	Bradford 735	Saxton, Cornwall
					(rebodied 10/59)					
	DKY 737	Karrier	W	50258	East Lancs	5600	H37/29F	3/46	Bradford 737	Bradford Industrial Museum
					(rebodied 12/59)					
	DRC 224	Sunbeam	F4	50750	Willowbrook	52007	H32/28R	12/52	Derby 224	London Trolleybus Preservation Society
	DRD 130	BUT	9611T	9611T069	Park Royal	B33239	H33/26RD	6/49	Reading 144	Sandtoft Transport Centre
	DUK 833	Sunbeam	W	50311	Roe	GO4715	H32/28R	6/46	Wolverhampton 433	Black Country Museum Transport Group, Dudley
					(rebodied -/59)					
	EBO 919	BUT	9641T	9641T098	East Lancs/Bruce	4209	H38/29D	11/49	Cardiff 262	Cardiff & South Wales Trolleybus Project
	EKU 743	BUT	9611T	9611T012	Roe	GO2835	H33/25R	12/49	Bradford 743	Sandtoft Transport Centre
	EKU 746	BUT	9611T	9611T015	Roe	G02833	H31/25R	12/49	Bradford 746	David Allen & Croft, Reading
	ELB 796	Leyland	LPTB70	14049	Metro-Cammell		H40/30R	2/38	London Transport 796	London Trolleybus Preservation Society
										(On loan from AMTUIR, Paris, France)
	ERD 145	Sunbeam	S7	70036	Park Royal	B34285	H38/30RD	10/50	Reading 174	Russell, Reading
	ERD 152	Sunbeam	S7	70043	Park Royal	B34292	H38/30RD	11/50	Reading 181	Harvey, Reading
	ERV 938	BUT	9611T	9611T147	Burlingham	4093	H28/24R	3/51	Portsmouth 313	London Trolleybus Preservation Society
	EXV 201	Leyland	LPTB70	300146	Leyland		H40/30R	2/39	London Transport 1201	London Trolleybus Preservation Society
	EXV 253	Leyland	LPTB70	300198	Leyland		H40/30R	3/39	London Transport 1253	London Transport Museum
	EXV 348	Leyland	LPTB70	300452	Leyland		H40/30R	6/39	London Transport 1348	Sandtoft Transport Centre
										(on long term loan fromTransport Museum Society of Ireland)
	FET 617	Daimler	CTE6	15886	Roe	GO4250	H40/30R	8/50	Rotherham 37	Rotherham Trolleybus Group
					(rebodied 5/56)					
	FET 618	Daimler	CTE6	15885	Roe	GO4454	H40/30R	8/50	Rotherham 44	Sandtoft Transport Centre
					(rebodied 1/57)					
	FJW 616	Sunbeam	F4	50647	Park Royal	B33173	H28/26R	3/49	Wolverhampton 616	BaMMOT, Wythall
	FJW 654	Guy	BT	BT37023	Park Royal	B33607	H28/26R	4/50	Wolverhampton 654	Trolleybus Museum Company
	FKU 758	BUT	9611T	9611T114	Weymann	M4518	H33/26R	1/51	Bradford 758	Bradford Trolleybus Association
	FWX 913	Sunbeam	F4	50566	*chassis only*			9/48	Mexborough & Swinton 29	Bowden & Collins, Nottingham
	FWX 914	Sunbeam	F4	50567	East Lancs	5890	H37/29F	9/48	Bradford 844	West Yorkshire PTE
					(rebodied 12/62)					*(in care of Keighley Bus Museum Trust)*
	FXH 521	Metro-Cammell			Metro-Cammell		H40/30R	6/40	London Transport 1521	London Trolleybus Preservation Society
	FYS 839	BUT	9613T	9613T044	Crossley	5826	H37/34R	3/58	Glasgow TB78	British Trolleybus Society

	Reg	Make	Model	Chassis no	Body	Body no	Layout	Date	First owner	Owner
	FYS 988	BUT	RETB1	580530	Burlingham	6523	B50F	11/58	Glasgow TBS13	Glasgow City Council
	FYS 996	BUT	RETB1	581124	Burlingham	6530	B50F	12/58	Glasgow TBS21	Roulston, Glasgow
	GAJ 12	Sunbeam	F4	50633	Roe	GO5965	H35/26R	6/50	Teesside 2	Price, Newcastle upon Tyne
					(rebodied 9/64)					
	GAJ 15	Sunbeam	F4	50636	Roe	GO5964	H35/26R	6/50	Teesside 5	Redcar & Cleveland Borough Council
					(rebodied 1/65)					
	GFU 692	BUT	9611T	9611T131	Northern Coachbuilders	228	H38/26R	7/50	Cleethorpes 59	Whitehead et al, Reading
	GHN 574	Karrier	W	50106	East Lancs	5489	H39/31F	11/44	Bradford 792	Stainforth, Hampshire
					(rebodied 11/58)					
	GKP 511	Sunbeam	W	50069	Roe	GO5172	H34/28R	5/44	Maidstone 56	Coates, Maidstone
					(rebodied 10/60)					
	GTV 666	Karrier	W	50188	Brush		H30/26R	7/45	Nottingham 466	Sandtoft Transport Centre
	HKR 11	→ see AFE 131A								
	HYM 768	BUT	9641T	9641T117	Metro-Cammell		H40/30R	2/48	London Transport 1768	London Transport Museum
	HYM 812	BUT	9641T	9641T161	Metro-Cammell		H40/30R	9/48	London Transport 1812	British Trolleybus Society
	JVU 755	Crossley	Dominion TDD64/1	94512	Crossley		H36/30R	-/51	Manchester 1250	Museum of Transport, Manchester
	JWW 375	Sunbeam	F4	50729	East Lancs	5888	H37/29F	8/50	Bradford 845	Sandtoft Transport Centre
					(rebodied 11/62)					
	JWW 376	Sunbeam	F4	50730	East Lancs	5893	H37/29F	8/50	Bradford 846	Yeomans, Bradford
					(rebodied 1/63)					
	JWW 377	Sunbeam	F4	50731	East Lancs	5894	H37/29F	8/50	Bradford 847	Sandtoft Transport Centre
					(rebodied 2/63)					
	KBO 961	BUT	9641T	9641T251	East Lancs	5094	B40R	-/55	Cardiff 243	Cardiff & South Wales Trolleybus Project
	KLJ 346	BUT	9641T	9641T438	Weymann	M4306	H31/25D	-/50	Bournemouth 212	Shears D, Winkleigh
	KTV 493	BUT	9611T	9611T060	Roe	GO2794	H31/25R	11/48	Nottingham 493	Thornton, Nottingham
	KTV 502	BUT	9641T	9641T341	Brush		H38/32R	2/50	Nottingham 502	Bowden, Nottingham
	KTV 506	BUT	9641T	9641T345	Brush		H38/32R	2/50	Nottingham 506	Needham, Carterton
	KTV 578	BUT	9641T	9641T506	Brush		H38/32R	12/51	Nottingham 578	Howard, Nottingham
	KVH 219	BUT	9641T	9641T601	East Lancs	-?-	H40/32R	1/57	Huddersfield 619	West Yorkshire Transport Circle
	LCD 52	BUT	9611T	9611T036	Weymann	M3820	H30/26R	5/50	Maidstone 52	London Trolleybus Preservation Society
	LHN 784	BUT	9611T	9611T025	East Lancs	5851	H37/29F	5/49	Bradford 834	Bentley & Whiteley, Bradford
					(rebodied 6/62)					
	LHN 785	BUT	9611T	9611T026	East Lancs	5853	H37/29F	4/49	Bradford 835	Munday, Huddersfield
					(rebodied 6/62)					
	LTC 774	Crossley	Empire TDD42/2	94442	Crossley		H30/26R	7/50	Ashton 80	Museum of Transport, Manchester
	LTN 501	Sunbeam	S7	70003	Northern Coachbuilders		H39/31R	9/48	Newcastle 501	North of England Open Air Museum, Beamish
	NBB 628	BUT	9641T	9641T499	Metro-Cammell		H40/30R	11/50	Newcastle 628	London Trolleybus Preservation Society
	NDH 959	Sunbeam	F4	50740	Brush		H34/31R	11/51	Walsall 342	British Trolleybus Society
	NNU 234	BUT	9611T	9611T126	Weymann	M4039	H32/26R	5/49	Notts & Derby 353	Shears D, Winkleigh
	NNU 238	BUT	9611T	9611T130	Weymann	M4047	H32/26R	5/49	Notts & Derby 357	Bowden, Nottingham
	ONE 744	BUT	9612T	9612T228	Burlingham	-?-	H32/28R	12/55	Manchester 1344	British Trolleybus Society
	PVH 931	Sunbeam	S7A	TFD74375	East Lancs	5590	H40/32R	12/59	Huddersfield 631	British Trolleybus Society
	SCH 237	Sunbeam	F4A	TFD74171	Roe	GO4985	H37/28R	3/60	Derby 237	Hopkinson, Nottingham
	TDH 912	Sunbeam	F4A	9031	Willowbrook	54182	H36/34RD	6/55	Walsall 862	Black Country Museum Transport Group, Dudley
(z)	TDH 914	Sunbeam	F4A	9035	Willowbrook	54184	H--/--RD	6/55	Walsall 864	Sandtoft Transport Centre
	VRD 186	Sunbeam	F4A	TFD74783	Burlingham	7078	H38/30F	7/61	Reading 186	Brown, Norwich
	VRD 193	Sunbeam	F4A	TFD74787	Burlingham	7085	H38/30F	6/61	Reading 193	Bilbé, Reading
	XDH 72	Sunbeam	F4A	9043	Willowbrook	55707	H36/34RD	10/56	Walsall 872	British Trolleybus Society

YLJ 286	Sunbeam	MF2B	STB80185	Weymann	M8574	H35/28D	8/59	Bournemouth 286	London Trolleybus Preservation Society
YTE 826	BUT	9612T	9612T252	Bond		H32/28R	9/56	Ashton 87	London Trolleybus Preservation Society
297 LJ	Sunbeam	MF2B	TFD80197	Weymann	M9519	H37/28D	9/62	Bournemouth 297	Bournemouth Heritage Transport Collection
299 LJ	Sunbeam	MF2B	TFD80200	Weymann	M9523	H37/28D	10/62	Bournemouth 299	Transport Museum Society of Ireland
301 LJ	Sunbeam	MF2B	TFD80202	Weymann	M9516	H37/28D	10/62	Bournemouth 301	Shears D, Winkleigh
2206 OI	Sunbeam	F4A	9045	Harkness		H36/32R	10/58	Belfast 246	London Trolleybus Preservation Society
AFE 131A	Sunbeam	W	50393	Northern Coachbuilders		H30/26R	4/47	Maidstone 72	Sandtoft Transport Centre
		(ex HKR 11) *(continues to display HKR 11)*							
LMP 657P	Henschel	uH111/s	6559/25288	Uerdingen		B32T	-/52	Solingen 1	Ward & Pearson, Enfield
		(ex SG 2030 *Germany*)							
LMP 658P	Henschel	uH111/s	6928/34503	Uerdingen		B28T	-/57	Solingen 40	Ward & Pearson, Enfield
		(ex SG 2111 *Germany*)							*(on loan to Pro OBus, Salzburg, Austria)*
C 45 HDT	Dennis	Dominator	DTA1401/101	Alexander	RHT/3084/1	H47/33F	9/85	South Yorkshire PTE 2450	Sandtoft Transport Centre
		(*sometimes displayed with registration B450 CKW*)							

Danish registration

AH 79505	Garrett	O	310	Strachan & Brown		B26D	9/26	NESA(Copenhagen) 5	London Trolleybus Preservation Society

French registration

964 H 87	Vetra-Berliet	CB60	-?-	CTL		B15D	7/43	Limoges 5	Nimmo, Bromley
7830 LG 69	Vetra	EH85	-?-	-?-		B22T	-/64	Lyon 1704	Sandtoft Transport Centre
8319 JD 13	Renault	ER100	10E0187	-?-		B26D	-/80	Marseilles 202	Sandtoft Transport Centre

German registrations

ES 234	Henschel	uH111/s	-?-	Uerdingen		B??	-/55	Esslingen	Ward & Pearson, Enfield
SG 2030	→ see LMP 657P								
SG 2111	→ see LMP 658P								
BAD 2054	Henschel	uH111/s	6890/29210	Uerdingen		B28T	-/54	Baden Baden 224	Ward & Pearson, Enfield
BAD 2091	Henschel	HS160 0SL	103065	Henschel		B33T	-/59	Baden Baden 231	Ward & Pearson, Enfield
AC-L 379	Henschel	562E	33552	Ludewig		RB17/44T	-/56	Aachen 22	British Trolleybus Society

Greek registration

5088	ZIU	682B10	00001708	ZIU		B24T	-/89	ILAP, Athens 5088	East Anglia Transport Museum Society

Portuguese registration

66	Lancia	?	120003	Dalfa		H43/25D	11/67	Oporto 140	Sandtoft Transport Centre

Unregistered

---	Berna	?	-?-	Hess		B37D	-/49	Biel (Switzerland) 39	Ward & Pearson, Enfield
---	BUT	9641T	9641T026	Bus Bodies	M135	H40/31D	5/48	Johannesburg (S.Africa) 589	Sandtoft Transport Centre
---	FN		?-	FN		B26D	-/32	Liege 425	Sandtoft Transport Centre
		(ex GKU 429E, EAK 563D, 5425 P *Belgium*)							
---	GMC	TGH5307	-?-	GMC		B35D	-/81	Edmonton (Canada) 189	Sandtoft Transport Centre

STEAM BUSES

DS 8768	Stanley	Mountain Wagon	7754	Stanley	T12	-/14	hotel bus, Colorado, USA	Williams, Chipperfield
GT 2827	Sentinel	DG6P	8590	replica	B30F	11/31	steam waggon	Smith {Northern Star}, Pickering (NY)
				(replica body -/05)				
JH 9994	Sentinel	S4	9151	replica	B??R	-/35	steam waggon	Bullen, -?-
				(replica body -/71)				
KG 1123	Sentinel	DG4P	8714	Appleby Heritage Centre	B32R	6/32	steam waggon	Saunders, Stotfold
				(replica body -/04)				
M 5798	Foden	5-ton	4258	replica	B14R	1/14	steam waggon	Painter, Congleton
				(replica body -/02)				
M 6359	Foden	C	11340	replica	B20R	12/23	steam waggon	Searle, Horsham
		(ex CD 8223)		*(replica body -/60)*				
Q231 RMA	replica		SABTVR0393110994E	replica	B14R	4/01	replica	Brogden, Macclesfield

(*replica of 1832 Walter Hancock steam carriage "Enterprise" operated by London & Paddington Steam Carriage Company*)

PRESERVED TRAMS

This list is presented in the following manner : -

Column 1 - operator
Column 2 - fleet number
Column 3 - truck configuration — 4w = 4 wheel) + C = Cable; 8w = 8 wheel) E = Electric; G = Gas; H = Horse; S = Steam; T = Trailer
Column 4 - Tram Builder
Column 5 - DT = double deck tram) ST = single deck tram) + seating capacity; TT = toastrack tram); O prefix for open top)
Column 6 - Year built
Column 7 - Location (if a museum) or owner

Aberdeen 1	4wH	Shinnie	ODT52	c1889	Grampian Transport Museum
Aberdeen Suburban 11	8wT	-?-	ST??	1911	Alford Valley Railway
Amsterdam 474	4wE	Beijnes	ST20	1929	East Anglia Transport Museum
Barrow 38	--E	Brush	ST--	1921	Stott, Widnes
Barrow 45	--E	Brush	ST--	1921	Stott, Widnes
Belfast 118	4wH	Belfast	ODT??	c1897	Ulster Folk & Transport Museum

Belfast 249	4wE Belfast	ODT??	1905	Ulster Folk & Transport Museum
Belfast 357	4wE Brush	DT68	1930	Ulster Folk & Transport Museum
Berlin 3006	4wE -?-	ST14	1969	Crich Tramway Village
Bessbrook & Newry 2	8wE Mather & Platt	ST??	1885	Ulster Folk & Transport Museum
Birkenhead 7	4wH Starbuck	ODT46	1876	Wirral Transport Museum
Birkenhead 20	4wE Milnes	ODT51	1901	Wirral Transport Museum
Birkenhead 69	4wE Taikoo	DT55	1992	Wirral Transport Museum
Birkenhead 70	4wE Taikoo	DT55	1992	Wirral Transport Museum
Birmingham 107	--E UEC	ODT--	1906	Aston Manor Road Transport Museum
Birmingham 395	4wE UEC	DT52	1911	Thinktank, Birmingham
Birmingham Central cable car	--C Falcon	ODT--	1888	Black Country Living Museum, Dudley
Birmingham & Midland 12	--E Brush	ST--	1904	Blists Hill Open Air Museum
Blackpool 2	4wE Blackpool	Works	1927	Crich Tramway Village (stored)
Blackpool 4	4wE Lancaster Carriage & Wagon	ODT32	1884	Crich Tramway Village
Blackpool 5	8wE Blackpool	ST48D	1972	Crich Tramway Village (stored)
Blackpool 8	8wE Blackpool	ST48D	1974	Lancastrian Transport Trust *(at Blackpool (LA))*
Blackpool 11	8wE English Electric	ST48C	1939	East Anglia Transport Museum
Blackpool 31	8wE Midland RCW	ODT50/36	1901	North of England Open Air Museum, Beamish
Blackpool 40	8wE Blackpool	DT46/32	1926	Crich Tramway Village
Blackpool 48	8wE Blackpool	DT46/32	1928	Willamette Shore Trolley, Oregon, USA
Blackpool 49	8wE Blackpool	DT46/32	1926	Crich Tramway Village
Blackpool 59	8wE Midland RCW	ODT49/44	1902	Crich Tramway Village (stored)
Blackpool 143 *(see Blackpool 753)*				
Blackpool 144	8wE Blackpool	DT46/32	1925	Seashore Trolley Museum, Maine, USA
Blackpool 147	8wE Hurst Nelson	DT46/32	1924	Blackpool (LA)
Blackpool 159	8wE Blackpool	DT46/32	1927	East Anglia Transport Museum
Blackpool 166	8wE Blackpool	ODT64	1927	Crich Tramway Village
Blackpool 167	8wE English Electric	ST52	1928	Crich Tramway Village *(on loan to Blackpool (LA))*
Blackpool 226	8wE English Electric	OST56	1934	Bay Area Electric Railway, Rio Vista, California, USA
Blackpool 228	8wE English Electric	OST56	1934	San Francisco Municipal Railway, California, USA
Blackpool 287	8wE Brush	ST--C	1937	Lancastrian Transport Trust
Blackpool 298	8wE Brush	ST48C	1937	Crich Tramway Village
Blackpool 304	8wE Roberts	ST56C	1952	Lancastrian Transport Trust *(stored c/o Blackpool (LA))*
Blackpool 605	8wE English Electric	OST52C	1934	Lancastrian Transport Trust
Blackpool 606	8wE English Electric	OST56C	1934	National Capital Trolley Museum, Washington, USA
Blackpool 607	8wE English Electrrc	OST56C	1934	Crich Tramway Village (stored)
Blackpool 619 *(as Heaton Park 7)*	8wE Bolton Trams	ST58	1987	Blackpool (LA) on loan to Heaton Park Tramway
Blackpool 621	8wE Brush	ST48C	1937	Friends of Fleetwood Trams
Blackpool 623	8wE Brush	ST48C	1937	Manchester Transport Museum Society
Blackpool 625	8wE Brush	ST48C	1937	Merseytravel, Birkenhead
Blackpool 626	8wE Brush	ST48C	1937	Merseytravel, Birkenhead
Blackpool 627	8wE Brush	ST48C	1937	Friends of Fleetwood Trams
Blackpool 630	8wE Brush	ST48C	1937	Crich Tramway Village
Blackpool 632	8wE Brush	ST48C	1937	Lancastrian Transport Trust *(may be used by Blackpool (LA))*
Blaclkpool 634	8wE Brush	ST48C	1937	Rushden Historical Transport Society member
Blackpool 663	8wE Roberts	ST56C	1953	Lancastrian Transport Trust
Blackpool 671	8wE English Electirc / Blackpool	ST53C	1935/60	Merseytravel, Birkenhead
Blackpool 676	8wE English Electric / Blackpool	ST53C	1935/58	Lancastrian Transport Trust

	Blackpool 678	8wE	English Electric / Blackpool	ST48C	1935/61	Friends of Fleetwood Trams
	Blackpool 679	8wE	English Electric / Blackpool	ST48C	1935/61	Lancastrian Transport Trust
	Blackpool 680	8wE	English Electric / Blackpool	ST48C	1935/60	Manchester Transport Museum Society
	Blackpool 681	8wT	Metro-Cammell	ST61C	1960	Merseytravel, Birkenhead
	Blackpool 686	8wT	Metro-Cammell	ST61C	1960	Lancastrian Transport Trust
(r)	Blackpool 687	8wT	Metro-Cammell	ST61C	1960	Lancastrian Transport Trust
	Blackpool 702	8wE	English Electric	DT44/40C	1934	Manchester Transport Museum Society
	Blackpool 703	8wE	English Electric	DT54/40C	1934	Lancastrian Transport Trust
						(on loan to North of England Open Air Museum as Sunderland 101)
	Blackpool 704	8wE	English Electric	DT54/40C	1934	Lancastrian Transport Trust
	Blackpool 708	8wE	English Electiric	DT54/40C	1934	Manchester Transport Museum Society
	Blackpool 719	8wE	English Electric	DT54/40C	1934	Friends of Fleetwood Trams
	Blackpool 712	8wE	English Electric	DT54/40C	1934	Crich Tramway Village
	Blackpool 715	8wE	English Electric	DT54/40C	1935	Lancastrian Transport Trust *(loaned back to Blackpool (LA))*
	Blackpool 726	8wE	English Electric	DT54/40C	1935	Friends of Fleetwood Trams
	Blackpool 731	8wE	Blackpool	Float-36	1959	Streetcar Investment Group, Oregon, USA
	Blackpool 732	8wE	Blackpool	Float-47	1961	Lancastrian Transport Trust
	Blackpool 735	8wE	Blackpool	Float-99	1963	Transport Preservation Trust, Beith
	Blackpool 752	4wE	Blackpool	Works	c1928	Manchester Transport Museum Society
	Blackpool 753	8wE	Blackpool	ODT--	1924	Lancastrian Transport Trust *(c/o Blackpool (LA))*
	Blackpool 761	8wE	English Electric/MetSec	DT56/48F	1979	Friends of Fleetwood Trams
	Blackpool 762	8wE	English Electric/MetSec	DT56/34D	1982	Crich Tramway Village
	Blackpool Loco	4wE	English Electric	Loco	1927	Crich Tramway Village
	Blackpool & Fleetwood 2	8wE	Milnes	TT56	1898	Crich Tramway Village
	Blackpool & Fleetwood 40	8wE	UEC	ST44	1914	Blackpool (LA) (on loan from Crich Tramway Village)
	Bolton 66	8wE	ERTCW	DT74	1901	Blackpool (LA) (on loan from Bolton 66 Trust)
	Bournemouth 85	8wE	UEC	ODT66	1914	Southern Electric Museum of Electricity, Christchurch
	Bournemouth 86	--E	UEC	ODT--	1914	Llandudno & Colwyn Bay Tramway Society
						(*to be restored as Llandudno & Colwyn Bay 6*)
	Bournemouth 113		-?-	-?-	19??	Park Farm Museum, Milton Abbas
	Bournemouth 126	--E	Brush	ODT--	c1926	Llandudno & Colwyn Bay Tramway Society
						(*to be restored as Llandudno & Colwyn Bay 7*)
	Bradford 40	4wH	WGH (replica)	ST18	1992	Bradford Industrial Museum
	Bradford 104	4wE	Bradford	DT43/19	1925	Bradford Industrial Museum
	Bradford & Shelf -?-	4wS	Green	Loco	c1895	Big Hole Museum, Kimberley, South Africa *(as Kimberley 2: Beaconsfield)*
						(UK identity to be confirmed)
	Brighton 53	--E	Brighton	ODT--	1937	Tram 53 Society, Brighton
	Bristol horse car	--H	?Starbuck?	-?-	18??	M Shed, Bristol
	Bristol (1 of 101-115)	--T	Milnes	ODT--/18	1895	Bristol Aero Collection
	Brussels 96	4wE	Brill	Works	c1905	Crich Tramway Village
	Budapest 2576	4wE	Ganz	ST16	1904	Munday, Huddersfield
	Budapest 2577	4wE	Ganz	ST16	1904	Munday, Huddersfield
	Burton & Ashby 14	?wE	Brush	ODT??	1906	Detroit Department of Tourism, USA
	Cambridge 1 (or 7)	--H	Starbuck	ODT??	1880	Ipswich Transport Museum
	Cardiff 21	4wH	Falcon	ODT42	1880	National Museum of Wales *(on loan to Crich Tramway Village)*
	Cardiff 131	4wE	Brush	Works	1905	Crich Tramway Village
	Carlisle -?-	--E	-?-	-?-	c1912	Workington Transport Heritage Trust
	Charleroi 38	4wT	-?-	ST??	1944	Gaeltacht Train Committee, Fintown

Charleroi 41	4wT -?-	ST??	1944	Gaeltacht Train Committee, Fintown
Charleroi 42	4wT -?-	ST??	1944	Gaeltacht Train Committee, Fintown
(Note: 1 of the 3 Charleroi trams is now with Southwold Railway)				
Cheltenham District 21	4wE English Electric	ODT52	1921	Cheltenham Art Gallery & Museums
Chesterfield 7	4wE Brush	ODT56	1904	Crich Tramway Village
Chesterfield 8	4wH Milnes	ST16	1899	Crich Tramway Village
Colchester 10	--E ERTCW	ODT--	1904	Harvey, Walton-on-the-Naze
Coventry 71	--E Brush	DT--	1931	-?-, Coventry
Cruden Bay 2	4wE GNSR	ST16	1899	Grampian Transport Museum
Derby 1	4wE Brush	ODT45	1903	Crich Tramway Village
Douglas 11	4wH Starbuck	OTT32	1886	Isle of Man Railway & Tramway Preservation Company
Douglas 14	4wH Metropolitan	ODT44	1883	Manx Museum, Douglas
Douglas 22	4wH Milnes	ST--	1890	Jurby Transport Museum
Douglas 46	4wH Milnes Voss	TT40	1909	Wirral Transport Museum
Douglas 47	4wH UEC	TT40	1911	Isle of Man Railway & Tramway Preservation Company
Douglas 49	4wH Vulcan	ST34	1935	Isle of Man Railway & Tramway Preservation Company
Douglas 72/73	8wC Milnes	TT36	1896	Douglas Corporation Transport
Douglas Southern 1	4wE New General Traction	ODT75	1896	Crich Tramway Village
Dublin 22	--E -?-	-?-	1935	Transport Museum Society of Ireland
Dublin 224	4wT Brush	ODT--	c1900	Transport Museum Society of Ireland
Dublin 253	--E Dublin United	DT--	1928	Transport Museum Society of Ireland
Dublin 284	--E Dublin United	DT--	1928	Transport Museum Society of Ireland
Dublin Directors Car	--E Dublin United	ODT--	1901	Transport Museum Society of Ireland
Dublin & Blessington -?-	8wT Drewry	ST40	192?	Ulster Folk & Transport Museum
Dudley & Stourbridge 5	4wE Tividale	ST32	1920	Black Country Living Museum, Dudley
Dudley & Stourbridge 75	--E Brush	ST--	1919	Black Country Living Museum, Dudley
Dudley & Stourbridge -?- (1 of 23-28)	--E ERTCW	ODT--	1901	Black Country Living Museum, Dudley
Dundee & District 2	--T Starbuck	ODT--	1882	Wirral Leisure Services
Dundee & District 21	8wT Milnes	ODT38/28	1895	Crich Tramway Village
Dusseldorf 392	?wE -?-	ST??	19??	Summerlee : Museum of Scottish Industrial Life
Edinburgh 23	4wH Edinburgh Street Tranways	ODT--	c1885	Edinburgh Horse Tram Trust
Edinburgh 35	4wE Edinburgh	DT62	1948	Crich Tramway Village
Edinburgh 79	--C Milnes	ODT--	1900	City of Edinburgh Council
Edinburgh 226	--E Dick Kerr	DT--	1903	City of Edinburgh Council
Falkirk 14	8wE Brush	ST28	1931	Falkirk Museums
Frankfurt 210	8wE Duwag	ST28	1956	-?-, Essex
Gateshead 5	8wE Gateshead	ST48	1927	Crich Tramway Village
Gateshead 10	8wE Gateshead	ST48	1925	North of England Open Air Museum, Beamish
Gateshead 51	--E ERTCW	ST--	1901	North of England Open Air Museum, Beamish
Gateshead 52	4wE ERTCW/Gateshead	ST32	1901/20	Crich Tramway Village (stored)
Giants Causeway 2	4wT Midland RCW	ST??	1882	Ulster Folk & Transport Museum
Giants Causeway 5	4wT Midland RCW	ST24	1882	Ulster Folk & Transport Museum
Giants Causeway 9	--T -?-	ST??	1887	Transport Museum Society of Ireland
Giants Causeway	4wT -?- (replica)	TT??	1986	Giants Causeway Centre
Glasgow 1	4wE Glasgow	Works	1905	Crich Tramway Village (stored)
Glasgow 21	--E Glasgow	Works	c1903	Crich Tramway Village (stored)
Glasgow 22	4wE Glasgow	DT62	1922	Crich Tramway Village
Glasgow 488	4wE Glasgow	DT??	1903	AMTUIR, Paris, France

Glasgow 543	4wH	North Metropolitan	ODT42	1894	Riverside Museum, Glasgow
Glasgow 585	4wE	Glasgow	DT59	1901	Science Museum, Wroughton
Glasgow 672	8wE	Glasgow	ST50C	1898	Riverside Museum, Glasgow
Glasgow 779	4wE	Glasgow	DT66	1900	Riverside Museum, Glasgow
Glasgow 812	4wE	Glasgow	DT59	1900	Crich Tramway Village
Glasgow 1016	--E	BEC	ST--	1904	Glasgow Vintage Vehicle Trust
Glasgow 1017	4wE	BEC	ST18	1904	Summerlee : Museum of Scottish Industrial Life
Glasgow 1088	4wE	Glasgow	DT59	1924	Riverside Museum, Glasgow
Glasgow 1089	8wE	Glasgow	ST21	1926	Riverside Museum, Glasgow
Glasgow 1100	8wE	Hurst Nelson	DT69	1928	Crich Tramway Village (stored)
Glasgow 1115	8wE	Hurst Nelson	DT68	1929	Crich Tramway Village
Glasgow 1173	8wE	Glasgow	DT64	1938	Riverside Museum, Glasgow (stored)
Glasgow 1245	8wE	Glasgow	DT64	1939	Summerlee : Museum of Scottish Industrial Life
Glasgow 1274	8wE	Glasgow	DT64	1940	Seashore Trolley Museum, Maine, USA
Glasgow 1282	8wE	Glasgow	DT64	1940	Crich Tramway Village
Glasgow 1297	8wE	Glasgow	DT40/30	1948	Crich Tramway Village
Glasgow 1392	8wE	Glasgow	DT66	1952	Riverside Museum, Glasgow
Gloucester horse car	4wH	Starbuck	ST16	187?	Gloucester Folk Museum (stored)
Graz 210	4wE	-?-	ST??	19??	Munday, Huddersfield
Graz 225	4wE	Simmering	ST16	1950	Tram 53 Society, Brighton
Great Northern Railway 381	4wH	Metropolitan	ODT48	1883	Ulster Folk & Transport Museum
Grimsby & Immingham 14	8wE	Great Central Railway	ST72	1915	Crich Tramway Village
Guernsey 3	--E	Milnes	ODT--	1897	Guernsey Museum & Art Gallery & Heritage Service
Guernsey 17	--T	-?-	ST--	????	Carman, Guernsey
den Haag 1147	8wE	La Brugeoise et Nivelles	ST36	1957	Crich Tramway Village
Halle 902	8wE	CKD Tatra	ST??	c1975	Crich Tramway Village
Hastings 48	--E	UEC	ODT--	1906	South Eastern Tramways Society, Eastbourne
Hastings 56	--E	UEC	ODT--	1906	South Eastern Tramways Society, Eastbourne
Heaton Park 7 *(see Blackpool 619)*					
Hill of Howth 2	8wE	Brush	ODT67	1901	Orange Empire Trolley Museum, California, USA
Hill of Howth 4	8wE	Brush	ODT67	1901	Ulster Folk & Transport Museum
Hill of Howth 9	8wE	Milnes	ODT41/33	1902	Transport Museum Society of Ireland
Hill of Howth 10	8wE	Milnes	ODT73	1902	Crich Tramway Village
Hull 96 *(see Leeds 6)*					
Hull 132	4wE	Hull	DT36/20	1910	Streetlife (Hull Museum of Transport)
Hull -?-	--E	Milnes	ODT--	1899	Crich Tramway Village (stored)
Ipswich 33	4wE	Brush	ODT--	1904	Ipswich Transport Museum
Johannesburg 60	4wE	UEC	DT62	1905	Crich Tramway Village
Krefeld 41	4wT	Duwag	ST24	1956	Pump House Museum, Walthamstow
Krefeld 412	8wE	Duwag	ST30	1957	Pump House Museum, Walthamstow
Lanarkshire Tramways 53	4wE	UEC	ODT55	1908	Summerlee : Museum of Scottish Industrial Life
Leamington & Warwick 1	4wH	Metropolitan	ODT18/18	1881	Crich Tramway Village
Leamington & Warwick 8	4wH	Midland RCW	ODT--	c1890	Summerlee : Museum of Scottish Industrial Life
Leeds 2	4wE	Leeds	Works	1932	Crich Tramway Village
Leeds 6	4wE	Hurst Nelson	ST22	1901	Manchester Transport Museum Society *(on loan to North of England Open Air Museum, Beamish)*
Leeds 107	--H	Milnes	ODT--	1898	Leeds Transport Historical Society
Leeds 180	4wE	Brush	DT60	1931	Crich Tramway Village

Tram	Type	Builder	Body	Date	Location
Leeds 345	4wE	Leeds	DT62	1921	Crich Tramway Village
Leeds 399	4wE	Leeds	DT70	1925	Crich Tramway Village
Leeds 600	8wE	Brush/Leeds	ST34C	1931/54	Crich Tramway Village (stored)
Leeds 602	8wE	Roe	ST34C	1953	Crich Tramway Village
Leicester 59	--E	ERTCW	ODT--	1904	-?-, -?-
Leicester 76	4wE	ERTCW	DT34/22	1904	Crich Tramway Village
Lisbon 305	8wE	-?-	ST??	19??	Llandudno & Colwyn Bay Tramway Society *(carries livery of Llandudno & Colwyn Bay 25)*
Lisbon 361	8wE	-?-	ST??	1906	Black Country Living Museum, Dudley
Lisbon 715	4wE	-?-	ST??	19??	Southampton City Museums
Lisbon 730	4wE	-?-	ST??	19??	Wirral Transport Museum
Liverpool 43	4wH	Liverpool Tramways	ODT43	c1879	Wirral Transport Museum
Liverpool 245	4wE	Liverpool	DT70	1938	Wirral Transport Museum
Liverpool 293	4wE	Liverpool	DT70	1939	Seashore Trolley Museum, Maine, USA
Liverpool 762	8wE	Liverpool	DT70	1930	Wirral Transport Museum
Liverpool 869	8wE	Liverpool	DT78	1936	Crich Tramway Village
Llandudno & Colwyn Bay 6 *(see Bournemouth 86)*					
Llandudno & Colwyn Bay 7 *(see Bournemouth 126)*					
Llandudno & Colwyn Bay 25 *(see Lisbon 305)*					
London County Council 106	4wE	ERTCW	ODT57	1903	Crich Tramway Village
London County Council T66	--T	BEEC	ODT--	1913	London Transport Museum
London Street Tramways 707	--H	?Falcon?	ODT--	c1887	Oxford Bus Musuem (Oxfordshire County Museums)
London Tramways Company 284	4wH	Stephenson	ODT24/20	1881	London Transport Museum
London Tramways Company -?-	--H	London Tramways	ODT--	c1895	Crich Tramway Village (stored)
London Transport 1	8wE	LCC	DT38/28	1932	Crich Tramway Village
London Transport 290 *(see West Ham 102)*					
London Transport 1025	8wE	LCC	DT73	1908	London Transport Museum
London Transport 1622	8wE	Brush	DT46/27	1912	Crich Tramway Village
London Transport 1858	8wE	LCC	DT46/28	1930	East Anglia Transport Museum
London Transport 2085	8wE	UCC	DT64	1931	Seashore Trolley Museum, Maine, USA
London United Tramways -?-	4wH	Milnes	ODT26/20	1895	Caister Castle Motor Museum
London United Tramways 159	-?-	Milnes	ODT--	c1902	Crich Tramway Village
Lowestoft 14	4wE	Milnes	ODT26/22	1904	East Anglia Transport Museum
Lowestoft -?- (one of 21-23)	--E	Milnes	ST--	1903	East Anglia Transport Museum
Luton 6	4wE	UEC	DT--	1908	Luton Museum
Maidstone 18	--E	UEC	ST--	1909	Dover Transport Museum
Manchester 173	4wE	Brush	ODT--	1901	Manchester Transport Museum Society, Museum of Transport, Manchester
Manchester 765	8wE	Manchester	ST40	1913	Manchester Transport Museum Society, Heaton Park Tramway
Manchester L53	4wH	Manchester Carriage & Tramways	ODT38	1877	Manchester Transport Museum Society, Bury Transport Museum
Manchester, Bury, Rochdale & Oldham 84	4wS	Beyer Peacock	Loco	1886	Crich Tramway Village (stored)
Manx Electric 23	8wE	Manx Electric	Loco	1899	Isle of Man Railway & Tramway Preservation Company
Manx Electric 26	8wE	Milnes	ST-goods	1895	Isle of Man Railway & Tramway Preservation Company
Manx Electric 59	8wT	Milnes	ST18	1895	Manx Electric Railway Visitor Centre, Ramsey
Metropolitan 331	8wE	UCC	DT70C	1929	Crich Tramway Village
Metropolitan 355	8wE	UCC	DT64	1931	London Transport Museum
Modern Electric Tramways 3	4wE	Modern Electric Tramways	ODT??	1952	Sorenson, Wilton, Connecticut, USA
Modern Electric Tramways 23	8wE	C Lane	DT??	1949	Butler, Penketh
Modern Electric Tramways 225	8wE	Modern Electric Tramways	OST??	1950	Sorenson, Wilton, Connecticut, USA

Modern Electric Tramways 238	8wE	Modern Electric Tramways	ST??	1954	Sorenson, Wilton, Connecticut, USA
Neath -?-	4wG	Ashbury	ODT40	1896	Cefn Colliery Museum
Newcastle 102	8wE	Hurst Nelson	ODT84	1901	Crich Tramway Village
Newcastle 114	4wE	WGH (replica)	ODT29/24	1993	North of England Open Air Museum, Beamish
Newcastle & Gosforth 49	--H	Midland RCW	ST--	1873	North of England Open Air Museum, Beamish
New South Wales 2	4wS	Beyer Peacock	Loco	1885	Crich Tramway Village
New York 3rd Avenue 674	8wE	3rd Avenue	ST48	1939	Crich Tramway Village
North Metropolitan 39	--H	-?-	ODT--	????	North Metropolitan 39 Trust
Nottingham 45	--E	English Electric	ODT--	1923	Nottingham Transport Heritage Centre
Nottingham 92	--E	ERTCW	ODT--	1902	Nottingham Industrial Museum
Nottingham 101	--E	Brush	-?-	1923	Great Central Railway Group, Nottingham
Nottingham 166	--E	UEC	DT--	1920	Crich Tranway Village (stored)
Oporto 9	4wH	Starbuck	ST20	1873	Crich Tramway Village
Oporto 176	4wE	-?-	ST23	1926	Harrison, Lanchester *(fitted with road wheels and towed to events)*
Oporto 196 *(in Gateshead livery)*	4wE	CCF do Porto	ST28	1935	North of England Open Air Museum, Beamish
Oporto 273	8wE	CCF do Porto	ST30	1928	Crich Tramway Village
Oporto C65	?wE	-?-	ST-goods	19??	Crich Tramway Village (stored)
Oxford 6	--H	London Tramways Co	ODT--	c1882	Oxford Bus Museum (Oxfordshire County Museums)
Oxford 20	--H	?Milnes?	ODT--	1898	Oxford Bus Museum (Oxfordshire County Museums)
Paisley 68	4wE	Hurst Nelson	ODT63	1919	Crich Tramway Village
Portsdown & Horndean 5	--E	BEC	ODT--	1903	Portsmouth City Museums
Portsdown & Horndean 13	--E	BEC	ODT--	1903	Portsmouth City Museums
Portsmouth 84	4wE	Milnes	ODT26/20	1880	Milestones, Basingstoke
Portsmouth ?	(4w)H	?Milnes?	ST--	c1872	Brickfields Horse Centre, Isle of Wight
Portstewart 1	4wS	Kitson	Loco	1882	Streetlife (Hull Museum of Transport)
Portstewart 2	4wS	Kitson	Loco	1883	Ulster Folk & Transport Museum
Prague 180	4wE	Ringhoffer	ST24	1905	Crich Tramway Village
Pwllheli 4	4wH	Falcon	ST16	1899	Welsh Highland Railway, Porthmadoc
Rawtenstall 23	--E	UEC	ST--	1910	Manchester Transport Museum Society
Rotterdam 109	8wE	Allan	ST28	1950	-?-, Selby area
Ryde Pier 1	4wE	Pollards	ST20	1911	Isle of Wight Bus Museum (Isle of Wight Council)
Ryde Pier 3	4wH	?Starbuck?	ST24	1871	Streetlife (Hull Museum of Transport)
Sheffield 15	4wH	Starbuck	ST16	1874	Crich Tramway Village
Sheffield 46	4wE	Milnes	ST22	1899	Crich Tramway Village (stored)
Sheffield 74	4wE	ERTCW	DT30/22	1900	Crich Tramway Village
Sheffield 189	4wE	Sheffield	DT61	1934	Crich Tramway Village
Sheffield 264	4wE	UEC	DT32/22	1907	North of England Open Air Museum, Beamish
Sheffield 264	4wE	Sheffield	DT61	1937	Crich Tramway Village
Sheffield 330	4wE	English Electric	Works	1920	Crich Tramway Village
Sheffield 419	--E	Brush	DT--	1922	Trolleybus Museum at Sandtoft
Sheffield 422	--E	Brush	DT--	1922	Trolleybus Museum at Sandtoft
Sheffield 460	--E	Cravens	DT--	1926	South Yorkshire Transport Museum
Sheffield 510	4wE	Roberts	DT36/26	1950	Crich Tramway Village
Sheffield 513	4wE	Roberts	DT36/26	1950	East Anglia Transport Museum *(on loan from North of England Open Air Museum)*
Southampton 11	--E	Southampton	DT--	1924	Southampton City Museums
Southampton 38	--E	Hurst Nelson	ODT--	1902	Southampton City Museums

Southampton 45	4wE Hurst Nelson	ODT56	1903	Crich Tramway Village
Southampton 57	--E Southampton	ODT--	1909	Southampton City Museums
Southampton 87	--E English Electric	DT--	1919	Southampton City Museums
South Lancs 65	--E Brush	ODT--	1906	Museum of Transport, Manchester
South Staffs 102	--E Tividale	ST--	1920	Black Country Living Museum, Dudley
Stockport 5	4wE ERTCW	ODT33/22	1901	Heaton Park Tramway (on loan from Stockport 5 Tramcar Trust)
Sunderland 16	--E ERTCW	DT--	1900	North of England Open Air Museum, Beamish
Sunderland 100 *(see Metropolitan 331)*				
Sunderland 101 *(see Blackpool 703)*				
Swansea 14	--E Brush	DT--	1924	Swansea Industrial & Maritime Museum
Swindon 13	--E English Electric	ODT--	1921	GWR Heritage Society, Swindon
Wallasey 78	4wE Brush	DT42/24	1920	Wirral Transport Museum
Warrington 2	--E Milnes	ODT--	1902	Wirral Transport Museum
West Ham 102	4wE UEC	DT54	1910	London Transport Museum
Wolverhampton 23	4wH Falcon	ODT26/18	1892	Black Country Living Museum, Dudley
Wolverhampton 49	--E UEC	ODT--	1909	Black Country Living Museum, Dudley
Wolverhampton & District 19	--E Brush	Works	1902	Black Country Living Museum, Dudley
Wolverhampton & District 34	4wE Tividale	ST32	1919	Black Country Living Museum, Dudley
Wolverton & Stony Stratford 2	--T Midland RCT	DT100	1887	Milton Keynes Museum
Wolverton & Stony Stratford 5	--T ?	DT--	1887	Milton Keynes Museum
York -?-	--E Brush	ODT--	c1910	Sutcliffe, Totternhoe

PRESERVED HORSE BUSES

Note: The H numbers are PSV Circle references numbers used to identify individual horse buses in subsequent reports in the British Journal.

H41	1840s	horse bus	-?-, -?-
H36	c1850	16-seat Favorite horse bus	Mossman Collection, Luton
H9	1863	horse bus	Ulster Folk & Transport Museum
H1	c1875	24-seat Thomas Tilling Times knifeboard	London Transport Museum
H11	c1875	London General knifeboard	London Bus Preservatioon Trust, London Bus Museum, Brooklands
H23	c1880	The Leatherhead 3-light garden seat	Drewitt, Epsom
H13	c1885	26-seat London General garden seat	London Bus Preservation Trust (*on loan to North of England Open Air Museum, Beamish*)
H14	c1885	London Road car garden seat	Gawsworth Hall Collection
H15	c1885	London General garden seat	Gawsworth Hall Collection
H2	1886	26-seat London General garden seat	London Transport Museum
H40	1880s	Star Omnibus garden-seat horse bus	-?-, -?-
H5	1890	38-seat Manchester Carriage Company garden seat	Museum of Transport, Manchester
H39	c1890	horse wagonette	Science Museum, Wroughton
H20	c1890	26-seat Patsy Hearn garden seat	Reckitt & Coleman, Norwich
H42	c1890	Andrews patent spring horse bus	Shire Horse Farm & Carriage Museum, Treskillard
H48	c1890	Star Omnibus 3-light garden seat	London Bus Preservation Trust, London Bus Museum, Brooklands
H21	1891	19-seat horse bus, Falmouth area	Stewart, Cornwall
H22	1893	horse bus, Callington area	Stewart, Cornwall
H33	1894	26-seat horse bus, Ross-on-Wye area	Gallifords, Wolbey
H44	1894	garden seat horse bus	Thompson, Startforth
H47	1895	26-seat horse bus	Roulston, Glasgow
H6	1896	26-seat Edinburgh & District garden seat	British Commercial Vehicle Museum, Leyland
H16	c1898	private estate horse bus	Tyrwhitt-Drake Museum of Carriages, Maidstone
H4	1900	Kent & East Sussex Railway station bus	National Railway Museum, York
H35	c1900	26-seat London General garden seat	Mossman Collection, Luton
H34	c1900	Glasgow Tramway & Omnibus horse bus	Summerlee : Museum of Scottish Industrial Life
H3	1929	replica of 1829 Shillibeer horse bus	London Transport Museum
H31	1935	replica of Leicester horse bus	Leicestershire Museums, Snibston Discovery Park
H8		10-seat Lawson Omnibuses station bus	Riverside Museum, Glasgow
H37		20-seat horse charabanc	Mossman Collection, Luton
H7		24-seat Ardrishaig Belle charabanc	Riverside Museum, Glasgow
H10		horse bus	Ulster Folk & Transport Museum
H24		horse bus	Campbell, Harrogate
H45		horse bus	Sandwell Farm, West Bromwich
H30		horse bus found in Aldershot	Drewitt, Epsom
H46		knifeboard horse bus	Foxdell Carriages, Bromsgrove
H17		Lion Hotel station bus	Hereford & Worcester County Museum, Hartlebury Castle
H29		London horse bus found in Suffolk	-?-, -?-
H50		Manchester horse bus	Manchester Transport Museum Society
H49		replica horse bus “Spirit of Bradford”	Bradford Industrial Museum
H38		Progressive horse cart with seats	Leicestershire Museums, Snibston Discovery Park
H18		station bus	Buckland Abbey, Yelverton
H19		station bus	Shuttleworth Collection

SELF POWERED MINIATURE PSVs

CB 9384	miniature coach styled on AEC Regal			-?-	19??	NT Horton Coachworks, Nottingham
JP 8179	Johnstone Midget	JM14	Harrington	-4-	1950	Dodds, Ayr (SW)
	(AEC Regal Harrington no fin style)					
LA 983	Farrington & Watson			O??RO	1985	Wilcock, Morecambe
	(LGOC B-type)					
LA 9848	Farrington & Watson			O??RO	19??	Gulliver's World, Warrington
	(LGOC B-type B470)					
LA 9927	1/3 scale LGOC B339 on Swift car chassis			O16RO	1956	Seaton & District Electric Tramway Company
LE 9061	miniature LGOC B-type			O??RO	19??	Pump House Museum, Walthamstow
	(may be unpowered)					
TR 6170	Lion Omnibus	PLSC3/47704	Lion Omnibus	B8	1972	Scoular, Edinburgh
	(5/8 scale Leyland Lion)					
BCM 650	Johnstone Midget		Johnstone	-2-	1950	Price, Walsall
	(Commer Avenger style)					
BDV 343	freelance on Lanchester car chassis			B5	1960	-?-, -?-
BRT 86	miniature coach syled on AEC Regal / Duple			-?-	c1986	-?-, -?-
BUS 1910	Lion Omnibus		Lion Omnibus	O??RO	19??	Marlow, Leicestershire
DMT 61	miniature Bedord OB based on mobility scooter			-?-	2009	Padfield, Trealaw
DUF 3	Johnstone Midget		Johnstone	-4-	1936	Johnstone, Brighton
	(Leyland TS style)					
FNJ 478	Johnstone Midget		Harrington	-4-	1950	Wren, Kingsbury
	(AEC Regal Harrington no fin style)					
FPM 404	Johnstone Midget	50-29	Harrington	-4-	19??	Price, Walsall
	(AEC Regal Harrington no fin style)					
GNP 1	Johnstone Midget		Harrington	-2-	1949	Price, Walsall
	(AEC Regal Harrington fin style)					
GUF 72	freelance miniature bus styled on Southdown Guy Arab			O?	2002	Littlehampton Bus Gathering
GUF 729	miniature Leyland PS1		Southdown apprentices	-?-	1947	Price, Walsall
HSF 1	Miniature bus in Northern Scottish livery			-?-	19??	Forrest, Cruden Bay
HTM 112	Johnstone Midget	-?-	Harrington	-4-	1950	Costin, Dunstable
	(AEC Regal Harrington no fin style)					
JCD 202	Johnstone Midget		Johnstone	-0-	1947	-?-, -?-
	(Leyland PS style)					
JMC 1	Johnston Midget		Johnstone	-0-	1958	Price, Walsall
	(Leyland PSUC self-drive style)					
JMC 2	Johnstone Midget		Johnstone	-0-	1958	Booth, Rolvenden Motor Museum
	(Leyland PSUC self-drive style)					
JMC 6	Johnstone Midget		Johnstone	-0-	1958	Price, Walsall
	(Leyland PSUC self-drive style)					
KOX 555	Johnstone Midget	50-31	Johnstone	-2-	1950	Skelding, Worcester
	(Leyland PSU Harrington style)					
KTG 24	Johnstone Midget	50-28	Harrington	-2-	1950	Buckle, Great Yarmouth
	(AEC Regal Harrington fin style)					
LEY 26	Miniature coach styled on Midland Red Leyland half cab			-?-	19??	Blue Bird Classic Realistic Models, High Wycombe
LUF 1	Johnstone Midget		Johnstone	-6-	1951	Price, Walsall
	(Leyland PSU Duple style)					

MSD 799	miniature bus			-?-	19??	-?-, Aberdeen
MTB 982	Johnstone Midget	JM56	Harrington	-2-	19??	Roberts, -?-
	(AEC Regal Harrington fin style)					
SCD 2	Johnstone Midget		Johnstone	-6-	195?	Kerr, Arbroath
	(Yeates Riviera style)					
TUF 3	Johnstone Midget		Johnstone	-6-	195?	Kerr, Arbroath
	(Yeates Riviera style)					
VBX 333	freelance miniature bus with VW running units	5031624		O??RO	1996	Lewis, Brynamman
VRD 182	1/3 scale Reading trolleybus 182			-?-	c1962	Lepine-Smith, Great Bookham
VRE 150	Johnstone Midget		Johnstone	-2-	1951	Happy Days, Stafford (ST)
	(Leyland PSU Harrington style)					
WFN 513	1/4 scale East Kent AEC Reliance Park Royal			-?-	2002	Richards, Canterbury
2677 PH	Farrington & Watson	M/AWSD1019043		O18RO	1983	Whittaker, West Bromwich
	(LGOC B55; based on Morris Minor rinning units)					
217 MDV	→ see VBX 333					
BNK 217A	freelance miniature bus with Mini running units	SABTVR03528033107		O??RO	19??	Ensign, Purfleet (EX)
BUF 426C	Miniature Ld PD3/ NC based on Batricar			O2	199?	Littlehampton Bus Gathering
	(formerly carried PRX 190B)					
XLH 485G	freelance styled on LGOC B-type			O??RO	1986	-?-, -?-
	(based on Fd Cargo BL05GP18236 new 8/68)					
WIG 570N	miniature bus in 'Urban Fox' livery			-?-	19??	-?-, Wigston
UUA 550P	1/2 scale Leyland TD1			O??RO	1972	Farmer, Southampton
BUS 1T	freelance miniature bus			O15DO	19??	-?-, Surrey
A100 QMH	freelance coach styled on Plaxton Paramount			-?-	19??	Whittaker, West Bromwich
C 36 JUD	freelance miniature bus with Mini running units	SAXXL2S1N20315843		B7F	2004	Whitmore, Chesterfield
E561 MKV	Lion Omnibus	87SLBH007	Lion Omnibus	O??RO	1990	Whittaker, West Bromwich
	(LGOC B550)					
L100 BJT	Ford Transit	BDVARU54102	Brijan	O8/6RO	2009	Brijan Tours, Curdridge (HA)
	(ex M28 ALT) *(converted from Fd Tt van new 7/94)*					
Q255 AFG	Lion Omnibus	G1H002	Lion Omnibus	O??RO	`1986	-?-, -?-
Q785 OVL	Lion Omnibus	87GH009	Lion Omnibus	O??RO	1985	Hollier, Norfolk
	(LGOC B1445)					
Q897 PVL	$4^{1}/_{2}$" scale miniature Foden steam bus	R04897		B??	1999	Pickles & Bacon, Scunthorpe
Q597 VOE	Farrington & Watson	Y73145		O18RO	1989	Whittaker, West Bromwich
	(LGOC B54; based on Morris Minor running units)					
J 8721	Lion Omnibus	85GH005	Lion Omnibus	O??RO	1986	Fantastic Tropical Gardens, Jersey
	(ex Q924 OTL)					
BERTIE	Lion Omnibus		Lion Omnibus	O??RO	198?	Rotary Club, Keighley
	(LGOC B-type)					
LION 1	freelance miniature bus			O??RO	19??	Bourne Lions, Bourne
---	Johnstone Midget		Harrington	-4-	1950	Booth, Rolvenden Motor Museum
	(ex KCD 311) *(Guy Arab style)*					
---	Johnstone Midget		Johnstone	-?-	195?	Boot, High Wycombe
	(Leyland PSU Duple style)					
---	Lion Omnibus		Lion Omnibus	O??RO	1970	Fraser, Spalding
	(LGOC B341)					
---	Lion Omnibus		Lion Omnibus	O??RO	1970	Ridpath, Storrington
	(LGOC B342)					

---	Lion Omnibus *(LGOC B342)*	Lion Omnibus	O??RO	198?	Werbe Mobil, Dusseldorf, Germany
---	Lion Omnibus *(LGOC B1345)*	Lion Omnibus	O??RO	1986	Scott Price, Blackpool
---	Lion Omnibus *(LGOC B-type)*	Lion Omnibus	O??RO	198?	Wickstead Park, Kettering
---	Lion Omnibus *(LGOC B-type)*	Lion Omnibus	O??RO	1988	Doncaster Lions
---	Lion Omnibus *(LGOC B-type; lettered 'Fairground Organs')*	Lion Omnibus	O??RO	1987	-?-, -?-
---	freelance built by Docherty, Auchterarder (SE) with Honda components		-4-	????	Docherty, Auchterarder (SE)
---	freelance miniature bus based on BMC Mini running units		O??RO	2005	Norton, Hull
---	freelance saloon in Maidstone & District livery		-8-	19??	-?-, Faversham
---	miniature bus styled on LGOC B87		-?-	19??	Price, Walsall
---	miniature bus styled on LGOC B340		O??RO	1988	Scott Price, Blackpool
---	miniature LGOC B-type		O??RO	19??	-?-, -?-
---	normal control charabus based on Austin A35 parts		C10	19??	Haynes, Sidcup
---	1/3 scale UTA Leyland PD2		-?-	1947	Ulster Folk & Transport Museum
---	¼-scale LGOC B-type based on Triumph Herald running units		O??RO	19??	-?-, Clwyd
---	6” scale Foden steam bus		-?-	????	Maskell, Wilstead

PRESERVED COMMERCIAL VEHICLES ON PSV CHASSIS

Note: Buses and coaches converted for use as service vehicles with bus and coach operators are listed in the main section.

Reg	Make	Model	Chassis no	Body	Body no	Type	Date	History	Owner
AB 4693	Ford	T	R517P	--		van	-/11	ex country bus	Dunster Farms, Bury
AH 9282	Crossley	Type 8	CC6/1922	--		van	-/18	ex charabanc	Banfield, Staplehurst
		(see also main section)							
AP 7595	Ford	TT	4369889	--		lorry	-/20	ex country bus	Taylor, Otterbourne
BC 2365	McCurd	5-ton	371			box van	-/14	Beedon, Northampton (chara)	Tate & Lyle, London
CK 4033	Leyland	Lion LSC3	46341	--		lorry	-/28	Ribble 566	Wright & Agar, Camerton
CU 5705	Maudslay	Regent III	D62032R	Park Royal	B34839	fire appliance	10/51	South Shields Fire Brigade	Pearson, Chester-le-Street
DD 9061	Morris Commercial	T	8395	Healey		lorry	3/26	Smith, Churchdown (lorry/bus)	Smith W, Churchdown
ED 1709	Caledon	E	E530	--		lorry	-/15	-?-, Warrington (charabanc)	Baldwin, Ilminster
GN 7317	AEC	Mercury	640069	--		tanker	3/31	Timpson 317	Pring, -?-
HF 9126	Leyland	Titan TD7c	304397	--		control unit	7/40	Wallasey 74	Hoare, Chepstow
HY 1801	Leyland	Lioness LTB1	51555	--		fire appliance	5/31	Bristol Fire Brigade	Berry, Swindon
KF 6683	Leyland	Lioness LTB1	51674	--		fire appliance	12/31	Liverpool Fire Brigade	Metz Museum, -?-
NH 5403	AEC	Y	7798	--		flat lorry	-/17	Beedon, Northampton (chara)	Shipley, Scunthorpe
PT 6047	Bean	25cwt	7916	--		lorry	12/25	ex wagonette	Seear, Tewkesbury
PW 104	Daimler	CB22	2047	--		lorry	-/15	United C72	Watts, Lydney
RR 3593	Garford	25	25270			lorry	-/19	Howlett, Newark	Banfield, Staplehurst
SU 5861	Leyland	LT5B	4120			lorry	7/34	Alexander P157	Richards, -?-
		(ex WG 2361)							
TW 2736	Morris-Commercial	D3	8899T	--		lorry	4/26	Eastern National	-?-, -?-
UV 6025	Leyland	O	12364	--		lorry	-/22	Maidstone & District 166	Longthorne, Skipton
		(ex KE 9677)							
XW 8997	Tilling-Stevens	TS3A	3247	--		lorry	-/24	London Fire Brigade	Hughes, Maidstone
YG 8984	Bristol	GO5G	GO5G.6	Eastern Counties	3508	showmans van	3/35	West Yorkshire 304	Redpath et al, Greenlaw
AHF 365	Leyland	Titan PD1A	481103	--		float	9/48	Wallasey 27	-?-, Beith
BAE 592	Bristol	4-ton	1270	--		lorry	10/20	Bristol Tramways	Amey Roadstone, Mere
BEN 114	Maudslay	Regent III	D62055R	Park Royal	B35486	fire appliance	4/52	Bury Fire Brigade	Cadlow & Winterbourn, Bury
BHW 432	Bristol	JNW	JNW70	ECW	3339	showmans van	8/35	Bristol N70	Harris & Scrivens, Shrewsbury
				(rebodied 10/49)					
CBV 703	AEC	Regal III	9621E804			asphalt patcher	7/49	Ribbledale, Blackburn 31	-?-, -?-
CFH 604	Bristol	L5G	48059	Bristol		mobile caravan	5/39	Bristol 1254	Carter, Maidenhead
				(rebodied 5/49)					
CFN 73	Leyland	Tiger PS1	462475	Park Royal	B32579	mobile caravan	5/47	East Kent	Walker, Ashbourne
DHL 999	Maudslay	Regent III	D62038R	Park Royal	B35471	fire appliance	3/52	Wakefield Fire Brigade	Thackray, Malton
ERD 158	Crossley	DD42/8	95301	--		flat transporter	11/50	Reading 89	Ragsdale, Retford
FGE 678	Thornycroft	Nippy HF/ER4	48410			flatbed lorry	1/48	MacBrayne 79	Smith, Basingstoke
FKG 50	Maudslay	Regent III	D62012R	Merryweather		fire appliance	11/50	Cardiff Fire Brigade	Hoare, Chepstow (CS)
GAW 86	Foden	PVFE6	29668	--		lorry	5/50	Salopia, Whitchurch 80	Sample, Brereton
GDV 802	Guy	Vixen	LV29603	--		box van	8/47	Sidmouth Motor Company	Kemp, Kent/Sussex
GLW 410	Leyland	Titan TD7	307129	Merryweather		fire appliance	4/42	National Fire Service	Huckle, Wilstead
GLW 411	Leyland	Titan TD7	-?-	Merryweather		fire appliance	-/42	National Fire Service	Manahan, Dublin
GLW 416	Leyland	Titan TD7	-?-	Merryweather		fire appliance	-/42	National Fire Service	Fire Services National Museum Trust
GLW 419	Leyland	Titan TD7	307135	Merryweather		fire appliance	642	National Fire Service	Lincolnshire Vintage Vehicle Society

GLW 422	Leyland	Titan TD7	307121	Merryweather		fire appliance	-/42	National Fire Service	-?-, -?-
GLW 425	Leyland	Titan TD7	307115	Merryweather		fire appliance	8/42	National Fire Service	Llewellyn, Eastbourne
GLW 427	Leyland	Titan TD7	307125	Merryweather		fire appliance	9/42	National Fire Service	Senior, Weybridge
HDG 402	Foden	PVSC5	27376	--		horsebox	9/48	Febry, Chipping Sodbury	Williams, Llanerchymedd
HVS 474	Leyland	Tiger Cub PSUC1/1	535096	--		flat lorry	-/53	Clayton Dewandre, Lincoln	-?-, -?-
		(ex HTP 943, unregistered)							
HXW 626	Maudslay	Marathon II	60051	Harrington		horsebox	-/47	Southern Railway	Parker, Holbeach
JFS 372	Maudslay	Regent III	D63001R	Merryweather		fire appliance	7/51	Edinburgh Fire Brigade	Hebard, Squirrel Heath
KOM 150	Daimler	CVD6SD	16910	Wilsdon		mobile press	6/50	Birmingham Post & Mail	Coventry Transport Museum
KSG 977	Maudslay	Regent III	D63006R	Merryweather		fire appliance	1/54	SE Scotland Fire Brigade	McCormick, Bishopstoke
LVE 562	Bedford	SB	16470	Wilsdon		fire appliance	1/54	Cambridgeshire Fire Brigade	Fire Services National Museum Trust
LVP 118	Bedford	SB	3151	Wilsdon		fire appliance	3/52	Birmingham Fire Brigade	BaMMOT, Wythall
OXT 779	Maudslay	Regent III	D62106R	Merryweather		fire appliance	6/54	London Fire Brigade	Cotton, -?-
SLO 24	Commer	Avenger III	T84A0032	Harrington	1827	telegraph unit	5/56	Post Office 54325	Leah, Huthwaite
TMK 637	AEC	Regent III	9621E502	--		dropside lorry	4/49	Davis, Streatham	Walls, Ireland
TOA 584	Bedford	SB3	37897	Wilsdon		fire appliance	-/55	Dunlop Tyres	Welsh Area Fire Engine Restoration Society, Skewen
VMK 200	Bedford	OB	143812	Duple	48550	mobile carvan	5/51	Grosvenor, Enfield	Grimes, Kimpton
WVE 63	Leyland	Worldmaster LRT3/1	593129	Marshall		transporter	c6/60	Owen Racing Organisation	Donington Collection
WWV 439	Bedford	SB3	84878	-?-		fire appliance	c9/60	Wiltshire Fire Brigade	Fire Services National Museum Trust
YKP 177	Maudslay	Regent III	D63010R	Merryweather		fire appliance	4/57	Kent Fire Brigade	Adby, Watlington
4166 RA	Leyland	Titan PD2/10	531744	Wilsdon		fire appliance	5/55	Nottinghamshire Fire Brigade	Spalding, Mansfield
		(ex PRR 1)							
453 AUP	AEC	Reliance	MU3RV1593	Plaxton	2362	horsebox	7/58	Wilkinson, Sedgefield 53	Evans, Newton-le-Willows
72 MMJ	Bedford	VAL14	1349	Harrington	2918	transporter	3/64	Taylor, Meppershall 72	Thomas, Southrepps
483 XUN	Bedford	SB3	86246	Hampshire Car Bodies		fire appliance	3/61	Lindsey Fire Brigade	-?-, -?-
		(ex WFW 958)							
ALM 842B	Leyland	Titan PD3A/1	L00472	Mann Egerton	7226	van	3/64	London Transport 1279LD	Doggett P, Purley
FFM 105C	Bedford	VAL14	1860	Boalloy		caravan transporter	6/65	Cheshire Caravan Transport	Webb, Armscote (WK)
LMG 952C	Bedford	VAL14	1596	Harrington	3079	C50F	2/65	Interline, London	Davis, Lower Earley
				(to be converted to car transporter)					
PNW 179C	AEC	Reliance	2U3RA5687	Van Plan		horsebox	5/65	East Kent	Bamford, Southowram
		(ex UBA 121X, DJG 618C)		*(rebodied 10/81)*					
FVO 67D	AEC	Reliance	2U3RA6450	Plaxton	669466	transporter	7/66	Barton 1067	Walsh, Ashton-under-Lyne
JLA 72D	Leyland	Titan PD3A/1	L42961	Mann Egerton	-?-	van	6/66	London Transport 1416LD	Lovett, Barking
GNF 951E	Bedford	VAL14	1847	RTS	4030	outside broadcast unit	3/67	ABC Television	Burford, Wootton
KJU 267E	Bedford	SB3 *(diesel engine)*	6877126	CSC		mobile cinema	c5/67	Ministry of Technology	Halls, Dunkeswell
LVF 480E	AEC	Swift	MP2R071	Norwich Coachworks		transporter	5/67	Team Lotus	Willenpart, Austria
SMY 843F	Bedford	VAM5	6867131	Papworth Industries		outside broadcast unit	8/67	ATV Television	Graham, Tring
WPX 135F	Albion	Viking VK41L	53071C	Sparshatt		removals van	5/68	Tullett, Bognor Regis	Biggar Albion Foundation
OOW 999G	Bedford	VAL70	7853351	Dell		outside broadcast unit	10/68	Southern Television	Marshall, Newark
EDM 893J	Maudslay	Regent III	D62018R	Park Royal	B34572	fire appliance	2/51	Douglas Fire Brigade	Shrimpton, Banstead
		(ex NMN 50)							
YAF 79J	Ford	R192	BC04KA46528	Booker	18953.3238	mobile clinic	4/71	-?-, -?-	-?-, -?-
GNR 844L	Bedford	VAL70	2T473224	GC Smith	34617.73	horsebox	2/73	-?-, -?-	Webb, Armscote (WK)
JAH 1L	Leyland	Leopard PSU3B/4R	7200626	Marshall		transporter	3/73	Team Lotus	-?-, -?-
MBK 390R	Bedford	VAS3	EW455166	-?-		control unit	-/77	Hampshire Fire Brigade	Mayell, -?-
OYT 517R	Ford	R1014	BC04RD67915	Willowbrook/Anglo	75136	control unit	8/76	London Fire Brigade	Rowley, Ringwood
ERR 1V	Leyland	Leopard PSU3F/5R	8030400	Yeates		van	5/81	City of Birmingham Symphony Orchestra	

		(ex UUS 666W)							Williams, Merthyr Tydfil
EBB 846W	Dennis	Dominator	SDA130A/204	Angloco		contol unit	10/80	Tyne & Wear Fire Brigade	-?-, -?_
211 JIF	Ford	R1114	-?-	Murphy		mobile library	-/??	Cork County Council	Kells Transport Museum, Cork
-?-	BMC	5K/CFECDE/3 (ex BMC 25)	89926	Marshall		transporter	-/60	BMC racing team	Stanworth, Droitwich
unregistered	Dodge	VK62B	8840521	Mulliner		transporter	-/40	RAF	Jones, Nantwich
unregistered	Maudslay	Regent III (ex ???? NI, KTX 333)	D62031R	Park Royal	B34838	fire appliance	10/51	Glamorgan Fire Brigade	Welsh Area Fire Engine Restoration Society, Skewen

PRESERVED POSTBUS CARS

A971 LSH	Ford	Sierra	DP34455	Ford	car4	5/84	Royal Mail 3760019	Cott, Winfarthing
B887 JSS	Landrover		LBAAG1AA157467	Landrover	car4	8/84	Royal Mail 1770011	Cott, Winfarthing
D454 DAS	Ford	Fiesta	BAFBFE51868	Ford	car4	8/86	Royal Mail 5920351	Cott, Winfarthing
J841 VUJ	Peugeot	405GLD	7043389	Peugeot	car4	3/92	Royal Mail 1760018	Croasdale, Burnley
K408 BSG	Landrover	110	919731	Landrover	car8	10/92	Royal Mail 2770015	Cott, Winfarthing
L232 LSC	Peugeot	405GLD	271161222	Peugeot	car4	6/94	Royal Mail 3760002	Cott, Winfarthing
M587 AEH	Ford	Mondeo	BBDNSC55414	Ford	car4	7/95	Royal Mail 5760002	Cott, Winfarthing
P678 OEH	Ford	Courier Combi	BAJ5TB21544	Ford	car4	c9/96	Royal Mail 5890268	Cott, Winfarthing
X432 AHT	Vauxhall	Brava	7102440	Vauxhall	car4	11/00	Royal Mail 0110003	Cott, Winfarthing
HX55 KWR	Renault	Kangoo Trekka 4x4	VF1KCAVAK3442567	Renault	car4	11/05	Royal Mail 5110045	Cott, Winfarthing

BRITISH OPERATED BUSES PRESERVED ABROAD

Note: Vehicles are listed under their UK registrations; some may now carry registrations issued in their country of residence.

AE 778	Berliet	18CV Model CAT	47	replica *(replica body by9/74)*		O11/11RO	-/09	Bristol Tramways	Automobiles Berliet, Venissieux, France
CP 3838	Morris-Commercial 1-ton		3119	Caseley *(body transferred by9/99 from UO 7095)*		T13	-/25	Sidmouth Motor Co *(body)*	Taylor, Nelson, New Zealand
DS 7653	Morris-Commercial R		-?-	Harris (Clanfield) *(replica body by6/88)*		B10	1929	-?-, -?-	-?-, Germany
DS 8251	International Harvester		-?-	Harris (Clanfield) *(replica body built by12/91)*		B10F	-/28	-?-, -?-	-?-, Germany
GO 5164	AEC	Regent	6611443	LGOC *(body new 3/30)*	10405	H--/--	5/31	London General ST798	Clandestine Immigration & Naval Museum, Haifa, Israel

Reg	Make	Model	Chassis no	Body	Body no	Layout	Date	Original operator	Location
HR 8868	Ford	T	6493659	?		B13	-/23	station bus	-?-, Denmark
KW 6025	Leyland	Lion LC1	47768	Wyatt		B??D	5/29	Bradford 380	-?-, USA
				(replica body -/81)					
LC 3185	Milnes-Daimler		-?-	Wyatt		O18/16RO	5/05	Brighton Hove & Preston United	Louwman Museum, den Haag, Netherlands
		(ex D 1959)		*(replica body 5/76)*				*(liveried as Tilling)*	
LN 314	Milnes-Daimler		5431	UECC		O18/16RO	-/07	Vanguard 181	Mercedes-Benz, Stuttgart, Germany
		(ex A 9164)							
XH 4004	UNIC	MIA2	20717	Anscomb		Ch14	-/22	Williams, Hove	museum, Spain
				(replica body -/96)					
XM 215	Thames Ironworks		-?-	Thrupp & Maberley		O16/8	-/13	Universal, London	Louwman Museum, den Haag, Netherlands
		(ex PB 9895, XM 215, -?-)							
AGX 517	AEC	Regent	6612320	Chalmers		van	6/33	London Transport 739J	Geenty, Daytona Beach, Florida, USA
				(rebodied from bus to van 2/50)					
BHN 237	Bristol	JO5G	JO5G173	*chassis/cab only*			-/36	United BJO41	Atkinson, Queensland, Australia
BYJ 904	Austin	K8CVC	23365	Plaxton	1882	C14F	7/52	Dickson, Dundee	Louwman Museum, den Haag, Netherlands
		*(Dutch registration BE-62-33_*							
CAP 211	Bristol	K5G	55073	ECW	6933	O30/26R	9/40	Brighton Hove & District 6356	-?-, Netherlands/Belgium
DFK 214	AEC	Regal III	6821A174	Burlingham	3651	C33F	7/49	Burnham, Worcester	De Kuiperberg, Ootmarsum, Netherlands
		(Dutch registration BG-TP-21)							
DJD 217	Bedford	OB	138326	Mulliner	AL16	B30F	6/50	Dr Barnado, Woodford Bridge	van de Merwe, Dordrecht, Netherlands
		(Dutch registration BE-67-57)							
EBE 259	AEC	Regent II	O6617819	Burlingham	-?-	H30/26R	6/47	Enterprise,Scunthorpe 75	Museum of Transportation, St Louis, USA
FCO 314	Austin	CXB	143401	Plaxton	224	C29F	4/50	Born, Northlew	Abela, Zejtun, Malta
FET 344	Daimler	CTC6	15852	East Lancs	-?-	B22D	1/50	Rotherham 84	Ejea Tramway, Spain
FFY 405	Leyland	Titan PD2/3	472245	Leyland		O30/26R	11/47	Southport 88	Woodland Museum, Cooperstown, USA
FSR 807	Commer	Q4	18B2189S	Harrington	595	C30F	9/49	Ritchie, Forfar	Lubbers, Zwolle, Netherlands
		(Dutch registration BE-63-91)							
FXT 257	AEC	Regent	O6616830	LPTB	398	H30/26R	-/40	London Transport RT82	Pommer, Boston, Massachusetts, USA
HYM 836	BUT	9641T	9641T185	Metro-Cammell		H36/18D	1/49	London Transport 1836	Ejea Tramway, Spain
HYM 837	BUT	9641T	9641T186	Metro-Cammell		H36/18D	12/48	London Transport 1837	Basque Railway Collection, Azpertia, Spain
HYM 839	BUT	9641T	9641T190	Metro-Cammell		H36/18D	1/49	London Transport 1839	TUZSA, Zaragoza, Spain
JEL 249	Bristol	K6A	76067	ECW	3577	L27/28R	9/49	Hants & Dorest 1230	McAbee, Birmingham, Alabama, USA
JHT 833	Bristol	L5G	61070	Bristol		B35R	12/46	Bristol 2180	Mutare Museum, Mutare, Zimbabwe
				(rebodied 6/57 with body new 2/51)					
JRX 822	Bristol	KSW6B	106025	ECW	7475	L27/28R	-/55	Thames Valley 747	McAbee, Birmingham, Alabama, USA
JWO 355	AEC	Regal III	9621A854	Bruce		B35R	2/51	Bedwas & Machen 7	
									Sandstone Heritage Foundation, Ficksburg, South Africa
JXC 27	AEC	Regent III	O961982	Weymann	W1570	H30/26R	6/48	London Transport RT664	Norddeutsches Auto und Motrorrad Museum, Bad Oyenhausen, Germany
JXC 103	AEC	Regent III	O961967	Weymann	W1402	H30/26R	7/48	London Transport RT740	James, Portland, Oregon, USA
JXC 155	AEC	Regent III	O9611089	Weymann	W1278	H30/26R	8/48	London Transport RT792	Wee, Flakkagjerd, Norway
JXN 52	AEC	Regent III	O961099	Weymann	W1131	H30/26R	11/48	London Transport RT1024	Churn, Beechboro, Western Australia
JXN 182	AEC	Regent III	O9611158	Park Royal	L1351	H30/26R	8/48	London Transport RT804	LondonBus Transport Oy, Esposo, Finland
JXN 225	AEC	Regent III	O9611397	Park Royal	L2701	H30/26R	9/48	London Transport RT847	
									Pate Museum of Transport, Fort Worth, Texas, USA
JXN 391	Leyland	7RT	485356	Park Royal	L358	H30/26R	1/49	LondonTransport RTL68	Goodwin, New Plymouth, New Zealand
KAG 840	Leyland	Titan PD3/3	571861	Northern Counties	5154	L35/32RD	11/57	Western SMT 1359	Historic Vehicle Society of Ontario, Canada
KDB 499	Leyland	Titan PD2/21	556153	Weymann	M7347	L30/28RD	-/56	North Western 666	Donaghue, Mississauga, Canada

		(ex KDB 666)							
KGU 76	Leyland	7RT	494909	Weymann	W861	H30/26R	12/49	London Transport RTL626	Musée Communal de l'Automobiles Mahymobiles, Leuse-en-Hainault, Belgium
KLB 539	AEC	Regent III	O9613263	Weymann	W1915	H30/26R	12/49	London Transport RT1290	Museo Del Transporte de Cataluna, Spain
KLB 755	AEC	Regent III	O9613239	Park Royal	L1021	H30/26R	10/49	London Transport RT2376	Gilmore Car Museum, Hickory Corners, Michigan, USA
KUM 386	AEC	Regal I	O6625309	Duple	54594	C37F	-/47	Wallace Arnold Tours	Malta Historic Vehicle Trust, Malta
				(being rebodied with Du 54594 C37F new 7/51 originally on Bl LL6B LTA 741)					
KXW 241	AEC	Regent III	O9613669	Weymann	W847	H30/26R	4/50	London Transport RT3132	Ferrymead Tramway Park, Christchurch, New Zealand
KXW 247	AEC	Regent III	O9613767	Weymann	W954	H30/26R	5/50	London Transport RT3138	Timson, Rohnert Park, California, USA
KXW 307	AEC	Regent III	O9613781	Weymann	W884	H30/26R	3/50	London Transport RT1661	Jysk Automobile Museum, Gjern, Denmark
KYY 520	AEC	Regent III	9612E5041	Weymann	M4366	L27/26R	7/50	London Transport RLH20	Pommer, Boston, Massachusetts USA
KYY 704	AEC	Regent III	O9614095	Park Royal	L1459	H30/26R	7/50	London Transport RT1849	Schnidrig, Gresham, Oregon, USA
KYY 811	Leyland	7RT	502091	Metro-Cammell		H30/26R	7/50	London Transport RTL841	Rawdon, Matjiesfontein, South Africa
KYY 965	AEC	Regent III	O9614070	Weymann	W1032	H30/26R	7/50	London Transport RT3236	Scott, Tamworth, Australia
LLU 899	Leyland	7RT	502820	Metro-Cammell		H30/26R	9/50	London Transport RTL909	Dufresne, Azay-le-Rideau, France
LRO 296	Bedford	OB	137102	Duple	48824	C29F	5/50	Picton & Gibbs, Garston	Giken Seisakusho, Kochi, , Japan
LTA 948	Bristol	KS5G	80169	ECW	4354	L27/28R	-/50	Southern National 1838	-?-, North/South Dakota, USA
LUC 33	AEC	Regent III	O9615260	Park Royal	L79	H??/??F	10/50	London Transport RT1947	Green, Pietermaritzberg, South Africa
LUC 462	AEC	Regent III	O9615756	Weymann	W1029	H30/26R	4/51	London Transport RT4113	Burdock, San Marcos, Texas, USA
								(*located at Central Texas Museum of Automotive History, Rosanky, Texas*)	
LYF 187	AEC	Regent III	O9615881	Park Royal	L110	H30/26R	5/51	London Transport RT2538	Murphy, East London, South Africa
		(*may be LYF 361 - RT2636*)							
LYF 248	AEC	Regent III	O9615925	Wetmann	W1413	H30/26R	6/51	London Transport RT4189	Foxton Trolleybus Museum, New Zealand
LYF 329	AEC	Regent III	O9615986	Weymann	W161	H30/26R	6/51	London Transport RT2604	Motor museum, Port Elizabeth, South Africa
LYF 359	AEC	Regent III	O9615996	Weymann	W121	H30/26R	7/51	London Transport RT2634	James Hall Museum of Transport, Johannesburg, South Africa
LYR 641	AEC	Regent III	O9616056	Park Royal	L276	H30/26R	8/51	London Transport RT2657	AMTUIR, Paris, France
MAS 427	Bedford	OB	92760	Duple	52287	C29F	11/48	St James School, Burnt Oak	Tap, Amersfoort, Netherlands
		(ex KJH 91) *(Dutch registration BE-50-08)*							
MFF 509	AEC	Routemaster	RM1312	Park Royal	L4391	H36/28R	12/62	London Transport RM1312	Haags Bus Museum,den Haag,Netherlands
		(ex 312 CLT)							
MUF 457	Leyland	Titan PD2/12	530377	Northern Counties	4767	H??/??RD	5/53	Southdown 757	Industrial Museum, Ankara, Turkey
MWY 120	Bristol	Lodekka LD6B	100142	ECW	6669	H33/25R	11/54	West Yorkshire DX11	Harold Le May Collection, Tacoma, Washington, USA
MXX 250	AEC	Regent III	9613E6977	Weymann	M5553	L27/26R	11/52	London Transport RLH50	Welch, Kaukpakapa, New Zealand
MXX 262	AEC	Regent III	9613E6992	Weymann	M5545	L27/26R	11/52	London Transport RLH62	Pullen, Westminster, Maryland, USA
NAE 63	Bristol	KSW6B	80112	ECW	4510	H32/28R	1/51	Bristol 8003	Egeskov Castle, Kvaerndrup, Denmark
NLE 815	AEC	Regent III	O9616878	Park Royal	L3192	H30/26R	5/53	London Transport RT3708	HCVA, Sydney Bus Museum, Sydney, Australia
NLP 528	AEC	Regent III	O9617369	Weymann	W1873	H30/26R	8/53	London Transport RT4363	Blystad, Oslo, Norway
OLD 857	Leyland	7RT	541265	Park Royal	L3279	H30/26R	10/54	London Transport RTL1628	Seashore Trolley Museum, Kennebunkport, Maine, USA
OWX 163	Bristol	Lodekka LD6B	108154	ECW	8118	H33/27RD	11/55	West Yorkshire DX19	Harold Le May Collection, Tacoma, Washington, USA
PHJ 951	Leyland	Titan PD3/6	580829	Massey	2303	O41/33R	6/58	Southend 312	Jesadatechnik, Nakhonpathom, Thailand
PRN 143	Leyland	Atlantean PDR1/1	610599	Metro-Cammell		H44/33F	6/61	Scout, Preston 3	Jeffriess & Blacklock, Newcastle, NSW, Australia
RVS 432	Leyland	Titan PD3/1	581025	Park Royal	B41206	H41/33R	6/58	Leicester 162	Augusta Richmond County Museum, Georgia, USA
		(ex TBC 162)							

SAX 186	Leyland	Titan PD2/40	571959	Willowbrook	57966	L27/28RD	10/57	West Monmouthshire 9	-?-, Tokyo, Japan
SRC 373	Leyland	Atlantean PDR1/1	591909	Weymann	M9337	L39/34F	3/60	Trent 1373	HCVA, Sydney Bus Museum, Sydney, Australia
TAS 466	AEC	Routemaster (ex WLT 883)	RML883	Park Royal	L4255	H40/32R	8/61	London Transport RML883	Billette, Czech Republic
TWY 610	Bristol	Lodekka LD6B	134239	ECW	9595	H33/27RD	5/58	West Yorkshire DX68	Charity Plus, British Columbia, Canada
VDR 943	Leyland	Atlantean PDR1/1	610531	Metro-Cammell		H44/33F	10/61	Plymouth 143	Doherty, -?-, Australia
VLT 58	AEC	Routemaster	RM58	Park Royal	L3309	H36/28R	11/59	London Transport RM58	Musée de l'Auto, Le Mans, France
VLT 232	AEC	Routemaster	RM232	Park Royal	L3916	H36/28R	4/60	London Transport RM232	Stormyri, Ritell, Bjugn, nr Trondheim, Norway
WFF 582	Bedford	OB (ex EY 9392) *(Belgian registration 5695 P)*	126578	Duple	44257	C29F	1/50	Jones, Menai Bridge	de Zigeuner, Diepenbeek, Belgium
WFF 583	Bedford	OB (ex EY 9025) *(Belgian registration BCK 893)*	100169	Duple	44258	C29F	3/49	Jones, Menai Bridge	de Zigeuner, Diepenbeek, Belgium
WFF 599	Bedford	SB3 (ex UDL 453) *(Belgian registration FUA 272)*	81191	Duple	1120/518	C37F	6/60	West Wight, Totland Bay	de Zigeuner, Diepenbeek, Belgium
WLT 428	AEC	Routemaster	RM428	Park Royal	L3907	O36/28R	8/60	London Transport RM428	de Zigeuner, Diepenbeek, Belgium
WLT 496	AEC	Routemaster	RM496	Park Royal	L4662	H36/28R	2/61	London Transport RM496	Matsuda Collection, Matsuda, Japan
7512 UA	Daimler	CVG6LX30DD	30055	Roe	GO4955	H38/32R	11/59	Leeds 512	Lille Museum of Transport, France
797 BAL	Leyland	Tiger PS1/B (ex EJU 439)	B471112	Northern Counties *(rebuilt and rebodied 8/59)*	5434	FL33/30F	12/47	Barton 759	British Bus Club, Pleasant Mount, Pennsylvania, USA
510 BTA	Bristol	Lodekka LD6G	154021	ECW	11078	H33/27RD	11/59	Western National 1958	-?-, -?-, USA
180 CLT	AEC	Routemaster *(Luxembourg registration B1180)*	RM1180	Park Royal	L4520	H36/28R	12/62	London Transport RM1180	Routemaster Association, Luxembourg
248 CLT	AEC	Routemaster	RM1248	Park Royal	L4616	H36/28R	12/62	London Transport RM1248	Matsuda Collection, Matsuda, Japan
282 CLT	AEC	Routemaster	RM1282	Park Royal	L4376	H36/28R	12/62	London Transport RM1282	Rahmi M Koc Musuem, Istanbul, Turkey
512 DKT	Leyland	Atlantean PDR1/1	590421	Metro-Cammell	H051194/23	H44/34F	5/59	Maidstone & District DH512	Smith, Sawtell, New South Wales, Australia
299 DWU	Bedford	SB5	91093	Duple Northern	130/2	C8F	5/63	Longster, Pateley Bridge	Lucas, Brittany, France
708 DYE	AEC	Routemaster	RM1708	Park Royal	L4417	H36/28R	10/63	London Transport RM1708	HCVA, Sydney Bus Museum, Sydney, Australia
884 GFU	Bedford	J2SZ10	190648	Plaxton	642116	C20F	3/64	Appleby, Conisholme	Jesadatechnik, Nakhonpathom, Thailand
334 GNN	AEC	Regent V	2D2RA942	East Lancs	5669	H35/28R	9/60	West Bridgford 35	Charity Plus, British Columbia, Canada
416 HDV	Bristol	SUL4A	190012	ECW	12759	B--F	10/61	Western National 647	Rivera, Mexico City, Mexico
52 JAL	Bristol	Lodekka FSF6G	179007	ECW	12339	H34/26F	2/62	Mansfield District 536	British Bus Club, Pleasant Mount, Pennsylvania, USA
136 NAL	AEC	Regent V	2D2RA1142	East Lancs	5828	H37/28R	5/62	West Bridgford 36	Charity Plus, British Columbia, Canada
340 TJO	AEC	Renown	3B3RA086	Park Royal	B50628	H38/27F	11/64	City of Oxford 340	Kieback, Gerstetten-Dettingen, Germany
787 UXA	AEC	Routemaster (ex WLT 894)	RML894	Park Royal	L4320	H40/32R	11/61	London Transport RML894	Vetra BV, De Rijke transport museum, Spijkenisse, Netherlands
NRH 802A	AEC	Routemaster (ex WLT 798)	RM798	Park Royal	L4027	H36/28R	7/61	London Transport RM798	Griffiths, Zamek Borec, Czech Republic
NSG 636A	AEC	Routemaster (ex 164 CLT)	RM1164	Park Royal	L4360	H36/28R	5/62	London Transport RM1164	`-?-, Japan
XMC 168A	Leyland	Titan PD3/3 (ex XMN 345)	580998	Metro-Cammell		O--/--R	6/58	Isle of Man Road Services 31	Reol, Madrid, Spain
XWV 942A	Autocar	UF21 (ex DS 7132)	-?-	?		B??	-/12	-?-, -?-	Autotron Rosmalen, Den Bosch, Netherlands
AED 31B	Leyland	Titan PD2/40	L21837	East Lancs	6194	H37/28R	9/64	Warrington 16	Griffiths, Zamec Borec, Czech Republic
ALD 897B	AEC	Routemaster *(Belgian registration GUS 594)*	RM1897	Park Royal	L5272	H36/28R	5/64	London Transport RM1897	Staf Cars. Lommel, Belgium
BCH 159B	Daimler	CVG6DD	20077	Roe	GO5888	H37/28R	10/64	Derby 159	Charity Plus, British Columbia, Canada
BOD 39C	Bristol	Lodekka FLF6G	229169	ECW	15080	H38/32F	10/65	Western National 2097	

									Harold Le May Collection, Tacoma, Washington, USA
CLJ 868C	Bristol	Lodekka FLF6B	224163	ECW	14784	H38/32F	2/65	Hants & Dorset 1517	-?-, Melbourne, Australia
JFM 234D	Bristol	Lodekka FS6G	230067	ECW	15411	H33/27RD	12/66	Crosville DFG234	van der Valk, Alphen aan den Rijn, Netherlands
		(Dutch registration BE-21-78)							
KGJ 611D	AEC	Routemaster	R2RH/2/2817	Park Royal	B54303	H32/24F	12/66	British European Airways 8218	Ustecka 130 Bus Historic Group, Czech Republic
HFR 513E	Leyland	Titan PD3A/1	700323	Metro-Cammell		H41/30R	6/67	Blackpool 513	Hermansson, Borgholm, Sweden
HGM 339E	Bristol	Lodekka FLF6G	236112	ECW	16676	H44/34F	5/67	Central SMT BL339	Ethnographic Museum, Addis Ababa, Ethiopia
NML 602E	AEC	Routemaster	RML2602	Park Royal	L5930	H40/32R	3/67	London Transport RML2602	AMTUIR, Paris, France
NML 622E	AEC	Routemaster	RML2622	Park Royal	L5895	H40/32R	5/67	London Transport RML2622	Jesadatechnik, Nakhonpathom, Thailand
URO 913E	Bedford	VAL14	6876646	Plaxton	672559	C52F	6/67	Fox, Hayes	Hard Rock Café, Orlando, Florida, USA
SMK 707F	AEC	Routemaster	RML2707	Park Royal	L5972	H40/32R	9/67	London Transport RML2707	Jesadatechnik, Nakhonpathom, Thailand
UWP 154F	Bedford	SB3	7T459769	Duple	1224/1	C41F	7/68	Blue Coach Tours, St Helier 11	de Zigeuner, Diepenbeck, Belgium
		(ex J 8697)							
SEL 241H	Leyland	Atlantean PDR1A/1	902851	Alexander	J14/3268/2	H43/31F	12/69	Bournemouth 241	Museum, Lucerne, Switzerland
YTF 162J	Bedford	OB	135777	Duple	51125	C29F	3/50	Corkill, Onchan	Hotel Kasteel de Vanenburg, Putten, Netherlands
		(ex MMN 57) *(Dutch registration BE-02-31)*							
RBY 764K	Bedford	VAS3	1T460014	Willowbrook	71137	DP20F	12/71	Royal Household	Bleckman, Kamp-Lintort, Germany
		(ex u/reg, WCO 466M, NLT 4)							
KJD 201P	Scania	BR111DH	543371	MCW		H43/29D	3/75	London Transport MD1	Saab-Scania, Sodertalje, Sweden
KJD 513P	Leyland	National 10351A/2R	03491	Leyland National		B36D	5/76	London Transport LS13	Norman, Sydney, Australia
LED 72P	Bristol	RESL6G	RESL-8-469	East Lancs	5304	B44F	1/76	Warrington 72	Griffiths, Zamek Borec, Czech Republic
LHC 919P	Bedford	YLQ	FW453786	Duple	615/2053	C45F	5/76	Warren, Ticehurst	Ustecka 130 Bus Historic Group, Czech Republic
NSJ 19R	Seddon	Pennine 7	60053	Alexander	93AY/4874/19	B53F	10/76	Western SMT 2602	Billette, Czech Republic
OJD 67R	Bristol	LH6L	LH-1322	ECW	21922	B41F	1/77	London Transport BL67	Bos, Nieuwegein, Netherlands
		(ex 24018, 5579, 10488, OJD 67R)							
OJD 426R	Leyland	Fleetline FE30ALR	7605827	Park Royal	B61025	H44/24D	5/77	London Transport DMS2426	Speedybus Services, Hong Kong
OTN 458R	Scania	BR111DH	544375	MCW		H46/30F	7/77	Tyne & Wear PTE 458	Hunter Transport Museum, Newcastle, Australia
PKM 111R	Bristol	VRT/SL3/6LXB	VRT/SL3/454	ECW	22077	O43/31F	9/76	Maidstone & District 5111	Ustecka 130 Bus Historic Group,Czech Republic
SDX 33R	Leyland	Atlantean AN68A/1R	7606366	Roe	GO7809	H43/29D	3/77	Ipswich 33	Ustecka 130 Bus Historic Group,Czech Republic
YDS 650S	Leyland	Atlantean AN68A/1R	7700609	Alexander	AL61/2273/3	H45/33F	12/77	Graham, Paisley L10	Billette, Czech Republic
BTB 23T	Leyland	National 11351A/1R	06001	Leyland National		B52F	3/79	Halton 23	Dopravni podnik mesta Usti nad Labem,Czech Republic
WYW 82T	MCW	Metrobus DR101/9	MB5155	MCW		H43/28D	7/79	London Transport M82	Ustecka 130 Bus Historic Group,Czech Republic
ERU 153V	Leyland	Fleetline FE30ALR	7805229	Alexander	AL80/1774/3	H43/31F	10/79	Bournemouth 153	-?-, Austria
OTB 26W	Leyland	Atlantean AN68C/1R	8003507	East Lancs	1505	H45/33F	6/81	Warrington 26	Griffiths, Zamek Borec,Czech Republic
NFS 172Y	Leyland	Leopard PSU3G/4R	8230085	Alexander	24AT/881/3	C49F	10/82	Alexander Fife FPE172	Billette, Czech Republic
C177 ECK	Leyland	Olympian ONLXB/1R	ON2070	ECW	26096	H42/30F	11/85	Ribble 2177	Foxton Trolleybus Museum, New Zealand
G901 TWS	Leyland	Olympian ONCL10/1RZ	ON11081	Leyland	DD1067	H47/31F	10/89	Badgerline 9001	Foxton Trolleybus Museum, New Zealand
1950 MN	Bedford	OB	142371	Duple	47572	C29F	3/51	Wents, Boxted	Kinnear, -?-, South Africa
		(ex RHK 843)							
3324	Albion	Victor FT39AN	73821C	Heaver		B--F	-/56	Guernsey Railway 59	-?-, Dinan, Cotes d'Armor, France
---	Bedford	A	-?-	-?-		B??F	?/?	Royal Navy	Malta Historic Vehicle Trust
---	Bedford	OB	-?-	Nicolau		C29F	?/?	unknown UK operator	Apollo 11, Larnaca, Cyprus
		(ex -?-)		*(rebodied 4/99-3/07 or heavy rebuild of Duple original)*					
---	Pierce-Arrow		-?-	?		O18/16RO	c-/17	-?-, -?-	-?-, Netherlands

MUSEUMS LISTINGS

The following vehicles are normally resident at, or associated with, each of the Transport Museums listed below. Please note the opening arrangements vary from daily to occasional and intending visitors are advised to check opening times before visiting. Vehicles on display may change from time to time, be displayed in rotation, be absent at rallies, or be kept in workshop areas not open to the public. Visitors wishing to inspect particular vehicles are advised to check with the museum before visiting.

Vehicles marked '*' are known to be off site or off display at the time of compilation.

Amberley Chalk Pits Museum (www.amberleymuseum.co.uk)

BP 9822	DL 621	KJ 1930	UF 1517	UF 6805	EUF 184
CD 4867	IB 552	KL 7796	UF 4813	UF 7428	XMD 47A
CD 5125	JG 683	MO 9324	UF 6473	ECD 524	

u/r Milnes-Daimler

Black Country Living Museum (www.bcmtg.co.uk)

EA 4181	RR 3116	DKY 731	DUK 833	KTT 689	6342 HA
MR 3879	UK 9978	DKY 735	GEA 174	TDH 912	Q340 GVC *

Birmingham Central ?	Dudley & Stourbridge 75	South Staffs 102	Wolverhampton 49	Wolverhampton & District 34
Dudley & Stourbridge 5	Lisbon 361	Wolverhampton 23	Wolverhampton & District 19	

Bradford Industrial Museum (www.bradfordmuseums.org/bim)

AK 9627	DKY 737

Bradford 40	Bradford 104	Horse bus H49

Bridgeton Bus Garage (www.gvvt.org)

GM 6384	MSD 407	YYS 174	HFR 501E	XGM 450L	RSD 973R	FSL 615W	FLD 447Y	D741 WRC
WG 2373	MSD 408	198 CUS	HGM 346E	NMS 576M	EFS 229S	KSD 103W	LUS 436Y	E186 BNS
WG 4445	NMS 358	522 XUT	JMS 452E	SCS 335M	SSN 248S	LMS 168W	MNS 10Y	G571 PNS
BUS 181	NSF 757	415 VYA	WPX 135F	VSB 164M	XUS 575S	RMS 400W	RSC 194Y	G567 PRM
FVA 854	RAG 411	EDS 288A	NDL 375G	CST 703N	GGE 173T	UGB 196W	A735 PSU	G545 RDS
FYS 8	SGD 65	YTS 916A	VMP 8G	JGA 189N	EMS 362V	WFS 145W	A25 VDS	L201 UNS
FYS 998	SGD 448	BJX 848C	VMP 10G	JUS 774N	GCS 50V	FGE 423X	B177 FFS	6769
FYS 999	SGD 500	CUV 121C	NRG 26H	KFF 586P	HSD 73V	KYV 781X	B100 PKS	47638
GUS 926	TVS 367	GYS 896D	XGA 15J	MSF 122P	JPA 82V	SSA 5X	B105 PKS	
HGG 359	WSK 509	HGA 983D	WSD 756K	MSJ 385P	LHS 747V	TSO 16X	C177 VSF	
KAG 856	XSA 620	GRS 334E	BSG 537L	PSJ 825R	UHG 141V	ALS 102Y	D902 CSH	

Glasgow 1016	Docherty miniature

Bristol Aero Collection (www.bristolaero.i12.com)

BAE 592	TWS 910T

Bristol tram

British Commercial Vehicle Museum (www.bcvm.co.uk)

LF 9967	XW 9892	JOJ 548	KGU 284
RN 8622	YT 3738	JRN 29	

Horse bus H6

Brooklands Museum (www.brooklandsmuseum.com)

MFB 724	JJD 504D	LYF 307D	LLH 809K

Bury Transport Museum (http://burytransportmuseum.org.uk/)

MTB 848	466 FTJ	FBN 232C	JRJ 281E
UWH 185	116 JTD	FEN 588E *	

Manchester L53

Bus Depot, Barry (www.thebusdepotbarry.org)

CUH 856 *	TUH 13	964 DTJ	EDW 68D	PAX 466F	WUH 585K	VHB 678S	G258 HUH
HWO 323	XNY 416	AAX 305A	FUH 370D	OUH 177G	NNY 817L	WVJ 181T	N143 PTG
LKG 678	XUH 368	ABO 434B	KNY 495D	UTG 313G	PKG 587M *	NDW 407X	P164 TNY
LNY 903	889 AAX	GNY 432C	JKG 497F	PKG 532H	LUH 105P	C42 GKG	
TAX 235	408 DBO	EDV 505D	MBO 512F	TKG 518J	OJD 45R	C101 HKG	

Caister Motor Museum

NN 373

LCC tram

Castle Point Transport Museum (www.castlepointtransportmuseum.co.uk)

CFV 851	MPU 52	PTW 110	XVX 19	217 MHK	GJN 509D	GNM 232N
FOP 429	NEH 453	SGD 407	381 BKM	28 TKR	OWC 182D	YEV 308S
JVW 430	ONO 49	VLT 44	138 CLT	373 WPU	AVX 975G	
LYR 997	PHJ 954	WNO 478	236 LNO	NTW 942C	CPU 979G	

Cavan & Leitrim Railway, Dromod

3945 UE	ZJ 5904	ZY 1715	EZH 170	KID 154	71 AHI	78-D-824
IY 7383	ZO 6960	AZD 203	FCI 323	UZH 258	643 MIP	85-D-2412
IY 8044	ZU 5000	EZH 155	ILI 98	177 IK	78-D-140	

Coventry Transport Museum (www.transport-museum.com)

SR 1266	EKV 966	JNB 416	KOM 150	PBC 734	SRB 424	333 CRW	PDU 125M	K232 DAC

Crich Tramway Village (www.tramway.co.uk)

UB 7931 *	CWJ 410 *						

Berlin 3006	Blackpool Loco	Gateshead 52 *	Johannesburg 60	London United 159	Sheffield 15
Blackpool 4	Blackpool & Fleetwood 2	Glasgow 21 *	Leamington & Warwick 1	Manchester Bury etc 84 *	Sheffield 46 *
Blackpool 5 *	Blackpool & Fleetwood 40 *	Glasgow 22	Leeds 180	Metropolitan 331	Sheffield 74
Blackpool 40	Brussels 96	Glasgow 812	Leeds 345	Newcastle 102	Sheffield 189
Blackpool 49	Cardiff 21	Glasgow 1100 *	Leeds 399	North Metropolitan 39 *	Sheffield 264
Blackpool 59 *	Cardiff 131	Glasgow 1115	Leeds 600 *	Nottingham 92 *	Sheffield 330
Blackpool 166	Chesterfield 7	Glasgow 1282	Leeds 602	Nottingham 166 *	Sheffield 510
Blackpool 167	Chesterfield 8	Glasgow 1297	Leeds Works 2	New South Wales 2	Southampton 45
Blackpool 298	den Haag 1147	Glasgow Works 1 *	Leicester 76	New York 674	
Blackpool 607 *	Derby 1	Grimsby & Immingham 14	Liverpool 869	Oporto 9	
Blackpool 630	Douglas Southern 1	Halle 902	London County Council 106	Oporto 273	
Blackpool 712	Dundee 21	Hill of Howth 10	London Tramways -?- *	Oporto C65 *	
Blackpool 762	Edinburgh 35	Hull 132 *	London Transport 1	Paisley 68	
Blackpool Works 2 *	Gateshead 5	Hull -?- *	London Transport 1622	Prague 180	

Dewsbury Bus Museum (www.dewsburybusmuseum.co.uk)

CCX 801	EHL 344	JHL 983	TWY 8	CUV 208C	NWW 89E *	XUA 73X	J377 AWT *
BHL 682	JHL 708	PJX 35	WHL 970	JJD 524D	LHL 164F	D901 MWR	

Dover Transport Museum (www.dovertransportmuseum.homestead.com)

CC 9305	WFN 912	569 KKK	GJG 751D		

Maidstone 18

East Anglia Transport Museum (www.eatm.org.uk)

EX 1128 *	CUL 260	FXH 521	LLU 829	557 BNG	VHK 177L	K62 KEX
EX 6566	DRC 224	GBJ 192	NBB 628	918 NRT	LMP 657P *	AH 79505
WX 3567 *	ELB 796	KAH 408 *	YLJ 286	AEX 85B	LMP 658P *	BAD 2054 *
ALJ 986	ERV 938	KXW 234	YTE 826	YRT 898H	NRO 229V *	BAD 2091 *
BDY 809 *	EXV 201	LCD 52	2206 OI	OCK 985K	D103 DAJ	5088

u/r Berna *	Blackpool 11	London 1858	Lowestoft -?-	
Amsterdam 474	Blackpool 159	Lowestoft 14	Sheffield 513	

Grampian Transport Museum (www.gtm.org.uk)

RG 1173	CRG 325C	JRS 22F	SRS 56K	KSO 74P	EFP 521T	K1 GRT	
CWG 273	JFM 238D	LRG 14G	NRG 154M	ORS 209R	URS 318X		
WTS 937A	GRS 10E	PRG 40J	HSO 61N	SBK 740S	E131 DRS		

Aberdeen 1	Cruden Bay 2

Heaton Park Tramway (www.heatonparktramway.btik.com)

Blackpool 619	Blackpool 752 *	Leeds works 6 *	Manchester 765	Stockport 5

Ipswich Transport Museum (www.ipswichtransportmuseum.co.uk)

DX 3988	DX 5629	PV 8270 *	VV 7255	BPV 9 *	KAH 407	APW 829B	MRT 6P
DX 5610	DX 6591 *	PV 9371	WV 1209	CAH 923	KNG 374	GNG 125C	
DX 5617	DX 7812 *	VF 2788 *	ADX 1	CDX 516	MAH 744 *	DPV 68D *	
DX 5621	PV 817	VF 8157	ADX 196	CVF 874 *	ADX 63B	JRT 82K	

Cambridge 1 (or 7)	Ipswich 33

Isle of Wight Bus Museum (www.iowbusmuseum.org.uk)

DL 5084	EDL 657	HDL 279 *	VJW 882 *	FDL 927D	VDL 264K *	YDL 135T *
JT 8077 *	FDL 676	ODL 400	519 SLG *	KDL 885F	NDL 637M *	RDL 309X *
NG 1109 *	FLJ 538	PDL 515 *	ADL 459B	SDL 638J *	MDL 880R *	A700 DDL *
DDL 50	GDL 764	SDL 268	CDL 479C	TDL 564K	UDL 673S *	B259 MDL *

Ryde Pier 1	

Jurby Transport Museum (http://mtt.fplc.co.uk/)

CCZ 5919	HMN 787	MMN 302	697 HMN	CMN 44C	DMN 16R	D440 MAN
SCZ 2658	KMN 504	WMN 487	410 LMN	MAN 691D	BMN 64V	EBY 565
XKC 862K	KMN 835	XMN 346	67 UMN	BMN 83G	BMN 193V	
MN 5454	MAN 1927	3680 MN	CMN 34C	MAN 32N	C57 MAN	

Douglas 22	Douglas 72/73

Keighley Bus Museum (www.kbmt.org.uk)

KW 2260	GJX 331	MNW 86	VTU 76	7514 UA	JCR 383E	TKU 467K	CBM 13X
KY 9106 *	HUM 401	MTE 635	WBR 246	CUB 331C	KVH 473E	WFM 801K	NKU 245X
TF 6860	JWU 886	NNW 492	XLG 477	PNW 179C	TWW 766F	XAK 355L	C147 KBT
WT 7101	LIL 7960	PFN 865	XYJ 418	ENW 980D	YLG 717F	GWY 690N	D275 OOJ
ANW 682	LYR 533	PJX 232	6203 KW	HNW 131D	LAK 309G	DNW 840T	N801 DNE
FWX 914	MAZ 7584	UUA 214	6220 KW	NWU 265D	LAK 313G	JUM 505V	

Lancastrian Transport Trust (www.ltt.org.uk)

BTB 928	OJI 4371	561 TD	CUV 290C	SMK 734F	OCK 997K	NKU 214X	N590 GRN
CCK 663	PFR 346	583 CLT	HFR 512E	LFR 540G	STJ 847L	A362 HHG	
DFV 146	RRN 405	760 CTD	HFR 515E	PFR 554H	OFR 970M	A542 PCW	
GTB 903	UIB 3987	OWJ 353A	HFR 516E	ATD 281J	HRN 99N	F575 RCW	
KUI 2269	YFR 351	CTF 627B	LFR 529F	OCK 366K	AHG 334V	H 3 FBT	

Blackpool 8	Blackpool 605	Blackpool 676	Blackpool 704	Blackpool 753
Blackpool 287 *	Blackpool 632	Blackpool 679	Blackpool 715	
Blackpool 304 *	Blackpool 663	Blackpool 686	Blackpool 732 *	

Leicester: Abbey Pumping Station (www.leicester.gov.uk/museums)

CBC 921	MTL 750	TBC 164

Lincolnshire Aviation Heritage Centre (www.lincsaviation.co.uk)

FW 2378	TMM 788

Lincolnshire Road Transport Museum (www.lvvs.org.uk)

FW 5698	TE 8318	WH 1553	DFE 383	GLW 419	LFW 326	RFE 416	UVL 873M
KW 474	TF 818	AHE 163 *	FDO 573	HPW 133	OHK 432 *	952 JUB	NFW 36V
KW 7604	VL 1263	BFE 419	FFU 860	JDN 668	OLD 714	CVL 850D	PFE 542V
RC 2721	VV 8934	DBE 187	FHN 833	KDT 393	ONO 59	EVL 549E	KTL 45Y

London Bus Museum (formerly Cobham Bus Museum) (www.lbpt.org)

GJ 2098	XO 7696	AGX 520	ELP 228	JXC 288	LYR 910	UMP 227	WYV 23T
GN 8242	XU 7498	AXM 693	EYK 396	KGK 803	MLL 763	461 CLT	WYW 6T
GO 5170	XX 9591	CGJ 188	FJJ 764	KGU 142	MXX 283	EGN 369J	Horse H11
UU 6646	YH 1173	CXX 171	FXT 122	LUC 381	MXX 334	JPA 190K	Horse H48
XO 1038	YN 3772	EGO 426	HGC 130	LYR 826	SLT 58	OJD 172R	

London Transport Museum (including The Depot, Acton) (www.ltmuseum.co.uk) **C = vehicle on display at Covent Garden**

GK 3192	LA 9928 C	YR 3844	EXV 253 C	NLE 537	737 DYE C	EGP 1J C	F115 PHM
GK 5323	LC 3701	AXM 649	FJJ 774	NXP 997	CUV 229C	KJD 401P	LK 53 MBV
GK 5486	MN 2615	AYV 651	HYM 768	OLD 589 C	CUV 360C	TPJ 61S	117 QDV 75
GO 5198	XC 8059	BXD 576	JDZ 2315	SLT 56	KGY 4D	NUW 567Y	Unreg Optare C
HX 2756	XM 7399	CLE 122	MXX 364	SLT 57	AML 582H	C526 DYT	

London Tramways 284 C	Metropolitan 355	Horse bus H1 C	Horse bus H3 C
London Transport 1025	West Ham 102 C	Horse bus H2	

M Shed, Bristol (www.bristol-city.gov.uk/museums)

HU 6618 *	TOI 2288 *	FHW 158D

Bristol horse tram *

Midland Railway - Butterley (www.midlandrailwaycentre.co.uk)

ESV 811	KRR 255	BNU 679G	RCH 629L	UOA 322L	NNU 124M	UHG 353Y
HVO 937	RCH 518F	PNU 114K *	SHN 80L	NNU 123M	LRA 801P	D278 FAS

Milestones, Basingstoke (www.milestones-museum.com)

BK 2986	EY 5218	RV 6368						

Portsmouth 84

Museum Of Transport, Manchester (www.gmts.co.uk)

CK 3825	BEN 177	FBU 827	JVU 755	TNA 496	414 CLT	HVM 901F	XVU 352M	D 62 NOF *
JA 7585 *	BJA 425 *	FTB 11 *	LMA 284	TNA 520	122 JTD	KDB 408F	GNC 276N	D 63 NOF
JP 4712	CDB 224	HEK 705 *	LTC 774	TRJ 112	YTS 743A *	KJA 871F	HVU 244N *	M939 XKA
VR 5742	CWG 206	HTB 656 *	NBU 494 *	UMA 370	BND 874C	MJA 891G	ORJ 83W	
VY 957	CWH 717	HTF 586	NDK 980	UNB 629	DBA 214C	MJA 897G	A706 LNC	
AJA 152	DBU 246	JBN 153	NNB 125	YDK 590	DDB 174C	SRJ 328H	B 65 PJA	
ANB 851	DJP 754	JNA 467	PND 460	3655 NE *	PTC 114C	TTD 386H	C208 FVU	
AXJ 857	EDB 562	JND 646 *	REN 116	4632 VM	PTE 944C	TXJ 507K	D674 NNE *	
BBA 560	EDB 575	JND 791	SDK 442	8860 VR	FRJ 254D *	VNB 101L	D676 NNE	

Manchester 173	South Lancs 65	Horse bus H5

Myreton Motor Museum, Aberlady

GA 3560	PP 8805							

National Motor Museum (www.beaulieu.co.uk/motormuseum)

CJ 5052	KYY 663	OHO 2L					

North of England Open Air Museum (www.beamish.org.uk)

J 2503	UP 551	VK 5401	WT 7108	LTN 501 *	DET 720D			

Blackpool 31	Gateshead 51	Newcastle & Gosforth 49	Sheffield 513 *
Blackpool 703	Leeds works 6	Oporto 196	Sunderland 16
Gateshead 10	Newcastle 114	Sheffield 264	Horse bus H13

North West Museum of Road Transport (formerly St Helens Transport Museum) (www.hallstreetdepot.info)

RV 6360	GDJ 435	TDJ 612	HTJ 521B	RFM 453F	OFM 957K	XTB 728N	XLV 140W *	H 35 HBG
AFY 971	HDJ 753	TRJ 109	JTD 300B	SMK 701F	DKC 301L	XTB 729N	YMA 99W	K853 MTJ
AJD 959	KDJ 999	XTC 684	BCK 367C	HCK 204G	DKC 365L	LED 73P	XGS 771X	S112 GUB
ATD 683	KRN 422	574 TD	BED 731C	KJA 299G	PDJ 269L	TMB 880R	DEM 779Y	ANQ 778
CDJ 878	KTD 768	1975 TJ	BED 732C	DFM 347H	RTC 645L	CFM 86S	A462 LFV	
CIW 708	LDJ 985	434 BTE	FFM 135C	EFM181H	WFM 808L	WYV 21T	A910 SYE	
DED 797	MXX 421	562 RTF	UTC 768D	JFM 650J	PKH 600M	GEK 14V	C214 CBU	
EWM 358	NTF 466	201 YTE	KUS 607E	LRN 60J	RFM 61N	RMA 435V	C101 UBC	
FFY 404	RFM 641	AJA 139B	MDJ 554E	PFY 72J	HEN 868N	SDM 94V	F98 STB	
FHF 456	RFM 644 *	HTF 644B	MDJ 555E	JMC 123K	HTU 155N	BMA 521W	G186 JHG	

Nottingham Transport Heritage Centre (www.nthc.co.uk)

VO 8846 | JVO 230 | OTV 161 | 866 HAL | KVO 429P | ARC 666T
DJF 349 * | MAL 310 | 444 EBE | CUV 218C | ORC 545P |

Nottingham 45 |

Oxford Bus Museum (www.oxfordbusmuseum.org.uk)

BM 2856 | YL 740 | OFC 393 | 850 ABK | 14 LFC | VER 262L | B106 XJO |
DU 4838 | DBW 613 | PWL 413 | 956 AJO | FWL 371E | HUD 476S | C724 JJO |
FC 2602 | JVF 528 | SFC 609 | 304 KFC | NAC 416F | BBW 21V | D122 PTT |
JO 5032 | NJO 703 | SFC 610 | 305 KFC | EUD 256K | JUD 597W | L247 FDV |
JO 5403 | OFC 205 | TWL 928 | 756 KFC | UFC 430K | BBW 214Y | |

London Street 707 | Oxford 6 | Oxford 20 |

Pump House Museum, Walthamstow (www.leavalleyexperience.co.uk)

MLL 600 | MXX 312 | VUP 442 | WLT 642 | ALM 23B | JJD 463D | RCD 108G | AML 91H | EGP 132J

Krefeld 41 * | Krefeld 412 | Miniature LE 9061

Rhondda Heritage Park, Trehafod (www.rhonddaheritagepark.com)

457 KTG | BTX 332J * | | | | | | |

Riverside Museum, Glasgow (formerly Glasgow Museu m of Transport) (www.glasgowlife.org.uk/museums/)

EGA 79 | | | | GFN 546N *

Glasgow 543 | Glasgow 779 | Glasgow 1089 | Glasgow 1392 | Horse bus H8 |
Glasgow 672 | Glasgow 1088 | Glasgow 1173 * | Horse bus H7 | |

Rushden Transport Museum (www.rhts.co.uk)

651 EBD | BNH 250C | ORP 273F | | | | |
Blackpool 634

Science Museum, Wroughton (www.sciencemuseum.org.uk/wroughton)

DR 4902 | CPM 61 | KPT 909 | OTT 55 | LMJ 653G | B232 XEU | |
DX 8871 | DHR 192 | NLP 645 | 504 EBL | BCD 820L | LK 53 MBO | |
VO 6806 | HET 513 | OLJ 291 | JCP 60F | HVF 455L | | |

u/r Moulton | Glasgow 585 | Horse bus H39

Scottish Vintage Bus Museum (www.busweb.co.uk/svbm)

CD 7045 | CU 4740 | GE 2446 | RU 8678 | SO 3740 | SS 7501 | VD 3433 | WG 3260 | WG 8790
CS 3364 | EK 8867 | HF 9126 | SJ 1340 | SS 7486 | TR 6170 | WG 1620 | WG 8107 | WG 9180

WS 4522	DCK 219	KHW 630	XOI 2258	DMS 325C	LUS 524E	SCS 333M	JTU 588T	NFS 176Y
XG 9304	DCS 616	LFS 480	YSG 101	DMS 359C	KGM 664F	SCS 366M	RLS 469T	A108 CFS
AAA 756	DGS 536	LIL 9929	YYJ 914	ESF 801C	LFS 288F	LSX 16P	SAS 859T	B349 LSO
ACB 904	DGS 625	LVS 175	7424 SP	EWS 130D	LFS 294F	MSF 750P	ULS 658T	B509 YAT
ATF 477	DMS 820	NMS 366	990 EHY	EWS 168D	NTY 416F	NCS 16P	WTS 266T	C777 SFS
AWG 393	DMS 823	NSJ 502	ABV 33A	EWS 812D	NAG 120G	SMS 120P	DSD 936V	E187 HSF
AWG 623	DSG 169	OFS 777	DRS 122A	FFV 447D	XFM 42G	NDL 656R	GSO 80V	K117 CSG
AWG 639	DTF 269	OFS 798	EDS 50A	FGS 59D	SSF 237H	OJD 903R	SSX 602V	
AYJ 379	DWG 526	OWS 620	EDS 320A	KBD 714D	TMS 585H	OSJ 629R	ESF 647W	
BDJ 67	ESG 652	RAG 578	LDS 201A	GRS 343E	RSX 84J	PRA 113R	FES 831W	
BMS 222	FKG 50	RCS 382	AFS 91B	HDV 634E	TGM 214J	XMS 252R	LMS 374W	
BMS 405	FSC 182	SWS 671	ARG 17B	HDV 639E	XWS 165K	CSG 773S	YFS 310W	
BRS 37	FWG 846	SWS 715	ASC 665B	HGM 335E	BFS 1L	CSG 792S	GSC 667X	
BWG 39	GSU 378	TYD 888	AWA 124B	HGM 346E	BFS 463L	GLS 265S	KSX 102X	
CDR 679	HDZ 5488	UCS 659	BXA 464B	HGM 351E	BFS 476L	UWV 611S	RRM 386X	
CMS 200	HRG 209	UFF 178	BCS 256C	JSC 854E	BWG 833L	EGT 458T	ULS 615X	
CMS 371	HWS 775	VSC 86	CSG 29C	JSC 869E	BWS 105L	JSF 928T	ULS 716X	
CYJ 252	JWS 594	WAJ 112	CSG 43C	JSC 900E	YSD 350L	JSX 595T	ULS 717X	

Edinburgh Street 23

Snibston Discovery Park (www.leics.gov.uk/index/community/museums/snibston)

B401 NJF

Horse bus H31 | Horse bus H38

South Yorkshire Transport Museum (formerly Sheffield Bus Museum) (www.sytm.co.uk)

HD 7905	KET 220	OWE 116	VDV 760	3904 WE	DWB 54H
HE 6762	KWE 255	RWB 87	WRA 12	6330 WJ	CWG 756V
GWJ 724	MHY 765	TDK 322	1322 WA	388 KDT	B674 GWJ
JWB 416	NIB 5232	TET 135	3156 WE	BWB 148H	C 53 HDT

Sheffield 460

Stondon Transport Museum & Garden Centre (www.transportmuseum.co.uk)

VA 5777 | JXN 263

Streetlife (formerly Hull Transport Museum) (www.hullcc.gov.uk/museums/streetlife)

KKH 650 * | KRH 338 | BKH 172B *

Hull 132 | Portstewart 1 | Ryde Pier 3

Summerlee : Museum of Scottish Industrial Life (www.monklands.co.uk/summerlee)

Dusseldorf 392	Glasgow 1245	Leamington & Warwick 8		
Glasgow 1017	Lanarkshire 53	Horse bus H34		

Swansea Bus Museum (www.swanseabusmuseum.com)

GCY 740	SWO 986	YTH 815	ABO 424B	RTH 931S	FTH 992W	E304 VEP	
JWN 908	UCY 837	824 BWN	GWN 864D	WTH 961T	KEP 829X	G166 LWN	
KTX 631	VLT 66	154 FCY	GWN 867E	AWN 815V	NTH 263X	L501 HCY	
MCY 407	WLT 308	375 GWN	KKG 215F	BEP 978V	YLW 895X	M109 PWN	
NCY 626	WNO 484	423 HCY	JMA 413L	CCY 820V	C207 HTH		
SWN 159	WWN 191	431 HCY	JTH 756P	FTH 991W	D230 LCY		

Tameside Transport Collection

DBN 978	FRJ 511	7209 PW	105 UTU	NMA 328D				
DNF 204	JND 728	422 CAX	BWO 585B					

Transport Museum, Wythall (www.bammot.org.uk)

CC 7745	CVP 207	HWO 334	ORB 277	5073 HA	BHA 656C	MHA 901F *	UTU 596J	PTT 75R
CN 2870	FDM 724	JOJ 245	ORF 130	5212 HA	BON 472C	NEA 101F	OWE 271K	SDA 757S *
HA 3501	FFY 402	JOJ 533	PDH 808	6341 HA	BON 474C	NOV 796G	YOX 235K	WDA 4T
HA 8047	FJW 616	JOJ 976	RDH 505	6360 HA	CUV 219C	SHA 645G	NHR 156M	WDA 835T
O 9926	FRC 956	JRA 634	SBF 233 *	6545 HA	DAX 610C *	XDH 56G	NOB 413M	WDA 956T *
OC 527	GHA 333	JRR 404	SHA 431	750 BHA	EHA 767D	XDH 516G *	PDU 135M	DOC 26V *
OV 4090	GHA 337	JUE 349	SUK 3	759 CTD	GHA 415D	AML 588H	PHA 370M	B811 AOP
OV 4486	GUE 247	KAL 579	UHA 255	819 HHA	GRY 60D	FRB 211H	GCL 349N	D553 NOE
RC 4615	HDG 448	KFM 775	VVP 911	871 KHA	HBF 679D	SOE 913H *	JOV 613P	
AHA 582	HHA 26	LVP 118	WDF 569	943 KHA	JHA 868E	UHA 941H	JOV 738P *	
AUF 670	HHA 637	MXX 23	XHA 482	802 MHW	KHW 306E	UHA 956H	KON 311P	
CKO 988	HHA 640	NHA 744	XHA 496	248 NEA	NJW 719E	UHA 981H *	NEN 965R	
CVP 122	HOV 685	NHA 795	3016 HA *	BHA 399C	KOX 780F	AHA 451J *	NOE 544R	

u/r Morrison Electricar

Transport Museum Society of Ireland - Heritage Depot, Howth (www.nationaltransportmuseum.org)

AZ 5078	MZ 7396	ZH 3937	ZO 6857	EZL 1	VZI 44	Unreg. Bd VAL	
GZ 8547	OZ 6686	ZH 4538	ZY 79	GUX 188	WZJ 724		
IY 7384	ZC 714	ZJ 5933	EZH 64	HZA 230	694 ZO		

Dublin 224	Dublin 253	Dublin Directors Car	Giants Causeway 9	Hill of Howth 9

Trolleybus Museum at Sandtoft (www.sandtoft.org.uk)

CU 3593	WW 4688	DRD 130	FET 618	HKR 11	LTN 501	VRD 186	UDT 455F	8319 JD 13
DY 5584	ALJ 973	EDT 703	FKU 758	HYM 812	LYR 542	VRD 193	WWJ 754M	66
FW 8990	ARD 676	EKU 743	FTO 614	JWW 375	MDT 222	WLT 529 *	C 45 HDT	Edmonton 189
JV 9901	AVH 470	EKU 746	FYS 839	JWW 376	NDH 959	XWX 795	D 472 OWE	Jo'burg 589 *
KW 6052	BDJ 87	EKY 558	GDT 421	JWW 377	ONE 744	297 LJ	D 473 OWE	Liege 425
RC 8472	CDT 636	ERD 145	GFU 692	KTV 493	OTV 137	9629 WU	F100 AKB	
RC 8575 *	CKG 193	ERD 152	GHN 574	KTV 506	PVH 931	657 BWB	ACL 379	
TV 4484	CVH 741	EXV 348	GKP 511	KVH 219	SVS 281	433 MDT	964 H 87	
TV 9333	DKY 706	FET 617	GTV 666	LHN 784	TDH 914	JTF 920B	7830 LG 69	

Sheffield 419	Sheffield 442

Ulster Folk & Transport Museum (www.magni.org.uk)

CZ 7013 *	FZ 7897	GZ 1882 *	IL 2849 *	EOI 4857				
FZ 7883 *	GZ 783	GZ 4696 *	ZD 726 *	KIJ 4035 *				

Belfast 118	Bessbrook & Newry 2	Giants Causeway 5	Portstewart 2	1/3 scale Ulsterbus PD2
Belfast 249	Dublin & Blessington -?-	Great Northern Railway 381	Horse bus H9	
Belfast 357	Giants Causeway 2	Hill of Howth 4	Horse bus H10	

West Of England Transport Collection, Winkleigh

DR 7100	UO 2331 *	EFJ 666	JLJ 403	MCO 669	YLJ 147	ALJ 340B	KTT 38P	RLN 237W
FV 5737 *	VH 6217	EMW 893	KEL 110	NLJ 268	YYK 765	CCP 524C	MOD 820P	YUY 94W
JA 7591	AAX 27	ETJ 108	KEL 127	NLJ 272	8154 EL	CRU 103C	MPX 945R	TPL 762X
JK 5605	ADR 813	ETT 946	KEL 133	NNU 234	301 LJ	CRU 180C	VDV 122S	YNW 33X
JK 9115	ADV 128	EUF 182	KGU 434	ONV 425	6162 RU	CTT 513C	AFJ 760T	A749 NTA
JY 124	ATT 922	EUF 204	KHU 624	PSL 234	6167 RU	KRU 55F	CRM 927T	G645 WDV
LJ 500	BOW 162	FRU 224	KLJ 346	ROD 765	252 BKM	UYO 91F	FWR 218T	K361 LWS
OD 5489	BOW 169	GLJ 957	LFM 717	RRU 904	484 EFJ	ORU 230G	YPL 448T	L512 BOD
OD 5868	DKY 703	GTA 395	LTA 741	TFJ 808	201 HOU	VTY 543J	FWA 450V	L401 VCV
OD 7500	DKY 712	HHP 755	LTA 958	VDV 817	815 KDV	XRU 277K	VJY 141V	Q995 CPE
RU 2266	DOD 474	JFJ 606	LTV 702	VFJ 995	991 MDV	WUO 439K	DBV 43W	
UF 8837	EFJ 241	JFJ 875	LUO 595	WRL 16	AEL 170B	OAE 957M	LFJ 855W	

Wirral Transport Museum (www.wirraltransportmuseum.org)

BG 8557	AHF 850	FBG 910	HKF 820	GCM 152E	B926 KWM		
BG 9225	CHF 565	FHF 451	RCM 493	UFM 52F			

Birkenhead 7	Birkenhead 69	Douglas 46	Liverpool 43	Liverpool 762	Warrington 2
Birkenhead 20	Birkenhead 70	Lisbon 730	Liverpool 245	Wallasey 78	

Yeldham Transport Museum (http://yeldhamtransportmuseum.co.uk/)

IUI 2142	VLT 40	JJD 492D	GHV 2N	NPK 257R	FRA 534V	UAR 597W	L802 MEV
KYY 970	WNO 479	NML 625E	GHV 51N	AYJ 97T	FYX 817W	KYV 447X	
MLL 992	860 UXC	TCD 490J	KJD 524P	WYV 40T	GYE 394W	A714 THV	
NLE 538	LDS 164A	GHM 818N	KJD 535P	CUL 96V	KPJ 264W	G642 BPH	

Frankfurt 210

PB, 12 March 2012